Decision Making

- **Decision making simulations** – place your students in the role of a key decision-maker where they are asked to make a series of decisions. The simulation will change and branch based on the decisions students make, providing a variation of scenario paths. Upon completion of each simulation, students receive a grade, as well as a detailed report of the choices they made during the simulation and the associated consequences of those decisions.

Critical Thinking

- **Writing Space** – better writers make great learners—who perform better in their courses. Providing a single location to develop and assess concept mastery and critical thinking, the Writing Space offers automatic graded, assisted graded and create your own writing assignments; allowing you to exchange personalized feedback with students quickly and easily.

  Writing Space can also check students' work for improper citation or plagiarism by comparing it against the world's most accurate text comparison database available from **Turnitin**.

PEARSON

What's Out?

Models, concepts, and topics that don't pass a simple test:
"Does this help students analyze cases and real business situations?"

What's In?

"VRIO" – an integrative framework (see next page for details).

- Broad enough to apply in analyzing a variety of cases and real business settings.
- Simple enough to understand and teach.

The Results?

Provides students with the tools they need to do strategic analysis.
Nothing more. Nothing less.

What Is It?

This book is not just a list of concepts, models, and theories. It is the first undergraduate textbook to introduce a **theory-based, multi-chapter organizing framework** to add additional structure to the field of strategic management.

"VRIO" is a mechanism that integrates two existing theoretical frameworks: the positioning perspective and the resource-based view. It is the primary tool for accomplishing internal analysis. It stands for four questions one must ask about a resource or capability to determine its competitive potential:

1. **The Question of Value:** Does a resource enable a firm to exploit an environmental opportunity, and/or neutralize an environmental threat?

2. **The Question of Rarity:** Is a resource currently controlled by only a small number of competing firms?

3. **The Question of Imitability:** Do firms without a resource face a cost disadvantage in obtaining or developing it?

4. **The Question of Organization:** Are a firm's other policies and procedures organized to support the exploitation of its valuable, rare, and costly-to-imitate resources?

What's the Benefit of the VRIO Framework?

The VRIO framework is the organizational foundation of the text. **It creates a decision-making framework for students** to use in analyzing case and business situations.

Students tend to view concepts, models, and theories (in all of their coursework) as fragmented and disconnected. Strategy is no exception. This view encourages rote memorization, not real understanding. VRIO, by serving as a consistent framework, connects ideas together. This encourages real understanding, not memorization.

This understanding enables students to better analyze business cases and situations—the goal of the course.

The VRIO framework makes it possible to discuss the formulation and implementation of a strategy simultaneously, within each chapter.

Because the VRIO framework provides a simple integrative structure, we are actually able to address issues in this book that are largely ignored elsewhere—including discussions of vertical integration, outsourcing, real options logic, and mergers and acquisitions, to name just a few.

EDITION

5

Strategic Management *and* Competitive Advantage

Concepts

Jay B. Barney

The University of Utah

William S. Hesterly

The University of Utah

PEARSON

Boston   Columbus   Hoboken   Indianapolis   New York   San Francisco
Amsterdam   Cape Town   Dubai   London   Madrid   Milan   Munich   Paris   Montréal   Toronto
Delhi   Mexico City   São Paulo   Sydney   Hong Kong   Seoul   Singapore   Taipei   Tokyo

Editor in Chief: Stephanie Wall
Acquisitions Editor: Daniel Tylman
Program Management Lead: Ashley Santora
Program Manager: Sarah Holle
Editorial Assistant: Linda Albelli
VP, Marketing: Maggie Moylan
Product Marketing Manager: Anne Fahlgren
Field Marketing Manager: Lenny Raper
Strategic Marketing Manager: Erin Gardner
Project Management Lead: Judy Leale

Project Manager: Karalyn Holland
Procurement Specialist: Michelle Klein
Cover Designer: Karen Quigley
Cover Art & Interior Illustrations:
  Gary Hovland
**Full-Service Project Management, Interior
Design, Composition:** Integra
Printer/Binder: RR Donnelley/Willard
Cover Printer: Phoenix Color/Hagerstown
Text Font: 10/12 Palatino LT Std Roman

Credits and acknowledgments borrowed from other sources and reproduced, with permission, in this textbook appear on the appropriate page within text.

Many of the designations by manufacturers and sellers to distinguish their products are claimed as trademarks. Where those designations appear in this book, and the publisher was aware of a trademark claim, the designations have been printed in initial caps or all caps.

Library of Congress Cataloging-in-Publication Data
Barney, Jay B.
  Strategic management and competitive advantage: concepts/Jay B. Barney,
The University of Utah, William S. Hesterly, The University of Utah.—5th edition.
    pages cm
Includes bibliographical references and index.
ISBN-13: 978-0-13-312930-4
ISBN-10:   0-13-312930-6
1. Strategic planning. 2. Business planning. 3. Industrial management. 4. Competition.
I. Hesterly, William S. II. Title.
HD30.28.B36834 2015
658.4′012—dc23

                                                      2014001795

10 9 8 7 6 5 4 3 2 1

ISBN 10:   0-13-312930-6
ISBN 13: 978-0-13-312930-4

This book is dedicated to my family: my wife, Kim; our children, Lindsay, Kristian, and Erin, and their spouses; and, most of all, our nine grandchildren, Isaac, Dylanie, Audrey, Chloe, Lucas, Royal, Lincoln, Nolan, and Theo. They all help me remember that no success could compensate for failure in the home.

Jay B. Barney
Salt Lake City, Utah

This book is for my family who has taught me life's greatest lessons about what matters most. To my wife, Denise; my daughters, sons, and their spouses: Lindsay, Matt, Jessica, John, Alex, Brittany, Austin, Julia, Ian, and Drew.; and my grandchildren, Ellie, Owen, Emerson, Cade, Elizabeth, Amelia, Eden, Asher, Lydia, and Scarlett.

William Hesterly
Salt Lake City, Utah

Brief Contents

Part 1: THE TOOLS of STRATEGIC ANALYSIS

Part 2: BUSINESS-LEVEL STRATEGIES

Part 3: CORPORATE STRATEGIES

Contents

Part 1: THE TOOLS of STRATEGIC ANALYSIS

Part 2: BUSINESS-LEVEL STRATEGIES

Part 3: CORPORATE STRATEGIES

Preface

The first thing you will notice as you look through this edition of our book is that it continues to be much shorter than most textbooks on strategic management. There is not the usual "later edition" increase in number of pages and bulk. We're strong proponents of the philosophy that, often, less is more. The general tendency is for textbooks to get longer and longer as authors make sure that their books leave out nothing that is in other books. We take a different approach. Our guiding principle in deciding what to include is: "Does this concept help students analyze cases and real business situations?" For many concepts we considered, the answer is no. But, where the answer is yes, the concept is in the book.

New to This Edition

This edition includes many new chapter-opening cases, including:

- Chapter 1: A case on the video app "Angry Birds"
- Chapter 2: A case on the music streaming industry
- Chapter 3: A case on how Google keeps going
- Chapter 8: A case on Berkshire-Hathaway's corporate strategy
- Chapter 9: A case on the alliance between Apple and Samsung
- Chapter 10: A case on Google's acquisition strategy
- Chapter 11: A case on the infant formula business in China

All the other opening cases have been reused and updated, along with all the examples throughout the book.

Two newer topics in the field have also been included in this edition of the book: the business model canvas (in Chapter 1) and blue ocean strategies (in Chapter 5).

VRIO Framework and Other Hallmark Features

One thing that has not changed in this edition is that we continue to have a point of view about the field of strategic management. In planning for this book, we recalled our own educational experience and the textbooks that did and didn't work for us then. Those few that stood out as the best did not merely cover all of the different topics in a field of study. They provided a framework that we could carry around in our heads, and they helped us to see what we were studying as an integrated whole rather than a disjointed sequence of loosely related subjects. This text continues to be integrated around the VRIO framework. As those of you familiar with the resource-based theory of strategy recognize, the VRIO framework addresses the central questions around gaining and sustaining competitive advantage. After it is introduced in Chapter 3, the VRIO logic of competitive advantage is applied in every chapter. It is simple enough to understand and teach yet broad enough to apply to a wide variety of cases and business settings.

Our consistent use of the VRIO framework does not mean that any of the concepts fundamental to a strategy course are missing. We still have all of the core ideas and theories that are essential to a strategy course. Ideas such as the study of environmental threats, value chain analysis, generic strategies, and corporate strategy are all in the book. Because the VRIO framework provides a single integrative structure, we are able to address issues in this book that are largely ignored elsewhere—including discussions of vertical integration, outsourcing, real options logic, and mergers and acquisitions, to name just a few.

We also have designed flexibility into the book. Each chapter has four short sections that present specific issues in more depth. These sections allow instructors to adapt the book to the particular needs of their students. "Strategy in Depth" examines the intellectual foundations that are behind the way managers think about and practice strategy today. "Strategy in the Emerging Enterprise" presents examples of strategic challenges faced by new and emerging enterprises. "Ethics and Strategy" delves into some of the ethical dilemmas that managers face as they confront strategic decisions. "Research Made Relevant" includes recent research related to the topics in that chapter.

We have also included cases—including many new cases in this edition—that provide students an opportunity to apply the ideas they learn to business situations. The cases include a variety of contexts, such as entrepreneurial, service, manufacturing, and international settings. The power of the VRIO framework is that it applies across all of these settings. Applying the VRIO framework to many topics and cases throughout the book leads to real understanding instead of rote memorization. The end result is that students will find that they have the tools they need to do strategic analysis. Nothing more. Nothing less.

Supplements

At the Instructor Resource Center, at www.pearsonhighered.com/irc, instructors can download a variety of digital and presentation resources. Registration is simple and gives you immediate access to all of the available supplements. As a registered faculty member, you also can receive immediate access to and instructions for installing course management content on your campus server. In case you ever need assistance, our dedicated technical support team is ready to help with the media supplements that accompany this text. Visit http://247.pearsoned.custhelp.com for answers to frequently asked questions and toll-free user support phone numbers.

The following supplements are available for download to adopting instructors:

- Instructor's Manual
- Case Teaching Notes
- Test Item File
- TestGen® Computerized Test Bank
- PowerPoint Slides

Videos

Videos illustrating the most important subject topics are available in two formats:

- ON DVD—available for in classroom use by instructors, includes videos mapped to Pearson textbooks.
- IN MyLab—available for instructors and students, provides round-the-clock instant access to videos and corresponding assessment and simulations for Pearson textbooks.

Contact your local Pearson representative to request access to either format.

Other Benefits

Element	Description	Benefit	Example
Chapter Opening Cases	We have chosen firms that are familiar to most students. Opening cases focus on whether or not Rovio Entertainment, Ltd.—maker of the popular video game "Angry Birds"—can sustain its success, how Ryanair has become the lowest cost airline in the world, how Victoria's Secret has differentiated its products, how ESPN has diversified its operations, and so forth.	By having cases tightly linked to the material, students can develop strategic analysis skills by studying firms familiar to them.	2–3
Strategy in Depth	For professors and students interested in understanding the full intellectual underpinnings of the field, we have included an optional Strategy in Depth feature in every chapter. Knowledge in strategic management continues to evolve rapidly, in ways that are well beyond what is normally included in introductory texts.	Customize your course as desired to provide enrichment material for advanced students.	223
Research Made Relevant	The Research Made Relevant feature highlights very current research findings related to some of the strategic topics discussed in that chapter.	Shows students the evolving nature of strategy.	47
Challenge Questions	These might be of an ethical or moral nature, forcing students to apply concepts across chapters, apply concepts to themselves, or extend chapter ideas in creative ways.	Requires students to think critically.	125
Problem Set	Problem Set asks students to apply theories and tools from the chapter. These often require calculations. They can be thought of as homework assignments. If students struggle with these problems they might have trouble with the more complex cases. These problem sets are largely diagnostic in character.	Sharpens quantitative skills and provides a bridge between chapter material and case analysis.	157–158
Ethics and Strategy	Highlights some of the most important dilemmas faced by firms when creating and implementing strategies.	Helps students make better ethical decisions as managers.	208
Strategy in the Emerging Enterprise	A growing number of graduates work for small and medium-sized firms. This feature presents an extended example, in each chapter, of the unique strategic problems facing those employed in small and medium-sized firms.	This feature highlights the unique challenges of doing strategic analysis in emerging enterprises and small and medium-sized firms.	53

Acknowledgments

Obviously, a book like this is not written in isolation. We owe a debt of gratitude to all those at Pearson who have supported its development. In particular, we want to thank Stephanie Wall, Editor-in-Chief; Dan Tylman, Acquisitions Editor; Sarah Holle, Program Manager; Erin Gardner, Marketing Manager; Judy Leale, Project Manager Team Lead; and Karalyn Holland, Senior Project Manager.

Many people were involved in reviewing drafts of each edition's manuscript. Their efforts undoubtedly improved the manuscript dramatically. Their efforts are largely unsung but very much appreciated.

Thank you to these professors who participated in manuscript reviews:

Yusaf Akbar—Southern New Hampshire University

Joseph D. Botana II—Lakeland College

Pam Braden—West Virginia University at Parkersburg

Erick PC Chang—Arkansas State University

Mustafa Colak—Temple University

Ron Eggers—Barton College

Michael Frandsen—Albion College

Swapnil Garg—University of Florida

Michele Gee—University of Wisconsin, Parkside

Peter Goulet—University of Northern Iowa

Rebecca Guidice—University of Nevada Las Vegas

Laura Hart—Lynn University, College of Business & Management

Tom Hewett—Kaplan University

Phyllis Holland—Valdosta State University

Paul Howard—Penn State University

Richard Insinga—St. John Fisher College

Homer Johnson—Loyola University Chicago

Marilyn Kaplan—University of Texas at Dallas

Joseph Leonard—Miami University

Paul Maxwell—St. Thomas University, Miami

Stephen Mayer—Niagara University

Richard Nemanick—Saint Louis University

Hossein Noorian—Wentworth Institute of Technology

Ralph Parrish—University of Central Oklahoma

Raman Patel—Robert Morris College

Jiten Ruparel—Otterbein College

Roy Simerly—East Carolina University

Sally Sledge—Christopher Newport University

David Stahl—Montclair State University

David Stephens—Utah State University

Philip Stoeberl—Saint Louis University

Ram Subramanian—Grand Valley State University

William W. Topper—Curry College

Thomas Turk—Chapman University

Henry Ulrich—Central Connecticut State (soon to be UCONN)

Floyd Willoughby—Oakland University

Reviewers of the Fourth Edition

Terry Adler—New Mexico State University

Jorge Aravelo—William Patterson University

Asli M. Arikan—The Ohio State University

Scott Brown—Chapman University

Carlos Ferran—Governors State University

Samual Holloway—University of Portland

Paul Longenecker—Otterbein University

Shelly McCallum—Saint Mary's University

Jeffrey Stone—CAL State–Channel Islands

Edward Taylor—Piedmont College

Les Thompson—Missouri Baptist University

Zhe Zhang—Eastern Kentucky University

All these people have given generously of their time and wisdom. But, truth be told, everyone who knows us knows that this book would not have been possible without Kathy Zwanziger and Rachel Snow.

Author Biographies

JAY B. BARNEY

Jay Barney is a Presidential Professor of strategic management and the Lassonde Chair of Social Entrepreneurship of the Entrepreneurship and Strategy Department in the David Eccles Business School, The University of Utah. He received his Ph.D. from Yale and has held faculty appointments at UCLA, Texas A&M, and OSU [The Ohio State University]. He joined the faculty at The University of Utah in summer of 2013. Jay has published more than 100 journal articles and books; has served on the editorial boards of *Academy of Management Review, Strategic Management Journal*, and *Organization Science;* has served as an associate editor of *The Journal of Management* and senior editor at *Organization Science;* and currently serves as co-editor at the *Strategic Entrepreneurship Journal*. He has received honorary doctorate degrees from the University of Lund (Sweden), the Copenhagen Business School (Denmark), and the Universidad Pontificia Comillas (Spain) and has been elected to the Academy of Management Fellows and Strategic Management Society Fellows. He has held honorary visiting professor positions at Waikato University (New Zealand), Sun Yat-Sen University (China), and Peking University (China). He has also consulted for a wide variety of public and private organizations, including Hewlett-Packard, Texas Instruments, Arco, Koch Industries Inc., and Nationwide Insurance, focusing on implementing large-scale organizational change and strategic analysis. He has received teaching awards at UCLA, Texas A&M, and Ohio State. Jay served as assistant program chair and program chair, chair elect, and chair of the Business Policy and Strategy Division. In 2005, he received the Irwin Outstanding Educator Award for the BPS Division of the Academy of Management, and in 2010, he won the Academy of Management's Scholarly Contribution to Management Award. In 2008, he was elected as the President-elect of the Strategic Management Society, where he currently serves as past-president.

WILLIAM S. HESTERLY

William Hesterly is the Associate Dean for Faculty and Research as well as the Dumke Family Endowed Presidential Chair in Management in the David Eccles School of Business, University of Utah. After studying at Louisiana State University, he received bachelors and masters degrees from Brigham Young University and a Ph.D. from the University of California, Los Angeles. Professor Hesterly has been recognized multiple times as the outstanding teacher in the MBA Program at the David Eccles School of Business and has also been the recipient of the Student's Choice Award. He has taught in a variety of executive programs for both large and small companies. Professor Hesterly's research on organizational economics, vertical integration, organizational forms, and entrepreneurial networks has appeared in top journals including the *Academy of Management Review, Organization Science, Strategic Management Journal, Journal of Management*, and the *Journal of Economic Behavior and Organization*. Currently, he is studying the sources of value creation in firms and also the determinants of who captures the value from a firm's competitive advantage. Recent papers in this area have appeared in the *Academy of Management Review* and *Managerial and Decision Economics.* Professor Hesterly's research was recognized with the Western Academy of Management's Ascendant Scholar Award in 1999. Dr. Hesterly has also received best paper awards from the Western Academy of Management and the Academy of Management. Dr. Hesterly currently serves as the senior editor of *Long Range Planning* and has served on the editorial boards of *Strategic Organization, Organization Science*, and the *Journal of Management*. He has served as Department Chair and also as Vice-President and President of the faculty at the David Eccles School of Business at the University of Utah.

1 THE TOOLS OF STRATEGIC ANALYSIS

What Is Strategy and the Strategic Management Process?

LEARNING OBJECTIVES *After reading this chapter, you should be able to:*

1. Define strategy.

2. Describe the strategic management process.

3. Define competitive advantage and explain its relationship to economic value creation.

4. Describe two different measures of competitive advantage.

5. Explain the difference between emergent and intended strategies.

6. Discuss the importance of understanding a firm's strategy even if you are not a senior manager in a firm.

MyManagementLab®

⭐ **Improve Your Grade!**
Over 10 million students improved their results using the Pearson MyLabs.
Visit **mymanagementlab.com** for simulations, tutorials, and end-of-chapter problems.

Why Are These Birds So Angry?

Rarely can the beginning on an entire industry be traced to a single event on a specific day. But this is the case with the smart phone applications industry.

On June 29, 2007, Apple first introduced the iPhone. A central feature of the iPhone was that it would be able to run a wide variety of applications, or "apps." And, most importantly for the evolution of the apps industry, Apple decided that while it would evaluate and distribute these applications—through the online Apple App Store—it would not develop them. Instead, Apple would "crowd source" most applications from outside developers.

And, thus, the smart phone applications industry began. By April 24, 2009, iPhone users had downloaded more than 1 billion apps from the Apple App Store. During 2012, more than 45.6 billion smart phone apps were downloaded from all sources, generating revenues in excess of $25 billion. Projections suggest double-digit growth in this industry for at least another five years.

Of course, much has changed since 2007. For example, Apple now has six competitors for its Apple App Store, including Amazon App Store, Google Play Store, BlackBerry World, and Windows Phone Store. Some of these stores distribute apps for non-Apple phone operating systems developed by Google (Android), BlackBerry, and Windows. But all of these distributors have adopted Apple's original model for developing applications: mostly outsource it to independent development companies.

These development companies fall into four categories: (1) Internet companies—including Google—who have developed smart phone versions of popular Internet sites—including, for example, YouTube and Google Maps; (2) traditional video game companies—including Sega—who have developed smart phone versions of popular video games—including, for example, Sonic Dash; (3) diversified media companies—including Disney—who have built apps featuring characters and stories developed in their far-flung media operations—including, for example, Monster's University; and (4) companies who have been formed to develop entirely new apps.

There are, of course, literally thousands—maybe hundreds of thousands—of this last type of app development firm. The proliferation of these firms—sometimes no more than one person with an idea—has led to a proliferation of apps across all smart phone platforms. Currently, there are 1.5 million downloadable apps available on both the Apple App Store and Google Play Store.

Among these thousands of independent developers, a few have been unusually successful. None exemplifies this "rag to riches" dynamic more than Rovio, an app development company headquartered outside Helsinki, Finland. Rovio is best known for an amazingly simple game involving enraged avians—yes, Angry Birds.

The challenge facing Rovio, and all these successful independent app developers, is: Can they go beyond developing a single "killer app," or will they be "one-hit wonders?" Rovio is trying to avoid this fate by leveraging the Angry Birds franchise into a series of related apps—Angry Birds Star Wars, Bad Piggies; by developing apps that build on new characters—The Croods; by diversifying into related non-app businesses—Angry Birds Toons; and by licensing Angry Birds characters to toy manufactures—including Mattel.

Rovio has even begun crowd sourcing new app ideas that it can bring to market. Independent developers can pitch games and apps to Rovio online. Whether this effort will lead to the next generation of Rovio apps is not yet known.

What is known is that the smart phone applications industry—an industry that was created only in 2007—is likely to grow and evolve dramatically over the next few years. And firms as diverse as Google, Apple, Disney, Sega—and even Rovio—will have to evolve with it.

Sources: www.rovio.com accessed August 23, 2013; www.distimo.com accessed August 23, 2013; www.newrelic.com accessed August 23, 2013

Firms in the smart phone applications industry—whether they have entered this business from another media industry—like Google and Disney—or not—like Rovio—face classic strategic questions. How is this industry likely to evolve? What actions can be taken to change this evolution? How can firms gain advantages in this industry? How sustainable are these advantages?

The process by which these, and related, questions are answered is the strategic management process, and the answers that firms develop for these questions help determine a firm's strategy.

Strategy and the Strategic Management Process

Although most can agree that a firm's ability to survive and prosper depends on choosing and implementing a good strategy, there is less agreement about what a strategy is and even less agreement about what constitutes a good strategy. Indeed, there are almost as many different definitions of these concepts as there are books written about them.

Defining Strategy

In this book, a firm's **strategy** is defined as its theory about how to gain competitive advantages.[1] A good strategy is a strategy that actually generates such advantages. Disney's theory of how to gain a competitive advantage in the apps industry is to leverage characters from its movie business. Rovio's theory is to develop entirely new content for its apps.

Each of these theories—like all theories—is based on a set of assumptions and hypotheses about the way competition in this industry is likely to evolve and how that evolution can be exploited to earn a profit. The greater the extent to which these assumptions and hypotheses accurately reflect how competition in this industry actually evolves, the more likely it is that a firm will gain a competitive advantage from implementing its strategies. If these assumptions and hypotheses turn out not to be accurate, then a firm's strategies are not likely to be a source of competitive advantage.

But here is the challenge. It is usually very difficult to predict how competition in an industry will evolve, and so it is rarely possible to know for sure that a firm is choosing the right strategy. This is why a firm's strategy is almost always a theory: It's a firm's best bet about how competition is going to evolve and how that evolution can be exploited for competitive advantage.

The Strategic Management Process

Although it is usually difficult to know for sure that a firm is pursuing the best strategy, it is possible to reduce the likelihood that mistakes are being made. The best way to do this is for a firm to choose its strategy carefully and systematically and to follow the strategic management process. The **strategic management process** is a sequential set of analyses and choices that can increase the likelihood that a firm will choose a good strategy; that is, a strategy that generates competitive advantages. An example of the strategic management process is presented in Figure 1.1. Not surprisingly, this book is organized around this strategic management process.

Figure 1.1   The Strategic Management Process

A Firm's Mission

The strategic management process begins when a firm defines its mission. A firm's **mission** is its long-term purpose. Missions define both what a firm aspires to be in the long run and what it wants to avoid in the meantime. Missions are often written down in the form of **mission statements**.

Some Missions May Not Affect Firm Performance.   Most mission statements incorporate common elements. For example, many define the businesses within which a firm will operate—medical products for Johnson and Johnson; adhesives and substrates for 3M—or they can very simply state how a firm will compete in those businesses. Many even define the core values that a firm espouses.

Indeed, mission statements often contain so many common elements that some have questioned whether having a mission statement even creates value for a firm.[2] Moreover, even if a mission statement does say something unique about a company, if that mission statement does not influence behavior throughout an organization, it is unlikely to have much impact on a firm's actions. After all, while Enron was engaging in wide ranging acts of fraud[3], it had a mission statement that emphasized the importance of honesty and integrity.[4]

Some Missions Can Improve Firm Performance.   Despite these caveats, research has identified some firms whose sense of purpose and mission permeates all that they do. These firms include, for example, 3M, IBM, Philip Morris, Wal-Mart, and Disney. Some of these **visionary firms**, or firms whose mission is central to all they do have enjoyed long periods of high performance.[5] From 1926 through 1995, an investment of $1 in one of these firms would have increased in value to $6,536. That same dollar invested in an average firm over this same time period would have been worth $415 in 1995.

These visionary firms earned substantially higher returns than average firms even though many of their mission statements suggest that profit maximizing, although an important corporate objective, is not their primary reason for existence. Rather, their primary reasons for existence are typically reflected in a widely held set of values and beliefs that inform day-to-day decision making. While, in other firms, managers may be tempted to sacrifice such values and beliefs to gain short-term advantages, in these special firms, the pressure for short-term performance is balanced by widespread commitment to values and beliefs that focus more on a firm's long-term performance.[6]

Of course, that these firms had performed well for many decades does not mean they will do so forever. Some previously identified visionary firms have stumbled more recently, including American Express, Ford, Hewlett-Packard, Motorola, and Sony. Some of these financial problems may be attributable to the fact that these formally mission-driven companies have lost focus on their mission.

Some Missions Can Hurt Firm Performance.   Although some firms have used their missions to develop strategies that create significant competitive advantages, missions can hurt a firm's performance as well. For example, sometimes a firm's mission will be very inwardly focused and defined only with reference to the personal values and priorities of its founders or top managers, independent of whether those values and priorities are consistent with the economic realities facing a firm. Strategies derived from such missions are not likely to be a source of competitive advantage.

For example, Ben & Jerry's Ice Cream was founded in 1977 by Ben Cohen and Jerry Greenfield, both as a way to produce super-premium ice cream and as a way to create an organization based on the values of the 1960s' counterculture. This strong sense of mission led Ben & Jerry's to adopt some very unusual human resource and other policies. Among these policies, the company adopted a compensation system whereby the highest-paid firm employee could earn no more than five times the income of the lowest-paid firm employee. Later, this ratio was adjusted to seven to one. However, even at this level, such a compensation policy made it very difficult to acquire the senior management talent needed to ensure the growth and profitability of the firm without grossly overpaying the lowest-paid employees in the firm. When a new CEO was appointed to the firm in 1995, his $250,000 salary violated this compensation policy.

Indeed, though the frozen dessert market rapidly consolidated through the late 1990s, Ben & Jerry's Ice Cream remained an independent firm, partly because of Cohen's and Greenfield's commitment to maintaining the social values that their firm embodied. Lacking access to the broad distribution network and managerial talent that would have been available if Ben & Jerry's had merged with another firm, the company's growth and profitability lagged. Finally, in April 2000, Ben & Jerry's Ice Cream was acquired by Unilever. The 66 percent premium finally earned by Ben & Jerry's stockholders in April 2000 had been delayed for several years. In this sense, Cohen's and Greenfield's commitment to a set of personal values and priorities was at least partly inconsistent with the economic realities of the frozen dessert market in the United States.[7]

Obviously, because a firm's mission can help, hurt, or have no impact on its performance, missions by themselves do not necessarily lead a firm to choose and implement strategies that generate competitive advantages. Indeed, as suggested in Figure 1.1, while defining a firm's mission is an important step in the strategic management process, it is only the first step in that process.

Objectives

Whereas a firm's mission is a broad statement of its purpose and values, its **objectives** are specific measurable targets a firm can use to evaluate the extent to which it is realizing its mission. High-quality objectives are tightly connected to elements of a firm's mission and are relatively easy to measure and track over time. Low-quality objectives either do not exist or are not connected to elements of a firm's mission, are not quantitative, or are difficult to measure or difficult to track over time. Obviously, low-quality objectives cannot be used by management to evaluate how well a mission is being realized. Indeed, one indication that a firm is not that serious about realizing part of its mission statement is when there are no objectives, or only low-quality objectives, associated with that part of the mission.

External and Internal Analysis

The next two phases of the strategic management process—external analysis and internal analysis—occur more or less simultaneously. By conducting an

external analysis, a firm identifies the critical threats and opportunities in its competitive environment. It also examines how competition in this environment is likely to evolve and what implications that evolution has for the threats and opportunities a firm is facing. A considerable literature on techniques for and approaches to conducting external analysis has evolved over the past several years. This literature is the primary subject matter of Chapter 2 of this book.

Whereas external analysis focuses on the environmental threats and opportunities facing a firm, **internal analysis** helps a firm identify its organizational strengths and weaknesses. It also helps a firm understand which of its resources and capabilities are likely to be sources of competitive advantage and which are less likely to be sources of such advantages. Finally, internal analysis can be used by firms to identify those areas of its organization that require improvement and change. As with external analysis, a considerable literature on techniques for and approaches to conducting internal analysis has evolved over the past several years. This literature is the primary subject matter of Chapter 3 of this book.

Strategic Choice

Armed with a mission, objectives, and completed external and internal analyses, a firm is ready to make its strategic choices. That is, a firm is ready to choose its theory of how to gain competitive advantage.

The strategic choices available to firms fall into two large categories: business-level strategies and corporate-level strategies. **Business-level strategies** are actions firms take to gain competitive advantages in a single market or industry. These strategies are the topic of Part 2 of this book. The two most common business-level strategies are cost leadership (Chapter 4) and product differentiation (Chapter 5).

Corporate-level strategies are actions firms take to gain competitive advantages by operating in multiple markets or industries simultaneously. These strategies are the topic of Part 3 of this book. Common corporate-level strategies include vertical integration strategies (Chapter 6), diversification strategies (Chapters 7 and 8), strategic alliance strategies (Chapter 9), merger and acquisition strategies (Chapter 10), and global strategies (Chapter 11).

Obviously, the details of choosing specific strategies can be quite complex, and a discussion of these details will be delayed until later in the book. However, the underlying logic of strategic choice is not complex. Based on the strategic management process, the objective when making a strategic choice is to choose a strategy that (1) supports the firm's mission, (2) is consistent with a firm's objectives, (3) exploits opportunities in a firm's environment with a firm's strengths, and (4) neutralizes threats in a firm's environment while avoiding a firm's weaknesses. Assuming that this strategy is implemented—the last step of the strategic management process—a strategy that meets these four criteria is very likely to be a source of competitive advantage for a firm.

Strategy Implementation

Of course, simply choosing a strategy means nothing if that strategy is not implemented. **Strategy implementation** occurs when a firm adopts organizational policies and practices that are consistent with its strategy. Three specific organizational policies and practices are particularly important in implementing a strategy: a firm's formal organizational structure, its formal and informal management control systems, and its employee compensation policies. A firm that adopts an organizational structure, management controls, and compensation policy that are consistent with and reinforce its strategies is more likely to be able to implement those strategies than a firm that adopts an organizational structure, management controls, and compensation policy that are inconsistent with its strategies. Specific organizational structures, management controls, and compensation policies used to implement the business-level strategies of cost leadership and product differentiation are discussed in Chapters 4 and 5. How organizational structure, management controls, and compensation can be used to implement corporate-level strategies, including vertical integration, strategic alliance, merger and acquisition, and global strategies, is discussed in Chapters 6, 9, 10, and 11, respectively. However, there is so much information about implementing diversification strategies that an entire chapter, Chapter 8, is dedicated to the discussion of how this corporate-level strategy is implemented.

What Is Competitive Advantage?

Of course, the ultimate objective of the strategic management process is to enable a firm to choose and implement a strategy that generates a competitive advantage. But what is a competitive advantage? In general, a firm has a **competitive advantage** when it is able to create more economic value than rival firms. **Economic value** is simply the difference between the perceived benefits gained by a customer that purchases a firm's products or services and the full economic cost of these products or services. Thus, the size of a firm's competitive advantage is the difference between the economic value a firm is able to create and the economic value its rivals are able to create.[8]

Consider the two firms presented in Figure 1.2. Both these firms compete in the same market for the same customers. However, Firm I generates $180 of economic value each time it sells a product or service, whereas Firm II generates $150 of economic value each time it sells a product or service. Because Firm I generates more economic value each time it sells a product or service, it has a competitive advantage over Firm II. The size of this competitive advantage is equal to the difference in the economic value these two firms create, in this case, $30($180 − $150 = $30).

However, as shown in the figure, Firm I's advantage may come from different sources. For example, it might be the case that Firm I creates greater perceived benefits for its customers than Firm II. In panel A of the figure, Firm I creates perceived customer benefits worth $230, whereas Firm II creates perceived customer benefits worth only $200. Thus, even though both firms' costs are the same (equal to $50 per unit sold), Firm I creates more economic value ($230 − $50 = $180) than Firm II ($200 − $50 = $150). Indeed, it is possible for Firm I, in this situation, to have higher costs than Firm II and still create more economic value than Firm II if these higher costs are offset by Firm I's ability to create greater perceived benefits for its customers.

Alternatively, as shown in panel B of the figure, these two firms may create the same level of perceived customer benefit (equal to $210 in this example) but have different costs. If Firm I's costs per unit are only $30, it will generate $180 worth of economic value ($210 − $30 = $180). If Firm II's costs are $60, it will generate only $150 of economic value ($210 − $60 = $150). Indeed, it might be possible for Firm I to create a lower level of perceived benefits for its customers than Firm II and still create more economic value than Firm II, as long

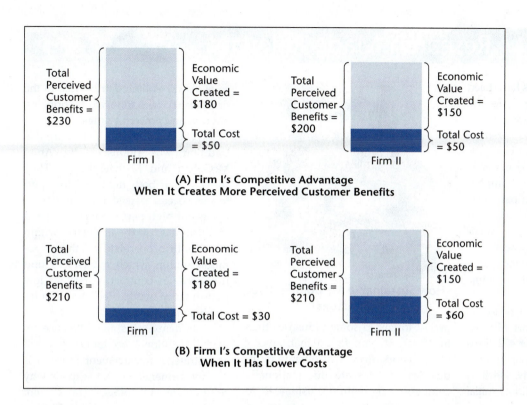

Figure 1.2   The Sources of a Firm's Competitive Advantage

Total Perceived Customer Benefits = $230

Economic Value Created = $180

Total Cost = $50

Firm I

Total Perceived Customer Benefits = $200

Economic Value Created = $150

Total Cost = $50

Firm II

(A) Firm I's Competitive Advantage When It Creates More Perceived Customer Benefits

Total Perceived Customer Benefits = $210

Economic Value Created = $180

Total Cost = $30

Firm I

Total Perceived Customer Benefits = $210

Economic Value Created = $150

Total Cost = $60

Firm II

(B) Firm I's Competitive Advantage When It Has Lower Costs

as its disadvantage in perceived customer benefits is more than offset by its cost advantage.

A firm's competitive advantage can be temporary or sustained. As summarized in Figure 1.3, a **temporary competitive advantage** is a competitive advantage that lasts for a very short period of time. A **sustained competitive advantage**, in contrast, can last much longer. How long sustained competitive advantages can last is discussed in the Research Made Relevant feature. Firms that create the same economic value as their rivals experience **competitive parity**. Finally, firms that generate less economic value than their rivals have a **competitive disadvantage**. Not surprisingly, competitive disadvantages can be either temporary or sustained, depending on the duration of the disadvantage.

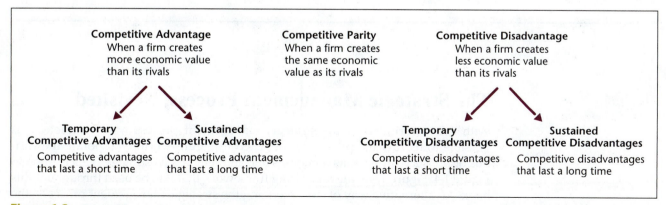

Competitive Advantage
When a firm creates more economic value than its rivals

Competitive Parity
When a firm creates the same economic value as its rivals

Competitive Disadvantage
When a firm creates less economic value than its rivals

Temporary Competitive Advantages
Competitive advantages that last a short time

Sustained Competitive Advantages
Competitive advantages that last a long time

Temporary Competitive Disadvantages
Competitive disadvantages that last a short time

Sustained Competitive Disadvantages
Competitive disadvantages that last a long time

Figure 1.3   Types of Competitive Advantage

Research Made Relevant

For some time, economists have been interested in how long firms are able to sustain competitive advantages. Traditional economic theory predicts that such advantages should be short-lived in highly competitive markets. This theory suggests that any competitive advantages gained by a particular firm will quickly be identified and imitated by other firms, ensuring competitive parity in the long run. However, in real life, competitive advantages often last longer than traditional economic theory predicts.

One of the first scholars to examine this issue was Dennis Mueller. Mueller divided a sample of 472 firms into eight categories, depending on their level of performance in 1949. He then examined the impact of a firm's initial performance on its subsequent performance. The traditional economic hypothesis was that all firms in the sample would converge on an average level of performance. This did not occur. Indeed, firms that were performing well in an earlier time period tended to perform well in later time periods, and firms that performed poorly in an earlier time period tended to perform poorly in later time periods as well.

Geoffrey Waring followed up on Mueller's work by explaining why competitive advantages seem to

How Sustainable Are Competitive Advantages?

persist longer in some industries than in others. Waring found that, among other factors, firms that operate in industries that (1) are informationally complex, (2) require customers to know a great deal in order to use an industry's products, (3) require a great deal of research and development, and (4) have significant economies of scale are more likely to have sustained competitive advantages compared to firms that operate in industries without these attributes.

Peter Roberts studied the persistence of profitability in one particular industry: the U.S. pharmaceutical industry. Roberts found that not only can firms sustain competitive advantages in this industry, but that the ability to do

so is almost entirely attributable to the firms' capacity to innovate by bringing out new and powerful drugs.

The most recent work in this tradition was published by Anita McGahan and Michael Porter. They showed that both high and low performance can persist for some time. Persistent high performance is related to attributes of the industry within which a firm operates and the corporation within which a business unit functions. In contrast, persistent low performance was caused by attributes of a business unit itself.

In many ways, the difference between traditional economics research and strategic management research is that the former attempts to explain why competitive advantages should not persist, whereas the latter attempts to explain when they can. Thus far, most empirical research suggests that firms, in at least some settings, can sustain competitive advantages.

Sources: D. C. Mueller (1977). "The persistence of profits above the norm." *Economica*, 44, pp. 369–380; P. W. Roberts (1999). "Product innovation, product-market competition, and persistent profitability in the U.S. pharmaceutical industry." *Strategic Management Journal*, 20, pp. 655–670; G. F. Waring (1996). "Industry differences in the persistence of firm-specific returns." *The American Economic Review*, 86, pp. 1253–1265; A. McGahan and M. Porter (2003). "The emergence and sustainability of abnormal profits." *Strategic Organization*, 1(1), pp. 79–108.

The Strategic Management Process, Revisited

With this description of the strategic management process now complete, it is possible to redraw the process, as depicted in Figure 1.1, to incorporate the various options a firm faces as it chooses and implements its strategy. This is done in Figure 1.4. Figure 1.4 is the organizing framework that will be used throughout this book. An alternative way of characterizing the strategic management process—the business model canvas—is described in the Strategy in Depth feature.

Figure 1.4   Organizing Framework

Measuring Competitive Advantage

A firm has a *competitive advantage* when it creates more economic value than its rivals. *Economic value* is the difference between the perceived customer benefits associated with buying a firm's products or services and the full cost of producing and selling these products or services. These are deceptively simple definitions. However, these concepts are not always easy to measure directly. For example, the benefits of a firm's products or services are always a matter of customer perception, and perceptions are not easy to measure. Also, the total costs associated with producing a particular product or service may not always be easy to identify or associate with a particular product or service. Despite the very real challenges associated with measuring a firm's competitive advantage, two approaches have emerged. The first estimates a firm's competitive advantage by examining its accounting performance; the second examines the firm's economic performance. These approaches are discussed in the following sections.

Accounting Measures of Competitive Advantage

A firm's **accounting performance** is a measure of its competitive advantage calculated by using information from a firm's published profit and loss and balance sheet statements. A firm's profit and loss and balance sheet statements, in turn, are typically created using widely accepted accounting standards and principles. The application of these standards and principles makes it possible to compare the accounting performance of one firm to the accounting performance of other firms, even if those firms are not in the same industry. However, to the extent that these standards and principles are not applied in generating a firm's accounting statements or to the extent that different firms use different accounting standards and principles in generating their statements, it can be difficult to compare the accounting performance of firms. These issues can be particularly challenging when comparing the performance of firms in different countries around the world.

One way to use a firm's accounting statements to measure its competitive advantage is through the use of accounting ratios. **Accounting ratios** are simply numbers taken from a firm's financial statements that are manipulated in ways that describe various aspects of a firm's performance. Some of the most

Strategy in Depth

Recently, some strategic management scholars have developed an alternative approach to characterizing the strategic management process. Rather than starting with mission statements and objectives and then proceeding through the different kinds of analyses that need to be done to choose and implement a strategy, this approach starts by identifying activities that have an impact on the ability of a firm to create and appropriate economic value and then specifying exactly how a particular firm accomplishes these activities. That set of activities that a firm engages in to create and appropriate economic value, in this approach, is called a firm's **business model**.

Probably the most influential approach to identifying a firm's business model was developed by Alex Osterwalder and Yves Pigneur in their book *Business Model Generator*. In the book, a generic business model—not unrelated to the generic value chains that will be introduced in Chapter 3 of this book—is presented. Because this approach enables managers to see the entire landscape of their business in a single page, this model is called the *business model canvas*. This canvas is reproduced in this feature.

The center of the canvas is dominated by a box labeled *Value Propositions*. A firm's value propositions are statements about how it will attempt to create value for its customers, customer problems it is trying to solve through its business operations, which customers it will focus on, and so forth. Identifying a firm's value propositions is very close to identifying its strategy, as presented in Figure 1.4.

Once a firm's value propositions are identified, they have important

The Business Model Canvas

implications for the *Key Activities* a firm needs to engage in, the *Key Resources* it needs to control to engage in those activities, and the *Key Partners* it needs to have to gain access to those resources. The value propositions also help determine critical *Customer Relationships*, the *Channels* a firm needs to use to reach those critical customers, and which *Customer Segments* a firm will address with its products or services.

If a firm's key activities, resources, and partners, on the one hand, and its customer relationships, channels, and segments, on the other hand, all support the execution of its value propositions, then these activities—collectively—will improve a firm's cost structure and revenue streams. Consistent with the definitions presented in this chapter, the difference between a firm's revenues and costs is a measure of the economic value created by a firm.

Different business models—as summarized by the business model canvas—have been given labels to help distinguish them. For example, a "bricks and clicks" business model

(where online retail is integrated with off-line retail) implies a very different set of business activities than a "franchise" business model (where quasi-independent entrepreneurs own and operate retail outlets), which are also different from a "direct" retail model (where firms eliminate in-process inventory by having customers order each product sold), and so forth.

Some scholars have objected to the introduction of the canvas, arguing that it does not add anything fundamental to our understanding of the strategic management process. Others have suggested that some important components of that process—including, for example, organizing to implement a firm's strategy—are left out of the canvas. Others argue that competition is not well represented in the canvas—if numbers of competing firms all adopt the same business model canvas, how is that canvas supposed to enhance the competitive position of any one of those firms? On the other hand, the canvas is a convenient way to summarize a wide variety of firm activities, how those activities are related to one another, and how they ultimately affect a firm's costs and revenues. And while the framework presented in Figure 1.4 will be used to organize the material in the rest of this book, insights from the canvas approach will be incorporated throughout the book as appropriate.

Sources: A. Osterwalder and Y. Pigneur (2010). Business Model Generator. NY: Wiley. G. George and A. J. Bock (2011). The business model in practice and its implications for entrepreneurial research. *Entrepreneurship: Theory and Practice*, 35(1), 83–111. C. Zott, R. Amit, and L. Massa. (2010). The Business Model: Theoretical Roots, Recent Development, and Future Research. Working Paper 862, IESE, Barcelona, Spain.

The Business Model Canvas

Designed for:

Designed by:

On:

Iteration:

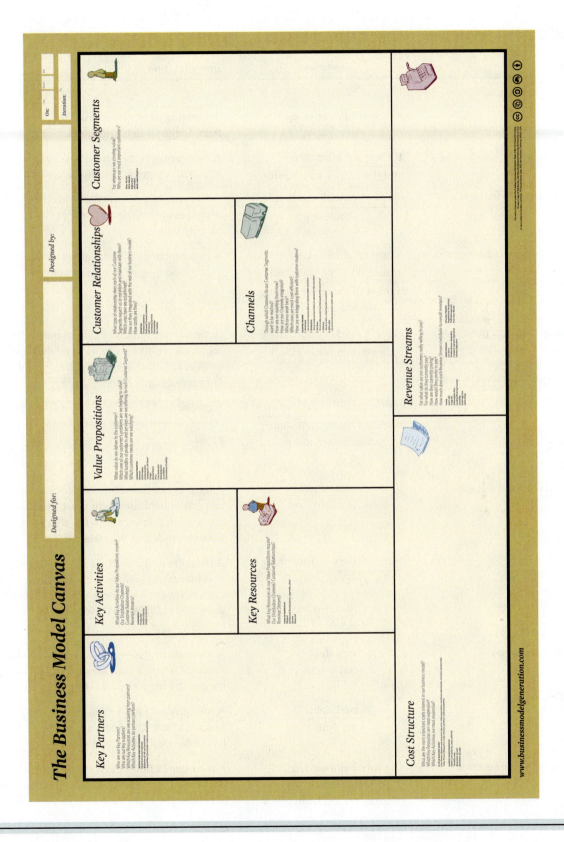

Key Partners

Who are our Key Partners?
Who are our key suppliers?
Which Key Resources are we acquiring from partners?
Which Key Activities do partners perform?

MOTIVATIONS FOR PARTNERSHIPS
Optimization and economy
Reduction of risk and uncertainty
Acquisition of particular resources and activities

Key Activities

What Key Activities do our Value Propositions require?
Our Distribution Channels?
Customer Relationships?
Revenue streams?

CATEGORIES
Production
Problem Solving
Platform/Network

Key Resources

What Key Resources do our Value Propositions require?
Our Distribution Channels? Customer Relationships?
Revenue Streams?

TYPES OF RESOURCES
Physical
Intellectual (brand patents, copyrights, data)
Human
Financial

Value Propositions

What value do we deliver to the customer?
Which one of our customer's problems are we helping to solve?
What bundles of products and services are we offering to each Customer Segment?
Which customer needs are we satisfying?

CHARACTERISTICS
Newness
Performance
Customization
"Getting the Job Done"
Design
Brand/Status
Price
Cost Reduction
Risk Reduction
Accessibility
Convenience/Usability

Customer Relationships

What type of relationship does each of our Customer
Segments expect us to establish and maintain with them?
Which ones have we established?
How are they integrated with the rest of our business model?
How costly are they?

EXAMPLES
Personal assistance
Dedicated Personal Assistance
Self-Service
Automated Services
Communities
Co-creation

Channels

Through which Channels do our Customer Segments
want to be reached?
How are we reaching them now?
How are our Channels integrated?
Which ones work best?
Which ones are most cost-efficient?
How are we integrating them with customer routines?

CHANNEL PHASES
1. Awareness
How do we raise awareness about our company's products and services?
2. Evaluation
How do we help customers evaluate our organization's Value Proposition?
3. Purchase
How do we allow customers to purchase specific products and services?
4. Delivery
How do we deliver a Value Proposition to customers?
5. After sales
How do we provide post-purchase customer support?

Customer Segments

For whom are we creating value?
Who are our most important customers?

Mass Market
Niche Market
Segmented
Diversified
Multi-sided Platform

Cost Structure

What are the most important costs inherent in our business model?
Which Key Resources are most expensive?
Which Key Activities are most expensive?

IS YOUR BUSINESS MORE
Cost Driven (leanest cost structure, low price value proposition, maximum automation, extensive outsourcing)
Value Driven (focused on value creation, premium value proposition)
SAMPLE CHARACTERISTICS
Fixed Costs (salaries, rents, utilities)
Variable costs
Economies of scale
Economies of scope

Revenue Streams

For what value are our customers really willing to pay?
For what do they currently pay?
How are they currently paying?
How would they prefer to pay?
How much does each Revenue Stream contribute to overall revenues?

TYPES
Asset sale
Usage fee
Subscription Fees
Lending/Renting/Leasing
Licensing
Brokerage fees
Advertising

FIXED PRICING
List Price
Product feature dependent
Customer segment dependent
Volume dependent

DYNAMIC PRICING
Negotiation (bargaining)
Yield Management
Real-time-Market

www.businessmodelgeneration.com

TABLE 1.1 Common Ratios to Measure a Firm's Accounting Performance

Ratio	Calculation	Interpretation
Profitability Ratios		
1. ROA	$\dfrac{\text{profit after taxes}}{\text{total assets}}$	A measure of return on total investment in a firm. Larger is usually better.
2. ROE	$\dfrac{\text{profit after taxes}}{\text{total stockholder's equity}}$	A measure of return on total equity investment in a firm. Larger is usually better.
3. Gross profit margin	$\dfrac{\text{sales} - \text{cost of goods sold}}{\text{sales}}$	A measure of sales available to cover operating expenses and still generate a profit. Larger is usually better.
4. Earnings per share (EPS)	$\dfrac{\text{profits (after taxes)} - \text{preferred stock dividends}}{\text{number of shares of common stock outstanding}}$	A measure of profit available to owners of common stock. Larger is usually better.
5. Price earnings ratio (p/e)	$\dfrac{\text{current market price/share}}{\text{after-tax earnings/share}}$	A measure of anticipated firm performance—a high p/e ratio tends to indicate that the stock market anticipates strong future performance. Larger is usually better.
6. Cash flow per share	$\dfrac{\text{after-tax profit} + \text{depreciation}}{\text{number of common shares stock outstanding}}$	A measure of funds available to fund activities above current level of costs. Larger is usually better.
Liquidity Ratios		
1. Current ratio	$\dfrac{\text{current assets}}{\text{current liabilities}}$	A measure of the ability of a firm to cover its current liabilities with assets that can be converted into cash in the short term. Recommended in the range of 2 to 3.
2. Quick ratio	$\dfrac{\text{current assets} - \text{inventory}}{\text{current liabilities}}$	A measure of the ability of a firm to meet its short-term obligations without selling off its current inventory. A ratio of 1 is thought to be acceptable in many industries.
Leverage Ratios		
1. Debt to assets	$\dfrac{\text{total debt}}{\text{total assets}}$	A measure of the extent to which debt has financed a firm's business activities. The higher, the greater the risk of bankruptcy.
2. Debt to equity	$\dfrac{\text{total debt}}{\text{total equity}}$	A measure of the use of debt versus equity to finance a firm's business activities. Generally recommended less than 1.
3. Times interest earned	$\dfrac{\text{profit before interest and taxes}}{\text{total interest charges}}$	A measure of how much a firm's profits can decline and still meet its interest obligations. Should be well above 1.

Ratio	Calculation	Interpretation
Activity Ratios		
1. Inventory turnover	$\dfrac{\text{sales}}{\text{inventory}}$	A measure of the speed with which a firm's inventory is turning over.
2. Accounts receivable turnover	$\dfrac{\text{annual credit sales}}{\text{accounts receivable}}$	A measure of the average time it takes a firm to collect on credit sales.
3. Average collection period	$\dfrac{\text{accounts receivable}}{\text{average daily sales}}$	A measure of the time it takes a firm to receive payment after a sale has been made.

common accounting ratios that can be used to characterize a firm's performance are presented in Table 1.1. These measures of firm accounting performance can be grouped into four categories: (1) **profitability ratios**, or ratios with some measure of profit in the numerator and some measure of firm size or assets in the denominator; (2) **liquidity ratios**, or ratios that focus on the ability of a firm to meet its short-term financial obligations; (3) **leverage ratios**, or ratios that focus on the level of a firm's financial flexibility, including its ability to obtain more debt; and (4) **activity ratios**, or ratios that focus on the level of activity in a firm's business.

Of course, these ratios, by themselves, say very little about a firm. To determine how a firm is performing, its accounting ratios must be compared with some standard. In general, that standard is the average of accounting ratios of other firms in the same industry. Using ratio analysis, a firm earns **above average accounting performance** when its performance is greater than the industry average. Such firms typically have competitive advantages, sustained or otherwise. A firm earns **average accounting performance** when its performance is equal to the industry average. These firms generally enjoy only competitive parity. A firm earns **below average accounting performance** when its performance is less than the industry average. These firms generally experience competitive disadvantages.

Consider, for example, the performance of Apple Inc. Apple's financial statements for 2011 and 2012 are presented in Table 1.2. Losses in this table would be presented in parentheses. Several ratio measures of accounting performance are calculated for Apple in these two years in Table 1.2.

Apple's sales increased dramatically from 2011 to 2012, from just over $108 billion to just over $156 billion. Profitability accounting ratios suggest its profitability during this same time period, from a return on total assets (ROA) of 0.217 to 0.237 and from a return on equity (ROE) of 0.33 to 0.353. Much of this increase may be attributable to Apple's increase in its gross profit margin from 0.408 to 0.439. So its sales went up, its overall profitability up, as did its gross profit margin. This pattern suggests that Apple was able to increase the prices of the products it was selling in 2012 compared with 2011, either by introducing new products or more expensive versions of its current products or both.

Apple's liquidity and leverage ratios remained largely unchanged over these two years. With current and quick ratios well over 1, it's pretty clear that Apple had enough cash on hand to respond to any short-term financial needs. And its leverage ratios suggest that it still had some opportunities to borrow money for long-term investments should the need arise.

Overall, the information in Tables 1.2 and 1.3 suggests that Apple Inc., in 2011 and 2012, was, financially speaking, very healthy.

TABLE 1.2 Apple Inc.'s Financial Statements for 2011 and 2012 (numbers in millions of dollars)

	2011	2012
Net sales	108,249	156,508
Cost of goods sold	64,431	87,846
Gross margin	43,818	68,662
Selling, general, and administrative expenses	7,599	10,040
R & D expense	2,429	3,381
Total operating expenses	10,028	13,421
Operating income (loss)	33,790	55,241
Total income (loss), before taxes	33,375	55,763
Provision for taxes	8,076	14,052
Net income, after taxes	25,299	41,711
Inventories	776	791
Total current assets	44,988	57,653
Total assets	116,371	176,064
Total current liabilities	27,970	38,542
Total debt	39,756	57,756
Total shareholders' equity	76,615	118,210
Retained earnings	62,841	

Economic Measures of Competitive Advantage

The great advantage of accounting measures of competitive advantage is that they are relatively easy to compute. All publicly traded firms must make their accounting statements available to the public. Even privately owned firms will typically release some information about their accounting performance. From these statements, it is quite easy to calculate various accounting ratios. One can learn a lot about a firm's competitive position by comparing these ratios to industry averages.

However, accounting measures of competitive advantage have at least one significant limitation. Earlier, economic profit was defined as the difference between the perceived benefit associated with purchasing a firm's products or services and the cost of producing and selling that product or service. However, one important component of cost typically is not included in most accounting measures of competitive advantage: the cost of the capital a firm employs to produce and sell its products. The **cost of capital** is the rate of return that a firm promises

TABLE 1.3 Some Accounting Ratios for Apple Inc. in 2011 and 2012

	2011	2012
ROA	$25{,}299/116{,}371 = 0.217$	$41{,}711/176{,}064 = 0.237$
ROE	$25{,}299/76{,}615 = 0.353$	$41{,}711/118{,}210 = 0.353$
Gross profit margin	$\dfrac{108{,}249 - 64{,}431}{108{,}249} = 0.405$	$\dfrac{156{,}508 - 87{,}846}{156{,}508} = 0.439$
Current ratio	$44{,}988/27{,}976 = 1.61$	$57{,}653/653 = 1.50$
Quick ratio	$\dfrac{44{,}988 - 776}{27{,}970} = 1.58$	$\dfrac{57{,}653 - 791}{38{,}542} = 1.48$
Debt to assets	$39{,}756/116.371 = 0.341$	$057{,}756/176{,}064 = 0.323$
Debt to equity	$39{,}756/76{,}615 = 0.519$	$57{,}756/118{,}210 = 0.489$

to pay its suppliers of capital to induce them to invest in the firm. Once these investments are made, a firm can use this capital to produce and sell products and services. However, a firm must provide the promised return to its sources of capital if it expects to obtain more investment capital in the future. **Economic measures of competitive advantage** compare a firm's level of return to its cost of capital instead of to the average level of return in the industry.

Generally, there are two broad categories of sources of capital: **debt** (capital from banks and bondholders) and **equity** (capital from individuals and institutions that purchase a firm's stock). The **cost of debt** is equal to the interest that a firm must pay its debt holders (adjusted for taxes) in order to induce those debt holders to lend money to a firm. The **cost of equity** is equal to the rate of return a firm must promise its equity holders in order to induce these individuals and institutions to invest in a firm. A firm's **weighted average cost of capital (WACC)** is simply the percentage of a firm's total capital, which is debt times the cost of debt plus the percentage of a firm's total capital; that is, equity times the cost of equity.

Conceptually, a firm's cost of capital is the level of performance a firm must attain if it is to satisfy the economic objectives of two of its critical stakeholders: debt holders and equity holders. A firm that earns above its cost of capital is likely to be able to attract additional capital because debt holders and equity holders will scramble to make additional funds available for this firm. Such a firm is said to be earning **above normal economic performance** and will be able to use its access to cheap capital to grow and expand its business. A firm that earns its cost of capital is said to have **normal economic performance**. This level of performance is said to be "normal" because this is the level of performance that most of a firm's equity and debt holders expect. Firms that have normal economic performance are able to gain access to the capital they need to survive, although they are not prospering. Growth opportunities may be somewhat limited for these firms. In general, firms with competitive parity usually have normal economic performance. A firm that earns less than its cost of capital is in the process of liquidating. **Below normal economic performance** implies that a firm's debt and equity holders will be looking for alternative ways to invest their money, someplace where they can earn at least what they expect to earn; that is, normal economic performance. Unless a firm with below normal performance changes, its long-term viability will come into question. Obviously, firms that have a competitive disadvantage generally have below normal economic performance.

Measuring a firm's performance relative to its cost of capital has several advantages for strategic analysis. Foremost among these is the notion that a firm that earns at least its cost of capital is satisfying two of its most important stakeholders: debt holders and equity holders. Despite the advantages of comparing a firm's performance to its cost of capital, this approach has some important limitations as well. For example, it can sometimes be difficult to calculate a firm's cost of capital. This is especially true if a firm is **privately held**—that is, if it has stock that is not traded on public stock markets or if it is a division of a larger company. In these situations, it may be necessary to use accounting ratios to measure a firm's performance. Moreover, some have suggested that although accounting measures of competitive advantage understate the importance of a firm's equity and debt holders in evaluating a firm's performance, economic measures of competitive advantage exaggerate the importance of these two particular stakeholders, often to the disadvantage of other stakeholders in a firm. These issues are discussed in more detail in the Ethics and Strategy feature.

Figure 1.5 Competitive Advantage and Firm Performance

The Relationship Between Economic and Accounting Performance Measures

The correlation between economic and accounting measures of competitive advantage is high. That is, firms that perform well using one of these measures usually perform well using the other. Conversely, firms that do poorly using one of these measures normally do poorly using the other. Thus, the relationships among competitive advantage, accounting performance, and economic performance depicted in Figure 1.5 generally hold.

However, it is possible for a firm to have above average accounting performance and simultaneously have below normal economic performance. This could happen, for example, when a firm is not earning its cost of capital but has above industry average accounting performance. Also, it is possible for a firm to have below average accounting performance and above normal economic performance. This could happen when a firm has a very low cost of capital and is earning at a rate in excess of this cost, but still below the industry average.

Emergent Versus Intended Strategies

The simplest way of thinking about a firm's strategy is to assume that firms choose and implement their strategies exactly as described by the strategic management process in Figure 1.1. That is, they begin with a well-defined mission and objectives, they engage in external and internal analyses, they make their strategic choices, and then they implement their strategies. And there is no doubt that this describes the process for choosing and implementing a strategy in many firms.

For example, FedEx, a world leader in the overnight delivery business, entered this industry with a very well-developed theory about how to gain competitive advantages in this business. Indeed, Fred Smith, the founder of FedEx (originally known as Federal Express), first articulated this theory as a student in a term paper for an undergraduate business class at Yale University. Legend has it that he received only a "C" on the paper, but the company that was founded on the theory of competitive advantage in the overnight delivery business developed in that paper has done extremely well. Founded in 1971, FedEx had 2013 sales just over $44 billion and profits of $2.5 billion.[9]

Other firms have also begun operations with a well-defined, well-formed strategy but have found it necessary to modify this strategy so much once it is actually implemented in the marketplace that it bears little resemblance to the theory with which the firm started. **Emergent strategies** are theories of how to gain competitive advantage in an industry that emerge over time or that have been radically reshaped once they are initially implemented.[10] The relationship between a firm's intended and emergent strategies is depicted in Figure 1.6.

Figure 1.6 Mintzberg's Analysis of the Relationship Between Intended and Realized Strategies

Source: Reprinted from "Strategy formation in an adhocracy," by H. Mintzberg and A. McHugh, published in *Administrative Science Quarterly*, 30, No. 2, June 1985, by permission of Administrative Science Quarterly. Copyright © 1985 by Administrative Science Quarterly.

Several well-known firms have strategies that are, at least partly, emergent. For example, J&J was originally a supplier of antiseptic gauze and medical plasters. It had no consumer business at all. Then, in response to complaints about irritation caused by some of its medical plasters, J&J began enclosing a small packet of talcum powder with each of the medical plasters it sold. Soon customers were asking to purchase the talcum powder by itself, and the company introduced "Johnson's Toilet and Baby Powder." Later, an employee invented a ready-to-use bandage for his wife. It seems she often cut herself while using knives in the kitchen. When J&J marketing managers learned of this invention, they decided to introduce it into the marketplace. J&J's Band-Aid products have since become the largest-selling brand category at J&J. Overall, J&J's intended strategy was to compete in the medical products market, but its emergent consumer products strategies now generate more than 40 percent of total corporate sales.

Another firm with what turns out to be an emergent strategy is the Marriott Corporation. Marriott was originally in the restaurant business. In the late 1930s, Marriott owned and operated eight restaurants. However, one of these restaurants was close to a Washington, D.C., airport. Managers at this restaurant noticed that airline passengers would come into the restaurant to purchase food to eat on their trip. J. Willard Marriott, the founder of the Marriott Corporation, noticed this trend and negotiated a deal with Eastern Airlines whereby Marriott's restaurant would deliver prepackaged lunches directly to Eastern's planes. This arrangement was later extended to include American Airlines. Over time, providing food service to airlines became a major business segment for Marriott. Although Marriott's initial intended strategy was to operate in the restaurant business, it became engaged in the emergent food service business at more than 100 airports throughout the world.[11]

Some firms have almost entirely emergent strategies. PEZ Candy, Inc., for example, manufactures and sells small plastic candy dispensers with cartoon and movie character heads, along with candy refills. This privately held firm has made few efforts to speed its growth, yet demand for current and older PEZ products continues to grow. In the 1990s, PEZ doubled the size of its manufacturing operation to keep up with demand. Old PEZ dispensers have become something of a collector's item. Several national conferences on PEZ collecting have been held, and some rare PEZ dispensers were once

Ethics and Strategy

Considerable debate exists about the role of a firm's equity and debt holders versus its other stakeholders in defining and measuring a firm's performance. These other stakeholders include a firm's suppliers, its customers, its employees, and the communities within which it does business. Like equity and debt holders, these other stakeholders make investments in a firm. They, too, expect some compensation for making these investments.

On the one hand, some argue that if a firm maximizes the wealth of its equity holders, it will automatically satisfy all of its other stakeholders. This view of the firm depends on what is called the *residual claimants* view of equity holders. This view is that equity holders only receive payment on their investment in a firm after all legitimate claims by a firm's other stakeholders are satisfied. Thus, a firm's equity holders, in this view, only receive payment on their investments after the firm's employees are compensated, its suppliers are paid, its customers are satisfied, and its obligations to the communities within which it does business have been met. By maximizing returns to its equity holders, a firm is ensuring that its other stakeholders are fully compensated for investing in a firm.

Stockholders Versus Stakeholders

On the other hand, some argue that the interests of equity holders and a firm's other stakeholders often collide and that a firm that maximizes the wealth of its equity holders does not necessarily satisfy its other stakeholders. For example, whereas a firm's customers may want it to sell higher-quality products at lower prices, a firm's equity holders may want it to sell low-quality products at higher prices; this obviously would increase the amount of money left over to pay off a firm's equity holders. Also, whereas a firm's employees may want it to adopt policies that lead to steady performance over long periods of time—because this will lead to stable employment—a firm's equity holders may be more interested in its

maximizing its short-term profitability, even if this hurts employment stability. The interests of equity holders and the broader community may also clash, especially when it is very costly for a firm to engage in environmentally friendly behaviors that could reduce its short-term performance.

This debate manifests itself in a variety of ways. For example, many groups that oppose the globalization of the U.S. economy do so on the basis that firms make production, marketing, and other strategic choices in ways that maximize profits for equity holders, often to the detriment of a firm's other stakeholders. These people are concerned about the effects of globalization on workers, on the environment, and on the cultures in the developing economies where global firms sometimes locate their manufacturing and other operations. Managers in global firms respond by saying that they have a responsibility to maximize the wealth of their equity holders. Given the passions that surround this debate, it is unlikely that these issues will be resolved soon.

Sources: T. Copeland, T. Koller, and J. Murrin (1995). *Valuation: Measuring and managing the value of companies.* New York: Wiley; L. Donaldson (1990). "The ethereal hand: Organizational economics and management theory." *Academy of Review,* 15, pp. 369–381.

auctioned at Christie's. This demand has enabled PEZ to raise its prices without increases in advertising, sales personnel, and movie tie-ins so typical in the candy industry.[12]

Of course, one might argue that emergent strategies are only important when a firm fails to implement the strategic management process effectively. After all, if this process is implemented effectively, then would it ever be necessary to fundamentally alter the strategies that a firm has chosen?

In reality, it will often be the case that at the time a firm chooses its strategies, some of the information needed to complete the strategic management

Strategy in the Emerging Enterprise

Every entrepreneur—and would-be entrepreneur—is familiar with the drill: If you want to receive financial support for your idea, you need to write a business plan. Business plans are typically 25 to 30 pages long. Most begin with an Executive Summary; then move quickly to describing an entrepreneur's business idea, why customers will be interested in this idea, how much it will cost to realize this idea; and usually end with a series of charts that project a firm's cash flows over the next five years.

Of course, because these business ideas are often new and untried, no one—including the entrepreneur—really knows if customers will like the idea well enough to buy from this firm. No one really knows how much it will cost to build these products or produce these services—they've never been built or produced before. And, certainly, no one really knows what a firm's cash flows will look like over the next five years or so. Indeed, it is not unusual for entrepreneurs to constantly revise their business plan to reflect new information they have obtained about their business idea and its viability. It is not even unusual for entrepreneurs to fundamentally revise their central business idea as they begin to pursue it in earnest.

Emergent Strategies and Entrepreneurship

The truth is, most decisions about whether to create an entrepreneurial firm take place under conditions of high uncertainty and high unpredictability. In this setting, the ability to adjust on the fly, to be flexible, and to recast a business idea in ways that are more consistent with customer interests may be a central determinant of a firm's ultimate success. This, of course, suggests that emergent strategies are likely to be very important for entrepreneurial firms.

This view of entrepreneurship is different from the popular stereotype. In the popular view, entrepreneurs are assumed to be hit by a "blinding rush of insight" about a previously unexploited market opportunity. In reality, entrepreneurs are more likely to experience a series of smaller insights about market opportunities.

But, typically, these periods of insight will be preceded by periods of disappointment, as an entrepreneur discovers that what he or she thought was a new and complete business model is, in fact, either not new or not complete or both. In the popular view, entrepreneurship is all about creativity, about being able to see opportunities others cannot see. In reality, entrepreneurship may be more about tenacity than creativity because entrepreneurs build their firms step by step out of the uncertainty and unpredictability that plague their decision making. In the popular view, entrepreneurs can envision their success well before it occurs. In reality, although entrepreneurs may dream about financial and other forms of success, they usually do not know the exact path they will take, nor what success will actually look like, until after they have arrived.

Sources: S. Alvarez and J. Barney (2005). "How do entrepreneurs organize firms under conditions of uncertainty?" *Journal of Management*, 31(5), pp. 776–793; S. Alvarez and J. Barney (2004). "Organizing rent generation and appropriation: Toward a theory of the entrepreneurial firm," *Journal of Business Venturing*, 19, pp. 621–636; W. Gartner (1988). "Who is the entrepreneur? is the wrong question." *American Journal of Small Business*, 12, pp. 11–32; S. Sarasvathy (2001). "Causation and effectuation: Toward a theoretical shift from economic inevitability to entrepreneurial contingency." *Academy of Management Review*, 26, pp. 243–264.

process may simply not be available. As suggested earlier, in this setting a firm simply has to make its "best bet" about how competition in an industry is likely to emerge. In such a situation, a firm's ability to change its strategies quickly to respond to emergent trends in an industry may be as important a source of competitive advantage as the ability to complete the strategic management process. For all these reasons, emergent strategies may be particularly important for entrepreneurial firms, as described in the Strategy in the Emerging Enterprise feature.

Why You Need to Know About Strategy

At first glance, it may not be obvious why students would need to know about strategy and the strategic management process. After all, the process of choosing and implementing a strategy is normally the responsibility of senior managers in a firm, and most students are unlikely to be senior managers in large corporations until many years after graduation. Why study strategy and the strategic management process now?

In fact, there are at least three very compelling reasons why it is important to study strategy and the strategic management process now. First, it can give you the tools you need to evaluate the strategies of firms that may employ you. We have already seen how a firm's strategy can have a huge impact on its competitive advantage. Your career opportunities in a firm are largely determined by that firm's competitive advantage. Thus, in choosing a place to begin or continue your career, understanding a firm's theory of how it is going to gain a competitive advantage can be essential in evaluating the career opportunities in a firm. Firms with strategies that are unlikely to be a source of competitive advantage will rarely provide the same career opportunities as firms with strategies that do generate such advantages. Being able to distinguish between these types of strategies can be very important in your career choices.

Second, once you are working for a firm, understanding that firm's strategies, and your role in implementing those strategies, can be very important for your personal success. It will often be the case that expectations of how you perform your function in a firm will change, depending on the strategies a firm is pursuing. For example, as we will see in Part 2 of this book, the accounting function plays a very different role in a firm pursuing a cost leadership strategy versus a product differentiation strategy. Marketing and manufacturing also play very different roles in these two types of strategies. Your effectiveness in a firm can be reduced by doing accounting, marketing, and manufacturing as if your firm were pursuing a cost leadership strategy when it is actually pursuing a product differentiation strategy.

Finally, although it is true that strategic choices are generally limited to very experienced senior managers in large organizations, in smaller and entrepreneurial firms many employees end up being involved in the strategic management process. If you choose to work for one of these smaller or entrepreneurial firms—even if it is not right after graduation—you could very easily find yourself to be part of the strategic management team, implementing the strategic management process and choosing which strategies this firm should implement. In this setting, a familiarity with the essential concepts that underlie the choice and implementation of a strategy may turn out to be very helpful.

Summary

A firm's strategy is its theory of how to gain competitive advantages. These theories, like all theories, are based on assumptions and hypotheses about how competition in an industry is likely to evolve. When those assumptions and hypotheses are consistent with the actual evolution of competition in an industry, a firm's strategy is more likely to be able to generate a competitive advantage.

One way that a firm can choose its strategies is through the strategic management process. This process is a set of analyses and decisions that increase the likelihood that a firm will be able to choose a "good" strategy, that is, a strategy that will lead to a competitive advantage.

The strategic management process begins when a firm identifies its mission, or its long-term purpose. This mission is often written down in the form of a mission statement. Mission statements, by themselves, can have no impact on performance, enhance a firm's performance, or hurt a firm's performance. Objectives are measurable milestones firms use to evaluate whether they are accomplishing their missions. External and internal analyses are the processes through which a firm identifies its environmental threats and opportunities and organizational strengths and weaknesses. Armed with these analyses, it is possible for a firm to engage in strategic choice. Strategies can be classified into two categories: business-level strategies (including cost leadership and product differentiation) and corporate-level strategies (including vertical integration, strategic alliances, diversification, and mergers and acquisitions). Strategy implementation follows strategic choice and involves choosing organizational structures, management control policies, and compensation schemes that support a firm's strategies.

The ultimate objective of the strategic management process is the realization of competitive advantage. A firm has a competitive advantage if it is creating more economic value than its rivals. Economic value is defined as the difference between the perceived customer benefits from purchasing a product or service from a firm and the total economic cost of developing and selling that product or service. Competitive advantages can be temporary or sustained. Competitive parity exists when a firm creates the same economic value as its rivals. A competitive disadvantage exists when a firm creates less economic value than its rivals, and it can be either temporary or sustained.

Two popular measures of a firm's competitive advantage are accounting performance and economic performance. Accounting performance measures competitive advantage using various ratios calculated from a firm's profit and loss and balance sheet statements. A firm's accounting performance is compared with the average level of accounting performance in a firm's industry. Economic performance compares a firm's level of return with its cost of capital. A firm's cost of capital is the rate of return it had to promise to pay to its debt and equity investors to induce them to invest in the firm.

Although many firms use the strategic management process to choose and implement strategies, not all strategies are chosen this way. Some strategies emerge over time, as firms respond to unanticipated changes in the structure of competition in an industry.

Students need to understand strategy and the strategic management process for at least three reasons. First, it can help in deciding where to work. Second, once you have a job it can help you to be successful in that job. Finally, if you have a job in a small or entrepreneurial firm you may become involved in strategy and the strategic management process from the very beginning.

MyManagementLab®

Go to **mymanagementlab.com** to complete the problems marked with this icon ⭐.

Challenge Questions

1.1. Some firms publicize their corporate mission statements by including them in annual reports, on company letterheads, and in corporate advertising. What, if anything, does this practice say about the ability of these mission statements to be sources of sustained competitive advantage for a firm?

⭐**1.2.** Why would including a corporate mission statement on company letterhead or in corporate advertising be seen as a source of sustained competitive advantage?

1.3. Little empirical evidence indicates that having a formal, written mission statement improves a firm's performance. Yet many firms spend a great deal of time and money developing mission statements. Why?

1.4. Explain if it is possible to distinguish between an emergent strategy and an ad hoc rationalization of a firm's past decisions.

1.5. Both external and internal analyses are important in the strategic management process. Is the order in which these analyses are conducted important?

1.6. If the order of analyses is important, which should come first: external analysis or internal analysis?

1.7. Concerning external analysis and internal analysis, if the order of analyses is not important, why not?

1.8. Will a firm that has a sustained competitive disadvantage necessarily go out of business?

1.9. Will a firm with below average accounting performance over a long period of time necessarily go out of business?

1.10. Will a firm with below normal economic performance over a long period of time necessarily go out of business?

1.11. Can more than one firm have a competitive advantage in an industry at the same time?

⭐ **1.12.** Is it possible for a firm to simultaneously have a competitive advantage and a competitive disadvantage?

Problem Set

1.13. Write objectives for each of the following mission statements.

(a) We will be a leader in pharmaceutical innovation.
(b) Customer satisfaction is our primary goal.
(c) We promise on-time delivery.
(d) Product quality is our first priority.

1.14. Rewrite each of the following objectives to make them more helpful in guiding a firm's strategic management process.

(a) We will introduce five new drugs.
(b) We will understand our customers' needs.
(c) Almost all of our products will be delivered on time.
(d) The number of defects in our products will fall.

1.15. Do firms with the following financial results have below normal, normal, or above normal economic performance?

(a) ROA = 14.3%, WACC = 12.8%
(b) ROA = 4.3%, WACC = 6.7%
(c) ROA = 6.5%, WACC = 9.2%
(d) ROA = 8.3%, WACC = 8.3%

1.16. Do these same firms have below average, average, or above average accounting performance?

(a) ROA = 14.3%, Industry Avg. ROA = 15.2%
(b) ROA = 4.3%, Industry Avg. ROA = 4.1%
(c) ROA = 6.5%, Industry Avg. ROA = 6.1%
(d) ROA = 8.3%, Industry Avg. ROA = 9.4%

1.17. Is it possible for a firm to simultaneously earn above normal economic returns and below average accounting returns? What about below normal economic returns and above average accounting returns? Why or why not? If this can occur, which measure of performance is more reliable: economic performance or accounting performance? Explain.

1.18. Examine the following corporate Web sites and determine if the strategies pursued by these firms were emergent, deliberate, or both emergent and deliberate. Justify your answer with facts from the Web sites.

(a) www.walmart.com
(b) www.homedepot.com
(c) www.cardinal.com

1.19. Using the information provided, calculate this firm's ROA, ROE, gross profit margin, and quick ratio. If this firm's WACC is 6.6 percent and the average firm in its industry has an ROA of 8 percent, is this firm earning above or below normal economic performance and above or below average accounting performance?

Net sales	6,134	Operating cash	3,226	Net other operating assets	916
Cost of goods sold	(4,438)	Accounts receivable	681	Total assets	5,161
Selling, general administrative expenses	(996)	Inventories	20	Net current liabilities	1,549
Other current assets	0	Long-term debt	300	Other expenses	(341)
Total current assets	3,927	Deferred income taxes	208	Interest income	72
Gross properties, plant, equipment	729	Preferred stock	0	Interest expense	(47)
Retained earnings	0	Provision for taxes	(75)	Accumulated depreciation	(411)
Common stock	3,104	Other income	245	Book value of fixed assets	318
Other liabilities	0	Net income	554	Goodwill	0
Total liabilities and equity	5,161				

MyManagementLab®

Go to **mymanagementlab.com** for Auto-graded writing questions as well as the following Assisted-graded writing questions:

⭐ **1.20.** Describe what visionary firms may do to earn substantially higher returns than average firms.

⭐ **1.21.** What is the relationship between a firm's business model and its value proposition?

End Notes

1. This approach to defining strategy was first suggested in Drucker, P. (1994). "The theory of business." *Harvard Business Review*, 75, September–October, pp. 95–105.
2. This approach to defining strategy was first suggested in Drucker, P. (1994). "The theory of business." *Harvard Business Review*, 75, September–October, pp. 95–105.
3. See www.enron.com.
4. See Emshwiller, J., D. Solomon, and R. Smith. (2004). "Lay is indicted for his role in Enron collapse." *The Wall Street Journal*, July 8, pp. A1+; Gilmartin, R. (2005). "They fought the law." *BusinessWeek*, January 10, pp. 82–83.
5. These performance results were presented originally in Collins, J. C., and J. I. Porras. (1997). *Built to last: Successful habits of visionary companies*. New York: HarperCollins.
6. Collins, J. C., and J. I. Porras. (1997). *Built to last: successful habits of visionary companies*. New York: HarperCollins.
7. See Theroux, J., and J. Hurstak. (1993). "Ben & Jerry's Homemade Ice Cream Inc.: Keeping the mission(s) alive." Harvard Business School Case No. 9-392-025; Applebaum, A. (2000). "Smartmoney.com: Unilever feels hungry, buys Ben & Jerry's." *The Wall Street Journal*, April 13, pp. B1+.
8. This definition of competitive advantage has a long history in the field of strategic management. For example, it is closely related to the definitions provided in Barney (1986, 1991) and Porter (1985). It is also consistent with the value-based approach described in Peteraf (2001), Brandenburger and Stuart (1999), and Besanko, Dranove, and Shanley (2000). For more discussion on this definition, see Peteraf and Barney (2004).
9. FedEx's history is described in Trimble, V. (1993). *Overnight success: Federal Express and Frederick Smith, its renegade creator*. New York: Crown.
10. Mintzberg, H. (1978). "Patterns in strategy formulation." *Management Science*, 24(9), pp. 934–948; and Mintzberg, H. (1985). "Of strategies, deliberate and emergent." *Strategic Management Journal*, 6(3), pp. 257–272. Mintzberg has been most influential in expanding the study of strategy to include emergent strategies.
11. The J&J and Marriott emergent strategy stories can be found in Collins, J. C., and J. I. Porras. (1997). *Built to last: Successful habits of visionary companies*. New York: HarperCollins.
12. See McCarthy, M. J. (1993). "The PEZ fancy is hard to explain, let alone justify." *The Wall Street Journal*, March 10, p. A1, for a discussion of PEZ's surprising emergent strategy.

2

Evaluating a Firm's External Environment

LEARNING OBJECTIVES *After reading this chapter, you should be able to:*

1. Describe the dimensions of the general environment facing a firm and how this environment can affect a firm's opportunities and threats.

2. Describe how the structure-conduct-performance (S-C-P) model suggests that industry structure can influence a firm's competitive choices.

3. Describe the five environmental threats and indicators of when each of these forces will improve or reduce the attractiveness of an industry.

4. Describe how rivals and substitutes differ.

5. Discuss the role of complements in analyzing competition within an industry.

6. Describe four generic industry structures and specific strategic opportunities in those industries.

7. Describe the impact of tariffs, quotas, and other non-tariff barriers to entry on the cost of entry into new geographic markets.

MyManagementLab®

⭐ **Improve Your Grade!**

Over 10 million students improved their results using the Pearson MyLabs.
Visit **mymanagementlab.com** for simulations, tutorials, and end-of-chapter problems.

---

iTunes and the Streaming Challenge

It was a normal Wednesday, February 24, 2010. Seventy-one-year-old Louie Sulce, from Woodstock, Georgia, had just finished downloading a song from one of his favorite country artists—Johnny Cash's "Guess Things Happen that Way"—from the iTunes store. Suddenly, the phone rang.

It was Steve Jobs, CEO of Apple calling to congratulate Mr. Sulce for downloading the 10 billionth song from the iTunes store. For being "Mr. 10 Billion," Mr. Sulce received a $10,000 iTunes store gift card.

This story is interesting on several dimensions. First, it signaled the remarkable growth of iTunes. Founded on April 28, 2003, iTunes grew steadily, reaching the 1 billion download mark less than three years later, on February 23, 2006. But with the growing popularity of Apple's iPod MP3 player and, later, its iPhone and iPad, iTunes downloads began to take off. It took less than a year to go from 1 billion to 2 billion downloads, less than six months to get to 3 billion, and so forth. By February 6, 2013, more than 25 billion songs had been downloaded from iTunes. By September 12, 2006, iTunes had 88 percent of the legal download market in the United States.

And this growth wasn't limited to just downloaded songs. Over the years, the range of products sold by iTunes has expanded from songs to movies, television shows, video games, and other media products.

Not surprisingly, iTunes revenues grew right along with the growth in iTunes downloads. With first-year revenues of $278 million, iTunes revenues had grown to $2.4 billion in the first *quarter* of 2013.

But Mr. Sulce's story is interesting in another way as well—a 71-year-old man was using iTunes to download music. By 2010, iTunes was no longer a Web site for technologically sophisticated young people to buy their music; it was the place where everyone bought their music. By June 2013, iTunes had more than 575 million active accounts supporting 315 million mobile devices in 119 countries. It has been the largest music vendor in the United States since April 2008 and the largest in the world since February 2010.

But such success and growth were bound to attract competition. In 2007, Amazon became an important rival for iTunes as it began selling on-line music downloads at a price lower than iTunes. In 2013, Amazon's share of the U.S. music download market had risen to 22 percent—still smaller than iTunes' share, but significant growth nevertheless.

Perhaps even more importantly, some important substitutes for iTunes had begun to emerge. In particular, music streaming services—where consumers listen to but do not buy music—were beginning to grow. In 2013, two versions of these streaming services existed: subscription services—including one Spotify service, Rdio, and Rhapsody—where consumers paid a monthly fee for unlimited music access and advertising-supported services—including a second Spotify service and Pandora—that provided unlimited access for free but required consumers to listen to commercials periodically.

Streaming services had several perceived advantages over iTunes. For example, these services provided instant access to a much wider variety of music than in most people's purchased collections. Also, users of these services did not have to use so much of the memory in their devices storing music. By 2013, iTunes' share of the music download business had dropped from 69 percent to 63 percent, mostly due to the increased popularity of music streaming services.

Indeed, in 2013, iTunes announced that it would introduce an advertising-supported streaming product on the iTunes store. Whether this will be enough to enable iTunes to retain its dominant position in the download industry remains to be seen.

Sources: Andy Fixmer. April 25, 2013. "Apple's 10-Year-Old iTunes Loses Ground to Streaming," http://www.businessweek.com/articles/2013-04-25/apples-10-year-old-itunes-loses-ground-to-streaming. Accessed July 3, 2013; Apple Press Release. "iTunes Serves Up 10 Billionth Song Download," February 2010. Accessed July 3, 2013; E. Smith (2006) "Can Anybody Catch iTunes?" *Wall Street Journal*, November 27, pp. R1+.

The strategic management process described in Chapter 1 suggested that one of the critical determinants of a firm's strategies is the threats and opportunities in its competitive environment. If a firm understands these threats and opportunities, it is one step closer to being able to choose and implement a "good strategy"; that is, a strategy that leads to competitive advantage.

iTunes is clearly in this position in the music download industry. Despite its dominant position, rivals—like Amazon—and substitutes—like Spotify and Pandora—have both emerged.

Of course, it is not enough to recognize that it is important to understand the threats and opportunities in a firm's competitive environment. A set of tools that managers can apply to systematically complete this external analysis as part of the strategic management process is also required. These tools must be rooted in a strong theoretical base, so that managers know that they have not been developed in an arbitrary way. Fortunately, such tools exist and will be described in this chapter.

Understanding a Firm's General Environment

Any analysis of the threats and opportunities facing a firm must begin with an understanding of the general environment within which a firm operates. This **general environment** consists of broad trends in the context within which a firm operates that can have an impact on a firm's strategic choices. As depicted in Figure 2.1, the general environment consists of six interrelated elements: technological change, demographic trends, cultural trends, the economic climate, legal and political conditions, and specific international events. Each of these elements of the general environment is discussed in this section.

In 1899, Charles H. Duell, commissioner of the U.S. patent office, said, "Everything that can be invented has been invented."[1] He was wrong. Technological changes over the past few years have had significant impacts on the ways firms do business and on the products and services they sell.

Figure 2.1 The General Environment Facing Firms

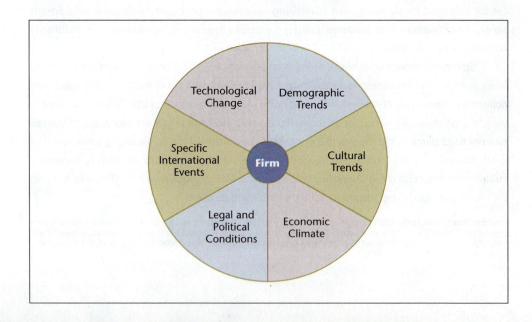

These impacts have been most obvious for technologies that build on digital information—computers, the Internet, cell phones, and so forth. Many of us routinely use digital products or services that did not exist just a few years ago. However, rapid technological innovation has not been restricted to digital technologies. Biotechnology has also made rapid progress over the past 10 years. New kinds of medicines are now being created. As important, biotechnology holds the promise of developing entirely new ways of both preventing and treating disease.[2]

Technological change creates both opportunity, as firms begin to explore how to use technology to create new products and services, and threats, as technological change forces firms to rethink their technological strategies.

A second element of the general environment facing firms is demographic trends. **Demographics** is the distribution of individuals in a society in terms of age, sex, marital status, income, ethnicity, and other personal attributes that may determine buying patterns. Understanding this basic information about a population can help a firm determine whether its products or services will appeal to customers and how many potential customers for these products or services it might have.

Some demographic trends are very well known. For example, everyone has heard of the "baby boomers"—those who were born shortly after World War II. This large population has had an impact on the strategies of many firms, especially as the boomers have grown older and have had more disposable income. However, other demographic groups have also had an impact on firm strategies. This is especially true in the automobile industry. For example, minivans were invented to meet the demands of "soccer moms"—women who live in the suburbs and have young children. The Nissan Xterra seems to have been designed for the so-called Generation Y—young men and women currently in their 20s and either just out of college or anticipating graduation shortly.

In the United States, an important demographic trend over the past 20 years has been the growth of the Hispanic population. In 1990, the percentage of the U.S. population that was African American was greater than the percentage that was Hispanic. However, by 2000, people of Latin descent outnumbered African Americans. Currently, Hispanics constitute almost 15 percent of the U.S. population, whereas the percentage of African Americans remains constant at less than 8 percent. These trends are particularly notable in the South and Southwest. For example, more than 36 percent of children under 18 in Houston are Hispanic, 39 percent in Miami and San Diego, 53 percent in Los Angeles, and more than 61 percent in San Antonio.[3]

Of course, firms are aware of this growing population and its buying power. Indeed, Hispanic disposable income in the United States jumped 29 percent, to $652 billion, from 2001 to 2003. In response, firms have begun marketing directly to the U.S. Hispanic population. In one year, Procter & Gamble spent $90 million marketing directly to Spanish-speaking customers. Procter & Gamble has also formed a 65-person bilingual team to manage the marketing of products to Hispanics. Indeed, Procter & Gamble expects that the Hispanic population will be the cornerstone of its sales growth in North America.[4]

Firms can try to exploit their understanding of a particular demographic segment of the population to create a competitive advantage—as Procter & Gamble is doing with the U.S. Hispanic population—but focusing on too narrow a demographic segment can limit demand for a firm's products. The WB, the alternative television network created by Time Warner in 1995, faced this dilemma. Initially, the

WB found success in producing shows for teens—classics such as *Dawson's Creek* and *Buffy the Vampire Slayer*. However, in 2003, the WB saw an 11 percent drop in viewership and a $25 million drop in advertising revenues. Although it did not leave its traditional demographic behind, the WB began producing some programs intended to appeal to older viewers. Ultimately, the WB merged with UPN to form a new network, the CW network. CW is a joint venture between CBS (owner of UPN) and Time Warner (owner of the WB).[5]

A third element of a firm's general environment is cultural trends. **Culture** is the values, beliefs, and norms that guide behavior in a society. These values, beliefs, and norms define what is "right and wrong" in a society, what is acceptable and unacceptable, what is fashionable and unfashionable. Failure to understand changes in culture, or differences between cultures, can have a very large impact on the ability of a firm to gain a competitive advantage.

This becomes most obvious when firms operate in multiple countries simultaneously. Even seemingly small differences in culture can have an impact. For example, advertisements in the United States that end with a person putting their index finger and thumb together mean that a product is "okay"; in Brazil, the same symbol is vulgar and offensive. Ads in the United States that have a bride dressed in white may be very confusing to the Chinese because, in China, white is the traditional color worn at funerals. In Germany, women typically purchase their own engagement rings, whereas in the United States, men purchase engagement rings for their fiancées. And what might be appropriate ways to treat women colleagues in Japan or France would land most men in U.S. firms in serious trouble. Understanding the cultural context within which a firm operates is important in evaluating the ability of a firm to generate competitive advantages.[6]

A fourth element of a firm's general environment is the current economic climate. The **economic climate** is the overall health of the economic systems within which a firm operates. The health of the economy varies over time in a distinct pattern: Periods of relative prosperity, when demand for goods and services is high and unemployment is low, are followed by periods of relatively low prosperity, when demand for goods and services is low and unemployment is high. When activity in an economy is relatively low, the economy is said to be in **recession**. A severe recession that lasts for several years is known as a **depression**. This alternating pattern of prosperity followed by recession, followed by prosperity, is called the **business cycle**.

Throughout the 1990s, the world, and especially the United States, enjoyed a period of sustained economic growth. Some observers even speculated that the government had become so skilled at managing demand in the economy through adjusting interest rates that a period of recession did not necessarily have to follow a period of sustained economic growth. Of course, the business cycle has reared its ugly head twice since the 1990s—first with the technology bubble-burst around 2001 and, more recently, in the credit crunch in 2008. Most observers now agree that although government policy can have a significant impact on the frequency and size of economic downturns, these policies are unlikely to be able prevent these downturns altogether.

A fifth element of a firm's general environment is **legal and political conditions**. The legal and political dimensions of an organization's general environment are the laws and the legal system's impact on business, together with the general nature of the relationship between government and business. These laws and the relationship between business and government can vary significantly around the world. For example, in Japan, business and the government are generally seen as having a consistently close and cooperative relationship. Indeed, some have observed that one reason that the Japanese economy has been growing so slowly over the past decade has been the government's reluctance to impose economic restructuring that would hurt the performance of some Japanese firms—especially the largest Japanese banks. In the United States, however, the quality of the relationship between business and the government tends to vary over time. In some administrations, rigorous antitrust regulation and tough environmental standards—both seen as inconsistent with the interests of business—dominate. In other administrations, antitrust regulation is less rigorous and the imposition of environmental standards is delayed, suggesting a more business-friendly perspective.

A final attribute of a firm's general environment is **specific international events**. These include events such as civil wars, political coups, terrorism, wars between countries, famines, and country or regional economic recessions. All of these specific events can have an enormous impact on the ability of a firm's strategies to generate competitive advantage.

Of course, one of the most important of these specific events to have occurred over the past several decades was the terrorist attacks on New York City and Washington, D.C., on September 11, 2001. Beyond the tragic loss of life, these attacks had important business implications as well. For example, it took more than five years for airline demand to return to pre–September 11 levels. Insurance companies had to pay out billions of dollars in unanticipated claims as a result of the attacks. Defense contractors saw demand for their products soar as the United States and some of its allies began waging war in Afghanistan and then Iraq.

A firm's general environment defines the broad contextual background within which it operates. Understanding this general environment can help a firm identify some of the threats and opportunities it faces. However, this general environment often has an impact on a firm's threats and opportunities through its impact on a firm's more local environment. Thus, while analyzing a firm's general environment is an important step in any application of the strategic management process, this general analysis must be accompanied by an analysis of a firm's more local environment if the threats and opportunities facing a firm are to be fully understood. The next section discusses specific tools for analyzing a firm's local environment and the theoretical perspectives from which these tools have been derived.

The Structure-Conduct-Performance Model of Firm Performance

In the 1930s, a group of economists began developing an approach for understanding the relationship among a firm's environment, behavior, and performance. The original objective of this work was to describe conditions under which competition in an industry would *not* develop. Understanding when competition was not developing in an industry assisted government regulators in identifying industries where competition-enhancing regulations should be implemented.[7]

Ethics and Strategy

One of the basic tenets of economic theory is that society is better off when industries are very competitive. Industries are very competitive when there are large numbers of firms operating in an industry, when the products and services that these firms sell are similar to each other, and when it is not very costly for firms to enter into or exit these industries. Indeed, as is described in more detail in the Strategy in Depth feature, these industries are said to be *perfectly competitive.*

The reasons that society is better off when industries are perfectly competitive are well known. In such industries, firms must constantly strive to keep their costs low, keep their quality high, and, when appropriate, innovate if they are to even survive. Low costs, high quality, and appropriate innovation are generally consistent with the interests of a firm's customers and, thus, consistent with society's overall welfare.

Indeed, concern for **social welfare,** or the overall good of society, is the primary reason the S-C-P model was developed. This model was to be used to identify industries where perfect competition was not occurring and, thus, where social welfare was not being maximized. With these industries identified, the government

Is a Firm Gaining a Competitive Advantage Good for Society?

could then engage in activities to increase the competitiveness of these industries, thereby increasing social welfare.

Strategic management scholars turned the S-C-P model upside down by using it to describe industries where firms could gain competitive advantages and attain above-average performance. However, some have asked that if strategic management is all about creating and exploiting competitive imperfections in industries, is strategic management also all about reducing the overall good of society for advantages to be gained by a few firms? It is not surprising that individuals who are more interested in improving society

than improving the performance of a few firms question the moral legitimacy of the field of strategic management.

However, there is another view about strategic management and social welfare. The S-C-P model assumes that any competitive advantages a firm has in an industry must hurt society. The alternative view is that at least some of the competitive advantages exist because a firm addresses customer needs more effectively than its competitors. From this perspective, competitive advantages are not bad for social welfare; they are actually good for social welfare.

Of course, both perspectives can be true. For example, a firm such as Microsoft has engaged in activities that at least some courts have concluded are inconsistent with social welfare. However, Microsoft also sells applications software that is routinely ranked among the best in the industry, an action that is consistent with meeting customer needs in ways that maximize social welfare.

Sources: J. B. Barney (1986). "Types of competition and the theory of strategy." *Academy of Management Review,* 11, pp. 791–800; H. Demsetz (1973). "Industry structure, market rivalry, and public policy." *Journal of Law and Economics,* 16, pp. 1–9; M. Porter (1981). "The contribution of industrial organization to strategic management." *Academy of Management Review,* 6, pp. 609–620.

The theoretical framework that developed out of this effort became known as the **structure-conduct-performance (S-C-P) model**; it is summarized in Figure 2.2. The term **structure** in this model refers to industry structure, measured by such factors as the number of competitors in an industry, the heterogeneity of products in an industry, the cost of entry and exit in an industry, and so forth. **Conduct** refers to the strategies that firms in an industry implement. **Performance** in the S-C-P model has two meanings: (1) the performance of individual firms and (2) the performance of the economy as a whole. Although both definitions of performance in the S-C-P model are important, as suggested in Chapter 1, the strategic

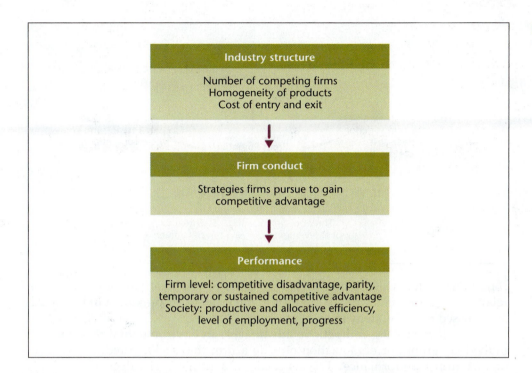

Figure 2.2 The Structure-Conduct-Performance Model

management process is much more focused on the performance of individual firms than on the performance of the economy as a whole. That said, the relationship between these two types of performance can sometimes be complex, as described in the Ethics and Strategy feature.

The logic that links industry structure to conduct and performance is well known. Attributes of the industry structure within which a firm operates define the range of options and constraints facing a firm. In some industries, firms have very few options and face many constraints. In general, firms in these industries can only gain competitive parity. In this setting, industry structure completely determines both firm conduct and long-run firm performance.

However, in other, less competitive industries, firms face fewer constraints and a greater range of conduct options. Some of these options may enable them to obtain competitive advantages. However, even when firms have more conduct options, industry structure still constrains the range of options. Moreover, as will be shown in more detail later in this chapter, industry structure also has an impact on how long firms can expect to maintain their competitive advantages in the face of increased competition.

A Model of Environmental Threats

As a theoretical framework, the S-C-P model has proven to be very useful in informing both research and government policy. However, the model can sometimes be awkward to use to identify threats in a firm's local environment. Fortunately, several scholars have developed models of environmental threats based on the S-C-P model that are highly applicable in identifying threats facing a particular firm.[8] These models identify the five most common threats, presented in Figure 2.3, faced by firms in their local competitive environments and the

Figure 2.3   Environmental
Threats and the Profit Potential
of Industries

conditions under which these threats are more or less likely to be present. The relationship between the S-C-P model and the framework presented in Figure 2.3 is discussed in the Strategy in Depth feature.

To a firm seeking competitive advantages, an **environmental threat** is any individual, group, or organization outside a firm that seeks to reduce the level of that firm's performance. Threats increase a firm's costs, decrease a firm's revenues, or in other ways reduce a firm's performance. In S-C-P terms, environmental threats are forces that tend to increase the competitiveness of an industry and force firm performance to competitive parity level. The five common environmental threats identified in the literature are: (1) threat from new competition, (2) threat from competition among existing competitors, (3) threat from superior or low-cost substitutes, (4) threat of supplier leverage, and (5) threats from buyers' influence.

Threat from New Competition

The first environmental threat identified in Figure 2.3 is the threat of new competitors. **New competitors** are firms that have either recently started operating in an industry or that threaten to begin operations in an industry soon. For the music download industry, Amazon is a new competitor. For televised sports, Fox Sports, NBC Sports Network, and CBS Sports Network are new competitors.[9]

According to the S-C-P model, new competitors are motivated to enter into an industry by the superior profits that some incumbent firms in that industry may be earning. Firms seeking these high profits enter the industry, thereby increasing the level of industry competition and reducing the performance of incumbent firms. With the absence of any barriers, entry will continue as long as any firms in the industry are earning competitive advantages, and entry will cease when all incumbent firms are earning competitive parity.

The extent to which new competitors act as a threat to an incumbent firm's performance depends on the cost of entry. If the cost of entry into an industry is greater than the potential profits a new competitor could obtain by entering, then entry will not be forthcoming, and new competitors are not a threat to incumbent firms. However, if the cost of entry is lower than the return from entry, entry will occur until the profits derived from entry are less than the costs of entry.

Strategy in Depth

The relationship between environmental threats and the S-C-P model turns on the relationship between the CE threats and the nature of competition in an industry. When all five threats are very high, competition in an industry begins to approach what economists call *perfect competition*. When all five threats are very low, competition in an industry begins to approach what economists call a *monopoly*. Between perfect competition and monopoly, economists have identified two other types of competition in an industry—*monopolistic competition* and *oligopoly*—where the five threats identified in the literature are moderately high. These four types of competition, and the expected performance of firms in these different industries, are summarized in the table below.

Industries are **perfectly competitive** when there are large numbers of competing firms, the products being sold are homogeneous with respect to cost and product attributes, and entry and exit costs are very low. An example of a perfectly competitive industry is the spot market for crude oil. Firms

Environmental Threats and the S-C-P Model

in perfectly competitive industries can expect to earn only competitive parity.

In **monopolistically competitive industries**, there are large numbers of competing firms and low-cost entry into and exit from the industry. However, unlike the case of perfect competition, products in these industries are not homogeneous with respect to costs or product attributes. Examples of monopolistically competitive industries include toothpaste, shampoo, golf balls, and automobiles. Firms in such industries can earn competitive advantages.

Oligopolies are characterized by a small number of competing firms, by homogeneous products, and by high entry and exit costs. Examples of oligopolistic industries include the U.S. automobile and steel industries in the 1950s and the U.S. breakfast cereal market today. Currently, the top four producers of breakfast cereal account for about 90 percent of the breakfast cereal sold in the United States. Firms in such industries can earn competitive advantages.

Finally, **monopolistic industries** consist of only a single firm. Entry into this type of industry is very costly. There are few examples of purely monopolistic industries. Historically, for example, the U.S. Post Office had a monopoly on home mail delivery. However, this monopoly has been challenged in small-package delivery by FedEx, in larger-package delivery by UPS, and in mail delivery by e-mail. Monopolists can generate competitive advantages—although they are sometimes managed very inefficiently.

Source: J. Barney (2007). *Gaining and sustaining competitive advantage*, 3rd ed. Upper Saddle River, NJ: Pearson Higher Education.

Types of Competition and Expected Firm Performance

Type of Competition	Attributes	Examples	Expected Firm Performance
Perfect competition	Large number of firms Homogeneous products Low-cost entry and exit	Stock market Crude oil	Competitive parity
Monopolistic competition	Large number of firms Heterogeneous products Low-cost entry and exit	Toothpaste Shampoo Golf balls Automobiles	Competitive advantage
Oligopoly	Small number of firms Homogenous products Costly entry and exit	U.S. steel and autos in the 1950s U.S. breakfast cereal	Competitive advantage
Monopoly	One firm Costly entry	Home mail delivery	Competitive advantage

TABLE 2.1 Possible Barriers to Entry into an Industry	1. Economies of scale 2. Product differentiation 3. Cost advantages independent of scale 4. Government regulation of entry

The threat of new competitors depends on the cost of entry, and the cost of entry, in turn, depends on the existence and "height" of barriers to entry. **Barriers to entry** are attributes of an industry's structure that increase the cost of entry. The greater the cost of entry, the greater the height of these barriers. When there are significant barriers to entry, potential new competitors will not enter into an industry even if incumbent firms are earning competitive advantages.

Four important barriers to entry have been identified in the S-C-P and strategy literatures. These four barriers, listed in Table 2.1, are (1) economies of scale, (2) product differentiation, (3) cost advantages independent of scale, and (4) government regulation of entry.[10]

Economies of Scale as a Barrier to Entry

Economies of scale exist in an industry when a firm's costs fall as a function of its volume of production. **Diseconomies of scale** exist when a firm's costs rise as a function of its volume of production. The relationship among economies of scale, diseconomies of scale, and a firm's volume of production is summarized in Figure 2.4. As a firm's volume of production increases, its costs begin to fall. This is a manifestation of economies of scale. However, at some point a firm's volume of production becomes too large and its costs begin to rise. This is a manifestation of diseconomies of scale. For economies of scale to act as a barrier to entry, the relationship between the volume of production and firm costs must have the shape of the line in Figure 2.4. This curve suggests that any deviation, positive or negative, from an optimal level of production (point X in Figure 2.4) will lead a firm to experience much higher costs of production.

Figure 2.4 Economies of Scale and the Cost of Production

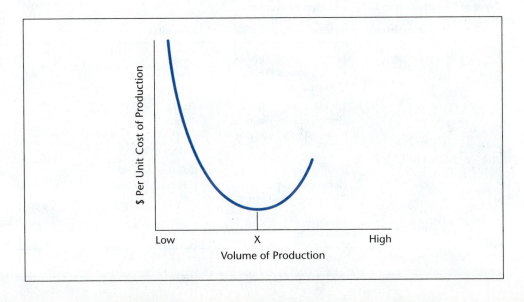

To see how economies of scale can act as a barrier to entry, consider the following scenario. Imagine an industry with the following attributes: The industry has five incumbent firms (each firm has only one plant); the optimal level of production in each of these plants is 4,000 units (X = 4,000 units); total demand for the output of this industry is fixed at 22,000 units; the economies-of-scale curve is as depicted in Figure 2.4; and products in this industry are very homogeneous. Total demand in this industry (22,000 units) is greater than total supply (5 × 4,000 units = 20,000). Everyone knows that when demand is greater than supply, prices go up. This means that the five incumbent firms in this industry will have high levels of profit. The S-C-P model suggests that, absent barriers, these superior profits should motivate entry.

However, look at the entry decision from the point of view of potential new competitors. Certainly, incumbent firms are earning superior profits, but potential entrants face an unsavory choice. On the one hand, new competitors could enter the industry with an optimally efficient plant and produce 4,000 units. However, this form of entry will lead industry supply to rise to 24,000 units (20,000 + 4,000). Suddenly, supply will be greater than demand (24,000 > 22,000), and all the firms in the industry, including the new entrant, will earn negative profits. On the other hand, the new competitor might enter the industry with a plant of smaller-than-optimal size (e.g., 1,000 units). This kind of entry leaves total industry demand larger than industry supply (22,000 > 21,000). However, the new competitor faces a serious cost disadvantage in this case because it does not produce at the low-cost position on the economies-of-scale curve. Faced with these bleak alternatives, the potential entrant simply does not enter even though incumbent firms are earning positive profits.

Of course, potential new competitors have other options besides entering at the efficient scale and losing money or entering at an inefficient scale and losing money. For example, potential entrants can attempt to expand the total size of the market (i.e., increase total demand from 22,000 to 24,000 units or more) and enter at the optimal size. Potential entrants can also attempt to develop new production technology, shift the economies-of-scale curve to the left (thereby reducing the optimal plant size), and enter. Or potential new competitors may try to make their products seem very special to their customers, enabling them to charge higher prices to offset higher production costs associated with a smaller-than-optimal plant.[11]

Any of these actions may enable a firm to enter an industry. However, these actions are costly. If the cost of engaging in these "barrier-busting" activities is greater than the return from entry, entry will not occur, even if incumbent firms are earning positive profits.

Historically, economies of scale acted as a barrier to entry into the world-wide steel market. To fully exploit economies of scale, traditional steel plants had to be very large. If new entrants into the steel market had built these efficient and large steel-manufacturing plants, they would have had the effect of increasing the steel supply over the demand for steel, and the outcome would have been reduced profits for both new entrants and incumbent firms. This discouraged new entry. However, in the 1970s, the development of alternative mini-mill technology shifted the economies-of-scale curve to the left by making smaller plants very efficient in addressing some segments of the steel market. This shift had the effect of decreasing barriers to entry into the steel industry. Recent entrants, including Nucor Steel and Chaparral Steel, now have significant cost advantages over firms still using outdated, less efficient production technology.[12]

Product Differentiation as a Barrier to Entry

Product differentiation means that incumbent firms possess brand identification and customer loyalty that potential new competitors do not. Brand identification and customer loyalty serve as entry barriers because new competitors not only have to absorb the standard costs associated with starting production in a new industry; they also have to absorb the costs associated with overcoming incumbent firms' differentiation advantages. If the cost of overcoming these advantages is greater than the potential return from entering an industry, entry will not occur, even if incumbent firms are earning positive profits.

Numerous examples exist of industries in which product differentiation tends to act as a barrier to entry. In the brewing industry, for example, substantial investments by Budweiser, Miller, and Coors (among other incumbent firms) in advertising (will we ever forget the Budweiser frogs?) and brand recognition have made large-scale entry into the U.S. brewing industry very costly.[13] Indeed, rather than attempting to enter the U.S. market, InBev, a large brewer headquartered in Belgium, decided to purchase Anheuser Busch.[14]

E. & J. Gallo Winery, a U.S. winemaker, faced product differentiation barriers to entry in its efforts to sell Gallo wine in the French market. The market for wine in France is huge—the French consume 16.1 gallons of wine per person per year, for a total consumption of more than 400 million cases of wine, whereas U.S. consumers drink only 1.8 gallons of wine per person per year, for a total consumption of less than 200 million cases. Despite this difference, intense loyalties to local French vineyards have made it very difficult for Gallo to break into the huge French market—a market where American wines are still given as "gag gifts" and only American theme restaurants carry U.S. wines on their menus. Gallo is attempting to overcome this product differentiation advantage of French wineries by emphasizing its California roots—roots that many French consider to be exotic—and downplaying the fact that it is a U.S. company; corporate origins that are less attractive to many French consumers.[15]

Cost Advantages Independent of Scale as Barriers to Entry

In addition to the barriers that have been cited, incumbent firms may have a whole range of cost advantages, independent of economies of scale, compared to new competitors. These cost advantages can act to deter entry because new competitors will find themselves at a cost disadvantage vis-à-vis incumbent firms with these cost advantages. New competitors can engage in activities to overcome the cost advantages of incumbent firms, but as the cost of overcoming them increases, the economic profit potential from entry is reduced. In some settings, incumbent firms enjoying cost advantages, independent of scale, can earn superior profits and still not be threatened by new entry because the cost of overcoming those advantages can be prohibitive. Examples of these cost advantages, independent of scale, are presented in Table 2.2; they include (1) proprietary technology, (2) managerial know-how, (3) favorable access to raw materials, and (4) learning-curve cost advantages.

Proprietary Technology.   In some industries, **proprietary** (i.e., secret or patented) **technology** gives incumbent firms important cost advantages over potential entrants. To enter these industries, potential new competitors must develop their own substitute technologies or run the risks of copying another firm's patented technologies. Both of these activities can be costly. Numerous firms in a wide variety of industries have discovered the sometimes substantial economic costs

Proprietary technology. When incumbent firms have secret or patented technology that reduces their costs below the costs of potential entrants, potential new competitors must develop substitute technologies to compete. The cost of developing this technology can act as a barrier to entry.

Managerial know-how. When incumbent firms have taken-for-granted knowledge, skills, and information that take years to develop and that is not possessed by potential new competitors. The cost of developing this know-how can act as a barrier to entry.

Favorable access to raw materials. When incumbent firms have low-cost access to critical raw materials not enjoyed by potential new competitors. The cost of gaining similar access can act as a barrier to entry.

Learning-curve cost advantages. When the cumulative volume of production of incumbent firms gives them cost advantages not enjoyed by potential new competitors. These cost disadvantages of potential entrants can act as a barrier to entry.

TABLE 2.2 Sources of Cost Advantage, Independent of Scale, That Can Act as Barriers to Entry

associated with violating another firm's patented proprietary technology. Indeed, the number of patent infringement suits continues to increase, especially in industries—such as consumer electronics—where products apply technologies developed by many different companies. In the past few years, Intertrust has sued Apple, Yahoo! has sued Facebook, Google has sued BT, Boston University has sued Apple, Nokia has sued HTC, Samsung has sued Apple, and Apple has sued Samsung.[16] In 2012, a total of 5,778 patent infringement suits were filed in the United States.[17]

Managerial Know-How. Even more important than technology per se as a barrier to entry is the managerial know-how built up by incumbent firms over their history.[18] **Managerial know-how** is the often-taken-for-granted knowledge and information that are needed to compete in an industry on a day-to-day basis.[19] Know-how includes information that it has taken years, sometimes decades, for a firm to accumulate that enables it to interact with customers and suppliers, to be innovative and creative, to manufacture quality products, and so forth. Typically, new entrants will not have access to this know-how, and it will often be costly for them to build it quickly.

One industry where this kind of know-how is a very important barrier to entry is the pharmaceutical industry. Success in this industry depends on having high-quality research and development skills. The development of world-class research and development skills—the know-how—takes decades to accumulate. New competitors face enormous cost disadvantages for decades as they attempt to develop these abilities, and thus entry into the pharmaceutical industry has been quite limited.[20]

Favorable Access to Raw Materials. Incumbent firms may also have cost advantages, compared to new entrants, based on favorable access to raw materials. If, for example, only a few sources of high-quality iron ore are available in a specific geographic region, steel firms that have access to these sources may have a cost advantage over those that must ship their ore in from distant sources.[21]

Learning-Curve Cost Advantages. It has been shown that in certain industries (such as airplane manufacturing) the cost of production falls with the cumulative volume of production. Over time, as incumbent firms gain experience in manufacturing, their costs fall below those of potential entrants. Potential new competitors, in this context, must endure substantially higher costs while they gain experience, and thus they may not enter the industry despite the superior profits being earned by incumbent firms. These learning-curve economies are discussed in more detail in Chapter 4.

Government Policy as a Barrier to Entry

Governments, for their own reasons, may decide to increase the cost of entry into an industry. This occurs most frequently when a firm operates as a government-regulated monopoly. In this setting, the government has concluded that it is in a better position to ensure that specific products or services are made available to the population at reasonable prices than competitive market forces. Industries such as electric power generation and elementary and secondary education have been (and, to some extent, continue to be) protected from new competitors by government restrictions on entry.

Threat from Existing Competitors

New competitors are an important threat to the ability of firms to maintain or improve their level of performance, but they are not the only threat in a firm's environment. A second environmental threat comes from the intensity of competition among a firm's current direct competitors. Amazon and iTunes are direct competitors. ESPN, CBS, NBC, Fox, USA Networks, and TNN—to name a few—are all direct competitors in televised sports.

Direct competition threatens firms by reducing their economic profits. High levels of direct competition are indicated by such actions as frequent price cutting by firms in an industry (e.g., price discounts in the airline industry), frequent introduction of new products by firms in an industry (e.g., continuous product introductions in consumer electronics), intense advertising campaigns (e.g., Pepsi versus Coke advertising), and rapid competitive actions and reactions in an industry (e.g., competing airlines quickly matching the discounts of other airlines).

Some of the attributes of an industry that are likely to generate high levels of direct competition are listed in Table 2.3. First, direct competition tends to be high when there are numerous firms in an industry and these firms tend to be roughly the same size. Such is the case in the laptop personal computer industry. Worldwide, more than 120 firms have entered the laptop computer market, and no one firm dominates in market share. Since the early 1990s, prices in the laptop market have been declining 25 to 30 percent a year. Profit margins for laptop personal computer firms that used to be in the 10 to 13 percent range have rapidly fallen to 3 to 4 percent.[22]

Second, direct competition tends to be high when industry growth is slow. When industry growth is slow, firms seeking to increase their sales must often acquire market share from established competitors. This tends to increase competition. Intense price rivalry emerged in the U.S. fast-food industry—with 99-cent Whoppers at Burger King and "dollar menus" at Wendy's and McDonald's—when the growth in this industry declined.[23]

TABLE 2.3 Attributes of an Industry That Increase the Threat of Direct Competition

1. Large number of competing firms that are roughly the same size
2. Slow industry growth
3. Lack of product differentiation
4. Capacity added in large increments

Third, direct competition tends to be high when firms are unable to differentiate their products in an industry. When product differentiation is not a viable strategic option, firms are often forced to compete only on the basis of price. Intense price competition is typical of high-competition industries. In the airline industry, for example, intense competition on longer routes—such as between Los Angeles and New York and Los Angeles and Chicago—has kept prices on these routes down. These routes have relatively few product differentiation options. However, by creating hub-and-spoke systems, certain airlines (American, United, Delta) have been able to develop regions of the United States where they are the dominant carrier. These hub-and-spoke systems enable airlines to partially differentiate their products geographically, thus reducing the level of competition in segments of this industry.[24]

Finally, direct competition tends to be high when production capacity is added in large increments. If, in order to obtain economies of scale, production capacity must be added in large increments, an industry is likely to experience periods of oversupply after new capacity comes online. This overcapacity often leads to price cuts. Much of the growing rivalry in the commercial jet industry between Boeing and AirBus can be traced to the large manufacturing capacity additions made by AirBus when it entered the industry.[25]

Threat of Substitute Products

A third environmental threat is the threat of substitute products. The products or services provided by a firm's direct competitors meet approximately the same customer needs in the same ways as the products or services provided by the firm itself. **Substitutes** meet approximately the same customer needs, but do so in different ways. Substitutes for downloaded music include Spotify, Pandora, and other music-streaming firms. Substitutes for televised sports include sports magazines, sports pages in the newspapers, and actually attending sporting events.

Substitutes place a ceiling on the prices firms in an industry can charge and on the profits firms in an industry can earn. In the extreme, substitutes can ultimately replace an industry's products and services. This happens when a substitute is clearly superior to previous products. Examples include electronic calculators as substitutes for slide rules and mechanical calculators, electronic watch movements as substitutes for pin–lever mechanical watch movements, and compact discs as substitutes for long-playing (LP) records (although some audiophiles continue to argue for the sonic superiority of LPs).

Substitutes are playing an increasingly important role in reducing the profit potential in a variety of industries. For example, in the legal profession private mediation and arbitration services are becoming viable substitutes for lawyers. Computerized texts are becoming viable substitutes for printed books in the publishing industry. Television news programs, especially services such as CNN and Fox News, are very threatening substitutes for weekly newsmagazines, including *Time* and *Newsweek*. In Europe, so-called superstores are threatening smaller food shops. Minor league baseball teams are partial substitutes for major league teams. Cable television is a substitute for broadcast television. Groups of "big box" retailers are substitutes for traditional shopping centers. Private mail delivery systems (such as those in the Netherlands and Australia) are substitutes for government postal services. Home financial planning software is a partial substitute for professional financial planners.[26]

Threat of Supplier Leverage

A fourth environmental threat is supplier leverage. **Suppliers** make a wide variety of raw materials, labor, and other critical assets available to firms. Suppliers can threaten the performance of firms in an industry by increasing the price of their supplies or by reducing the quality of those supplies. Any profits that were being earned in an industry can be transferred to suppliers in this way. In music downloading, record labels and, to a lesser extent, artists are critical suppliers. In televised sports, critical suppliers include sports leagues—such as the NFL and the NHL—as well as TV personalities.

Some supplier attributes that can lead to high levels of threat are listed in Table 2.4. First, suppliers are a greater threat if the *suppliers'* industry is dominated by a small number of firms. In this setting, a firm has little choice but to purchase supplies from these firms. These few firms thus have enormous flexibility to charge high prices, to reduce quality, or in other ways to squeeze the profits of the firms in the industry to which they sell. Much of Microsoft's power in the software industry reflects its dominance in the operating system market, where Windows remains the de facto standard for most personal computers. For now, at least, if a company wants to sell personal computers, it is going to need to interact with Microsoft. It will be interesting to see if Linux-based PCs become more powerful, thereby limiting some of Microsoft's leverage as a supplier.

Conversely, when a firm has the option of purchasing from a large number of suppliers, suppliers have less leverage to threaten a firm's profits. For example, as the number of lawyers in the United States has increased over the years (up 40 percent since 1981, currently more than 1 million), lawyers and law firms have been forced to begin competing for work. Some corporate clients have forced law firms to reduce their hourly fees and to handle repetitive simple legal tasks for low flat fees.[27]

Second, suppliers are a greater threat when what they supply is unique or highly differentiated. There is only one LeBron James. As a basketball player, as a spokesperson, and as a celebrity, his unique status gives him enormous bargaining power as a supplier and enables him to extract some of the economic profit that would otherwise have been earned by the Miami Heat and Nike. In the same way, Intel's unique ability to develop, manufacture, and sell microprocessors gives it significant bargaining power as a supplier in the personal computer industry.

The uniqueness of suppliers can operate in almost any industry. For example, in the highly competitive world of television talk shows, some guests, as suppliers, can gain surprising fame for their unique characteristics. For example, one woman was a guest on eight talk shows. Her claim to fame: She was the tenth wife of a gay, con-man bigamist.

Third, suppliers are a greater threat to firms in an industry when suppliers are *not* threatened by substitutes. When there are no effective substitutes, suppliers can

TABLE 2.4 Indicators of the Threat of Supplier Leverage in an Industry

1. Suppliers' industry is dominated by small number of firms.
2. Suppliers sell unique or highly differentiated products.
3. Suppliers are *not* threatened by substitutes.
4. Suppliers threaten forward vertical integration.
5. Firms are *not* important customers for suppliers.

take advantage of their position to extract economic profits from firms they supply. Both Intel (in microprocessors) and Microsoft (in PC operating systems) have been accused of exploiting their unique product positions to extract profits from customers.

When there are substitutes for supplies, supplier power is checked. In the metal can industry, for example, steel cans are threatened by aluminum and plastic containers as substitutes. In order to continue to sell to can manufacturers, steel companies have had to keep their prices lower than would otherwise have been the case. In this way, the potential power of the steel companies is checked by the existence of substitute products.[28]

Fourth, suppliers are a greater threat to firms when they can credibly threaten to enter into and begin competing in a firm's industry. This is called **forward vertical integration**; in this situation, suppliers cease to be suppliers only and become suppliers *and* rivals. The threat of forward vertical integration is partially a function of barriers to entry into an industry. When an industry has high barriers to entry, suppliers face significant costs of forward vertical integration, and thus forward integration is not as serious a threat to the profits of incumbent firms. (Vertical integration is discussed in detail in Chapter 6.)

Finally, suppliers are a threat to firms when firms are *not* an important part of suppliers' business. Steel companies, for example, are not too concerned with losing the business of a sculptor or of a small construction company. However, they are very concerned about losing the business of the major can manufacturers, major white-goods manufacturers (i.e., manufacturers of refrigerators, washing machines, dryers, and so forth), and automobile companies. Steel companies, as suppliers, are likely to be very accommodating and willing to reduce prices and increase quality for can manufacturers, white-goods manufacturers, and auto companies. Smaller, "less important" customers, however, are likely to be subject to greater price increases, lower-quality service, and lower-quality products.

Threat from Buyers' Influence

The final environmental threat is buyers. **Buyers** purchase a firm's products or services. Whereas powerful suppliers act to increase a firm's costs, powerful buyers act to decrease a firm's revenues. In music downloads, consumers are the ultimate buyer. In televised sports, buyers include all those who watch sports on television as well as those who purchase advertising space on networks. Some of the important indicators of the threat of buyers are listed in Table 2.5.

First, if a firm has only one buyer or a small number of buyers, these buyers can be very threatening. Firms that sell a significant amount of their output to the U.S. Department of Defense recognize the influence of this buyer on their operations. Reductions in defense spending have forced defense companies to try even harder to reduce costs and increase quality to satisfy government

1. Number of buyers is small.
2. Products sold to buyers are undifferentiated and standard.
3. Products sold to buyers are a significant percentage of a buyer's final costs.
4. Buyers are *not* earning significant economic profits.
5. Buyers threaten backward vertical integration.

TABLE 2.5 Indicators of the Threat of Buyers' Influence in an Industry

demands. All these actions reduce the economic profits of these defense-oriented companies.[29] Firms that sell to large retail chains have also found it difficult to maintain high levels of profitability. Powerful retail firms—such as Wal-Mart and Home Depot—can make significant and complex logistical and other demands on their suppliers, and if suppliers fail to meet these demands, buyers can "fire" their suppliers. These demands can have the effect of reducing the profits of suppliers.

Second, if the products or services that are being sold to buyers are standard and not differentiated, then the threat of buyers can be greater. For example, farmers sell a very standard product. It is very difficult to differentiate products such as wheat, corn, or tomatoes (although this can be done to some extent through the development of new strains of crops, the timing of harvests, pesticide-free crops, and so forth). In general, wholesale grocers and food brokers can always find alternative suppliers of basic food products. These numerous alternative suppliers increase the threat of buyers and force farmers to keep their prices and profits low. If any one farmer attempts to raise prices, wholesale grocers and food brokers simply purchase their supplies from some other farmer.

Third, buyers are likely to be more of a threat when the supplies they purchase are a significant portion of the costs of their final products. In this context, buyers are likely to be very concerned about the costs of their supplies and constantly on the lookout for cheaper alternatives. For example, in the canned food industry, the cost of the can itself can constitute up to 40 percent of a product's final price. Not surprisingly, firms such as Campbell Soup Company are very concerned about keeping the price of the cans they purchase as low as possible.[30]

Fourth, buyers are likely to be more of a threat when they are *not* earning significant economic profits. In these circumstances, buyers are likely to be very sensitive to costs and insist on the lowest possible cost and the highest possible quality from suppliers. This effect can be exacerbated when the profits suppliers earn are greater than the profits buyers earn. In this setting, a buyer would have a strong incentive to enter into its supplier's business to capture some of the economic profits being earned by the supplier. This strategy of **backward vertical integration** is discussed in more detail in Chapter 6.

Finally, buyers are more of a threat to firms in an industry when they have the ability to vertically integrate backward. In this case, buyers become both buyers and rivals and lock in a certain percentage of an industry's sales. The extent to which buyers represent a threat to vertically integrate, in turn, depends on the barriers to entry that are not in place in an industry. If there are significant barriers to entry, buyers may not be able to engage in backward vertical integration, and their threat to firms is reduced.

Environmental Threats and Average Industry Performance

The five environmental threats have three important implications for managers seeking to choose and implement strategies. First, they describe the most common sources of local environmental threat in industries. Second, they can be used to characterize the overall level of threat in an industry. Finally, because the overall level of threat in an industry is, according to S-C-P logic, related to the average level of performance of a firm in an industry, they can also be used to anticipate the average level of performance of firms in an industry.

	Industry I	Industry II	Industry III	Industry IV
Threat of new competitors	High	Low	High	Low
Threat of direct competition	High	Low	Low	High
Threat of superior or low cost product substitutes	High	Low	High	Low
Threat of supplier leverage	High	Low	Low	High
Threat of buyers; influence	High	Low	High	Low
Expected average firm performance	Low	High	Mixed	Mixed

TABLE 2.6 Estimating the Level of Average Performance in an Industry

Of course, it will rarely be the case that all five threats in an industry will be equally threatening at the same time. This can sometimes complicate the anticipation of the average level of firm performance in an industry. Consider, for example, the four industries in Table 2.6. It is easy to anticipate the average level of performance of firms in the first two industries: In Industry I, this performance will be low; in Industry II, this performance will be high; however, in Industries III and IV it is somewhat more complicated. In these mixed situations, the real question to ask in anticipating the average performance of firms in an industry is, "Are one or more threats in this industry powerful enough to appropriate most of the profits that firms in this industry might generate?" If the answer to this question is yes, then the anticipated average level of performance will be low. If the answer is no, then the anticipated performance will be high.

Even more fundamentally, this type of analysis can be used only to anticipate the average level of firm performance in an industry. This is acceptable if a firm's industry is the primary determinant of its overall performance. However, as described in the Research Made Relevant feature, research suggests that the industry a firm operates in is far from the only determinant of its performance.

Another Environmental Force: Complementors

Professors Adam Brandenburger and Barry Nalebuff have suggested that another force needs to be added to the analysis of the profit potential of industries.[31] These authors distinguish between competitors and what they call a firm's *complementors*. If you were the chief executive officer of a firm, the following is how you could tell the difference between your competitors and your complementors: Another firm is a **competitor** if your customers value your product less when they have the other firm's product than when they have your product alone. Direct competitors, new competitors, and substitutes are all examples of competitors. In contrast, another firm is a **complementor** if your customers value your product more when they have this other firm's product than when they have your product alone.

Consider, for example, the relationship between producers of television programming and cable television companies. The value of these firms' products partially depends on the existence of one another. Television producers need outlets for their programming. The growth in the number of channels on cable television provides more of these outlets and thus increases the value of these production firms. Cable television companies can continue to add channels, but those channels need content. So, the value of cable television companies depends partly on the existence of television production firms. Because the value of program-producing companies is greater when cable television firms exist and because the value of cable television companies is greater when program-producing companies exist, these types of firms are complements.

Brandenburger and Nalebuff go on to argue that an important difference between complementors and competitors is that a firm's complementors help to increase the size of a firm's market, whereas a firm's competitors divide this market among a set of firms. Based on this logic, these authors suggest that, although it is usually the case that a firm will want to discourage the entry of competitors into its market, it will usually want to encourage the entry of complementors. Returning to the television producers/cable television example, television producers will actually want cable television companies to grow and prosper and constantly add new channels, and cable television firms will want television show producers to grow and constantly create new and innovative programming. If the growth of either of these businesses slows, it hurts the growth of the other.

Of course, the same firm can be a complementor for one firm and a competitor for another. For example, the invention of satellite television and increased popularity of DirecTV and the Dish Network represent a competitive challenge to cable television companies. That is, DirecTV and, say, Time Warner Cable are competitors. However, DirecTV and television production companies are complementors to each other. In deciding whether to encourage the entry of new complementors, a firm has to weigh the extra value these new complementors will create against the competitive impact of this entry on a firm's current complementors.

It is also the case that a single firm can be both a competitor and a complementor to the same firm. This is very common in industries where it is important to create technological standards. Without standards for, say, the size of a CD, how information on a CD will be stored, how this information will be read, and so forth, consumers will often be unwilling to purchase a CD player. With standards in place, however, sales of a particular technology can soar. To develop technology standards, firms must be willing to cooperate. This cooperation means that, with respect to the technology standard, these firms are complementors. And, indeed, when these firms act as complementors, their actions have the effect of increasing the total size of the market. However, once these firms cooperate to establish standards, they begin to compete to try to obtain as much of the market they jointly created as possible. In this sense, these firms are also competitors.

Understanding when firms in an industry should behave as complementors and when they should behave as competitors is sometimes very difficult. It is even more difficult for a firm that has interacted with other firms in its industry as a competitor to change its organizational structure, formal and informal control systems, and compensation policy and start interacting with these firms as a complementor, at least for some purposes. Learning to manage what Brandenburger and Nalebuff call the "Jekyll and Hyde" dilemma associated with competitors and complementors can distinguish excellent from average firms.

Research Made Relevant

For some time now, scholars have been interested in the relative impact of the attributes of the industry within which a firm operates and the attributes of the firm itself on its performance. The first work in this area was published by Richard Schmalansee. Using a single year's worth of data, Schmalansee estimated the variance in the performance of firms that was attributable to the industries within which firms operated versus other sources of performance variance. Schmalansee's conclusion was that approximately 20 percent of the variance in firm performance was explained by the industry within which a firm operated—a conclusion consistent with the S-C-P model and its emphasis on industry as a primary determinant of a firm's performance.

Richard Rumelt identified some weaknesses in Schmalansee's research. Most important of these was that Schmalansee had only one year's worth of data with which to examine the effects of industry and firm attributes on firm performance. Rumelt was able to use four years' worth of data, which allowed him to distinguish between stable and transient industry and firm effects on firm performance.

The Impact of Industry and Firm Characteristics on Firm Performance

Rumelt's results were consistent with Schmalansee's in one sense: Rumelt also found that about 16 percent of the variance in firm performance was due to industry effects, versus Schmalansee's 20 percent. However, only about half of this industry effect was stable. The rest represented year-to-year fluctuations in the business conditions in an industry. This result is broadly inconsistent with the S-C-P model.

Rumelt also examined the impact of firm attributes on firm performance and found that more than 80 percent of the variance in firm performance was due to these firm attributes, but that more than half of this 80 percent (46.38 percent) was due to stable firm effects. The importance of stable firm differences in explaining differences in firm performance is also inconsistent with the S-C-P framework. These results are consistent with another model of firm performance called the *resource-based view*, which will be described in Chapter 3.

Since Rumelt's research, efforts to identify the factors that explain variance in firm performance have accelerated. At least nine articles addressing this issue have been published in the literature. One of the most recent of these suggests that, while the impact of the industry and the corporation on business unit performance can vary across industries and across corporations, overall, business unit effects are larger than either corporate or industry effects.

Sources: R. P. Rumelt (1991). "How much does industry matter?" *Strategic Management Journal*, 12, pp. 167–185; R. Schmalansee (1985). "Do markets differ much?" *American Economic Review*, 75, pp. 341–351; V. F. Misangyi, H. Elms, T. Greckhamer, and J. A. Lepine (2006). "A new perspective on a fundamental debate: A multilevel approach to industry, corporate, and business unit effects." *Strategic Management Journal*, 27(6), pp. 571–590.

Industry Structure and Environmental Opportunities

Identifying environmental threats is only half the task in accomplishing an external analysis. Such an analysis must also identify opportunities. Fortunately, the same S-C-P logic that made it possible to develop tools for the analysis of environmental threats can also be used to develop tools for the analysis of environmental opportunities. However, instead of identifying the threats that are common in most industries, opportunity analysis begins by identifying several generic industry structures and then describing the strategic opportunities that are available in each of these different kinds of industries.[32]

TABLE 2.7 Industry
Structure and Environmental
Opportunities

Industry Structure	Opportunities
Fragmented industry	Consolidation
Emerging industry	First-mover advantages
Mature industry	Product refinement
	Investment in service quality
	Process innovation
Declining industry	Leadership
	Niche
	Harvest
	Divestment

Of course, there are many different generic industry structures. However, four are very common and will be the focus of opportunity analysis in this book: (1) fragmented industries, (2) emerging industries, (3) mature industries, and (4) declining industries. A fifth industry structure—international industries—will be discussed later in the chapter. The kinds of opportunities typically associated with these industry structures are presented in Table 2.7.

Opportunities in Fragmented Industries: Consolidation

Fragmented industries are industries in which a large number of small or medium-sized firms operate and no small set of firms has dominant market share or creates dominant technologies. Most service industries, including retailing, fabrics, and commercial printing, to name just a few, are fragmented industries.

Industries can be fragmented for a wide variety of reasons. For example, the fragmented industry may have few barriers to entry, thereby encouraging numerous small firms to enter. The industry may have few, if any, economies of scale, and even some important diseconomies of scale, thus encouraging firms to remain small. Also, close local control over enterprises in an industry may be necessary—for example, local movie houses and local restaurants—to ensure quality and to minimize losses from theft.

The major opportunity facing firms in fragmented industries is the implementation of strategies that begin to consolidate the industry into a smaller number of firms. Firms that are successful in implementing this **consolidation strategy** can become industry leaders and obtain benefits from this kind of effort, if they exist.

Consolidation can occur in several ways. For example, an incumbent firm may discover new economies of scale in an industry. In the highly fragmented funeral home industry, Service Corporation International (SCI) found that the development of a chain of funeral homes gave it advantages in acquiring key supplies (coffins) and in the allocation of scarce resources (morticians and hearses). By acquiring numerous previously independent funeral homes, SCI was able to substantially reduce its costs and gain higher levels of economic performance.[33]

Incumbent firms sometimes adopt new ownership structures to help consolidate an industry. Kampgrounds of America (KOA) uses franchise agreements with local operators to provide camping facilities to travelers in the fragmented private campgrounds industry. KOA provides local operators with professional training, technical skills, and access to its brand-name reputation.

Local operators, in return, provide KOA with local managers who are intensely interested in the financial and operational success of their campgrounds. Similar franchise agreements have been instrumental in the consolidation of other fragmented industries, including fast food (McDonald's), muffler repair (Midas), and motels (La Quinta, Holiday Inn, Howard Johnson's).[34]

The benefits of implementing a consolidation strategy in a fragmented industry turn on the advantages larger firms in such industries gain from their larger market share. As will be discussed in Chapter 4, firms with large market share can have important cost advantages. Large market share can also help a firm differentiate its products.

Opportunities in Emerging Industries: First-Mover Advantages

Emerging industries are newly created or newly re-created industries formed by technological innovations, changes in demand, the emergence of new customer needs, and so forth. Over the past 30 years, the world economy has been flooded by emerging industries, including the microprocessor industry, the personal computer industry, the medical imaging industry, and the biotechnology industry, to name a few. Firms in emerging industries face a unique set of opportunities, the exploitation of which can be a source of superior performance for some time for some firms.

The opportunities that face firms in emerging industries fall into the general category of first-mover advantages. **First-mover advantages** are advantages that come to firms that make important strategic and technological decisions early in the development of an industry. In emerging industries, many of the rules of the game and standard operating procedures for competing and succeeding have yet to be established. First-moving firms can sometimes help establish the rules of the game and create an industry's structure in ways that are uniquely beneficial to them. In general, first-mover advantages can arise from three primary sources: (1) technological leadership, (2) preemption of strategically valuable assets, and (3) the creation of customer-switching costs.[35]

First-Mover Advantages and Technological Leadership

Firms that make early investments in particular technologies in an industry are implementing a **technological leadership strategy**. Such strategies can generate two advantages in emerging industries. First, firms that have implemented these strategies may obtain a low-cost position based on their greater cumulative volume of production with a particular technology. These cost advantages have had important competitive implications in such diverse industries as the manufacture of titanium dioxide by DuPont and Procter & Gamble's competitive advantage in disposable diapers.[36]

Second, firms that make early investments in a technology may obtain patent protections that enhance their performance.[37] Xerox's patents on the xerography process and General Electric's patent on Edison's original lightbulb design were important for these firms' success when these two industries were emerging.[38] However, although there are some exceptions (e.g., the pharmaceutical industry and specialty chemicals), patents, per se, seem to provide relatively small profit opportunities for first-moving firms in most emerging industries. One group of researchers found that imitators can duplicate first movers' patent-based advantages for about 65 percent of the first mover's costs.[39] These researchers also found that 60 percent of all patents are imitated within four years of being granted—without legally violating patent rights obtained by first movers. As we will discuss in detail in Chapter 3, patents are rarely a source of sustained competitive advantage for firms, even in emerging industries.

First-Mover Advantages and Preemption of Strategically Valuable Assets

First movers that invest only in technology usually do not obtain sustained competitive advantages. However, first movers that move to tie up strategically valuable resources in an industry before their full value is widely understood can gain sustained competitive advantages. **Strategically valuable assets** are resources required to successfully compete in an industry. Firms that are able to acquire these resources have, in effect, erected formidable barriers to imitation in an industry. Some strategically valuable assets that can be acquired in this way include access to raw materials, particularly favorable geographic locations, and particularly valuable product market positions.

When an oil company such as Royal Dutch Shell (because of its superior exploration skills) acquires leases with greater development potential than was expected by its competition, the company is gaining access to raw materials in a way that is likely to generate sustained competitive advantages. When Wal-Mart opens stores in medium-sized cities before the arrival of its competition, Wal-Mart is making it difficult for the competition to enter into this market. And when breakfast cereal companies expand their product lines to include all possible combinations of wheat, oats, bran, corn, and sugar, they, too, are using a first-mover advantage to deter entry.[40]

First-Mover Advantages and Creating Customer-Switching Costs

Firms can also gain first-mover advantages in an emerging industry by creating customer-switching costs. **Customer-switching costs** exist when customers make investments in order to use a firm's particular products or services. These investments tie customers to a particular firm and make it more difficult for customers to begin purchasing from other firms.[41] Such switching costs are important factors in industries as diverse as applications software for personal computers, prescription pharmaceuticals, and groceries.[42]

In applications software for personal computers, users make significant investments to learn how to use a particular software package. Once computer users have learned how to operate particular software, they are unlikely to switch to new software, even if that new software system is superior to what they currently use. Such a switch would require learning the new software and determining how it is similar to and different from the old software. For these reasons, some computer users will continue to use outdated software, even though new software performs much better.

Similar switching costs can exist in some segments of the prescription pharmaceutical industry. Once medical doctors become familiar with a particular drug, its applications, and side effects, they are sometimes reluctant to change to a new drug, even if that new drug promises to be more effective than the older, more familiar one. Trying the new drug requires learning about its properties and side effects. Even if the new drug has received government approvals, its use requires doctors to be willing to "experiment" with the health of their patients. Given these issues, many physicians are unwilling to rapidly adopt new drug therapies. This is one reason that pharmaceutical firms spend so much time and money using their sales forces to educate their physician customers. This kind of education is necessary if a doctor is going to be willing to switch from an old drug to a new one.

Customer-switching costs can even play a role in the grocery store industry. Each grocery store has a particular layout of products. Once customers learn where different products in a particular store are located, they are not likely to change stores because they would then have to relearn the location of products. Many customers want to avoid the time and frustration associated with wandering around a new store looking for some obscure product. Indeed, the cost of switching stores may be large enough to enable some grocery stores to charge higher prices than would be the case without customer-switching costs.

First-Mover Disadvantages

Of course, the advantages of first moving in emerging industries must be balanced against the risks associated with exploiting this opportunity. Emerging industries are characterized by a great deal of uncertainty. When first-moving firms are making critical strategic decisions, it may not be at all clear what the right decisions are. In such highly uncertain settings, a reasonable strategic alternative to first moving may be retaining flexibility. Where first-moving firms attempt to resolve the uncertainty they face by making decisions early and then trying to influence the evolution of an emerging industry, they use flexibility to resolve this uncertainty by delaying decisions until the economically correct path is clear and then moving quickly to take advantage of that path.

Opportunities in Mature Industries: Product Refinement, Service, and Process Innovation

Emerging industries are often formed by the creation of new products or technologies that radically alter the rules of the game in an industry. However, over time, as these new ways of doing business become widely understood, as technologies diffuse through competitors, and as the rate of innovation in new products and technologies drops, an industry begins to enter the mature phase of its development. As described in the Strategy in the Emerging Enterprise feature, this change in the nature of a firm's industry can be difficult to recognize and can create both strategic and operational problems for a firm.

Common characteristics of **mature industries** include (1) slowing growth in total industry demand, (2) the development of experienced repeat customers, (3) a slowdown in increases in production capacity, (4) a slowdown in the introduction of new products or services, (5) an increase in the amount of international competition, and (6) an overall reduction in the profitability of firms in the industry.[43]

The fast-food industry in the United States has matured over the last several years. In the 1960s, the United States had only three large national fast-food chains: McDonald's, Burger King, and Dairy Queen. Through the 1980s, all three of these chains grew rapidly, although the rate of growth at McDonald's outstripped the growth rate of the other two firms. During this time period, however, other fast-food chains also entered the market. These included some national chains, such as Kentucky Fried Chicken, Wendy's, and Taco Bell, and some strong regional chains, such as Jack in the Box and In and Out Burger. By the early 1990s, growth in this industry had slowed considerably. McDonald's announced that it was having difficulty finding locations for new McDonald's that did not impinge on the sales of already existing McDonald's. Except for non–U.S. operations, where competition in the fast-food industry is not as mature, the profitability of most U.S. fast-food companies did not grow as much in the 1990s as it did in the 1960s through the 1980s. Indeed, by 2002, all the major fast-food chains were either not making very much money or, like McDonald's, actually losing money.[44]

Opportunities for firms in mature industries typically shift from the development of new technologies and products in an emerging industry to a greater emphasis on refining a firm's current products, an emphasis on increasing the quality of service, and a focus on reducing manufacturing costs and increased quality through process innovations.

Refining Current Products

In mature industries, such as home detergents, motor oil, and kitchen appliances, few, if any, major technological breakthroughs are likely. However, this does not mean that innovation is not occurring in these industries. Innovation in these industries focuses on extending and improving current products and technologies. In home detergents, innovation recently has focused on changes in packaging and on selling more highly concentrated detergents. In motor oil, packaging changes (from fiber foil cans to plastic containers), additives that keep oil cleaner longer, and oil formulated to operate in four-cylinder engines are recent examples of this kind of innovation. In kitchen appliances, recent improvements include the availability of refrigerators with crushed ice and water through the door, commercial-grade stoves for home use, and dishwashers that automatically adjust the cleaning cycle depending on how dirty the dishes are.[45] In fast foods, firms like McDonald's and Wendy's have introduced healthy, more adult-oriented food to complement their kid-friendly hamburger-heavy menus. This movement has helped restore the profitability of these firms.

Emphasis on Service

When firms in an industry have only limited ability to invest in radical new technologies and products, efforts to differentiate products often turn toward the quality of customer service. A firm that is able to develop a reputation for high-quality customer service may be able to obtain superior performance even though its products are not highly differentiated.

This emphasis on service has become very important in a wide variety of industries. For example, in the convenience food industry, one of the major reasons for slower growth in the fast-food segment has been growth in the so-called "casual dining" segment. This segment includes restaurants such as Chili's and Applebee's. The food sold at fast-food restaurants and casual dining restaurants overlaps—they both sell burgers, soft drinks, salads, chicken, desserts, and so forth—although many consumers believe that the quality of food is superior in the casual dining restaurants. In addition to any perceived differences in the food, however, the level of service in the two kinds of establishments varies significantly. At fast-food restaurants, food is handed to consumers on a tray; in casual dining restaurants, waitstaff actually bring food to consumers on a plate. This level of service is one reason that casual dining is growing in popularity.[46]

On the other hand, the fastest-growing segment of the U.S. restaurant industry is the "fast casual" segment—Panera Bread, Café Rio (a regional Mexican restaurant), and Chipotle. These restaurants deliver high-quality food but avoid the delays often associated with full-service restaurants.

Process Innovation

A firm's **processes** are the activities it engages in to design, produce, and sell its products or services. **Process innovation**, then, is a firm's effort to refine and

Strategy in the Emerging Enterprise

It began with a 5,000-word e-mail sent by Steve Balmer, CEO of Microsoft, to all 57,000 employees. Whereas previous e-mails from Microsoft founder Bill Gates—including one in 1995 calling on the firm to learn how to "ride the wave of the Internet"—inspired the firm to move on to conquer more technological challenges, Balmer's e-mail focused on Microsoft's current state and called on the firm to become more focused and efficient. Balmer also announced that Microsoft would cut its costs by $1 billion during the next fiscal year. One observer described it as the kind of e-mail you would expect to read at Procter & Gamble, not at Microsoft.

Then the other shoe dropped. In a surprise move, Balmer announced that Microsoft would distribute a large portion of its $56 billion cash reserve in the form of a special dividend to stockholders. In what is believed to be the largest such cash dispersion ever, Microsoft distributed $32 billion to its stockholders and used an additional $30 billion to buy back stock. Bill Gates received a $3.2 billion cash dividend. These changes meant that Microsoft's capital structure was more similar to, say, Procter & Gamble's than to an entrepreneurial, high-flying software company.

What happened at Microsoft? Did Microsoft's management conclude that the PC software industry

Microsoft Grows Up

was no longer emerging, but had matured to the point that Microsoft would have to alter some of its traditional strategies? Most observers believe that Balmer's e-mail, and the decision to reduce its cash reserves, signaled that Microsoft had come to this conclusion. In fact, although most of Microsoft's core businesses—its Windows operating systems, its PC applications software, and its server software—are still growing at the rate of about $3 billion a year, if they were growing at historical rates these businesses would be generating $7 billion in new revenues each year. Moreover, Microsoft's new businesses—video games, Internet services, business software, and software for phones and handheld computers—are adding less than $1 billion in new revenues each year. That is, growth in Microsoft's new businesses is not offsetting slower growth in its traditional businesses.

Other indicators of the growing maturity of the PC software industry, and Microsoft's strategic changes, also exist. For example, during 2003 and 2004, Microsoft resolved most of the outstanding antitrust litigation it was facing, abandoned its employee stock option plan in favor of a stock-based compensation scheme popular with slower-growth firms, improved its systems for receiving and acting on feedback from customers, and improved the quality of its relationships with some of its major rivals, including Sun Microsystems, Inc. These are all the actions of a firm that recognizes that the rapid growth opportunities that existed in the software industry when Microsoft was a new company do not exist anymore.

At this point, Microsoft has to choose whether it is going to jump-start its growth through a series of large acquisitions or accept the lower growth rates in its core markets. It has tried to jump-start its growth through acquisitions, a strong indicator that Microsoft, while acknowledging slower growth in its core, has not completely abandoned the idea of growing quickly in some parts of its business.

Sources: J. Greene (2004). "Microsoft's midlife crisis." *BusinessWeek*, April 19, 2004, pp. 88+; R. Guth and S. Thurm (2004). "Microsoft to dole out its cash hoard." *The Wall Street Journal*, Wednesday, July 21, 2004, pp. A1+; S. Hamm (2004). "Microsoft's worst enemy: Success." *BusinessWeek*, July 19, 2004, p. 33; Accessed July 12, 2006.

improve its current processes. Several authors have studied the relationship between process innovation, product innovation, and the maturity of an industry.[47] This work suggests that, in the early stages of industry development, product innovation is very important. However, over time product innovation becomes less important, and process innovations designed to reduce manufacturing costs, increase product quality, and streamline management become more important.

In mature industries, firms can often gain an advantage by manufacturing the same product as competitors, but at a lower cost. Alternatively, firms can manufacture a product that is perceived to be of higher quality and do so at a competitive cost. Process innovations facilitate both the reduction of costs and the increase in quality.

The role of process innovation in more mature industries is perhaps best exemplified by the improvement in quality in U.S. automobiles. In the 1980s, Japanese firms such as Nissan, Toyota, and Honda sold cars that were of significantly higher quality than those produced by U.S. firms General Motors, Ford, and Chrysler. In the face of that competitive disadvantage, the U.S. firms engaged in numerous process reforms to improve the quality of their cars. In the 1980s, U.S. manufacturers were cited for car body panels that did not fit well, bumpers that were hung crookedly on cars, and the wrong engines being placed in cars. Today, the differences in quality between newly manufactured U.S. and Japanese automobiles are very small. Indeed, one well-known judge of initial manufacturing quality—J. D. Powers—now focuses on items such as the quality of a car's cup holders and the maximum distance at which a car's keyless entry system still works to establish quality rankings. The really significant quality issues of the 1980s are virtually gone.[48]

Opportunities in Declining Industries: Leadership, Niche, Harvest, and Divestment

A **declining industry** is an industry that has experienced an absolute decline in unit sales over a sustained period of time.[49] Obviously, firms in a declining industry face more threats than opportunities. Rivalry in a declining industry is likely to be very high, as is the threat of buyers, suppliers, and substitutes. However, even though threats are significant, firms do have opportunities they can exploit. The major strategic opportunities that firms in this kind of industry face are leadership, niche, harvest, and divestment.

Market Leadership

An industry in decline is often characterized by overcapacity in manufacturing, distribution, and so forth. Reduced demand often means that firms in a declining industry will have to endure a significant **shakeout period** until overcapacity is reduced and capacity is brought in line with demand. After the shakeout, a smaller number of lean and focused firms may enjoy a relatively benign environment with few threats and several opportunities. If the industry structure that is likely to exist after a shakeout is quite attractive, firms in an industry before the shakeout may have an incentive to weather the storm of decline—to survive until the situation improves to the point that they can begin to earn higher profits.

If a firm has decided to wait out the storm of decline in hopes of better environmental conditions in the future, it should consider various steps to increase its chances of survival. Most important of these is that a firm must establish itself as a **market leader** in the pre-shakeout industry, most typically by becoming the firm with the largest market share in that industry. The purpose of becoming a market leader is *not* to facilitate tacit collusion (see Chapter 9) or to obtain lower costs from economies of scale (see Chapter 6). Rather, in a declining industry the leader's objective should be to try to facilitate the exit of firms that are not likely to survive a shakeout, thereby obtaining a more favorable competitive environment as quickly as possible.

Market leaders in declining industries can facilitate exit in a variety of ways, including purchasing and then deemphasizing competitors' product lines, purchasing and retiring competitors' manufacturing capacity, manufacturing spare parts for competitors' product lines, and sending unambiguous signals of their intention to stay in an industry and remain a dominant firm. For example, overcapacity problems in the European petrochemical industry were partially resolved when Imperial Chemical Industries (ICI) traded its polyethylene plants to British Petroleum for BP's polyvinylchloride (PVC) plants. In this case, both firms were able to close some excess capacity in specific markets (polyethylene and PVC), while sending clear signals of their intention to remain in these markets.[50]

Market Niche

A firm in a declining industry following a leadership strategy attempts to facilitate exit by other firms, but a firm following a **niche strategy** in a declining industry reduces its scope of operations and focuses on narrow segments of the declining industry. If only a few firms choose a particular niche, then these firms may have a favorable competitive setting, even though the industry as a whole is facing shrinking demand.

Two firms that used the niche approach in a declining market are GTE Sylvania and General Electric (GE) in the vacuum tube industry. Yes, vacuum tubes! The invention of the transistor followed by the semiconductor just about destroyed demand for vacuum tubes in new products. GTE Sylvania and GE rapidly recognized that new product sales in vacuum tubes were drying up. In response, these firms began specializing in supplying *replacement* vacuum tubes to the consumer and military markets. To earn high profits, these firms had to refocus their sales efforts and scale down their sales and manufacturing staffs. Over time, as fewer and fewer firms manufactured vacuum tubes, GTE Sylvania and GE were able to charge very high prices for replacement parts.[51]

Harvest

Leadership and niche strategies, though differing along several dimensions, have one attribute in common: Firms that implement these strategies intend to remain in the industry despite its decline. Firms pursuing a **harvest strategy** in a declining industry do not expect to remain in the industry over the long term. Instead, they engage in a long, systematic, phased withdrawal, extracting as much value as possible during the withdrawal period.

The extraction of value during the implementation of a harvest strategy presumes that there is some value to harvest. Thus, firms that implement this strategy must ordinarily have enjoyed at least some profits at some time in their history, before the industry began declining. Firms can implement a harvest strategy by reducing the range of products they sell, reducing their distribution network, eliminating less profitable customers, reducing product quality, reducing service quality, deferring maintenance and equipment repair, and so forth. In the end, after a period of harvesting in a declining industry, firms can either sell their operations (to a market leader) or simply cease operations.

In principle, the harvest opportunity sounds simple, but in practice it presents some significant management challenges. The movement toward a harvest strategy often means that some of the characteristics of a business that have long been a source of pride to managers may have to be abandoned. Thus, where prior to harvest a firm may have specialized in high-quality service, quality products, and excellent customer value, during the harvest period service quality may fall, product quality may deteriorate, and prices may rise. These changes may be difficult for managers to accept, and higher turnover may be the result. It is also difficult to hire quality managers into a harvesting business because such individuals are likely to seek greater opportunities elsewhere.

For these reasons, few firms explicitly announce a harvest strategy. However, examples can be found. GE seems to be following a harvest strategy in the electric turbine business. Also, United States Steel and the International Steel Group seem to be following this strategy in certain segments of the steel market.[52]

Divestment

The final opportunity facing firms in a declining industry is divestment. Like a harvest strategy, the objective of **divestment** is to extract a firm from a declining industry. However, unlike harvest, divestment occurs quickly, often soon after a pattern of decline has been established. Firms without established competitive advantages may find divestment a superior option to harvest because they have few competitive advantages they can exploit through harvesting.

In the 1980s, GE used this rapid divestment approach to virtually abandon the consumer electronics business. Total demand in this business was more or less stable during the 1980s, but competition (mainly from Asian manufacturers) increased substantially. Rather than remain in this business, GE sold most of its consumer electronics operations and used the capital to enter into the medical imaging industry, where this firm has found an environment more conducive to superior performance.[53]

In the defense business, divestment is the stated strategy of General Dynamics, at least in some of its business segments. General Dynamics' managers recognized early on that the changing defense industry could not support all the incumbent firms. When General Dynamics concluded that it could not remain a leader in some of its businesses, it decided to divest those and concentrate on a few remaining businesses. Since 1991, General Dynamics has sold businesses worth more than $2.83 billion, including its missile systems business, its Cessna aircraft division, and its tactical aircraft division (maker of the very successful F-16 aircraft and partner in the development of the next generation of fighter aircraft, the F-22). These divestitures have left General Dynamics in just three businesses: armored tanks, nuclear submarines, and space launch vehicles. During this time, the market price of General Dynamics stock has returned almost $4.5 billion to its investors, has seen its stock go from $25 per share to a high of $110 per share and has provided a total return to stockholders of 555 percent.[54]

Of course, not all divestments are caused by industry decline. Sometimes firms divest certain operations to focus their efforts on remaining operations, sometimes they divest to raise capital, and sometimes they divest to simplify operations. These types of divestments reflect a firm's diversification strategy and are explored in detail in Chapter 11.

Summary

The strategic management process requires that a firm engage in an analysis of threats and opportunities in its competitive environment before a strategic choice can be made. This analysis begins with an understanding of the firm's general environment. This general environment has six components: technological change, demographic trends, cultural trends, economic climate, legal and political conditions, and specific international events. Although some of these components of the general environment can affect a firm directly, more frequently they affect a firm through their impact on its local environment.

The S-C-P model can be used to develop tools for analyzing threats in a firm's competitive environment. The most influential of these tools focuses on five environmental threats to the profitability of firms in an industry. The five threats are: threat from new competitors, threat from existing direct competitors, threat from superior or low cost substitutes, threat of supplier leverage, and the threat from buyers' influence. The threat of new competition depends on the existence and "height" of barriers to entry. Common barriers to entry include economies of scale, product differentiation, cost advantages independent of scale, and government regulation. The threat of current direct competitors depends on the number and competitiveness of firms in an industry. This threat is high in an industry when there are large numbers of competing firms, competing firms are roughly the same size and have the same influence, growth in an industry is slow, there is no product differentiation, and productive capacity is added in large increments. The threat of superior substitutes depends on how close substitute products and services are—in performance and cost—to products and services in an industry. Whereas direct competitors meet the same customer needs in approximately the same way, substitutes meet the same customer needs, but do so in very different ways. The threat of supplier leverage in an industry depends on the number and distinctiveness of the products suppliers provide to an industry. The threat of supplier leverage increases when a supplier's industry is dominated by a few firms, when suppliers sell unique or highly differentiated products, when suppliers are not threatened by substitutes, when suppliers threaten forward vertical integration, and when firms are not important customers for suppliers. Finally, the threat of buyers' influence depends on the number and size of an industry's customers. The threat of buyers' influence is greater when the number of buyers is small, products sold to buyers are undifferentiated and standard, products sold to buyers are a significant percentage of a buyer's final costs, buyers are not earning significant profits, and buyers threaten backward vertical integration. Taken together, the level of these threats in an industry can be used to determine the expected average performance of firms in an industry.

One additional force in a firm's environment is complementors. Where competitors compete with a firm to divide profits in a market, complementors increase the total size of the market. If you are a CEO of a firm, you know that another firm is a complementor when the value of your products to your customers is higher in combination with this other firm's products than when customers use your products alone. Where firms have strong incentives to reduce the entry of competitors, they can sometimes have strong incentives to increase the entry of complementors.

The S-C-P model can also be used to develop tools for analyzing strategic opportunities in an industry. This is done by identifying generic industry structures and the strategic opportunities available in these different kinds of industries. Four common industry structures are fragmented industries, emerging industries, mature industries, and declining industries. The primary opportunity in fragmented industries is consolidation. In emerging industries, the most important opportunity is first-mover advantages from technological leadership, preemption of strategically valuable assets, or creation of customer-switching costs. In mature industries, the primary opportunities are product refinement, service, and process innovation. In declining industries, opportunities include market leadership, niche, harvest, and divestment.

MyManagementLab®

Go to **mymanagementlab.com** to complete the problems marked with this icon ✪.

Challenge Questions

2.1. Your former college roommate calls you and asks to borrow $10,000 so that he can open a pizza restaurant in his hometown. In justifying this request, he argues that there must be significant demand for pizza and other fast food in his hometown because there are lots of such restaurants already there and three or four new ones are opening each month. He also argues that demand for convenience food will continue to increase, and he points to the large number of firms that now sell frozen dinners in grocery stores. What are the risks involved in choosing to lend him money?

⭐ **2.2.** One potential threat in an industry is buyers' influence. Yet unless buyers are satisfied, they are likely to look for satisfaction elsewhere. Can the fact that buyers can be threats be reconciled with the need to satisfy buyers?

2.3. Government policies can have a significant impact on the average profitability of firms in an industry. Government, however, is not included as a potential threat. Why should the model be expanded to include government? Why or why not?

2.4. In particular, if an industry has large numbers of complementors, does that make it more attractive or less attractive or does it have no impact on the industry's attractiveness? Justify your answer.

⭐ **2.5.** Opportunities analysis seems to suggest that strategic opportunities are available in almost any industry, including declining ones. If that is true, is it fair to say that there is really no such thing as an unattractive industry?

2.6. If there is really no such thing as an unattractive industry, what implications does this have for the applicability of environmental threat analysis?

2.7. Describe an industry that has no opportunities.

2.8. Describe when the evolution of industry structure from an emerging industry to a mature industry to a declining industry is inevitable.

Problem Set

2.9. Perform an analysis of the profit potential on the following two industries:

The Pharmaceutical Industry

The pharmaceutical industry consists of firms that develop, patent, and distribute drugs. Although this industry does not have significant production economies, it does have important economies in research and development. Product differentiation exists as well because firms often sell branded products. Firms compete in research and development. However, once a product is developed and patented, competition is significantly reduced. Recently, the increased availability of generic, nonbranded drugs has threatened the profitability of some drug lines. Once an effective drug is developed, few, if any, alternatives to that drug usually are available. Drugs are manufactured from commodity chemicals that are available from numerous suppliers. Major customers include doctors and patients. Recently, increased costs have led the federal government and insurance companies to pressure drug companies to reduce their prices.

The Textile Industry

The textile industry consists of firms that manufacture and distribute fabrics for use in clothing, furniture, carpeting, and so forth. Several firms have invested heavily in sophisticated manufacturing technology, and many lower-cost firms located in Asia have begun fabric production. Textiles are not branded products. Recently, tariffs on some imported textiles have been implemented. The industry has numerous firms; the largest have less than 10 percent market share. Traditional fabric materials (such as cotton and wool) have recently been threatened by the development of alternative chemical-based materials (such as nylon and rayon), although many textile companies have begun manufacturing with these new materials as well. Most raw materials are widely available, although some synthetic products periodically may be in short supply. There are numerous textile customers, but textile costs are usually a large percentage of their final product's total costs. Many users shop around the world for the lowest textile prices.

2.10. Perform an opportunities analysis on the following industries:

(a) The U.S. airline industry
(b) The U.S. beer industry
(c) The U.S. property and casualty insurance industry
(d) The worldwide portable digital media (e.g., flash drives) industry
(e) The worldwide small-package overnight delivery industry

2.11. For each of the following firms, identify at least two competitors (rivals, new entrants, or substitutes) and two complementors.

(a) Yahoo!
(b) Microsoft
(c) Dell
(d) Boeing
(e) McDonald's

MyManagementLab®

Go to **mymanagementlab.com** for Auto-graded writing questions as well as the following Assisted-graded writing questions:

2.12. Describe a case when a single firm can be both a competitor and a complementor to the same firm.

2.13. Under what constraints can firms also gain first-mover advantages in an emerging industry?

End Notes

1. See (2003). *The big book of business quotations*. New York: Basic Books, p. 209.
2. See Weintraub, A. (2004). "Repairing the engines of life." *BusinessWeek*, May 24, 2004, pp. 99+ for a discussion of recent developments in biotechnology research and the business challenges they have created.
3. See Grow, B. (2004). "Hispanic nation." *BusinessWeek*, March 15, 2004, pp. 59+.
4. Ibid.
5. Barnes, B. (2004). "The WB grows up." *The Wall Street Journal*, July 19, 2004, pp. B1+; money.cnn.com/2006/01/24/news/companies/cbs_warner. Accessed February 2007.
6. These and other cultural differences are described in Rugman, A., and R. Hodgetts. (1995). *International business*. New York: McGraw-Hill. A discussion of the dimensions along which country cultures can vary is presented in a later chapter.
7. Early contributors to the structure-conduct-performance model include Mason, E. S. (1939). "Price and production policies of large scale enterprises." *American Economic Review*, 29, pp. 61–74; and Bain, J. S. (1956). *Barriers to new competition*. Cambridge, MA: Harvard

University Press. The major developments in this framework are summarized in Bain, J. S. (1968). *Industrial organization*. New York: John Wiley & Sons, Inc.; and Scherer, F. M. (1980). *Industrial market structure and economic performance*. Boston: Houghton Mifflin. The links between this framework and work in strategic management are discussed by Porter, M. E. (1981a). "The contribution of industrial organization to strategic management." *Academy of Management Review*, 6, pp. 609–620; and Barney, J. B. (1986c). "Types of competition and the theory of strategy: Toward an integrative framework." *Academy of Management Review*, 1, pp. 791–800.
8. See, for example, Porter, M. E. (1979). "How competitive forces shape strategy." *Harvard Business Review*, March–April, pp. 137–156; and Porter, M. E. (1980). *Competitive strategy*. New York: Free Press.
9. Sharma, A., and M. Fatterman. (2013). "Fox, latest underdog, takes on ESPN." *The Wall Street Journal*, Friday, July 26, pp. B1+.
10. These barriers were originally proposed by Bain, J. S. (1968). *Industrial organization*. New York: John Wiley & Sons, Inc. It is actually possible to estimate the "height" of barriers to entry in an industry by comparing the cost of entry into an industry with

barriers and the cost of entry into that industry if barriers did not exist. The difference between these costs is the "height" of the barriers to entry.

11. Another alternative would be for a firm to own and operate more than one plant. If there are economies of scope in this industry, a firm might be able to enter and earn above-normal profits. An economy of scope exists when the value of operating in two businesses simultaneously is greater than the value of operating in these two businesses separately. The concept of economy of scope is explored in more detail in Part 3 of this book.

12. See Ghemawat, P., and H. J. Stander III. (1992). "Nucor at a crossroads." Harvard Business School Case No. 9-793-039.

13. See Montgomery, C. A., and B. Wernerfelt. (1991). "Sources of superior performance: Market share versus industry effects in the U.S. brewing industry." *Management Science*, 37, pp. 954–959.

14. Sorkin, A. R., and M. Merced. (2008). "Brewer bids $46 billion for Anheuser-Busch." *New York Times*, June 12. http://www.nytimes.com/2008/06/12/business/worldbusiness/12beer.html?_r=0

15. Stecklow, S. (1999). "Gallo woos French, but don't expect Bordeaux by the jug." *The Wall Street Journal*, March 26, pp. A1+.

16. Wingfield, N. (2013). "Intertrust sues Apple over patent violations." Bcts.blogs. NYTimes.com, March 20; Swisler, K. (2012). "Yahoo sues Facebook for patent infringement." Allthings.com, March 12; Fingas, J. (2013). "Google countersues BT." www.engadget.com, February 13; "Boston University sues Apple for patent infringement." (2013). www.macworld.com, July 3; "Nokia taking HTC to court over patent violations." (2013). www.mobilemg.com, May 25;Dobie, A. (2013). "Apple looks to add Sony Galaxy 54 to patent infringement suit."www.androidcentral.com, May 14; "Bad Apple." (2013). www.catholic.org, June 5.

17. www.patstats.org. Accessed July 3, 2013.

18. See Kogut, B., and U. Zander. (1992). "Knowledge of the firm, combinative capabilities, and the replication of technology." *Organization Science*, 3, pp. 383–397; and Dierickx, I., and K. Cool. (1989). "Asset stock accumulation and sustainability of competitive advantage." *Management Science*, 35, pp. 1504–1511. Both emphasize the importance of know-how as a barrier to entry into an industry. More generally, intangible resources are seen as particularly important sources of sustained competitive advantage. This will be discussed in more detail in Chapter 5.

19. See Polanyi, M. (1962). *Personal knowledge: Towards a post-critical philosophy.* London: Routledge & Kegan Paul; and Itami, H. (1987). *Mobilizing invisible assets.* Cambridge, MA: Harvard University Press.

20. See Henderson, R., and I. Cockburn. (1994). "Measuring competence: Exploring firm effects in pharmaceutical research." *Strategic Management Journal*, 15, pp. 361–374.

21. See Scherer, F. M. (1980). *Industrial market structure and economic performance.* Boston: Houghton Mifflin.

22. See Saporito, B. (1992). "Why the price wars never end." *Fortune*, March 23, pp. 68–78; and Allen, M., and M. Siconolfi. (1993). "Dell Computer drops planned share offering." *The Wall Street Journal*, February 25, p. A3.

23. Chartier, John. (2002). "Burger battles." CNN/Money, http://money.cnn.com, December 11.

24. See Ghemawat, P., and A. McGahan. (1995). "The U.S. airline industry in 1995." Harvard Business School Case No. 9-795-113.

25. Labich, K. (1992). "Airbus takes off." *Fortune*, June 1, pp. 102–108.

26. See Pollock, E. J. (1993). "Mediation firms alter the legal landscape." *The Wall Street Journal*, March 22, p. B1; Cox, M. (1993). "Electronic campus: Technology threatens to shatter the world of college textbooks." *The Wall Street Journal*, June 1, p. A1; Reilly, P. M. (1993). "At a crossroads: The instant-new age leaves *Time* magazine searching for a mission." *The Wall Street Journal*, May 12, p. A1; Rohwedder, C. (1993). "Europe's smaller food shops face finis." *The Wall Street Journal*, May 12, p. B1; Fatsis, S. (1995). "Major leagues keep minors at a distance." *The Wall Street Journal*, November 8, pp. B1+; Norton, E., and G. Stem. (1995). "Steel and aluminum vie over every ounce in a car's construction." *The Wall Street Journal*, May 9, pp. A1+; Paré, T. P. (1995). "Why the banks lined up against Gates." *Fortune*, May 29, p. 18; "Hitting the mail on the head." *The Economist*, April 30, 1994, pp. 69–70; Pacelle,

M. (1996). "'Big Boxes' by discounters are booming." *The Wall Street Journal*, January 17, p. A2; and Pope, K., and L. Cauley. (1998). "In battle for TV ads, cable is now the enemy." *The Wall Street Journal*, May 6, pp. B1+.

27. Tully, S. (1992). "How to cut those #$%* legal costs." *Fortune*, September 21, pp. 119–124.

28. See DeWitt, W. (1997). "Crown Cork & Seal/Carnaud Metalbox." Harvard Business School Case No. 9-296-019.

29. Perry, N. J. (1993). "What's next for the defense industry." *Fortune*, February 22, pp. 94–100.

30. See "Crown Cork and Seal in 1989." Harvard Business School Case No. 5-395-224.

31. See Brandenburger, A., and B. Nalebuff. (1996). *Co-opetition.* New York: Doubleday.

32. This approach to studying opportunities was also first suggested in Porter, M. E. (1980). *Competitive strategy.* New York: Free Press.

33. Jacob, R. (1992). "Service Corp. International: Acquisitions done the right way." *Fortune*, November 16, p. 96.

34. Porter, M. E. (1980). *Competitive strategy.* New York: Free Press.

35. For the definitive discussion of first-mover advantages, see Lieberman, M., and C. Montgomery. (1988). "First-mover advantages." *Strategic Management Journal*, 9, pp. 41–58.

36. See Ghemawat, P. (1991). *Commitment.* New York: Free Press.

37. See Gilbert, R. J., and D. M. Newbery. (1982). "Preemptive patenting and the persistence of monopoly." *American Economic Review*, 72(3), pp. 514–526.

38. See Bresnahan, T. F. (1985). "Post-entry competition in the plain paper copier market." *American Economic Review*, 85, pp. 15–19, for a discussion of Xerox's patents; and Bright, A. A. (1949). *The electric lamp industry.* New York: Macmillan, for a discussion of General Electric's patents.

39. See Mansfield, E., M. Schwartz, and S. Wagner. (1981). "Imitation costs and patents: An empirical study." *Economic Journal*, 91, pp. 907–918.

40. See Main, O. W. (1955). *The Canadian nickel industry.* Toronto: University of Toronto Press, for a discussion of asset preemption in the oil and gas industry; Ghemawat, P. (1986). "Wal-Mart store's discount operations." Harvard Business School Case No. 9-387-018, for Wal-Mart's preemption strategy; Schmalansee, R. (1978). "Entry deterrence in the ready-to-eat breakfast cereal industry." *Bell Journal of Economics*, 9(2), pp. 305–327; and Robinson, W. T., and C. Fornell. (1985). "Sources of market pioneer advantages in consumer goods industries." *Journal of Marketing Research*, 22(3), pp. 305–307, for a discussion of preemption in the breakfast cereal industry. In this latter case, the preempted valuable asset is shelf space in grocery stores.

41. Klemperer, P. (1986). "Markets with consumer switching costs." Doctoral thesis, Graduate School of Business, Stanford University; and Wernerfelt, B. (1986). "A special case of dynamic pricing policy." *Management Science*, 32, pp. 1562–1566.

42. See Gross, N. (1995). "The technology paradox." *BusinessWeek*, March 6, pp. 691–719; Bond, R. S., and D. F. Lean. (1977). *Sales, promotion, and product differentiation in two prescription drug markets.* Washington, D.C.: U.S. Federal Trade Commission; Montgomery, D. B. (1975). "New product distribution: An analysis of supermarket buyer decision." *Journal of Marketing Research*, 12, pp. 255–264; Ries, A., and J. Trout. (1986). *Marketing warfare.* New York: McGraw-Hill; and Davidson, J. H. (1976). "Why most new consumer brands fail." *Harvard Business Review*, 54, March–April, pp. 117–122, for a discussion of switching costs in these industries.

43. Porter, M. E. (1980). *Competitive strategy.* New York: Free Press.

44. Gibson, R. (1991). "McDonald's insiders increase their sales of company's stock." *The Wall Street Journal*, June 14, p. A1; and Chartier, J. (2002). "Burger battles." http://money.cnn.com, December 11. McDonald's lost money for only one quarter. It has since repositioned itself with nice upscale fast foods and has returned to profitability.

45. Descriptions of these product refinements can be found in Demetrakakes, P. (1994). "Household-chemical makers concentrate on downsizing." *Packaging*, 39(1), p. 41; Reda, S. (1995). "Motor oil: Hands-on approach." *Stores*, 77(5), pp. 48–49; and Quinn, J. (1995). "KitchenAid." *Incentive*, 169(5), pp. 46–47.

46. Chartier, J. (2002). "Burger battles." CNN/Money, http://money.cnn.com, December 11.
47. See Hayes, R. H., and S. G. Wheelwright. (1979). "The dynamics of process-product life cycles." *Harvard Business Review*, March–April, p. 127.
48. See www.jdpowers.com.
49. See Porter, M. E. (1980). *Competitive strategy*. New York: Free Press; and Harrigan, K. R. (1980). *Strategies for declining businesses*. Lexington, MA: Lexington Books.
50. See Aguilar, F. J., J. L. Bower, and B. Gomes-Casseres. (1985). "Restructuring European petrochemicals: Imperial Chemical Industries, P.L.C." Harvard Business School Case No. 9-385-203.
51. See Harrigan, K. R. (1980). *Strategies for declining businesses*. Lexington, MA: Lexington Books.
52. See Klebnikov, P. (1991). "The powerhouse." *Forbes*, September 2, pp. 46–52; and Rosenbloom, R. S., and C. Christensen. (1990). "Continuous casting investments at USX corporation." Harvard Business School Case No. 9-391-121.
53. Finn, E. A. (1987). "General Eclectic." *Forbes*, March 23, pp. 74–80.
54. See Smith, L. (1993). "Can defense pain be turned to gain?" *Fortune*, February 8, pp. 84–96; Perry, N. J. (1993). "What's next for the defense industry?" *Fortune*, February 22, pp. 94–100; and Dial, J., and K. J. Murphy. (1995). "Incentive, downsizing, and value creation at General Dynamics." *Journal of Financial Economics*, 37, pp. 261–314.

3 Evaluating a Firm's Internal Capabilities

After reading this chapter, you should be able to:

1. Describe the critical assumptions of the resource-based view.

2. Describe four types of resources and capabilities.

3. Apply the VRIO framework to identify the competitive implications of a firm's resources and capabilities.

4. Apply value chain analysis to identify a firm's valuable resources and capabilities.

5. Describe the kinds of resources and capabilities that are likely to be costly to imitate.

6. Describe how a firm uses its structure, formal and informal control processes, and compensation policy to exploit its resources.

7. Discuss how the decision of whether to imitate a firm with a competitive advantage affects the competitive dynamics in an industry.

MyManagementLab®

⭐ **Improve Your Grade!**

Over 10 million students improved their results using the Pearson MyLabs.
Visit **mymanagementlab.com** for simulations, tutorials, and end-of-chapter problems.

When a Noun Becomes a Verb

Google wasn't the first Internet search engine. At least 19 search engines existed—including Lycos, Alta Vista, Excite, Yahoo!, and Ask Jeeves—before Google was introduced in 1998. Nor is Google the only Internet search engine currently operating. Currently, at least 32 Internet search engines exist, including Ask.com, Bing, Baidu, and DuckDuckGo.

However, despite what appears to be an incredibly competitive industry, Google reigns supreme, with a U.S. and worldwide market share in excess of 60 percent of all Internet searches.

Indeed, Google has been so successful that it has been "verbicized." Now, to "google" something means to look something up on the Internet. This is the case even if you don't use Google to search the Web.

Many have wondered what has made Google so successful and whether it will be able to maintain—and even extend—its success. Three attributes of Google have been most widely cited.

First, Google is technically very competent. In the mid-1990s, all other search engines counted key words on Web pages and then reported which Web sites had the most key words. Google conceptualized the search process differently and used the relationship among pages as a way to guide users to those Web sites that were most helpful to them. Most people agree that Google's approach to Internet search was superior.

This technical competence has enabled Google to buy the technologies of several firms—including Keyhole and Global IP Solutions—and then to leverage those technologies into successful Google products—including Google Earth and Google Hangout.

Second, Google has been unusually successful in monetizing its software—that is, finding ways to make the software it gives to customers for free generate revenues for Google. Perhaps the best example of this is Google's AdWords program—a system that uses demand for Google advertising to precisely price the value of clicking onto a Web site. In 2012, Google advertising generated $10.42 billion in revenue.

Finally, Google's founders—Larry Page and Sergey Brin—are convinced that Google's unique organizational culture is central to their success. Google has a playful yet demanding

© FocusDigital/Alamy

culture. Developers are held to the highest standards of performance but are also encouraged to spend at least 20 percent of their time working on their own personal projects—many of which have turned into great products for Google. Google expects to meet its product announcement dates, but when it issued some new shares in 2005, it sold 14,159,265 shares, exactly. Why? Because those are the first eight numbers after the decimal point in pi (3.14159265). Google's unofficial slogan—a not-very-subtle dig on Microsoft—is "Don't Do Evil." So, Google doesn't develop proprietary software that it then attempts to sell to users for high prices. Instead, Google trusts its users, follows their lead in developing new products, and adopts an open approach to developing software.

Whether or not these three attributes of Google are sources of sustained competitive advantage is still up for debate. On the one hand, Google has used all three to develop an open source smart phone operating system—Android—that has emerged as a serious competitor for Apple's operating system. Moreover, Google seems to have figured out how to begin to monetize the success of one of its best-known acquisitions, YouTube.

On the other hand, Google's acquisition of Motorola Mobile for $12.5 billion seems to have created new challenges for the firm. Justified based on the mobile phone patents owned by Motorola, Google must nevertheless find a way to make money manufacturing cell phones. Motorola failed in this effort the last few years it owned Motorola Mobile. And Google has never before owned a business that actually made tangible products, like phones.

There are, of course, lots of different opinions about Google, and it's easy to find them—just "google" Google on the Web, and in less than half a second, you will see more than 2 billion Web sites that are related to Google.

Sources: www.Google.com; D. Vise and M. Malseed (2005). The Google Story. NY: Bantam //Wikipedia/history-of-internet-search-engines. Accessed July 5, 2013.

Google has been extremely successful, first in the Internet search engine market and later in related markets. What, if anything, about Google's resources and capabilities make it likely that this firm will be able to continue its success? The ideas presented in this chapter help answer this question.

The Resource-Based View of the Firm

In Chapter 2, we saw that it was possible to take some theoretical models developed in economics—specifically the structure-conduct-performance (S-C-P) model—and apply them to develop tools for analyzing a firm's external threats and opportunities. The same is true for analyzing a firm's internal strengths and weaknesses. However, whereas the tools described in Chapter 2 were based on the S-C-P model, the tools described in this chapter are based on the **resource-based view (RBV)** of the firm. The RBV is a model of firm performance that focuses on the resources and capabilities controlled by a firm as sources of competitive advantage.[1]

What Are Resources and Capabilities?

Resources in the RBV are defined as the tangible and intangible assets that a firm controls that it can use to conceive and implement its strategies. Examples of resources include a firm's factories (a tangible asset), its products (a tangible asset), its reputation among customers (an intangible asset), and teamwork among its managers (an intangible asset). eBay's tangible assets include its Web site and associated software. Its intangible assets include its brand name in the auction business.

Capabilities are a subset of a firm's resources and are defined as the tangible and intangible assets that enable a firm to take full advantage of the other resources it controls. That is, capabilities alone do not enable a firm to conceive and implement its strategies, but they enable a firm to use other resources to conceive and implement such strategies. Examples of capabilities might include a firm's marketing skills and teamwork and cooperation among its managers. At eBay, the cooperation among software developers and marketing people that made it possible for eBay to dominate the online action market is an example of a capability.

A firm's resources and capabilities can be classified into four broad categories: financial resources, physical resources, individual resources, and organizational resources. **Financial resources** include all the money, from whatever source, that firms use to conceive and implement strategies. These financial resources include cash from entrepreneurs, equity holders, bondholders, and banks. **Retained earnings**, or the profit that a firm made earlier in its history and invests in itself, are also an important type of financial resource.

Physical resources include all the physical technology used in a firm. This includes a firm's plant and equipment, its geographic location, and its access to raw materials. Specific examples of plant and equipment that are part of a firm's physical resources are a firm's computer hardware and software technology, robots used in manufacturing, and automated warehouses. Geographic location, as a type of physical resource, is important for firms as diverse as Wal-Mart (with its operations in rural markets generating, on average, higher returns than its operations in more competitive urban markets) and L. L. Bean (a catalogue retail firm that believes that its rural Maine location helps its employees identify with the outdoor lifestyle of many of its customers).[2]

Human resources include the training, experience, judgment, intelligence, relationships, and insight of *individual* managers and workers in a firm.[3] The importance of the human resources of well-known entrepreneurs such as Bill Gates (Microsoft) and Steve Jobs (formerly at Apple) is broadly understood. However, valuable human resources are not limited to just entrepreneurs or senior managers. Each employee at a firm like Southwest Airlines is seen as essential for the overall success of the firm. Whether it is the willingness of the gate agent to joke with the harried traveler, or a baggage handler hustling to get a passenger's bag into a plane, or even a pilot's decision to fly in a way that saves fuel—all of these human resources are part of the resource base that has enabled Southwest to gain competitive advantages in the very competitive U.S. airline industry.[4]

Whereas human resources are an attribute of single individuals, **organizational resources** are an attribute of groups of individuals. Organizational resources include a firm's formal reporting structure; its formal and informal planning, controlling, and coordinating systems; its culture and reputation; and informal relations among groups within a firm and between a firm and those in its environment. At Southwest Airlines, relationships among individual resources are an important organizational resource. For example, it is not unusual to see the pilots at Southwest helping to load the bags on an airplane to ensure that the plane leaves on time. This kind of cooperation and dedication shows up in an intense loyalty between Southwest employees and the firm—a loyalty that manifests itself in low employee turnover and high employee productivity, even though more than 80 percent of Southwest's workforce is unionized.

Critical Assumptions of the Resource-Based View

The RBV rests on two fundamental assumptions about the resources and capabilities that firms may control. First, different firms may possess different bundles of resources and capabilities, even if they are competing in the same industry. This is the assumption of firm **resource heterogeneity**. Resource heterogeneity implies that for a given business activity, some firms may be more skilled in accomplishing this activity than other firms. In manufacturing, for example, Toyota continues to be more skilled than, say, General Motors. In product design, Apple continues to be more skilled than, say, IBM. In motorcycles, Harley Davidson's reputation for big, bad, and loud rides separates it from its competitors.

Second, some of these resource and capability differences among firms may be long lasting because it may be very costly for firms without certain resources and capabilities to develop or acquire them. This is the assumption of **resource immobility**. For example, Toyota has had its advantage in manufacturing for at least 30 years. Apple has had product design advantages over IBM since Apple was founded in the 1980s. And eBay has been able to retain its brand reputation since the beginning of the online auction industry. It is not that GM, IBM, and eBay's competitors are unaware of their disadvantages. Indeed, some of these firms—notably GM and IBM—have made progress in addressing their disadvantages. However, despite these efforts, Toyota, Apple, and, to a lesser extent, eBay continue to enjoy advantages over their competition.

Taken together, these two assumptions make it possible to explain why some firms outperform other firms, even if these firms are all competing in the same industry. If a firm possesses valuable resources and capabilities that few other firms possess and if these other firms find it too costly to imitate these resources and capabilities, the firm that possesses these tangible and intangible assets can gain a sustained competitive advantage. The economic logic that underlies the RBV is described in more detail in the Strategy in Depth feature.

Strategy in Depth

The theoretical roots of the resource-based view can be traced to research done by David Ricardo in 1817. Interestingly, Ricardo was not even studying the profitability of firms; he was interested in the economic consequences of owning more or less fertile farm land.

Unlike many other inputs into the production process, the total supply of land is relatively fixed and cannot be significantly increased in response to higher demand and prices. Such inputs are said to be **inelastic in supply** because their quantity of supply is fixed and does not respond to price increases. In these settings, it is possible for those who own higher-quality inputs to gain competitive advantages.

Ricardo's argument concerning land as a productive input is summarized in Figure 3.1. Imagine that there are many parcels of land suitable for growing wheat. Also, suppose that the fertility of these different parcels varies from high fertility (low costs of production) to low fertility (high costs of production). It seems obvious that when the market price for wheat is low, it will only pay farmers with the most fertile land to grow wheat. Only these farmers will have costs low enough to make money when the market price

Ricardian Economics and the Resource-Based View

for wheat is low. As the market price for wheat increases, then farmers with progressively less fertile land will be able to use it to grow wheat. These observations lead to the market supply curve in panel A of Figure 3.1: As prices (P) go up, supply (S) also goes up. At some point on this supply curve, supply will equal demand (D). This point determines the market price for wheat, given supply and demand. This price is called P^* in the figure.

Now consider the situation facing two different kinds of farmers. Ricardo assumed that both these farmers follow traditional economic logic by producing a quantity (q) such that their marginal cost (MC) equals their marginal revenue (MR); that is, they produce enough wheat so that the cost of producing the last bushel of wheat equals the revenue they will get from selling that last bushel. However, this decision for the farm with less fertile land (in panel B of the figure) generates revenues that exactly equal the average total cost (ATC) of the only capital this farmer is assumed to employ, the cost of his land. In contrast, the farmer with more fertile land (in panel C of the figure) has an average total cost (ATC) less than the market-determined price and thus is able to earn an above-normal economic profit. This is because at the market-determined price, P^*, MC equals ATC for the farmer with less fertile land, whereas MC is greater than ATC for the farmer with more fertile land.

In traditional economic analysis, the profit earned by the farmer with more fertile land should lead other farmers to enter into this market, that is, to obtain some land and produce wheat. However, all the land that can be used to produce wheat in a way that generates at least a normal return given the market price P^* is already in production. In particular, no more very fertile land is available, and fertile land (by assumption) cannot be created. This is what is

The VRIO Framework

Armed with the RBV, it is possible to develop a set of tools for analyzing all the different resources and capabilities a firm might possess and the potential of each of these to generate competitive advantages. In this way, it will be possible to identify a firm's internal strengths and its internal weaknesses. The primary tool for accomplishing this internal analysis is called the VRIO framework.[5] The acronym, *VRIO*, in **VRIO framework** stands for four questions one must ask about a resource or capability to determine its competitive potential: the question of **Value**, the question of **Rarity**, the question of **Imitability**, and the question of **Organization**. These four questions are summarized in Table 3.1.

A. Market supply and demand, market quantity (Q*) and market-determined price (P*)

B. Performance of firm with less fertile land (higher average total cost – ATC)

C. Performance of firm with more fertile land (lower average total cost – ATC)

MC = marginal costs, ATC = average total costs, Q = aggregate quantity produced in the industry, q = quantity produced by each firm in the industry

Figure 3.1
The Economics of Land with Different Levels of Fertility

meant by land being inelastic in supply. Thus, the farmer with more fertile land and lower production costs has a sustained competitive advantage over those farmers with less fertile land and higher production costs. Therefore, the farmer with the more fertile land is able to earn an above-normal economic profit.

Of course, at least two events can threaten this sustained competitive advantage. First, market demand may shift down and to the left. This would force farmers with less fertile land to cease production and would also reduce the profit of those with more fertile land. If demand shifted far enough, this profit might disappear altogether.

Second, farmers with less fertile land may discover low-cost ways of increasing their land's fertility, thereby reducing the competitive advantage of farmers with more fertile land. For example, farmers with less fertile land may be able to use inexpensive fertilizers to increase their land's fertility. The existence of such low-cost fertilizers suggests that, although *land* may be in fixed supply, *fertility* may not be. If enough farmers can increase the fertility of their land, then the profits originally earned by the farmers with the more fertile land will disappear.

Of course, what the RBV does is recognize that land is not the only productive input that is inelastic in supply and that farmers are not the only firms that benefit from having such resources at their disposal.

Source: D. Ricardo (1817). *Principles of political economy and taxation.* London: J. Murray.

The Question of Value

The **question of value** is: "Do resources and capabilities enable a firm to exploit an external opportunity or neutralize an external threat?" If a firm answers this question with a "yes," then its resources and capabilities are valuable and can be considered *strengths*. If a firm answers this question with a "no," its resources and capabilities are *weaknesses*. There is nothing inherently valuable about a firm's resources and capabilities. Rather, they are only valuable to the extent that they enable a firm to enhance its competitive position. Sometimes, the same resources and capabilities can be strengths in one market and weaknesses in another.

TABLE 3.1 Questions Needed to Conduct a Resource-Based Analysis of a Firm's Internal Strengths and Weaknesses

1. *The Question of Value.* Does a resource enable a firm to exploit an environmental opportunity and/or neutralize an environmental threat?
2. *The Question of Rarity.* Is a resource currently controlled by only a small number of competing firms?
3. *The Question of Imitability.* Do firms without a resource face a cost disadvantage in obtaining or developing it?
4. *The Question of Organization.* Are a firm's other policies and procedures organized to support the exploitation of its valuable, rare, and costly-to-imitate resources?

Valuable Resources and Firm Performance

Sometimes it is difficult to know for sure whether a firm's resources and capabilities really enable it to exploit its external opportunities or neutralize its external threats. Sometimes this requires detailed operational information that may not be readily available. Other times, the full impact of a firm's resources and capabilities on its external opportunities and threats may not be known for some time.

One way to track the impact of a firm's resources and capabilities on its opportunities and threats is to examine the impact of using these resources and capabilities on a firm's revenues and costs. In general, firms that use their resources and capabilities to exploit opportunities or neutralize threats will see an increase in their net revenues, or a decrease in their net costs, or both, compared to the situation in which they were not using these resources and capabilities to exploit opportunities or neutralize threats. That is, the value of these resources and capabilities will generally manifest itself in either higher revenues or lower costs or both, once a firm starts using them to exploit opportunities or neutralize threats.

Applying the Question of Value

For many firms, the answer to the question of value has been "yes." That is, many firms have resources and capabilities that are used to exploit opportunities and neutralize threats, and the use of these resources and capabilities enables these firms to increase their net revenues or decrease their net costs. For example, historically Sony had a great deal of experience in designing, manufacturing, and selling miniaturized electronic technology. Sony used these resources and capabilities to exploit opportunities, including video games, digital cameras, computers and peripherals, handheld computers, home video and audio, portable audio, and car audio. 3M has used its resources and capabilities in substrates, coatings, and adhesives, along with an organizational culture that rewards risk-taking and creativity, to exploit opportunities in office products, including invisible tape and Post-It notes. Sony's and 3M's resources and capabilities—including their specific technological skills and their creative organizational cultures—have made it possible for these firms to respond to, and even create, new opportunities.[6]

Unfortunately, for other firms the answer to the question of value appears to be "no." The merger of AOL and Time Warner was supposed to create a new kind of entertainment and media company; it is now widely recognized that Time Warner has been unable to marshal the resources necessary to create economic value. Time Warner wrote off $90 billion in value in 2002; its stock price has been at record lows, and there have been rumors that it will be broken up. Ironically, many of the segments of this diverse media conglomerate continue to create value. However, the company as a whole has not realized the synergies that it was expected to generate when it was created. Put differently, these synergies—as resources and capabilities—are apparently not valuable.[7]

Strategy in the Emerging Enterprise

Entrepreneurial firms, like all other firms, must be able to answer "yes" to the question of value. That is, decisions by entrepreneurs to organize a firm to exploit an opportunity must increase revenues or reduce costs beyond what would be the case if they did not choose to organize a firm to exploit an opportunity.

However, entrepreneurs often find it difficult to answer the question of value before they actually organize a firm and try to exploit an opportunity. This is because the impact of exploiting an opportunity on a firm's revenues and costs often cannot be known, with certainty, before that opportunity is exploited.

Despite these challenges, entrepreneurs often are required to not only estimate the value of any opportunities they are thinking about exploiting, but to do so in some detail and in a written form. Projections about how organizing a firm to exploit an opportunity will affect a firm's revenues and costs are often the centerpiece of an entrepreneur's **business plan**—a document that summarizes how an entrepreneur will organize a firm to exploit an opportunity, along with the economic implications of exploiting that opportunity.

Two schools of thought exist as to the value of entrepreneurs writing business plans. On the one hand, some authors argue that writing a business plan is likely to be helpful for entrepreneurs because

Are Business Plans Good for Entrepreneurs?

it forces them to be explicit about their assumptions, exposes those assumptions to others for critique and analysis, and helps entrepreneurs focus their efforts on building a new organization and exploiting an opportunity. On the other hand, other authors argue that writing a business plan may actually hurt an entrepreneur's performance because writing such a plan may divert an entrepreneur's attention from more important activities, may give entrepreneurs the illusion that they have more control of their business than they actually do, and may lead to decision-making errors.

Research supports both points of view. Scott Shane and Frederic Delmar have shown that writing a business plan significantly enhances the probability that an entrepreneurial firm will survive. In contrast, Amar Bhide shows that most entrepreneurs go through many different business plans

before they land on one that describes a business opportunity that they actually support. For Bhide, writing the business plan is, at best, a means of helping to create a new opportunity. Because most business plans are abandoned soon after they are written, writing business plans has limited value.

One way to resolve the conflicts among these scholars is to accept that writing a business plan may be very useful in some settings and not so useful in others. In particular, when it is possible for entrepreneurs to collect sufficient information about a potential market opportunity so as to be able to describe the probability of different outcomes associated with exploiting that opportunity—a setting described as *risky* in the entrepreneurship literature—business planning can be very helpful. However, when such information cannot be collected—a setting described as *uncertain* in the entrepreneurship literature—then writing a business plan would be of only limited value, and its disadvantages might outweigh any advantages it might create.

Sources: S. Shane and F. Delmar (2004). "Planning for the market: Business planning before marketing and the continuation of organizing efforts." *Journal of Business Venturing,* 19, pp. 767–785; A. Bhide (2000). *The origin and evolution of new businesses.* New York: Oxford; F. H. Knight (1921). *Risk, uncertainty, and profit.* Chicago: University of Chicago Press; S. Alvarez and J. Barney (2006). "Discovery and creation: Alternative theories in the field of entrepreneurship." *Strategic Entrepreneurship Journal,* 1(1), pp. 11–26.

Using Value Chain Analysis to Identify Potentially Valuable Resources and Capabilities

One way to identify potentially valuable resources and capabilities controlled by a firm is to study that firm's value chain. A firm's **value chain** is the set of business activities in which it engages to develop, produce, and market its products or services. Each step in a firm's value chain requires the application and integration of different resources and capabilities. Because different firms may make different choices about which value chain activities they will engage in, they can end up developing different sets of resources and capabilities. This can be the case even if these firms are all operating in the same industry. These choices can have implications for a firm's strategies, and, as described in the Ethics and Strategy feature, they can also have implications for society more generally.

Consider, for example, the oil industry. Figure 3.2 provides a simplified list of all the business activities that must be completed if crude oil is to be turned into consumer products, such as gasoline. These activities include exploring for crude oil, drilling for crude oil, pumping crude oil, shipping crude oil, buying crude oil, refining crude oil, selling refined products to distributors, shipping refined products, and selling refined products to final customers.

Different firms may make different choices about which of these stages in the oil industry they want to operate. Thus, the firms in the oil industry may have very different resources and capabilities. For example, exploring for crude oil is very expensive and requires substantial financial resources. It also requires access to land (a physical resource), the application of substantial scientific and technical knowledge (individual resources), and an organizational commitment to risk-taking and exploration (organizational resources). Firms that operate in this stage of the oil business are likely to have very different resources and capabilities than those that, for example, sell refined oil products to final customers. To be successful in the retail stage of this industry, a firm needs retail outlets (such as stores and gas stations), which are costly to build and require both financial and physical resources. These outlets, in turn, need to be staffed by salespeople—individual resources—and marketing these products to customers through advertisements and other means can require a commitment to creativity—an organizational resource.

However, even firms that operate in the same set of value chain activities in an industry may approach these activities very differently and therefore may

Figure 3.2   A Simplified Value Chain of Activities of Oil-Based Refined Products such as Gasoline and Motor Oil

Ethics and Strategy

Strategic management adopts the perspective of a firm's owners in discussing how to gain and sustain competitive advantages. Even when adopting a stakeholder perspective (see the Ethics and Strategy feature in Chapter 1), how a firm can improve its performance and increase the wealth of its owners still takes center stage.

However, an exclusive focus on the performance of a firm and the wealth of its owners can sometimes have broader effects—on society and on the environment—that are not fully recognized. Economists call these broader effects "externalities" because they are external to the core issue in economics and strategic management of how firms can maximize their performance. They are external to this issue because firms generally do not bear the full costs of the externalities their profit-maximizing behavior creates.

Externalities can take many forms. The most obvious of these has to do with pollution and the environment. If, for example, in the process of maximizing its performance a firm engages in activities that pollute the environment, the impact of that pollution is an externality. Such pollution reduces our quality of life and hurts the environment, but the firm creating this pollution often does not bear the full costs of doing so.

Other externalities have to do with a firm's impact on the public's health. For example, when tobacco companies maximize their profits by selling tobacco to children, they are also creating a public health externality. Getting children hooked on tobacco

Externalities and the Broader Consequences of Profit Maximization

early on might be good for the bottom line of a tobacco company, but it increases the chances of these children developing lung cancer, emphysema, heart disease, and the other ailments associated with tobacco. Obviously, these individuals absorb most of the adverse consequences of these diseases, but society suffers as well from the high health care costs that are engendered.

Put differently, while adopting a simple profit-maximizing perspective in choosing and implementing strategies can have positive impacts for a firm, its owners, and its stakeholders, it can also have negative consequences for society as a whole. Two broad solutions to this problem of externalities have been proposed. First, governments can take on the responsibility of directly monitoring and regulating the behavior of firms in areas where these kinds of externalities are likely to develop. Second, governments can use lawsuits and regulations to ensure that firms directly bear more

of the costs of any externalities their behavior might generate. Once these externalities are "internalized," it is then a matter of self-interest for firms not to engage in activities that generate negative externalities.

Consumers can sometimes also help internalize the externalities generated by a firm's behavior by adjusting their consumption patterns to buy products or services only from companies that do not generate negative externalities. Consumers can even be more proactive and let firms know which of their strategies are particularly troubling. For example, many consumers united to boycott firms with operations in South Africa when South Africa was still implementing a policy of apartheid. Ultimately, this pressure not only changed the strategies of many firms; it also helped change South Africa's domestic policies. More recently, consumer pressures on pharmaceutical companies forced these firms to make their AIDS drugs more accessible in less developed countries in Africa; similar pressures forced Nike to adjust the wages and working conditions of the individuals who manufacture Nike's shoes. To the extent that sufficient demand for "socially responsible firms" exists in the marketplace, it may make profit-maximizing sense for a firm to engage in socially responsible behavior by reducing the extent to which its actions generate negative externalities.

Sources: "AIDS in Africa." *British Medical Journal,* June 1, p. 456; J. S. Friedman (2003). "Paying for apartheid." *Nation,* June 6, pp. 7+; L. Lee (2000). "Can Nike still do it?" *BusinessWeek,* February 21, pp. 121+.

Technology development	Product design	Manufacturing	Marketing	Distribution	Service

Source
Sophistication
Patents
Product/process
  choices
	Function
	Physical
	  characteristics
	Aesthetics
	Quality
		Integration
		Raw materials
		Capacity
		Location
		Procurement
		Parts production
		Assembly
			Prices
			Advertising/
			  promotion
			Sales force
			Package
			Brand
				Channels
				Integration
				Inventory
				Warehousing
				Transport
					Warranty Speed
					Captive/independent
					Prices

Figure 3.3

The Generic Value Chain Developed by McKinsey and Company

develop very different resources and capabilities associated with these activities. For example, two firms may sell refined oil products to final customers. However, one of these firms may sell only through retail outlets it owns, whereas the second may sell only through retail outlets it does not own. The first firm's financial and physical resources are likely to be very different from the second firm's, although these two firms may have similar individual and organizational resources.

Studying a firm's value chain forces us to think about firm resources and capabilities in a disaggregated way. Although it is possible to characterize a firm's resources and capabilities more broadly, it is usually more helpful to think about how each of the activities a firm engages in affects its financial, physical, individual, and organizational resources. With this understanding, it is possible to begin to recognize potential sources of competitive advantage for a firm in a much more detailed way.

Because this type of analysis can be so helpful in identifying the financial, physical, individual, and organizational resources and capabilities controlled by a firm, several generic value chains for identifying them have been developed. One of these, proposed by the management-consulting firm McKinsey and Company, is presented in Figure 3.3.[8] This relatively simple model suggests that the creation of value almost always involves six distinct activities: technology development, product design, manufacturing, marketing, distribution, and service. Firms can develop distinctive capabilities in any one or any combination of these activities.

The Question of Rarity

Understanding the value of a firm's resources and capabilities is an important first consideration in understanding a firm's internal strengths and weaknesses. However, if a particular resource or capability is controlled by numerous competing firms, then that resource is unlikely to be a source of competitive advantage for any one of them. Instead, valuable but common (i.e., not rare) resources and capabilities are sources of competitive parity. Only when a resource is not controlled by numerous other firms is it likely to be a source of competitive advantage. These observations lead to the **question of rarity**: "How many competing firms already possess particular valuable resources and capabilities?"

Consider, for example, competition among television sports channels. All the major networks broadcast sports. In addition, several sports-only cable channels are available, including the best-known all-sports channel, ESPN. Several years ago, ESPN began televising what were then called alternative sports—skateboarding, snowboarding, mountain biking, and so forth. The surprising popularity of these programs led ESPN to package them into an annual competition called the "X-Games." "X" stands for "extreme," and ESPN has definitely gone to the extreme in including sports in the X-Games. The X-Games have included sports such as sky-surfing, competitive high diving, competitive bungee cord jumping, and so forth. ESPN broadcasts both a summer X-Games and a winter X-Games. No other sports outlet has yet made such a commitment to so-called extreme sports, and it has paid handsome dividends for ESPN—extreme sports have very low-cost broadcast rights and draw a fairly large audience. This commitment to extreme sports—as an example of a valuable and rare capability—has been a source of at least a temporary competitive advantage for ESPN.

Of course, not all of a firm's resources and capabilities have to be valuable and rare. Indeed, most firms have a resource base that is composed primarily of valuable but common resources and capabilities. These resources cannot be sources of even temporary competitive advantage, but are essential if a firm is to gain competitive parity. Under conditions of competitive parity, although no one firm gains a competitive advantage, firms do increase their probability of survival.

Consider, for example, a telephone system as a resource or capability. Because telephone systems are widely available and because virtually all organizations have access to telephone systems, these systems are not rare and thus are not a source of competitive advantage. However, firms that do not possess a telephone system are likely to give their competitors an important advantage and place themselves at a competitive disadvantage.

How rare a valuable resource or capability must be in order to have the potential for generating a competitive advantage varies from situation to situation. It is not difficult to see that, if a firm's valuable resources and capabilities are absolutely unique among a set of current and potential competitors, they can generate a competitive advantage. However, it may be possible for a small number of firms in an industry to possess a particular valuable resource or capability and still obtain a competitive advantage. In general, as long as the number of firms that possess a particular valuable resource or capability is less than the number of firms needed to generate perfect competition dynamics in an industry, that resource or capability can be considered rare and a potential source of competitive advantage.

The Question of Imitability

Firms with valuable and rare resources are often strategic innovators because they are able to conceive and engage in strategies that other firms cannot because they lack the relevant resources and capabilities. These firms may gain the first-mover advantages discussed in Chapter 2.

Valuable and rare organizational resources, however, can be sources of sustained competitive advantage only if firms that do not possess them face a cost disadvantage in obtaining or developing them, compared to firms that already possess them. These kinds of resources are **imperfectly imitable**.[9] These observations lead to the **question of imitability**: "Do firms without a resource or capability face a cost disadvantage in obtaining or developing it compared to firms that already possess it?"

Imagine an industry with five essentially identical firms. Each of these firms manufactures the same products, uses the same raw materials, and sells the products to the same customers through the same distribution channels. It is not hard to see that firms in this kind of industry will have normal economic performance. Now, suppose that one of these firms, for whatever reason, discovers or develops a heretofore unrecognized valuable resource and uses that resource either to exploit an external opportunity or to neutralize an external threat. Obviously, this firm will gain a competitive advantage over the others.

This firm's competitors can respond to this competitive advantage in at least two ways. First, they can ignore the success of this one firm and continue as before. This action, of course, will put them at a competitive disadvantage. Second, these firms can attempt to understand why this one firm is able to be successful and then duplicate its resources to implement a similar strategy. If competitors have no cost disadvantages in acquiring or developing the needed resources, then this imitative approach will generate competitive parity in the industry.

Sometimes, however, for reasons that will be discussed later, competing firms may face an important cost disadvantage in duplicating a successful firm's valuable resources. If this is the case, this one innovative firm may gain a sustained competitive advantage—an advantage that is not competed away through strategic imitation. Firms that possess and exploit costly-to-imitate, rare, and valuable resources in choosing and implementing their strategies may enjoy a period of sustained competitive advantage.[10]

For example, other sports networks have observed the success of ESPN's X-Games and are beginning to broadcast similar competitions. NBC, for example, developed its own version of the X-Games, called the "Gravity Games," and even the Olympics now include sports that were previously perceived as being "too extreme" for this mainline sports competition. Several Fox sports channels broadcast programs that feature extreme sports, and at least one new cable channel (Fuel) broadcasts only extreme sports. Fuel was recently acquired by Fox to provide another outlet for extreme sports on a Fox channel. Whether these efforts will be able to attract the competitors that the X-Games attract, whether winners at these other competitions will gain as much status in their sports as do winners of the X-Games, and whether these other competitions and programs will gain the reputation among viewers enjoyed by ESPN will go a long way to determining whether ESPN's competitive advantage in extreme sports is temporary or sustained.[11]

Forms of Imitation: Direct Duplication and Substitution

In general, imitation occurs in one of two ways: **direct duplication** or **substitution**. Imitating firms can attempt to directly duplicate the resources possessed by the firm with a competitive advantage. Thus, NBC sponsoring an alternative extreme games competition can be thought of as an effort to directly duplicate the resources that enabled ESPN's X-Games to be successful. If the cost of this direct duplication is too high, then a firm with these resources and capabilities may obtain a sustained competitive advantage. If this cost is not too high, then any competitive advantages in this setting will be temporary.

Imitating firms can also attempt to substitute other resources for a costly-to-imitate resource possessed by a firm with a competitive advantage. Extreme sports shows and an extreme sports cable channel are potential substitutes for ESPN's X-Games strategy. These shows appeal to much the same audience as the X-Games, but they do not require the same resources as an X-Games strategy requires (i.e., because they are not competitions, they do not require the network to bring together a large number of athletes all at once). If substitute resources exist and if imitating firms do not face a cost disadvantage in obtaining them, then the competitive advantage of other firms will be temporary. However, if these resources have no substitutes or if the cost of acquiring these substitutes is greater than the cost of obtaining the original resources, then competitive advantages can be sustained.

Why Might It Be Costly to Imitate Another Firm's Resources or Capabilities?

A number of authors have studied why it might be costly for one firm to imitate the resources and capabilities of another. Four sources of costly imitation have been noted.[12] They are summarized in Table 3.2 and discussed in the following text.

Unique Historical Conditions.   It may be the case that a firm was able to acquire or develop its resources and capabilities in a low-cost manner because of its unique historical conditions. The ability of firms to acquire, develop, and use resources often depends on their place in time and space. Once time and history pass, firms that do not have space-and-time-dependent resources face a significant cost disadvantage in obtaining and developing them because doing so would require them to re-create history.[13]

ESPN's early commitment to extreme sports is an example of these unique historical conditions. The status and reputation of the X-Games were created because ESPN happened to be the first major sports outlet that took these competitions seriously. The X-Games became the most important competition in many of these extreme sports. Indeed, for snowboarders, winning a gold medal in the X-Games is almost as important as—if not more important than—winning a gold medal in the Winter Olympics. Other sports outlets that hope to be able to compete with the X-Games will have to overcome both the status of ESPN as "the worldwide leader in sports" and its historical advantage in extreme sports. Overcoming these advantages is likely to be costly, making competitive threats from direct duplication, at least, less significant.

Of course, firms can also act to increase the costliness of imitating the resources and capabilities they control. ESPN is doing this by expanding its

TABLE 3.2 Sources of Costly Imitation

Unique Historical Conditions. When a firm gains low-cost access to resources because of its place in time and space, other firms may find these resources to be costly to imitate. Both first-mover advantages and path dependence can create unique historical conditions.

Causal Ambiguity. When competitors cannot tell, for sure, what enables a firm to gain an advantage, that advantage may be costly to imitate. Sources of causal ambiguity include when competitive advantages are based on "taken-for-granted" resources and capabilities, when multiple non-testable hypotheses exist about why a firm has a competitive advantage, and when a firm's advantages are based on complex sets of interrelated capabilities.

Social Complexity. When the resources and capabilities a firm uses to gain a competitive advantage involve interpersonal relationships, trust, culture, and other social resources that are costly to imitate in the short term.

Patents. Only a source of sustained competitive advantage in a few industries, including pharmaceuticals and specialty chemicals.

coverage of extreme sports and by engaging in a "grassroots" marketing campaign that engages young "extreme athletes" in local competitions. The purpose of these efforts is clear: to keep ESPN's status as the most important source of extreme sports competitions intact.[14]

Unique historical circumstances can give a firm a sustained competitive advantage in at least two ways. First, it may be that a particular firm was the first in an industry to recognize and exploit an opportunity, and being first gave the firm one or more of the first-mover advantages discussed in Chapter 2. Thus, although in principle other firms in an industry could have exploited an opportunity, that only one firm did so makes it more costly for other firms to imitate the original firm.

A second way that history can have an impact on a firm builds on the concept of **path dependence**.[15] A process is said to be path dependent when events early in the evolution of a process have significant effects on subsequent events. In the evolution of competitive advantage, path dependence suggests that a firm may gain a competitive advantage in the current period based on the acquisition and development of resources in earlier periods. In these earlier periods, it is often not clear what the full future value of particular resources will be. Because of this uncertainty, firms are able to acquire or develop these resources for less than what will turn out to be their full value. However, once the full value of these resources is revealed, other firms seeking to acquire or develop these resources will need to pay their full known value, which (in general) will be greater than the costs incurred by the firm that acquired or developed these resources in some earlier period. The cost of acquiring both duplicate and substitute resources would rise once their full value became known.

Consider, for example, a firm that purchased land for ranching some time ago and discovered a rich supply of oil on this land in the current period. The difference between the value of this land as a supplier of oil (high) and the value of this land for ranching (low) is a source of competitive advantage for this firm. Moreover, other firms attempting to acquire this or adjacent land will now have to pay for the full value of the land in its use as a supply of oil (high) and thus will be at a cost disadvantage compared to the firm that acquired it some time ago for ranching.

Causal Ambiguity.   A second reason why a firm's resources and capabilities may be costly to imitate is that imitating firms may not understand the relationship between the resources and capabilities controlled by a firm and that firm's competitive advantage. In other words, the relationship between firm resources and capabilities and competitive advantage may be **causally ambiguous**.

At first, it seems unlikely that causal ambiguity about the sources of competitive advantage for a firm would ever exist. Managers in a firm seem likely to understand the sources of their own competitive advantage. If managers in one firm understand the relationship between resources and competitive advantage, then it seems likely that managers in other firms would also be able to discover these relationships and thus would have a clear understanding of which resources and capabilities they should duplicate or seek substitutes for. If there are no other sources of cost disadvantage for imitating firms, imitation should lead to competitive parity and normal economic performance.[16]

However, it is not always the case that managers in a particular firm will fully understand the relationship between the resources and capabilities they control and competitive advantage. This lack of understanding could occur for at least three reasons. First, it may be that the resources and capabilities that generate competitive advantage are so taken for granted, so much a part of the day-to-day experience of managers in a firm, that these managers are unaware of them.[17] Organizational resources and capabilities such as teamwork among top managers, organizational culture, relationships among other employees, and relationships with customers and suppliers may be almost "invisible" to managers in a firm.[18] If managers in firms that have such capabilities do not understand their relationship to competitive advantage, managers in other firms face significant challenges in understanding which resources they should imitate.

Second, managers may have multiple hypotheses about which resources and capabilities enable their firm to gain a competitive advantage, but they may be unable to evaluate which of these resources and capabilities, alone or in combination, actually create the competitive advantage. For example, if one asks successful entrepreneurs what enabled them to be successful, they are likely to reply with several hypotheses, such as "hard work, willingness to take risks, and a high-quality top management team." However, if one asks what happened to unsuccessful entrepreneurs, they, too, are likely to suggest that their firms were characterized by "hard work, willingness to take risks, and a high-quality top management team." It may be the case that "hard work, willingness to take risks, and a high-quality top management team" are important resources and capabilities for entrepreneurial firm success, but other factors may also play a role. Without rigorous experiments, it is difficult to establish which of these resources have a causal relationship with competitive advantage and which do not.

Finally, it may be that not just a few resources and capabilities enable a firm to gain a competitive advantage, but that literally thousands of these organizational attributes, bundled together, generate these advantages. When the resources and capabilities that generate competitive advantage are complex networks of relationships between individuals, groups, and technology, imitation can be costly.

Whenever the sources of competitive advantage are widely diffused across people, locations, and processes in a firm, those sources will be costly to imitate. Perhaps the best example of such a resource is knowledge itself. To the extent that valuable knowledge about a firm's products, processes, customers, and so on is widely diffused throughout an organization, competitors will have difficulty imitating that knowledge, and it can be a source of sustained competitive advantage.[19]

Social Complexity. A third reason that a firm's resources and capabilities may be costly to imitate is that they may be socially complex phenomena, beyond the ability of firms to systematically manage and influence. When competitive advantages are based on such complex social phenomena, the ability of other firms to imitate these resources and capabilities, either through direct duplication or substitution, is significantly constrained. Efforts to influence these kinds of phenomena are likely to be much more costly than they would be if these phenomena developed in a natural way over time in a firm.[20]

A wide variety of firm resources and capabilities may be **socially complex**. Examples include the interpersonal relations among managers in a firm, a firm's culture, and a firm's reputation among suppliers and customers.[21] Notice that in most of these cases it is possible to specify how these socially complex resources add value to a firm. Thus, there is little or no causal ambiguity surrounding the link between these firm resources and capabilities and competitive advantage. However, understanding that an organizational culture with certain attributes or quality relations among managers can improve a firm's efficiency and effectiveness does not necessarily imply that firms lacking these attributes can engage in systematic efforts to create them or that low-cost substitutes for them exist. For the time being, such social engineering may be beyond the abilities of most firms. At the very least, such social engineering is likely to be much more costly than it would be if socially complex resources evolved naturally within a firm.[22]

It is interesting to note that firms seeking to imitate complex physical technology often do not face the cost disadvantages of imitating complex social phenomena. A great deal of physical technology (machine tools, robots, and so forth) can be purchased in supply markets. Even when a firm develops its own unique physical technology, reverse engineering tends to diffuse this technology among competing firms in a low-cost manner. Indeed, the costs of imitating a successful physical technology are often lower than the costs of developing a new technology.[23]

Although physical technology is usually not costly to imitate, the application of this technology in a firm is likely to call for a wide variety of socially complex organizational resources and capabilities. These organizational resources may be costly to imitate, and if they are valuable and rare, the combination of physical and socially complex resources may be a source of sustained competitive advantage. The importance of socially complex resources and capabilities for firm performance has been studied in detail in the field of strategic human resource management, as described in the Research Made Relevant feature.

Patents.   At first glance, it might appear that a firm's patents would make it very costly for competitors to imitate its products.[24] Patents do have this effect in some industries. For example, patents in the pharmaceutical and specialty chemical industry effectively foreclose other firms from marketing the same products until a firm's patents expire. As suggested in Chapter 2, patents can raise the cost of imitation in a variety of other industries as well.

However, from another point of view a firm's patents may decrease, rather than increase, the costs of imitation. When a firm files for patent protection, it is forced to reveal a significant amount of information about its product. Governments require this information to ensure that the technology in question is patentable. By obtaining a patent, a firm may provide important information to competitors about how to imitate its technology.

Moreover, most technological developments in an industry are diffused throughout firms in that industry in a relatively brief period of time, even if the technology in question is patented, because patented technology is not immune from low-cost imitation. Patents may restrict direct duplication for a time, but they may actually increase the chances of substitution by functionally equivalent technologies.[25]

The Question of Organization

A firm's potential for competitive advantage depends on the value, rarity, and imitability of its resources and capabilities. However, to fully realize this potential, a firm must be organized to exploit its resources and capabilities. These observations lead to the **question of organization**: "Is a firm organized to exploit the full competitive potential of its resources and capabilities?"

Numerous components of a firm's organization are relevant to the question of organization, including its formal reporting structure, its formal and informal management control systems, and its compensation policies. A firm's **formal reporting**

Research Made Relevant

Most empirical tests of the RBV have focused on the extent to which history, causal ambiguity, and social complexity have an impact on the ability of firms to gain and sustain competitive advantages. Among the most important of these tests has been research that examines the extent to which human resource practices that are likely to generate socially complex resources and capabilities are related to firm performance. This area of research is known as *strategic human resources management*.

The first of these tests was conducted as part of a larger study of efficient low-cost manufacturing in the worldwide automobile industry. A group of researchers from Massachusetts Institute of Technology developed rigorous measures of the cost and quality of more than 70 manufacturing plants that assembled mid-size sedans around the world. They discovered that at the time of their study only six of these plants had simultaneous low costs and high-quality manufacturing—a position that obviously would give these plants a competitive advantage in the marketplace.

Strategic Human Resource Management Research

In trying to understand what distinguished these six plants from the others in the sample, the researchers found that, not surprisingly, these six plants had the most modern and up-to-date manufacturing technology. However, so did many of the less effective plants. What distinguished these effective plants was not their manufacturing technology, per se, but their human resource (HR) practices. These six plants all implemented a bundle of such practices that included participative decision making, quality circles, and an emphasis on team production. One of the results of these efforts—and

another distinguishing feature of these six plants—was a high level of employee loyalty and commitment to a plant, as well as the belief that plant managers would treat employees fairly. These socially complex resources and capabilities are the types of resources that the RBV suggests should be sources of sustained competitive advantage.

Later work has followed up on this approach and has examined the impact of HR practices on firm performance outside the manufacturing arena. Using a variety of measures of firm performance and several different measures of HR practices, the results of this research continue to be very consistent with RBV logic. That is, firms that are able to use HR practices to develop socially complex human and organizational resources are able to gain competitive advantages over firms that do not engage in such practices.

Sources: J. P. Womack, D. I. Jones, and D. Roos (1990). *The machine that changed the world.* New York: Rawson; M. Huselid (1995). "The impact of human resource management practices on turnover, productivity, and corporate financial performance." *Academy of Management Journal,* 38, pp. 635–672; J. B. Barney and P. Wright (1998). "On becoming a strategic partner." *Human Resource Management,* 37, pp. 31–46.

structure is a description of whom in the organization reports to whom; it is often embodied in a firm's **organizational chart**. **Management control systems** include a range of formal and informal mechanisms to ensure that managers are behaving in ways consistent with a firm's strategies. **Formal management controls** include a firm's budgeting and reporting activities that keep people higher up in a firm's organizational chart informed about the actions taken by people lower down in a firm's organizational chart. **Informal management controls** might include a firm's culture and the willingness of employees to monitor each other's behavior. **Compensation policies** are the ways that firms pay employees. Such policies create incentives for employees to behave in certain ways.

These components of a firm's organization are often called **complementary resources and capabilities** because they have limited ability to generate competitive advantage in isolation. However, in combination with other resources and capabilities they can enable a firm to realize its full potential for competitive advantage.[26]

For example, it has already been suggested that ESPN may have a sustained competitive advantage in the extreme sports segment of the sports broadcasting industry. However, if ESPN's management had not taken advantage of its opportunities in extreme sports by expanding coverage, ensuring that the best competitors come to ESPN competitions, adding additional competitions, and changing up older competitions, then its potential for competitive advantage would not have been fully realized. Of course, the reason that ESPN has done all these things is because it has an appropriate organizational structure, management controls, and employee compensation policies. By themselves, these attributes of ESPN's organization could not be a source of competitive advantage; however, they were essential for ESPN to realize its full competitive advantage potential.

Having an appropriate organization in place has enabled ESPN to realize the full competitive advantage potential of its other resources and capabilities. Having an inappropriate organization in place prevented Sony from exploiting its valuable, rare, and costly-to-imitate resources and capabilities.

Earlier in this chapter, it was suggested that Sony had unusual experience in designing and building a wide variety of consumer electronics products. In the process of building this giant consumer electronics company, managers at Sony developed and acquired two substantial businesses: Sony Consumer Electronics and Sony Records.

Among the many products developed by the Consumer Electronics business was an early MP3 player (i.e., a portable device that played music and other digital media from a hard drive). The key to MP3 technology was compression—taking analog signals and storing them in a way that they did not take up disproportionate space on the hard drive. Without compression, you could only store a few songs on an MP3 player; with compression, you can store thousands. Sony was a leader in compression technology.

Of course, to be effective, MP3 players must have content to play. Here, the Sony Records Division should have been very helpful to the Consumer Electronics Division: Records had recording contracts with many famous artists, and Consumer Products had the MP3 player (along with compression technology) to play that music.

So, why does Apple—with iPods, iTunes, iPhones, and iPads—dominate the portable music listening market? Apple had no advantages. It was late to the MP3 market (although it did introduce an MP3 player with a particularly elegant interface), it did not own any content, and it had a limited online presence.

One explanation of Apple's success is Sony's failure—despite having the potential to dominate this market, despite its history of dominating similar markets in the past (e.g., the Sony Walkman portable tape player), Sony could not find a way for its two divisions—Consumer Electronics and Music—to cooperate. Put differently, Sony's failure was a failure in organization. The engineers in the Consumer Electronics business could never find a way to work with the artists in the music business.

Of course, Apple had to do a great deal more to take advantage of the opportunity that Sony's organization failure had created for them. Nevertheless, despite its potential, Sony failed to gain or sustain any significant competitive advantages in this lucrative MP3 market.[27]

Applying the VRIO Framework

The questions of value, rarity, imitability, and organization can be brought together into a single framework to understand the return potential associated with exploiting any of a firm's resources or capabilities. This is done in Table 3.3. The relationship of the VRIO framework to strengths and weaknesses is presented in Table 3.4.

If a resource or capability controlled by a firm is not valuable, it will not enable a firm to choose or implement strategies that exploit environmental opportunities or neutralize environmental threats. Organizing to exploit this resource will increase a firm's costs or decrease its revenues. These types of resources are weaknesses. Firms will either have to fix these weaknesses or avoid using them when choosing and implementing strategies. If firms do exploit these kinds of resources and capabilities, they can expect to put themselves at a competitive disadvantage compared to those that either do not possess these nonvaluable resources or do not use them in conceiving and implementing strategies.

If a resource or capability is valuable but not rare, exploitation of this resource in conceiving and implementing strategies will generate competitive parity. Exploiting these types of resources will generally not create competitive advantages, but failure to exploit them can put a firm at a competitive disadvantage. In this sense, valuable-but-not-rare resources can be thought of as organizational strengths.

If a resource or capability is valuable and rare but not costly to imitate, exploiting this resource will generate a temporary competitive advantage for a firm. A firm that exploits this kind of resource is, in an important sense, gaining a first-mover advantage because it is the first firm that is able to exploit a particular resource. However, once competing firms observe this competitive advantage, they will be able to acquire or develop the resources needed to implement this strategy through direct duplication or substitution at no cost disadvantage, compared to the first-moving firm. Over time, any competitive advantage that the first mover obtained would be competed away as other firms imitate the resources needed to compete. Consequently, this type of resource or capability can be thought of as an organizational strength and as a **distinctive competence**.

If a resource or capability is valuable, rare, and costly to imitate, exploiting it will generate a sustained competitive advantage. In this case, competing firms

TABLE 3.3 The VRIO Framework

Is a resource or capability:				
Valuable?	**Rare?**	**Costly to imitate?**	**Exploited by organization?**	**Competitive implications**
No	—	—	No	Competitive disadvantage
Yes	No	—		Competitive parity
Yes	Yes	No		Temporary competitive advantage
Yes	Yes	Yes	Yes	Sustained competitive advantage

TABLE 3.4 **TABLE 3.4** The Relationship Between the VRIO Framework and Organizational Strengths and Weaknesses

Is a resource or capability:				
Valuable?	Rare?	Costly to imitate?	Exploited by organization?	Strength or weakness
No	—	—	No	Weakness
Yes	No	—	↑	Strength
Yes	Yes	No		Strength and distinctive competence
Yes	Yes	Yes	Yes	Strength and sustainable distinctive competence

face a significant cost disadvantage in imitating a successful firm's resources and capabilities. As suggested earlier, this competitive advantage may reflect the unique history of the successful firm, causal ambiguity about which resources to imitate, the socially complex nature of these resources and capabilities, or any patent advantages a firm might possess. In any case, attempts to compete away the advantages of firms that exploit these resources will not generate competitive advantage, or even competitive parity, for imitating firms. Even if these firms are able to acquire or develop the resources or capabilities in question, the very high costs of doing so would put them at a competitive disadvantage. These kinds of resources and capabilities are organizational strengths and **sustainable distinctive competencies**.

The question of organization operates as an adjustment factor in the VRIO framework. For example, if a firm has a valuable, rare, and costly-to-imitate resource and capability but fails to organize itself to take full advantage of this resource, some of its potential competitive advantage could be lost (this is the Sony example). Extremely poor organization, in this case, could actually lead a firm that has the potential for competitive advantage to gain only competitive parity or competitive disadvantages.

Applying the VRIO Framework to Southwest Airlines

To examine how the VRIO framework can be applied in analyzing real strategic situations, consider the competitive position of Southwest Airlines. Southwest Airlines has been the only consistently profitable airline in the United States over the past 30 years. While many U.S. airlines have gone in and out of bankruptcy, Southwest has remained profitable. How has it been able to gain this competitive advantage?

Potential sources of this competitive advantage fall into two big categories: operational choices Southwest has made and Southwest's approach to managing its people. On the operational side, Southwest has chosen to fly only a single type of aircraft (Boeing 737), only flies into smaller airports, has avoided complicated hub-and-spoke route systems, and, instead, flies a point-to-point system. On the people-management side, despite being highly unionized, Southwest has been able to develop a sense of commitment and loyalty among its employees. It is not unusual to see Southwest employees go well beyond their narrowly defined job responsibilities, helping out in whatever way is necessary to get a plane off the ground safely and on time. Which of these—operational choices or Southwest's approach to managing its people—is more likely to be a source of sustained competitive advantage?

Southwest's Operational Choices and Competitive Advantage

Consider first Southwest's operational choices. First, do these operational choices reduce Southwest's costs or increase the willingness of its customers to pay—that is, are these operational choices valuable? It can be shown that most of Southwest's operational choices have the effect of reducing its costs. For example, by flying only one type of airliner, Southwest is able to reduce the cost of training its maintenance staff, reduce its spare parts inventory, and reduce the time its planes are being repaired. By flying into smaller airports, Southwest reduces the fees it would otherwise have to pay to land at larger airports. Its point-to-point system of routes avoids the costs associated with establishing large hub-and-spoke systems. Overall, these operational choices are valuable.

Second, are these operational choices rare? For most of its history, Southwest's operational choices have been rare. Only recently have large incumbent airlines and smaller new entrants begun to implement similar operational choices.

Third, are these operational choices costly to imitate? Several incumbent airline firms have set up subsidiaries designed to emulate most of Southwest's operational choices. For example, Continental created the Continental Lite division, United created the Ted division, and Delta created the Song division. All of these divisions chose a single type of airplane to fly, flew into smaller airports, adopted a point-to-point route structure, and so forth.

In addition to these incumbent airlines, many new entrants into the airline industry—both in the United States and elsewhere—have adopted similar operational choices as Southwest. In the United States, these new entrants include AirTran Airlines (recently purchased by Southwest), Allegiant Airlines, JetBlue, Skybus Airlines (now bankrupt), Spirit Airlines, and Virgin American Airlines.

Thus, while Southwest's operational choices are valuable and have been rare, they are apparently not costly to imitate. This is not surprising because these operational choices have few of the attributes of resources or capabilities that are costly to imitate. They do not derive from a firm's unique history, they are not path dependent, they are not causally ambiguous, and they are not socially complex.

Finally, is Southwest organized to fully exploit its operational choices? Most observers agree that Southwest's structure, management controls, and compensation policies are consistent with its operational choices.

Taken together, this analysis of Southwest's operational choices suggests that they are valuable, have been rare, but are not costly to imitate. While Southwest is organized to exploit these opportunities, they are likely to be only a source of temporary competitive advantage for Southwest.

Southwest's People-Management and Competitive Advantage

A similar VRIO analysis can be conducted for Southwest's approach to people management. First, is this approach valuable; that is, does it reduce Southwest's costs or increase the willingness of its customers to pay?

Employee commitment and loyalty at Southwest is one explanation of why Southwest is able to get higher levels of employee productivity than most other U.S. airlines. This increased productivity shows up in numerous ways. For example, the average turnaround time for Southwest flights is around 18 minutes. The average turnaround time for the average U.S. airline is 45 minutes. Southwest Airline employees are simply more effective in unloading and loading luggage, fueling, and catering their airplanes than employees in other airlines. This means that Southwest Airlines airplanes are on the ground for less time and in the air more time than its competitors. Of course, an airplane is only making money if it is in the air. This seemingly simple idea is worth hundreds of millions of dollars in lower costs to Southwest.

Have such loyalty and teamwork been rare in the U.S. airline industry? Over the past 15 years, the U.S. airline industry has been wracked by employment strife. Many airlines have had to cut employment, reduce wages, and in other ways strain their relationship with their employees. Overall, in comparison to incumbent airlines, the relationship that Southwest enjoys with its employees has been rare.

Is this relationship costly to imitate? Certainly, relationships between an airline and its employees have many of the attributes that should make them costly to imitate. They emerge over time; they are path dependent, causally ambiguous, and socially complex. It is reasonable to expect that incumbent airlines, airlines that already have strained relationships with their employees, would have difficulty imitating the relationship Southwest enjoys with its employees. Thus, in comparison to incumbent airlines, Southwest's approach to managing its people is probably valuable, rare, and costly to imitate. Assuming it is organized appropriately (and this seems to be the case), this would mean that—relative to incumbent airlines—Southwest has a sustained competitive advantage.

The situation may be somewhat different for new entrants into the U.S. airline industry. These airlines may not have a history of strained employee relationships. As new firms, they may be able to develop more valuable employee relationships from the very beginning. This suggests that, relative to new entrants, Southwest's approach to people management may be valuable and rare, but not costly to imitate. Again, assuming Southwest is organized appropriately, relative to new entrants into the U.S. airline industry, Southwest's people-management capabilities may be a source of only a temporary competitive advantage.

Imitation and Competitive Dynamics in an Industry

Suppose a firm in an industry has conducted an analysis of its resources and capabilities, concludes that it possesses some valuable, rare, and costly-to-imitate resources and capabilities, and uses these to choose a strategy that it implements with the appropriate organizational structure, formal and informal management controls, and compensation policies. The RBV suggests that this firm will gain a competitive advantage even if it is operating in what an environmental threat analysis (see Chapter 2) would suggest is a very unattractive industry. Examples of firms that have competitive advantages in unattractive industries include Southwest Airlines, Nucor Steel, and Wal-Mart, to name a few.

Given that a particular firm in an industry has a competitive advantage, how should other firms respond? Decisions made by other firms given the strategic choices of a particular firm define the nature of the **competitive dynamics** that exist in an industry. In general, other firms in an industry can respond to the advantages of a competitor in one of three ways. First, they can choose to limit their response. For example, when Wal-Mart entered the discount grocery market with the creation of Super Walmarts, some competitors (e.g., Safeway) ignored Wal-Mart's moves and continued on as before. Other competitors (e.g., Kroger) modified some of their tactics, including, for example, selling more prepared foods and more specialty foods than before. Finally, other firms fundamentally altered their strategies (e.g., Target began building stores that also sold discount groceries).

Not Responding to Another Firm's Competitive Advantage

A firm might not respond to another firm's competitive advantage for at least three reasons. First, this firm might have its own competitive advantage. By responding to another firm's competitive advantage, it might destroy, or at least compromise, its own sources of competitive advantage. For example, digital time-keeping has made accurate watches available to most consumers at reasonable prices. A firm such as Casio has a competitive advantage in this market because of its miniaturization and electronic capabilities. Indeed, Casio's market share and performance in the watch business continue to climb although demand for watches, overall, has gone down. How should Rolex—a manufacturer of very expensive, non-electronic watches—respond to Casio? Rolex's decision has been: *Not at all*. Rolex appeals to a very different market segment than Casio. Should Rolex change its strategies—even if it replaced its mechanical self-winding design with the technologically superior digital design—it could easily compromise its competitive advantage in its own niche market.[28] In general, when a firm already possesses its own sources of competitive advantage, it will not respond to different sources of competitive advantage controlled by another firm.

Second, a firm may not respond to another firm's competitive advantage because it does not have the resources and capabilities to do so. A firm with insufficient or inappropriate resources and capabilities—be they physical, financial, human, or organizational—typically will not be able to imitate a successful firm's resources either through direct duplication or substitution. This may very well be the case with US Airways and Southwest Airlines. It may simply be beyond the ability of US Airways to imitate Southwest's managerial resources and capabilities. In this setting, US Airways is likely to find itself at a sustained competitive disadvantage.[29]

Finally, a firm may not respond to the advantages of a competitor because it is trying to reduce the level of rivalry in an industry. Any actions a firm takes that have the effect of reducing the level of rivalry in an industry and that also do not require firms in an industry to directly communicate or negotiate with each other can be thought of as **tacit cooperation**. Explicit cooperation, where firms do directly communicate and negotiate with each other, is discussed in detail in Chapter 9's analysis of strategic alliances.

Reducing the level of rivalry in an industry can benefit all firms operating in that industry. This decision can have the effect of reducing the quantity of goods and services provided in an industry to below the competitive level, actions that will have the effect of increasing the prices of these goods or services. When tacit cooperation has the effect of reducing supply and increasing prices, it is known as **tacit collusion**. Tacit collusion can be illegal in some settings. However, firms can also tacitly cooperate along other dimensions besides quantity and price. These actions can also benefit all the firms in an industry and typically are not illegal.[30]

For example, it may be that firms can tacitly agree not to invest in certain kinds of research and development. Some forms of research and development are very expensive, and although these investments might end up generating products or services that could benefit customers, firms might still prefer to avoid the expense and risk. Firms can also tacitly agree not to market their products in certain ways. For example, before regulations compelled them to do so, most tobacco companies had already decided not to put cigarette vending machines in locations usually frequented by children, even though these machines could have generated significant revenues. Also, firms can tacitly cooperate by agreeing not

TABLE 3.5 Attributes of
Industry Structure That Facilitate
the Development of Tacit
Cooperation

1. Small number of competing firms
2. Homogeneous products and costs
3. Market-share leader
4. High barriers to entry

to engage in certain manufacturing practices, such as outsourcing to developing countries and engaging in environmentally unsound practices.

All of these actions can have the effect of reducing the level of rivalry in an industry. And reducing the level of rivalry can have the effect of increasing the average level of performance for a firm in an industry. However, tacit cooperative relationships among firms are sometimes difficult to maintain. Typically, in order for tacit cooperation to work, an industry must have the structural attributes described in Table 3.5. First, the industry must have relatively few firms. Informally communicating and coordinating strategies among a few firms is difficult enough; it is even more difficult when the industry has a large number of firms. For this reason, tacit cooperation is a viable strategy only when an industry is an oligopoly (see Chapter 2).

Second, firms in this industry must be homogeneous with respect to the products they sell and their cost structure. Having heterogeneous products makes it too easy for a firm to "cheat" on its tacitly cooperative agreements by modifying its products, and heterogeneous cost means that the optimal level of output for a particular firm may be very different from the level agreed to through tacit cooperation. In this setting, a firm might have a strong incentive to increase its output and upset cooperative agreements.

Third, an industry typically has to have at least one strong market-share leader if firms are going to tacitly cooperate. This would be a relatively large firm that has established an example of the kind of behavior that will be mutually beneficial in the industry, and other firms in the industry sometimes fall into line with this example. Indeed, it is often the market-share leader that will choose not to respond to the competitive actions of another firm in the industry in order to maintain cooperative relations.

Finally, the maintenance of tacit cooperation in an industry almost always requires the existence of high barriers to entry. If tacit cooperation is successful, the average performance of firms in an industry will improve. However, this higher level of performance can induce other firms to enter into this industry (see Chapter 2). Such entry will increase the number of firms in an industry and make it very difficult to maintain tacitly cooperative relationships. Thus, it must be very costly for new firms to enter into an industry for those in that industry to maintain their tacit cooperation. The higher these costs, the higher the barriers to entry.

Changing Tactics in Response to Another Firm's Competitive Advantage

Tactics are the specific actions a firm takes to implement its strategies. Examples of tactics include decisions firms make about various attributes of their products—including size, shape, color, and price—specific advertising approaches adopted by a firm, and specific sales and marketing efforts. Generally, firms change their tactics much more frequently than they change their strategies.[31]

When competing firms are pursuing approximately the same strategies, the competitive advantages that any one firm might enjoy at a given point in time are most likely due to the tactics that that firm is pursuing. In this setting, it is not unusual for competing firms to change their tactics by imitating the tactics of the firm with an advantage in order to reduce that firm's advantage. Although changing one's tactics in this manner will only generate competitive parity, this is usually better than the competitive disadvantage these firms were experiencing.

Several industries provide excellent examples of these kinds of tactical interactions. In consumer goods, for example, if one company increases its sales by adding a "lemon scent" to laundry detergent, then lemon scents start showing up in everyone's laundry detergent. If Coke starts selling a soft drink with half the sugar and half the carbs of regular Coke, can Pepsi's low-sugar/low-carb product be far behind? And when Delta Airlines cuts it airfares, can American and United be far behind? Not surprisingly, these kinds of tactical changes, because they initially may be valuable and rare, are seldom costly to imitate and thus are typically only sources of temporary competitive advantage.

Sometimes, rather than simply imitating the tactics of a firm with a competitive advantage, a firm at a disadvantage may "leapfrog" its competitors by developing an entirely new set of tactics. Procter & Gamble engaged in this strategy when it introduced its laundry detergent, Tide, in a new, concentrated formula. This new formulation required new manufacturing and packaging equipment—the smaller box could not be filled in the current manufacturing lines in the industry—which meant that Tide's competitors had to take more time in imitating the concentrated laundry detergent tactic than other tactics pursued in this industry. Nevertheless, within just a few weeks other firms in this market were introducing their own versions of concentrated laundry detergent.

Indeed, some firms can become so skilled at innovating new products and other tactics that this innovative capability can be a source of sustained competitive advantage. Consider, for example, Sony during its heydays. Most observers agree that Sony possessed some special management and innovation skills that enabled it to conceive, design, and manufacture high-quality miniaturized consumer electronics. However, virtually every time Sony brought out a new miniaturized product several of its competitors quickly duplicated that product through reverse engineering, thereby reducing Sony's technological advantage. In what way can Sony's socially complex miniaturization resources and capabilities be a source of sustained competitive advantage when most of Sony's products were quickly imitated through direct duplication?

After Sony introduced each new product, it experienced a rapid increase in profits attributable to the new product's unique features. This increase, however, leads other firms to reverse-engineer the Sony product and introduce their own versions. Increased competition resulted in a reduction in the profits associated with a new product. Thus, at the level of individual products, Sony apparently enjoys only temporary competitive advantages. However, looking at the total returns earned by Sony across all of its new products over time makes clear the source of Sony's sustained competitive advantage: By exploiting its resources and capabilities in miniaturization, Sony was able to constantly introduce new and exciting personal electronics products. No single product generated a sustained competitive advantage, but, over time, across several such product introductions, Sony's resource and capability advantages led to sustained competitive advantages.[32]

Changing Strategies in Response to Another Firm's Competitive Advantage

Finally, firms sometimes respond to another firm's competitive advantage by changing their strategies. Obviously, this does not occur very often, and it typically only occurs when another firm's strategies usurp a firm's competitive advantage. In this setting, a firm will not be able to gain even competitive parity if it maintains its strategy, even if it implements that strategy very effectively.

Changes in consumer tastes, in population demographics, and in the laws that govern a business can all have the effect of rendering what once was a valuable strategy as valueless. However, the most frequent impact is changes in technology. For example, no matter how well made a mechanical calculator is, it is simply inferior to an electronic calculator. No matter how efficient the telegraph was in its day, it is an inferior technology to the telephone. And no matter how quickly one's fingers can move the beads on an abacus, an electronic cash register is a better way of keeping track of sales and making change in a store.

When firms change their strategies, they must proceed through the entire strategic management process, as described in Chapter 1. However, these firms will often have difficulty abandoning their traditional strategies. For most firms, their strategy helps define what they do and who they are. Changing its strategy often requires a firm to change its identity and its purposes. These are difficult changes to make, and many firms wait to change their strategy until absolutely forced to do so by disastrous financial results. By then, these firms not only have to change their strategy—with all that implies—they have to do so in the face of significant financial pressures.

The ability of virtually all strategies to generate competitive advantages typically expires, sooner or later. In general, it is much better for a firm to change its strategy before that strategy is no longer viable. In this way, a firm can make a planned move to a new strategy that maintains whatever resources and capabilities it still possesses while it develops the new resources and capabilities it will need to compete in the future.

Implications of the Resource-Based View

The RBV and the VRIO framework can be applied to individual firms to understand whether these firms will gain competitive advantages, how sustainable these competitive advantages are likely to be, and what the sources of these competitive advantages are. In this way, the RBV and the VRIO framework can be understood as important complements to the threats and opportunities analyses described in Chapter 2.

However, beyond what these frameworks can say about the competitive performance of a particular firm, the RBV has some broader implications for managers seeking to gain competitive advantages. Some of these broader implications are listed in Table 3.6 and discussed in the following section.

Where Does the Responsibility for Competitive Advantage in a Firm Reside?

First, the RBV suggests that competitive advantages can be found in several of the different resources and capabilities controlled by the firm. These resources and capabilities are not limited to those that are controlled directly by a firm's

1. The responsibility for competitive advantage in a firm:
   Competitive advantage is every employee's responsibility.
2. Competitive parity and competitive advantage:
   If all a firm does is what its competition does, it can gain only competitive parity. In gaining competitive advantage, it is better for a firm to exploit its own valuable, rare, and costly-to-imitate resources than to imitate the valuable and rare resources of a competitor.
3. Difficult to implement strategies:
   As long as the cost of strategy implementation is less than the value of strategy implementation, the relative cost of implementing a strategy is more important for competitive advantage than the absolute cost of implementing a strategy.
   Firms can systematically overestimate and underestimate their uniqueness.
4. Socially complex resources:
   Not only can employee empowerment, organizational culture, and teamwork be valuable, they can also be sources of sustained competitive advantage.
5. The role of the organization:
   Organization should support the use of valuable, rare, and costly-to-imitate resources. If conflicts between these attributes of a firm arise, change the organization.

TABLE 3.6 Broader Implications of the Resource-Based View

senior managers. Thus, the responsibility for creating, nurturing, and exploiting valuable, rare, and costly-to-imitate resources and capabilities for competitive advantage is not restricted to senior managers, but falls on every employee in a firm. Therefore, employees should go beyond defining their jobs in functional terms and instead define their jobs in competitive and economic terms.

Consider a simple example. In a recent visit to a very successful automobile manufacturing plant, the plant manager was asked to describe his job responsibilities. He said, "My job is to manage this plant in order to help the firm make and sell the best cars in the world." In response to a similar question, the person in charge of the manufacturing line said, "My job is to manage this manufacturing line in order to help the firm make and sell the best cars in the world." A janitor was also asked to describe his job responsibilities. Although he had not been present in the two earlier interviews, the janitor responded, "My job is to keep this facility clean in order to help the firm make and sell the best cars in the world."

Which of these three employees is most likely to be a source of sustained competitive advantage for this firm? Certainly, the plant manager and the manufacturing line manager *should* define their jobs in terms of helping the firm make and sell the best cars in the world. However, it is unlikely that their responses to this question would be any different than the responses of other senior managers at other manufacturing plants around the world. Put differently, although the definition of these two managers' jobs in terms of enabling the firm to make and sell the best cars in the world is valuable, it is unlikely to be rare, and thus it is likely to be a source of competitive parity, not competitive advantage. However, a janitor who defines her job as helping the firm make and sell the best cars in the world instead of simply to clean the facility is, most would agree, quite unusual. Because it is rare, it might be a source of at least a temporary competitive advantage.[33]

The value created by one janitor defining her job in competitive terms rather than functional terms is not huge, but suppose that all the employees in this plant defined their jobs in these terms. Suddenly, the value that might be created could be substantial. Moreover, the organizational culture and tradition in a firm that would lead employees to define their jobs in this way are likely to be costly for other firms to imitate. Thus, if this approach to defining job responsibilities is broadly diffused in a particular plant, it seems likely to be valuable, rare, and costly to imitate and thus a source of sustained competitive advantage, assuming the firm is organized to take advantage of this unusual resource.

In the end, it is clear that competitive advantage is too important to remain the sole property of senior management. To the extent that employees throughout an organization are empowered to develop and exploit valuable, rare, and costly-to-imitate resources and capabilities in the accomplishment of their job responsibilities, a firm may actually be able to gain sustained competitive advantages.

Competitive Parity and Competitive Advantage

Second, the RBV suggests that, if all a firm does is create value in the same way as its competitors, the best performance it can ever expect to gain is competitive parity. To do better than competitive parity, firms must engage in valuable and rare activities. They must do things to create economic value that other firms have not even thought of, let alone implemented.

This is especially critical for firms that find themselves at a competitive disadvantage. Such a firm certainly should examine its more successful competition, understand what has made this competition so successful, and, where imitation is very low cost, imitate the successful actions of its competitors. In this sense, benchmarking a firm's performance against the performance of its competitors can be extremely important.

However, if this is all that a firm does, it can only expect to gain competitive parity. Gaining competitive advantage depends on a firm discovering its own unique resources and capabilities and how they can be used in choosing and implementing strategies. For a firm seeking competitive advantage, it is better to be excellent in how it develops and exploits its own unique resources and capabilities than it is to be excellent in how it imitates the resources and capabilities of other firms.

This does not imply that firms must always be first movers to gain competitive advantages. Some firms develop valuable, rare, and costly-to-imitate resources and capabilities in being efficient second movers—that is, in rapidly imitating and improving on the product and technological innovations of other firms. Rather than suggesting that firms must always be first movers, the RBV suggests that, in order to gain competitive advantages, firms must implement strategies that rely on valuable, rare, and costly-to-imitate resources and capabilities, whatever those strategies or resources might be.

Difficult-to-Implement Strategies

Third, as firms contemplate different strategic options, they often ask how difficult and costly it will be to implement different strategies. As long as the cost of implementing a strategy is less than the value that a strategy creates, the RBV suggests that the critical question facing firms is not "Is a strategy easy to implement or not?" but rather "Is this strategy easier for us to implement than it is for our competitors to implement?" Firms that already possess the valuable, rare, and costly-to-imitate resources needed to implement a strategy will, in general, find it easier (i.e., less costly) to implement a strategy than firms that first have to develop the required resources and then implement the proposed strategy. For firms that already possess a resource, strategy implementation can be natural and swift.

In understanding the relative costs of implementing a strategy, firms can make two errors. First, they can overestimate the uniqueness of the resources they control. Although every firm's history is unique and no two management teams are exactly the same, this does not always mean that a firm's resources and capabilities will be rare. Firms with similar histories operating in similar industries will often develop similar capabilities. If a firm overestimates the rarity of its resources and capabilities, it can overestimate its ability to generate competitive advantages.

For example, when asked what their most critical sources of competitive advantage are, many firms will cite the quality of their top management team, the quality of their technology, and their commitment to excellence in all that they do. When pushed about their competitors, these same firms will admit that they too have high-quality top management teams, high-quality technology, and a commitment to excellence in all that they do. Although these three attributes can be sources of competitive parity, they cannot be sources of competitive advantage.

Second, firms can sometimes underestimate their uniqueness and thus underestimate the extent to which the strategies they pursue can be sources of sustained competitive advantage. When firms possess valuable, rare, and costly-to-imitate resources, strategy implementation can be relatively easy. In this context, it seems reasonable to expect that other firms will be able to quickly imitate this "easy-to-implement" strategy. Of course, this is not the case if these resources controlled by a firm are, in fact, rare and costly to imitate.

In general, firms must take great care not to overestimate or underestimate their uniqueness. An accurate assessment of the value, rarity, and imitability of a firm's resources is necessary to develop an accurate understanding of the relative costs of implementing a firm's strategies and, thus, the ability of those strategies to generate competitive advantages. Often, firms must employ outside assistance in helping them describe the rarity and imitability of their resources, even though managers in firms will generally be much more familiar with the resources controlled by a firm than outsiders. However, outsiders can provide a measure of objectivity in evaluating the uniqueness of a firm.

Socially Complex Resources

Over the past several decades, much has been written about the importance of employee empowerment, organizational culture, and teamwork for firm performance. Most of this work suggests that firms that empower employees, that have an enabling culture, and that encourage teamwork will, on average, make better strategic choices and implement them more efficiently than firms without these organizational attributes. Using the language of the RBV, most of this work has suggested that employee empowerment, organizational culture, and teamwork, at least in some settings, are economically valuable.[34]

Resource-based logic acknowledges the importance of the value of these organizational attributes. However, it also suggests that these socially complex resources and capabilities can be rare and costly to imitate—and it is these attributes that make it possible for socially complex resources and capabilities to be sources of sustained competitive advantage. Put differently, the RBV actually extends and broadens traditional analyses of the socially complex attributes of firms. Not only can these attributes be valuable, but they can also be rare and costly to imitate and, thus, sources of sustained competitive advantage.

The Role of Organization

Finally, resource-based logic suggests that an organization's structure, control systems, and compensation policies should support and enable a firm's efforts to fully exploit the valuable, rare, and costly-to-imitate resources and capabilities it controls. These attributes of organization, by themselves, are usually not sources of sustained competitive advantage.

These observations suggest that if there is a conflict between the resources a firm controls and that firm's organization, the organization should be changed. However, it is often the case that once a firm's structure, control systems, and compensation policies are put in place they tend to remain, regardless of whether they are consistent with a firm's underlying resources and capabilities. In such settings, a firm will not be able to realize the full competitive potential of its underlying resource base. To the extent that a firm's resources and capabilities are continuously evolving, its organizational structure, control systems, and compensation policies must also evolve. For these attributes of organization to evolve, managers must be aware of their link with a firm's resources and capabilities and of organizational alternatives.

Summary

The RBV is an economic theory that suggests that firm performance is a function of the types of resources and capabilities controlled by firms. Resources are the tangible and intangible assets a firm uses to conceive and implement its strategies. Capabilities are a subset of resources that enable a firm to take advantage of its other resources. Resources and capabilities can be categorized into financial, physical, human, and organizational resources categories.

The RBV makes two assumptions about resources and capabilities: the assumption of resource heterogeneity (that some resources and capabilities may be heterogeneously distributed across competing firms) and the assumption of resource immobility (that this heterogeneity may be long lasting). These two assumptions can be used to describe conditions under which firms will gain competitive advantages by exploiting their resources.

A tool for analyzing a firm's internal strengths and weaknesses can be derived from the RBV. Called the VRIO framework, this tool asks four questions about a firm's resources and capabilities in order to evaluate their competitive potential. These questions are the question of value, the question of rarity, the question of imitability, and the question of organization.

A firm's resources and capabilities are valuable when they enable it to exploit external opportunities or neutralize external threats. Such valuable resources and capabilities are a firm's strengths. Resources and capabilities that are not valuable are a firm's weaknesses. Using valuable resources to exploit external opportunities or neutralize external threats will have the effect of increasing a firm's net revenues or decreasing its net costs.

One way to identify a firm's valuable resources and capabilities is by examining its value chain. A firm's value chain is the list of business activities it engages in to develop, produce, and sell its products or services. Different stages in this value chain require different resources and capabilities, and differences in value chain choices across firms can lead to important differences among the resources and capabilities controlled by different companies. A generic value chain has been developed by McKinsey and Company.

Valuable and common (i.e., not rare) resources and capabilities can be a source of competitive parity. Failure to invest in such resources can create a competitive disadvantage for a firm. Valuable and rare resources can be a source of at least a temporary competitive advantage. There are fewer firms able to control such a resource and still exploit it as a source of at least temporary competitive advantage than there are firms that will generate perfect competition dynamics in an industry.

Valuable, rare, and costly-to-imitate resources and capabilities can be a source of sustained competitive advantage. Imitation can occur through direct duplication or through substitution. A firm's resources and capabilities may be costly to imitate for at least four reasons: unique historical circumstances, causal ambiguity, socially complex resources and capabilities, and patents.

To take full advantage of the potential of its resources and capabilities, a firm must be appropriately organized. A firm's organization consists of its formal reporting structure, its formal and informal control processes, and its compensation policy. These are complementary resources in that they are rarely sources of competitive advantage on their own.

The VRIO framework can be used to identify the competitive implications of a firm's resources and capabilities—whether they are a source of competitive disadvantage, competitive parity, temporary competitive advantage, or sustained competitive advantage—and the extent to which these resources and capabilities are strengths or weaknesses.

When a firm faces a competitor that has a sustained competitive advantage, the firm's options are to not respond, to change its tactics, or to change its strategies. A firm may choose not to respond in this setting for at least three reasons. First, a response might weaken its own sources of sustained competitive advantage. Second, a firm may not have the resources required to respond. Third, a firm may be trying to create or maintain tacit cooperation within an industry.

The RBV has a series of broader managerial implications as well. For example, resource-based logic suggests that competitive advantage is every employee's responsibility. It also suggests that if all a firm does is what its competition does, it can gain only competitive parity, and that in gaining competitive advantage it is better for a firm to exploit its own valuable, rare, and costly-to-imitate resources than to imitate the valuable and rare resources of a competitor. Also, resource-based logic implies that as long as the cost of strategy implementation is less than the value of strategy implementation, the relative cost of implementing a strategy is more important for competitive advantage than the absolute cost of implementing a strategy. It also implies that firms can systematically overestimate and underestimate their uniqueness. With regard to a firm's resources and capabilities, resource-based logic suggests that not only can employee empowerment, organizational culture, and teamwork be valuable; they can also be sources of sustained competitive advantage. Also, if conflicts arise between a firm's valuable, rare, and costly-to-imitate resources and its organization, the organization should be changed.

MyManagementLab®

Go to **mymanagementlab.com** to complete the problems marked with this icon ⭐.

Challenge Questions

3.1. Explain which of the following approaches to strategy formulation is more likely to generate economic profits: (a) evaluating external opportunities and threats and then developing resources and capabilities to exploit these opportunities and neutralize these threats or (b) evaluating internal resources and capabilities and then searching for industries where they can be exploited?

3.2. Which firm will have a higher level of economic performance: (a) a firm with valuable, rare, and costly-to-imitate resources and capabilities operating in a very attractive industry or (b) a firm with valuable, rare, and costly-to-imitate resources and capabilities operating in a very unattractive industry? Assume both these firms are appropriately organized. Explain your answer.

3.3. Considering which is more critical to sustaining human life—water or diamonds—why do firms that provide water to customers generally earn lower economic performance than firms that provide diamonds?

⭐ **3.4.** Why would a firm currently experiencing competitive parity be able to gain sustained competitive advantages by studying another firm that is currently experiencing sustained competitive advantages?

3.5. Your former college roommate calls you and asks to borrow $10,000 so that he can open a pizza restaurant in his hometown. He acknowledges that there is a high degree of direct competition in this market, that the cost of entry is low, and that there are numerous substitutes for pizza, but he believes that his pizza restaurant will have some sustained competitive advantages. For example, he is going to have sawdust on his floor, a variety of imported beers, and a late-night delivery service. What are the risks in lending him the money?

3.6. In the text, it is suggested that Boeing did not respond to Airbus's announcement of the development of a super-jumbo aircraft. Assuming this aircraft will give Airbus a competitive advantage in the segment of the airliner business that supplies airplanes for long international flights, why did Boeing not respond?

3.7. Boeing did not respond to Airbus's announcement of the development of a super-jumbo aircraft. Does it have its own competitive advantage that it does not want to abandon? Explain.

3.8. Boeing did not respond to Airbus's announcement of the development of a super-jumbo aircraft. Does it not have the resources and capabilities needed to respond? Explain.

3.9. Boeing did not respond to Airbus's announcement of the development of a super-jumbo aircraft. Is it trying to reduce the level of rivalry in this industry? Explain.

⭐ **3.10.** Between the following two firms, which one is more likely to be successful in exploiting its sources of sustained competitive advantage in its home market than in a highly competitive, nondomestic market: (a) a firm from a less competitive home country or (b) a firm from a more competitive home country? Why?

Problem Set

3.11. Apply the VRIO framework in the following settings. Will the actions described be a source of competitive disadvantage, parity, temporary advantage, or sustained competitive advantage? Explain your answers.

(a) Procter & Gamble introduces new, smaller packaging for its Tide laundry detergent.
(b) American Airlines announces a 5 percent across-the-board reduction in airfares.
(c) The Korean automobile firm Hyundai announces a 10-year, 100,000-mile warranty on its cars.
(d) Microsoft makes it easier to transfer data and information from Microsoft Word to Microsoft Excel.
(e) Merck is able to coordinate the work of its chemists and biologists in the development of new drugs.
(f) Ford patents a new kind of brake pad for its cars.
(g) Ashland Chemical, a specialty chemical company, patents a new chemical.

(h) The New York Yankees sign All-Star pitcher Randy Johnson to a long-term contract.

(i) Michael Dell uses the money he has made from Dell to purchase the Dallas Cowboys football team.

(j) Ted Turner uses the money he has made from his broadcasting empire to purchase the Atlanta Braves baseball team.

3.12. Identify three firms you might want to work for. Using the VRIO framework, evaluate the extent to which the resources and capabilities of these firms give them the potential to realize competitive disadvantages, parity, temporary advantages, or sustained advantages. What implications, if any, does this analysis have for the company you might want to work for?

3.13. You have been assigned to estimate the present value of a potential construction project for your company. How would you use the VRIO framework to construct the cash-flow analysis that is a part of any present-value calculation?

MyManagementLab®

Go to **mymanagementlab.com** for Auto-graded writing questions as well as the following Assisted-graded writing questions:

⭐ **3.14.** Give an example of how you would apply value chain analysis to identify a firm's valuable resources and capabilities.

⭐ **3.15.** What is required for a firm to gain a sustained competitive advantage from a resource considered rare?

End Notes

1. The term *the resource-based view* was coined by Wernerfelt, B. (1984). "A resource-based view of the firm." *Strategic Management Journal*, 5, pp. 171–180. Some important early contributors to this theory include Rumelt, R. P. (1984). "Toward a strategic theory of the firm." In R. Lamb (ed.), *Competitive strategic management* (pp. 556–570). Upper Saddle River, NJ: Prentice Hall; and Barney, J. B. (1986). "Strategic factor markets: Expectations, luck and business strategy." *Management Science*, 32, pp. 1512–1514. A second wave of important early resource-based theoretical work includes Barney, J. B. (1991). "Firm resources and sustained competitive advantage." *Journal of Management*, 7, pp. 49–64; Dierickx, I., and K. Cool. (1989). "Asset stock accumulation and sustainability of competitive advantage." *Management Science*, 35, pp. 1504–1511; Conner, K. R. (1991). "A historical comparison of resource-based theory and five schools of thought within industrial organization economics: Do we have a new theory of the firm?" *Journal of Management*, 17(1), pp. 121–154; and Peteraf, M. A. (1993). "The cornerstones of competitive advantage: A resource-based view." *Strategic Management Journal*, 14, pp. 179–191. A review of much of this early theoretical literature can be found in Mahoney, J. T., and J. R. Pandian. (1992). "The resource-based view within the conversation of strategic management." *Strategic Management Journal*, 13, pp. 363–380. The theoretical perspective has also spawned a growing body of empirical work, including Brush, T. H., and K. W. Artz. (1999). "Toward a contingent resource-based theory." *Strategic Management Journal*, 20, pp. 223–250; Marcus, A., and D. Geffen. (1998). "The dialectics of competency acquisition." *Strategic Management Journal*, 19, pp. 1145–1168; Brush, T. H., P. Bromiley, and M. Hendrickx. (1999). "The relative influence of industry and corporation on business segment performance." *Strategic Management Journal*, 20, pp. 519–547; Yeoh, P.-L., and K. Roth. (1999). "An empirical analysis of sustained advantage in the U.S. pharmaceutical industry." *Strategic Management Journal*, 20, pp. 637–653; Roberts, P. (1999). "Product innovation, product-market competition and persistent profitability in the U.S. pharmaceutical industry."

Strategic Management Journal, 20, pp. 655–670; Gulati, R. (1999). "Network location and learning." *Strategic Management Journal*, 20, pp. 397–420; Lorenzoni, G., and A. Lipparini. (1999). "The leveraging of interfirm relationships as a distinctive organizational capability." *Strategic Management Journal*, 20, pp. 317–338; Majumdar, S. (1998). "On the utilization of resources." *Strategic Management Journal*, 19(9), pp. 809–831; Makadok, R. (1997). "Do inter-firm differences in capabilities affect strategic pricing dynamics?" *Academy of Management Proceedings '97*, pp. 30–34; Silverman, B. S., J. A. Nickerson, and J. Freeman. (1997). "Profitability, transactional alignment, and organizational mortality in the U.S. trucking industry." *Strategic Management Journal*, 18 (Summer special issue), pp. 31–52; Powell, T. C., and A. Dent-Micallef. (1997). "Information technology as competitive advantage." *Strategic Management Journal*, 18(5), pp. 375–405; Miller, D., and J. Shamsie. (1996). "The Resource-based view of the firm in two environments." *Academy of Management Journal*, 39(3), pp. 519–543; and Maijoor, S., and A. Van Witteloostuijn. (1996). "An empirical test of the resource-based theory." *Strategic Management Journal*, 17, pp. 549–569; Barnett, W. P., H. R. Greve, and D. Y. Park. (1994). "An evolutionary model of organizational performance." *Strategic Management Journal*, 15 (Winter special issue), pp. 11–28; Levinthal, D., and J. Myatt. (1994). "Co-evolution of capabilities and industry: The evolution of mutual fund processing." *Strategic Management Journal*, 17, pp. 45–62; Henderson, R., and I. Cockburn. (1994). "Measuring competence? Exploring firm effects in pharmaceutical research." *Strategic Management Journal*, 15, pp. 63–84; Pisano, G. P. (1994). "Knowledge, integration, and the locus of learning: An empirical analysis of process development." *Strategic Management Journal*, 15, pp. 85–100; and Zajac, E. J., and J. D. Westphal. (1994). "The costs and benefits of managerial incentives and monitoring in large U.S. corporations: When is more not better?" *Strategic Management Journal*, 15, pp. 121–142.

2. Ghemawat, P. (1986). "Wal-Mart stores' discount operations." Harvard Business School Case No. 9-387-018, on Wal-Mart; Kupfer, A. (1991).

"The champion of cheap clones." *Fortune*, September 23, pp. 115–120; and Holder, D. (1989). "L. L. Bean, Inc.—1974." Harvard Business School Case No. 9-676-014, on L. L. Bean. Some of Wal-Mart's more recent moves, especially its international acquisitions, are described in Laing, J. R. (1999). "Blimey! Wal-Mart." *Barron's*, 79, p. 14. L. L. Bean's lethargic performance in the 1990s, together with its turnaround plan, is described in Symonds, W. (1998). "Paddling harder at L. L. Bean." *BusinessWeek*, December 7, p. 72.

3. For an early discussion of the importance of human capital in firms, see Becker, G. S. (1964). *Human capital.* New York: Columbia University Press.

4. Heskett, J. L., and R. H. Hallowell. (1993). "Southwest Airlines: 1993 (A)." Harvard Business School Case No. 9-695-023.

5. See Barney, J. (1991). "Firm resources and sustained competitive advantage." *Journal of Management*, 17, pp. 99–120.

6. See Schlender, B. R. (1992). "How Sony keeps the magic going." *Fortune*, February 24, pp. 75–84; and (1999). "The weakling kicks back." *The Economist*, July 3, p. 46, for a discussion of Sony. See Krogh, L., J. Praeger, D. Sorenson, and J. Tomlinson. (1988). "How 3M evaluates its R&D programs." *Research Technology Management*, 31, pp. 10–14.

7. Anders, G. (2002). "AOL's true believers." *Fast Company*, July pp. 96+. In a recent *Wall Street Journal* article, managers of AOL Time Warner admitted they are no longer seeking synergies across their businesses. See Karnitschnig, M. (2006). "That's all, folks: After years of pushing synergy, Time Warner, Inc. says enough." *The Wall Street Journal*, June 2, A1+.

8. See Grant, R. M. (1991). *Contemporary strategy analysis.* Cambridge, MA: Basil Blackwell.

9. Lipman, S., and R. Rumelt. (1982). "Uncertain imitability: An analysis of interfirm differences in efficiency under competition." *Bell Journal of Economics*, 13, pp. 418–438; Barney, J. B. (1986). "Strategic factor markets: Expectations, luck and business strategy." *Management Science*, 32, pp. 1512–1514; and Barney, J. B. (1986). "Organizational culture: Can it be a source of sustained competitive advantage?" *Academy of Management Review*, 11, pp. 656–665.

10. Note that the definition of sustained competitive advantage presented here, though different, is consistent with the definition given in Chapter 1. In particular, a firm that enjoys a competitive advantage for a long period of time (the Chapter 1 definition) does not have its advantage competed away through imitation (the Chapter 3 definition).

11. See Breen, B. (2003). "What's selling in America." *Fast Company*, January, pp. 80+.

12. These explanations of costly imitation were first developed by Dierickx, I., and K. Cool. (1989). "Asset stock accumulation and sustainability of competitive advantage." *Management Science*, 35, pp. 1504–1511; Barney, J. B. (1991). "Firm resources and sustained competitive advantage." *Journal of Management*, 7, pp. 49–64; Mahoney, J. T., and J. R. Pandian. (1992). "The resource-based view within the conversation of strategic management." *Strategic Management Journal*, 13, pp. 363–380; and Peteraf, M. A. (1993). "The cornerstones of competitive advantage: A resource-based view." *Strategic Management Journal*, 14, pp. 179–191.

13. Dierickx, I., and K. Cool. (1989). "Asset stock accumulation and sustainability of competitive advantage." *Management Science*, 35, pp. 1504–1511. In economics, the role of history in determining competitive outcomes was first examined by Arthur, W. B. (1989). "Competing technologies, increasing returns, and lock-in by historical events." *Economic Journal*, 99, pp. 116–131.

14. See Breen, B. (2003). "What's selling in America." *Fast Company*, January, pp. 80+.

15. This term was first suggested by Arthur, W. B. (1989). "Competing technologies, increasing returns, and lock-in by historical events." *Economic Journal*, 99, pp. 116–131. A good example of path dependence is the development of Silicon Valley and the important role that Stanford University and a few early firms played in creating the network of organizations that has since become the center of much of the electronics business. See Alley, J. (1997). "The heart of Silicon Valley." *Fortune*, July 7, pp. 86+.

16. Reed, R., and R. J. DeFillippi. (1990). "Causal ambiguity, barriers to imitation, and sustainable competitive advantage." *Academy of Management Review*, 15(1), pp. 88–102, suggest that causal ambiguity about the sources of a firm's competitive advantage need only exist among a firm's competitors for it to be a source of sustained competitive advantage. Managers in a firm, they argue, may

fully understand the sources of their advantage. However, in a world where employees freely and frequently move from firm to firm, such special insights into the sources of a firm's competitive advantage would not remain proprietary for very long. For this reason, for causal ambiguity to be a source of sustained competitive advantage, both the firm trying to gain such an advantage and those trying to imitate it must face similar levels of causal ambiguity. Indeed, Wal-Mart sued Amazon for trying to steal some of its secrets by hiring employees away from Wal-Mart. See Nelson, E. (1998). "Wal-Mart accuses Amazon.com of stealing its secrets in lawsuit." *The Wall Street Journal*, October 19, p. B10. For a discussion of how difficult it is to maintain secrets, especially in a world of the World Wide Web, see Farnham, A. (1997). "How safe are your secrets?" *Fortune*, September 8, pp. 114+. The international dimensions of the challenges associated with maintaining secrets are discussed in Robinson, E. (1998). "China spies target corporate America." *Fortune*, March 30, pp. 118+.

17. Itami, H. (1987). *Mobilizing invisible assets.* Cambridge, MA: Harvard University Press.

18. See Barney, J. B., and B. Tyler. (1990). "The attributes of top management teams and sustained competitive advantage." In M. Lawless and L. Gomez-Mejia (eds.), *Managing the high technology firm* (pp. 33–48). Greenwich, CT: JAI Press, on teamwork in top management teams; Barney, J. B. (1986). "Organizational culture: Can it be a source of sustained competitive advantage?" *Academy of Management Review*, 11, pp. 656–665, on organizational culture; Henderson, R. M., and I. Cockburn. (1994). "Measuring competence? Exploring firm effects in pharmaceutical research." *Strategic Management Journal*, 15, pp. 63–84, on relationships among employees; and Dyer, J. H., and H. Singh. (1998). "The relational view: Cooperative strategy and sources of interorganizational competitive advantage." *Academy of Management Review*, 23(4), pp. 660–679, on relationships with suppliers and customers.

19. For a discussion of knowledge as a source of competitive advantage in the popular business press, see Stewart, T. (1995). "Getting real about brain power." *Fortune*, November 27, pp. 201+; Stewart, T. (1995). "Mapping corporate knowledge." *Fortune*, October 30, pp. 209+. For the academic version of this same issue, see Simonin, B. L. (1999). "Ambiguity and the process of knowledge transfer in strategic alliances." *Strategic Management Journal*, 20(7), pp. 595–623; Spender, J. C. (1996). "Making knowledge the basis of a dynamic theory of the firm." *Strategic Management Journal*, 17 (Winter special issue), pp. 109–122; Hatfield, D. D., J. P. Liebeskind, and T. C. Opler. (1996). "The effects of corporate restructuring on aggregate industry specialization." *Strategic Management Journal*, 17, pp. 55–72; and Grant, R. M. (1996). "Toward a knowledge-based theory of the firm." *Strategic Management Journal*, 17 (Winter special issue), pp. 109–122.

20. Porras, J., and P. O. Berg. (1978). "The impact of organizational development." *Academy of Management Review*, 3, pp. 249–266, have done one of the few empirical studies on whether systematic efforts to change socially complex resources are effective. They found that such efforts are usually not effective. Although this study is getting older, it is unlikely that current change methods will be any more effective than the methods examined by these authors.

21. See Hambrick, D. (1987). "Top management teams: Key to strategic success." *California Management Review*, 30, pp. 88–108, on top management teams; Barney, J. B. (1986). "Organizational culture: Can it be a source of sustained competitive advantage?" *Academy of Management Review*, 11, pp. 656–665, on culture; Porter, M. E. (1980). *Competitive strategy.* New York: Free Press; and Klein, B., and K. Leffler. (1981). "The role of market forces in assuring contractual performance." *Journal of Political Economy*, 89, pp. 615–641, on relations with customers.

22. See Harris, L. C., and E. Ogbonna. (1999). "Developing a market oriented culture: A critical evaluation." *Journal of Management Studies*, 36(2), pp. 177–196.

23. Lieberman, M. B. (1987). "The learning curve, diffusion, and competitive strategy." *Strategic Management Journal*, 8, pp. 441–452, has a very good analysis of the cost of imitation in the chemical industry. See also Lieberman, M. B., and D. B. Montgomery. (1988). "First-mover advantages." *Strategic Management Journal*, 9, pp. 41–58.

24. Rumelt, R. P. (1984). "Toward a strategic theory of the firm." In R. Lamb (ed.), *Competitive strategic management* (pp. 556–570). Upper Saddle River, NJ: Prentice Hall, among others, cites patents as a source of costly imitation.

25. Significant debate surrounds the patentability of different kinds of products. For example, although typefaces are not patentable (and cannot be copyrighted), the process for displaying typefaces may be. See Thurm, S. (1998). "Copy this typeface? Court ruling counsels caution." *The Wall Street Journal*, July 15, pp. B1+.

26. For an insightful discussion of these complementary resources, see Amit, R., and P. J. H. Schoemaker. (1993). "Strategic assets and organizational rent." *Strategic Management Journal*, 14(1), pp. 33–45.

27. See H. Tabuchi (2012) How the tech parade passed Sony by. April 15, 2012. *New York Times*. http://www.nytimes.com/2012/04/15/technology/how-sony-fell-behind in the tech parade. Accessed January 27, 2014.

28. (2004). "Casio." *Marketing*, May 6, p. 95; Weisul, K. (2003). "When time is money—and art." *BusinessWeek*, July 21, p. 86.

29. That said, there have been some "cracks" in Southwest's capabilities armor lately. Its CEO suddenly resigned, and its level of profitability dropped precipitously in 2004. Whether these are indicators that Southwest's core strengths are being dissipated or there are short-term problems is not yet known. However, Southwest's stumbling would give US Airways some hope. Trottman, M., S. McCartney, and J. Lublin. (2004). "Southwest's CEO abruptly quits 'draining job.'" *The Wall Street Journal*, July 16, pp. A1+.

30. One should consult a lawyer before getting involved in these forms of tacit cooperation.

31. This aspect of the competitive dynamics in an industry is discussed in Smith, K. G., C. M. Grimm, and M. J. Gannon. (1992). *Dynamics of competitive strategy*. Newberry Park, CA: Sage.

32. Schlender, B. R. (1992). "How Sony keeps the magic going." *Fortune*, February 24, pp. 75–84.

33. Personal communication.

34. See, for example, Peters, T., and R. Waterman. (1982). *In search of excellence*. New York: Harper Collins; Collins, J., and J. Porras. (1994). *Built to last*. New York: Harper Business; Collins, J. (2001). *Good to great*. New York: Harper Collins; and Bennis, W. G., and R. Townsend. (2006). *Reinventing leadership*. New York: Harper Collins.

2 BUSINESS-LEVEL STRATEGIES

4 Cost Leadership

LEARNING OBJECTIVES *After reading this chapter, you should be able to:*

1. Define cost leadership.

2. Identify six reasons firms can differ in their costs.

3. Identify four reasons economies of scale can exist and four reasons diseconomies of scale can exist.

4. Explain the relationship between cost advantages due to learning-curve economies and a firm's market share, as well as the limitations of this logic.

5. Identify how cost leadership helps neutralize each of the major threats in an industry.

6. Identify the bases of cost leadership that are more likely to be rare and costly to imitate.

7. Explain how firms use a functional organizational structure to implement business-level strategies, such as cost leadership.

8. Describe the formal and informal management controls and compensation policies firms use to implement cost leadership strategies.

MyManagementLab®

⭐ **Improve Your Grade!**
Over 10 million students improved their results using the Pearson MyLabs.
Visit **mymanagementlab.com** for simulations, tutorials, and end-of-chapter problems.

The World's Lowest-Cost Airline

Everyone's heard of low-cost airlines—Southwest, EasyJet, and JetBlue, for example. But have you heard of the world's lowest-cost airline? This airline currently gives 25 percent of its seats away for free. Its goal is to double that within a couple of years. And yet, in 2013, this airline announced record annual profits of €569 million, up 13 percent; an increase in passenger traffic of 5 percent (from €75.8 million to €79.3 million); and an increase in revenues of 13 percent (from €4325 million to €4884 million). And this in spite of continued increases in jet fuel prices during this same time period!

The name of this airline is Ryanair. Headquartered in Dublin, Ireland, Ryanair flies short flights throughout Western Europe. In 1985, Ryanair's founders started a small airline to fly between Ireland and England. For six years, this airline barely broke even. Then, in 1991, Michael O'Leary—current CEO at Ryanair—was brought on board. O'Leary traveled to the United States and studied the most successful low-cost airline in the world at that time: Southwest Airlines. O'Leary became convinced that, once European airspace was deregulated, an airline that adopted Southwest's model of quick turnarounds, no frills, no business class, flying into smaller regional airports, and using only a single kind of aircraft could be extremely successful. Prices in the European air market were fully deregulated in 1997.

Since then, Ryanair has become an even lower-cost airline than Southwest. Indeed, it calls itself the only "ultra-low cost carrier."

For example, like Southwest, Ryanair only flies a single type of aircraft—a Boeing 737–800. However, to save on the cost of its airplanes, Ryanair orders them without window shades and with seats that do not recline. This saves several hundred thousand dollars per plane and also reduces ongoing maintenance costs. Both Southwest and Ryanair try to make it easy for consumers to order tickets online, thereby avoiding the costs of call centers and travel agents. However, just 59 percent of Southwest's tickets are sold online; 98 percent of Ryanair's tickets are sold online.

© imagebroker/Alamy

This focus on low costs allows Ryanair to have the lowest prices possible for a seat on its airplanes. The average fare on Southwest is $92; the average fare on Ryanair is $53. But, even at those low prices, Ryanair is still able to earn comfortable margins.

However, those net margins don't come just from Ryanair's low costs. They also reflect the fact that the fare you pay Ryanair includes only the seat and virtually no other services. If you want any other services, you have to pay extra for them. For example, you want to check bags? It will cost $9.95 per bag. You want a snack on the airplane? It will cost you $5.50. For that, you get a not-very-tasty hot dog. You want a bottle of water? It will cost you $3.50. You want a blanket or pillow—they cost $2.50 each.

In addition, flight attendants will sell you all sorts of extras to keep you occupied during your flight. These include scratch-card games, perfume, digital cameras ($137.50), and MP3 players ($165). During 2007, Ryanair began offering in-flight mobile telephone service. Not only did this enable passengers to call their friends and family, Ryanair also used this service to introduce mobile gambling on its planes. Now, on your way from London to Paris, you can play blackjack, poker, and slot machines.

Finally, to further increase revenues, Ryanair sells space on its planes to advertisers. When your seat tray is up, you may see an ad for a cell phone from Vodaphone. When the tray is down, you may see an ad from Hertz.

All of these actions enable Ryanair to keep its profits up while keeping its fares as low as possible. And the results of this strategy have been impressive—from near bankruptcy in 1991, Ryanair is now among the largest international airlines in the world.

Of course, this success did not happen without some controversy. For example, in October 2006, Ryanair was chosen as the most disliked European airline in a poll of some 4,000 readers of TripAdvisor, a British Web site for frequent travelers. Ryanair's response: These frequent travelers usually have their companies pay for their travel. If they had to pay for their own tickets, they would prefer Ryanair. Also, Ryanair's strong anti-union stance has caused it political problems in many of the union-dominated countries where it flies. Finally, Ryanair has been criticized for some of its lax security and safety procedures, for how it treats disabled passengers, and for the cleanliness of its planes.

However, if you want to fly from London to Barcelona for $49 round trip, it's hard to beat Ryanair.

Source: K. Capell (2006). "Wal-Mart with wings." *BusinessWeek*, November 27, pp. 44–46; www//en.wikipedia.org/wiki/Ryanair; and Peter Arnold, Inc. www.Ryanair.com

Ryanair has been profitable in an industry—the airline industry—that has historically been populated by bankrupt firms. It does this by implementing an aggressive low-cost strategy.

What Is Business-Level Strategy?

Part 1 of this book introduced the basic tools required to conduct a strategic analysis: tools for analyzing external threats and opportunities (in Chapter 2) and tools for analyzing internal strengths and weaknesses (in Chapter 3). Once these two analyses have been completed, it is possible to begin making strategic choices. As explained in Chapter 1, strategic choices fall into two large categories: business strategies and corporate strategies. **Business-level strategies** are actions firms take to gain competitive advantages in a single market or industry. **Corporate-level strategies** are actions firms take to gain competitive advantages by operating in multiple markets or industries simultaneously.

The two business-level strategies discussed in this book are cost leadership (this chapter) and product differentiation (Chapter 5). The importance of these two business-level strategies is so widely recognized that they are often called **generic business strategies**.

What Is Cost Leadership?

A firm that chooses a **cost leadership business strategy** focuses on gaining advantages by reducing its costs to below those of all its competitors. This does not mean that this firm abandons other business or corporate strategies. Indeed, a single-minded focus on *just* reducing costs can lead a firm to make low-cost products that no one wants to buy. However, a firm pursuing a cost leadership strategy focuses much of its effort on keeping its costs low.

Numerous firms have pursued cost leadership strategies. Ryanair clearly follows this strategy in the airline industry, Timex and Casio in the watch industry, and BIC in the disposable pen and razor market. All these firms advertise their products. However, these advertisements tend to emphasize reliability and low prices—the kinds of product attributes that are usually emphasized by firms pursuing cost leadership strategies.

In automobiles, Fiat has implemented a cost leadership strategy with its emphasis on low-priced cars for basic transportation. Like Ryanair, Timex, Casio, and BIC, Fiat spends a significant amount of money advertising its products, but its advertisements tend to emphasize its sporty sexy styling and low price. Fiat has positioned its cars as fun and inexpensive, not a high-performance sports car or a luxurious status symbol. Fiat's ability to sell these fun and inexpensive automobiles depends on its design choices (keep it simple) and its low manufacturing costs.[1]

Sources of Cost Advantages

An individual firm may have a cost advantage over its competitors for a number of reasons. Cost advantages are possible even when competing firms produce similar products. Some of the most important of these sources of cost advantage are listed in Table 4.1 and discussed in this section.

TABLE 4.1 Important Sources of Cost Advantages for Firms

Size Differences and Economies of Scale

One of the most widely cited sources of cost advantages for a firm is its size. When there are significant economies of scale in manufacturing, marketing, distribution, service, or other functions of a business, larger firms (up to some point) have a cost advantage over smaller firms. The concept of economies of scale was first defined in Chapter 2. **Economies of scale** are said to exist when the increase in firm size (measured in terms of volume of production) is associated with lower costs (measured in terms of average costs per unit of production), as depicted in Figure 4.1. As the volume of production in a firm increases, the average cost per unit decreases until some optimal volume of production (point X) is reached, after which the average costs per unit of production begins to rise because of **diseconomies of scale** (a concept discussed in more detail later in this chapter).

If the relationship between volume of production and average costs per unit of production depicted in Figure 4.1 holds, and if a firm in an industry has the largest volume of production (but not greater than the optimal level, X), then that firm will have a cost advantage in that industry. Increasing the volume of production can reduce a firm's costs for several reasons. Some of the most important of these reasons are summarized in Table 4.2 and discussed in the following text.

Volume of Production and Specialized Machines.   When a firm has high levels of production, it is often able to purchase and use specialized manufacturing tools that cannot be kept in operation in small firms. Manufacturing managers at BIC

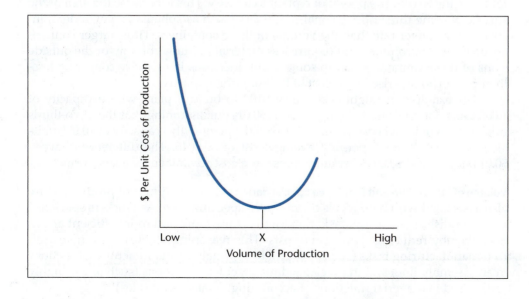

Figure 4.1   Economies of Scale

TABLE 4.2 Why Higher Volumes of Production in a Firm Can Lead to Lower Costs

With higher production volume . . .

1. firms can use specialized machines . . .
2. firms can build larger plants . . .
3. firms can increase employee specialization . . .
4. firms can spread overhead costs across more units produced . . .

. . . which can lower per-unit production costs.

Corporation, for example, have emphasized this important advantage of high volumes of production. A former director of manufacturing at BIC once observed:

> We are in the automation business. Because of our large volume, one tenth of 1 cent in savings turns out to be enormous. . . . One advantage of the high-volume business is that you can get the best equipment and amortize it entirely over a short period of time (4 to 5 months). I'm always looking for new equipment. If I see a cost-savings machine, I can buy it. I'm not constrained by money.[2]

Only firms with BIC's level of production in the pen industry have the ability to reduce their costs in this manner.

Volume of Production and the Cost of Plant and Equipment.   High volumes of production may also enable a firm to build larger manufacturing operations. In some industries, the cost of building these manufacturing operations per unit of production is lower than the cost of building smaller manufacturing operations per unit of production. Thus, large-volume firms, other factors being equal, will be able to build lower-per-unit-cost manufacturing operations and will have lower average costs of production.

The link between volume of production and the cost of building manufacturing operations is particularly important in industries characterized by **process manufacturing**—chemical, oil refining, paper and pulp manufacturing, and so forth. Because of the physical geometry of process manufacturing facilities, the costs of constructing a processing plant with increased capacity can be expected to rise as the two-thirds power of a plant's capacity. This is because the area of the surface of some three-dimensional containers (such as spheres and cylinders) increases at a slower rate than the volume of these containers. Thus, larger containers hold greater volumes and require less material per unit volume for the outside skins of these containers. Up to some point, increases in capacity come at a less-than-proportionate rise in the cost of building this capacity.[3]

For example, it might cost a firm $100 to build a plant with a capacity of 1,000 units, for a per-unit average cost of $0.01. But, assuming that the "two-thirds rule" applies, it might cost a firm $465 to build a plant with a capacity of 10,000 units ($465 = 10,000^{2/3}$), for a per-unit average cost of $0.0046. The difference between $0.01 per unit and $0.0046 per unit represents a cost advantage for a large firm.

Volume of Production and Employee Specialization.   High volumes of production are also associated with high levels of employee specialization. As workers specialize in accomplishing a narrow task, they can become more and more efficient at this task, thereby reducing their firm's costs. This reasoning applies both in specialized manufacturing tasks (such as the highly specialized manufacturing functions in an assembly line) and in specialized management functions (such as the highly specialized managerial functions of accounting, finance, and sales).

Smaller firms often do not possess the volume of production needed to justify this level of employee specialization. With smaller volumes of production, highly specialized employees may not have enough work to keep them busy an entire workday. This low volume of production is one reason why smaller firms often have employees that perform multiple business functions and often use outside contract employees and part-time workers to accomplish highly specialized functions, such as accounting, taxes, and human resource management.

Volume of Production and Overhead Costs.   A firm with high volumes of production has the luxury of spreading its overhead costs over more units and thereby reducing the overhead costs per unit. Suppose, in a particular industry, that the operation of a variety of accounting, control, and research and development functions, regardless of a firm's size, is $100,000. Clearly, a firm that manufactures 1,000 units is imposing a cost of $100 per unit to cover overhead expenses. However, a firm that manufactures 10,000 units is imposing a cost of $10 per unit to cover overhead. Again, the larger-volume firm's average per-unit costs are lower than the small-volume firm's average per-unit cost.

Size Differences and Diseconomies of Scale

Just as economies of scale can generate cost advantages for larger firms, important diseconomies of scale can actually increase costs if firms grow too large. As Figure 4.1 shows, if the volume of production rises beyond some optimal point (point X in the figure), this can actually lead to an increase in per-unit costs. If other firms in an industry have grown beyond the optimal firm size, a smaller firm (with a level of production closer to the optimal) may obtain a cost advantage even when all firms in the industry are producing very similar products. Some important sources of diseconomies of scale for a firm are listed in Table 4.3 and discussed in this section.

Physical Limits to Efficient Size.   Applying the two-thirds rule to the construction of manufacturing facilities seems to imply, for some industries at least, that larger is always better. However, there are some important physical limitations to the size of some manufacturing processes. Engineers have found, for example, that cement kilns develop unstable internal aerodynamics at capacities of above 7 million barrels per year. Others have suggested that scaling up nuclear reactors from small installations to huge facilities generates forces and physical processes that, though undetectable in smaller facilities, can become significant in larger operations. These physical limitations on manufacturing processes reflect the underlying physics and engineering in a manufacturing process and suggest when the cost curve in Figure 4.1 will begin to rise.[4]

Managerial Diseconomies.   Although the underlying physics and engineering in a manufacturing process have an important impact on a firm's costs, managerial diseconomies are perhaps an even more important cause of these cost increases.

When the volume of production gets too large . . .
1. physical limits to efficient size . . .
2. managerial diseconomies . . .
3. worker de-motivation . . .
4. distance to markets and suppliers . . .
. . . can increase per-unit costs.

TABLE 4.3 Major Sources of Diseconomies of Scale

As a firm increases in size, it often increases in complexity, and the ability of managers to control and operate it efficiently becomes limited.

One well-known example of a manufacturing plant that grew too large and thus became inefficient is Crown, Cork and Seal's can-manufacturing plant in Philadelphia. Through the early part of this century, this Philadelphia facility handled as many as 75 different can-manufacturing lines. The most efficient plants in the industry, however, were running from 10 to 15 lines simultaneously. The huge Philadelphia facility was simply too large to operate efficiently and was characterized by large numbers of breakdowns, a high percentage of idle lines, and poor-quality products.[5]

Worker De-Motivation.   A third source of diseconomies of scale depends on the relationship between firm size, employee specialization, and employee motivation. It has already been suggested that one of the advantages of increased volumes of production is that it allows workers to specialize in smaller and more narrowly defined production tasks. With specialization, workers become more and more efficient at the particular task facing them.

However, a significant stream of research suggests that these types of very specialized jobs can be unmotivating for employees. Based on motivational theories taken from social psychology, this work suggests that as workers are removed further from the complete product that is the end result of a manufacturing process, the role that a worker's job plays in the overall manufacturing process becomes more and more obscure. As workers become mere "cogs in a manufacturing machine," worker motivation wanes, and productivity and quality can both suffer.[6]

Distance to Markets and Suppliers.   A final source of diseconomies of scale can be the distance between a large manufacturing facility and where the goods in question are to be sold or where essential raw materials are purchased. Any reductions in cost attributable to the exploitation of economies of scale in manufacturing may be more than offset by large transportation costs associated with moving supplies and products to and from the manufacturing facility. Firms that build highly efficient plants without recognizing these significant transportation costs may put themselves at a competitive disadvantage compared to firms with slightly less efficient plants that are located closer to suppliers and key markets.

Experience Differences and Learning-Curve Economies

A third possible source of cost advantages for firms in a particular business depends on their different cumulative levels of production. In some circumstances, firms with the greatest experience in manufacturing a product or service will have the lowest costs in an industry and thus will have a cost-based advantage. The link between cumulative volumes of production and cost has been formalized in the concept of the **learning curve**. The relationship between cumulative volumes of production and per-unit costs is graphically represented in Figure 4.2.

The Learning Curve and Economies of Scale.   As depicted in Figure 4.2, the learning curve is very similar to the concept of economies of scale. However, there are two important differences. First, whereas economies of scale focus on the relationship between the volume of production at a given point in time and average unit costs, the learning curve focuses on the relationship between the *cumulative* volume of production—that is, how much a firm has produced over time—and average unit costs. Second, where diseconomies of scale are presumed to exist if a firm gets too

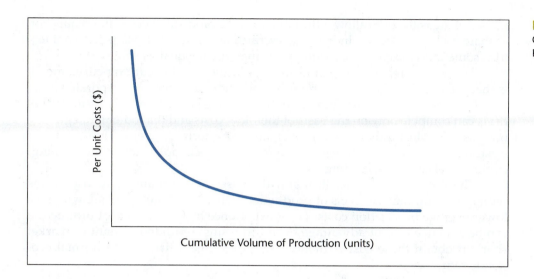

Figure 4.2   The Learning Curve and the Cost of Production

large, there is no corresponding increase in costs in the learning-curve model as the cumulative volume of production grows. Rather, costs continue to fall until they approach the lowest technologically possible cost.

The Learning Curve and Cost Advantages.   The learning-curve model is based on the empirical observation that the costs of producing a unit of output fall as the cumulative volume of output increases. This relationship was first observed in the construction of aircraft before World War II. Research showed that the labor costs per aircraft fell by 20 percent each time the cumulative volume of production doubled.[7] A similar pattern has been observed in numerous industries, including the manufacture of ships, computers, spacecraft, and semiconductors. In all these cases, increases in cumulative production have been associated with detailed learning about how to make production as efficient as possible.

However, learning-curve cost advantages are not restricted to manufacturing. Learning can be associated with any business function, from purchasing raw materials to distribution and service. Service industries can also experience important learning effects. The learning curve applies whenever the cost of accomplishing a business activity falls as a function of the cumulative number of times a firm has engaged in that activity.[8]

The Learning Curve and Competitive Advantage.   The learning-curve model summarized in Figure 4.2 has been used to develop a model of cost-based competitive advantage that links learning with market share and average production costs.[9]

The logic behind this application of the learning-curve model is straightforward: The first firm that successfully moves down the learning curve will obtain a cost advantage over rivals. To move a production process down the learning curve, a firm needs to have higher levels of cumulative volume of production. Of course, firms successful at producing high volumes of output need to sell that output to customers. In selling this output, firms are increasing their market share. Thus, to drive down the learning curve and obtain a cost advantage, firms must aggressively acquire market share.

This application of learning-curve logic has been criticized by a wide variety of authors.[10] Two criticisms are particularly salient. First, although the acquisition of market share is likely to allow a firm to reduce its production costs, the acquisition of share itself is expensive. Indeed, as described in the Research Made Relevant feature, sometimes the cost of acquiring share may rise to equal its value.

The second major criticism of this application of the learning-curve model is that there is, in this logic, no room for any other business or corporate strategies. In other words, this application of the learning curve implicitly assumes that firms can compete only on the basis of their low costs and that other strategies are not possible. Most industries, however, are characterized by opportunities for at least some of these other strategies, and thus this strict application of the learning-curve model can be misleading.[11]

These criticisms aside, it is still the case that in many industries firms with larger cumulative levels of production, other things being equal, will have lower average production costs. Thus, experience in all the facets of production can be a source of cost advantage even if the single-minded pursuit of market share to obtain these cost reductions may not give a firm above normal economic returns.

Differential Low-Cost Access to Productive Inputs

Besides economies of scale, diseconomies of scale, and learning-curve cost advantages, differential low-cost access to productive inputs may create cost differences among firms producing similar products in an industry. **Productive inputs** are any supplies used by a firm in conducting its business activities; they include, among other things, labor, capital, land, and raw materials. A firm that has differential low-cost access to one or more of these factors is likely to have lower economic costs compared to rivals.

Consider, for example, an oil company with fields in Saudi Arabia compared to an oil company with fields in the North Sea. The cost of obtaining crude oil for the first firm is considerably less than the cost of obtaining crude oil for the second. North Sea drilling involves the construction of giant offshore drilling platforms, housing workers on floating cities, and transporting oil across an often-stormy sea. Drilling in Saudi Arabia requires only the simplest drilling technologies because the oil is found relatively close to the surface.

Of course, in order to create a cost advantage, the cost of acquiring low-cost productive inputs must be less than the cost savings generated by these factors. For example, even though it may be much less costly to drill for oil in Saudi Arabia than in the North Sea, if it is very expensive to purchase the rights to drill in Saudi Arabia compared to the costs of the rights to drill in the North Sea, the potential cost advantages of drilling in Saudi Arabia can be lost. As with all sources of cost advantages, firms must be careful to weigh the cost of acquiring that advantage against the value of that advantage for the firm.

Differential access to raw materials such as oil, coal, and copper ore can be important determinants of a cost advantage. However, differential access to other productive inputs can be just as important. For example, it may be easier (i.e., less costly) to recruit highly trained electronics engineers for firms located near where these engineers receive their schooling than for firms located some distance away. This lower cost of recruiting is a partial explanation of the development of geographic technology centers such as Silicon Valley in California, Route 128 in Massachusetts, and the Research Triangle in North Carolina. In all three cases, firms are located physically close to several universities that train the engineers that are the lifeblood of high-technology companies. The search for low-cost labor can create ethical dilemmas, as described in the Ethics and Strategy feature.

Research Made Relevant

Research on the relationship between market share and firm performance has continued over many decades. Early work identified market share as the primary determinant of firm performance. Indeed, one particularly influential article identified market share as being *the key* to firm profitability.

This initial conclusion about the relationship between market share and firm performance was based on the observed positive correlation between these two variables. That is, firms with large market share tend to be highly profitable; firms with low market share tend to be less profitable. The logical conclusion of this empirical finding seems to be that if a firm wants to increase its profitability, it should increase its market share.

Not so fast. It turns out that the relationship between market share and firm profits is not that simple. Consider the following scenario: Suppose that 10 companies all conclude that the key to their profitability is gaining market share. To acquire share from each other, each firm will probably increase its advertising and other marketing expenses as well as reduce its prices. This has the effect of putting a price on the market share that a firm seeks to acquire—that is, these competing firms are creating what might be called a "market-for-market share." And because there

How Valuable Is Market Share—Really?

are 10 firms competing for share in this market, this market is likely to be highly competitive. Returns to acquiring share in such competitive markets for market share should fall to a normal economic level.

All this analysis suggests that although there may be a cross-sectional positive correlation between market share and firm performance—that is, at a given point in time, market share and firm performance may be positively correlated—this correlation may not be positive over time, as firms seek to increase their market share. Several papers have examined this hypothesis. Two of the most influential of these papers—by Dick Rumelt and Robin Wensley and by Cynthia Montgomery and Birger Wernerfelt—have shown

that markets for market share often do emerge in industries, that these markets are often very competitive, and that acquiring market share in these competitive markets does not improve a firm's economic performance. Indeed, in their study of the consolidation of the beer industry Montgomery and Wernerfelt showed that firms such as Anheuser-Busch and Miller paid so much for the market share they acquired that it actually reduced their profitability.

The general consensus in the literature now seems to be that large market share is an outcome of a competitive process within an industry, not an appropriate objective of firm managers, per se. Thus, firms with particularly valuable strategies will naturally attract more customers, which, in turn, suggests that they will often have higher market share. That is, a firm's valuable strategies generate both high levels of firm performance and large market share. This, in turn, explains the positive correlation between market share and firm performance.

Sources: R. D. Buzzell, B. T. Gale, and R. M. Sultan (1975). "Market share—the key to profitability." *Harvard Business Review,* 53, pp. 97–106; R. Rumelt and R. Wensley (1981). "In search of the market share effect." *Proceedings of the Academy of Management Meetings, 1981,* pp. 2–6; C. Montgomery and B. Wernerfelt (1991). "Sources of superior performance: Market share versus industry effects in the U.S. brewing industry." *Management Science,* 37, pp. 954–959.

Technological Advantages Independent of Scale

Another possible source of cost advantage in an industry may be the different technologies that firms employ to manage their business. It has already been suggested that larger firms may have technology-based cost advantages that reflect their ability to exploit economies of scale (e.g., the two-thirds rule).

Traditionally, discussion of technology-based cost advantages has focused on the machines, computers, and other physical tools that firms use to manage their business. Clearly, in some industries, these physical technology differences between firms can create important cost differences—even when the firms in question are approximately the same size in terms of volume of production. In the steel industry, for example, technological advances can substantially reduce the cost of producing steel. Firms with the latest steel-manufacturing technology will typically enjoy some cost advantage compared to similar-sized firms that do not have the latest technology. The same applies in the manufacturing of semiconductors, automobiles, consumer electronics, and a wide variety of other products.[12]

These physical technology cost advantages apply in service firms as well as in manufacturing firms. For example, early in its history Charles Schwab, a leading discount brokerage, purchased a computer system that enabled it to complete customer transactions more rapidly and at a lower cost than its rivals.[13] Kaiser-Permanente, the largest HMO in the United States, has invested in information technology that doctors can use to avoid incorrect diagnoses and procedures that can adversely affect a patient's health. By avoiding these medical mistakes, Kaiser-Permanente can substantially reduce its costs of providing medical service.[14]

However, the concept of technology can be easily broadened to include not just the physical tools that firms use to manage their business, but any processes within a firm used in this way. This concept of firm technology includes not only the **technological hardware** of companies—the machines and robots—but also the **technological software** of firms—things such as the quality of relations between labor and management, an organization's culture, and the quality of managerial controls. All these characteristics of a firm can have an impact on a firm's economic costs.[15]

Policy Choices

Thus far, this discussion has focused on reasons why a firm can gain a cost advantage despite producing products that are similar to competing firms' products. When firms produce essentially the same outputs, differences in economies of scale, learning-curve advantages, differential access to productive inputs, and differences in technology can all create cost advantages (and disadvantages) for them. However, firms can also make choices about the kinds of products and services they will sell—choices that have an impact on their relative cost position. These choices are called **policy choices**.

In general, firms that are attempting to implement a cost leadership strategy will choose to produce relatively simple standardized products that sell for relatively low prices compared to the products and prices firms pursuing other business or corporate strategies choose. These kinds of products often tend to have high volumes of sales, which (if significant economies of scale exist) tend to reduce costs even further.

These kinds of choices in product and pricing tend to have a very broad impact on a cost leader's operations. In these firms, the task of reducing costs is not delegated to a single function or a special task force within the firm, but is the responsibility of every manager and employee. Cost reduction sometimes becomes the central objective of the firm. Indeed, in this setting management must be constantly alert to cost-cutting efforts that reduce the ability of the firm to meet customers' needs. This kind of cost-cutting culture is central to Ryanair's ability to implement its cost leadership strategy.

Ethics and Strategy

One of the most important productive inputs in almost all companies is labor. Getting differential low-cost access to labor can give a firm a cost advantage.

This search for low labor costs has led some firms to engage in an international "race to the bottom." It is well known that the wage rates of most U.S. and Western European workers are much higher than the wage rates of workers in other, less developed parts of the world. While a firm might have to pay its employees $20 per hour (in wages and benefits) to make sneakers and basketball shoes in the United States, that same firm may only have to pay an employee in the Philippines or Malaysia or China $1.00 per day to make the same sneakers and basketball shoes—shoes the firm might be able to sell for $250 a pair in the United States and Europe. Thus, many firms look to overseas manufacturing as a way to keep their labor cost low.

But this search for low labor cost has some important unintended consequences. First, the location of the lowest cost labor rates in the world changes over time. It used to be that Mexico had the lowest labor rates, then Korea and the Philippines, then Malaysia, then China, now Vietnam. As the infrastructures of each of these countries evolve to the point that they

The Race to the Bottom

can support worldwide manufacturing, firms abandon their relationships with firms in prior countries in search of still lower costs in new countries. The only way former "low-cost centers" can compete is to drive their costs even lower.

This sometimes leads to a second unintended consequence of the "race to the bottom": horrendous working conditions and low wages in these low-cost manufacturing settings. Employees earning $1 for working a 10-hour day, six days a week may look good on the corporate bottom line, but many observers are deeply concerned about the moral and ethical issues associated with this strategy. Indeed, several companies—including Nike and Kmart—have been forced to increase the wages and improve the

working conditions of many of their overseas employees.

An even more horrific result of this "race to the bottom" has been the reemergence of what amounts to slavery in some Western European countries and some parts of the United States. In search of the promise of a better life, illegal immigrants are sometimes brought to Western European countries or the United States and forced to work in illegal, underground factories. These illegal immigrants are sometimes forced to work as many as 20 hours a day, for little or no pay—supposedly to "pay off" the price of bringing them out of their less developed countries. And because of their illegal status and language barriers, they often do not feel empowered to go to the local authorities.

Of course, the people who create and manage these facilities are criminals and deserve contempt. But what about the companies that purchase the services of these illegal and immoral manufacturing operations? Aren't they also culpable, both legally and morally?

Sources: R. DeGeorge (2000). "Ethics in international business—A contradiction in terms?" *Business Credit*, 102, pp. 50+; G. Edmondson, K. Carlisle, I. Resch, K. Nickel Anhalt, and H. Dawley (2000). "Workers in bondage." *BusinessWeek*, November 27, pp. 146+; D. Winter (2000). "Facing globalization." *Ward's Auto World*, 36, pp. 7+.

The Value of Cost Leadership

There is little doubt that cost differences can exist among firms, even when those firms are selling very similar products. Policy choices about the kinds of products firms in an industry choose to produce can also create important cost differences. But under what conditions will these kinds of cost advantages actually create value for a firm?

Cost Leadership and Environmental Threats

It was suggested in Chapter 3 that one way to tell if a resource or capability—such as the ability of a firm to have a cost advantage—actually creates value for a firm is by whether that resource or capability enables a firm to neutralize its external threats or exploit its external opportunities. The ability of a cost leadership position to neutralize external threats will be examined here. The ability of such a position to enable a firm to exploit opportunities will be left as an exercise. The specific economic consequences of cost leadership are discussed in the Strategy in Depth feature.

A cost leadership competitive strategy helps reduce the threat of new entrants by creating cost-based barriers to entry. Recall that many of the barriers to entry cited in Chapter 2, including economies of scale and cost advantages independent of scale, assume that incumbent firms have lower costs than potential entrants. If an incumbent firm is a cost leader, for any of the reasons just listed, then new entrants may have to invest heavily to reduce their costs prior to entry. Often, new entrants will enter using another business strategy (e.g., product differentiation) rather than attempting to compete on costs.

Firms with a low-cost position also reduce the threat of rivalry. The threat of rivalry is reduced through pricing strategies that low-cost firms can engage in and through their relative impact on the performance of a low-cost firm and its higher-cost rivals.

As suggested in Chapter 2, substitutes become a threat to a firm when their cost and performance, relative to a firm's current products or services, become more attractive to customers. Thus, when the price of crude oil goes up, substitutes for crude oil become more attractive. When the cost and performance of electronic calculators improve, demand for mechanical adding machines disappears.

In this situation, cost leaders have the ability to keep their products and services attractive relative to substitutes. While high-cost firms may have to charge high prices to cover their costs, thus making substitutes more attractive, cost leaders can keep their prices low and still earn normal or above-normal economic profits.

Suppliers can become a threat to a firm by charging higher prices for the goods or services they supply or by reducing the quality of those goods or services. However, when a supplier sells to a cost leader, that firm has greater flexibility in absorbing higher-cost supplies than does a high-cost firm. Higher supply costs may destroy any above-normal profits for high-cost firms but still allow a cost leader firm to earn an above-normal profit.

Cost leadership based on large volumes of production and economies of scale can also reduce the threat of suppliers. Large volumes of production imply large purchases of raw materials and other supplies. Suppliers are not likely to jeopardize these sales by threatening their customers. Indeed, as was suggested earlier, buyers are often able to use their purchasing volume to extract volume discounts from suppliers.

Cost leadership can also reduce the threat of buyers. Powerful buyers are a threat to firms when they insist on low prices or higher quality and service from their suppliers. Lower prices threaten firm revenues; higher quality can increase a firm's costs. Cost leaders can have their revenues reduced by buyer threats and still have normal or above-normal performance. These firms can also absorb the greater costs of increased quality or service and still have a cost advantage over their competition.

Strategy in Depth

Another way to demonstrate that cost leadership can be a source of economic value is to directly examine the economic profits generated by a firm with a cost advantage operating in an otherwise very competitive industry. This is done in Figure 4.3.

The firms depicted in this figure are **price takers**—that is, the price of the products or services they sell is determined by market conditions and not by individual decisions of firms. This implies that there is effectively no product differentiation in this market and that no one firm's sales constitute a large percentage of this market.

The price of goods or services in this type of market (P^*) is determined by aggregate industry supply and demand. This industry price determines the demand facing an individual firm in this market. Because these firms are price takers, the demand facing an individual firm is horizontal—that is, firm decisions about levels of output have a negligible impact on overall industry supply and thus a negligible impact on the market-determined price. A firm in this setting maximizes its economic performance by

The Economics of Cost Leadership

producing a quantity of output (Q) so that marginal revenue equals marginal cost (MC). The ability of firms to earn economic profits in this setting depends upon the relationship between the market-determined price (P^*) and the average total cost (ATC) of a firm at the quantity it chooses to produce.

Firms in the market depicted in Figure 4.3 fall into two categories. All but one firm have the average-total-cost curve ATC_2 and marginal-cost curve MC_2. However, one firm in this industry has the average-total-cost

curve ATC_1 and marginal-cost curve MC_1. Notice that ATC_1 is less than ATC_2 at the performance-maximizing quantities produced by these two kinds of firms (Q_1 and Q_2, respectively). In this particular example, firms with common average-total-cost curves are earning zero economic profits, while the low-cost firm is earning an economic profit (equal to the shaded area in the figure). A variety of other examples could also be constructed: The cost leader firm could be earning zero economic profits, while other firms in the market are incurring economic losses; the cost leader firm could be earning substantial economic profits, while other firms are earning smaller economic profits; the cost leader firm could be incurring small economic losses, while the other firms are incurring substantial economic losses; and so forth. However, in all these examples the cost leader's economic performance is greater than the economic performance of other firms in the industry. Thus, cost leadership can have an important impact on a firm's economic performance.

Figure 4.3   Cost Leadership and Economic Performance

Buyers can also be a threat through backward vertical integration. Being a cost leader deters backward vertical integration by buyers because a buyer that vertically integrates backward will often not have costs as low as an incumbent cost leader. Rather than vertically integrating backward and increasing its cost of supplies, powerful buyers usually prefer to continue purchasing from their low-cost suppliers.

Finally, if cost leadership is based on large volumes of production, then the threat of buyers may be reduced because buyers may depend on just a few firms for the goods or services they purchase. This dependence reduces the willingness of buyers to threaten a selling firm.

Cost Leadership and Sustained Competitive Advantage

Given that cost leadership can be valuable, an important question becomes "Under what conditions will firms implementing this business strategy be able to maintain that leadership to obtain a sustained competitive advantage?" If cost leadership strategies can be implemented by numerous firms in an industry or if no firms face a cost disadvantage in imitating a cost leadership strategy, then being a cost leader will not generate a sustained competitive advantage for a firm. As suggested in Chapter 3, the ability of a valuable cost leadership competitive strategy to generate a sustained competitive advantage depends on that strategy being rare and costly to imitate, either through direct duplication or substitution. As suggested in Tables 4.4 and 4.5, the rarity and imitability of a cost leadership strategy depend, at least in part, on the sources of that cost advantage.

The Rarity of Sources of Cost Advantage

Some of the sources of cost advantage listed in Table 4.4 are likely to be rare among a set of competing firms; others are less likely to be rare. Sources of cost advantage that are likely to be rare include learning-curve economies (at least in emerging industries), differential low-cost access to productive inputs, and technological "software." The remaining sources of cost advantage are less likely to be rare.

TABLE 4.4 The Rarity of Sources of Cost Advantage

Likely-to-be-rare sources of cost advantage	Less-likely-to-be-rare sources of cost advantage
Learning-curve economies of scale (especially in emerging businesses)	Economies of scale (except when efficient plant size approximately equals total industry demand)
Differential low-cost access to productive inputs	Diseconomies of scale
Technological "software"	Technological hardware (unless a firm has proprietary hardware development skills)
	Policy choices

"economies of scale"

firms w/ large volume of production have lower cost than those w/ smaller volumes of production

what actions can firms take to ensure they realize econ of scale are created by their Volume of Production

ial differences in the cumulative vol-
unusual. Indeed, this was one of the
ntages, discussed in Chapter 2. These
on, in combination with substantial
e settings, learning-curve advantages
rary competitive advantage.
productive inputs implies that this
s of competing firms have this same
ve advantage.
be rare among a set of competing
ach firm's path through history. If
cal software they create may also be
perience similar paths through his-
is less likely to be rare.

Less Rare Sources of Cost Advantage

When the efficient size of a firm or plant is significantly smaller than the total size of an industry, there will usually be numerous efficient firms or plants in that industry, and a cost leadership strategy based on economies of scale will not be rare. For example, if the efficient firm or plant size in an industry is 500 units, and the total size of the industry (measured in units produced) is 500,000 units, then there are likely to be numerous efficient firms or plants in this industry, and economies of scale are not likely to give any one firm a cost-based competitive advantage.

Cost advantages based on diseconomies of scale are also not likely to be rare. It is unusual for numerous firms to adopt levels of production in excess of optimal levels. If only a few firms are too large in this sense, then several competing firms in an industry that are *not* too large will have cost advantages over the firms that are too large. However, because several firms will enjoy these cost advantages, they are not rare.

One important exception to this generalization may be when changes in technology significantly reduce the most efficient scale of an operation. Given such changes in technology, several firms may be inefficiently large. If a small number of firms happen to be sized appropriately, then the cost advantages these firms obtain in this way may be rare. Such changes in technology have made large integrated steel producers "too big" relative to smaller mini-mills. Thus, mini-mills have a cost advantage over larger integrated steel firms.

Technological hardware is also not likely to be rare, especially if it is developed by suppliers and sold on the open market. However, if a firm has proprietary technology development skills, it may possess rare technological hardware that creates cost advantages.

Finally, policy choices by themselves are not likely to be a rare source of cost advantage, particularly if the product or service attributes in question are easy to observe and describe.

The Imitability of Sources of Cost Advantage

Even when a particular source of cost advantage is rare, it must be costly to imitate in order to be a source of sustained competitive advantage. Both direct duplication and substitution, as forms of imitation, are important. Again, the imitability of a cost advantage depends, at least in part, on the source of that advantage.

TABLE 4.5 Direct Duplication of Cost Leadership

		Basis for costly duplication		
	Source of Cost Advantage	History	Uncertainty	Social Complexity
Low-cost duplication possible	1. Economies of scale	—	—	—
	2. Diseconomies of scale	—	—	—
May be costly to duplicate	3. Learning-curve economies	*	—	—
	4. Technological "hardware"	—	*	*
	5. Policy choices	*	—	—
Usually costly to duplicate	6. Differential low-cost access to productive inputs	***	—	**
	7. Technological "software"	***	**	***

— = not a source of costly imitation, * = somewhat likely to be a source of costly imitation, ** = likely to be a source of costly imitation, *** = very likely to be a source of costly imitation

Easy-to-Duplicate Sources of Cost Advantage

In general, economies of scale and diseconomies of scale are relatively easy-to-duplicate bases of cost leadership. As can be seen in Table 4.5, these sources of cost advantage do not build on history, uncertainty, or socially complex resources and capabilities and thus are not protected from duplication for these reasons.

For example, if a small number of firms obtain a cost advantage based on economies of scale and if the relationship between production scale and costs is widely understood among competing firms, then firms at a cost disadvantage will rapidly adjust their production to exploit these economies of scale. This can be done by either growing a firm's current operations to the point that the firm exploits economies or by combining previously separate operations to obtain these economies. Both actions enable a firm at a cost disadvantage to begin using specialized machines, reduce the cost of plant and equipment, increase employee specialization, and spread overhead costs more effectively.

Indeed, perhaps the only time economies of scale are not subject to low-cost duplication is when the efficient size of operations is a significant percentage of total demand in an industry. Of course, this is the situation described in Chapter 2's discussion of economies of scale as a barrier to entry. For example, as suggested earlier, BIC Corporation, with its dominant market share in the disposable pen market, has apparently been able to gain and retain an important cost advantage in that market based on economies of scale. BIC's ability to retain this advantage reflects the fact that the optimal plant size in the disposable pen market is a significant percentage of the pen market, and thus economies of scale act as a barrier to entry in that market.

Like economies of scale, in many settings diseconomies of scale will not be a source of sustained competitive advantage for firms that have *not* grown too large. In the short run, firms experiencing significant diseconomies can shrink the size of their operations to become more efficient. In the long run, firms that fail to adjust their size will earn below-normal economic performance and cease operations.

Although in many ways reducing the size of operations to improve efficiency seems like a simple problem for managers in firms or plants, in practice it is often a difficult change to implement. Because of uncertainty, managers in a firm or plant that is too large may not understand that diseconomies of scale have increased their costs. Sometimes, managers conclude that the problem is that employees are not working hard enough, that problems in production can be fixed, and so forth. These firms or plants may continue their inefficient operations for some time, despite costs that are higher than the industry average.[16]

Other psychological processes can also delay the abandonment of operations that are too large. One of these phenomena is known as **escalation of commitment**: Sometimes, managers committed to an incorrect (cost-increasing or revenue-reducing) course of action *increase* their commitment to this action as its limitations become manifest. For example, a manager who believes that the optimal firm size in an industry is larger than the actual optimal size may remain committed to large operations despite costs that are higher than the industry average.[17]

For all these reasons, firms suffering from diseconomies of scale must often turn to outside managers to assist in reducing costs. Outsiders bring a fresh view to the organization's problems and are not committed to the practices that generated the problems in the first place.[18]

Bases of Cost Leadership That May Be Costly to Duplicate

Although cost advantages based on learning-curve economies are rare (especially in emerging industries), they are usually not costly to duplicate. As suggested in Chapter 2, for learning-curve cost advantages to be a source of sustained competitive advantage the learning obtained by a firm must be proprietary. Most recent empirical work suggests that in most industries learning is not proprietary and thus can be rapidly duplicated as competing firms move down the learning curve by increasing their cumulative volume of production.[19]

However, the fact that learning is not costly to duplicate in *most* industries does not mean it is never costly to duplicate. In some industries, the ability of firms to learn from their production experience may vary significantly. For example, some firms treat production errors as failures and systematically punish employees who make those errors. These firms effectively reduce risk-taking among their production employees and thus reduce the chances of learning how to improve their production process. Alternatively, other firms treat production errors as opportunities to learn how to improve their production process. These firms are likely to move rapidly down the learning curve and retain cost advantages, despite the cumulative volume of production of competing firms. These different responses to production errors reflect the organizational cultures of these different firms. Because organizational cultures are socially complex, they can be very costly to duplicate.[20]

Because technological hardware can usually be purchased across supply markets, it is also not likely to be difficult to duplicate. Sometimes, however, technological hardware can be proprietary or closely bundled with other unique, costly-to-duplicate resources controlled by a firm. In this case, technological hardware *can* be costly to duplicate.

It is unusual, but not impossible, for policy choices, per se, to be a source of sustained competitive cost advantages for a firm. As suggested earlier, if the policies in question focus on easy to observe and easy to describe product characteristics, then duplication is likely, and cost advantages based on policy choices will be temporary. However, if policy choices reflect complex decision processes within a firm, teamwork among different parts of the design and manufacturing process, or any of the software commitments discussed previously, then policy choices can be a source of sustained competitive advantage, as long as only a few firms have the ability to make these choices.

Indeed, most of the successful firms that operate in unattractive industries make policy choices that are costly to imitate because they reflect historical, causally ambiguous, and socially complex firm processes. Thus, for example, Wal-Mart's supply chain management strategy—a policy with clear low-cost implications—actually reflects Wal-Mart's unique history, its socially complex relations with suppliers, and its unique organizational culture. And Ryanair's low-price pricing strategy—a strategy that reflects its low-cost position—is possible because of the kind of airplane fleet Ryanair has built over time, the commitment of its employees to Ryanair's success, a charismatic founder, and its unique organizational culture. Because these policies reflect costly-to-imitate attributes of these firms, they can be sources of sustained competitive advantage.

However, for these and other firms, it is not these policy choices, per se, that create sustainable cost leadership advantages. Rather, it is how these policies flow from the historical, causally ambiguous, and socially complex processes within a firm that makes them costly to duplicate. This has been the case for the Oakland A's baseball team, as described in the Strategy in the Emerging Enterprise feature.

Costly-to-Duplicate Sources of Cost Advantage

Differential access to low-cost productive inputs and technological software is usually a costly-to-duplicate basis of cost leadership. This is because these inputs often build on historical, uncertain, and socially complex resources and capabilities. As suggested earlier, differential access to productive inputs often depends on the location of a firm. Moreover, to be a source of economic profits, this valuable location must be obtained before its full value is widely understood. Both these attributes of differential access to productive inputs suggest that if, in fact, it is rare, it will often be costly to duplicate. First, some locations are unique and cannot be duplicated. For example, most private golf clubs would like to own courses with the spectacular beauty of Pebble Beach in Monterey, California, but there is only one Pebble Beach—a course that runs parallel to some of the most beautiful oceanfront scenery in the world. Although "scenery" is an important factor of production in running and managing a golf course, the re-creation of Pebble Beach's scenery at some other location is simply beyond our technology.

Second, even if a location is not unique, once its value is revealed, acquisition of that location is not likely to generate economic profits. Thus, for example, although being located in Silicon Valley provides access to some important low-cost productive inputs for electronics firms, firms that moved to this location after its value was revealed have substantially higher costs than firms that moved there before its full value was revealed. These higher costs effectively reduce the economic profit that otherwise could have been generated. Referring to the discussion in Chapter 3, these arguments suggest that gaining differential access to productive inputs in a way that generates economic profits may reflect a firm's unique path through history.

Technological software is also likely to be difficult to duplicate and often can be a source of sustained competitive advantage. As suggested in Chapter 3, the values, beliefs, culture, and teamwork that constitute this software are socially complex and may be immune from competitive duplication. Firms with cost advantages rooted in these socially complex resources incorporate cost savings in every aspect of their organization; they constantly focus on improving the quality and cost of their operations, and they have employees who are firmly committed to, and understand, what it takes to be a cost leader. Other firms may talk about low costs; these firms live cost leadership. Ryanair, Dell, Wal-Mart, and Southwest are all examples of such firms. If there are few firms in an industry with these kinds of beliefs and commitments, then they can gain a sustained competitive advantage from their cost advantage.

Substitutes for Sources of Cost Advantage

In an important sense, all of the sources of cost advantage listed in this chapter are at least partial substitutes for each other. Thus, for example, one firm may reduce its cost through exploiting economies of scale in large-scale production, and a competing firm may reduce its costs through exploiting learning-curve economies and large cumulative volume of production. If these different activities have similar effects on a firm's cost position and if they are equally costly to implement, then they are strategic substitutes for each other.

Because of the substitute effects of different sources of cost advantage, it is not unusual for firms pursuing cost leadership to simultaneously pursue *all* the cost-reduction activities discussed in this chapter. Implemention of this *bundle* of cost-reducing activities may have few substitutes. If duplicating this bundle of activities is also rare and difficult, then a firm may be able to gain a sustained competitive advantage from doing so.

Several of the other strategies discussed in later chapters can also have the effect of reducing a firm's costs and thus may be substitutes for the sources of cost reduction discussed in this chapter. For example, one common motivation for firms implementing strategic alliance strategies is to exploit economies of scale in combination with other firms. Thus, a strategic alliance that reduces a firm's costs may be a substitute for a firm exploiting economies of scale on its own to reduce its costs. As is discussed in more detail in Chapter 8, many of the strategic alliances among aluminum mining and smelting companies are motivated by realizing economies of scale and cost reduction. Also, corporate diversification strategies often enable firms to exploit economies of scale across different businesses within which they operate. In this setting, each of these businesses—treated separately—may have scale disadvantages, but collectively their scale creates the same low-cost position as that of an individual firm that fully exploits economies of scale to reduce costs in a single business (see Chapter 9).

Organizing to Implement Cost Leadership

As with all strategies, firms seeking to implement cost leadership strategies must adopt an organizational structure, management controls, and compensation policies that reinforce this strategy. Some key issues associated with using these organizing tools to implement cost leadership are summarized in Table 4.6.

Baseball in the United States has a problem. Most observers agree that it is better for fans if there is competitive balance in the league—that is, if, at the beginning of the year, the fans of several teams believe that their team has a chance to go to the World Series and win it all. However, the economic reality of competition in baseball is that only a small number of financially successful teams in large cities—the New York Yankees, the Los Angeles Dodgers, the Chicago Cubs, the Los Angeles Angels—have the resources necessary to compete for a spot in the World Series year after year. So-called "small-market teams," such as the Pittsburgh Pirates or the Milwaukee Brewers, may be able to compete every once in a while, but these exceptions prove the general rule—teams from large markets usually win the World Series.

And then there is Oakland and the Oakland A's. Oakland (with a population of just over 400,000) is the smallest— and least glamorous—of the three cities in the San Francisco Bay Area, the other two being San Francisco and San Jose. The A's play in an outdated stadium to an average crowd of 25,586 fans—ranking twenty-fourth among the 30 major league baseball teams in the United States. In 2013, the A's player payroll was $65 million, about one-fifth of the Yankees' player payroll.

Despite these liabilities, from 1999 to 2012, the A's either won their division or placed second in all but four years. This compares favorably to any major league team during this time period, including teams with much higher payrolls. And the team made money!

What is the "secret" to the A's success? Their general manager, William Lamar Beane, says that it has to do with three factors: how players are evaluated, making sure that every personnel decision in the organization is consistent with this approach to evaluation, and

The Oakland A's: Inventing a New Way to Play Competitive Baseball

ensuring that all personnel decisions are thought of as business decisions.

The criteria used by the A's to evaluate players are easy enough to state. For batters, the A's focus on on-base percentage (i.e., how often a batter reaches base) and total bases (a measure of the ability of a batter to hit for power); that is, they focus on the ability of players to get on base and score. For pitchers, the A's focus on the percentage of first pitches that are strikes and the quality of a pitcher's fast ball. First-pitch strikes and throwing a good fast ball are correlated with keeping runners off base. Thus, not surprisingly, the A's criteria for evaluating pitchers are the reverse of their criteria for evaluating hitters.

Although these evaluation criteria are easy to state, getting the entire organization to apply them consistently in scouting, choosing, developing, and managing players is much more difficult. Almost every baseball player and fan has his or her own favorite way to evaluate players. However, if you want to work in the A's organization, you must be willing to let go of your personal favorite and evaluate players the A's way. The result is that players that come through the A's farm system— the minor leagues where younger players are developed until they are ready to play in the major leagues—learn a single way of playing baseball instead of learning a new approach to the game

every time they change managers or coaches. One of the implications of this consistency has been that the A's farm system has been among the most productive in baseball.

This consistent farm system enables the A's to treat personnel decisions—including decisions about whether they should re-sign a star player or let him go to another team—as business decisions. The A's simply do not have the resources necessary to play the personnel game the same way as the Los Angeles Dodgers or the New York Yankees. When these teams need a particular kind of player, they go and sign one. Oakland has to rely more on its farm system. But because its farm system performs so well, the A's can let so-called "superstars" go to other teams, knowing that they are likely to have a younger— and cheaper—player in the minor leagues, just waiting for the chance to play in "the show"—the players' nickname for the major leagues. This allows the A's to keep their payroll costs down and remain profitable, despite relatively small crowds, while still fielding a team that competes virtually every year for the right to play in the World Series.

Of course, an important question becomes: How sustainable is the A's competitive advantage? The evaluation criteria themselves are not a source of sustained competitive advantage. However, the socially complex nature of how these criteria are consistently applied throughout the A's organization may be a source of sustained competitive advantage in enabling the A's to gain the differential access to low-cost productive inputs—in this case, baseball players.

Sources: K. Hammonds (2003). "How to play Beane ball." *Fast Company,* May, pp. 84+; M. Lewis (2003). *Moneyball.* New York: Norton; A. McGahan, J. F. McGuire, and J. Kou (1997). "The baseball strike." Harvard Business School Case No. 9-796-059; www.cbssports.com/mlb/story/21989238/baseball-payrolls-list. Accessed August 21, 2013; espn.go.com/mlb/attendance/-/sort/Allavg. Accessed August 21, 2013.

TABLE 4.6 Organizing to Realize the Full Potential of Cost Leadership Strategies

Organization structure: Functional structure with

1. Few layers in the reporting structure
2. Simple reporting relationships
3. Small corporate staff
4. Focus on narrow range of business functions

Management control systems

1. Tight cost control systems
2. Quantitative cost goals
3. Close supervision of labor, raw material, inventory, and other costs
4. A cost leadership philosophy

Compensation policies

1. Reward for cost reduction
2. Incentives for all employees to be involved in cost reduction

Organizational Structure in Implementing Cost Leadership

As suggested in Table 4.6, firms implementing cost leadership strategies will generally adopt what is known as a **functional organizational structure**.[21] An example of a functional organization structure is presented in Figure 4.4. Indeed, this functional organizational structure is the structure used to implement all business-level strategies a firm might pursue, although this structure is modified when used to implement these different strategies.

In a functional structure, each of the major business functions is managed by a **functional manager**. For example, if manufacturing, marketing, finance, accounting, and sales are all included within a functional organization, then a manufacturing manager leads that function, a marketing manager leads that function, a finance manager leads that function, and so forth. In a functional organizational structure, all these functional managers report to one person. This person has many different titles—including *president, CEO, chair,* or *founder.* However, for purposes of this discussion, this person will be called the **chief executive officer (CEO)**.

The CEO in a functional organization has a unique status. Everyone else in this company is a functional specialist. The manufacturing people manufacture, the marketing people market, the finance people finance, and so forth. Indeed, only one person in the functional organization has to have a multifunctional perspective: the CEO. This role is so important that sometimes the functional organization is called a **U-form structure**, where the "U" stands for "unitary"— because there is only one person in this organization that has a broad, multifunctional corporate perspective.

Figure 4.4   An Example of the U-form Organizational Structure

When used to implement a cost leadership strategy, this U-form structure is kept as simple as possible. As suggested in Table 4.6, firms implementing cost leadership strategies will have relatively few layers in their reporting structure. Complicated reporting structures, including **matrix structures** where one employee reports to two or more people, are usually avoided.[22] Corporate staff in these organizations is kept small. Such firms do not operate in a wide range of business functions, but instead operate only in those few business functions where they have valuable, rare, and costly-to-imitate resources and capabilities.

One excellent example of a firm pursuing a cost leadership strategy is Nucor Steel. A leader in the mini-mill industry, Nucor has only five layers in its reporting structure, compared to 12 to 15 in its major higher-cost competitors. Most operating decisions at Nucor are delegated to plant managers, who have full profit-and-loss responsibility for their operations. Corporate staff at Nucor is small and focuses its efforts on accounting for revenues and costs and on exploring new manufacturing processes to further reduce Nucor's operating expenses and expand its business opportunities. Nucor's former president Ken Iverson believed that Nucor does only two things well: build plants efficiently and run them effectively. Thus, Nucor focuses its efforts in these areas and subcontracts many of its other business functions, including the purchase of its raw materials, to outside vendors.[23]

Responsibilities of the CEO in a Functional Organization

The CEO in a U-form organization has two basic responsibilities: (1) to formulate the strategy of the firm and (2) to coordinate the activities of the functional specialists in the firm to facilitate the implementation of this strategy. In the special case of a cost leadership strategy, the CEO must decide on which bases such a strategy should be founded—including any of those listed in Table 4.1—and then coordinate functions within a firm to make sure that the economic potential of this strategy is fully realized.

Strategy Formulation.   The CEO in a U-form organization engages in strategy formulation by applying the strategic management process described in Chapter 1. A CEO establishes the firm's mission and associated objectives, evaluates environmental threats and opportunities, understands the firm's strengths and weaknesses, and then chooses one or more of the business and corporate strategies discussed in this book. In the case of a cost leadership strategy, the application of the strategic management process must lead a CEO to conclude that the best chance for achieving a firm's mission is for that firm to adopt a cost leadership business-level strategy.

Although the responsibility for strategy formulation in a U-form organization ultimately rests with the CEO, this individual needs to draw on the insights, analysis, and involvement of functional managers throughout the firm. CEOs who fail to involve functional managers in strategy formulation run several risks. First, strategic choices made in isolation from functional managers may be made without complete information. Second, limiting the involvement of functional managers in strategy formulation can limit their understanding of, and commitment to, the chosen strategy. This can severely limit their ability, and willingness, to implement any strategy—including cost leadership—that is chosen.[24]

Coordinating Functions for Strategy Implementation.   Even the best-formulated strategy is competitively irrelevant if it is not implemented. And the only way that strategies can be effectively implemented is if all the functions within a firm are aligned in a way consistent with this strategy.

For example, compare two firms pursuing a cost leadership strategy. All but one of the first firm's functions—marketing—are aligned with this cost leadership strategy. All of the second firm's functions—including marketing—are aligned with this cost leadership strategy. Because marketing is not aligned with the first firm's cost leadership strategy, this firm is likely to advertise products that it does not sell. That is, this firm might advertise its products on the basis of their style and performance, but sell products that are reliable (but not stylish) and inexpensive (but not high performers). A firm that markets products it does not actually sell is likely to disappoint its customers. In contrast, the second firm that has all of its functions—including marketing—aligned with its chosen strategy is more likely to advertise products it actually sells and thus is less likely to disappoint its customers. In the long run, it seems reasonable to expect this second firm to outperform the first, at least with respect to implementing a cost leadership strategy.

Of course, alignment is required of all of a firm's functional areas, not just marketing. Also, misalignment can emerge in any of a firm's functional areas. Some common misalignments between a firm's cost leadership strategy and its functional activities are listed in Table 4.7.

Management Controls in Implementing Cost Leadership

As suggested in Table 4.6, cost leadership firms are typically characterized by very tight cost-control systems; frequent and detailed cost-control reports; an emphasis on quantitative cost goals and targets; and close supervision of labor, raw materials, inventory, and other costs. Again, Nucor Steel is an example of a cost leadership firm that has implemented these kinds of control systems. At Nucor, groups of employees are given weekly cost and productivity improvement goals. Groups that meet or exceed these goals receive extra compensation. Plant managers are held responsible for cost and profit performance. A plant manager who does not meet corporate performance expectations cannot expect a long career

TABLE 4.7 Common Misalignments Between Business Functions and a Cost Leadership Strategy

	When Function Is *Aligned* with Cost Leadership Strategies	When Function Is *Misaligned* with Cost Leadership Strategies
Manufacturing	Lean, low cost, good quality	Inefficient, high cost, poor quality
Marketing	Emphasize value, reliability, and price	Emphasize style and performance
Research and Development	Focus on product extensions and process improvements	Focus on radical new technologies and products
Finance	Focus on low cost and stable financial structure	Focus on nontraditional financial instruments
Accounting	Collect cost data and adopt conservative accounting principles	Collect no-cost data and adopt very aggressive accounting principles
Sales	Focus on value, reliability, and low price	Focus on style and performance and high price

at Nucor. Similar group-oriented cost-reduction systems are in place at some of Nucor's major competitors, including Chaparral Steel.[25]

Less formal management control systems also drive a cost-reduction philosophy at cost leadership firms. For example, although Wal-Mart is one of the most successful retail operations in the world, its Arkansas headquarters is plain and simple. Indeed, some have suggested that Wal-Mart's headquarters looks like a warehouse. Its style of interior decoration was once described as "early bus station." Wal-Mart even involves its customers in reducing costs by asking them to "help keep your costs low" by returning shopping carts to the designated areas in Wal-Mart's parking lots.[26]

Compensation Policies and Implementing Cost Leadership Strategies

As suggested in Table 4.6, compensation in cost leadership firms is usually tied directly to cost-reducing efforts. Such firms often provide incentives for employees to work together to reduce costs and increase or maintain quality, and they expect *every* employee to take responsibility for both costs and quality. For example, an important expense for retail stores like Wal-Mart is "shrinkage"—a nice way of saying people steal stuff. About half the shrinkage in most stores comes from employees stealing their own companies' products.

Wal-Mart used to have a serious problem with shrinkage. Among other solutions (including hiring "greeters" whose real job is to discourage shoplifters), Wal-Mart developed a compensation scheme that took half the cost savings created by reduced shrinkage and shared it with employees in the form of a bonus. With this incentive in place, Wal-Mart's shrinkage problems dropped significantly.

Summary

Firms producing essentially the same products can have different costs for several reasons. Some of the most important of these are: (1) size differences and economies of scale, (2) size differences and diseconomies of scale, (3) experience differences and learning-curve economies, (4) differential access to productive inputs, and (5) technological advantages independent of scale. In addition, firms competing in the same industry can make policy choices about the kinds of products and services to sell that can have an important impact on their relative cost position. Cost leadership in an industry can be valuable by assisting a firm in reducing the threat of each of the five environmental threats in an industry outlined in Chapter 2.

Each of the sources of cost advantage discussed in this chapter can be a source of sustained competitive advantage if it is rare and costly to imitate. Overall, learning-curve economies, differential access to productive inputs, and technological "software" are more likely to be rare than other sources of cost advantage. Differential access to productive inputs and technological "software" is more likely to be costly to imitate—either through direct duplication or through substitution—than the other sources of cost advantage. Thus, differential access to productive inputs and technological "software" will often be more likely to be a source of sustained competitive advantage than cost advantages based on other sources.

Of course, to realize the full potential of these competitive advantages, a firm must be organized appropriately. Organizing to implement a strategy always involves a firm's organizational structure, its management control systems, and its compensation policies. The organizational structure used to implement cost leadership—and other business strategies—is called a *functional,* or *U-form,* structure. The CEO is the only person in this structure who has a corporate perspective. The CEO has two responsibilities: to formulate a firm's strategy and to implement it by coordinating functions within a firm. Ensuring that a firm's functions are aligned with its strategy is essential to successful strategy implementation.

When used to implement a cost leadership strategy, the U-form structure generally has few layers, simple reporting relationships, and a small corporate staff. It focuses on a narrow range of business functions. The management control systems used to implement these strategies generally include tight cost controls; quantitative cost goals; close supervision of labor, raw materials, inventory, and other costs; and a cost leadership culture and mentality. Finally, compensation policies in these firms typically reward cost reduction and provide incentives for everyone in the organization to be part of the cost-reduction effort.

MyManagementLab®

Go to **mymanagementlab.com** to complete the problems marked with this icon ⭐.

Challenge Questions

4.1. Ryanair, Wal-Mart, Timex, Casio, and Hyundai are all cited as examples of firms pursuing cost leadership strategies, but these firms make substantial investments in advertising, which seems more likely to be associated with a product differentiation strategy. Are these firms really pursuing a cost leadership strategy, or are they pursuing a product differentiation strategy by emphasizing their lower costs?

⭐ **4.2.** When economies of scale exist, firms with large volumes of production will have lower costs than those with smaller volumes of production. The realization of these economies of scale, however, is far from automatic. What actions can firms take to ensure that they realize whatever economies of scale are created by their volume of production?

4.3. Firms engage in an activity called "forward pricing" when they establish, during the early stages of the learning curve, a price for their products that is lower than their actual costs, in anticipation of lower costs later on, after significant learning has occurred. Under what conditions, if any, does forward pricing make sense?

⭐ **4.4.** When firms do engage in "forward pricing" what risks, if any, do they face?

4.5. One way of thinking about organizing to implement cost leadership strategies is that firms pursuing this strategy should be highly centralized, have high levels of direct supervision, and keep employee wages to an absolute minimum. Another approach is to decentralize decision-making authority—to ensure that individuals who know the most about reducing costs make decisions about how to reduce costs. This, in turn, would imply less direct supervision and somewhat higher levels of employee wages. Why is this?

4.6. Which of the two approaches used to implement cost leadership strategies seems more reasonable?

4.7. Under what conditions would the two different approaches for implementing cost leadership strategies make more or less sense?

Problem Set

4.8. The economies of scale curve in Figure 4.1 can be represented algebraically in the following equation:

$$\text{Average costs} = a + bQ + cQ^2$$

where Q is the quantity produced by a firm and a, b, and c are coefficients that are estimated from industry data. For example, it has been shown that the economies of scale curve for U.S. savings and loans is:

$$\text{Average costs} = 2.38 - .615A + .54A^2$$

where A is a savings and loan's total assets. Using this equation, what is the optimal size of a savings and loan? (Hint: Plug in different values of A and calculate average costs. The lowest possible average cost is the optimal size for a savings and loan.)

4.9. The learning curve depicted in Figure 4.2 can be represented algebraically by the following equation:

$$\text{Average time to produce } x \text{ units} = ax^{-\beta}$$

where x is the total number of units produced by a firm in its history, a is the amount of time it took a firm to produce its first unit, and β is a coefficient that describes the rate of learning in a firm.

Suppose it takes a team of workers 45 hours to assemble its first product ($a = 45$) and 40.5 hours to assemble the second. When a firm doubles its production (in this case, from one to two units) and cuts its production time (in this case, from 45 hours to 40.5 hours), learning is said to have occurred (in this case, a 40.5/45, or 90 percent, learning curve). The β for a 90 percent learning curve is 0.3219. Thus, this firm's learning curve is:

$$\text{Average time to produce } x \text{ units} = 45x^{-0.3219}$$

What is the average amount of time it will take this firm to produce six products? (Hint: Simply plug "6" in for x in the equation and solve.) What is the total time it took this firm to produce these six products? (Hint: Simply multiply the number of units produced, 6, by the average time it will take to produce these six products.) What is the average time it will take this firm to produce five products? What is the total time it will take this firm to produce five products? So, what is the total time it will take this firm to produce its sixth product? (Hint: Subtract the total time needed to produce five products from the total time needed to produce six products.)

Suppose a new firm is going to start producing these same products. Assuming this new firm does not learn anything from established firms, what will its cost disadvantage be when it assembles its first product? (Hint: Compare the costs of the experienced firm's sixth product with the cost of the new firm's first product.)

MyManagementLab®

Go to **mymanagementlab.com** for Auto-graded writing questions as well as the following Assisted-graded writing questions:

⭐ **4.10.** What are the implications and considerations for a small business that chooses a cost leadership business strategy?

⭐ **4.11.** Discuss the impact of a cost leadership strategy on environmental threats.

End Notes

1. Kiley, D. (2011). "Fiat headed back to U.S. after 27 years." http://autos.aol.com/article/fiat-500-coming-to-america/ Accessed Aug 21, 2013.
2. Christensen, C. R., N. A. Berg, and M. S. Salter. (1980). *Policy formulation and administration: A casebook of senior management problems in business,* 8th ed. Homewood, IL: Irwin, p. 163.
3. Scherer, F. M. (1980). *Industrial market structure and economic performance.* Boston: Houghton Mifflin; Moore, F. T. (1959). "Economies of scale: Some statistical evidence." *Quarterly Journal of Economics,* 73, pp. 232–245; and Lau, L. J., and S. Tamura. (1972). "Economies of scale, technical progress, and the nonhomothetic leontief production function." *Journal of Political Economy,* 80, pp. 1167–1187.
4. Scherer, F. M. (1980). *Industrial market structure and economic performance.* Boston: Houghton Mifflin; and Perrow, C. (1984). *Normal accidents: Living with high-risk technologies.* New York: Basic Books.
5. Hamermesh, R. G., and R. S. Rosenbloom. (1989). "Crown Cork and Seal Co., Inc." Harvard Business School Case No. 9-388-096.
6. See Hackman, J. R., and G. R. Oldham. (1980). *Work redesign.* Reading, MA: Addison-Wesley.
7. This relationship was first noticed in 1925 by the commander of Wright-Patterson Air Force Base in Dayton, Ohio.
8. Learning curves have been estimated for numerous industries. Boston Consulting Group. (1970). "Perspectives on experience." Boston: BCG, presents learning curves for over 20 industries while Lieberman, M. (1984). "The learning curve and pricing in the chemical processing industries." *Rand Journal of Economics,* 15, pp. 213–228, estimates learning curves for 37 chemical products.
9. See Henderson, B. (1974). *The experience curve reviewed III—How does it work?* Boston: Boston Consulting Group; and Boston Consulting Group. (1970). "Perspectives on experience." Boston: BCG.
10. Hall, G., and S. Howell. (1985). "The experience curve from the economist's perspective." *Strategic Management Journal,* 6, pp. 197–212.
11. Hill, C. W. L. (1988). "Differentiation versus low-cost or differentiation and low-cost: A contingency framework." *Academy of Management Review,* 13(3), pp. 401–412.
12. See Ghemawat, P., and H. J. Stander III. (1992). "Nucor at a crossroads." Harvard Business School Case No. 9-793-039 on technology in steel manufacturing and cost advantages; Shaffer, R. A. (1995). "Intel as conquistador." *Forbes,* February 27, p. 130 on technology in semiconductor manufacturing and cost advantages; Monteverde, K., and D. Teece. (1982). "Supplier switching costs and vertical integration in the automobile industry." *Rand Journal of Economics,* 13(1), pp. 206–213; and McCormick, J., and N. Stone. (1990). "From national champion to global competitor: An interview with Thomson's Alain Gomez." *Harvard Business Review,* May/June, pp. 126–135 on technology in consumer electronic manufacturing and cost advantages.
13. Schultz, E. (1989). "Climbing high with discount brokers." *Fortune,* Fall (special issue), pp. 219–223.
14. Schonfeld, E. (1998). "Can computers cure health care?" *Fortune,* March 30, pp. 111+.
15. Ibid.
16. See Meyer, M. W., and L. B. Zucker. (1989). *Permanently failing organizations.* Newbury Park, CA: Sage.
17. Staw, B. M. (1981). "The escalation of commitment to a course of action." *Academy of Management Review,* 6, pp. 577–587.
18. Hesterly, W. S. (1989). *Top management succession as a determinant of firm performance and de-escalation: An agency problem.* Unpublished doctoral dissertation, University of California, Los Angeles.
19. Barney, J. B. (1986). "Organizational culture: Can it be a source of sustained competitive advantage?" *Academy of Management Review,* 11, pp. 656–665.
20. See Spence, A. M. (1981). "The learning curve and competition." *Bell Journal of Economics,* 12, pp. 49–70, on why learning needs to be proprietary; Mansfield, E. (1985). "How rapidly does new industrial technology leak out?" *Journal of Industrial Economics,* 34(2), pp. 217–223; Lieberman, M. B. (1982). *The learning-curve, pricing and market structure in the chemical processing industries.* Unpublished doctoral dissertation, Harvard University; Lieberman, M. B. (1987). "The learning curve, diffusion, and competitive strategy." *Strategic Management Journal,* 8, pp. 441–452, on why it usually is not proprietary.
21. Williamson, O. (1975). *Markets and hierarchies.* New York: Free Press.
22. Davis, S. M., and P. R. Lawrence. (1977). *Matrix.* Reading, MA: Addison-Wesley.
23. See Ghemawat, P., and H. J. Stander III. (1992). "Nucor at a crossroads." Harvard Business School Case No. 9-793-039.
24. See Floyd, S. W., and B. Woldridge. (1992). "Middle management involvement in strategy and its association with strategic type: A research note." *Strategic Management Journal,* 13, pp. 153–167.
25. Ibid.
26. Walton, S. (1992). *Sam Walton, Made in America: My story.* New York: Doubleday.

5 Product Differentiation

LEARNING OBJECTIVES *After reading this chapter, you should be able to:*

1. Define product differentiation.

2. Describe 11 bases of product differentiation and how they can be grouped into three categories.

3. Describe how product differentiation is ultimately limited only by managerial creativity.

4. Describe how product differentiation can be used to neutralize environmental threats and exploit environmental opportunities.

5. Describe those bases of product differentiation that are not likely to be costly to duplicate, those that may be

costly to duplicate, and those that will often be costly to duplicate.

6. Describe the main substitutes for product differentiation strategies.

7. Describe how organizational structure, control processes, and compensation policies can be used to implement product differentiation strategies.

8. Discuss whether it is possible for a firm to implement cost leadership and product differentiation strategies simultaneously.

MyManagementLab®

⭐ **Improve Your Grade!**
More than 10 million students improved their results using the Pearson MyLabs.
Visit **mymanagementlab.com** for simulations, tutorials, and end-of-chapter problems.

Who Is Victoria, and What Is Her Secret?

Sexy. Glamorous. Mysterious. Victoria's Secret is the world's leading specialty retailer of lingerie and beauty products. With 2012 sales of $6.12 billion and operating income of $1 billion, Victoria's Secret sells its mix of sexy lingerie, prestige fragrances, and fashion-inspired collections through more than 1,000 retail stores and the almost 400 million catalogues it distributes each year.

But all this glamour and success leaves the two central questions about this firm unanswered: "Who is Victoria?" and "What is her secret?"

It turns out that Victoria is a retired fashion model who lives in an up-and-coming fashionable district in London. She has a committed relationship and is thinking about starting a family. However, these maternal instincts are balanced by Victoria's adventurous and sexy side. She loves good food, classical music, and great wine. She travels frequently and is as much at home in New York, Paris, and Los Angeles as she is in London. Her fashion tastes are edgy enough to never be boring, but practical enough to never be extreme. Her lingerie is an essential part of her wardrobe. Sexy and alluring, but never cheap, trashy, or vulgar, Victoria's lingerie is the perfect complement to her overall lifestyle. Most important, while Victoria knows she is beautiful and sexy, she also knows that it is her brains, not her looks, that have enabled her to succeed in life.

This is who Victoria is. This is the woman that Victoria's Secret's designers design for, the woman Victoria's Secret marketers create advertising for, and the woman to whom all Victoria's Secret sales associates are trained to sell.

And this is her secret—Victoria doesn't really exist. Or, more precisely, the number of real women in the entire world who are like Victoria is very small—no more than a handful. So why would a company like Victoria's Secret organize all of its design, marketing, and sales efforts around meeting the lingerie needs of a woman who, for all practical purposes, doesn't really exist?

Image Source/Getty

Victoria's Secret knows how few of its actual customers are like Victoria. However, it is convinced that many of its customers would like to be treated as if they were Victoria, if only for a time, when they come into a Victoria's Secret store. Victoria's Secret is not just selling lingerie; it is selling an opportunity, almost a fantasy, to be like Victoria—to live in an exciting and sexy city, to travel the world, to have refined, yet edgy, tastes. To buy and wear Victoria's Secret lingerie is—if only for a moment or two—an opportunity to experience life as Victoria experiences it.

Practically speaking, building an entire company around meeting the needs of a customer who does not actually exist creates some interesting problems. You can't just call Victoria on the phone and ask her about trends in her lifestyle; you can't form a focus group of people like Victoria and ask them to evaluate new lines of lingerie. In a sense, not only has Victoria's Secret invented Victoria; it also had to invent Victoria's lifestyle—and the lingerie, fragrances, and accessories that go along with that lifestyle. And as long as the lifestyle that it invents for Victoria is desirable to, but just beyond the reach of, its actual customers, Victoria's Secret will continue to be able to sell a romantic fantasy—along with its bras and panties.

Sources: www.limitedbrands.com accessed August 24, 2013; www.victoriassecret.com accessed August 24, 2013.

Victoria's Secret uses the fictional character "Victoria" to help implement its product differentiation strategy. As successful as this effort is, however, this is only one of many ways that firms can try to differentiate their products.

What Is Product Differentiation?

Whereas RyanAir exemplifies a firm pursuing a cost leadership strategy, Victoria's Secret exemplifies a firm pursuing a product differentiation strategy. **Product differentiation** is a business strategy where firms attempt to gain a competitive advantage by increasing the perceived value of their products or services relative to the perceived value of other firms' products or services. These other firms can be rivals or firms that provide substitute products or services. By increasing the perceived value of its products or services, a firm will be able to charge a higher price than it would otherwise. This higher price can increase a firm's revenues and generate competitive advantages.

A firm's attempts to create differences in the relative perceived value of its products or services often are made by altering the objective properties of those products or services. Rolex attempts to differentiate its watches from Timex and Casio watches by manufacturing them with solid gold cases. Mercedes attempts to differentiate its cars from Fiat's cars through sophisticated engineering and high performance. Victoria's Secret attempts to differentiate its shopping experience from Wal-Mart, and other retailers, through the merchandise it sells and the way it sells it.

Although firms often alter the objective properties of their products or services in order to implement a product differentiation strategy, the existence of product differentiation, in the end, is *always* a matter of customer perception. Products sold by two different firms may be very similar, but if customers believe the first is more valuable than the second, then the first product has a differentiation advantage.

In the world of "craft" or "microbrewery" beers, for example, the consumers' image of how a beer is brewed may be very different from how it is actually brewed. Boston Beer Company, for example, sells Samuel Adams Beer. Customers can tour the Boston Beer Company, where they will see a small row of fermenting tanks and two 10-barrel kettles being tended by a brewmaster wearing rubber boots. However, Samuel Adams Beer was not actually brewed in this small factory. Instead, it was, for much of its history, brewed—in 200-barrel steel tanks—in Cincinnati, Ohio, by the Hudepohl-Schoenling Brewing Company, a contract brewing firm that also manufactured Hudy Bold Beer and Little Kings Cream Ale. Maui Beer Company's Aloha Lager brand was brewed in Portland, Oregon, and Pete's Wicked Ale (a craft beer that claims it is brewed "one batch at a time. Carefully.") was brewed in batches of 400 barrels each by Stroh Brewery Company, makers of Old Milwaukee Beer. However, the more consumers believe there are important differences between these "craft" beers and more traditional brews—despite many of their common manufacturing methods—the more willing they will be to pay more for a craft beer. This willingness to pay more suggests that an important "perceptual" basis of product differentiation exists for these craft beers.[1] If products or services are *perceived* as being different in a way that is valued by consumers, then product differentiation exists.

Just as perceptions can create product differentiation between products that are essentially identical, the lack of perceived differences between products with very different characteristics can prevent product differentiation. For example, consumers with an untrained palate may not be able to distinguish between two different wines, even though expert wine tasters would be very much aware of their differences. Those who are not aware of these differences, even if they exist, will not be willing to pay more for one wine over the other. In this sense, for these consumers at least, these two wines, though different, are not differentiated.

Product differentiation is always a matter of customer perceptions, but firms can take a variety of actions to influence these perceptions. These actions can be thought of as different bases of product differentiation.

Bases of Product Differentiation

A large number of authors, drawing on both theory and empirical research, have developed lists of ways firms can differentiate their products or services.[2] Some of these are listed in Table 5.1. Although the purpose of all these bases of product differentiation is to create the perception that a firm's products or services are unusually valuable, different bases of product differentiation attempt to accomplish this objective in different ways. For example, the first four bases of product differentiation listed in Table 5.1 attempt to create this perception by focusing directly on the attributes of the products or services a firm sells. The second three attempt to create this perception by developing a relationship between a firm and its customers. The last five attempt to create this perception through linkages within and between firms. Of course, these bases of product differentiation are not mutually exclusive. Indeed, firms will often attempt to differentiate their products or services along multiple dimensions simultaneously. An empirical method for identifying ways that firms have differentiated their products is discussed in the Research Made Relevant feature.

Focusing on the Attributes of a Firm's Products or Services

The first group of bases of product differentiation identified in Table 5.1 focuses on the attributes of a firm's products or services.

TABLE 5.1 Ways Firms Can Differentiate Their Products

To differentiate its products, a firm can focus directly on the attributes of its products or services:

1. Product features
2. Product complexity
3. Timing of product introduction
4. Location

or on relationships between itself and its customers:

5. Product customization
6. Consumer marketing
7. Product reputation

or on linkages within or between firms:

8. Linkages among functions within a firm
9. Linkages with other firms
10. Product mix
11. Distribution channels
12. Service and support

Sources: M. E. Porter (1980). *Competitive strategy.* New York: Free Press; R. E. Caves and P. Williamson (1985). "What is product differentiation, really?" *Journal of Industrial Economics*, 34, pp. 113–132.

Product Features.   The most obvious way that firms can try to differentiate their products is by altering the features of the products they sell. One industry in which firms are constantly modifying product features to attempt to differentiate their products is the automobile industry. Chrysler, for example, introduced the "cab forward" design to try to give its cars a distinctive look, whereas Audi went with a more radical flowing and curved design to differentiate its cars. For emergency situations, General Motors (GM) introduced the "On Star" system, which instantly connects drivers to GM operators 24 hours a day, while Mercedes-Benz continued to develop its "crumple zone" system to ensure passenger safety in a crash. In body construction, General Motors continues to develop its "uni-body" construction system where different parts of a car are welded to each other rather than built on a single frame—while Jaguar introduced a 100 percent aluminum body to help differentiate its top-of-the-line model from other luxury cars. Mazda continues to tinker with the motor and suspension of its sporty Miata, while Nissan introduced the 370Z—a continuation of the famous 240Z line—and Porsche changed from air-cooled to water-cooled engines in its 911 series of sports cars. All these—and many more—changes in the attributes of automobiles are examples of firms trying to differentiate their products by altering product features.

Product Complexity.   Product complexity can be thought of as a special case of altering a product's features to create product differentiation. In a given industry, product complexity can vary significantly. The BIC "crystal pen," for example, has only a handful of parts, whereas a Cross or a Mont Blanc pen has many more parts. To the extent that these differences in product complexity convince consumers that the products of some firms are more valuable than the products of other firms, product complexity can be a basis of product differentiation.

Timing of Product Introduction.   Introducing a product at the right time can also help create product differentiation. As suggested in Chapter 2, in some industry settings (e.g., in emerging industries) *the* critical issue is to be a first mover—to introduce a new product before all other firms. Being first in emerging industries can enable a firm to set important technological standards, preempt strategically valuable assets, and develop customer-switching costs. These first-mover advantages can create a perception among customers that the products or services of the first-moving firm are somehow more valuable than the products or services of other firms.[3]

Timing-based product differentiation, however, does not depend only on being a first mover. Sometimes, a firm can be a later mover in an industry but introduce products or services at just the right time and thereby gain a competitive advantage. This can happen when the ultimate success of a product or service depends on the availability of complementary products or technologies. For example, the domination of Microsoft's MS-DOS operating system, and thus ultimately the domination of Windows, was only possible because IBM introduced its version of the personal computer. Without the IBM PC, it would have been difficult for any operating system—including MS-DOS—to have such a large market presence.[4]

Location.   The physical location of a firm can also be a source of product differentiation.[5] Consider, for example, Disney's operations in Orlando, Florida. Beginning with The Magic Kingdom and EPCOT Center, Disney built a world-class destination resort in Orlando. Over the years, Disney has added numerous attractions to its core entertainment activities, including Disney Studios, more than 11,000 Disney-owned hotel rooms, a $100 million sports center, an automobile racing track, an after-hours entertainment district, and, most recently, a $1 billion theme park called

Research Made Relevant

Of all the possible bases of product differentiation that might exist in a particular market, how does one pinpoint those that have actually been used? Research in strategic management and marketing has shown that the bases of product differentiation can be identified using multiple regression analysis to estimate what are called **hedonic prices.** A hedonic price is that part of the price of a product or service that is attributable to a particular characteristic of that product or service.

The logic behind hedonic prices is straightforward. If customers are willing to spend more for a product with a particular attribute than they are willing to spend for that same product without that attribute, then that attribute differentiates the first product from the second. That is, this attribute is a basis of product differentiation in this market.

Consider, for example, the price of used cars. The market price of a used car can be determined through the use of a variety of used car buying guides. These guides typically establish the base price of a used car. This base price typically includes product features that are common to almost all cars—a radio, a standard engine, a heater/defroster. Because these

Discovering the Bases of Product Differentiation

product attributes are common to virtually all cars, they are not a basis for product differentiation.

However, in addition to these common features, the base price of an automobile is adjusted based on some less common features—a high-end stereo system, a larger engine, air-conditioning. How much the base price of the car is adjusted when these features are added—$300 for a high-end stereo, $500 for a larger engine, $200 for air-conditioning—are the hedonic prices of these product attributes. These product attributes differentiate well-equipped cars from less-well-equipped cars and, because consumers are willing to pay more for

well-equipped cars, can be thought of as bases of product differentiation in this market.

Multiple regression techniques are used to estimate these hedonic prices in the following way. For our simple car example, the following regression equation is estimated:

$$Price = a_1 + b_1(Stereo) + b_2(Engine) + b_3(AC)$$

where *Price* is the retail price of cars, *Stereo* is a variable describing whether a car has a high-end stereo, *Engine* is a variable describing whether a car has a large engine, and *AC* is a variable describing whether a car has air-conditioning. If the hedonic prices for these features are those suggested earlier, the results of running this regression analysis would be:

$$Price = \$7,800 + \$300(Stereo) + \$500(Engine) + \$200(AC)$$

where $7,800 is the base price of this type of used car.

Sources: D. Hay and D. Morris (1979). *Industrial economics: Theory and evidence.* Oxford: Oxford University Press; K. Cowling and J. Cubbin (1971). "Price, quality, and advertising competition." *Economica,* 38, pp. 378–394.

"The Animal Kingdom"—all in and around Orlando. Now, families can travel from around the world to Orlando, knowing that in a single location they can enjoy a full range of Disney adventures.[6]

Focusing on the Relationship Between a Firm and Its Customers

The second group of bases of product differentiation identified in Table 5.1 focuses on relationships between a firm and its customers.

Product Customization.   Products can also be differentiated by the extent to which they are customized for particular customer applications. Product customization is an important basis for product differentiation in a wide variety of industries, from enterprise software to bicycles.

Enterprise software is software that is designed to support all of a firm's critical business functions, including human resources, payroll, customer service, sales, quality control, and so forth. Major competitors in this industry include Oracle and SAP. However, although these firms sell basic software packages, most firms find it necessary to customize these basic packages to meet their specific business needs. The ability to build complex software packages that can also be customized to meet the specific needs of a particular customer is an important basis of product differentiation in this marketplace.

In the bicycle industry, consumers can spend as little as $50 on a bicycle, and as much as—well, almost as much as they want on a bicycle, easily in excess of $10,000. High-end bicycles use, of course, the very best components, such as brakes and gears. But what really distinguishes these bicycles is their feel when they are ridden. Once a serious rider becomes accustomed to a particular bicycle, it is very difficult for that rider to switch to alternative suppliers.

Consumer Marketing.   Differential emphasis on consumer marketing has been a basis for product differentiation in a wide variety of industries. Through advertising and other consumer marketing efforts, firms attempt to alter the perceptions of current and potential customers, whether or not specific attributes of a firm's products or services are actually altered.

For example, in the soft drink industry, Mountain Dew—a product of PepsiCo—was originally marketed as a fruity, lightly carbonated drink that tasted "as light as a morning dew in the mountains." However, beginning in the late 1990s Mountain Dew's marketing efforts changed dramatically. "As light as a morning dew in the mountains" became "Do the Dew," and Mountain Dew focused its marketing efforts on young, mostly male, extreme-sports–oriented consumers. Young men riding snowboards, roller blades, mountain bikes, and skateboards—mostly upside down—became central to most Mountain Dew commercials. Mountain Dew became a sponsor of a wide variety of extreme sports contests and an important sponsor of the X Games on ESPN. Note that this radical repositioning of Mountain Dew depended entirely on changes in consumer marketing. The features of the underlying product were not changed.

Reputation.   Perhaps the most important relationship between a firm and its customers depends on a firm's reputation in its marketplace. Indeed, a firm's **reputation** is really no more than a socially complex relationship between a firm and its customers. Once developed, a firm's reputation can last a long time, even if the basis for that reputation no longer exists.[7]

A firm that has tried to exploit its reputation for cutting-edge entertainment is MTV, a division of Viacom, Inc. Although several well-known video artists—including Madonna—have had their videos banned from MTV, it has still been able to develop a reputation for risk-taking on television. MTV believes that its viewers have come to expect the unexpected in MTV programming. One of the first efforts to exploit, and reinforce, this reputation for risk-taking was *Beavis and Butthead*, an animated series starring two teenage boys with serious social and emotional development problems. More recently, MTV exploited its reputation by inventing an entirely new genre of television—"reality TV"—through its *Real World* and *Road Rules* programs. Not only are these shows cheap to produce, they build on the reputation that MTV has for providing entertainment that is a little risky, a little sexy, and a little controversial. Indeed, MTV has been so successful in providing this kind of entertainment that it had to form an entirely new cable station—MTV 2—to actually show music videos.[8]

Focusing on Links Within and Between Firms

The third group of bases of product differentiation identified in Table 5.1 focuses on links within and between firms.

Linkages Between Functions.   A less obvious but still important way in which a firm can attempt to differentiate its products is through linking different functions within the firm. For example, research in the pharmaceutical industry suggests that firms vary in the extent to which they are able to integrate different scientific specialties—such as genetics, biology, chemistry, and pharmacology—to develop new drugs. Firms that are able to form effective multidisciplinary teams to explore new drug categories have what some have called an **architectural competence,** that is, the ability to use organizational structure to facilitate coordination among scientific disciplines to conduct research. Firms that have this competence are able to more effectively pursue product differentiation strategies—by introducing new and powerful drugs—than those that do not have this competence. And in the pharmaceutical industry, where firms that introduce such drugs can experience very large positive returns, the ability to coordinate across functions is an important source of competitive advantage.[9]

Links with Other Firms.   Another basis of product differentiation is linkages with other firms. Here, instead of differentiating products or services on the basis of linkages between functions within a single firm or linkages between different products, differentiation is based on explicit linkages between one firm's products and the products or services of other firms.

This form of product differentiation has increased in popularity over the past several years. For example, with the growth in popularity of stock car racing in the United States, more and more corporations are looking to link their products or services with famous names and cars in NASCAR. Firms such as Burger King, McDonald's Target, Taco Bell, GEICO, Farmers Insurance, Lowe's, FedEx, 5-Hour Energy, and Miller Lite have all been major sponsors of NASCAR teams. In one year, the Coca-Cola Corporation filled orders for more than 200,000 NASCAR-themed vending machines. Visa struggled to keep up with demand for its NASCAR affinity cards, and more than 1 million NASCAR Barbies were sold by Mattel—generating revenues of about $50 million. Notice that none of these firms, except GEICO and Farmers, sells products for automobiles. Rather, these firms seek to associate themselves with NASCAR because of the sport's popularity.[10]

In general, linkages between firms that differentiate their products are examples of cooperative strategic alliance strategies. The conditions under which cooperative strategic alliances create value and are sources of sustained competitive advantage are discussed in detail in Chapter 9.

Product Mix.   One of the outcomes of links among functions within a firm and links between firms can be changes in the mix of products a firm brings to the market. This mix of products or services can be a source of product differentiation, especially when (1) those products or services are technologically linked or (2) when a single set of customers purchases several of a firm's products or services.

For example, technological interconnectivity is an extremely important selling point in the information technology business and, thus, an important basis of potential product differentiation. However, seamless interconnectivity—where Company A's computers talk to Company B's computers across Company C's data line merging a database created by Company D's software with a database created by Company E's software to be used in a calling center that operates with

Company F's technology—has been extremely difficult to realize. For this reason, some information technology firms try to realize the goal of interconnectivity by adjusting their product mix, that is, by selling a bundle of products whose interconnectivity they can control and guarantee to customers. This goal of selling a bundle of interconnected technologies can influence a firm's research and development, strategic alliance, and merger and acquisition strategies because all these activities can influence the set of products a firm brings to market.

Shopping malls are an example of the second kind of linkage among a mix of products—where products have a common set of customers. Many customers prefer to go to one location, to shop at several stores at once, rather than travel to a series of locations to shop. This one-stop shopping reduces travel time and helps turn shopping into a social experience. Mall development companies have recognized that the value of several stores brought together in a particular location is greater than the value of those stores if they were isolated, and they have invested to help create this mix of retail shopping opportunities.[11]

Distribution Channels. Linkages within and between firms can also have an impact on how a firm chooses to distribute its products, and distribution channels can be a basis of product differentiation. For example, in the soft drink industry, Coca-Cola, PepsiCo, and 7-Up all distribute their drinks through a network of independent and company-owned bottlers. These firms manufacture key ingredients for their soft drinks and ship these ingredients to local bottlers, who add carbonated water, package the drinks in bottles or cans, and distribute the final product to soft drink outlets in a given geographic area. Each local bottler has exclusive rights to distribute a particular brand in a geographic location.

Canada Dry has adopted a completely different distribution network. Instead of relying on local bottlers, Canada Dry packages its soft drinks in several locations and then ships them directly to wholesale grocers, who distribute the product to local grocery stores, convenience stores, and other retail outlets.

One of the consequences of these alternative distribution strategies is that Canada Dry has a relatively strong presence in grocery stores but a relatively small presence in soft drink vending machines. The vending machine market is dominated by Coca-Cola and PepsiCo. These two firms have local distributors that maintain and stock vending machines. Canada Dry has no local distributors and is able to get its products into vending machines only when they are purchased by local Coca-Cola or Pepsi distributors. These local distributors are likely to purchase and stock Canada Dry products such as Canada Dry ginger ale, but they are contractually prohibited from purchasing Canada Dry's various cola products.[12]

Service and Support. Finally, products have been differentiated by the level of service and support associated with them. For example, some personal computer firms have very low levels of service provided by independent service dealers. Others have outsourced service and support functions to overseas companies, often in India. On the other hand, some firms continue to staff support centers with highly qualified individuals, thereby providing a high level of support.[13]

Product Differentiation and Creativity

The bases of product differentiation listed in Table 5.1 indicate a broad range of ways in which firms can differentiate their products and services. In the end, however, any effort to list all possible ways to differentiate products and services is doomed to failure. Product differentiation is ultimately an expression of the creativity of individuals and groups within firms. It is limited only by the opportunities that exist, or that can be created, in a particular industry and by the willingness and ability of firms to creatively explore ways to take advantage of those opportunities. It is not unreasonable to expect that the day some academic researcher claims to have developed the definitive list of bases of product differentiation, some creative engineer, marketing specialist, or manager will think of yet another way to differentiate his or her product.

The Value of Product Differentiation

In order to have the potential for generating competitive advantages, the bases of product differentiation upon which a firm competes must be valuable. The market conditions under which product differentiation can be valuable are discussed in the Strategy in Depth feature. More generally, in order to be valuable, bases of product differentiation must enable a firm to neutralize its threats and/or exploit its opportunities.

Product Differentiation and Environmental Threats

Successful product differentiation helps a firm respond to each of the environmental threats identified. For example, product differentiation helps reduce the threat of new entry by forcing potential entrants to an industry to absorb not only the standard costs of beginning business, but also the additional costs associated with overcoming incumbent firms' product differentiation advantages. The relationship between product differentiation and new entry has already been discussed in Chapter 2.

Product differentiation reduces the threat of rivalry because each firm in an industry attempts to carve out its own unique product niche. Rivalry is not reduced to zero because these products still compete with one another for a common set of customers, but it is somewhat attenuated because the customers each firm seeks are different. For example, both a Rolls-Royce and a Fiat satisfy the same basic consumer need—transportation—but it is unlikely that potential customers of Rolls-Royce will also be interested in purchasing a Fiat or vice versa.

Product differentiation also helps firms reduce the threat of substitutes by making a firm's current products appear more attractive than substitute products. For example, fresh food can be thought of as a substitute for frozen processed foods. In order to make its frozen processed foods more attractive than fresh foods, products such as Stouffer's and Swanson are marketed heavily through television advertisements, newspaper ads, point-of-purchase displays, and coupons.

Product differentiation can also reduce the threat of powerful suppliers. Powerful suppliers can raise the prices of the products or services they provide. Often, these increased supply costs must be passed on to a firm's customers in the form of higher prices if a firm's profit margin is not to deteriorate. A firm without a highly differentiated product may find it difficult to pass its increased costs on to customers because these customers will have numerous other ways to purchase similar products or services from a firm's competitors. However, a firm with a highly differentiated product may have loyal customers or customers who

Strategy in Depth

The two classic treatments of the relationship between product differentiation and firm value, developed independently and published at approximately the same time, are by Edward Chamberlin and Joan Robinson.

Both Chamberlin and Robinson examine product differentiation and firm performance relative to perfect competition. As explained in Chapter 2, under perfect competition, it is assumed that there are numerous firms in an industry, each controlling a small proportion of the market, and the products or services sold by these firms are assumed to be identical. Under these conditions, firms face a horizontal demand curve (because they have no control over the price of the products they sell), and they maximize their economic performance by producing and selling output such that marginal revenue equals marginal costs. The maximum economic performance a firm in a perfectly competitive market can obtain, assuming no cost differences across firms, is normal economic performance.

When firms sell differentiated products, they gain some ability to adjust their prices. A firm can sell its output at very high prices and produce relatively smaller amounts of output, or it can sell its output at very low prices and produce relatively greater amounts of output. These

The Economics of Product Differentiation

trade-offs between price and quantity produced suggest that firms selling differentiated products face a downward-sloping demand curve, rather than the horizontal demand curve for firms in a perfectly competitive market. Firms selling differentiated products and facing a downward-sloping demand curve are in an industry structure described by Chamberlin as **monopolistic competition.** It is as if, within the market niche defined by a firm's differentiated product, a firm possesses a monopoly.

Firms in monopolistically competitive markets still maximize their economic profit by producing and selling a quantity of products such that marginal revenue equals

marginal cost. The price that firms can charge at this optimal point depends on the demand they face for their differentiated product. If demand is large, then the price that can be charged is greater; if demand is low, then the price that can be charged is lower. However, if a firm's average total cost is below the price it can charge (i.e., if average total cost is less than the demand-determined price), then a firm selling a differentiated product can earn an above-normal economic profit.

Consider the example presented in Figure 5.1. Several curves are relevant in this figure. First, note that a firm in this industry faces downward-sloping demand (D). This means that the industry is not perfectly competitive and that a firm has some control over the prices it will charge for its products. Also, the marginal-revenue curve (MR) is downward sloping and everywhere lower than the demand curve. Marginal revenue is downward sloping because in order to sell additional levels of output of a single product, a firm must be willing to lower its price. The marginal-revenue curve is lower than the demand curve because this lower price applies to all the products sold by a firm, not just to any additional products the firm

are unable to purchase similar products or services from other firms. These types of customers are more likely to accept increased prices. Thus, a powerful supplier may be able to raise its prices, but, up to some point, these increases will not reduce the profitability of a firm selling a highly differentiated product.

Finally, product differentiation can reduce the threat of powerful buyers. When a firm sells a highly differentiated product, it enjoys a "quasi-monopoly" in that segment of the market. Buyers interested in purchasing this particular product must buy it from a particular firm. Any potential buyer power is reduced by the ability of a firm to withhold highly valued products or services from a buyer.

sells. The marginal-cost curve (MC) is upward sloping, indicating that in order to produce additional outputs a firm must accept additional costs. The average-total-cost curve (ATC) can have a variety of shapes, depending on the economies of scale, the cost of productive inputs, and other cost phenomena described in Chapter 4.

These four curves (demand, marginal revenue, marginal cost, and average total cost) can be used to determine the level of economic profit for a firm under monopolistic competition. To maximize profit, the firm produces an amount (Q_e) such that marginal costs equal marginal revenues. To determine the price of a firm's output at this level of production, a vertical line is drawn from the point where marginal costs equal marginal revenues. This line will intersect with the demand curve. Where this vertical line intersects demand, a horizontal line is drawn to the vertical (price) axis to determine the price a firm can

charge. In the figure, this price is P_e. At the point P_e, average total cost is less than the price. The total revenue obtained by the firm in this situation (price × quantity) is indicated by the shaded area in the figure. The economic profit portion of this total revenue is indicated by the crosshatched section of the shaded portion of the figure. Because this crosshatched section is above average total costs in the figure, it represents a competitive advantage. If this section was below average total costs, it would represent a competitive disadvantage.

Chamberlin and Robinson go on to discuss the impact of entry into the market niche defined by a firm's differentiated product. As discussed in Chapter 2, a basic assumption of S-C-P models is that the existence of above-normal economic performance motivates entry into an industry or into a market niche within an industry. In monopolistically competitive industries, such entry means that the demand curve facing incumbent firms shifts downward and to the left. This implies that an incumbent firm's customers will buy less of its output if it maintains its prices or (equivalently) that a firm will have to lower its prices to maintain its current volume of sales. In the long run, entry into this market niche can lead to a situation where the price of goods or services sold when a firm produces output such that marginal cost equals marginal revenue is exactly equal to that firm's average total cost. At this point, a firm earns zero economic profits even if it still sells a differentiated product.

Sources: E. H. Chamberlin (1933). *The economics of monopolistic competition.* Cambridge, MA: MIT Press; J. Robinson (1934). "What is perfect competition?" *Quarterly Journal of Economics,* 49, pp. 104–120.

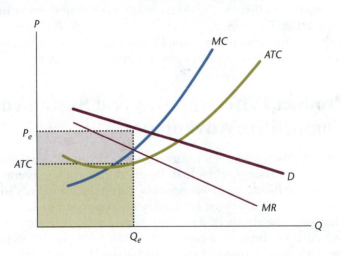

Figure 5.1 Product Differentiation and Firm Performance: The Analysis of Monopolistic Competition

Product Differentiation and Environmental Opportunities

Product differentiation can also help a firm take advantage of environmental opportunities. For example, in fragmented industries firms can use product differentiation strategies to help consolidate a market. In the office-paper industry, Xerox has used its brand name to become the leading seller of paper for office copy machines and printers. Arguing that its paper is specially manufactured to avoid jamming in its own copy machines, Xerox was able to brand what had been a commodity product and facilitate the consolidation of what had been a very fragmented industry.[14]

The role of product differentiation in emerging industries was discussed in Chapter 2. By being a first mover in these industries, firms can gain product differentiation advantages based on perceived technological leadership, preemption of strategically valuable assets, and buyer loyalty due to high switching costs.

In mature industries, product differentiation efforts often switch from attempts to introduce radically new technologies to product refinement as a basis of product differentiation. For example, in the mature retail gasoline market firms attempt to differentiate their products by selling slightly modified gasoline (cleaner-burning gasoline, gasoline that cleans fuel injectors, and so forth) and by altering the product mix (linking gasoline sales with convenience stores). In mature markets, it is sometimes difficult to find ways to actually refine a product or service. In such settings, firms can sometimes be tempted to exaggerate the extent to which they have refined and improved their products or services. The implications of these exaggerations are discussed in the Ethics and Strategy feature.

Product differentiation can also be an important strategic option in a declining industry. Product-differentiating firms may be able to become leaders in this kind of industry (based on their reputation, unique product attributes, or some other product differentiation basis). Alternatively, highly differentiated firms may be able to discover a viable market niche that will enable them to survive despite the overall decline in the market.

Finally, the decision to implement a product differentiation strategy can have a significant impact on how a firm acts in a global industry. For example, several firms in the retail clothing industry with important product differentiation advantages in their home markets are beginning to enter into the U.S. retail clothing market. These firms include Sweden's H & M Hennes & Mauritz AB, with its emphasis on "cheap chic"; the Dutch firm Mexx; the Spanish company Zara; and the French sportswear company Lacoste.[15]

Product Differentiation and Sustained Competitive Advantage

Product differentiation strategies add value by enabling firms to charge prices for their products or services that are greater than their average total cost. Firms that implement this strategy successfully can reduce a variety of environmental threats and exploit a variety of environmental opportunities. However, as discussed in Chapter 3, the ability of a strategy to add value to a firm must be linked with rare and costly-to-imitate organizational strengths in order to generate a sustained competitive advantage. Each of the bases of product differentiation listed earlier in this chapter varies with respect to how likely it is to be rare and costly to imitate.

Rare Bases for Product Differentiation

The concept of product differentiation generally assumes that the number of firms that have been able to differentiate their products in a particular way is, at some point in time, smaller than the number of firms needed to generate perfect competition dynamics. Indeed, the reason that highly differentiated firms can charge a price for their product that is greater than average total cost is because these firms are using a basis for product differentiation that few competing firms are also using.

Ultimately, the rarity of a product differentiation strategy depends on the ability of individual firms to be creative in finding new ways to differentiate their

Ethics and Strategy

One of the most common ways to try to differentiate a product is to make claims about that product's performance. In general, high-performance products command a price premium over low-performance products. However, the potential price advantages enjoyed by high-performance products can sometimes lead firms to make claims about their products that, at the least, strain credibility and, at the most, simply lie about what their products can do.

Some of these claims are easily dismissed as harmless exaggerations. Few people actually believe that using a particular type of whitening toothpaste is going to make your in-laws like you or that not wearing a particular type of deodorant is going to cause patrons in a bar to collapse when you lift your arms in victory after a foosball game. These exaggerations are harmless and present few ethical challenges.

However, in the field of health care, exaggerated product performance claims can have serious consequences. This can happen when a patient takes a medication with exaggerated performance claims instead of a medication with more modest, although accurate, performance claims. A history of false medical performance claims in the United States led to the formation of the Food and Drug Administration (FDA), a federal regulatory agency charged with evaluating the efficacy of drugs before they are marketed. Historically, the

Product Claims and the Ethical Dilemmas in Health Care

FDA has adopted the "gold standard" of drug approval—not only must a drug demonstrate that it does what it claims, it must also demonstrate that it does not do any significant harm to the patient. Patients can be confident that drugs that pass the FDA approval process meet the highest standards in the world.

However, this "gold standard" of approval creates important ethical dilemmas—mostly stemming from the time it takes a drug to pass the FDA approval process. This process can take between five and seven years. During FDA trials, patients who might otherwise benefit from a drug are not allowed to use it because it has not yet received FDA approval. Thus, although the FDA approval process may work very well for people who may need a drug sometime in the future, it works less well for those who need a drug right now.

A growing suspicion among some consumers that the FDA process may prevent effective drugs from being marketed has helped feed the growth of alternative treatments—usually based on some herbal or more natural formula. Such treatments are careful to note that their claims—everything from regrowing hair to losing weight to enhancing athletic performance to quitting smoking—have not been tested by the FDA. And yet these claims are still made.

Some of these performance claims seem at least reasonable. For example, it is now widely accepted that ephedra does behave as an amphetamine and thus is likely to enhance strength and athletic performance. Others—including those that claim that a mixture of herbs can actually increase the size of male genitals—seem far-fetched, at best. Indeed, a recent analysis of herbal treatments making this claim found no ingredients that could have this effect, but did find an unacceptably high concentration of bacteria from animal feces that can cause serious stomach disorders. Firms that sell products on the basis of exaggerated and unsubstantiated claims face their own ethical dilemmas. And, without the FDA to ensure product safety and efficacy, the adage *caveat emptor*—let the buyer beware—seems like good advice.

Sources: J. Angwin (2003). "Some 'enlargement pills' pack impurities." *The Wall Street Journal*, April 8, p. B1; G. Pisano (1991). "Nucleon, Inc." Harvard Business School Case No. 9-692-041.

products. As suggested earlier, highly creative firms will be able to discover or create new ways to do this. These kinds of firms will always be one step ahead of the competition because rival firms will often be trying to imitate these firms' last product differentiation moves while creative firms are working on their next one.

The Imitability of Product Differentiation

Valuable and rare bases of product differentiation must be costly to imitate if they are to be sources of sustained competitive advantage. Both direct duplication and substitution, as approaches to imitation, are important in understanding the ability of product differentiation to generate competitive advantages.

Direct Duplication of Product Differentiation

As discussed in Chapter 4, firms that successfully implement a cost leadership strategy can choose whether they want to reveal this strategic choice to their competition by adjusting their prices. If they keep their prices high—despite their cost advantages—the existence of those cost advantages may not be revealed to competitors. Of course, other firms—such as Wal-Mart—that are confident that their cost advantages cannot be duplicated at low cost are willing to reveal their cost advantage through charging lower prices for their products or services.

Firms pursuing product differentiation strategies usually do not have this option. More often than not, the act of selling a highly differentiated product or service reveals the basis upon which a firm is trying to differentiate its products. In fact, most firms go to great lengths to let their customers know how they are differentiating their products, and in the process of informing potential customers they also inform their competitors. Indeed, if competitors are not sure how a firm is differentiating its product, all they need to do is purchase that product themselves. Their own experience with the product—its features and other attributes—will tell them all they need to know about this firm's product differentiation strategy.

Knowing how a firm is differentiating its products, however, does not necessarily mean that competitors will be able to duplicate the strategy at low cost. The ability to duplicate a valuable and rare product differentiation strategy depends on the basis upon which a firm is differentiating its products. As suggested in Table 5.2, some bases of product differentiation—including the use of product features—are almost always easy to duplicate. Others—including product mix, links with other firms, product customization, product complexity, and consumer marketing—can sometimes be costly to duplicate. Finally, still other bases of product differentiation—including links between functions, timing, location, reputation, distribution channels, and service and support—are usually costly to duplicate.

How costly it is to duplicate a particular basis of product differentiation depends on the kinds of resources and capabilities that basis uses. When those resources and capabilities are acquired in unique historical settings, when there is some uncertainty about how to build these resources and capabilities, or when these resources and capabilities are socially complex in nature, then product differentiation strategies that exploit these kinds of resources and capabilities will be costly to imitate. These strategies can be a source of sustained competitive advantage for a firm. However, when a product differentiation strategy exploits resources and capabilities that do not possess these attributes, then those strategies are likely to be less costly to duplicate and, even if they are valuable and rare, will only be sources of temporary competitive advantage.

Bases of Product Differentiation That Are Easy to Duplicate.   The one basis of product differentiation in Table 5.2 that is identified as almost always being easy to duplicate is product features. The irony is that product features are by far the most popular way for firms to try to differentiate their products. Rarely do product

TABLE 5.2 Bases of Product Differentiation and the Cost of Duplication

	History	Uncertainty	Social Complexity
Low-cost duplication usually possible			
1. Product features	—	—	—
May be costly to duplicate			
2. Product mix	*	*	*
3. Links with other firms	*	—	**
4. Product customization	*	—	**
5. Product complexity	*	—	*
6. Consumer marketing	—	**	—
Usually costly to duplicate			
7. Links between functions	*	*	**
8. Timing	***	*	—
9. Location	***	—	—
10. Reputation	***	**	***
11. Distribution channels	**	*	**
12. Service and support	*	*	**

— = Not likely to be a source of costly duplication, * = Somewhat likely to be a source of costly duplication,
** = Likely to be a source of costly duplication, *** = Very likely to be a source of costly duplication

features, by themselves, enable a firm to gain sustained competitive advantages from a product differentiation strategy.

For example, virtually every one of the product features used in the automobile industry to differentiate the products of different automobile companies has been duplicated. Chrysler's "cab forward" design has been incorporated into the design of many manufacturers. The curved, sporty styling of the Audi has surfaced in cars manufactured by Lexus and General Motors. GM's "On Star" system has been duplicated by Mercedes. Mercedes' crumple-zone technology has become the industry standard, as has GM's uni-body construction method. Indeed, only the Mazda Miata, Nissan 370Z, and Porsche 911 have remained unduplicated—and this has little to do with the product features of these cars and much more to do with their reputation.

The only time product features, per se, can be a source of sustained competitive advantage for a firm is when those features are protected by patents. However, as was discussed in Chapters 2 and 3, even patents provide only limited protection from direct duplication, except in very unusual settings.

Although product features, by themselves, are usually not a source of sustained competitive advantage, they can be a source of a temporary competitive advantage. During the period of time when a firm has a temporary competitive advantage from implementing a product differentiation strategy based on product features, it may be able to attract new customers. Once these customers try the product, they may discover other features of a firm's products that make them attractive. If these other features are costly to duplicate, then they can be a source of sustained competitive advantage, even though the features that originally attracted a customer to a firm's products will often be rapidly duplicated by competitors.

Bases of Product Differentiation That May Be Costly to Duplicate. Some bases of product differentiation may be costly to duplicate, at least in some circumstances. The first of these, listed in Table 5.2, is product mix.

Duplicating the features of another firm's products is usually not difficult. However, if that firm brings a series of products to market, if each of these products has unique features, and most important, if the products are highly integrated with each other, then this mix of products may be costly to duplicate. Certainly, the technological integration of the mix of information technology products sold by IBM and other firms has been relatively difficult to duplicate for firms that do not manufacture all these products themselves.

However, when this basis of a product mix advantage is a common customer, then duplication is often less difficult. Thus, although having a mall that brings several stores together in a single place is a source of competitive advantage over stand-alone stores, it is not a competitive advantage over other malls that provide the same service. Because there continue to be opportunities to build such malls, the fact that malls make it easier for a common set of customers to shop does not give any one mall a sustained competitive advantage.

Links with other firms may also be costly to duplicate, especially when those links depend on socially complex relationships. The extent to which inter-firm links can provide sources of sustained competitive advantage is discussed in more detail in Chapter 9.

In the same way, product customization and product complexity are often easy-to-duplicate bases of product differentiation. However, sometimes the ability of a firm to customize its products for one of its customers depends on the close relationships it has developed with those customers. Product customization of this sort depends on the willingness of a firm to share often-proprietary details about its operations, products, research and development, or other characteristics with a supplying firm. Willingness to share this kind of information, in turn, depends on the ability of each firm to trust and rely on the other. The firm opening its operations to a supplier must trust that that supplier will not make this information broadly available to competing firms. The firm supplying customized products must trust that its customer will not take unfair advantage of it. If two firms have developed these kinds of socially complex relationships, and few other firms have them, then links with other firms will be costly to duplicate and a source of sustained competitive advantage.

The product customization seen in both enterprise software and in high-end customized bicycles has these socially complex features. In a real sense, when these products are purchased, a relationship with a supplier is being established—a relationship that is likely to last a long period of time. Once this relationship is established, partners are likely to be unwilling to abandon it, unless, of course, a party to the exchange tries to take unfair advantage of another party to that exchange. This possibility is discussed in detail in Chapter 9.

Finally, consumer marketing, though a very common form of product differentiation, is often easy to duplicate. Thus, whereas Mountain Dew has established itself as the "extreme games" drink, other drinks, including Gatorade, have also begun to tap into this market segment. Of course, every once in a while an advertising campaign or slogan, a point-of-purchase display, or some other attribute of a consumer marketing campaign will unexpectedly catch on and create greater-than-expected product awareness. In beer, marketing campaigns such as "Tastes great, less filling," "Why ask why?," the "Budweiser Frogs," and "What's Up?" have had these unusual effects. If a firm, in relation with its various consumer marketing agencies, is systematically able to develop these superior consumer marketing campaigns, then it may be able to obtain a sustained competitive advantage. However, if such campaigns are unpredictable and largely a matter of a firm's good luck, they cannot be expected to be a source of sustained competitive advantage.

Bases of Product Differentiation That Are Usually Costly to Duplicate.   The remaining bases of product differentiation listed in Table 5.2 are usually costly to duplicate. Firms that differentiate their products on these bases may be able to obtain sustained competitive advantages.

Linkages across functions within a single firm are usually a costly-to-duplicate basis of product differentiation. Whereas linkages with other firms can be either easy or costly to duplicate, depending on the nature of the relationship that exists between firms, linkages across functions within a single firm usually require socially complex, trusting relations. There are numerous built-in conflicts between functions and divisions within a single firm. Organizations that have a history and culture that support cooperative relations among conflicting divisions may be able to set aside functional and divisional conflicts to cooperate in delivering a differentiated product to the market. However, firms with a history of conflict across functional and divisional boundaries face a significant, and costly, challenge in altering these socially complex, historical patterns.

Indeed, the research on architectural competence in pharmaceutical firms suggests that not only do some firms possess this competence, but that other firms do not. Moreover, despite the significant advantages that accrue to firms with this competence, firms without this competence have, on average, been unable to develop it. All this suggests that such a competence, if it is also rare, is likely to be costly to duplicate and thus a source of sustained competitive advantage.

Timing is also a difficult-to-duplicate basis of product differentiation. As suggested in Chapter 3, it is difficult (if not impossible) to re-create a firm's unique history. If that history endows a firm with special resources and capabilities it can use to differentiate its products, this product differentiation strategy can be a source of sustained competitive advantage. Rivals of a firm with such a timing-based product differentiation advantage may need to seek alternative ways to differentiate their products. Thus, it is not surprising that universities that compete with the oldest universities in the country find alternative ways to differentiate themselves—through their size, the quality of their extramural sports, their diversity—rather than relying on their age.

Location is often a difficult-to-duplicate basis of product differentiation. This is especially the case when a firm's location is unique. For example, research on the hotel preferences of business travelers suggests that location is a major determinant of the decision to stay in a hotel. Hotels that are convenient to both major transportation and commercial centers in a city are preferred, other things being equal, to hotels in other types of locations. Indeed, location has been shown to be a more important decision criterion for business travelers than price. If only a few hotels in a city have these prime locations and if no further hotel development is possible, then hotels with these locations can gain sustained competitive advantages.

Of all the bases of product differentiation listed in this chapter, perhaps none is more difficult to duplicate than a firm's reputation. As suggested earlier, a firm's reputation is actually a socially complex relationship between a firm and its customers, based on years of experience, commitment, and trust. Reputations are not built quickly, nor can they be bought and sold. Rather, they can only be developed over time by consistent investment in the relationship between a firm and its customers. A firm with a positive reputation can enjoy a significant competitive advantage, whereas a firm with a negative reputation, or no reputation, may have to invest significant amounts over long periods of time to match the differentiated firm.

Distribution channels can also be a costly-to-duplicate basis of product differentiation, for at least two reasons. First, relations between a firm and its distribution channels are often socially complex and thus costly to duplicate. Second, the supply of distribution channels may be limited. Firms that already have access to these channels may be able to use them, but firms that do not have such access may be forced to create their own or develop new channels. Creating new channels or developing entirely new means of distribution can be difficult and costly undertakings.[16] These costs are one of the primary motivations underlying many international joint ventures (see Chapter 9).

Finally, level of service and support can be a costly-to-duplicate basis of product differentiation. In most industries, it is usually not too costly to provide a minimum level of service and support. In home electronics, this minimum level of service can be provided by a network of independent electronic repair shops. In automobiles, this level of service can be provided by service facilities associated with dealerships. In fast foods, this level of service can be provided by a minimum level of employee training.

However, moving beyond this minimum level of service and support can be difficult for at least two reasons. First, increasing the quality of service and support may involve substantial amounts of costly training. McDonald's has created a sophisticated training facility (Hamburger University) to maintain its unusually high level of service in fast foods. General Electric has invested heavily in training for service and support over the past several years. Many Japanese automakers spent millions on training employees to help support auto dealerships before they opened U.S. manufacturing facilities.[17]

More important than the direct costs of the training needed to provide high-quality service and support, these bases of product differentiation often reflect the attitude of a firm and its employees toward customers. In many firms throughout the world, the customer has become "the bad guy." This is, in many ways, understandable. Employees tend to interact with their customers less frequently than they interact with other employees. When they do interact with customers, they are often the recipients of complaints directed at the firm. In these settings, hostility toward the customer can develop. Such hostility is, of course, inconsistent with a product differentiation strategy based on customer service and support.

In the end, high levels of customer service and support are based on socially complex relations between firms and customers. Firms that have conflicts with their customers may face some difficulty duplicating the high levels of service and support provided by competing firms.

Substitutes for Product Differentiation

The bases of product differentiation outlined in this chapter vary in how rare they are likely to be and in how difficult they are to duplicate. However, the ability of the bases of product differentiation to generate a sustained competitive advantage also depends on whether low-cost substitutes exist.

Substitutes for bases of product differentiation can take two forms. First, many of the bases of product differentiation listed in Table 5.1 can be partial substitutes for each other. For example, product features, product customization, and product complexity are all very similar bases of product differentiation and thus can act as substitutes for each other. A particular firm may try to develop a competitive advantage by differentiating its products on the basis of product customization only to find that its customization advantages are reduced as another firm alters the features of its products. In a similar way, linkages between functions, linkages between firms, and product mix, as bases of product differentiation, can also be substitutes for each other. IBM links its sales, service, and consulting functions to differentiate itself in the computer market. Other computer firms, however, may develop close relationships with computer service companies and consulting firms to close this product differentiation advantage. Given that different bases of product differentiation are often partial substitutes for each other, it is not surprising that firms pursue these multiple bases of product differentiation simultaneously.

Second, other strategies discussed throughout this book can be substitutes for many of the bases of product differentiation listed in Table 5.1. One firm may try to gain a competitive advantage through adjusting its product mix, and another firm may substitute strategic alliances to create the same type of product differentiation. For example, Southwest Airlines' continued emphasis on friendly, on-time, low-cost service and United Airlines' emphasis on its links to Lufthansa and other worldwide airlines through the Star Alliance can both be seen as product differentiation efforts that are at least partial substitutes.[18]

In contrast, some of the other bases of product differentiation discussed in this chapter have few obvious close substitutes. These include timing, location, distribution channels, and service and support. To the extent that these bases of product differentiation are also valuable, rare, and difficult to duplicate, they may be sources of sustained competitive advantage.

Organizing to Implement Product Differentiation

V R I O

As was suggested in Chapter 3, the ability to implement a strategy depends on the adjustment of a firm's structure, its management controls, and its compensation policies to be consistent with that strategy. Whereas strategy implementation for firms adopting a cost leadership strategy focuses on reducing a firm's costs and increasing its efficiency, strategy implementation for a firm adopting a product differentiation strategy must focus on innovation, creativity, and product performance. Whereas cost-leading firms are all about customer value, product-differentiating firms are all about style. How the need for style is reflected in a firm's structure, controls, and compensation policies is summarized in Table 5.3.

Organizational Structure:
1. Cross-divisional/cross-functional product development teams
2. Complex matrix structures
3. Isolated pockets of intense creative efforts: Skunk works

Management Control Systems:
1. Broad decision-making guidelines
2. Managerial freedom within guidelines
3. A policy of experimentation

Compensation Policies:
1. Rewards for risk-taking, not punishment for failures
2. Rewards for creative flair
3. Multidimensional performance measurement

TABLE 5.3 Organizing to Implement Product Differentiation Strategies

Organizational Structure and Implementing Product Differentiation

Both cost leadership and product differentiation strategies are implemented through the use of a functional, or U-form, organizational structure. However, whereas the U-form structure used to implement a cost leadership strategy has few layers, simple reporting relationships, a small corporate staff, and a focus on only a few business functions, the U-form structure for a firm implementing a product differentiation strategy can be somewhat more complex. For example, these firms often use temporary cross-divisional *and* cross-functional teams to manage the development and implementation of new, innovative, and highly differentiated products. These teams bring individuals from different businesses and different functional areas together to cooperate on a particular new product or service.

One firm that has used these cross-divisional and cross-functional teams effectively is the British advertising agency WPP. WPP owns several very large advertising agencies, several public relations firms, several market research companies, and so forth. Each of these businesses operates relatively independently in most areas. However, the corporation has identified a few markets where cross-divisional and cross-functional collaboration is important. One of these is the health care market. To exploit opportunities in the health care market, WPP, the corporation, forms teams of advertising specialists, market research specialists, public relations specialists, and so on, drawn from each of the businesses it owns. The resulting cross-divisional teams are given the responsibility of developing new and highly differentiated approaches to developing marketing strategies for their clients in the health care industry.[19]

The creation of cross-divisional or cross-functional teams often implies that a firm has implemented some form of matrix structure. As suggested in Chapter 4, a **matrix structure** exists when individuals in a firm have two or more "bosses" simultaneously. Thus, for example, if a person from one of WPP's advertising agencies is assigned temporarily to a cross-divisional team, that person has two bosses: the head of the temporary team and the boss back in the advertising agency. Managing two bosses simultaneously can be very challenging, especially when they have conflicting interests. And as we will see in Chapter 8, the interests of these multiple bosses *will* often conflict.

A particularly important form of the cross-divisional or cross-functional team exists when this team is relieved of all other responsibilities in the firm and focuses all its attention on developing a new innovative product or service. The best-known example of this approach to developing a differentiated product occurred at the Lockheed Corporation during the 1950s and 1960s when small groups of engineers were put on very focused teams to develop sophisticated and top-secret military aircraft. These teams would have a section of the Lockheed facility dedicated to their efforts and designated as off-limits to almost all other employees. The joke was that these intensive creative efforts were so engaging that members of these teams actually would forget to shower—hence the name **"skunk works."** Skunk works have been used by numerous firms to focus the creative energy required to develop and introduce highly differentiated products.[20]

Management Controls and Implementing Product Differentiation

The first two management controls helpful for implementing product differentiation listed in Table 5.3—broad decision-making guidelines and managerial freedom within those guidelines—often go together. How some firms have used

Strategy in the Emerging Enterprise

So much innovation in both small and large organizations focuses on repositioning a firm's products along established bases of competition—a more fuel-efficient car, a better-cleaning shampoo, a less expensive insurance policy. While these efforts can, for a time, be a source of product differentiation, for reasons discussed in Chapter 3, they are usually not sustainable.

For this reason, two scholars—W. Chan Kim and Renee Mauborgne—began studying firms that did not just reposition their products in well-established competitive markets but, instead, transcended their competition to identify entirely new markets. They called these markets "blue oceans" because they are not crowded with competitors seeking to improve their positions but instead are empty of competitors and give firms the opportunity to grow quickly. For these authors, blue oceans emerge when managers discover that the only way to beat the competition is to stop *trying* to beat the competition.

Examples of companies that have created blue oceans include Cirque du Soleil—a firm that redefined what a circus was to become an international entertainment sensation—and Casella Wines—a firm whose [yellow tail] brand made drinking wine a simple alternative to drinking beer. Both

Going in Search of Blue Oceans

these companies did not try to compete with established firms; they created a new competitive space where these firms were irrelevant.

So, how can a firm create a blue ocean? Kim and Mauborgne suggest that firms begin by understanding the bases of competition that exist within an industry already. In the U.S. wine industry, for example, Casella identified seven bases of competition: price, an elite image in packaging, consumer marketing, aging quality of wine, vineyard prestige, taste complexity, and a diverse range of wines. With these bases of product differentiation identified, firms should then ask four questions about competition in their industry:

1. Which factors that the industry currently competes on should be *eliminated*?
2. Which factors that the industry currently competes on should be *reduced well below* the industry's standard?
3. Which factors should be *raised well above* the industry's standard?
4. Which factors should be *created* that the industry has never offered?

By applying these four questions to the bases of competition identified by Casella, this firm decided that elite packaging, aging quality wine, vineyard prestige, and taste complexity all complicated the wine drinking experience and could be eliminated. They also created new bases for competition: easy drinking, ease of selection, and fun and adventure. The result was a wine brand—[yellow tail]—that has grown faster than any other wine over the past 10 years.

Some firms have found it difficult to apply these principles to develop blue oceans for their businesses. Nevertheless, by systematically seeking ways to redefine the bases of competition in an industry, some firms have been able to create entirely new markets where competition does not exist.

Source: W. Chan Kim and Renee Mauborgne (2005). *Blue ocean strategy.* Cambridge: Harvard Business School Press.

these kinds of controls to build entirely new markets is described in the Strategy in the Emerging Enterprise feature.

Broad decision-making guidelines help bring order to what otherwise might be a chaotic decision-making process. When managers have no constraints in their decision making, they can make decisions that are disconnected from each other and inconsistent with a firm's overall mission and objectives. This results in decisions that are either not implemented or not implemented well.

However, if these decision-making guidelines become too narrow, they can stifle creativity within a firm. As was suggested earlier, a firm's ability to differentiate its products is limited only by its creativity. Thus, decision guidelines must be narrow enough to ensure that the decisions made are consistent with a firm's mission and objectives. Yet these guidelines also must be broad enough so that managerial creativity is not destroyed. In well-managed firms implementing product differentiation strategies, as long as managerial decisions fall within the broad decision-making guidelines in a firm, managers have the right—in fact, are expected—to make creative decisions.

A firm that has worked hard to reach this balance between chaos and control is 3M. In an effort to provide guiding principles that define the range of acceptable decisions at 3M, its senior managers have developed a set of innovating principles. These are presented in Table 5.4 and define the boundaries of innovative chaos at 3M. Within these boundaries, managers and engineers are expected to be creative and innovative in developing highly differentiated products and services.[21]

Another firm that has managed this tension well is British Airways (BA). BA has extensive training programs to teach its flight attendants how to provide world-class service, especially for its business-class customers. This training constitutes standard operating procedures that give purpose and structure to BA's efforts to provide a differentiated service in the highly competitive airline industry. Interestingly, however, BA also trains its flight attendants in when to violate these standard policies and procedures. By recognizing that no set of management controls can ever anticipate all the special situations that can occur when providing service to customers, BA empowers its employees to meet specific customer needs. This enables BA to have both a clearly defined product differentiation strategy and the flexibility to adjust this strategy as the situation dictates.[22]

Firms can also facilitate the implementation of a product differentiation strategy by adopting a **policy of experimentation.** Such a policy exists when firms are committed to engaging in several related product differentiation efforts simultaneously. That these product differentiation efforts are related suggests that a firm has some vision about how a particular market is likely to unfold over time. However, that there are several of these product differentiation efforts occurring simultaneously suggests that a firm is not overly committed to a particular narrow vision about how a market is going to evolve. Rather, several different experiments facilitate the exploration of different futures in a marketplace. Indeed, successful experiments can actually help define the future evolution of a marketplace.

Consider, for example, Charles Schwab, the innovative discount broker. In the face of increased competition from full-service and Internet-based brokerage firms, Schwab engaged in a series of experiments to discover the next generation of products it could offer to its customers and the different ways it could differentiate those products. Schwab investigated software for simplifying online mutual fund selection, online futures trading, and online company research. It also formed an exploratory alliance with Goldman Sachs to evaluate the possibility of enabling Schwab customers to trade in initial public offerings. Not all of Schwab's experiments led to the introduction of highly differentiated products. For example, based on some experimental investments, Schwab decided not to enter the credit card market. However, by experimenting with a range of possible product differentiation moves, it was able to develop a range of new products for the fast-changing financial services industry.[23]

TABLE 5.4 Guiding Innovative Principles at 3M*

1. **Vision.** Declare the importance of innovation; make it part of the company's self-image.

   "Our efforts to encourage and support innovation are proof that we really do intend to achieve our vision of ourselves...that we intend to become what we want to be...as a business and as creative individuals."

2. **Foresight.** Find out where technologies and markets are going. Identify articulated and unarticulated needs of customers.

   "If you are working on a next-generation medical imaging device, you'll probably talk to radiologists, but you might also sit down with people who enhance images from interplanetary space probes."

3. **Stretch goals.** Set goals that will make you and the organization stretch to make quantum improvements. Although many projects are pursued, place your biggest bets on those that change the basis of competition and redefine the industry.

   "We have a number of stretch goals at 3M. The first states that we will drive 30 percent of all sales from products introduced in the past 4 years....To establish a sense of urgency, we've recently added another goal, which is that we want 10 percent of our sales to come from products that have been in the market for just 1 year....Innovation is time sensitive...you need to move quickly."

4. **Empowerment.** Hire good people and trust them, delegate responsibilities, provide slack resources, and get out of the way. Be tolerant of initiative and the mistakes that occur because of that initiative.

   "William McKnight [a former chairman of 3M] came up with one way to institutionalize a tolerance of individual effort. He said that all technical employees could devote 15 percent of their time to a project of their own invention. In other words, they could manage themselves for 15 percent of the time....The number is not so important as the message, which is this: The system has some slack in it. If you have a good idea, and the commitment to squirrel away time to work on it and the raw nerve to skirt your lab manager's expressed desires, then go for it.

   "Put another way, we want to institutionalize a bit of rebellion in our labs. We can't have all our people off totally on their own...we do believe in discipline...but at the same time 3M management encourages a healthy disrespect for 3M management. This is not the sort of thing we publicize in our annual report, but the stories we tell—with relish—are frequently about 3Mers who have circumvented their supervisors and succeeded.

   "We also recognize that when you let people follow their own lead...everyone doesn't wind up at the same place. You can't ask people to have unique visions and march in lockstep. Some people are very precise, detail-oriented people...and others are fuzzy thinkers and visionaries...and this is exactly what we want."

5. **Communications.** Open, extensive exchanges according to ground rules in forums that are present for sharing ideas and where networking is each individual's responsibility. Multiple methods for sharing information are necessary.

   "When innovators communicate with each other, you can leverage their discoveries. This is critically important because it allows companies to get the maximum return on their substantial investments in new technologies. It also acts as a stimulus to further innovation. Indeed, we believe that the ability to combine and transfer technologies is as important as the original discovery of a technology."

6. **Rewards and recognition.** Emphasize individual recognition more than monetary rewards through peer recognition and by choice of managerial or technical promotion routes. "Innovation is an intensely human activity."

   "I've laid out six elements of 3M's corporate culture that contribute to a tradition of innovation: vision, foresight, stretch goals, empowerment, communication, and recognition....The list is...too orderly. Innovation at 3M is anything but orderly. It is sensible, in that our efforts are directed at reaching our goals, but the organization...and the process...and sometimes the people can be chaotic. We are managing in chaos, and this is the right way to manage if you want innovation. It's been said that the competition never knows what we are going to come up with next. The fact is, neither do we."

*As expressed by W. Coyne (1996). *Building a tradition of innovation.* The Fifth U.K. Innovation Lecture, Department of Trade and Industry, London. Cited in Van de Ven et al. (1999), pp. 198–200.

Compensation Policies and Implementing Product Differentiation Strategies

The compensation policies used to implement product differentiation listed in Table 5.3 very much complement the organizational structure and managerial controls listed in that table. For example, a policy of experimentation has little impact on the ability of a firm to implement product differentiation strategies if every time an innovative experiment fails individuals are punished for taking risks. Thus, compensation policies that reward risk-taking and celebrate a creative flair help to enable a firm to implement its product differentiation strategy.

Consider, for example, Nordstrom. Nordstrom is a department store that celebrates the risk-taking and creative flair of its associates as they try to satisfy their customers' needs. The story is often told of a Nordstrom sales associate who allowed a customer to return a set of tires to the store because she wasn't satisfied with them. What makes this story interesting—whether or not it is true—is that Nordstrom doesn't sell tires. But this sales associate felt empowered to make what was obviously a risky decision, and this decision is celebrated within Nordstrom as an example of the kind of service that Nordstrom's customers should expect.

The last compensation policy listed in Table 5.3 is multidimensional performance measurement. In implementing a cost leadership strategy, compensation should focus on providing appropriate incentives for managers and employees to reduce costs. Various forms of cash payments, stock, and stock options can all be tied to the attainment of specific cost goals and thus can be used to create incentives for realizing cost advantages. Similar techniques can be used to create incentives for helping a firm implement its product differentiation advantage. However, because the implementation of a product differentiation strategy generally involves the integration of multiple business functions, often through the use of product development teams, compensation schemes designed to help implement this strategy must generally recognize its multifunctional character.

Thus, rather than focusing only on a single dimension of performance, these firms often examine employee performance along multiple dimensions simultaneously. Examples of such dimensions include not only a product's sales and profitability, but customer satisfaction, an employee's willingness to cooperate with other businesses and functions within a firm, an employee's ability to effectively facilitate cross-divisional and cross-functional teams, and an employee's ability to engage in creative decision making.

Can Firms Implement Product Differentiation and Cost Leadership Simultaneously?

The arguments developed in Chapter 4 and in this chapter suggest that cost leadership and product differentiation business strategies, under certain conditions, can both create sustained competitive advantages. Given the beneficial impact of both strategies on a firm's competitive position, an important question becomes: Can a single firm simultaneously implement both strategies? After all, if each separately can improve a firm's performance, wouldn't it be better for a firm to implement both?

No: These Strategies Cannot Be Implemented Simultaneously

A quick comparison of the organizational requirements for the successful implementation of cost leadership strategies and product differentiation strategies presented in Table 5.5 summarizes one perspective on the question of whether these strategies can be implemented simultaneously. In this view, the organizational requirements of these strategies are essentially contradictory. Cost leadership requires simple reporting relationships, whereas product differentiation requires cross-divisional/cross-functional linkages. Cost leadership requires intense labor supervision, whereas product differentiation requires less intense supervision of creative employees. Cost leadership requires rewards for cost reduction, whereas product differentiation requires rewards for creative flair. It is reasonable to ask "Can a single firm combine these multiple contradictory skills and abilities?"

Some have argued that firms attempting to implement both strategies will end up doing neither well. This logic suggests that there are often only two ways to earn superior economic performance within a single industry: (1) by selling high-priced products and gaining small market share (product differentiation) or (2) by selling low-priced products and gaining large market share (cost leadership). Firms that do not make this choice of strategies (medium price, medium market share) or that attempt to implement both strategies will fail. These firms are said to be "stuck in the middle."[24]

TABLE 5.5 The Organizational Requirements for Implementing Cost Leadership and Product Differentiation Strategies

Cost leadership	Product differentiation
Organizational structure	**Organizational structure**
1. Few layers in the reporting structure	1. Cross-divisional/cross-functional product development teams
2. Simple reporting relationships	2. Willingness to explore new structures to exploit new opportunities
3. Small corporate staff	3. Isolated pockets of intense creative efforts
4. Focus on narrow range of business functions	
Management control systems	**Management control systems**
1. Tight cost-control systems	1. Broad decision-making guidelines
2. Quantitative cost goals	2. Managerial freedom within guidelines
3. Close supervision of labor, raw material, inventory, and other costs	3. Policy of experimentation
4. A cost leadership philosophy	
Compensation policies	**Compensation policies**
1. Reward for cost reduction	1. Rewards for risk-taking, not punishment for failures
2. Incentives for all employees to be involved in cost reduction	2. Rewards for creative flair
	3. Multidimensional performance measurement

Yes: These Strategies Can Be Implemented Simultaneously

More recent work contradicts assertions about being "stuck in the middle." This work suggests that firms that are successful in both cost leadership and product differentiation can often expect to gain a sustained competitive advantage. This advantage reflects at least two processes.

Differentiation, Market Share, and Low-Cost Leadership

Firms able to successfully differentiate their products and services are likely to see an increase in their volume of sales. This is especially the case if the basis of product differentiation is attractive to a large number of potential customers. Thus, product differentiation can lead to increased volumes of sales. It has already been established (in Chapter 4) that an increased volume of sales can lead to economies of scale, learning, and other forms of cost reduction. So, successful product differentiation can, in turn, lead to cost reductions and a cost leadership position.[25]

This is the situation that best describes McDonald's. McDonald's has traditionally followed a product differentiation strategy, emphasizing cleanliness, consistency, and fun in its fast-food outlets. Over time, McDonald's has used its differentiated product to become the market share leader in the fast-food industry. This market position has enabled it to reduce its costs, so that it is now the cost leader in fast foods as well. Thus, McDonald's level of profitability depends both on its product differentiation strategy and its low-cost strategy. Either one of these two strategies by itself would be difficult to overcome; together they give McDonald's a very costly-to-imitate competitive advantage.[26]

Managing Organizational Contradictions

Product differentiation can lead to high market share and low costs. It may also be the case that some firms develop special skills in managing the contradictions that are part of simultaneously implementing low-cost and product differentiation strategies. Some recent research on automobile manufacturing helps describe these special skills.[27] Traditional thinking in automotive manufacturing was that plants could either reduce manufacturing costs by speeding up the assembly line or increase the quality of the cars they made by slowing the line, emphasizing team-based production, and so forth. In general, it was thought that plants could not simultaneously build low-cost/high-quality (i.e., low-cost *and* highly differentiated) automobiles.

Several researchers have examined this traditional wisdom. They began by developing rigorous measures of the cost and quality performance of automobile plants and then applied these measures to more than 70 auto plants throughout the world that assembled mid-size sedans. What they discovered was six plants in the entire world that had, at the time this research was done, very low costs *and* very high quality.[28]

In examining what made these six plants different from other auto plants, the researchers focused on a broad range of manufacturing policies, management practices, and cultural variables. Three important findings emerged. First, these six plants had the best manufacturing technology hardware available—robots, laser-guided paint machines, and so forth. However, because many of the plants in the study had these same technologies, manufacturing technology by itself was not enough to make these six plants special. In addition, policies and procedures at these plants implemented a range of highly participative, group-oriented management techniques, including participative management, team production, and total quality management. As important, employees in these plants had a sense of loyalty and commitment toward the plant they worked for—a belief that they would be treated fairly by their plant managers.

What this research shows is that firms *can* simultaneously implement cost leadership and product differentiation strategies if they learn how to manage the contradictions inherent in these two strategies. The management of these contradictions, in turn, depends on socially complex relations among employees, between employees and the technology they use, and between employees and the firm for which they work. These relations are not only valuable (because they enable a firm to implement cost leadership and differentiation strategies) but also socially complex and thus likely to be costly to imitate and a source of sustained competitive advantage.

Recently, many scholars have backed away from the original "stuck in the middle" arguments and now suggest that low-cost firms must have competitive levels of product differentiation to survive and that product differentiation firms must have competitive levels of cost to survive.[29] For example, the fashion design company Versace—the ultimate product differentiating firm—has hired a new CEO and controller to help control its costs.[30]

Summary

Product differentiation exists when customers perceive a particular firm's products to be more valuable than other firms' products. Although differentiation can have several bases, it is, in the end, always a matter of customer perception. Bases of product differentiation include: (1) attributes of the products or services a firm sells (including product features, product complexity, the timing of product introduction, and location); (2) relations between a firm and its customers (including product customization, consumer marketing, and reputation); and (3) links within and between firms (including links between functions, links with other firms, a firm's product mix, its distribution system, and its level of service and support). However, in the end, product differentiation is limited only by the creativity of a firm's managers.

Product differentiation is valuable to the extent that it enables a firm to set its prices higher than what it would otherwise be able to. Each of the bases of product differentiation identified can be used to neutralize environmental threats and exploit environmental opportunities. The rarity and imitability of bases of product differentiation vary. Highly imitable bases of product differentiation include product features. Somewhat imitable bases include product mix, links with other firms, product customization, and consumer marketing. Costly-to-imitate bases of product differentiation include linking business functions, timing, location, reputation, and service and support.

The implementation of a product differentiation strategy involves management of organizational structure, management controls, and compensation policies. Structurally, it is not unusual for firms implementing product differentiation strategies to use cross-divisional and cross-functional teams, together with teams that are focused exclusively on a particular product differentiation effort, so-called "skunk works." Managerial controls that provide free managerial decision making within broad decision-making guidelines can be helpful in implementing product differentiation strategies, as is a policy of experimentation. Finally, compensation policies that tolerate risk-taking and a creative flair and that measure employee performance along multiple dimensions simultaneously can also be helpful in implementing product differentiation strategies.

A variety of organizational attributes is required to successfully implement a product differentiation strategy. Some have argued that contradictions between these organizational characteristics and those required to implement a cost leadership strategy mean that firms that attempt to do both will perform poorly. More recent research has noted the relationship between product differentiation, market share, and low costs and has observed that some firms have learned to manage the contradictions between cost leadership and product differentiation.

MyManagementLab®

Go to **mymanagementlab.com** to complete the problems marked with this icon ⭐.

Challenge Questions

5.1. Although cost leadership is perhaps less relevant for firms pursuing product differentiation, costs are not totally irrelevant. What advice about costs would you give a firm pursuing a product differentiation strategy?

⭐ **5.2.** Product features are often the focus of product differentiation efforts. Yet product features are among the easiest-to-imitate bases of product differentiation and thus among the least likely bases of product differentiation to be a source of sustained competitive advantage. This appears paradoxical. How can you resolve this paradox?

5.3. What are the strengths and weaknesses of using regression analysis and hedonic prices to describe the bases of product differentiation?

5.4. Chamberlin used the term "monopolistic competition" to describe firms pursuing a product differentiation strategy in a competitive industry. However, it is usually the case that firms that operate in monopolies are less efficient and less competitive than those that operate in more competitive settings (see Chapter 3). Why would this same problem exist for

firms operating in a "monopolistic competition" context?

⭐ **5.5.** Implementing a product differentiation strategy seems to require just the right mix of control and creativity. How do you know if a firm has the right mix?

5.6. Is it possible to evaluate the mix of control and creativity when implementing a product differentiation strategy before problems associated with being out of balance manifest themselves? If yes, how? If no, why not?

5.7. A firm with a highly differentiated product can increase the volume of its sales. Increased sales volumes can enable a firm to reduce its costs. High volumes with low costs can lead a firm to have very high profits, some of which the firm can use to invest in further differentiating its products. What advice would you give a firm whose competition is enjoying this product differentiation and cost leadership advantage?

Problem Set

5-8. For each of the listed products, describe at least two ways they are differentiated.

(a) Ben & Jerry's ice cream
(b) The Hummer H2
(c) The X-Games
(d) The movies *Animal House* and *Caddyshack*
(e) Frederick's of Hollywood
(f) Taco Bell

5-9. Which, if any, of the bases of product differentiation in the previous question are likely to be sources of sustained competitive advantage? Why?

5-10. Suppose you obtained the following regression results, where the starred (*) coefficients are statistically significant. What could you say about the bases of product differentiation in this market? (Hint: A regression coefficient is statistically significant when it is so large that its effect is very unlikely to have emerged by chance.)

$$\text{House Price} = 125{,}000^* + 15{,}000^*(\text{More than three bedrooms})$$
$$+\ \$18{,}000^*(\text{More than 3,500 square feet})$$
$$+\ \$150(\text{Has plumbing}) + \$180(\text{Has lawn})$$
$$+\ 17{,}000^*(\text{Lot larger than 1/2 acre})$$

How much would you expect to pay for a four-bedroom, 3,800-square-foot house on a one-acre lot? How much for a four-bedroom, 2,700-square-foot house on a quarter-acre lot? Do these results say anything about the sustainability of competitive advantages in this market?

5-11. Which of the following management controls and compensation policies is consistent with implementing cost leadership? With product differentiation? With both cost leadership and product differentiation? With neither cost leadership nor product differentiation?

(a) Firm-wide stock options
(b) Compensation that rewards each function separately for meeting its own objectives
(c) A detailed financial budget plan
(d) A document that describes, in detail, how the innovation process will unfold in a firm
(e) A policy that reduces the compensation of a manager who introduces a product that fails in the market
(f) A policy that reduces the compensation of a manager who introduces several products that fail in the market
(g) The creation of a purchasing council to discuss how different business units can reduce their costs

5-12. Identify three industries or markets where it is unlikely that firms will be able to simultaneously implement cost leadership and product differentiation. Which firms in this industry are implementing cost leadership strategies? Which are implementing product differentiation strategies? Are any firms "stuck in the middle"? If yes, which ones? If no, why not? Are any firms implementing both cost leadership and product differentiation strategies? If yes, which ones? If no, why not?

MyManagementLab®

Go to **mymanagementlab.com** for Auto-graded writing questions as well as the following Assisted-graded writing questions:

5.13. How can product differentiation be used to neutralize environmental threats and exploit environmental opportunities?

5.14. How can organizational structure be used to implement product differentiation strategies?

End Notes

1. See Ono, Y. (1996). "Who really makes that cute little beer? You'd be surprised." *The Wall Street Journal*, April 15, pp. A1+. Since this 1996 article, some of these craft beer companies have changed the way they manufacture the beers to be more consistent with the image they are trying to project.
2. See Porter, M. E. (1980). *Competitive strategy.* New York: Free Press; and Caves, R. E., and P. Williamson. (1985). "What is product differentiation, really?" *Journal of Industrial Organization Economics*, 34, pp. 113–132.
3. Lieberman, M. B., and D. B. Montgomery. (1988). "First-mover advantages." *Strategic Management Journal*, 9, pp. 41–58.
4. Carroll, P. (1993). *Big blues: The unmaking of IBM.* New York: Crown Publishers.
5. These ideas were first developed in Hotelling, H. (1929). "Stability in competition." *Economic Journal*, 39, pp. 41–57; and Ricardo, D. (1817). *Principles of political economy and taxation.* London: J. Murray.
6. See Gunther, M. (1998). "Disney's call of the wild." *Fortune*, April 13, pp. 120–124.
7. The idea of reputation is explained in Klein, B., and K. Leffler. (1981). "The role of market forces in assuring contractual performance." *Journal of Political Economy*, 89, pp. 615–641.
8. See Robichaux M. (1995). "It's a book! A T-shirt! A toy! No, just MTV trying to be Disney." *The Wall Street Journal*, February 8, pp. A1+.
9. See Henderson, R., and I. Cockburn. (1994). "Measuring competence? Exploring firm effects in pharmaceutical research." *Strategic Management Journal*, 15, pp. 63–84.
10. See Johnson, R. (1999). "Speed sells." *Fortune*, April 12, pp. 56–70. In the last few years, NASCAR's popularity has begun to wane. For example, NASCAR television ratings have been consistently down since 2005. www.jayski.com/news/pages/story/NASCAR-television-ratings
11. Kotler, P. (1986). *Principles of marketing.* Upper Saddle River, NJ: Prentice Hall.
12. Porter, M. E., and R. Wayland. (1991). "Coca-Cola vs. Pepsi-Cola and the soft drink industry." Harvard Business School Case No. 9-391-179.
13. Ghemawat, P. (1993). "Sears, Roebuck and Company: The merchandise group." Harvard Business School Case No. 9-794-039.
14. Welsh, J. (1998). "Office-paper firms pursue elusive goal: Brand loyalty." *The Wall Street Journal*, September 21, p. B6.
15. See White, E., and K. Palmer. (2003). "U.S. retailing 101." *The Wall Street Journal*, August 12, pp. B1+.
16. See Hennart, J. F. (1988). "A transaction cost theory of equity joint ventures." *Strategic Management Journal*, 9, pp. 361–374.
17. Deutsch, C. H. (1991). "How is it done? For a small fee…" *New York Times*, October 27, p. 25; and Armstrong, L. (1991). "Services: The customer as 'Honored Guest.'" *BusinessWeek*, October 25, p. 104.
18. See Yoffie, D. (1994). "Swissair's alliances (A)." Harvard Business School Case No. 9-794-152.
19. "WPP—Integrating icons." Harvard Business School Case No. 9-396-249.
20. Orosz, J. J. (2002). "Big funds need a 'Skunk Works' to stir ideas." *Chronicle of Philanthropy*, June 27, p. 47.
21. Van de Ven, A., D. Polley, R. Garud, and S. Venkatraman. (1999). *The innovation journey.* New York: Oxford, pp. 198–200.
22. Prokesch, S. (1995). "Competing on customer service: An interview with British Airways' Sir Colin Marshall." *Harvard Business Review*, November–December, p. 101. Now if they wouldn't lose our luggage at Heathrow, they would be a great airline.
23. Position, L. L. (1999). "David S. Pottruck." *BusinessWeek*, September 27, EB 51.
24. Porter, M. E. (1980). *Competitive strategy.* New York: Free Press.
25. Hill, C. W. L. (1988). "Differentiation versus low cost or differentiation and low cost: A contingency framework." *Academy of Management Review*, 13(3), pp. 401–412.
26. Gibson, R. (1995). "Food: At McDonald's, new recipes for buns, eggs." *The Wall Street Journal*, June 13, p. B1.
27. Originally discussed in the Research Made Relevant feature in Chapter 3.
28. Womack, J. P., D. I. Jones, and D. Roos. (1990). *The machine that changed the world.* New York: Rawson.
29. Porter, M. E. (1985). *Competitive advantage.* New York: Free Press.
30. Agins, T., and A. Galloni. (2003). "Facing a squeeze, Versace struggles to trim the fat." *The Wall Street Journal*, September 30, pp. A1+.

3 CORPORATE STRATEGIES

6 Vertical Integration

LEARNING OBJECTIVES *After reading this chapter, you should be able to:*

1. Define vertical integration, forward vertical integration, and backward vertical integration.

2. Discuss how vertical integration can create value by reducing the threat of opportunism.

3. Discuss how vertical integration can create value by enabling a firm to exploit its valuable, rare, and costly-to-imitate resources and capabilities.

4. Discuss how vertical integration can create value by enabling a firm to retain its flexibility.

5. Describe conditions under which vertical integration may be rare and costly to imitate.

6. Describe how the functional organization structure, management controls, and compensation policies are used to implement vertical integration.

Outsourcing Research

First it was simple manufacturing—toys, dog food, and the like—that was outsourced to Asia. This was OK because even though manufacturing could be outsourced to China and India, the real value driver of the Western economy—services—could never be outsourced. Or at least that was what we thought.

And then firms started outsourcing call centers and tax preparation and travel planning and a host of other services to India and the Philippines. Anything that could be done on a phone or online, it seemed, could be done cheaper in Asia. Sometimes, the quality of the service was compromised, but with training and additional technological development, maybe even these problems could be addressed. And this was OK because the real value driver of the Western economy—research and intellectual property—could never be outsourced. Or at least that was what we thought.

Now, it turns out that some leading Western pharmaceutical firms—including Merck, Eli Lilly, and Johnson & Johnson—have begun outsourcing some critical aspects of the pharmaceutical research and development process to pharmaceutical firms in India. This seemed impossible just a few years ago.

In the 1970s, India announced that it would not honor international pharmaceutical patents. This policy decision had at least two important implications for the pharmaceutical industry in India. First, it led to the founding of thousands of generic drug manufacturers there—firms that reverse engineered patented drugs produced by U.S. and Western European pharmaceutical companies and then sold them on world markets for a fraction of their original price. Second, virtually no pharmaceutical research and development took place in India. After all, why spend all the time and money needed to develop a new drug when generic drug firms would instantly reverse engineer your technology and undercut your ability to make a profit?

All this changed in 2003 when the Indian government reversed its policies and began honoring global pharmaceutical patents. Now, for the first time in more than two decades, Indian firms could tap into their pool of highly educated scientists and engineers and begin engaging in original research. But developing the skills needed to do world-class pharmaceutical research on your own is difficult and time-consuming. So, Indian firms began searching for potential partners in the West.

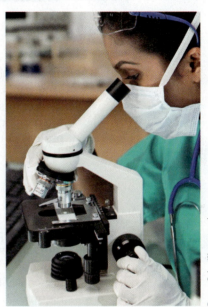

In the beginning, Western pharmaceutical companies outsourced only very routine lab work to their new Indian partners. But many of these firms found that their Indian partners were well-managed, with potentially significant technical capability, and willing to do more research-oriented kinds of work. Since 2007, a surprisingly large number of Western pharmaceutical firms have begun outsourcing progressively more important parts of the research and development process to their Indian partners.

And what do the Western firms get out of this outsourcing? Not surprisingly—low costs. It costs about $250,000 per year to employ a Ph.D. chemist in the West. That same $250,000 buys five such scientists in India. Five times as many scientists means that pharmaceutical firms can develop and test more compounds faster by working with their Indian partners than they could do on their own. The mantra in R&D—"fail fast and cheap"—is more easily realized when much of the early testing of potential drugs is done in India and not the West.

Of course, testing compounds developed by Western firms is not exactly doing basic research in pharmaceuticals. Early results indicate that Indian R&D efforts in pharmaceuticals have met with only limited success. For example, an alliance between Eli Lilly and its Indian partner, Zydus, was called off in early 2012. Disappointing results have also emerged in alliances between Merck and Novartis and their Indian partners. Also, recently the Indian government has begun to not recognize global pharmaceutical patents and is contemplating putting price limits on some drugs sold in India. All this will probably make it more difficult for true drug R&D to emerge in India. However, if Indian firms can develop R&D capabilities, their lower costs may make them attractive outsourcing parties for international pharmaceutical firms.

Sources: M. Kripalani and P. Engardio (2003). "The rise of India." *BusinessWeek*, December 8, pp. 66+; K. J. Delaney (2003). "Outsourcing jobs—and workers—to India." *The Wall Street Journal*, October 13, pp. B1+; B. Eihhorn (2006). "A dragon in R&D." *BusinessWeek*, November 6, pp. 44+; P. Engardio and A. Weintraub (2008). "Outsourcing the drug industry." *BusinessWeek*, September 5, 2008, pp. 48–52; Peter Arnold, Inc. (2012). "Zydus, Eli Lilly drug discovery deal off." *The Economic Times*, January 2; J. Lamattina (2012). "It's time to stop outsourcing Pharma R&D to India." www.forbes.com/sites/Johnlamattina/2012/10/11/its-time-to-stop-outsourcing-pharma-RD-to-india. Accessed August 20, 2013.

Τhe decision to hire an offshore company to accomplish a specific business function is an example of a decision that determines the level of a firm's vertical integration. This is the case whether the company that is hired to perform these services is located in the United States or India.

What Is Corporate Strategy?

Vertical integration is the first corporate strategy examined in detail in this book. As suggested in Chapter 1, **business strategy** is a firm's theory of how to gain competitive advantage in a single business or industry. The two business strategies discussed in this book are cost leadership and product differentiation. **Corporate strategy** is a firm's theory of how to gain competitive advantage by operating in several businesses simultaneously. Decisions about whether to vertically integrate often determine whether a firm is operating in a single business or industry or in multiple businesses or industries. Other corporate strategies discussed in this book include strategic alliances, diversification, and mergers and acquisitions.

What Is Vertical Integration?

The concept of a firm's value chain was first introduced in Chapter 3. As a reminder, a **value chain** is that set of activities that must be accomplished to bring a product or service from raw materials to the point that it can be sold to a final customer. A simplified value chain of the oil and gas industry, originally presented in Figure 3.2, is reproduced in Figure 6.1.

A firm's level of **vertical integration** is simply the number of steps in this value chain that a firm accomplishes within its boundaries. Firms that are more vertically integrated accomplish more stages of the value chain within their boundaries than firms that are less vertically integrated. A more sophisticated approach to measuring the degree of a firm's vertical integration is presented in the Strategy in Depth feature.

A firm engages in **backward vertical integration** when it incorporates more stages of the value chain within its boundaries and those stages bring it closer to the beginning of the value chain, that is, closer to gaining access to raw materials. When computer companies developed all their own software, they were engaging in backward vertical integration because these actions are close to the beginning of the value chain. When they began using independent companies operating in India to develop this software, they were less vertically integrated backward.

A firm engages in **forward vertical integration** when it incorporates more stages of the value chain within its boundaries and those stages bring it closer to the end of the value chain; that is, closer to interacting directly with final customers. When companies staffed and operated their own call centers in the United States, they were engaging in forward vertical integration because these activities brought them closer to the ultimate customer. When they started using independent companies in India to staff and operate these centers, they were less vertically integrated forward.

Of course, in choosing how to organize its value chain, a firm has more choices than whether to vertically integrate or not vertically integrate. Indeed, between these two extremes a wide range of somewhat vertically integrated options exists. These alternatives include various types of strategic alliances and joint ventures, the primary topic of Chapter 9.

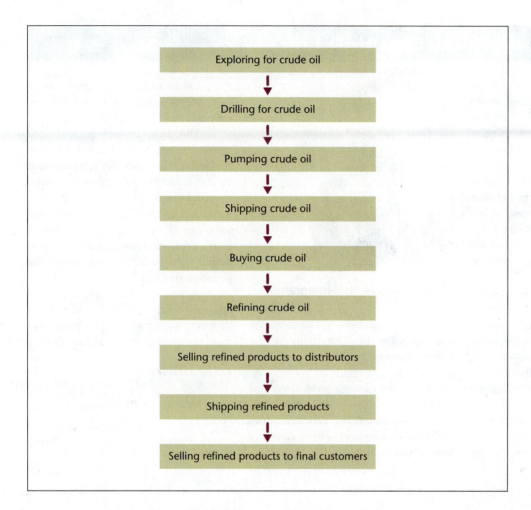

Figure 6.1 A Simplified Value Chain of Activities in the Oil and Gas Industry

The Value of Vertical Integration

The question of vertical integration—which stages of the value chain should be included within a firm's boundaries and why—has been studied by many scholars for almost 100 years. The reason this question has been of such interest was first articulated by Nobel Prize–winning economist Ronald Coase. In a famous article originally published in 1937, Coase asked a simple question: Given how efficiently markets can be used to organize economic exchanges among thousands, even hundreds of thousands, of separate individuals, why would markets, as a method for managing economic exchanges, ever be replaced by firms? In markets, almost as if by magic, Adam Smith's "invisible hand" coordinates the quantity and quality of goods and services produced with the quantity and quality of goods and services demanded through the adjustment of prices—all without a centralized controlling authority. However, in firms, centralized bureaucrats monitor and control subordinates who, in turn, battle each other for "turf" and control of inefficient internal "fiefdoms." Why would the "beauty" of the invisible hand ever be replaced by the clumsy "visible hand" of the modern corporation?[1]

Strategy in Depth

It is sometimes possible to observe which stages of the value chain a firm is engaging in and, thus, the level of that firm's vertical integration. Sometimes, however, it is more difficult to directly observe a firm's level of vertical integration. This is especially true when a firm believes that its level of vertical integration is a potential source of competitive advantage. In this case, the firm would not likely reveal this information freely to competitors.

In this situation, it is possible to get a sense of the degree of a firm's vertical integration—though not a complete list of the steps in the value chain integrated by the firm—from a close examination of the firm's **value added as a percentage of sales.** Valued added as a percentage of sales measures that percentage of a firm's sales that is generated by activities done within the boundaries of a firm. A firm

Measuring Vertical Integration

with a high ratio between value added and sales has brought many of the value-creating activities associated with its business inside its boundaries, consistent with a high level of vertical integration. A firm with a low ratio between value added and sales does not have, on average, as high a level of vertical integration.

Value added as a percentage of sales is computed using the following equation in Exhibit 1.

The sum of net income and income taxes is subtracted in both the numerator and the denominator in this equation to control for inflation and changes in the tax code over time. Net income, income taxes, and sales can all be taken directly from a firm's profit and loss statement. Value added can be calculated using the equation in Exhibit 2.

Again, most of the numbers needed to calculate value added can be found either in a firm's profit and loss statement or in its balance sheet.

Sources: A. Laffer (1969). "Vertical integration by corporations: 1929–1965." *Review of Economics and Statistics,* 51, pp. 91–93; I. Tucker and R. P. Wilder (1977). "Trends in vertical integration in the U.S. manufacturing sector." *Journal of Industrial Economics,* 26, pp. 81–94; K. Harrigan (1986). "Matching vertical integration strategies to competitive conditions." *Strategic Management Journal,* 7, pp. 535–555.

Exhibit 1

$$\text{vertical integration}_i = \frac{\text{value added}_i - (\text{net income}_i + \text{income taxes}_i)}{\text{sales}_i - (\text{net income}_i + \text{income taxes}_i)}$$

where,

$\text{vertical integration}_i$ = the level of vertical integration for firm$_i$

value added_i = the level of value added for firm$_i$

net inform_i = the level of net income for firm$_i$

income taxes_i = firm$_i$'s income taxes

sales_i = firm$_i$'s sales

Exhibit 2

value added = depreciation + amortization + fixed charges + interest expense
+ labor and related expenses + pension and retirement
expenses + income taxes + net income (after taxes)
+ rental expense

Coase began to answer his own question when he observed that sometimes the cost of using a market to manage an economic exchange must be higher than the cost of using vertical integration and bringing an exchange within the boundary of a firm. Over the years, efforts have focused on identifying the conditions under which this would be the case. The resulting work has described several different situations where vertical integration can either increase a firm's revenues or decrease its costs compared with not vertically integrating, that is, several situations where vertical integration can be valuable. The following sections present three of the most influential of these explanations of when vertical integration can create value for a firm.

Vertical Integration and the Threat of Opportunism

One of the best-known explanations of when vertical integration can be valuable focuses on using vertical integration to reduce the threat of opportunism.[2] **Opportunism** exists when a firm is unfairly exploited in an exchange. Examples of opportunism include when a party to an exchange expects a high level of quality in a product it is purchasing, only to discover it has received a lower level of quality than it expected; when a party to an exchange expects to receive a service by a particular point in time and that service is delivered late (or early); and when a party to an exchange expects to pay a price to complete this exchange and its exchange partner demands a higher price than what was previously agreed.

Obviously, when one of its exchange partners behaves opportunistically, this reduces the economic value of a firm. One way to reduce the threat of opportunism is to bring an exchange within the boundary of a firm, that is, to vertically integrate into this exchange. This way, managers in a firm can monitor and control this exchange instead of relying on the market to manage it. If the exchange that is brought within the boundary of a firm brings a firm closer to its ultimate suppliers, it is an example of backward vertical integration. If the exchange that is brought within the boundary of a firm brings a firm closer to its ultimate customer, it is an example of forward vertical integration.

Of course, firms should only bring market exchanges within their boundaries when the cost of vertical integration is less than the cost of opportunism. If the cost of vertical integration is greater than the cost of opportunism, then firms should not vertically integrate into an exchange. This is the case for both backward and forward vertical integration decisions.

So, when will the threat of opportunism be large enough to warrant vertical integration? Research has shown that the threat of opportunism is greatest when a party to an exchange has made transaction-specific investments. A **transaction-specific investment** is any investment in an exchange that has significantly more value in the current exchange than it does in alternative exchanges. Perhaps the easiest way to understand the concept of a transaction-specific investment is through an example.

Consider the economic exchange between an oil refining company and an oil pipeline building company, which is depicted in Figure 6.2. As can be seen in the figure, this oil refinery is built on the edge of a deep-water bay. Because of this, the refinery has been receiving supplies of crude oil from large tanker ships. However, an oil field exists several miles distant from the refinery, but the only way to transport crude oil from the oil field to the refinery is with trucks—a very expensive way to move crude oil, especially compared to large tankers. But if the oil refining company could find a way to get crude oil from this field cheaply, it would probably make this refinery even more valuable.

Figure 6.2   The Exchange Between an Oil Refinery and an Oil Pipeline Company

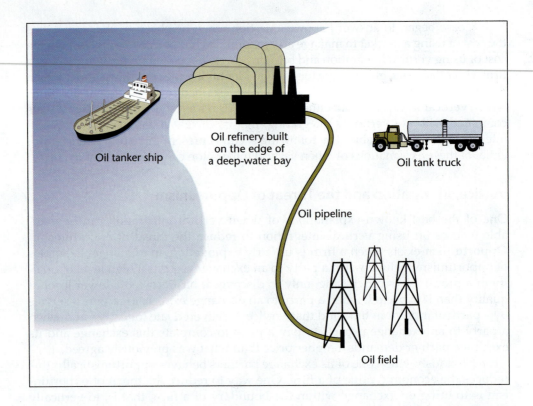

Oil tanker ship

Oil refinery built on the edge of a deep-water bay

Oil tank truck

Oil pipeline

Oil field

Enter the pipeline company. Suppose this pipeline company approaches the refinery and offers to build a pipeline from the oil field to the refinery. In return, all the pipeline company expects is for the refinery to promise to buy a certain number of barrels of crude at an agreed-to price for some period of time, say, five years, through the pipeline. If reasonable prices can be negotiated, the oil refinery is likely to find this offer attractive, for the cost of crude oil carried by the pipeline is likely to be lower than the cost of crude oil delivered by ship or by truck. Based on this analysis, the refinery and the oil pipeline company are likely to cooperate and the pipeline is likely to be built.

Now, five years go by, and it is time to renegotiate the contract. Which of these two firms has made the largest transaction-specific investments? Remember that a transaction-specific investment is any investment in an exchange that is more valuable in that particular exchange than in alternative exchanges.

What specific investments has the refinery made? Well, how much is this refinery worth if this exchange with the pipeline company is not renewed? Its value would probably drop some because oil through the pipeline is probably cheaper than oil through ships or trucks. So, if the refinery doesn't use the pipeline any longer, it will have to use these alternative supplies. This will reduce its value some—say, from $1 million to $900,000. This $100,000 difference is the size of the transaction-specific investment made by the refining company.

However, the transaction-specific investment made by the pipeline firm is probably much larger. Suppose the pipeline is worth $750,000 as long as it is pumping oil to the refinery. But if it is not pumping oil, how much is it worth? Not very much. An oil pipeline that is not pumping oil has limited alternative uses. It has value either as scrap or (perhaps) as the world's largest enclosed water slide. If the value of the pipeline is only $10,000 if it is not pumping oil to the refinery, then the level of transaction-specific investment made by the pipeline firm is substantially larger than that made by the firm that owns the refinery: $750,000 − $10,000, or $740,000, for the pipeline company versus $100,000 for the refining company.

So, which company is at greater risk of opportunism when the contract is renegotiated—the refinery or the pipeline company? Obviously, the pipeline company has more to lose. If it cannot come to an agreement with the oil refining company, it will lose $740,000. If the refinery cannot come to an agreement with the pipeline company, it will lose $100,000. Knowing this, the refining company can squeeze the pipeline company during the renegotiation by insisting on lower prices or more timely deliveries of higher-quality crude oil, and the pipeline company really cannot do much about it.

Of course, managers in the pipeline firm are not stupid. They know that after the first five years of their exchange with the refining company they will be in a very difficult bargaining position. So, in anticipation, they will insist on much higher prices for building the oil pipeline in the first place than would otherwise be the case. This will drive up the cost of building the pipeline, perhaps to the point that it is no longer cheaper than getting crude oil from ships. If this is the case, then the pipeline will not be built, even though if it could be built and the threat of opportunism eliminated, both the refining company and the pipeline company would be better off.

One way to solve this problem is for the oil refining company to buy the oil pipeline company—that is, for the oil refinery to backward vertically integrate.[3] When this happens, the incentive for the oil refinery to exploit the vulnerability of the pipeline company will be reduced. After all, if the refinery business tries to rip off the pipeline business, it only hurts itself because it owns the pipeline business.

This, then, is the essence of opportunism-based explanations of when vertical integration creates value: Transaction-specific investments make parties to an exchange vulnerable to opportunism, and vertical integration solves this vulnerability problem. Using language developed in Chapter 3, this approach suggests that vertical integration is valuable when it reduces threats from a firm's powerful suppliers or powerful buyers due to any transaction-specific investments a firm has made.

This logic explains part of the vertical integration decisions made by U.S. pharmaceutical firms discussed in the opening case of this chapter. As the risks of opportunism associated with outsourcing to Indian partners fell, U.S. pharmaceutical companies felt more comfortable gaining access to the low costs of Indian firms, and outsourcing increased.

Vertical Integration and Firm Capabilities

A second approach to vertical integration decisions focuses on a firm's capabilities and its ability to generate sustained competitive advantages.[4] This approach has two broad implications. First, it suggests that firms should vertically integrate into those business activities where they possess valuable, rare, and costly-to-imitate resources and capabilities. This way, firms can appropriate at least some of the profits that using these capabilities to exploit environmental opportunities will create. Second, this approach also suggests that firms should not vertically integrate into business activities where they do not possess the resources necessary to gain competitive advantages. Such vertical integration decisions would not be a source of profits to a firm, because it does not possess any of the valuable, rare, or costly-to-imitate resources needed to gain competitive advantages in these business activities. Indeed, to the extent that some other firms have competitive advantages in these business activities, vertically integrating into them could put a firm at a competitive disadvantage.

This, then, is the essence of the capabilities approach to vertical integration: If a firm possesses valuable, rare, and costly-to-imitate resources in a business activity, it should vertically integrate into that activity; otherwise, no vertical integration. This perspective can sometimes lead to vertical integration decisions that conflict with decisions derived from opportunism-based explanations of vertical integration.

Consider, for example, firms acting as suppliers to Wal-Mart. Wal-Mart has a huge competitive advantage in the discount retail industry. In principle, firms that sell to Wal-Mart could vertically integrate forward into the discount retail market to sell their own products. That is, these firms could begin to compete against Wal-Mart. However, such efforts are not likely to be a source of competitive advantage for these firms. Wal-Mart's resources and capabilities are just too extensive and costly to imitate for most of these suppliers. So, instead of forward vertical integration, most of these firms sell their products through Wal-Mart.

Of course, the problem is that by relying so much on Wal-Mart, these firms are making significant transaction-specific investments. If they stop selling to Wal-Mart, they may go out of business. However, this decision will have a limited impact on Wal-Mart. Wal-Mart can go to any number of suppliers around the world that are willing to replace this failed firm. So, Wal-Mart's suppliers are at risk of opportunism in this exchange, and indeed, it is well-known that Wal-Mart can squeeze its suppliers, in terms of the quality of the products it purchases, the price at which it purchases them, and the way in which these products are delivered.

So the tension between these two approaches to vertical integration becomes clear. Concerns about opportunism suggest that Wal-Mart's suppliers should vertically integrate forward. Concerns about having a competitive disadvantage if they do vertically integrate forward suggest that Wal-Mart's suppliers should not vertically integrate. So, should they or shouldn't they vertically integrate?

Not many of Wal-Mart's suppliers have been able to resolve this difficult problem. Most do not vertically integrate into the discount retail industry. However, they try to reduce the level of transaction-specific investment they make with Wal-Mart by supplying other discount retailers, both in the United States and abroad. They also try to use their special capabilities to differentiate their products so much that Wal-Mart's customers insist on Wal-Mart selling these products. And these firms constantly search for cheaper ways to make and distribute higher-quality products.

This capabilities analysis explains why outsourcing all of U.S. pharmaceutical research to low-cost Indian companies—discussed in the opening case of this chapter—has not occurred. It turns out that those basic R&D capabilities are very difficult to develop, and while Indian firms can engage in less sophisticated compound testing, they are not yet sufficiently skilled to engage in basic R&D. The result—U.S. pharmaceutical firms are very tentative about outsourcing their basic R&D.

Vertical Integration and Flexibility

A third perspective on vertical integration focuses on the impact of this decision on a firm's flexibility. **Flexibility** refers to how costly it is for a firm to alter its strategic and organizational decisions. Flexibility is high when the cost of changing strategic choices is low; flexibility is low when the cost of changing strategic choices is high.

So, which is less flexible—vertical integration or no vertical integration? Research suggests that, in general, vertically integrating is less flexible than not vertically integrating.[5] This is because once a firm has vertically integrated, it has committed its organizational structure, its management controls, and its compensation policies to a particular vertically integrated way of doing business. Undoing this decision often means changing these aspects of an organization.

Suppose, for example, that a vertically integrated firm decides to get out of a particular business. To do so, the firm will have to sell or close its factories (actions that can adversely affect both the employees it has to lay off and those that remain), alter its supply relationships, hurt customers that have come to rely on it as a partner, and change its internal reporting structure. In contrast, if a non-vertically integrated firm decides to get out of a business, it simply stops. It cancels whatever contracts it might have had in place and ceases operations in that business. The cost of exiting a non-vertically integrated business is generally much lower than the cost of exiting a vertically integrated business.

Of course, flexibility is not always valuable. In fact, flexibility is only valuable when the decision-making setting a firm is facing is uncertain. A decision-making setting is **uncertain** when the future value of an exchange cannot be known when investments in that exchange are being made. In such settings, less vertical integration is better than more vertical integration. This is because vertically integrating into an exchange is less flexible than not vertically integrating into an exchange. If an exchange turns out not to be valuable, it is usually more costly for firms that have vertically integrated into an exchange to exit that exchange compared with those that have not vertically integrated.

Consider, for example, a pharmaceutical firm making investments in biotechnology. The outcome of biotechnology research is very uncertain. If a pharmaceutical company vertically integrates into a particular type of biotechnology research by hiring particular types of scientists, building an expensive laboratory, and developing the other skills necessary to do this particular type of biotechnology research, it has made a very large investment. Now suppose that this research turns out not to be profitable. This firm has made huge investments that now have little value. As important, it has failed to make investments in other areas of biotechnology that could turn out to be valuable.

A flexibility-based approach to vertical integration suggests that rather than vertically integrating into a business activity whose value is highly uncertain, firms should not vertically integrate but should instead form a strategic alliance to manage this exchange. A strategic alliance is more flexible than vertical integration but still gives a firm enough information about an exchange to estimate its value over time.

An alliance has a second advantage in this setting. The downside risks associated with investing in a strategic alliance are known and fixed. They equal the cost of creating and maintaining the alliance. If an uncertain investment turns out not to be valuable, parties to this alliance know the maximum amount they can lose—an amount equal to the cost of creating and maintaining the alliance. On the other hand, if this exchange turns out to be very valuable, then maintaining an alliance can give a firm access to this huge upside potential. This partially explains why, to the extent that U.S. pharmaceutical firms outsource basic R&D to Indian partners, they do so through joint ventures. These aspects of strategic alliances will be discussed in more detail in Chapter 9.

Each of these explanations of vertical integration has received significant empirical attention in the academic literature. Some of these studies are described in the Research Made Relevant feature.

Applying the Theories to the Management of Call Centers

One of the most common business functions to be outsourced, and even off-shored, is a firm's call center activities. So, what do these three theories say about how call centers should be managed: When should they be brought within the boundaries of a firm, and when should they be outsourced? Each of these theories will be discussed in turn.

Transaction-Specific Investments and Managing Call Centers

When applying opportunism-based explanations of vertical integration, start by looking for actual or potential transaction-specific investments that would need to be made in order to complete an exchange. High levels of such investments suggest the need for vertical integration; low levels of such investments suggest that vertically integrating this exchange is not necessary.

When the call-center approach to providing customer service was first developed in the 1980s, it required substantial levels of transaction-specific investment. First, a great deal of special-purpose equipment had to be purchased. And although this equipment could be used for any call center, it had little value except within a call center. Thus, this equipment was an example of a somewhat specific investment.

More important, in order to provide service in call centers, call-center employees would have to be fully aware of all the problems likely to emerge

Research Made Relevant

Of the three explanations of vertical integration discussed here, opportunism-based explanations are the oldest and thus have received the greatest empirical support. One review of this empirical work, by Professor Joe Mahoney of the University of Illinois, observes that the core assertion of this approach—that high levels of transaction-specific investment lead to higher levels of vertical integration—receives consistent empirical support.

More recent work has begun to examine the trade-offs among these three explanations of vertical integration by examining their effects on vertical integration simultaneously. For example, Professor Tim Folta of Purdue University examined the opportunism and flexibility approaches to vertical integration simultaneously. His results show that the basic assertion of the opportunism approach still holds. However, when he incorporates uncertainty into his empirical analysis,

Empirical Tests of Theories of Vertical Integration

he finds that firms engage in less vertical integration than predicted by opportunism by itself. In other words, firms apparently worry not only about transaction-specific investments when they make vertical integration choices; they also worry about how costly it is to reverse those investments in the face of high uncertainty.

An even more recent study by Michael Leiblein from The Ohio State University and Doug Miller from the University of Illinois examines all three of these explanations of vertical integration simultaneously. These authors studied vertical integration decisions in the semiconductor manufacturing industry and found that all three explanations hold. That is, firms in this industry worry about transaction-specific investment, the capabilities they possess, the capabilities they would like to possess, and the uncertainty of the markets within which they operate when they make vertical integration choices.

Sources: J. Mahoney (1992). "The choice of organizational form: Vertical financial ownership versus other methods of vertical integration." *Strategic Management Journal*, 13, pp. 559–584; T. Folta (1998). "Governance and uncertainty: The trade-off between administrative control and commitment." *Strategic Management Journal*, 19, pp. 1007–1028; M. Leiblein and D. Miller (2003). "An empirical examination of transaction- and firm-level influences on the vertical boundaries of the firm." *Strategic Management Journal*, 24(9), pp. 839–859.

with the use of a firm's products. This requires a firm to study its products very closely and then to train call-center employees to be able to respond to any problems customers might have. This training was sometimes very complex and time-consuming and represented substantial transaction-specific investments on the part of call-center employees. Only employees that worked full time for a large corporation—where job security was usually high for productive workers—would be willing to make these kinds of specific investments. Thus, vertical integration into call-center management made a great deal of sense.

However, as information technology improved, firms found it was possible to train call-center employees much faster. Now, all call-center employees had to do was follow scripts that were prewritten and preloaded onto their computers. By asking a few scripted questions, call-center employees could diagnose most problems. In addition, solutions to those problems were also included on an employee's computer. Only really unusual problems could not be handled by employees working off these computer scripts. Because the level of specific investment required to use these scripts was much lower, employees were willing to work for companies without the job security usually associated with large firms. Indeed, call centers became good part-time and temporary employment opportunities. Because the level of specific investment required to work in these call centers was much lower, not vertically integrating into call-center management made a great deal of sense.

Capabilities and Managing Call Centers

In opportunism-based explanations of vertical integration, you start by looking for transaction-specific investments and then make vertical integration decisions based on these investments. In capability-based approaches, you start by looking for valuable, rare, and costly-to-imitate resources and capabilities and then make vertical integration decisions appropriately.

In the early days of call-center management, how well a firm operated its call centers could actually be a source of competitive advantage. During this time period, the technology was new, and the training required to answer a customer's questions was extensive. Firms that developed special capabilities in managing these processes could gain competitive advantages and thus would vertically integrate into call-center management.

However, over time, as more and more call-center management suppliers were created and as the technology and training required to staff a call center became more widely available, the ability of a call center to be a source of competitive advantage for a firm dropped. That is, the ability to manage a call center was still valuable, but it was no longer rare or costly to imitate. In this setting, it is not surprising to see firms getting out of the call-center management business, outsourcing this business to low-cost specialist firms, and focusing on those business functions where they might be able to gain a sustained competitive advantage.

Flexibility and Managing Call Centers

Opportunism logic suggests starting with a search for transaction-specific investments; capabilities logic suggests starting with a search for valuable, rare, and costly-to-imitate resources and capabilities. Flexibility logic suggests starting by looking for sources of uncertainty in an exchange.

One of the biggest uncertainties in providing customer service through call centers is the question of whether the people staffing the phones actually help a firm's customers. This is a particularly troubling concern for firms that are selling complex products that can have numerous types of problems. A variety of technological solutions have been developed to try to address this uncertainty. But, if a firm vertically integrates into the call-center management business, it is committing to a particular technological solution. This solution may not work, or it may not work as well as some other solutions.

In the face of this uncertainty, maintaining relationships with several different call-center management companies—each of whom have adopted different technological solutions to the problem of how to use call-center employees to assist customers who are using very complex products—gives a firm technological flexibility that it would not otherwise have. Once a superior solution is identified, then a firm no longer needs this flexibility and may choose to vertically integrate into call-center management or not, depending on opportunism and capabilities considerations.

Integrating Different Theories of Vertical Integration

At first glance, having three different explanations about how vertical integration can create value seems troubling. After all, won't these explanations sometimes contradict each other?

The answer to this question is yes. We have already seen such a contradiction in the case of opportunism and capabilities explanations of whether Wal-Mart suppliers should forward vertically integrate into the discount retail industry.

However, more often than not, these three explanations are complementary in nature. That is, each approach generally leads to the same conclusion about how a firm should vertically integrate. Moreover, sometimes it is simply easier to apply one of these approaches to evaluate a firm's vertical integration choices than the other two. Having a "tool kit" that includes three explanations of vertical integration enables the analyst to choose the approach that is most likely to be a source of insight in a particular situation.

Even when these explanations make contradictory assertions about vertical integration, having multiple approaches can be helpful. In this context, having multiple explanations can highlight the trade-offs that a firm is making when choosing its vertical integration strategy. Thus, for example, if opportunism-based explanations suggest that vertical integration is necessary because of high transaction-specific investments, capabilities-based explanations caution about the cost of developing the resources and capabilities necessary to vertically integrate and flexibility concerns caution about the risks that committing to vertical integration imply, and the costs and benefits of whatever vertical integration decision is ultimately made can be understood very clearly.

Overall, having three explanations of vertical integration has several advantages for those looking to analyze the vertical integration choices of real firms. Of course, applying these explanations can create important ethical dilemmas for a firm, especially when it becomes clear that a firm needs to become less vertically integrated than it has historically been. Some of these dilemmas are discussed in the Ethics and Strategy feature.

Vertical Integration and Sustained Competitive Advantage

Of course, in order for vertical integration to be a source of sustained competitive advantage, not only must it be valuable (because it responds to threats of opportunism; enables a firm to exploit its own or other firms' valuable, rare, and costly-to-imitate resources; or gives a firm flexibility), it must also be rare and costly to imitate, and a firm must be organized to implement it correctly.

The Rarity of Vertical Integration

A firm's vertical integration strategy is rare when few competing firms are able to create value by vertically integrating in the same way. A firm's vertical integration strategy can be rare because it is one of a small number of competing firms that is able to vertically integrate efficiently or because it is one of a small number of firms that is able to adopt a non-vertically integrated approach to managing an exchange.

Rare Vertical Integration

A firm may be able to create value through vertical integration, when most of its competitors are not able to, for at least three reasons. Not surprisingly, these reasons parallel the three explanations of vertical integration presented in this chapter.

Ethics and Strategy

Imagine a firm that has successfully operated in a vertically integrated manner for decades. Employees come to work, they know their jobs, they know how to work together effectively, they know where to park. The job is not just the economic center of their lives; it has become the social center as well. Most of their friends work in the same company, in the same function, as they do. The future appears to be much as the past—stable employment and effective work, all aiming toward a comfortable and well-planned retirement. And then the firm adopts a new outsourcing strategy. It changes its vertical integration strategy by becoming less vertically integrated and purchasing services from outside suppliers that it used to obtain internally.

The economics of outsourcing can be compelling. Outsourcing can help firms reduce costs and focus their efforts on those business functions that are central to their competitive advantage. When done well, outsourcing creates value—value that firms can share with their owners, their stockholders.

Indeed, outsourcing is becoming a trend in business. Some observers

The Ethics of Outsourcing

predict that by 2015, an additional 3.3 million jobs in the United States will be outsourced, many to operations overseas.

But what of the employees whose jobs are taken away? What of their lifetime of commitment, their steady and reliable work? What of their stable and secure retirement? Outsourcing often devastates lives, even as it creates economic value. Of course, some firms go out of their way to soften the impact of outsourcing on their employees. Those that are near retirement age are often

given an opportunity to retire early. Others receive severance payments in recognition of their years of service. Other firms hire "outplacement" companies—firms that specialize in placing suddenly unemployed people in new jobs and new careers.

But all these efforts to soften the blow do not make the blow go away. Many employees assume that they have an implicit contract with the firms they work for. That contract is: "As long as I do my job well, I will have a job." That contract is being replaced with: "As long as a firm wants to employ me, I will have a job." In such a world, it is not surprising that many employees now look first to maintain their employability in their current job—by receiving additional training and experiences that might be valuable at numerous other employers—and are concerned less with what they can do to improve the performance of the firm they work for.

Sources: S. Steele-Carlin (2003). "Outsourcing poised for growth in 2002." *FreelanceJobsNews.com*, October 20; (2003). "Who wins in off-shoring?" *McKinseyQuarterly.com*, October 20.

Rare Transaction-Specific Investment and Vertical Integration. First, a firm may have developed a new technology or a new approach to doing business that requires its business partners to make substantial transaction-specific investments. Firms that engage in these activities will find it in their self-interest to vertically integrate, whereas firms that have not engaged in these activities will not find it in their self-interest to vertically integrate. If these activities are rare and costly to imitate, they can be a source of competitive advantage for a vertically integrating firm.

For example, many firms in the computer industry are offshoring some of their key business functions. However, one firm—Dell—brought one of these functions—its technical call center for business customers—back from India and re-vertically integrated it into its business function.[6] The problems faced by corporate customers are typically much more complicated than those faced by individual consumers. Thus, it is much more difficult to provide call-center employees with the training they need to address corporate problems. Moreover, because corporate technologies change more rapidly than many consumer technologies, keeping call-center employees up to date on how to service corporate customers is also more complicated than having call-center employees provide services to its noncorporate customers. Because Dell needs the people staffing its corporate call centers to make substantial specific investments in its technology and in understanding its customers, it has found it necessary to bring these individuals within the boundaries of the firm and to re-vertically integrate the operation of this particular type of service center.

If Dell, through this vertical integration decision, is able to satisfy its customers more effectively than its competitors and if the cost of managing this call center is not too high, then this vertical integration decision is both valuable and rare and thus a source of at least a temporary competitive advantage for Dell.

Rare Capabilities and Vertical Integration. A firm such as Dell might also conclude that it has unusual skills, either in operating a call center or in providing the training that is needed to staff certain kinds of call centers. If those capabilities are valuable and rare, then vertically integrating into businesses that exploit these capabilities can enable a firm to gain at least a temporary competitive advantage. Indeed, the belief that a firm possesses valuable and rare capabilities is often a justification for rare vertical integration decisions in an industry.

Rare Uncertainty and Vertical Integration. Finally, a firm may be able to gain an advantage from vertically integrating when it resolves some uncertainty it faces sooner than its competition. Suppose, for example, that several firms in an industry all begin investing in a very uncertain technology. Flexibility logic suggests that, to the extent possible, these firms will prefer to not vertically integrate into the manufacturing of this technology until its designs and features stabilize and market demand for this technology is well established.

However, imagine that one of these firms is able to resolve these uncertainties before any other firm. This firm no longer needs to retain the flexibility that is so valuable under conditions of uncertainty. Instead, this firm might be able to, say, design special-purpose machines that can efficiently manufacture this technology. Such machines are not flexible, but they can be very efficient.

Of course, outside vendors would have to make substantial transaction-specific investments to use these machines. Outside vendors may be reluctant to make these investments. In this setting, this firm may find it necessary to vertically integrate to be able to use its machines to produce this technology. Thus, this firm, by resolving uncertainty faster than its competitors, is able to gain some of the advantages of vertical integration sooner than its competitors. Whereas the competition is still focusing on flexibility in the face of uncertainty, this firm gets to focus on production efficiency in meeting customers' product demands. This can obviously be a source of competitive advantage.

Rare Vertical Dis-Integration

Each of the examples of vertical integration and competitive advantage described so far has focused on a firm's ability to vertically integrate to create competitive advantage. However, firms can also gain competitive advantages through their decisions to vertically dis-integrate, that is, through the decision to outsource an activity that used to be within the boundaries of the firm. Whenever a firm is among the first in its industry to conclude that the level of specific investment required to manage an economic exchange is no longer high, or that a particular exchange is no longer rare or costly to imitate, or that the level of uncertainty about the value of an exchange has increased, it may be among the first in its industry to vertically dis-integrate this exchange. Such activities, to the extent they are valuable, will be rare and, thus, a source of at least a temporary competitive advantage.

The Imitability of Vertical Integration

The extent to which these rare vertical integration decisions can be sources of sustained competitive advantage depends, as always, on the imitability of the rare resources that give a firm at least a temporary competitive advantage. Both direct duplication and substitution can be used to imitate another firm's valuable and rare vertical integration choices.

Direct Duplication of Vertical Integration

Direct duplication occurs when competitors develop or obtain the resources and capabilities that enable another firm to implement a valuable and rare vertical integration strategy. To the extent that these resources and capabilities are path dependent, socially complex, or causally ambiguous, they may be immune from direct duplication and, thus, a source of sustained competitive advantage.

With respect to offshoring business functions, it seems that the very popularity of this strategy suggests that it is highly imitable. Indeed, this strategy is becoming so common that firms that move in the other direction by vertically integrating a call center and managing it in the United States (like Dell) make news.

But the fact that many firms are implementing this strategy does not mean that they are all equally successful in doing so. These differences in performance may reflect some subtle and complex capabilities that some of these outsourcing firms possess but others do not. These are the kinds of resources and capabilities that may be sources of sustained competitive advantage.

Some of the resources that might enable a firm to implement a valuable and rare vertical integration strategy may not be susceptible to direct duplication. These might include a firm's ability to analyze the attributes of its economic exchanges and its ability to conceive and implement vertical integration strategies. Both of these capabilities may be socially complex and path dependent—built up over years of experience.

Substitutes for Vertical Integration

The major substitute for vertical integration—strategic alliances—is the major topic of Chapter 9. An analysis of how strategic alliances can substitute for vertical integration will be delayed until then.

Organizing to Implement Vertical Integration

Organizing to implement vertical integration involves the same organizing tools as implementing any business or corporate strategy: organizational structure, management controls, and compensation policies.

Organizational Structure and Implementing Vertical Integration

The organizational structure that is used to implement a cost leadership and product differentiation strategy—the functional, or U-form, structure—is also used to implement a vertical integration strategy. Indeed, each of the exchanges included within the boundaries of a firm as a result of vertical integration decisions are incorporated into one of the functions in a functional organizational structure. Decisions about which manufacturing activities to vertically integrate into determine the range and responsibilities of the manufacturing function within a functionally organized firm; decisions about which marketing activities to vertically integrate into determine the range and responsibilities of the marketing function within a functionally organized firm; and so forth. Thus, in an important sense, vertical integration decisions made by a firm determine the structure of a functionally organized firm.

The chief executive officer (CEO) in this vertically integrated, functionally organized firm has the same two responsibilities that were first identified in Chapter 4: strategy formulation and strategy implementation. However, these two responsibilities take on added dimensions when implementing vertical integration decisions. In particular, although the CEO must take the lead in making decisions about whether each individual function should be vertically integrated into a firm, this person must also work to resolve conflicts that naturally arise between vertically integrated functions. The particular roles of the CEO in smaller entrepreneurial firms are described in the Strategy in the Emerging Enterprise feature.

Resolving Functional Conflicts in a Vertically Integrated Firm

From a CEO's perspective, coordinating functional specialists to implement a vertical integration strategy almost always involves conflict resolution. Conflicts among functional managers in a U-form organization are both expected and normal. Indeed, if there is no conflict among certain functional managers in a U-form organization, then some of these managers probably are not doing their jobs. The task facing the CEO is not to pretend this conflict does not exist or to ignore it, but to manage it in a way that facilitates strategy implementation.

Consider, for example, the relationship between manufacturing and sales managers. Typically, manufacturing managers prefer to manufacture a single product with long production runs. Sales managers, however, generally prefer to sell numerous customized products. Manufacturing managers generally do not like large inventories of finished products; sales managers generally prefer large inventories of finished products that facilitate rapid deliveries to customers. If these various interests of manufacturing and sales managers do not, at least sometimes, come into conflict in a vertically integrated U-form organization, then the manufacturing manager is not focusing enough on cost reduction and quality improvement in manufacturing or the sales manager is not focusing enough on meeting customer needs in a timely way or both.

Numerous other conflicts arise among functional managers in a vertically integrated U-form organization. Accountants often focus on maximizing managerial accountability and close analysis of costs; research and development managers may fear that such accounting practices will interfere with innovation and creativity. Finance managers often focus on the relationship between a firm and its external capital markets; human resource managers are more concerned with the relationship between a firm and external labor markets.

In this context, the CEO's job is to help resolve conflicts in ways that facilitate the implementation of the firm's strategy. Functional managers do not have to "like" one another. However, if a firm's vertical integration strategy is correct, the reason that a function has been included within the boundaries of a firm is that this decision creates value for the firm. Allowing functional conflicts to get in the way of taking advantage of each of the functions within a firm's boundaries can destroy this potential value.

Strategy in the Emerging Enterprise

With a net worth of more than $2.8 billion, Oprah Winfrey heads one of the most successful multimedia organizations in the United States. One of the businesses she owns—Harpo Productions—produced one of the most successful daytime television shows ever (with revenues of more than $300 million a year); launched one of the most successful magazines ever (with 2.5 million paid subscribers it is larger than *Vogue* and *Fortune*); and a movie production unit. One investment banker estimates that if Harpo, Inc., was a publicly traded firm, it would be valued at $575 million. Other properties Oprah owns—including investments, real estate, a stake in the cable television channel Oxygen, and stock options in Viacom—generate another $468 million in revenues per year.

And Oprah Winfrey does not consider herself to be a CEO.

She heads a multimedia conglomerate that employs more than 12,000 people. Her film studio has produced more than 25 movies and more than a dozen television productions. The introduction of her magazine was once described as the most successful magazine product launch ever. She formed a joint venture with the Discovery Channel to introduce a new cable channel. And in 1985, she was nominated for an Academy Award. But Oprah Winfrey does not think of herself as a CEO.

Oprah, Inc.

Certainly, her decision-making style is not typical of most CEOs. She has been quoted as describing her business decision making as "leaps of faith" and "If I called a strategic planning meeting, there would be dead silence, and then people would fall out of their chairs laughing."

However, she has made other decisions that put her firmly in control of her empire. For example, in 1987, she hired a tough Chicago entertainment attorney—Jeff Jacobs—as president of her business empire, Harpo, Inc. Whereas Oprah's business decisions are made from her gut and from her heart, Jacobs makes sure that the numbers add up to more revenues and profits for Harpo. She has also been unwilling to license her name to other firms, unlike Martha Stewart, who licensed her name to Kmart. Oprah has made strategic alliances with King

World (to distribute her TV show), with ABC (to broadcast her movies), with Hearst (to distribute her magazine), with Oxygen (to distribute some other television programs), and with the Discovery Channel. But she has never given up control of her business. And she has not taken her firm public. She currently owns 90 percent of Harpo's stock. She was once quoted as saying, "If I lost control of my business, I'd lose myself—or at least the ability to be myself."

To help control this growing business, Oprah and Jacobs hired a chief operating officer (COO), Tim Bennett, who then created several functional departments, including accounting, legal, and human resources, to help manage the firm. With thousands of employees, offices in Chicago and Los Angeles, and a real organization, Harpo is a real company, and Oprah is a real CEO—albeit a CEO with a slightly different approach to making business decisions.

That said, when Oprah's television network, OWN, started losing money, Oprah quickly took over as CEO and chief creative officer. Such decisive action makes Oprah seem more CEO-like all the time.

Sources: P. Sellers (2002). "The business of being Oprah." *Fortune*, April 1, pp. 50+; Oprah.com accessed August 30, 2013; Hoovers.com/Harpo Inc.; accessed August 30, 2013.

Management Controls and Implementing Vertical Integration

Although having the correct organizational structure is important for firms implementing their vertical integration strategies, that structure must be supported by a variety of management control processes. Among the most important of these processes are the budgeting process and the management committee oversight process, which can also help CEOs resolve the functional conflicts that are common within vertically integrated firms.

The Budgeting Process

Budgeting is one of the most important control mechanisms available to CEOs in vertically integrated U-form organizations. Indeed, in most U-form companies enormous management effort goes into the creation of budgets and the evaluation of performance relative to budgets. Budgets are developed for costs, revenues, and a variety of other activities performed by a firm's functional managers. Often, managerial compensation and promotion opportunities depend on the ability of a manager to meet budget expectations.

Although budgets are an important control tool, they can also have unintended negative consequences. For example, the use of budgets can lead functional managers to overemphasize short-term behavior that is easy to measure and underemphasize longer-term behavior that is more difficult to measure. Thus, for example, the strategically correct thing for a functional manager to do might be to increase expenditures for maintenance and management training, thereby ensuring that the function will have both the technology and the skilled people needed to do the job in the future. An overemphasis on meeting current budget requirements, however, might lead this manager to delay maintenance and training expenditures. By meeting short-term budgetary demands, this manager may be sacrificing the long-term viability of this function, compromising the long-term viability of the firm.

CEOs can do a variety of things to counter the "short-termism" effects of the budgeting process. For example, research suggests that evaluating a functional manager's performance relative to budgets can be an effective control device when (1) the process used in developing budgets is open and participative, (2) the process reflects the economic reality facing functional managers and the firm, and (3) quantitative evaluations of a functional manager's performance are augmented by qualitative evaluations of that performance. Adopting an open and participative process for setting budgets helps ensure that budget targets are realistic and that functional managers understand and accept them. Including qualitative criteria for evaluation reduces the chances that functional managers will engage in behaviors that are very harmful in the long run but enable them to make budget in the short run.[7]

The Management Committee Oversight Process

In addition to budgets, vertically integrated U-form organizations can use various internal management committees as management control devices. Two particularly common internal management committees are the **executive committee** and the **operations committee** (although these committees have many different names in different organizations).

The executive committee in a U-form organization typically consists of the CEO and two or three key functional senior managers. It normally meets weekly and reviews the performance of the firm on a short-term basis. Functions represented on this committee generally include accounting, legal, and other functions (such as manufacturing or sales) that are most central to the firm's short-term business success. The fundamental purpose of the executive committee is to track the short-term performance of the firm, to note and correct any budget variances for functional managers, and to respond to any crises that might emerge. Obviously, the executive committee can help avoid many functional conflicts in a vertically integrated firm before they arise.

In addition to the executive committee, another group of managers meets regularly to help control the operations of the firm. Often called the *operations committee*, this committee typically meets monthly and usually consists of the CEO and each of the heads of the functional areas included in the firm. The executive committee is a subset of the operations committee.

The primary objective of the operations committee is to track firm performance over time intervals slightly longer than the weekly interval of primary interest to the executive committee and to monitor longer-term strategic investments and activities. Such investments might include plant expansions, the introduction of new products, and the implementation of cost-reduction or quality improvement programs. The operations committee provides a forum in which senior functional managers can come together to share concerns and opportunities and to coordinate efforts to implement strategies. Obviously, the operations committee can help resolve functional conflicts in a vertically integrated firm after they arise.

In addition to these two standing committees, various other committees and task forces can be organized within the U-form organization to manage specific projects and tasks. These additional groups are typically chaired by a member of the executive or operations committee and report to one or both of these standing committees, as warranted.

Compensation in Implementing Vertical Integration Strategies

Organizational structure and management control systems can have an important impact on the ability of a firm to implement its vertical integration strategy. However, a firm's compensation policies can be important as well.

We have already seen how compensation can play a role in implementing cost leadership and product differentiation and how compensation can be tied to budgets to help implement vertical integration. However, the three explanations of vertical integration presented in this chapter have important compensation implications as well. We will first discuss the compensation challenges these three explanations suggest and then discuss ways these challenges can be addressed.

Opportunism-Based Vertical Integration and Compensation Policy

Opportunism-based approaches to vertical integration suggest that employees who make firm-specific investments in their jobs will often be able to create more value for a firm than employees who do not. Firm-specific investments are a type of transaction-specific investment. Whereas transaction-specific investments are investments that have more value in a particular exchange than in alternative exchanges, **firm-specific investments** are investments made by employees that have more value in a particular firm than in alternative firms.[8]

Examples of firm-specific investments include an employee's understanding of a particular firm's culture, his or her personal relationships with others in the firm, and an employee's knowledge about a firm's unique business processes. All this knowledge can be used by an employee to create a great deal of value in a firm. However, this knowledge has almost no value in other firms. The effort to create this knowledge is thus a firm-specific investment.

Despite the value that an employee's firm-specific investments can create, opportunism-based explanations of vertical integration suggest that employees will often be reluctant to make these investments because, once they do, they become vulnerable in their exchange with this firm. For example, an employee who has made very significant firm-specific investments may not be able to quit and go to work for another company, even if he or she is passed over for promotion, does not receive a raise, or is even actively discriminated against. This is because by quitting this firm, this employee loses all the investment he or she made in this particular firm. Because this employee has few employment options other than his or her current firm, this firm can treat this employee badly and the employee can do little about it. This is why employees are often reluctant to make firm-specific investments.

But the firm needs its employees to make such investments if it is to realize its full economic potential. Thus, one of the tasks of compensation policy is to create incentives for employees whose firm-specific investments could create great value to actually make those investments.

Capabilities and Compensation

Capability explanations of vertical integration also acknowledge the importance of firm-specific investments in creating value for a firm. Indeed, many of the valuable, rare, and costly-to-imitate resources and capabilities that can exist in a firm are a manifestation of firm-specific investments made by a firm's employees. However, whereas opportunism explanations of vertical integration tend to focus on firm-specific investments made by individual employees, capabilities explanations tend to focus on firm-specific investments made by groups of employees.[9]

In Chapter 3, it was suggested that one of the reasons that a firm's valuable and rare resources may be costly to imitate is that these resources are socially complex in nature. Socially complex resources reflect the teamwork, cooperation, and culture that have evolved within a firm—capabilities that can increase the value of a firm significantly, but capabilities that other firms will often find costly to imitate, at least in the short to medium term. Moreover, these are capabilities that exist because several employees—not just a single employee—have made specific investments in a firm.

From the point of view of designing a compensation policy, capabilities analysis suggests that not only should a firm's compensation policy encourage employees whose firm-specific investments could create value to actually make those investments; it also recognizes that these investments will often be collective in nature—that, for example, until all the members of a critical management team make firm-specific commitments to that team, that team's ability to create and sustain competitive advantages will be significantly limited.

Flexibility and Compensation

Flexibility explanations of vertical integration also have some important implications for compensation. In particular, because the creation of flexibility in a firm depends on employees being willing to engage in activities that have fixed and known downside risks and significant upside potential, it follows that compensation that has fixed and known downside risks and significant upside potential would encourage employees to choose and implement flexible vertical integration strategies.

Compensation Alternatives

Table 6.1 lists several compensation alternatives and how they are related to each of the three explanations of vertical integration discussed in this chapter. Not

Opportunism explanations	Salary
	Cash bonuses for individual performance
	Stock grants for individual performance
Capabilities explanations	Cash bonuses for corporate or group performance
	Stock grants for corporate or group performance
Flexibility explanations	Stock options for individual, corporate, or group performance

TABLE 6.1 Types of Compensation and Approaches to Making Vertical Integration Decisions

surprisingly, opportunism-based explanations suggest that compensation that focuses on individual employees and how they can make firm-specific investments will be important for firms implementing their vertical integration strategies. Such individual compensation includes an employee's salary, cash bonuses based on individual performance, and **stock grants**—or payments to employees in a firm's stock—based on individual performance.

Capabilities explanations of vertical integration suggest that compensation that focuses on groups of employees making firm-specific investments in valuable, rare, and costly-to-imitate resources and capabilities will be particularly important for firms implementing vertical integration strategies. Such collective compensation includes cash bonuses based on a firm's overall performance and stock grants based on a firm's overall performance.

Finally, flexibility logic suggests that compensation that has a fixed and known downside risk and significant upside potential is important for firms implementing vertical integration strategies. **Stock options,** whereby employees are given the right, but not the obligation, to purchase stock at predetermined prices, are a form of compensation that has these characteristics. Stock options can be granted based on an individual employee's performance or the performance of the firm as a whole.

The task facing CEOs looking to implement a vertical integration strategy through compensation policy is to determine what kinds of employee behavior they need to have for this strategy to create sustained competitive advantages and then to use the appropriate compensation policy. Not surprisingly, most CEOs find that all three explanations of vertical integration are important in their decision making. Thus, not surprisingly, many firms adopt compensation policies that feature a mix of the compensation policies listed in Table 6.1. Most firms use both individual and corporate-wide compensation schemes along with salaries, cash bonuses, stock grants, and stock options for employees who have the greatest impact on a firm's overall performance.

Summary

Vertical integration is defined as the number of stages in an industry's value chain that a firm has brought within its boundaries. Forward vertical integration brings a firm closer to its ultimate customer; backward vertical integration brings a firm closer to the sources of its raw materials. In making vertical integration decisions for a particular business activity, firms can choose to be not vertically integrated, somewhat vertically integrated, or vertically integrated.

Vertical integration can create value in three different ways: First, it can reduce opportunistic threats from a firm's buyers and suppliers due to transaction-specific investments the firm may have made. A transaction-specific investment is an investment that has more value in a particular exchange than in any alternative exchanges. Second, vertical integration can create value by enabling a firm to exploit its valuable, rare, and costly-to-imitate resources and capabilities. Firms should vertically integrate into activities in which they enjoy such advantages and should not vertically integrate into other activities. Third, vertical integration typically only creates value under conditions of low uncertainty. Under high uncertainty, vertical integration can commit a firm to a costly-to-reverse course of action and the flexibility of a non-vertically integrated approach may be preferred.

Often, all three approaches to vertical integration will generate similar conclusions. However, even when they suggest different vertical integration strategies, they can still be helpful to management.

The ability of valuable vertical integration strategies to generate a sustained competitive advantage depends on how rare and costly to imitate the strategies are. Vertical integration strategies can be rare in two ways: (1) when a firm is vertically integrated while most competing firms are not vertically integrated and (2) when a firm is not vertically integrated while most competing firms are. These rare vertical integration strategies are possible when firms vary in the extent to which the strategies they pursue require transaction-specific investments; they vary in the resources and capabilities they control; or they vary in the level of uncertainty they face.

The ability to directly duplicate a firm's vertical integration strategies depends on how costly it is to directly duplicate the resources and capabilities that enable a firm to pursue these strategies. The closest substitute for vertical integration—strategic alliances—is discussed in more detail in Chapter 9.

Organizing to implement vertical integration depends on a firm's organizational structure, its management controls, and its compensation policies. The organizational structure most commonly used to implement vertical integration is the functional, or U-form, organization, which involves cost leadership and product differentiation strategies. In a vertically integrated U-form organization, the CEO must focus not only on deciding which functions to vertically integrate into, but also on how to resolve conflicts that inevitably arise in a functionally organized vertically integrated firm. Two management controls that can be used to help implement vertical integration strategies and resolve these functional conflicts are the budgeting process and management oversight committees.

Each of the three explanations of vertical integration suggests different kinds of compensation policies that a firm looking to implement vertical integration should pursue. Opportunism-based explanations suggest individual-based compensation—including salaries and cash bonus and stock grants based on individual performance; capabilities-based explanations suggest group-based compensation—including cash bonuses and stock grants based on corporate or group performance; and flexibility-based explanations suggest flexible compensation—including stock options based on individual, group, or corporate performance. Because all three approaches to vertical integration are often operating in a firm, it is not surprising that many firms employ all these devices in compensating employees whose actions are likely to have a significant impact on firm performance.

MyManagementLab®

Go to **mymanagementlab.com** to complete the problems marked with this icon ⭐.

Challenge Questions

6.1. Some firms have engaged in backward vertical integration strategies in order to appropriate the economic profits that would have been earned by suppliers selling to them. How is this motivation for backward vertical integration related to the opportunism logic for vertical integration described in this chapter? (Hint: Compare the competitive conditions under which firms may earn economic profits to the competitive conditions under which firms will be motivated to avoid opportunism through vertical integration.)

6.2. You are about to purchase a used car. What kinds of threats do you face in this purchase?

6.3. You are about to purchase a used car. What can you do to protect yourself from the threats in this situation?

6.4. How is buying a car like and unlike vertical integration decisions?

⭐ **6.5.** What are the competitive implications for firms if they assume that all potential exchange partners cannot be trusted?

6.6. Common conflicts between sales and manufacturing are men-

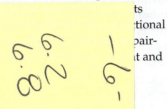

manufacturing; finance and manufacturing; marketing and sales; and accounting and everyone else?

⭐ **6.7.** What could a CEO do to help resolve the conflicts found between functional areas of the organization?

6.8. Under what conditions would you accept a lower-paying job over a higher-paying one?

6.9. What implications does your accepting a lower-paying job over a higher-paying one have for your potential employer's compensation policy?

Problem Set

6.10. Which of the following two firms is more vertically integrated? How can you tell?

(a) Firm A has included manufacturing, sales, finance, and human resources within its boundaries and has outsourced legal and customer service.
(b) Firm B has included manufacturing, sales, legal, and customer service within its boundaries and has outsourced finance and human resources.

6.11. What is the level of transaction-specific investment for each firm in the following transactions? Who in these transactions is at greater risk of being taken unfair advantage of?

(a) Firm I has built a plant right next door to Firm II. Firm I's plant is worth $5 million if it supplies Firm II. It is worth $200,000 if it does not supply Firm II. Firm II has three alternative suppliers. If it receives supplies from Firm I, it is worth $10 million. If it does not receive supplies from Firm I, it is worth $9.8 million.
(b) Firm A has just purchased a new computer system that is only available from Firm B. Firm A has redesigned its entire production process around this new computer system. The old production process is worth $1 million; the new process is worth $12 million. Firm B has several hundred customers for its new computer system.
(c) Firm Alpha, a fast-food restaurant company, has a contract with Firm Beta, a movie studio. After negotiating with several other potential partners, Firm Alpha agreed to a contract that requires Firm Alpha to pay Firm Beta $5 million per year for the right to use characters from Firm Beta's movies in its packaged meals for children. Demand for children's movies has recently dropped.

(d) Firm I owns and runs a printing press. Firm J uses the services of a printing press. Historically, Firm I has sold its services to many customers. However, it was recently approached by Firm J to become its exclusive supplier of printing-press services. Currently, Firm I is worth $1 million. If it became the sole supplier to Firm J, it would be worth $8 million. To complete this deal, Firm I would have to stop supplying its current customers and modify its machines to meet Firm J's needs. No other firm needs the same services as Firm J. Firm J contacted several other suppliers who said they would be willing to become a sole supplier for Firm J before deciding to propose this arrangement with Firm I.

6.12. In each of the following situations, would you recommend vertical integration or no vertical integration? Explain.

(a) Firm A needs a new and unique technology for its product line. No substitute technologies are available. Should Firm A make this technology or buy it?

(b) Firm I has been selling its products through a distributor for some time. It has become the market share leader. Unfortunately, this distributor has not been able to keep up with the evolving technology and customers are complaining. No alternative distributors are available. Should Firm I keep its current distributor, or should it begin distribution on its own?

(c) Firm Alpha has manufactured its own products for years. Recently, however, one of these products has become more and more like a commodity. Several firms are now able to manufacture this product at the same price and quality as Firm Alpha. However, they do not have Firm Alpha's brand name in the marketplace. Should Firm Alpha continue to manufacture this product, or should it outsource it to one of these other firms?

(d) Firm I is convinced that a certain class of technologies holds real economic potential. However, it does not know, for sure, which particular version of this technology is going to dominate the market. There are eight competing versions of this technology currently, but ultimately only one will dominate the market. Should Firm I invest in all eight of these technologies itself? Should it invest in just one of these technologies? Should it partner with other firms that are investing in these different technologies?

MyManagementLab®

Go to **mymanagementlab.com** for Auto-graded writing questions as well as the following Assisted-graded writing questions:

⭐ **6.13.** How can vertical integration create value by enabling a firm to retain its flexibility?

⭐ **6.14.** Describe how both direct duplication and substitution can be used to imitate another firm's valuable and rare vertical integration choices.

End Notes

1. Coase, R. (1937). "The nature of the firm." *Economica*, 4, pp. 386–405.
2. This explanation of vertical integration is known as transactions cost economics in the academic literature. See Williamson, O. (1975). *Markets and hierarchies: Analysis and antitrust implications.* New York: Free Press; Williamson, O. (1985). *The economic institutions of capitalism.*

New York: Free Press; and Klein, B., R. Crawford, and A. Alchian. (1978). "Vertical integration, appropriable rents, and the competitive contracting process." *Journal of Law and Economics*, 21, pp. 297–326.
3. Another option—forming an alliance between these two firms—is discussed in more detail in Chapter 9.

4. This explanation of vertical integration is known as the capabilities-based theory of the firm in the academic literature. It draws heavily from the resource-based view described in Chapter 3. See Barney, J. B. (1991). "Firm resources and sustained competitive advantage." *Journal of Management*, 17, pp. 99–120; Barney, J. B. (1999). "How a firm's capabilities affect boundary decisions." *Sloan Management Review*, 40(3); and Conner, K. R., and C. K. Prahalad. (1996). "A resource-based theory of the firm: Knowledge versus opportunism." *Organization Science*, 7, pp. 477–501.

5. This explanation of vertical integration is known as real-options theory in the academic literature. See Kogut, B. (1991). "Joint ventures and the option to expand and acquire." *Management Science*, 37, pp. 19–33.

6. Kripalani, M., and P. Engardio. (2003). "The rise of India." *BusinessWeek*, December 8, pp. 66+.

7. See Gupta, A. K. (1987). "SBU strategies, corporate-SBU relations and SBU effectiveness in strategy implementation." *Academy of Management Journal*, 30(3), pp. 477–500.

8. Becker, G. S. (1993). *Human capital: A theoretical and empirical analysis, with special reference to education.* Chicago: University of Chicago Press.

9. Barney, J. B. (1991). "Firm resources and sustained competitive advantage." *Journal of Management*, 17, pp. 99–120.

7 Corporate Diversification

LEARNING OBJECTIVES *After reading this chapter, you should be able to:*

1. Define corporate diversification and describe five types of corporate diversification.

2. Specify the two conditions that a corporate diversification strategy must meet in order to create economic value.

3. Define the concept of "economies of scope" and identify eight potential economies of scope a diversified firm might try to exploit.

4. Identify which of these economies of scope a firm's outside equity investors are able to realize on their own at low cost.

5. Specify the circumstances under which a firm's diversification strategy will be rare.

6. Indicate which of the economies of scope identified in this chapter are more likely to be subject to low-cost imitation and which are less likely to be subject to low-cost imitation.

7. Identify two potential substitutes for corporate diversification.

MyManagementLab®

⭐ **Improve Your Grade!**
Over 10 million students improved their results using the Pearson MyLabs.
Visit **mymanagementlab.com** for simulations, tutorials, and end-of-chapter problems.

The Worldwide Leader

The breadth of ESPN's diversification has even caught the attention of Hollywood writers. In the 2004 movie *Dodgeball: A True Underdog Story*, the championship game between the underdog Average Joes and the bad guy Purple Cobras is broadcast on the fictitious cable channel ESPN8. Also known as "the Ocho," ESPN8's theme is "If it's almost a sport, we've got it."

Here's the irony: ESPN has way more than eight networks currently in operation.

ESPN was founded in 1979 by Bill and Scott Rasmussen after the father and son duo was fired from positions with the New England Whalers, a National Hockey League team now playing in Raleigh, North Carolina. Their initial idea was to rent satellite space to broadcast sports from Connecticut—the University of Connecticut's basketball games, Whaler's hockey games, and so forth. But they found that it was cheaper to rent satellite space for 24 hours straight than to rent space a few hours during the week, and thus a 24-hour sports channel was born.

ESPN went on the air September 7, 1979. The first event broadcast was a slow-pitch softball game. Initially, the network broadcast sports that, at the time, were not widely known to U.S. consumers—Australian rules football, Davis Cup tennis, professional wrestling, minor league bowling. Early on, ESPN also gained the rights to broadcast early rounds of the NCAA basketball tournament. At the time, the major networks did not broadcast these early round games, even though we now know that some of these early games are among the most exciting in the entire tournament.

The longest-running ESPN program is, of course, *SportsCenter*. Although the first *SportsCenter* contained no highlights and a scheduled interview with the football coach at the University of

Colorado was interrupted by technical difficulties, *SportsCenter* and its familiar theme have become icons in American popular culture. The 50,000th episode of *SportsCenter* was broadcast on September 13, 2012.

ESPN was "admitted" into the world of big-time sports in 1987 when it signed with the National Football League to broadcast Sunday Night Football. Since then, ESPN has broadcast Major League Baseball, the National Basketball Association, and, at various times, the National Hockey League. These professional sports have been augmented by college football, basketball, and baseball games.

ESPN's first expansion was modest—in 1993, it introduced ESPN2. Originally, this station played nothing but rock music and scrolled sports scores. Within a few months, however, ESPN2 was broadcasting a full program of sports.

After this initial slow expansion, ESPN began to diversify its businesses rapidly. In 1996, it added ESPN News (an all-sports news channel); in 1997, it acquired a company and opened ESPN Classics (this channel shows old sporting events); and in 2005, it started ESPNU (a channel dedicated to college athletics).

However, these five ESPN channels represent only a fraction of ESPN's diverse business interests. In 1998, ESPN opened its first restaurant, the ESPN Zone. This chain has continued to expand around the world. Also, in 1998, it started a magazine to compete with the then-dominant *Sports Illustrated*. Called *ESPN The Magazine,* it now has more than 2 million subscribers. In 2001, ESPN went into the entertainment production business when it founded ESPN Original Entertainment. In 2005, ESPN started ESPN Deportes, a Spanish-language 24-hour sports channel. And, in 2006, it founded ESPN on ABC, a company that manages much of the sports content broadcast on ABC. (In 1984, ABC purchased ESPN. Subsequently, ABC was purchased by Capital Cities Entertainment, and most of Capital Cities Entertainment was then sold to Walt Disney Corporation. Currently, 80 percent of ESPN is owned by Disney.)

And none of this counts ESPN HD; ESPN2 HD; ESPN Pay Per View; ESPN3; ESPN Films; ESPN Plus; ESPN America; The Longhorn Network; the SEC Network; the ESPN Web site; city-based ESPN Web sites in Boston, New York, Chicago, and Los Angeles; ESPN Radio; and ESPN's retail operations on the Web—ESPN.com. In addition, ESPN owns 27 international sports networks that reach 190 countries in 11 languages.

Of all the expansion and diversification efforts, so far ESPN has only stumbled once. In 2006, it founded Mobile ESPN, a mobile telephone service. Not only would this service provide its customers mobile telephone service, it would also provide them up-to-the-minute scoring updates and a variety of other sports information. ESPN spent more than $40 million advertising its new service and more than $150 million on the technology required to make this service available. Unfortunately, it never signed up more than 30,000 subscribers. The breakeven point was estimated to be 500,000 subscribers.

Also, all of ESPN's success hasn't gone unnoticed by other broadcasters. Recently, NBC entered the 24-hour sports channel market with NBCSN. CBS also entered this market with the CBS Sports channel.

Despite these challenges, ESPN has emerged from being that odd little cable channel that broadcast odd little games to a multibillion-dollar company with operations around the world in cable and broadcast television, radio, restaurants, magazines, books, and movie and television production. Which of those numerous enterprises could be characterized as "the Ocho" is hard to tell.

Sources: T. Lowry (2006). "ESPN's cell-phone fumble." *BusinessWeek*, October 30, pp. 26+; en.wikipedia.org/wiki/ESPN accessed September 15, 2013; AP Wide World Photos.

ESPN is like most large firms in the United States and the world: It has diversified operations. Indeed, virtually all of the 500 largest firms in the United States and the 500 largest firms in the world are diversified, either by product or geographically. Large single-business firms are very unusual. However, like most of these large diversified firms, ESPN has diversified along some dimensions but not others.

What Is Corporate Diversification?

A firm implements a **corporate diversification strategy** when it operates in multiple industries or markets simultaneously. When a firm operates in multiple industries simultaneously, it is said to be implementing a **product diversification strategy**. When a firm operates in multiple geographic markets simultaneously, it is said to be implementing a **geographic market diversification strategy**. When a firm implements both types of diversification simultaneously, it is said to be implementing a **product-market diversification strategy**.

We have already seen glimpses of these diversification strategies in the discussion of vertical integration strategies in Chapter 6. Sometimes, when a firm vertically integrates backward or forward, it begins operations in a new product or geographic market. This happened to computer software firms when they began manning their own call centers. These firms moved from the "computer software development" business to the "call-center management" business when they vertically integrated forward. In this sense, when firms vertically integrate, they may also be implementing a diversification strategy. However, the critical difference between the diversification strategies studied here and vertical integration (discussed in Chapter 6) is that in this chapter product-market diversification is the primary objective of these strategies, whereas in Chapter 6 such diversification was often a secondary consequence of pursuing a vertical integration strategy.

Types of Corporate Diversification

Firms vary in the extent to which they have diversified the mix of businesses they pursue. Perhaps the simplest way of characterizing differences in the level of corporate diversification focuses on the relatedness of the businesses pursued by a firm. As shown in Figure 7.1, firms can pursue a strategy of **limited corporate diversification**, of **related corporate diversification**, or of **unrelated corporate diversification**.

Figure 7.1 Levels and Types of Diversification

Limited Corporate Diversification

A firm has implemented a strategy of **limited corporate diversification** when all or most of its business activities fall within a single industry and geographic market (see Panel A of Figure 7.1). Two kinds of firms are included in this corporate diversification category: **single-business firms** (firms with greater than 95 percent of their total sales in a single-product market) and **dominant-business firms** (firms with between 70 and 95 percent of their total sales in a single-product market).

Differences between single-business and dominant-business firms are represented in Panel A of Figure 7.1. The firm pursuing a single-business corporate diversification strategy engages in only one business, Business A. An example of a single-business firm is the WD-40 Company of San Diego, California. This company manufactures and distributes only one product: the spray cleanser and lubricant WD-40. The dominant-business firm pursues two businesses, Business E and a smaller Business F that is tightly linked to Business E. An example of a dominant-business firm is Donato's Pizza. Donato's Pizza does the vast majority of its business in a single product—pizza—in a single market—the United States. However, Donato's has begun selling non-pizza food products, including sandwiches, and also owns a subsidiary that makes a machine that automatically slices and puts pepperoni on pizzas. Not only does Donato's use this machine in its own pizzerias, it also sells this machine to food manufacturers that make frozen pepperoni pizza.

In an important sense, firms pursuing a strategy of limited corporate diversification are not leveraging their resources and capabilities beyond a single product or market. Thus, the analysis of limited corporate diversification is logically equivalent to the analysis of business-level strategies (discussed in Part 2 of this book). Because these kinds of strategies have already been discussed, the remainder of this chapter focuses on corporate strategies that involve higher levels of diversification.

Related Corporate Diversification

As a firm begins to engage in businesses in more than one product or market, it moves away from being a single-business or dominant-business firm and begins to adopt higher levels of corporate diversification. When less than 70 percent of a firm's revenue comes from a single-product market and these multiple lines of business are linked, the firm has implemented a strategy of **related corporate diversification**.

The multiple businesses that a diversified firm pursues can be related in two ways (see Panel B in Figure 7.1). If all the businesses in which a firm operates share a significant number of inputs, production technologies, distribution channels, similar customers, and so forth, this corporate diversification strategy is called **related-constrained.** This strategy is *constrained* because corporate managers pursue business opportunities in new markets or industries only if those markets or industries share numerous resource and capability requirements with the businesses the firm is currently pursuing. Commonalities across businesses in a strategy of related-constrained diversification are represented by the linkages among Businesses K, L, M, and N in the related-constrained section of Figure 7.1.

PepsiCo is an example of a related-constrained diversified firm. Although PepsiCo operates in multiple businesses around the world, all of its businesses focus on providing snack-type products, either food or beverages. PepsiCo is not in the business of making or selling more traditional types of food—such as pasta or cheese or breakfast cereal. Moreover, PepsiCo attempts to use a single, firm-wide capability to gain competitive advantages in each of its businesses—its ability to develop and exploit well-known brand names. Whether it's Pepsi, Doritos, Mountain Dew, or Big Red, PepsiCo is all about building brand names. In fact, PepsiCo has 16 brands that generate well over $1 billion or more in revenues each year.[1]

If the different businesses that a single firm pursues are linked on only a couple of dimensions or if different sets of businesses are linked along very different dimensions, the corporate diversification strategy is called **related-linked**. For example, Business Q and Business R may share similar production technology, Business R and Business S may share similar customers, Business S and Business T may share similar suppliers, and Business Q and Business T may have no common attributes. This strategy is represented in the related-linked section of Figure 7.1 by businesses with relatively few links between them and with different kinds of links between them (i.e., straight lines and curved lines).

An example of a related-linked diversified firm is Disney. Disney has evolved from a single-business firm (when it did nothing but produce animated motion pictures), to a dominant business firm (when it produced family-oriented motion pictures and operated a theme park), to a related-constrained diversified firm (when it produced family-oriented motion pictures, operated multiple theme parks, and sold products through its Disney Stores). Recently, it has become so diversified that it has taken on the attributes of related-linked diversification. Although much of the Disney empire still builds on characters developed in its animated motion pictures, it also owns and operates businesses—including several hotels and resorts that have little or nothing to do with Disney characters and a television network (ABC) that broadcasts non-Disney-produced content—that are less directly linked to these characters. This is not to suggest that Disney is pursuing an unrelated diversification strategy. After all, most of its businesses are in the entertainment industry, broadly defined. Rather, this is only to suggest that it is no longer possible to find a single thread—like a Mickey Mouse or a Lion King—that connects all of Disney's business enterprises. In this sense, Disney has become a related-linked diversified firm.[2]

Unrelated Corporate Diversification

Firms that pursue a strategy of related corporate diversification have some type of linkages among most, if not all, the different businesses they pursue. However, it is possible for firms to pursue numerous different businesses and for there to be *no* linkages among them (see Panel C of Figure 7.1). When less than 70 percent of a firm's revenues is generated in a single-product market and when a firm's businesses share few, if any, common attributes, then that firm is pursuing a strategy of **unrelated corporate diversification**.

General Electric (GE) is an example of a firm pursuing an unrelated diversification strategy. GE's mix of businesses includes appliances for business, aviation, capital, critical power, energy management, health care, industrial solutions, intelligent platforms, lighting, mining, oil and gas, power and water, software, and transportation. It is difficult to see how these businesses are closely related to each other. Indeed, GE tends to manage each of its businesses as if they were stand-alone entities—a management approach consistent with a firm implementing an unrelated diversified corporate strategy.[3]

The Value of Corporate Diversification

For corporate diversification to be economically valuable, two conditions must hold. First, there must be some valuable economy of scope among the multiple businesses in which a firm is operating. Second, it must be less costly for managers in a firm to realize these economies of scope than for outside equity holders on their own. If outside investors could realize the value of a particular economy of scope on their own and at low cost, then they would have few incentives to "hire" managers to realize this economy of scope for them. Each of these requirements for corporate diversification to add value for a firm will be considered below.

What Are Valuable Economies of Scope?

Economies of scope exist in a firm when the value of the products or services it sells increases as a function of the number of businesses in which that firm operates. In this definition, the term *scope* refers to the range of businesses in which a diversified firm operates. For this reason, only diversified firms can, by definition, exploit economies of scope. Economies of scope are valuable to the extent that they increase a firm's revenues or decrease its costs, compared with what would be the case if these economies of scope were not exploited.

A wide variety of potentially valuable sources of economies of scope have been identified in the literature. Some of the most important of these are listed in Table 7.1 and discussed in the following text. How valuable economies of scope actually are, on average, has been the subject of a great deal of research, which we summarize in the Research Made Relevant feature.

Diversification to Exploit Operational Economies of Scope

Sometimes, economies of scope may reflect operational links among the businesses in which a firm engages. **Operational economies of scope** typically take one of two forms: shared activities and shared core competencies.

Shared Activities.   In Chapter 3, it was suggested that value-chain analysis can be used to describe the specific business activities of a firm. This same value-chain

TABLE 7.1 Different Types of Economies of Scope

1. Operational economies of scope
   - Shared activities
   - Core competencies
2. Financial economies of scope
   - Internal capital allocation
   - Risk reduction
   - Tax advantages
3. Anticompetitive economies of scope
   - Multipoint competition
   - Exploiting market power
4. Employee and stakeholder incentives for diversification
   - Maximizing management compensation

Research Made Relevant

In 1994, Lang and Stulz published a sensational article that suggested that, on average, when a firm began implementing a corporate diversification strategy, it destroyed about 25 percent of its market value. Lang and Stulz came to this conclusion by comparing the market performance of firms pursuing a corporate diversification strategy with portfolios of firms pursuing a limited diversification strategy. Taken together, the market performance of a portfolio of firms that were pursuing a limited diversification strategy was about 25 percent higher than the market performance of a single diversified firm operating in all of the businesses included in this portfolio. These results suggested that not only were economies of scope not valuable, but, on average, efforts to realize these economies actually destroyed economic value. Similar results were published by Comment and Jarrell using different measures of firm performance.

How Valuable Are Economies of Scope, on Average?

Not surprisingly, these results generated quite a stir. If Lang and Stulz were correct, then diversified firms—no matter what kind of diversification strategy they engaged in—destroyed an enormous amount of economic value. This could lead to a fundamental restructuring of the U.S. economy.

However, several researchers questioned Lang and Stulz's conclusions. Two new findings suggest that, even if there is a 25 percent discount, diversification can still add value. First, Villalonga and others found that firms pursuing diversification strategies were generally performing more poorly before they began diversifying than firms that never pursued diversification strategies. Thus, although it might appear that diversification leads to a significant loss of economic value, in reality that loss of value occurred before these firms began implementing a diversification strategy. Indeed, some more recent research suggests that these relatively poor-performing firms may actually increase their market value over what would have been the case if they did not diversify.

Second, Miller found that firms that find it in their self-interest to diversify do so in a very predictable pattern. These firms tend to diversify analysis can also be used to describe the business activities that may be shared across several different businesses within a diversified firm. These **shared activities** are potential sources of operational economies of scope for diversified firms.

Consider, for example, the hypothetical firm presented in Figure 7.2. This diversified firm engages in three businesses: A, B, and C. However, these three businesses share a variety of activities throughout their value chains. For example, all three draw on the same technology development operation. Product design and manufacturing are shared in Businesses A and B and separate for Business C. All three businesses share a common marketing and service operation. Business A has its own distribution system.

These kinds of shared activities are quite common among both related-constrained and related-linked diversified firms. At Texas Instruments, for example, a variety of electronics businesses share some research and development activities and many share common manufacturing locations. Procter & Gamble's numerous consumer products businesses often share common manufacturing locations and rely on a common distribution network (through retail grocery stores).[4] Some of the most common shared activities in diversified firms and their location in the value chain are summarized in Table 7.2.

into the most profitable new business first, the second-most profitable business second, and so forth. Not surprisingly, the fiftieth diversification move made by these firms might not generate huge additional profits. However, these profits—it turns out—are still, on average, positive. Because multiple rounds of diversification increase profits at a decreasing rate, the overall average profitability of diversified firms will generally be less than the overall average profitability of firms that do not pursue a diversification strategy—thus, a substantial difference between the market value of non-diversified and diversified firms might exist. However, this discount, per se, does not mean that the diversified firm is destroying economic value. Rather, it may mean only that a diversifying firm is creating value in smaller increments as it continues to diversify.

However, more recent research suggests that Lang and Stulz's original "diversification discount" finding may be reemerging. It turns out that all the papers that show that diversification does not, on average, destroy value, and that it sometimes can add value, fail to consider all the investment options open to firms. In particular, firms that are generating free cash flow but have limited growth opportunities in their current businesses—that is, the kinds of firms that Villalonga and Miller suggest will create value through diversification—have other investment options besides diversification. In particular, these firms can return their free cash to their equity holders, either through a direct cash dividend or through buying back stock.

Mackey and Barney show that firms that do not pay out to shareholders destroy value compared with firms that do pay out. In particular, firms that use their free cash flow to pay dividends and buy back stock create value; firms that pay out and diversify destroy some value; and firms that just diversify destroy significant value.

Of course, these results are "on average." It is possible to identify firms that actually create value from diversification—about 17 percent of diversified firms in the United States create value from diversification. What distinguishes firms that destroy and create value from diversification is likely to be the subject of research for some time to come.

Sources: H. P. Lang and R. M. Stulz (1994). "Tobin's q, corporate diversification, and firm performance." *Journal of Political Economy*, 102, pp. 1248–1280; R. Comment and G. Jarrell (1995). "Corporate focus and stock returns." *Journal of Financial Economics*, 37, pp. 67–87; D. Miller (2006). "Technological diversity, related diversification, and firm performance." *Strategic Management Journal*, 27(7), pp. 601–620; B. Villalonga (2004). "Does diversification cause the 'diversification discount'?" *Financial Management*, 33(2), pp. 5–28; T. Mackey and J. Barney (2013). "Incorporating opportunity costs in strategic management research: The value of diversification and payout as opportunities forgone when reinvesting in the firm." *Strategic Organization*, online, May 8 2013.

Figure 7.2   A Hypothetical
Firm Sharing Activities Among
Three Businesses

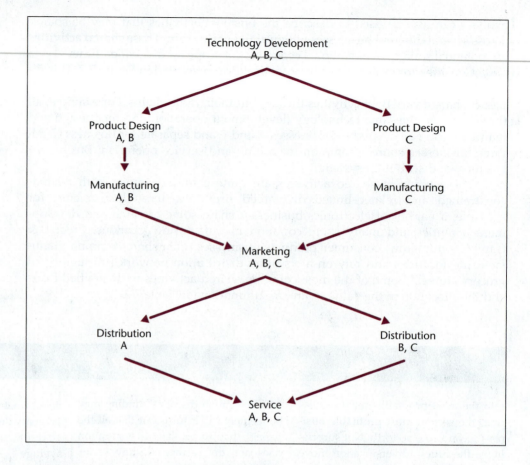

Many of the shared activities listed in Table 7.2 can have the effect of reducing a diversified firm's costs. For example, if a diversified firm has a purchasing function that is common to several of its different businesses, it can often obtain volume discounts on its purchases that would otherwise not be possible. Also, by manufacturing products that are used as inputs into several of a diversified firm's businesses, the total costs of producing these products can be reduced. A single sales force representing the products or services of several different businesses within a diversified firm can reduce the cost of selling these products or services. Firms such as IBM, HP, and General Motors (GM) have all used shared activities to reduce their costs in these ways.

Failure to exploit shared activities across businesses can lead to out-of-control costs. For example, Kentucky Fried Chicken, when it was a division of PepsiCo, encouraged each of its regional business operations in North America to develop its own quality improvement plan. The result was enormous redundancy and at least three conflicting quality efforts—all leading to higher-than-necessary costs. In a similar way, Levi Strauss's unwillingness to centralize and coordinate order processing led to a situation where six separate order-processing computer systems operated simultaneously. This costly redundancy was ultimately replaced by a single, integrated ordering system shared across the entire corporation.[5]

Shared activities can also increase the revenues in diversified firms' businesses. This can happen in at least two ways. First, it may be that shared product development and sales activities may enable two or more businesses in a

TABLE 7.2 Possible Shared Activities and Their Place in the Value Chain

Value Chain Activity	Shared Activities
Input activities	Common purchasing
	Common inventory control system
	Common warehousing facilities
	Common inventory delivery system
	Common quality assurance
	Common input requirements system
	Common suppliers
Production activities	Common product components
	Common product components manufacturing
	Common assembly facilities
	Common quality control system
	Common maintenance operation
	Common inventory control system
Warehousing and distribution	Common product delivery system
	Common warehouse facilities
Sales and marketing	Common advertising efforts
	Common promotional activities
	Cross-selling of products
	Common pricing systems
	Common marketing departments
	Common distribution channels
	Common sales forces
	Common sales offices
	Common order processing services
Dealer support and service	Common service network
	Common guarantees and warranties
	Common accounts receivable management systems
	Common dealer training
	Common dealer support services

Sources: M. E. Porter (1985). *Competitive advantage.* New York: Free Press; R. P. Rumelt (1974). *Strategy, structure, and economic performance.* Cambridge, MA: Harvard University Press; H. I. Ansoff (1965). *Corporate strategy.* New York: McGraw-Hill.

diversified firm to offer a bundled set of products to customers. Sometimes, the value of these "product bundles" is greater than the value of each product separately. This additional customer value can generate revenues greater than would have been the case if the businesses were not together and sharing activities in a diversified firm.

In the telecommunications industry, for example, separate firms sell telephones, access to telephone lines, equipment to route calls in an office, mobile telephones, and paging services. A customer that requires all these services could contact five different companies. Each of these five different firms would likely possess its own unique technological standards and software, making the development of an integrated telecommunications system for the customer difficult at best. Alternatively, a single diversified firm sharing sales activities across these businesses could significantly reduce the search costs of potential customers. This one-stop shopping is likely to be valuable to customers, who might be willing to pay a slightly higher price for this convenience than they would pay if they purchased these services from five separate firms. Moreover, if this diversified firm also shares some technology development activities across its businesses, it might be able to offer an integrated telecommunications network to potential customers. The extra value of this integrated network for customers is very likely to be reflected in prices that are higher than would have been possible if each of these businesses were independent or if activities among these businesses were not shared. Most of the regional telephone operating companies in the United States are attempting to gain these economies of scope.[6]

Such product bundles are important in other firms as well. Many grocery stores now sell prepared foods alongside traditional grocery products in the belief that busy customers want access to all kinds of food products—in the same location.[7]

Second, shared activities can enhance business revenues by exploiting the strong, positive reputations of some of a firm's businesses in other of its businesses. For example, if one business has a strong positive reputation for high-quality manufacturing, other businesses sharing this manufacturing activity will gain some of the advantages of this reputation. And, if one business has a strong positive reputation for selling high-performance products, other businesses sharing sales and marketing activities with this business will gain some of the advantages of this reputation. In both cases, businesses that draw on the strong reputation of another business through shared activities with that business will have larger revenues than they would were they operating on their own.

The Limits of Activity Sharing.   Despite the potential of activity sharing to be the basis of a valuable corporate diversification strategy, this approach has three important limits.[8] First, substantial organizational issues are often associated with a diversified firm's learning how to manage cross-business relationships. Managing these relationships effectively can be very difficult, and failure can lead to excess bureaucracy, inefficiency, and organizational gridlock. These issues are discussed in detail in Chapter 8.

Second, sharing activities may limit the ability of a particular business to meet its specific customers' needs. For example, if two businesses share manufacturing activities, they may reduce their manufacturing costs. However, to gain these cost advantages, these businesses may need to build products using somewhat standardized components that do not fully meet their individual customers' needs. Businesses that share distribution activities may have lower overall distribution costs but be unable to distribute their products to all their customers. Businesses that share sales activities may have lower overall sales costs but be unable to provide the specialized selling required in each business.

One diversified firm that has struggled with the ability to meet the specialized needs of customers in its different divisions is GM. To exploit economies of scope in the design of new automobiles, GM shared the design process across several automobile divisions. The result through much of the 1990s was "cookie-cutter" cars—the traditional distinctiveness of several GM divisions, including Oldsmobile and Cadillac, was all but lost.[9]

Third, if one business in a diversified firm has a poor reputation, sharing activities with that business can reduce the quality of the reputation of other businesses in the firm.

Taken together, these limits on activity sharing can more than offset any possible gains. Indeed, over the past decade more and more diversified firms have been abandoning efforts at activity sharing in favor of managing each business's activities independently. For example, ABB, Inc. (a Swiss engineering firm) and CIBA-Geigy (a Swiss chemicals firm) have adopted explicit corporate policies that restrict almost all activity sharing across businesses.[10] Other diversified firms, including Nestlé and GE, restrict activity sharing to just one or two activities (such as research and development or management training). However, to the extent that a diversified firm can exploit shared activities while avoiding these problems, shared activities can add value to a firm.

Core Competencies.   Recently, a second operational linkage among the businesses of a diversified firm has been described. Unlike shared activities, this linkage is based on different businesses in a diversified firm sharing less tangible resources such as managerial and technical know-how, experience, and wisdom. This source of operational economy of scope has been called a firm's core competence.[11] **Core competence** has been defined by Prahalad and Hamel as "the collective learning in the organization, especially how to coordinate diverse production skills and integrate multiple streams of technologies." Core competencies are complex sets of resources and capabilities that link different businesses in a diversified firm through managerial and technical know-how, experience, and wisdom.[12]

Two firms that have well-developed core competencies are 3M and Johnson & Johnson (J&J). 3M has a core competence in substrates, adhesives, and coatings. Collectively, employees at 3M know more about developing and applying adhesives and coatings on different kinds of substrates than do employees in any other organization. Over the years, 3M has applied these resources and capabilities in a wide variety of products, including Post-it notes, magnetic tape, photographic film, pressure-sensitive tape, and coated abrasives. At first glance, these widely diversified products seem to have little or nothing in common. Yet they all draw on a single core set of resources and capabilities in substrates, adhesives, and coatings.

Johnson & Johnson has a core competence in developing or acquiring pharmaceutical and medical products and then marketing them to the public. Many of J&J's products are dominant in their market segments—J&J's in baby powder, Ethicon in surgical sutures, and Tylenol in pain relievers. And although these products range broadly from those sold directly to consumers (e.g., the Band-Aid brand of adhesive bandages) to highly sophisticated medical technologies sold only to doctors and hospitals (e.g., Ethicon sutures), all of J&J's products build on the same ability to identify, develop, acquire, and market products in the pharmaceutical and medical products industry.

To understand how core competencies can reduce a firm's costs or increase its revenues, consider how core competencies emerge over time. Most firms begin operations in a single business. Imagine that a firm has carefully evaluated all of its current business opportunities and has fully funded all of those with a positive net present value. Any of the above-normal returns that this firm has left over after fully funding all its current positive net present value opportunities can be thought of as **free cash flow**.[13] Firms can spend this free cash in a variety of ways: They can spend it on benefits for managers; they can give it to shareholders through dividends or by buying back a firm's stock; they can use it to invest in new businesses.

Suppose a firm chooses to use this cash to invest in a new business. In other words, suppose this firm chooses to implement a diversification strategy. If this firm is seeking to maximize the return from implementing this diversification strategy, which of all the possible businesses that it could invest in should it invest in? Obviously, a profit-maximizing firm will choose to begin operations in a business in which it has a competitive advantage. What kind of business is likely to generate this competitive advantage for this firm? The obvious answer is a business in which the same underlying resources and capabilities that gave this firm an advantage in its original business are still valuable, rare, and costly to imitate. Consequently, this first diversification move sees the firm investing in a business that is closely related to its original business because both businesses will draw on a common set of underlying resources and capabilities that provide the firm with a competitive advantage.

Put another way, a firm that diversifies by exploiting its resource and capability advantages in its original business will have lower costs than those that begin a new business without these resource and capability advantages, or higher revenues than firms lacking these advantages, or both. As long as this firm organizes itself to take advantage of these resource and capability advantages in its new business, it should earn high profits in its new business, along with the profits it will still be earning in its original business.[14] This can be true for even relatively small firms, as described in the Strategy in the Emerging Enterprise feature.

Of course, over time this diversified firm is likely to develop new resources and capabilities through its operations in the new business. These new resources and capabilities enhance the entire set of skills that a firm might be able to bring to still another business. Using the profits it has obtained in its previous businesses, this firm is likely to enter another new business. Again, choosing from among all the new businesses it could enter, it is likely to begin operations in a business in which it can exploit its now-expanded resource and capability advantages to obtain a competitive advantage, and so forth.

After a firm has engaged in this diversification strategy several times, the resources and capabilities that enable it to operate successfully in several businesses become its core competencies. A firm develops these core competencies by transferring the technical and management knowledge, experience, and wisdom it developed in earlier businesses to its new businesses. A firm that has just begun this diversification process has implemented a dominant-business strategy. If all of a firm's businesses share the same core competencies, then that firm has implemented a strategy of related-constrained diversification. If different businesses exploit different sets of resources and capabilities, that firm has implemented a strategy of related-linked diversification. In any case, these core competencies enable firms to have lower costs or higher revenues as they include more businesses in their diversified portfolio, compared with firms without these competencies.

Of course, not all firms develop core competencies in this logical and rational manner. That is, sometimes a firm's core competencies are examples of the emergent strategies described in Chapter 1. Indeed, as described in Chapter 1, J&J is an example of a firm that has a core competence that emerged over time. However, no matter how a firm develops core competencies, to the extent that they enable a diversified firm to have lower costs or larger revenues in its business operations, these competencies can be thought of as sources of economies of scope.

Strategy in the Emerging Enterprise

W. L. Gore & Associates is best known for manufacturing a waterproof and windproof, but breathable, fabric that is used to insulate winter coats, hiking boots, and a myriad of other outdoor apparel products. This fabric—known as Gore-Tex—has a brand name in its market niche every bit as strong as any of the brand names controlled by PepsiCo or Procter & Gamble. The "Gore-Tex" label attached to any outdoor garment promises waterproof comfort in even the harshest conditions.

But W. L. Gore & Associates did not start out in the outdoor fabric business. Indeed, for the first 10 years of its existence, W. L. Gore sold insulation for wires and similar industrial products using a molecular technology originally developed by DuPont—a technology most of us know as Teflon. Only 10 years after its initial founding did the founder's son, Bob Gore, discover that it was possible to stretch the Teflon molecule to form a strong and porous material that is chemically inert, has a low friction coefficient, functions within a wide temperature range, does not age, and is extremely strong. This is the material called Gore-Tex.

Gore-Tex and Guitar Strings

By extending its basic technology, W. L. Gore and Associates has been able to diversify well beyond its original wire insulation business. With more than 8,000 employees and more than $2 billion in revenues, the company currently has operations in medical products (including synthetic blood vessels and patches for soft tissue regeneration), electronics products (including wiring board materials and computer chip components), industrial products (including filter bags for environmental protection and sealants for chemical manufacturing), and fabrics (including Gore-Tex fabric, Wind-Stopper fabric, and CleanStream filters).

And Gore continues to discover new ways to exploit its competence in the Teflon molecule. In 1997, a team of Gore engineers developed a cable made out of the Teflon molecule to control puppets at Disney's theme parks. Unfortunately, these cables did not perform up to expectations and were not sold to Disney. However, some guitar players discovered these cables and began using them as strings for their guitars. They found out that these "Gore-Tex" strings sounded great and lasted five times as long as alternative guitar strings. So Gore entered yet another market—the $100 million fretted-stringed-instrument business—with its Elixir brand of guitar strings. Currently, W. L. Gore is the second-largest manufacturer in this market.

The flexibility of the Teflon molecule—and W. L. Gore's ability to explore and exploit that flexibility—has created a diversified company whose original objective was simply to sell insulation for wires.

Sources: www.gore.com accessed July 15, 2012; D. Sacks (2003). "The Gore-Tex of guitar strings." *Fast Times*, December, p. 46.

Some diversified firms realize the value of these kinds of core competencies through shared activities. For example, as suggested earlier, 3M has a core competence in substrates, adhesives, and coatings. To exploit this, 3M has adopted a multitiered product innovation process. In addition to product innovations within each business unit separately, 3M also supports a corporate research and development lab that seeks to exploit and expand its core competence in substrates, adhesives, and coatings. Because the corporate research and development laboratory is shared by all of 3M's different businesses, it can be thought of as a shared activity.

However, other firms realize the value of their core competencies without shared activities. Although J&J has a core competence in developing, acquiring, and marketing pharmaceutical and medical products, it does not realize this core competence through shared activities. Indeed, each of J&J's businesses is run very independently. For example, although one of its most successful products is Tylenol, the fact that the company that manufactures and distributes Tylenol—McNeil—is actually a division of J&J and is not printed on any Tylenol packaging. If you did not know that Tylenol was a J&J product, you could not tell from the bottles of Tylenol you buy.

Although J&J does not use shared activities to realize the value of its core competencies, it does engage in other activities to realize this value. For example, it is not uncommon for members of the senior management team of each of the businesses in J&J's portfolio to have obtained managerial experience in some other J&J business. That is, J&J identifies high-potential managers in one of its businesses and uses this knowledge by giving these managers additional responsibilities in another J&J business. This ability to leverage its management talent across multiple businesses is an example of a firm's core competence, although the realization of the value of that competence does not depend on the existence of a shared activity.

Sometimes, because a firm's core competence is not reflected in specific shared activities, it is easy to conclude that it is not exploiting any economies of scope in its diversification strategy. Diversified firms that are exploiting core competencies as an economy of scope but are not doing so with any shared activities are sometimes called **seemingly unrelated diversified firms**. They may appear to be unrelated diversified firms but are, in fact, related diversified firms without any shared activities.

One example of a seemingly unrelated diversified firm is the British company Virgin Group. Operating in a wide variety of businesses—everything from record producing, music retailing, air and rail travel, soft drinks, spirits, mobile phones, cosmetics, retail bridal shops, financial services, and providing gas and electricity to hot air ballooning—the Virgin Group is clearly diversified. The firm has few, if any, shared activities. However, at least two core competencies cut across all the business activities in the group—the brand name "Virgin" and the eccentric marketing and management approach of Virgin's founder, Richard Branson. Branson is the CEO who walked down a "catwalk" in a wedding gown to help publicize the opening of Virgin Brides—the Virgin Group's line of retail bridal shops. Branson is also the CEO who had all of Virgin Air's airplanes repainted with the British "Union Jack" and the slogan "Britain's Real Airline" when British Airways eliminated the British flag from its airplanes. Whether these two core competencies create sufficient value to justify the Virgin Group's continued existence and whether they will continue beyond Branson's affiliation with the group are still open questions.

Limits of Core Competencies.   Just as there are limits to the value of shared activities as sources of economies of scope, so there are limits to core competencies as sources of these economies. The first of these limitations stems from important organizational issues to be discussed in Chapter 8. The way that a diversified firm is organized can either facilitate the exploitation of core competencies or prevent this exploitation from occurring.

A second limitation of core competencies is a result of the intangible nature of these economies of scope. Whereas shared activities are reflected in tangible operations in a diversified firm, core competencies may be reflected only in shared knowledge, experience, and wisdom across businesses. The intangible character of these relationships is emphasized when they are described as a **dominant logic** in a firm, or a common way of thinking about strategy across different businesses.[15]

The intangibility of core competencies can lead diversified firms to make two kinds of errors in managing relatedness. First, intangible core competencies can be illusory inventions by creative managers who link even the most completely unrelated businesses and thereby justify their diversification strategy. A firm that manufactures airplanes and running shoes can rationalize this diversification by claiming to have a core competence in managing transportation businesses. A firm operating in the professional football business and the movie business can rationalize this diversification by claiming to have a core competence in managing entertainment businesses. Such **invented competencies** are not real sources of economies of scope.

Second, a diversified firm's businesses may be linked by a core competence, but this competence may affect these businesses' costs or revenues in a trivial way. Thus, for example, all of a firm's businesses may be affected by government actions, but the impact of these actions on costs and revenues in different businesses may be quite small. A firm may have a core competence in managing relationships with the government, but this core competence will not reduce costs or enhance revenues for these particular businesses very much. Also, each of a diversified firm's businesses may use some advertising. However, if advertising does not have a major impact on revenues for these businesses, core competencies in advertising are not likely to significantly reduce a firm's costs or increase its revenues. In this case, a core competence may be a source of economies of scope, but the value of those economies may be very small.

Diversification to Exploit Financial Economies of Scope

A second class of motivations for diversification shifts attention away from operational linkages among a firm's businesses and toward financial advantages associated with diversification. Three financial implications of diversification have been studied: diversification and capital allocation, diversification and risk reduction, and tax advantages of diversification.

Diversification and Capital Allocation.   Capital can be allocated to businesses in one of two ways. First, businesses operating as independent entities can compete for capital in the external capital market. They do this by providing a sufficiently high return to induce investors to purchase shares of their equity, by having a sufficiently high cash flow to repay principal and interest on debt, and in other ways. Alternatively, a business can be part of a diversified firm. That diversified firm competes in the external capital market and allocates capital among its various businesses. In a sense, diversification creates an **internal capital market** in which businesses in a diversified firm compete for corporate capital.[16]

For an internal capital market to create value for a diversified firm, it must offer some efficiency advantages over an external capital market. It has been suggested that a potential efficiency gain from internal capital markets depends on the greater amount and quality of information that a diversified firm possesses about the businesses it owns, compared with the information that external suppliers of capital possess. Owning a business gives a diversified firm access to detailed and accurate information about the actual performance of the business, its true future prospects, and thus the actual amount and cost of the capital that should be allocated to it. External sources of capital, in contrast, have relatively limited access to information and thus have a limited ability to judge the actual performance and future prospects of a business.

Some have questioned whether a diversified firm, as a source of capital, actually has more and better information about a business it owns, compared with external sources of capital. After all, independent businesses seeking capital have a strong incentive to provide sufficient information to external suppliers of capital to obtain required funds. However, a firm that owns a business may have at least two informational advantages over external sources of capital.

First, although an independent business has an incentive to provide information to external sources of capital, it also has an incentive to downplay or even not report any negative information about its performance and prospects. Such negative information would raise an independent firm's cost of capital. External sources of capital have limited ability to force a business to reveal all information about its performance and prospects and thus may provide capital at a lower cost than they would if they had full information. Ownership gives a firm the right to compel more complete disclosure, although even here full disclosure is not guaranteed. With this more complete information, a diversified firm can allocate just the right amount of capital, at the appropriate cost, to each business.

Second, an independent business may have an incentive not to reveal all the positive information about its performance and prospects. In Chapter 3, the ability of a firm to earn economic profits was shown to depend on the imitability of its resources and capabilities. An independent business that informs external sources of capital about all of its sources of competitive advantage is also informing its potential competitors about these sources of advantage. This information sharing increases the probability that these sources of advantage will be imitated. Because of the competitive implications of sharing this information, firms may choose not to share it, and external sources of capital may underestimate the true performance and prospects of a business.

A diversified firm, however, may gain access to this additional information about its businesses without revealing it to potential competitors. This information enables the diversified firm to make more informed decisions about how much capital to allocate to a business and about the cost of that capital, compared with the external capital market.[17]

Over time, there should be fewer errors in funding businesses through internal capital markets, compared with funding businesses through external capital markets. Fewer funding errors, over time, suggest a slight capital allocation advantage for a diversified firm, compared with an external capital market. This advantage should be reflected in somewhat higher rates of return on invested capital for the diversified firm, compared with the rates of return on invested capital for external sources of capital.

However, the businesses within a diversified firm do not always gain cost-of-capital advantages by being part of a diversified firm's portfolio. Several authors have argued that because a diversified firm has lower overall risk (see the following discussion), it will have a lower cost of capital, which it can pass along to the businesses within its portfolio. Although the lower risks associated with a diversified firm may lower the firm's cost of capital, the appropriate cost of capital to businesses within the firm depends on the performance and prospects of each of those businesses. The firm's advantages in evaluating its businesses' performances and prospects result in more appropriate capital allocation, not just in lower cost of capital for those businesses. Indeed, a business's cost of capital may be lower than it could have obtained in the external capital market (because the firm is able to more fully evaluate the positive aspects of that business), or it may be higher than it could have obtained in the external capital market (because the firm is able to more fully evaluate the negative aspects of that business).

Of course, if these businesses also have lower cost or higher revenue expectations because they are part of a diversified firm, then those cost/revenue advantages will be reflected in the appropriate cost of capital for these businesses. In this sense, any operational economies of scope for businesses in a diversified firm may be recognized by a diversified firm exploiting financial economies of scope.

Limits on Internal Capital Markets.   Although internal capital allocation has several potential advantages for a diversified firm, this process also has several limits. First, the level and type of diversification that a firm pursues can affect the efficiency of this allocation process. A firm that implements a strategy of unrelated diversification, whereby managers have to evaluate the performance and prospects of numerous very different businesses, puts a greater strain on the capital allocation skills of its managers than does a firm that implements related diversification. Indeed, in the extreme, the capital allocation efficiency of a firm pursuing broad-based unrelated diversification will probably not be superior to the capital allocation efficiency of the external capital market.

Second, the increased efficiency of internal capital allocation depends on managers in a diversified firm having better information for capital allocation than the information available to external sources. However, this higher-quality information is not guaranteed. The incentives that can lead managers to exaggerate their performance and prospects to external capital sources can also lead to this behavior within a diversified firm. Indeed, several examples of business managers falsifying performance records to gain access to more internal capital have been reported.[18] Research suggests that capital allocation requests by managers are routinely discounted in diversified firms in order to correct for these managers' inflated estimates of the performance and prospects of their businesses.[19]

Finally, not only do business managers have an incentive to inflate the performance and prospects of their business in a diversified firm, but managers in charge of capital allocation in these firms may have an incentive to continue investing in a business despite its poor performance and prospects. The reputation and status of these managers often depend on the success of these business investments because often they initially approved them. These managers often continue throwing good money at these businesses in hope that they will someday improve, thereby justifying their original decision. Organizational psychologists call this process **escalation of commitment** and have presented numerous examples of managers becoming irrationally committed to a particular investment.[20]

Indeed, research on the value of internal capital markets in diversified firms suggests that, on average, the limitations of these markets often outweigh their advantages. For example, even controlling for firm size, excessive investment in poorly performing businesses in a diversified firm reduces the market value of the average diversified firm.[21] However, the fact that many firms do not gain the advantages associated with internal capital markets does not necessarily imply that no firms gain these advantages. If only a few firms are able to obtain the advantages of internal capital markets while successfully avoiding their limitations, this financial economy of scope may be a source of at least a temporary competitive advantage.

Diversification and Risk Reduction.   Another possible financial economy of scope for a diversified firm has already been briefly mentioned—the riskiness of the cash flows of diversified firms is lower than the riskiness of the cash flows of undiversified firms. Consider, for example, the riskiness of two businesses operating separately compared with the risk of a diversified firm operating in those same two businesses simultaneously. If both these businesses are very risky on their own and the cash flows from these businesses are not highly correlated over time, then combining these two businesses into a single firm will generate a lower level of overall risk for the diversified firm than for each of these businesses on their own.

This lower level of risk is due to the low correlation between the cash flows associated with these two businesses. If Business I is having a bad year, Business II might be having a good year, and a firm that operates in both of these businesses simultaneously can have moderate levels of performance. In another year, Business II might be off, while Business I is having a good year. Again, the firm operating in both these businesses can have moderate levels of performance. Firms that diversify to reduce risk will have relatively stable returns over time, especially as they diversify into many different businesses with cash flows that are not highly correlated over time.

Tax Advantages of Diversification.   Another financial economy of scope from diversification stems from possible tax advantages of this corporate strategy. These possible tax advantages reflect one or a combination of two effects. First, a diversified firm can use losses in some of its businesses to offset profits in others, thereby reducing its overall tax liability. Of course, substantial losses in some of its businesses may overwhelm profits in other businesses, forcing businesses that would have remained solvent if they were independent to cease operation. However, as long as business losses are not too large, a diversified firm's tax liability can be reduced. Empirical research suggests that diversified firms do, sometimes, offset profits in some businesses with losses in others, although the tax savings of these activities are usually small.[22]

Second, because diversification can reduce the riskiness of a firm's cash flows, it can also reduce the probability that a firm will declare bankruptcy. This can increase a firm's debt capacity. This effect on debt capacity is greatest when the cash flows of a diversified firm's businesses are perfectly and negatively correlated. However, even when these cash flows are perfectly and positively correlated, there can still be a (modest) increase in debt capacity.

Debt capacity is particularly important in tax environments where interest payments on debt are tax deductible. In this context, diversified firms can increase their leverage up to their debt capacity and reduce their tax liability accordingly. Of course, if interest payments are not tax deductible or if the marginal corporate tax rate is relatively small, then the tax advantages of diversification can be quite small. Empirical work suggests that diversified firms do have greater debt capacity than undiversified firms. However, low marginal corporate tax rates, at least in the United States, make the accompanying tax savings on average relatively small.[23]

Diversification to Exploit Anticompetitive Economies of Scope
A third group of motivations for diversification is based on the relationship between diversification strategies and various anticompetitive activities by firms. Two specific examples of these activities are (1) multipoint competition to facilitate mutual forbearance and tacit collusion and (2) exploiting market power.

Multipoint Competition.   Multipoint competition exists when two or more diversified firms simultaneously compete in multiple markets. For example, HP and

Dell compete in both the personal computer market and the market for computer printers. Michelin and Goodyear compete in both the U.S. automobile tire market and the European automobile tire market. Disney and AOL/Time Warner compete in both the movie production and book publishing businesses.

Multipoint competition can serve to facilitate a particular type of tacit collusion called **mutual forbearance**. Firms engage in **tacit collusion** when they cooperate to reduce rivalry below the level expected under perfect competition. Consider the situation facing two diversified firms, A and B. These two firms operate in the same businesses, I, II, III, and IV (see Figure 7.3). In this context, any decisions that Firm A might make to compete aggressively in Businesses I and III must take into account the possibility that Firm B will respond by competing aggressively in Businesses II and IV and vice versa. The potential loss that each of these firms may experience in some of its businesses must be compared with the potential gain that each might obtain if it exploits competitive advantages in other of its businesses. If the present value of gains does not outweigh the present value of losses from retaliation, then both firms will avoid competitive activity. Refraining from competition is mutual forbearance.[24]

Mutual forbearance as a result of multipoint competition has occurred in several industries. For example, this form of tacit collusion has been described as existing between Michelin and Goodyear, Maxwell House and Folger's, Caterpillar and John Deere, and BIC and Gillette.[25] Another clear example of such cooperation can be found in the airline industry. For example, America West (now part of US Air) began service into the Houston Intercontinental Airport with very low introductory fares. Continental Airlines (now part of United Airlines), the dominant firm at Houston Intercontinental, rapidly responded to America West's low Houston fares by reducing the price of its flights from Phoenix, Arizona, to several cities in the United States. Phoenix is the home airport of America West. Within just a few weeks, America West withdrew its low introductory fares in the Houston market, and Continental withdrew its reduced prices in the Phoenix market. The threat of retaliation across markets apparently led America West and Continental to tacitly collude on prices.[26]

However, sometimes multipoint competition does not lead to mutual forbearance. Consider, for example, a conflict between The Walt Disney Company and Time Warner. As mentioned earlier, Disney operates in the theme park, movie

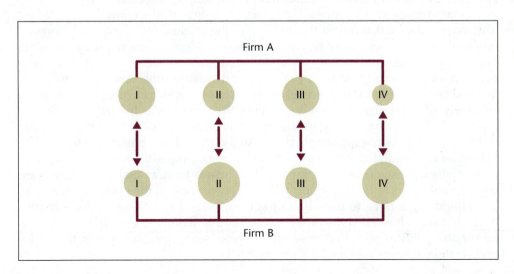

Firm A

Firm B

Figure 7.3 Multipoint Competition Between Hypothetical Firms A and B and television production, and television broadcasting industries. Time Warner operates in the theme park and movie and television production industries and also operates a very large magazine business (*Time, People, Sports Illustrated,* among others). From 1988 through 1993, Disney spent more than $40 million in advertising its theme parks in Time Warner magazines. Despite this substantial revenue, Time Warner began an aggressive advertising campaign aimed at wooing customers away from Disney theme parks to its own. Disney retaliated by canceling all of its advertising in Time Warner magazines. Time Warner responded to Disney's actions by canceling a corporate meeting to be held in Florida at Disney World. Disney responded to Time Warner's meeting cancellation by refusing to broadcast Time Warner theme park advertisements on its Los Angeles television station.[27]

Some recent research investigates the conditions under which mutual forbearance strategies are pursued, as well as conditions under which multipoint competition does not lead to mutual forbearance.[28] In general, the value of the threat of retaliation must be substantial for multipoint competition to lead to mutual forbearance. However, not only must the payoffs to mutual forbearance be substantial, but the firms pursuing this strategy must have strong strategic linkages among their diversified businesses. This suggests that firms pursuing mutual forbearance strategies based on multipoint competition are usually pursuing a form of related diversification.

Diversification and Market Power.   Internal allocations of capital among a diversified firm's businesses may enable it to exploit in some of its businesses the market power advantages it enjoys in other of its businesses. For example, suppose that a firm is earning monopoly profits in a particular business. This firm can use some of these monopoly profits to subsidize the operations of another of its businesses. This cross-subsidization can take several forms, including **predatory pricing**— that is, setting prices so that they are less than the subsidized business's costs. The effect of this cross-subsidy may be to drive competitors out of the subsidized business and then to obtain monopoly profits in that subsidized business. In a sense, diversification enables a firm to apply its monopoly power in several different businesses. Economists call this a **deep-pockets model** of diversification.[29]

Diversified firms with operations in regulated monopolies have been criticized for this kind of cross-subsidization. For example, most of the regional telephone companies in the United States are engaging in diversification strategies. The consent decree that forced the breakup of the original AT&T expressly forbade cross-subsidies between these regional companies' telephone monopolies and other business activities, under the assumption that such subsidies would give these firms an unfair competitive advantage in their diversified business activities.[30]

Although these market power economies of scope, in principle, may exist, relatively little empirical work documents their existence. Indeed, research on regulated utilities diversifying into nonregulated businesses in the 1980s suggests not that these firms use monopoly profits in their regulated businesses to unfairly subsidize nonregulated businesses, but that non-competition-oriented management skills developed in the regulated businesses tend to make diversification less profitable rather than more profitable.[31] Nevertheless, the potential that large diversified firms have to exercise market power and to behave in socially irresponsible ways has led some observers to call for actions to curtail both the economic and political power of these firms. These issues are discussed in the Ethics and Strategy feature.

Firm Size and Employee Incentives to Diversify

Employees may have incentives to diversify that are independent of any benefits from other sources of economies of scope. This is especially the case for employees in senior management positions and employees with long tenure in a particular firm. These employee incentives reflect the interest of employees to diversify because of the relationship between firm size and management compensation.

Research over the years demonstrates conclusively that the primary determinant of the compensation of top managers in a firm is not the economic performance of the firm but the size of the firm, usually measured in sales.[32] Thus, managers seeking to maximize their income should attempt to grow their firm. One of the easiest ways to grow a firm is through diversification, especially unrelated diversification through mergers and acquisitions. By making large acquisitions, a diversified firm can grow substantially in a short period of time, leading senior managers to earn higher incomes. All of this is independent of any economic profit that diversification may or may not generate. Senior managers need only worry about economic profit if the level of that profit is so low that unfriendly takeovers are a threat or so low that the board of directors may be forced to replace management.

Recently, the traditional relationship between firm size and management compensation has begun to break down. More and more, the compensation of senior managers is being tied to the firm's economic performance. In particular, the use of stock and other forms of deferred compensation makes it in management's best interest to be concerned with a firm's economic performance. These changes in compensation do not necessarily imply that firms will abandon all forms of diversification. However, they do suggest that firms will abandon those forms of diversification that do not generate real economies of scope.

Can Equity Holders Realize These Economies of Scope on Their Own?

Earlier in this chapter, it was suggested that for a firm's diversification strategies to create value, two conditions must hold. First, these strategies must exploit valuable economies of scope. Potentially valuable economies of scope were presented in Table 7.1 and discussed in the previous section. Second, it must be less costly for managers in a firm to realize these economies of scope than for outside equity holders on their own. If outside equity holders could realize a particular economy of scope on their own, without a firm's managers, at low cost, why would they want to hire managers to do this for them by investing in a firm and providing capital to managers to exploit an economy of scope?

Table 7.3 summarizes the discussion on the potential value of the different economies of scope listed in Table 7.1. It also suggests which of these economies of scope will be difficult for outside equity investors to exploit on their own and thus which bases of diversification are most likely to create positive returns for a firm's equity holders.

Most of the economies of scope listed in Table 7.3 cannot be realized by equity holders on their own. This is because most of them require activities that equity holders cannot engage in or information that equity holders do not possess. For example, shared activities, core competencies, multipoint competition, and exploiting market power all require the detailed coordination of business activities across multiple businesses in a firm. Although equity holders may own a portfolio of equities, they are not in a position to coordinate business activities across this portfolio. In a similar way, internal capital allocation requires information about a business's prospects that is simply not available to a firm's outside equity holders.

Ethics and Strategy

In 1999, a loose coalition of union members, environmentalists, youth, indigenous peoples, human rights activists, and small farmers took to the streets of Seattle, Washington, to protest a meeting of the World Trade Organization (WTO) and to fight against the growing global power of corporations. Government officials and corporate officers alike were confused by these protests. After all, hadn't world trade increased 19 times from 1950 to 1995 ($0.4 trillion to $7.6 trillion in constant 2003 dollars), and hadn't the total economic output of the entire world gone from $6.4 trillion in 1950 to $60.7 trillion in 2005 (again, in constant 2003 dollars)? Why protest a global economic system—a system that was enhancing the level of free trade and facilitating global economic efficiency—that was so clearly improving the economic well-being of the world's population? This 1999 protest turned out to be the first of many such demonstrations, culminating in the Occupy Movement after the financial crisis of 2007. And, still, many business and government leaders remain confused. Empirically, globalization has improved the world economy, so why the protests?

The protestors' message to government and big business was that these aggregate growth numbers masked more truth than they told. Yes, there has been economic growth. But that growth has benefited only a small percentage of the world's population. Most of the population still struggles to survive. The combined net worth of 358 U.S. billionaires in the early 1990s ($760 billion) was equal to the combined net worth of the 2.5 billion poorest people on the earth! Eighty-three percent of the world's total income

Globalization and the Threat of the Multinational Firm

goes to the richest fifth of the population while the poorest fifth of the world's population receives only 1.4 percent of the world's total income. Currently, 45 million to 70 million people worldwide have had to leave their home countries to find work in foreign lands, and approximately 1.4 billion people around the world live on less than $1 a day. Even in relatively affluent societies such as the United States, people find it increasingly difficult to meet their financial obligations. Falling real wages, economic insecurity, and corporate downsizing have led many people to work longer hours or to hold two or three jobs. While the number of billionaires in the world continues to grow, the number of people facing mind-numbing and strength-robbing poverty grows even faster.

The causes of this apparent contradiction—global economic growth linked with growing global economic decay—are numerous and complex. However, one explanation focuses on the growing economic power of the diversified multinational corporation.

The size of these institutions can be immense—many international diversified firms are larger than the entire economies of many nations. And these huge institutions, with a single-minded focus on maximizing their performance, can make profit-making decisions that adversely affect their suppliers, their customers, their employees, and the environment, all with relative impunity. Armed with the unspoken mantra that "Greed is good," these corporations can justify almost any action, as long as it increases the wealth of their shareholders.

Of course, even if one accepts this hypothesis—and it is far from being universally accepted—solutions to the growing power of internationally diversified firms are not obvious. The problem is that one way that firms become large and powerful is by being able to meet customer demands effectively. Thus, firm size, per se, is not necessarily an indication that a firm is behaving in ways inconsistent with the public good. Government efforts to restrict the size of firms simply because they are large could easily have the effect of making citizens worse off. However, once firms are large and powerful, they may very well be tempted to exercise that power in ways that benefit themselves at great cost to society.

Whatever the causes and solutions to these problems, protests that began in Seattle in 1999 have at least one clear message: global growth for growth's sake is no longer universally accepted as the correct objective of international economic policy.

Sources: D. C. Korten (2001). *When corporations rule the world*, 2nd ed. Bloomfield, CT: Kumarian Press; H. Demsetz (1973). "Industry structure, market rivalry, and public policy." *Journal of Law and Economics*, 16, pp. 1–9; J. Stiglitz (2007). *Making globalization work*. New York: Norton.

TABLE 7.3 The Competitive Implications of Different Economies of Scope

Types of Economy of Scope	Are They Valuable?	Can They Be Realized by Equity Holders on Their Own?	Positive Returns to Equity Holders?
1. *Operational economies of scope*			
Shared activities	Possible	No	Possible
Core competencies	Possible	No	Possible
2. *Financial economies of scope*			
Internal capital allocation	Possible	No	Possible
Risk reduction	Possible	Yes	No
Tax advantages	Possible—small	No	Possible—small
3. *Anticompetitive economies of scope*			
Multipoint competition	Possible	No	Possible
Exploiting market power	Possible	No	Possible
4. *Employee incentives for diversification*			
Maximizing management compensation	No	No	No

Indeed, the only two economies of scope listed in Table 7.3 that do not have the potential for generating positive returns for a firm's equity holders are diversification in order to maximize the size of a firm—because firm size, per se, is not valuable—and diversification to reduce risk—because equity holders can do this on their own at very low cost by simply investing in a diversified portfolio of stocks. Indeed, although risk reduction is often a published rationale for many diversification moves, this rationale, by itself, is not directly consistent with the interests of a firm's equity holders. However, some scholars have suggested that this strategy may directly benefit other of a firm's stakeholders and thus indirectly benefit its equity holders. This possibility is discussed in detail in the Strategy in Depth feature.

Overall, this analysis of possible bases of diversification suggests that related diversification is more likely to be consistent with the interests of a firm's equity holders than unrelated diversification. This is because the one economy of scope listed in Table 7.3 that is the easiest for outside equity holders to duplicate—risk reduction—is the only economy of scope that an unrelated diversified firm can try to realize. All the other economies of scope listed in Table 7.3 require coordination and information sharing across businesses in a diversified firm that are very difficult to realize in unrelated diversified firms. Indeed, the preponderance of empirical research suggests that related diversified firms outperform unrelated diversified firms.[33]

Corporate Diversification and Sustained Competitive Advantage

V R I O

Table 7.3 describes those economies of scope that are likely to create real economic value for diversifying firms. It also suggests that related diversification can be valuable, and unrelated diversification is usually not valuable. However, as we have seen with all the other strategies discussed in this book, the fact that a

Strategy in Depth

Although diversifying in order to reduce risk generally does not directly benefit outside equity investors in a firm, it can *indirectly* benefit outside equity investors through its impact on the willingness of other stakeholders in a firm to make firm-specific investments. A firm's **stakeholders** include all those groups and individuals who have an interest in how a firm performs. In this sense, a firm's equity investors are one of a firm's stakeholders. Other firm stakeholders include employees, suppliers, and customers.

Firm stakeholders make **firm-specific investments** when the value of the investments they make in a particular firm is much greater than the value of those same investments would be in other firms. Consider, for example, a firm's employees. An employee with a long tenure in a particular firm has generally made substantial **firm-specific human capital investments.** These investments include understanding a particular firm's culture, policies, and procedures; knowing the "right" people to contact to complete a task; and so forth. Such investments have significant value in the firm where they are made. Indeed, such firm-specific knowledge is generally necessary if an employee is to be able to help a firm conceive and implement valuable

Risk-Reducing Diversification and a Firm's Other Stakeholders

strategies. However, the specific investments that an employee makes in a particular firm have almost no value in other firms. If a firm were to cease operations, employees would instantly lose almost all the value of any of the firm-specific investments they had made in that firm.

Suppliers and customers can also make these firm-specific investments. Suppliers make these investments when they customize their products or services to the specific requirements of a particular customer. They also make firm-specific investments when they forgo opportunities to sell to other firms in order to sell to a particular firm. Customers make firm-specific investments when they customize their operations to fully utilize the products or services

of a particular firm. Also, by developing close relationships with a particular firm, customers may forgo the opportunity to develop relationships with other firms. These, too, are firm-specific investments made by customers. If a firm were to cease operations, suppliers and customers would instantly lose almost the entire value of the specific investments they have made in this firm.

Although the firm-specific investments made by employees, suppliers, and customers are risky—in the sense that almost their entire value is lost if the firm in which they are made ceases operations—they are extremely important if a firm is going to be able to generate economic profits. As was suggested in Chapter 3, valuable, rare, and costly-to-imitate resources and capabilities are more likely to be a source of sustained competitive advantage than resources and capabilities without these attributes. Firm-specific investments are more likely to have these attributes than non-firm-specific investments. Non-firm-specific investments are investments that can generate value in numerous different firms.

Thus, valuable, rare, and costly-to-imitate firm-specific investments made by a firm's employees, suppliers, and customers can be the source of economic profits. And because a

strategy is valuable does not necessarily imply that it will be a source of sustained competitive advantage. In order for diversification to be a source of sustained competitive advantage, it must be not only valuable but also rare and costly to imitate, and a firm must be organized to implement this strategy. The rarity and imitability of diversification are discussed in this section; organizational questions are deferred until the next.

firm's outside equity holders are residual claimants on the cash flows generated by a firm, these economic profits benefit equity holders. Thus, a firm's outside equity holders generally will want a firm's employees, suppliers, and customers to make specific investments in a firm because those investments are likely to be sources of economic wealth for outside equity holders.

However, given the riskiness of firm-specific investments, employees, suppliers, and customers will generally only be willing to make these investments if some of the riskiness associated with making them can be reduced. Outside equity holders have little difficulty managing the risks associated with investing in a particular firm because they can always create a portfolio of stocks that fully diversifies this risk at very low cost. This is why diversification that reduces the riskiness of a firm's cash flows does not generally directly benefit a firm's outside equity holders. However, a firm's employees, suppliers, and customers usually do not have these low-cost diversification opportunities. Employees, for example, are rarely able to make firm-specific human capital investments in a large enough number of different firms to fully diversify the risks associated with making them. And although

suppliers and customers can diversify their firm-specific investments to a greater degree than employees—through selling to multiple customers and through buying from multiple suppliers—the cost of this diversification for suppliers and customers is usually greater than the costs that are borne by outside equity holders in diversifying their risk.

Because it is often very costly for a firm's employees, suppliers, and customers to diversify the risks associated with making firm-specific investments on their own, these stakeholders will often prefer that a firm's managers help manage this risk for them. Managers in a firm can do this by diversifying the portfolio of businesses in which a firm operates. If a firm is unwilling to diversify its portfolio of businesses, then that firm's employees, suppliers, and customers will generally be unwilling to make specific investments in that firm. Moreover, because these firm-specific investments can generate economic profits and because economic profits can directly benefit a firm's outside equity holders, equity holders have an indirect incentive to encourage a firm to pursue a diversification strategy, even though that strategy does not directly benefit them.

Put differently, a firm's diversification strategy can be thought of

as compensation for the firm-specific investments that a firm's employees, suppliers, and customers make in a firm. Outside equity holders have an incentive to encourage this compensation in return for access to some of the economic profits that these firm-specific investments can generate. In general, the greater the impact of the firm-specific investment made by a firm's employees, suppliers, and customers on the ability of a firm to generate economic profits, the more likely that pursuing a corporate diversification strategy is indirectly consistent with the interests of a firm's outside equity holders. In addition, the more limited the ability of a firm's employees, suppliers, and customers to diversify the risks associated with making firm-specific investments at low cost, the more that corporate diversification is consistent with the interests of outside equity investors.

Sources: J. B. Barney (1991). "Firm resources and sustained competitive advantage." *Journal of Management*, 17, pp. 99–120; R. M. Stulz (1996). "Rethinking risk management." *Journal of Applied Corporate Finance*, Fall, pp. 8–24; K. Miller (1998). "Economic exposure and integrated risk management," *Strategic Management Journal*, 33, pp. 756–779; R. Amit and B. Wernerfelt (1990). "Why do firms reduce business risk?" *Academy of Management Journal*, 33, pp. 520–533; H. Wang and J. Barney (2006), "Employee incentives to make firm specific investments: Implications for resource-based theories of diversification." *Academy of Management Review*, 31(2), pp. 466–476.

The Rarity of Diversification

At first glance, it seems clear that diversification per se is usually not a rare firm strategy. Most large firms have adopted some form of diversification, if only the limited diversification of a dominant-business firm. Even many small and medium-sized firms have adopted different levels of diversification strategy.

However, the rarity of diversification depends not on diversification per se but on how rare the particular economies of scope associated with that diversification are. If only a few competing firms have exploited a particular economy of scope, that economy of scope can be rare. If numerous firms have done so, it will be common and not a source of competitive advantage.

The Imitability of Diversification

Both forms of imitation—direct duplication and substitution—are relevant in evaluating the ability of diversification strategies to generate sustained competitive advantages, even if the economies of scope that they create are rare.

Direct Duplication of Diversification

The extent to which a valuable and rare corporate diversification strategy is immune from direct duplication depends on how costly it is for competing firms to realize this same economy of scope. As suggested in Table 7.4, some economies of scope are, in general, more costly to duplicate than others.

Shared activities, risk reduction, tax advantages, and employee compensation as bases for corporate diversification are usually relatively easy to duplicate. Because shared activities are based on tangible assets that a firm exploits across multiple businesses, such as common research and development labs, common sales forces, and common manufacturing, they are usually relatively easy to duplicate. The only duplication issues for shared activities concern developing the cooperative cross-business relationships that often facilitate the use of shared activities—issues discussed in the next chapter. Moreover, because risk reduction, tax advantages, and employee compensation motives for diversifying can be accomplished through both related and unrelated diversification, these motives for diversifying tend to be relatively easy to duplicate.

Other economies of scope are much more difficult to duplicate. These difficult-to-duplicate economies of scope include core competencies, internal capital allocation efficiencies, multipoint competition, and exploitation of market power. Because core competencies are more intangible, their direct duplication is often challenging. The realization of capital allocation economies of scope requires very substantial information-processing capabilities. These capabilities are often very difficult to develop. Multipoint competition requires very close coordination between the different businesses in which a firm operates. This kind of coordination is socially complex and thus often immune from direct duplication. Finally, exploitation of market power may be costly to duplicate because it requires that a firm must possess significant market power in one of its lines of business. A firm that does not have this market power advantage would have to obtain it. The cost of doing so, in most situations, would be prohibitive.

TABLE 7.4 Costly Duplication of Economies of Scope	Less Costly-to-Duplicate Economies of Scope	Costly-to-Duplicate Economies of Scope
	Shared activities	Core competencies
	Risk reduction	Internal capital allocation
	Tax advantages	Multipoint competition
	Employee compensation	Exploiting market power

Substitutes for Diversification

Two obvious substitutes for diversification exist. First, instead of obtaining cost or revenue advantages from exploiting economies of scope *across* businesses in a diversified firm, a firm may decide to simply grow and develop each of its businesses separately. In this sense, a firm that successfully implements a cost leadership strategy or a product differentiation strategy in a single business can obtain the same cost or revenue advantages it could have obtained by exploiting economies of scope but without having to develop cross-business relations. Growing independent businesses within a diversified firm can be a substitute for exploiting economies of scope in a diversification strategy.

One firm that has chosen this strategy is Nestlé. Nestlé exploits few, if any, economies of scope among its different businesses. Rather, it has focused its efforts on growing each of its international operations to the point that they obtain cost or revenue advantages that could have otherwise been obtained in some form of related diversification. Thus, for example, Nestlé's operation in the United States is sufficiently large to exploit economies of scale in production, sales, and marketing, without reliance on economies of scope between U.S. operations and operations in other countries.[34]

A second substitute for exploiting economies of scope in diversification can be found in strategic alliances. By using a strategic alliance, a firm may be able to gain the economies of scope it could have obtained if it had carefully exploited economies of scope across its businesses. Thus, for example, instead of a firm exploiting research and development economies of scope between two businesses it owns, it could form a strategic alliance with a different firm and form a joint research and development lab. Instead of a firm exploiting sales economies of scope by linking its businesses through a common sales force, it might develop a sales agreement with another firm and obtain cost or revenue advantages in this way.

Summary

Firms implement corporate diversification strategies that range from limited diversification (single-business, dominant-business) to related diversification (related-constrained, related-linked) to unrelated diversification. In order to be valuable, corporate diversification strategies must reduce costs or increase revenues by exploiting economies of scope that outside equity holders cannot realize on their own at low cost.

Several motivations for implementing diversification strategies exist, including exploiting operational economies of scope (shared activities, core competencies), exploiting financial economies of scope (internal capital allocation, risk reduction, obtaining tax advantages), exploiting anticompetitive economies of scope (multipoint competition, market power advantages), and employee incentives to diversify (maximizing management compensation). All these reasons for diversifying, except diversifying to maximize management compensation, have the potential to create economic value for a firm. Moreover, a firm's outside equity holders will find it costly to realize all of these bases for diversification, except risk reduction. Thus, diversifying to maximize management compensation or diversifying to reduce risk is not consistent with the wealth-maximizing interests of a firm's equity holders. This analysis also suggests that, on average, related diversified firms will outperform unrelated diversified firms.

The ability of a diversification strategy to create sustained competitive advantages depends not only on the value of that strategy, but also on its rarity and imitability. The rarity of a diversification strategy depends on the number of competing firms that are exploiting the same economies of scope through diversification. Imitation can occur either through direct duplication or through substitutes. Costly-to-duplicate economies of scope include core competencies, internal capital allocation, multipoint competition, and exploitation of market power. Other economies of scope are usually less costly to duplicate. Important substitutes for diversification are when relevant economies are obtained through the independent actions of businesses within a firm and when relevant economies are obtained through strategic alliances. This discussion set aside important organizational issues in implementing diversification strategies. These issues are examined in detail in the next chapter.

MyManagementLab®

Go to **mymanagementlab.com** to complete the problems marked with this icon ⭐.

Challenge Questions

7.1. One simple way to think about relatedness is to look at the products or services a firm manufactures. The more similar these products or services are, the more related is the firm's diversification strategy. Why or why not would firms that exploit core competencies in their diversification strategies always produce products or services that are similar to each other?

7.2. A firm implementing a diversification strategy has just acquired what it claims is a strategically related target firm but announces that it is not going to change this recently acquired firm in any way. Why or why not would this type of diversifying

acquisition enable the firm to realize any valuable economies of scope that could not be duplicated by outside investors on their own?

⭐ **7.3.** One of the reasons why internal capital markets may be more efficient than external capital markets is that firms may not want to reveal full information about their sources of competitive advantage to external capital markets in order to reduce the threat of competitive imitation. This suggests that external capital markets may systematically undervalue firms with competitive advantages that are subject to imitation. If you agree with this analysis, how could you trade on

this information in your own investment activities?

7.4. A particular firm is owned by members of a single family. Most of the wealth of this family is derived from the operations of this firm, and the family does not want to "go public" with the firm by selling its equity position to outside investors. Will this firm choose to pursue a highly related diversification strategy or a somewhat less related diversification strategy?

⭐ **7.5.** Under what conditions will a related diversification strategy not be a source of competitive advantage for a firm?

Problem Set

7.6. Visit the corporate Web sites for the following firms. How would you characterize the corporate strategies of these companies? Are they following a strategy of limited diversification, related diversification, or unrelated diversification?

(a) ExxonMobil
(b) Google
(c) General Motors
(d) JetBlue
(e) Citigroup
(f) Entertainment Arts
(g) IBM
(h) Dell
(i) Berkshire Hathaway

7.7. Consider the following list of strategies. In your view, which are examples of potential economies of scope underlying a corporate diversification strategy? For those strategies that are an economy of scope, which economy of scope are they? For those strategies that are not an economy of scope, why aren't they?

(a) The Coca-Cola Corporation replaces its old diet cola drink (Tab) with a new diet cola drink called Diet Coke.

(b) Apple introduces an iPod MP3 player with a larger memory.

(c) PepsiCo distributes Lay's Potato Chips to the same stores where it sells Pepsi.

(d) Kmart extends its licensing arrangement with Martha Stewart for four years.

(e) Wal-Mart uses the same distribution system to supply its Wal-Mart stores, its Wal-Mart Supercenters (Wal-Mart stores with grocery stores in them), and its Sam's Clubs.

(f) Head Ski Company introduces a line of tennis rackets.

(g) General Electric borrows money from Bank of America at 3 percent interest and then makes capital available to its jet engine subsidiary at 8 percent interest.

(h) McDonald's acquires Boston Market and Chipotle (two restaurants where many customers sit in the restaurant to eat their meals).

(i) A venture capital firm invests in a firm in the biotechnology industry and a firm in the entertainment industry.

(j) Another venture capital firm invests in two firms in the biotechnology industry.

7.8. Consider the following facts. The standard deviation of the cash flows associated with Business I is 0.8. The larger this standard deviation, the riskier a business's future cash flows are likely to be. The standard deviation of the cash flows associated with Business II is 1.3. That is, Business II is riskier than Business I. Finally, the correlation between the cash flows of these two businesses over time is 0.8. This means that when Business I is up, Business II tends to be down, and vice versa. Suppose one firm owns both of these businesses.

(a) Assuming that Business I constitutes 40 percent of this firm's revenues and Business II constitutes 60 percent of its revenues, calculate the riskiness of this firm's total revenues using the following equation:

$$sd_{I,II} = \sqrt{w^2 sd_I^2 + (1 - w)^2 sd_{II}^2 + 2w(1 + w)(r_{I,II} sd_I sd_{II})}$$

Where $w = 0.40$; $sd_I = 0.8$, $sd_{II} = 1.3$, and $r_{I, II} = -8$.

(b) Given this result, does it make sense for this firm to own both Business I and Business II? Why or why not?

MyManagementLab®

Go to **mymanagementlab.com** for Auto-graded writing questions as well as the following Assisted-graded writing questions:

⭐ **7.9.** Not all firms will choose corporate diversification. Describe the benefits and challenges of the alternatives.

⭐ **7.10.** Internal capital markets have several limitations. When a firm is confronted by these limitations, what is it likely to do?

End Notes

1. See Sellers, P. (2004). "The brand king's challenge." *Fortune*, April 5, pp. 192+.
2. The Walt Disney Company. (1995). Harvard Business School Case No. 1-388-147.
3. Useem, J. (2004). "Another boss, another revolution." *Fortune*, April 5, pp. 112+.
4. See Rogers, A. (1992). "It's the execution that counts." *Fortune*, November 30, pp. 80–83; and Porter, M. E. (1981). "Disposable diaper industry in 1974." Harvard Business School Case No. 9-380-175. A more general discussion of the value of shared activities can be found in St. John, C. H., and J. S. Harrison. (1999). "Manufacturing-based relatedness, synergy, and coordination." *Strategic Management Journal*, 20, pp. 129–145.
5. See Fuchsberg, G. (1992). "Decentralized management can have its drawbacks." *The Wall Street Journal*, December 9, p. B1.
6. See Crockett, R. (2000). "A Baby Bell's growth formula." *BusinessWeek*, March 6, pp. 50–52; and Crockett, R. (1999). "The last monopolist." *BusinessWeek*, April 12, p. 76.
7. de Lisser, E. (1993). "Catering to cooking-phobic customers, supermarkets stress carryout." *The Wall Street Journal*, April 5, p. B1.
8. See, for example, Davis, P., R. Robinson, J. Pearce, and S. Park. (1992). "Business unit relatedness and performance: A look at the pulp and paper industry." *Strategic Management Journal*, 13, pp. 349–361.
9. Loomis, C. J. (1993). "Dinosaurs?" *Fortune*, May 3, pp. 36–42.
10. Rapoport, C. (1992). "A tough Swede invades the U.S." *Fortune*, June 29, pp. 776–779.
11. Prahalad, C. K., and G. Hamel. (1990). "The core competence of the organization." *Harvard Business Review*, 90, p. 82.
12. See also Grant, R. M. (1988). "On 'dominant logic' relatedness and the link between diversity and performance." *Strategic Management Journal*, 9, pp. 639–642; Chatterjee, S., and B. Wernerfelt. (1991). "The link between resources and type of diversification: Theory and evidence." *Strategic Management Journal*, 12, pp. 33–48; Markides, C., and P. J. Williamson. (1994). "Related diversification, core competencies, and corporate performance." *Strategic Management Journal*, 15, pp. 149–165; Montgomery, C. A., and B. Wernerfelt. (1991). "Sources of superior performance: Market share versus industry effects in the U.S. brewing industry." *Management Science*, 37, pp. 954–959; Liedtka, J. M. (1996). "Collaborating across lines of business for competitive advantage." *Academy of Management Executive*, 10(2), pp. 20–37; and Farjoun, M. (1998). "The independent and joint effects of the skill and physical bases of relatedness in diversification." *Strategic Management Journal*, 19, pp. 611–630.
13. Jensen, M. C. (1986). "Agency costs of free cash flow, corporate finance, and takeovers." *American Economic Review*, 76, pp. 323–329.
14. See Nayyar, P. (1990). "Information asymmetries: A source of competitive advantage for diversified service firms." *Strategic Management Journal*, 11, pp. 513–519; and Robins, J., and M. Wiersema. (1995). "A resource-based approach to the multibusiness firm: Empirical analysis of portfolio interrelationships and corporate financial performance." *Strategic Management Journal*, 16, pp. 277–299, for a discussion of the evolution of core competencies.
15. Prahalad, C. K., and R. A. Bettis. (1986). "The dominant logic: A new linkage between diversity and performance." *Strategic Management Journal*, 7(6), pp. 485–501.
16. See Williamson, O. E. (1975). *Markets and hierarchies: Analysis and antitrust implications*. New York: Free Press.
17. See Liebeskind, J. P. (1996). "Knowledge, strategy, and the theory of the firm." *Strategic Management Journal*, 17 (Winter Special Edition), pp. 93–107.
18. Perry, L. T., and J. B. Barney. (1981). "Performance lies are hazardous to organizational health." *Organizational Dynamics*, 9(3), pp. 68–80.
19. Bethel, J. E. (1990). *The capital allocation process and managerial mobility: A theoretical and empirical investigation*. Unpublished doctoral dissertation, University of California at Los Angeles.
20. Staw, B. M. (1981). "The escalation of commitment to a course of action." *Academy of Management Review*, 6, pp. 577–587.
21. See Comment, R., and G. Jarrell. (1995). "Corporate focus and stock returns." *Journal of Financial Economics*, 37, pp. 67–87; Berger, P. G., and E. Ofek. (1995). "Diversification's effect on firm value." *Journal of Financial Economics*, 37, pp. 39–65; Maksimovic, V., and G. Phillips. (1999). "Do conglomerate firms allocate resources inefficiently?"

Working paper, University of Maryland; Matsusaka, J. G., and V. Nanda. (1998). "Internal capital markets and corporate refocusing." Working paper, University of Southern California; Palia, D. (1998). "Division-level overinvestment and agency conflicts in diversified firms." Working paper, Columbia University; Rajan, R., H. Servaes, and L. Zingales. (1997). "The cost of diversity: The diversification discount and inefficient investment." Working paper, University of Chicago; Scharfstein, D. S. (1997). "The dark side of internal capital markets II: Evidence from diversified conglomerates." NBER [National Bureau of Economic Research]. Working paper; Shin, H. H., and R. M. Stulz. (1998). "Are internal capital markets efficient?" *The Quarterly Journal of Economics*, May, pp. 551–552. But Houston and James (1998) show that internal capital markets can create competitive advantages for firms: Houston, J., and C. James. (1998). "Some evidence that banks use internal capital markets to lower capital costs." *Journal of Applied Corporate Finance*, 11(2), pp. 70–78.
22. Scott, J. H. (1977). "On the theory of conglomerate mergers." *Journal of Finance*, 32, pp. 1235–1250.
23. See Brennan, M. (1979). "The pricing of contingent claims in discrete time models." *Journal of Finance*, 34, pp. 53–68; Cox, J., S. Ross, and M. Rubinstein. (1979). "Option pricing: A simplified approach." *Journal of Financial Economics*, 7, pp. 229–263; Stapleton, R. C. (1982). "Mergers, debt capacity, and the valuation of corporate loans." In M. Keenan and L. J. White. (eds.), *Mergers and acquisitions*. Lexington, MA: D. C. Heath, Chapter 2; and Galai, D., and R. W. Masulis. (1976). "The option pricing model and the risk factor of stock." *Journal of Financial Economics*, 3, pp. 53–82.
24. See Karnani, A., and B. Wernerfelt. (1985). "Multiple point competition." *Strategic Management Journal*, 6, pp. 87–96; Bernheim, R. D., and M. D. Whinston. (1990). "Multimarket contact and collusive behavior." *Rand Journal of Economics*, 12, pp. 605–617; Tirole, J. (1988). *The theory of industrial organization*. Cambridge, MA: MIT Press; Gimeno, J., and C. Y. Woo. (1999). "Multimarket contact, economies of scope, and firm performance." *Academy of Management Journal*, 43(3), pp. 239–259; Korn, H. J., and J. A. C. Baum. (1999). "Chance, imitative, and strategic antecedents to multimarket contact." *Academy of Management Journal*, 42(2), pp. 171–193; Baum, J. A. C., and H. J. Korn. (1999). "Dynamics of dyadic competitive interaction." *Strategic Management Journal*, 20, pp. 251–278; Gimeno, J. (1999). "Reciprocal threats in multimarket rivalry: Staking our 'spheres of influence' in the U.S. airline industry." *Strategic Management Journal*, 20, pp. 101–128; Gimeno, J., and C. Y. Woo. (1996). "Hypercompetition in a multimarket environment: The role of strategic similarity and multimarket contact in competitive de-escalation." *Organization Science*, 7(3), pp. 322–341; Ma, H. (1998). "Mutual forbearance in international business." *Journal of International Management*, 4(2), pp. 129–147; McGrath, R. G., and M.-J. Chen. (1998). "Multimarket maneuvering in uncertain spheres of influence: Resource diversion strategies." *Academy of Management Review*, 23(4), pp. 724–740; Chen, M.-J. (1996). "Competitor analysis and interfirm rivalry: Toward a theoretical integration." *Academy of Management Review*, 21(1), pp. 100–134; Chen, M.-J., and K. Stucker. (1997). "Multinational management and multimarket rivalry: Toward a theoretical development of global competition." *Academy of Management Proceedings 1997*, pp. 2–6; and Young, G., K. G. Smith, and C. M. Grimm. (1997). "Multimarket contact, resource heterogeneity, and rivalrous firm behavior." *Academy of Management Proceedings 1997*, pp. 55–59. This idea was originally proposed by Edwards, C. D. (1955). "Conglomerate bigness as a source of power." In *Business concentration and price policy*. NBER Conference Report. Princeton, NJ: Princeton University Press.
25. See Karnani, A., and B. Wernerfelt. (1985). "Multiple point competition." *Strategic Management Journal*, 6, pp. 87–96.
26. This was documented by Gimeno, J. (1994). "Multipoint competition, market rivalry and firm performance: A test of the mutual forbearance hypothesis in the United States airline industry, 1984–1988." Unpublished doctoral dissertation, Purdue University.
27. See Landro, L., P. M. Reilly, and R. Turner. (1993). "Cartoon clash: Disney relationship with Time Warner is a strained one." *The Wall Street Journal*, April 14, p. A1; and Reilly, P. M., and R. Turner. (1993). "Disney pulls ads in tiff with *Time*." *The Wall Street Journal*, April 2, p. B1. The growth and consolidation of the entertainment industry since the early 1990s have made Disney and Time Warner (especially

after its merger with AOL) large entertainment conglomerates. It will be interesting to see if these two larger firms will be able to find ways to tacitly collude or will continue the competition begun in the early 1990s.

28. The best work in this area has been done by Gimeno, J. (1994). "Multipoint competition, market rivalry and firm performance: A test of the mutual forbearance hypothesis in the United States airline industry, 1984–1988." Unpublished doctoral dissertation, Purdue University. See also Smith, F., and R. Wilson. (1995). "The predictive validity of the Karnani and Wernerfelt model of multipoint competition." *Strategic Management Journal*, 16, pp. 143–160.

29. See Tirole, J. (1988). *The theory of industrial organization.* Cambridge, MA: MIT Press.

30. Carnevale, M. L. (1993). "Ring in the new: Telephone service seems on the brink of huge innovations." *The Wall Street Journal*, February 10, p. A1. SBC acquired the remaining assets of the original AT&T and renamed the newly merged company AT&T.

31. See Russo, M. V. (1992). "Power plays: Regulation, diversification, and backward integration in the electric utility industry." *Strategic Management Journal*, 13, pp. 13–27. Work by Jandik and Makhija (1999) indicates that when a regulated utility diversifies out of a regulated industry, it often earns a more positive return than when an unregulated firm does this. Jandik, T., and A. K. Makhija. (1999). "An empirical examination of the atypical diversification practices of electric utilities: Internal capital markets and regulation." Fisher College of Business, Ohio State University, working paper (September). This work shows that regulators have the effect of making a regulated firm's internal capital market more efficient. Differences between Russo's (1992) findings and Jandik and Makhija's (1999) findings may have to do

with when this work was done. Russo's (1992) research may have focused on a time period before regulatory agencies had learned how to improve a firm's internal capital market. However, even though Jandik and Makhija (1999) report positive returns from regulated firms diversifying, these positive returns do not reflect the market power advantages of these firms.

32. Finkelstein, S., and D. C. Hambrick. (1989). "Chief executive compensation: A study of the intersection of markets and political processes." *Strategic Management Journal*, 10, pp. 121–134.

33. See William, J., B. L. Paez, and L. Sanders. (1988). "Conglomerates revisited." *Strategic Management Journal*, 9, pp. 403–414; Geringer, J. M., S. Tallman, and D. M. Olsen. (2000). "Product and international diversification among Japanese multinational firms." *Strategic Management Journal*, 21, pp. 51–80; Nail, L. A., W. L. Megginson, and C. Maquieira. (1998). "How stock-swap mergers affect shareholder (and bondholder) wealth: More evidence of the value of corporate 'focus.'" *Journal of Applied Corporate Finance*, 11(2), pp. 95–106; Carroll, G. R., L. S. Bigelow, M.-D. L. Seidel, and L. B. Tsai. (1966). "The fates of *De Novo* and *De Alio* producers in the American automobile industry 1885–1981." *Strategic Management Journal*, 17 (Special Summer Issue), pp. 117–138; Nguyen, T. H., A. Seror, and T. M. Devinney. (1990). "Diversification strategy and performance in Canadian manufacturing firms." *Strategic Management Journal*, 11, pp. 411–418; and Amit, R., and J. Livnat. (1988). "Diversification strategies, business cycles and economic performance." *Strategic Management Journal*, 9, pp. 99–110, for a discussion of corporate diversification in the economy over time.

34. The Nestlé story is summarized in Templeman, J. (1993). "Nestlé: A giant in a hurry." *BusinessWeek*, March 22, pp. 50–54.

8 Organizing to Implement Corporate Diversification

LEARNING OBJECTIVES *After reading this chapter, you should be able to:*

1. Describe the multidivisional, or M-form, structure and how it is used to implement a corporate diversification strategy.

2. Describe the roles of the board of directors, institutional investors, the senior executive, corporate staff, division general managers, and shared activity managers in making the M-form structure work.

3. Describe how three management control processes—measuring divisional performance, allocating corporate capital, and transferring intermediate products—are used to help implement a corporate diversification strategy.

4. Describe the role of management compensation in helping to implement a corporate diversification strategy.

MyManagementLab®
⭐ **Improve Your Grade!**
Over 10 million students improved their results using the Pearson MyLabs.
Visit **mymanagementlab.com** for simulations, tutorials, and end-of-chapter problems.

And Then There Is Berkshire Hathaway

Berkshire Hathaway is one of the largest and most profitable publicly traded diversified corporations in the world. With sales in excess of $162 billion, Berkshire Hathaway operates in four large segments: insurance; railroads; utilities and energy; and manufacturing, services, and retail. However, its businesses are run through literally hundreds of wholly owned subsidiaries. Some of these subsidiaries are relatively obscure and sell only to other companies—TTI, a Texas company that distributes components to electronics manufacturing firms. Other subsidiaries are well-known—GEICO, Fruit of the Loom, Russell Brands, Justin Brands, Benjamin Moore, Dairy Queen, RC Wiley, Helzberg Diamonds, and Net Jets to name just a few.

In addition to owning hundreds of businesses outright, Berkshire Hathaway also invests cash from its insurance businesses to take substantial, but not controlling, investments in a variety of other companies, including Mars, American Express, Coca-Cola, Wells Fargo, and IBM.

However, unlike many diversified firms, Berkshire Hathaway does not look to realize economics of scope across its businesses. According to its 2012 10K report: "Berkshire's operating businesses are managed on an unusually decentralized basis. There are essentially no centralized or integrated business functions (such as sales, marketing, purchasing, legal, or human resources) and there is minimal involvement by Berkshire's corporate headquarters in the day to day business activities of the operating businesses."

Thus, Berkshire Hathaway is an unrelated diversified firm. And, yet, it is so effectively managed as an unrelated diversified firm that it is able to generate significant value. For example, Berkshire employs 288,500 people worldwide, but—consistent with its unrelated diversification strategy—has only 24 employees at corporate headquarters.

In describing Berkshire's operating principles, founder and chair, Warren Buffett, has written: "Although our form is corporate, our attitude is partnership. Charlie Munger (Vice Chair of the Board) and I think of our shareholders as owner-partners, and ourselves as managing partners… We do not view the company as the ultimate owner of our business assets but instead view the company as a conduit through which our shareholders own the assets… Our long term economic goal is to maximize Berkshire's average annual rate of gain in intrinsic business value on a per-share basis. We do not measure the economic significance or performance of Berkshire by its size; we measure by per-share progress… Our preference would be to reach our goal by directly

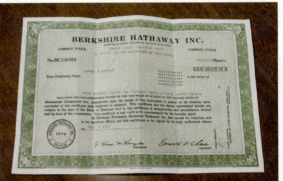

owning a diversified group of businesses…our second preference is to own parts of similar businesses… Accounting consequences do not influence our operating or capital allocation decisions. When acquisition costs are similar, we much prefer to purchase $2 of earnings that is not reportable by us under standard accounting procedures than to buy $1 of earnings that are reportable…Regardless of price, we have no interest in selling any good business Berkshire owns. We are also reluctant to sell sub-par businesses as long as we expect them to generate at least some cash… Gin Rummy managerial behavior (discard your least-promising business at each turn) is not our style."

These operating principles are quite different from many other diversified firms. General Electric, for example, for some time followed a simple operating principle: If a business unit was not number one or number two in a growing business, it would be divested. This is very much the "gin rummy" approach to management described by Warren Buffett. Also, most diversified firms seek to realize as many "integrated business activities" as they can. Certainly, ESPN—the diversified firm discussed at the beginning of Chapter 7—has many shared activities across its numerous networks.

But what works for GE or for ESPN may simply not work for Berkshire Hathaway, and vice versa. One of the many things we can learn from Berkshire Hathaway is how important it is to match a firm's corporate strategy with its organizing principles. One could argue that Berkshire Hathaway does this match very well.

Sources: (2012). *10K report for Berkshire Hathaway*; W. Buffet (2013). "An owner's manual, revised." www.berkshirehathaway.com. Accessed July 26, 2013.

This chapter is about how large diversified firms—like Berkshire Hathaway—are managed and governed efficiently. The chapter explains how these kinds of firms are managed in a way that is consistent with the interests of their owners—equity holders—as well as the interests of their other stakeholders. The three components of organizing to implement any strategy, which were first identified in Chapter 3—organizational structure, management controls, and compensation policy—are also important in implementing corporate diversification strategies.

Organizational Structure and Implementing Corporate Diversification

The most common organizational structure for implementing a corporate diversification strategy is the **M-form,** or **multidivisional,** structure. A typical M-form structure, as it would appear in a firm's annual report, is presented in Figure 8.1. This same structure is redrawn in Figure 8.2 to emphasize the roles and responsibilities of each of the major components of the M-form organization.[1]

In the multidivisional structure, each business that the firm engages in is managed through a **division.** Different firms have different names for these divisions—strategic business units (SBUs), business groups, companies. Whatever their names, the divisions in an M-form organization are true **profit-and-loss centers:** Profits and losses are calculated at the level of the division in these firms.

Different firms use different criteria for defining the boundaries of profit-and-loss centers. For example, General Electric defines its divisions in terms of the types of products each one manufactures and sells (e.g., aviation, capital, energy management, and health care). Nestlé defines its divisions with reference to the

Figure 8.1   An Example of M-Form Organizational Structure as Depicted in a Firm's Annual Report

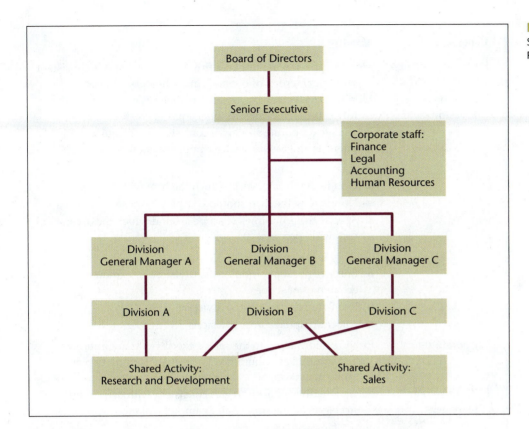

Figure 8.2 An M-Form Structure Redrawn to Emphasize Roles and Responsibilities

geographic scope of each of its businesses (North America, South America, and so forth). General Motors defines its divisions in terms of the brand names of its products (Cadillac, Chevrolet, and so forth). However they are defined, divisions in an M-form organization should be large enough to represent identifiable business entities but small enough so that each one can be managed effectively by a division general manager. Indeed, each division in an M-form organization typically adopts a U-form structure (see the discussion of the U-form structure in Chapters 4, 5, and 6), and the division general manager takes on the role of a U-form senior executive for his or her division.

The M-form structure is designed to create checks and balances for managers that increase the probability that a diversified firm will be managed in ways consistent with the interests of its equity holders. The roles of each of the major elements of the M-form structure in accomplishing this objective are summarized in Table 8.1 and discussed in the following text. Some of the conflicts of interest that might emerge between a firm's equity holders and its managers are described in the Strategy in Depth feature.

The Board of Directors

One of the major components of an M-form organization is a firm's **board of directors.** In principle, all of a firm's senior managers report to the board. The board's primary responsibility is to monitor decision making in the firm, ensuring that it is consistent with the interests of outside equity holders.

A board of directors typically consists of 10 to 15 individuals drawn from a firm's top management group and from individuals outside the firm. A firm's

Component	Activity
Board of directors	Monitor decision making in a firm to ensure that it is consistent with the interests of outside equity holders
Institutional investors	Monitor decision making to ensure that it is consistent with the interests of major institutional equity investors
Senior executives	Formulate corporate strategies consistent with equity holders' interests and assure strategy implementation Strategy formulation: ■ Decide the businesses in which the firm will operate ■ Decide how the firm should compete in those businesses ■ Specify the economies of scope around which the diversified firm will operate Strategy implementation: ■ Encourage cooperation across divisions to exploit economies of scope ■ Evaluate performance of divisions ■ Allocate capital across divisions
Corporate staff	Provide information to the senior executive about internal and external environments for strategy formulation and implementation
Division general managers	Formulate divisional strategies consistent with corporate strategies and assure strategy implementation Strategy formulation: ■ Decide how the division will compete in its business, given the corporate strategy Strategy implementation: ■ Coordinate the decisions and actions of functional managers reporting to the division general manager to implement divisional strategy ■ Compete for corporate capital allocations ■ Cooperate with other divisions to exploit corporate economies of scope
Shared activity managers	Support the operations of multiple divisions

senior executive (often identified by the title *president* or *chief executive officer* or *CEO*), its chief financial officer (CFO), and a few other senior managers are usually on the board—although managers on the board are typically outnumbered by outsiders. The firm's senior executive is often, but not always, the **chairman of the board** (a term used here to denote both female and male senior executives). The task of managerial board members—including the board chairman—is to provide other board members information and insights about critical decisions being made in the firm and the effect those decisions are likely to have on a firm's equity holders. The task of outsiders on the board is to evaluate the past, current, and future performance of the firm and of its senior managers to ensure that the actions taken in the firm are consistent with equity holders' interests.[2]

Strategy in Depth

In Chapter 7, it was suggested that sometimes it is in the best interest of equity holders to delegate to managers the day-to-day management of their equity investments in a firm. This will be the case when equity investors cannot realize a valuable economy of scope on their own, while managers *can* realize that economy of scope.

Several authors have suggested that whenever one party in an exchange delegates decision-making authority to a second party, an **agency relationship** has been created between these parties. The party delegating this decision-making authority is called the **principal;** the party to whom this authority is delegated is called the **agent.** In the context of corporate diversification, an agency relationship exists between a firm's outside equity holders (as principals) and its managers (as agents) to the extent that equity holders delegate the day-to-day management of their investment to those managers.

The agency relationship between equity holders and managers can be very effective as long as managers make investment decisions that are consistent with equity holders' interests. Thus, if equity holders are interested in maximizing the rate of return on their investment in a firm and if managers make their investment decisions with this objective in mind, then equity holders will have few concerns about delegating the day-to-day management of their investments to managers. Unfortunately, in numerous situations the interests of a firm's outside equity holders and its managers do not coincide. When parties in an agency relationship differ in their decision-making objectives,

Agency Conflicts Between Managers and Equity Holders

agency problems arise. Two common agency problems have been identified: investment in managerial perquisites and managerial risk aversion.

Managers may decide to take some of a firm's capital and invest it in **managerial perquisites** that do not add economic value to the firm but do directly benefit those managers. Examples of such investments include lavish offices, fleets of corporate jets, and corporate vacation homes. Dennis Kozlowski, former CEO of Tyco International, is accused of "stealing" $600 million in these kinds of managerial perquisites from his firm. The list of goods and services that Kozlowski lavished on himself and those close to him is truly astounding— a multimillion-dollar birthday party for his wife, a $6,000 wastebasket, a $15,000 umbrella stand, a $144,000 loan to a board member, toga-clad waiters at an event, and so on.

As outrageous as some of these managerial perquisites can be, the

second source of agency problems— **managerial risk aversion**—is probably more important in most diversified firms. As discussed in Chapter 7, equity holders can diversify their portfolio of investments at very low cost. Through their diversification efforts, they can eliminate all firm-specific risk in their portfolios. In this setting, equity holders would prefer that managers make more risky rather than less risky investments because the expected return on risky investments is usually greater than the expected return on less risky investments.

Managers, in contrast, have limited ability to diversify their human capital investments in their firm. Some portion of these investments is specific to a particular firm and has limited value in alternative uses. The value of a manager's human capital investment in a firm depends critically on the continued existence of the firm. Thus, managers are *not* indifferent to the riskiness of investment opportunities in a firm. Very risky investments may jeopardize a firm's survival and thus eliminate the value of a manager's human capital investments. These incentives can make managers more risk averse in their decision making than equity holders would like them to be.

One of the purposes of the M-form structure, and indeed of all aspects of organizing to implement corporate diversification, is to reduce these agency problems.

Sources: M. C. Jensen and W. H. Meckling (1976). "Theory of the firm: Managerial behavior, agency costs, and ownership structure." *Journal of Financial Economics,* 3, pp. 305–360; J. Useem (2003). "The biggest show." *Fortune,* December 8, pp. 157+; R. Lambert (1986). "Executive effort and selection of risky projects." *Rand Journal of Economics,* 13(2), pp. 369–378.

Research Made Relevant

A great deal of research has tried to determine when boards of directors are more or less effective in ensuring that firms are managed in ways consistent with the interests of equity holders. Three issues have received particular attention: (1) the roles of insiders (i.e., managers) and outsiders on the board, (2) whether the board chair and the senior executive should be the same or different people, and (3) whether the board should be active or passive.

With respect to insiders and outsiders on the board, in one way this seems like a simple problem. Because the primary role of the board of directors is to monitor managerial decisions to ensure that they are consistent with the interests of equity holders, it follows that the board should consist primarily of outsiders because they face no conflict of interest in evaluating managerial performance. Obviously, managers, as inside members of the board, face significant conflicts of interest in evaluating their own performance.

Research on outsider members of boards of directors tends to support this point of view. Outside directors,

The Effectiveness of Boards of Directors

as compared with insiders, tend to focus more on monitoring a firm's economic performance than on other measures of firm performance. Obviously, a firm's economic performance is most relevant to its equity investors. Outside board members are also more likely than inside members to dismiss CEOs for poor performance. Also, outside board members have a stronger incentive than inside members to maintain their reputations as effective monitors. This incentive by itself can lead to more effective monitoring by outside board members. Moreover, the monitoring effectiveness of outside

board members seems to be enhanced when they personally own a substantial amount of a firm's equity.

However, the fact that outside members face fewer conflicts of interest in evaluating managerial performance compared with management insiders on the board does not mean that there is no appropriate role for inside board members. Managers bring something to the board that cannot be easily duplicated by outsiders—detailed information about the decision-making activities inside the firm. This is precisely the information that outsiders need to effectively monitor the activities of a firm, and it is information available to them only if they work closely with insiders (managers). One way to gain access to this information is to include managers as members of the board of directors. Thus, while most research suggests that a board of directors should be composed primarily of outsiders, there is an important role for insiders/managers to play as members of a firm's board.

There is currently some debate about whether the roles of board chair and CEO should be combined

Boards of directors are typically organized into several subcommittees. An **audit committee** is responsible for ensuring the accuracy of accounting and financial statements. A **finance committee** maintains the relationship between the firm and external capital markets. A **nominating committee** nominates new board members. A **personnel and compensation committee** evaluates and compensates the performance of a firm's senior executive and other senior managers. Often, membership on these standing committees is reserved for external board members. Other standing committees reflect specific issues for a particular firm and are typically open to external and internal board members.[3]

Over the years, a great deal of research has been conducted about the effectiveness of boards of directors in ensuring that a firm's managers make decisions in ways consistent with the interests of its equity holders. Some of this work is summarized in the Research Made Relevant feature.

or separated and, if separated, what kinds of people should occupy these positions. Some have argued that the roles of CEO and board chair should definitely be separated and that the role of the chair should be filled by an outside (nonmanagerial) member of the board of directors. These arguments are based on the assumption that only an outside member of the board can ensure the independent monitoring of managerial decision making. Others have argued that effective monitoring often requires more information than would be available to outsiders, and thus the roles of board chair and CEO should be combined and filled by a firm's senior manager.

Empirical research on this question suggests that whether these roles of CEO and chairman should be combined depends on the complexity of the information analysis and monitoring task facing the CEO and board chair. Brian Boyd has found that combining the roles of CEO and chair is positively correlated with firm performance when firms operate in slow-growth and simple competitive environments—environments that do not overtax the cognitive capability

of a single individual. This finding suggests that combining these roles does not necessarily increase conflicts between a firm and its equity holders. This research also found that separating the roles of CEO and board chair is positively correlated with firm performance when firms operate in high-growth and very complex environments. In such environments, a single individual cannot fulfill all the responsibilities of both CEO and board chair, and thus the two roles need to be held by separate individuals.

Finally, with respect to active versus passive boards, historically the boards of major firms have been relatively passive and would take dramatic action, such as firing the senior executive, only if a firm's performance was significantly below expectations for long periods of time. However, more recently, boards have become more active proponents of equity holders' interests. This recent surge in board activity reflects a new economic reality: If a board does not become more active in monitoring firm performance, then other monitoring mechanisms will.

Consequently, the board of directors has become progressively more influential in representing the interests of a firm's equity holders.

However, board activity can go too far. To the extent that the board begins to operate a business on a day-to-day basis, it goes beyond its capabilities. Boards rarely have sufficient detailed information to manage a firm directly. When it is necessary to change a firm's senior executive, boards will usually not take on the responsibilities of that executive, but rather will rapidly identify a single individual—either an insider or outsider—to take over this position.

Sources: E. Zajac and J. Westphal (1994). "The costs and benefits of managerial incentives and monitoring in large U.S. corporations: When is more not better?" *Strategic Management Journal*, 15, pp. 121–142; P. Rechner and D. Dalton (1991). "CEO duality and organizational performance: A longitudinal analysis." *Strategic Management Journal*, 12, pp. 155–160; S. Finkelstein and R. D'Aveni (1994). "CEO duality as a double-edged sword: How boards of directors balance entrenchment avoidance and unity of command." *Academy of Management Journal*, 37, pp. 1079–1108; B. K. Boyd (1995). "CEO duality and firm performance: A contingency model." *Strategic Management Journal*, 16, pp. 301–312; I. F. Kesner and R. B. Johnson (1990). "An investigation of the relationship between board composition and stockholder suits." *Strategic Management Journal*, 11, pp. 327–336.

Institutional Owners

Historically, the typical large diversified firm has had its equity owned in small blocks by millions of individual investors. The exception to this general rule was family-owned or -dominated firms, a phenomenon that is relatively more common outside the United States. When a firm's ownership is spread among millions of small investors, it is difficult for any one of these investors to have a large enough ownership position to influence management decisions directly. The only course of action open to such investors if they disagree with management decisions is to sell their stock.

However, the growth of institutional owners has changed the ownership structure of many large diversified firms over the past several years. **Institutional owners** are usually pension funds, mutual funds, insurance companies, or other groups of individual investors that have joined together to manage their investments. In 1970, institutions owned 32 percent of the equity traded in the United States. By 1990, institutions owned 48 percent of this equity. In 2005, they owned 59 percent of all equity traded in the United States and 69 percent of the equity of the 1,000 largest firms in the United States.[4]

Institutional investors can use their investment clout to insist that a firm's management behaves in ways consistent with the interests of equity holders. Observers who assume that institutional investors are interested more in maximizing the short-term value of their portfolios than in the long-term performance of firms in those portfolios fear that such power will force firms to make only short-term investments. Research in the United States and Japan, however, suggests that institutional investors are not unduly myopic. Rather, as suggested earlier, these investors use approximately the same logic equity investors use when evaluating the performance of a firm. For example, one group of researchers examined the impact of institutional ownership on research and development investments in research and development (R&D)–intensive industries. R&D investments tend to be longer term in orientation. If institutional investors are myopic, they should influence firms to invest in relatively less R&D in favor of investments that generate shorter-term profits. This research showed that high levels of institutional ownership did not adversely affect the level of R&D in a firm. These findings are consistent with the notion that institutional investors are not inappropriately concerned with the short term in their monitoring activities.[5]

More generally, other researchers have shown that high levels of institutional ownership lead firms to sell strategically unrelated businesses. This effect of institutional investors is enhanced if, in addition, outside directors on a firm's board have substantial equity investments in the firm. Given the discussion of the value of unrelated diversification in Chapter 7, it seems clear that these divestment actions are typically consistent with maximizing the present value of a firm.[6]

The Senior Executive

As suggested in Table 8.1, the senior executive (the president or CEO) in an M-form organization has two responsibilities: strategy formulation and strategy implementation. *Strategy formulation* entails deciding which set of businesses a diversified firm will operate in; *strategy implementation* focuses on encouraging behavior in a firm that is consistent with this strategy. Each of these responsibilities of the senior executive is discussed in turn.

Strategy Formulation

At the broadest level, deciding which businesses a diversified firm should operate in is equivalent to discovering and developing valuable economies of scope among a firm's current and potential businesses. If these economies of scope are also rare and costly to imitate, they can be a source of sustained competitive advantage for a diversified firm.

The senior executive is uniquely positioned to discover, develop, and nurture valuable economies of scope in a diversified firm. Every other manager in this kind of firm either has a divisional point of view (e.g., division general managers and shared activity managers) or is a functional specialist (e.g., corporate staff and functional managers within divisions). Only the senior executive has a truly corporate perspective. However, the senior executive in an M-form organization should involve numerous other divisional and functional managers in strategy formulation to ensure complete and accurate information as input to the process and a broad understanding of and commitment to that strategy once it has been formulated.

Strategy Implementation

As is the case for senior executives in a U-form structure, strategy implementation in an M-form structure almost always involves resolving conflicts among groups of managers. However, instead of simply resolving conflicts between functional managers (as is the case in a U-form), senior executives in M-form organizations must resolve conflicts within and between each of the major managerial components of the M-form structure: corporate staff, division general managers, and shared activity managers. Various corporate staff managers may disagree about the economic relevance of their staff functions, corporate staff may come into conflict with division general managers over various corporate programs and activities, division general managers may disagree with how capital is allocated across divisions, division general managers may come into conflict with shared activity managers about how shared activities should be managed, shared activity managers may disagree with corporate staff about their mutual roles and responsibilities, and so forth.

Obviously, the numerous and often conflicting relationships among groups of managers in an M-form organization can place significant strategy implementation burdens on the senior executive.[7] While resolving these numerous conflicts, however, the senior executive needs to keep in mind the reasons why the firm began pursuing a diversification strategy in the first place: to exploit real economies of scope that outside investors cannot realize on their own. Any strategy implementation decisions that jeopardize the realization of these real economies of scope are inconsistent with the underlying strategic objectives of a diversified firm. These issues are analyzed in detail later in this chapter, in the discussion of management control systems in the M-form organization.

The Office of the President: Board Chair, CEO, and COO

It is often the case that the roles and responsibilities of the senior executive in an M-form organization are greater than can be reasonably managed by a single individual. This is especially likely if a firm is broadly diversified across numerous complex products and markets. In this situation, it is not uncommon for the tasks of the senior executive to be divided among two or three people: the **board chair,** the **chief executive officer,** and the **chief operating officer (COO).** The primary responsibilities of each of these roles in an M-form organization are listed in Table 8.2. Together, these roles are known as the **office of the president.** In general, as the tasks facing the office of the president become more demanding and complex, the more likely it is that the roles and responsibilities of this office will be divided among two or three people.

Corporate Staff

The primary responsibility of **corporate staff** is to provide information about the firm's external and internal environments to the firm's senior executive. This information is vital for both the strategy formulation and the strategy implementation responsibilities of the senior executive. Corporate staff functions that provide

Board chair	Supervision of the board of directors in its monitoring role
Chief executive officer	Strategy formulation
Chief operating officer	Strategy implementation

TABLE 8.2 Responsibilities of Three Different Roles in the Office of the President

information about a firm's external environment include finance, investor relations, legal affairs, regulatory affairs, and corporate advertising. Corporate staff functions that provide information about a firm's internal environment include accounting and corporate human resources. These corporate staff functions report directly to a firm's senior executive and are a conduit of information to that executive.

Corporate and Divisional Staff

Many organizations re-create some corporate staff functions within each division of the organization. This is particularly true for internally oriented corporate staff functions such as accounting and human resources. At the division level, divisional staff managers usually have a direct "solid-line" reporting relationship to their respective corporate staff functional managers and a less formal "dotted-line" reporting relationship to their division general manager. The reporting relationship between the divisional staff manager and the corporate staff manager is the link that enables the corporate staff manager to collect the information that the senior executive requires for strategy formulation and implementation. The senior executive can also use this corporate staff–division staff relationship to communicate corporate policies and procedures to the divisions, although these policies can also be communicated directly by the senior executive to division general managers.

Although divisional staff managers usually have a less formal relationship with their division general managers, in practice division general managers can have an important influence on the activities of divisional staff. After all, divisional staff managers may formally report to corporate staff managers, but they spend most of their time interacting with their division general managers and with the other functional managers who report to their division general managers. These divided loyalties can sometimes affect the timeliness and accuracy of the information transmitted from divisional staff managers to corporate staff managers and thus affect the timeliness and accuracy of the information the senior executive uses for strategy formulation and implementation.

Nowhere are these divided loyalties potentially more problematic than in accounting staff functions. Obviously, it is vitally important for the senior executive in an M-form organization to receive timely and accurate information about divisional performance. If the timeliness and accuracy of that information are inappropriately affected by division general managers, the effectiveness of senior management can be adversely affected. Moreover, in some situations division general managers can have very strong incentives to affect the timeliness and accuracy of divisional performance information, especially if a division general manager's compensation depends on this information or if the capital allocated to a division depends on this information.

Efficient monitoring by the senior executive requires that corporate staff, and especially the accounting corporate staff function, remains organizationally independent of division general managers—thus, the importance of the solid-line relationship between divisional staff managers and corporate staff managers. Nevertheless, the ability of corporate staff to obtain accurate performance information from divisions also depends on close cooperative working relationships between corporate staff, divisional staff, and division general managers—hence, the importance of the dotted-line relationship between divisional staff managers and division general managers. How one maintains the balance between the distance and objectivity needed to evaluate a division's performance on the one hand, and, on the other hand, the cooperation and teamwork needed to gain access to the information required to evaluate a division's performance distinguishes excellent from mediocre corporate staff managers.

Overinvolvement in Managing Division Operations

Over and above the failure to maintain a balance between objectivity and cooperation in evaluating divisional performance, the one sure way that corporate staff can fail in a multidivisional firm is to become too involved in the day-to-day operations of divisions. In an M-form structure, the management of such day-to-day operations is delegated to division general managers and to functional managers who report to division general managers. Corporate staff managers collect and transmit information; they do not manage divisional operations.

One way to ensure that corporate staff does not become too involved in managing the day-to-day operations of divisions is to keep corporate staff small. This is certainly true for some of the best-managed diversified firms in the world including (and described in the opening case) Berkshire Hathaway. For example, just 1.5 percent of Johnson & Johnson's more than 80,000 employees work at the firm's headquarters, and only some of those individuals are members of the corporate staff. Hanson Industries has in its U.S. headquarters 120 people who help manage a diversified firm with $8 billion in revenues. Clayton, Dubilier, and Rice, a management buyout firm, has only 11 headquarters staff members overseeing eight businesses with collective sales of more than $6 billion.[8]

Division General Manager

Division general managers in an M-form organization have primary responsibility for managing a firm's businesses from day to day. Division general managers have full profit-and-loss responsibility and typically have multiple functional managers reporting to them. As general managers, they have both strategy formulation and strategy implementation responsibilities. On the strategy formulation side, division general managers choose strategies for their divisions, within the broader strategic context established by the senior executive of the firm. Many of the analytical tools described in Parts 1 and 2 of this book can be used by division general managers to make these strategy formulation decisions.

The strategy implementation responsibilities of division general managers in an M-form organization parallel the strategy implementation responsibilities of senior executives in U-form organizations. In particular, division general managers must be able to coordinate the activities of often-conflicting functional managers in order to implement a division's strategies.

In addition to their responsibilities as a U-form senior executive, division general managers in an M-form organization have two additional responsibilities: to compete for corporate capital and to cooperate with other divisions to exploit corporate economies of scope. Division general managers compete for corporate capital by promising high rates of return on capital invested by the corporation in their business. In most firms, divisions that have demonstrated the ability to generate high rates of return on earlier capital investments gain access to more capital or to lower-cost capital, compared with divisions that have not demonstrated a history of such performance.

Division general managers cooperate to exploit economies of scope by working with shared activity managers, corporate staff managers, and the senior executive in the firm to isolate, understand, and use the economies of scope around which the diversified firm was originally organized. Division general managers can even become involved in discovering new economies of scope that were not anticipated when the firm's diversification strategy was originally implemented but nevertheless may be both valuable and costly for outside investors to create on their own.

Of course, a careful reader will recognize a fundamental conflict between the last two responsibilities of division general managers in an M-form organization. These managers are required to compete for corporate capital and to cooperate to exploit economies of scope at the same time. Competition is important because it leads division general managers to focus on generating high levels of economic performance from their divisions. If each division is generating high levels of economic performance, then the diversified firm as a whole is likely to do well also. However, cooperation is important to exploit economies of scope that are the economic justification for implementing a diversification strategy in the first place. If divisions do not cooperate in exploiting these economies, there are few, if any, justifications for implementing a corporate diversification strategy, and the diversified firm should be split into multiple independent entities. The need to simultaneously compete and cooperate puts significant managerial burdens on division general managers. It is likely that this ability is both rare and costly to imitate across most diversified firms.[9]

Shared Activity Managers

One of the potential economies of scope identified in Chapter 7 was shared activities. Divisions in an M-form organization exploit this economy of scope when one or more of the stages in their value chains are managed in common. Typical examples of activities shared across two or more divisions in a multidivisional firm include common sales forces, common distribution systems, common manufacturing facilities, and common research and development efforts (also see Table 7.2). The primary responsibility of the individuals who manage shared activities is to support the operations of the divisions that share the activity.

The way in which M-form structure is often depicted in company annual reports (as in Figure 8.1) tends to obscure the operational role of shared activities. In this version of the M-form organizational chart, no distinction is made between corporate staff functions and shared activity functions. Moreover, it appears that managers of shared activities report directly to a firm's senior executive, just like corporate staff. These ambiguities are resolved by redrawing the M-form organizational chart to emphasize the roles and responsibilities of different units within the M-form (as in Figure 8.2). In this more accurate representation of how an M-form actually functions, corporate staff groups are separated from shared activity managers, and each is shown reporting to its primary internal "customer." That "internal customer" is the senior executive for corporate staff groups and two or more division general managers for shared activity managers.

Shared Activities as Cost Centers

Shared activities are often managed as cost centers in an M-form structure. That is, rather than having profit-and-loss responsibility, **cost centers** are assigned a budget and manage their operations to that budget. When this is the case, shared activity managers do not attempt to create profits when they provide services to the divisions they support. Rather, these services are priced to internal customers in such a way that the shared activity just covers its cost of operating.

Because cost center shared activities do not have to generate profits from their operations, the cost of the services they provide to divisions can be less than the cost of similar services provided either by a division itself or by outside suppliers. If a shared activity is managed as a cost center, and the cost of services from this shared activity is *greater than* the cost of similar services provided by alternative sources, then either this shared activity is not being well managed or it was not a real economy of scope in the first place. However, when the cost of services from a shared activity is *less than* the cost of comparable services provided by a division itself or by an outside supplier, then division general managers have a strong incentive to use the services of shared activities, thereby exploiting an economy of scope that may have been one of the original reasons why a firm implemented a corporate diversification strategy.

Shared Activities as Profit Centers

Some diversified firms are beginning to manage shared activities as profit centers, rather than as cost centers. Moreover, rather than requiring divisions to use the services of shared activities, divisions retain the right to purchase services from internal shared activities or from outside suppliers or to provide services for themselves. In this setting, managers of shared activities are required to compete for their internal customers on the basis of the price and quality of the services they provide.[10]

One firm that has taken this profit-center approach to managing shared activities is ABB, Inc., a Swiss engineering firm. ABB eliminated almost all its corporate staff and reorganized its remaining staff functions into shared activities. Shared activities in ABB compete to provide services to ABB divisions. Not only do some traditional shared activities—such as research and development and sales—compete for internal customers, but many traditional corporate staff functions—such as human resources, marketing, and finance—do as well. ABB's approach to managing shared activities has resulted in a relatively small corporate staff and in increasingly specialized and customized shared activities.[11]

Of course, the greatest risk associated with treating shared activities as profit centers and letting them compete for divisional customers is that divisions may choose to obtain no services or support from shared activities. Although this course of action may be in the self-interest of each division, it may not be in the best interest of the corporation as a whole if, in fact, shared activities are an important economy of scope around which the diversified firm is organized.

In the end, the task facing the managers of shared activities is the same: to provide such highly customized and high-quality services to divisional customers at a reasonable cost that those internal customers will not want to seek alternative suppliers outside the firm or provide those services themselves. In an M-form organization, the best way to ensure that shared activity economies of scope are realized is for shared activity managers to satisfy their internal customers.

Management Controls and Implementing Corporate Diversification

The M-form structure presented in Figures 8.1 and 8.2 is complex and multifaceted. However, no organizational structure by itself is able to fully implement a corporate diversification strategy. The M-form structure must be supplemented with a variety of management controls. Three of the most important management controls in an M-form structure—systems for evaluating divisional performance, for allocating capital across divisions, and for transferring intermediate products between divisions—are discussed in this section.[12]

Evaluating Divisional Performance

Because divisions in an M-form structure are profit-and-loss centers, evaluating divisional performance should, in principle, be straightforward: Divisions that are very profitable should be evaluated more positively than divisions that are less profitable. In practice, this seemingly simple task is surprisingly complex. Two problems typically arise: (1) How should division profitability be measured? and (2) How should economy-of-scope linkages between divisions be factored into divisional performance measures?

Measuring Divisional Performance

Divisional performance can be measured in at least two ways. The first focuses on a division's accounting performance; the second on a division's economic performance.

Accounting Measures of Divisional Performance. Both accounting and economic measures of performance can be used in measuring the performance of divisions within a diversified firm. Common accounting measures of divisional performance include the return on the assets controlled by a division, the return on a division's sales, and a division's sales growth. These accounting measures of divisional performance are then compared with some standard to see if a division's performance exceeds or falls short of that standard. Diversified firms use three different standards of comparison when evaluating the performance of a division: (1) a hurdle rate that is common across all the different business units in a firm, (2) a division's budgeted level of performance (which may vary by division), and (3) the average level of profitability of firms in a division's industry.

Each of these standards of comparison has its strengths and weaknesses. For example, if a corporation has a single hurdle rate of profitability that all divisions must meet or exceed, there is little ambiguity about the performance objectives of divisions. However, a single standard ignores important differences in performance that might exist across divisions.

Comparing a division's actual performance to its budgeted performance allows the performance expectations of different divisions to vary, but the budgeting process is time-consuming and fraught with political intrigue. One study showed that corporate managers routinely discount the sales projections and capital requests of division managers on the assumption that division managers are trying to "game" the budgeting system.[13] Moreover, division budgets are usually based on a single set of assumptions about how the economy is going to evolve, how competition in a division's industry is going to evolve, and what actions that division is going to take in its industry. When these assumptions no longer hold, budgets are redone—a costly and time-consuming process that has little to do with generating value in a firm.

Finally, although comparing a division's performance with the average level of profitability of firms in a division's industry also allows performance expectations to vary across divisions within a diversified firm, this approach lets other firms determine what is and is not excellent performance for a division within a diversified firm. This approach can also be manipulated: By choosing just the "right" firms with which to compare a division's performance, almost any division can be made to look like it's performing better than its industry average.[14]

No matter what standard of comparison is used to evaluate a division's accounting performance, most accounting measures of divisional performance have a common limitation. All these measures have a short-term bias. This short-term bias reflects the fact that all these measures treat investments in resources and capabilities that have the potential for generating value in the long run as costs during a particular year. In order to reduce costs in a given year, division managers may sometimes forgo investing in these resources and capabilities, even if they could be a source of sustained competitive advantage for a division in the long run.

Economic Measures of Divisional Performance.   Given the limitations of accounting measures of divisional performance, several firms have begun adopting economic methods of evaluating this performance. Economic methods build on accounting methods but adjust those methods to incorporate short-term investments that may generate long-term benefits. Economic methods also compare a division's performance with a firm's cost of capital (see Chapter 1). This avoids some of the gaming that can characterize the use of other standards of comparison in applying accounting measures of divisional performance.

Perhaps the most popular of these economically oriented measures of division performance is known as **economic value added (EVA).**[15] EVA is calculated by subtracting the cost of capital employed in a division from that division's earnings in the following manner:

$$\text{EVA} = \text{adjusted accounting earnings}$$
$$(\text{weighted average cost of capital} \times \text{total capital employed by a division})$$

Several of the terms in the EVA formula require some discussion. For example, the calculation of economic value added begins with a division's "adjusted" accounting earnings. These are a division's traditional accounting earnings, adjusted so that they approximate a division's economic earnings. Several adjustments to a division's accounting statements have been described in the literature. For example, traditional accounting practices require R&D spending to be deducted each year from a division's earnings. This can lead division general managers to under-invest in longer-term R&D efforts. In the EVA measure of divisional performance, R&D spending is added back into a division's performance, and R&D is then treated as an asset and depreciated over some period of time.

One consulting firm (Stern Stewart) that specializes in implementing EVA-based divisional evaluation systems in multidivisional firms makes up to 40 "adjustments" to a division's standard accounting earnings so that they more closely approximate economic earnings. Many of these adjustments are proprietary to this consulting firm. However, the most important adjustments—such as how R&D should be treated—are broadly known.

The terms in parentheses in the EVA equation reflect the cost of investing in a division. Rather than using some alternative standard of comparison, EVA applies financial theory and multiplies the amount of money invested in a division by a firm's weighted average cost of capital. A firm's weighted average cost of capital is the amount of money a firm could earn if it invested in any of its other divisions. In this sense, a firm's weighted average cost of capital can be thought of as the opportunity cost of investing in a particular division, as opposed to investing in any other division in the firm.

By adjusting a division's earnings and accounting for the cost of investing in a division, EVA is a much more accurate estimate of a division's economic performance than are traditional accounting measures of performance. The number of diversified firms evaluating their divisions with EVA-based measures of divisional performance is impressive and growing. These firms include AT&T, Coca-Cola, Quaker Oats, CSX, Briggs and Stratton, and Allied Signal. At Allied Signal, divisions that do not earn their cost of capital are awarded the infamous "leaky bucket" award. If this performance is not improved, division general managers are replaced. The use of EVA has been touted as the key to creating economic wealth in a diversified corporation.[16]

Economies of Scope and the Ambiguity of Divisional Performance

Whether a firm uses accounting measures to evaluate the performance of a division or uses economic measures of performance such as EVA, divisional performance in a well-managed diversified firm can never be evaluated unambiguously. Consider a simple example.

Suppose that in a particular multidivisional firm there are only two divisions (Division A and Division B) and one shared activity (R&D). Also, suppose that the two divisions are managed as profit-and-loss centers and that the R&D shared activity is managed as a cost center. To support this R&D effort, each division pays $10 million per year and has been doing so for 10 years. Finally, suppose that after 10 years of effort (and investment) the R&D group develops a valuable new technology that perfectly addresses Division A's business needs.

Obviously, no matter how divisional performance is measured it is likely to be the case that Division A's performance will rise relative to Division B's performance. In this situation, what percentage of Division A's improved performance should be allocated to Division A, what percentage should be allocated to the R&D group, and what percentage should be allocated to Division B?

The managers in each part of this diversified firm can make compelling arguments in their favor. Division general manager A can reasonably argue that without Division A's efforts to exploit the new technology, the full value of the technology would never have been realized. The R&D manager can reasonably argue that, without the R&D effort, there would not have been a technology to exploit in the first place. Finally, division general manager B can reasonably argue that, without the dedicated long-term investment of Division B in R&D, there would have been no new technology and no performance increase for Division A.

That all three of these arguments can be made suggests that, to the extent that a firm exploits real economies of scope in implementing a diversification strategy, it will not be possible to unambiguously evaluate the performance of individual divisions in that firm. The fact that there are economies of scope in a diversified firm means that all of the businesses a firm operates in are more valuable bundled together than they would be if kept separate from one another. Efforts to evaluate the performance of these businesses as if they were separate from one another are futile.

One solution to this problem is to force businesses in a diversified firm to operate independently of each other. If each business operates independently, then it will be possible to unambiguously evaluate its performance. Of course, to the extent that this independence is enforced, the diversified firm is unlikely to be able to realize the very economies of scope that were the justification for the diversification strategy in the first place.

Divisional performance ambiguity is bad enough when shared activities are the primary economy of scope that a diversified firm is trying to exploit. This ambiguity increases dramatically when the economy of scope is based on intangible core competencies. In this situation, it is shared learning and experience that justify a firm's diversification efforts. The intangible nature of these economies of scope multiplies the difficulty of the divisional evaluation task.

Even firms that apply rigorous EVA measures of divisional performance are unable to fully resolve these performance ambiguity difficulties. For example, the Coca-Cola division of the Coca-Cola Company has made enormous investments in the Coke brand name over the years, and the Diet Coke division has exploited some of that brand name capital in its own marketing efforts. Of course, it is not clear that all of Diet Coke's success can be attributed to the Coke brand name. After all, Diet Coke has developed its own creative advertising, its own loyal group of customers, and so forth. How much of Diet Coke's success—as measured through that division's economic value added—should be allocated to the Coke brand name (an investment made long before Diet Coke was even conceived) and how much should be allocated to the Diet Coke division's efforts? EVA measures of divisional performance do not resolve ambiguities created when economies of scope exist across divisions.[17]

In the end, the quantitative evaluation of divisional performance—with either accounting or economic measures—must be supplemented by the experience and judgment of senior executives in a diversified firm. Only by evaluating a division's performance numbers in the context of a broader, more subjective evaluation of the division's performance can a true picture of divisional performance be developed.

Allocating Corporate Capital

Another potentially valuable economy of scope outlined in Chapter 7 (besides shared activities and core competencies) is internal capital allocation. In that discussion, it was suggested that for internal capital allocation to be a justification for diversification the information made available to senior executives allocating capital in a diversified firm must be superior, in both amount and quality, to the information available to external sources of capital in the external capital market. Both the quality and the quantity of the information available in an internal capital market depend on the organization of the diversified firm.

One of the primary limitations of internal capital markets is that division general managers have a strong incentive to overstate their division's prospects and understate its problems in order to gain access to more capital at lower costs. Having an independent corporate accounting function in a diversified firm can help address this problem. However, given the ambiguities inherent in evaluating divisional performance in a well-managed diversified firm, independent corporate accountants do not resolve all these informational problems.

In the face of these challenges, some firms use a process called **zero-based budgeting** to help allocate capital. In zero-based budgeting, corporate executives create a list of all capital allocation requests from divisions in a firm, rank them from "most important" to "least important," and then fund all the projects a firm can afford, given the amount of capital it has available. In principle, no project will receive funding for the future simply because it received funding in the past. Rather, each project has to stand on its own merits each year by being included among the important projects the firm can afford to fund.

Although zero-based budgeting has some attractive features, it has some important limitations as well. For example, evaluating and ranking all projects in a diversified firm from "most important" to "least important" is a very difficult task. It requires corporate executives to have a very complete understanding of the strategic role of each of the projects being proposed by a division, as well as an understanding of how these projects will affect the short-term performance of divisions.

In the end, no matter what process firms use to allocate capital, allocating capital inside a firm in a way that is more efficient than could be done by external capital markets requires the use of information that is not available to those external markets. Typically, that information will be intangible, tacit, and complex. Corporate managers looking to realize this economy of scope must find a way to use this kind of information effectively.[18] The difficulty of managing this process effectively may be one of the reasons why internal capital allocation often fails to qualify as a valuable economy of scope in diversified firms.[19]

Transferring Intermediate Products

The existence of economies of scope across multiple divisions in a diversified firm often means that products or services produced in one division are used as inputs for products or services produced by a second division. Such products or services are called **intermediate products or services.** Intermediate products or services can be transferred between any of the units in an M-form organization. This transfer is perhaps most important and problematic when it occurs between profit center divisions.

The transfer of intermediate products or services among divisions is usually managed through a **transfer-pricing system:** One division "sells" its product or service to a second division for a transfer price. Unlike a market price, which is typically determined by market forces of supply and demand, transfer prices are set by a firm's corporate management to accomplish corporate objectives.

Setting Optimal Transfer Prices

From an economic point of view, the rule for establishing the optimal transfer price in a diversified firm is quite simple: The transfer price should be the value of the opportunities forgone when one division's product or service is transferred to another division. Consider the following example. Division A's marginal cost of production is $5 per unit, but Division A can sell all of its output to outside customers for $6 per unit. If Division A can sell all of its output to outside customers for $6 per unit, the value of the opportunity forgone of transferring a unit of production from Division A to Division B is $6—the amount of money that Division A forgoes by transferring its production to Division B instead of selling it to the market.

However, if Division A is selling all the units it can to external customers for $6 per unit but still has some excess manufacturing capacity, the value of the opportunity forgone in transferring the product from Division A to Division B is only $5 per unit—Division A's marginal cost of production. Because the external market cannot absorb any more of Division A's product at $6 per unit, the value of the opportunity forgone when Division A transfers units of production to Division B is not $6 per unit (Division A can't get that price), but only $5 per unit.[20]

When transfer prices are set equal to opportunity costs, selling divisions will produce output up to the point that the marginal cost of the last unit produced equals the transfer price. Moreover, buying divisions will buy units from other divisions in the firm as long as the net revenues from doing so just cover the transfer price. These transfer prices will lead profit-maximizing divisions to optimize the diversified firm's profits.

Difficulties in Setting Optimal Transfer Prices

Setting transfer prices equal to opportunity costs sounds simple enough, but it is very difficult to do in real diversified firms. Establishing optimal transfer prices requires information about the value of the opportunities forgone by the "selling" division. This, in turn, requires information about this division's marginal costs, its manufacturing capacity, external demand for its products, and so forth. Much of this information is difficult to obtain. Moreover, it is rarely stable. As market conditions change, demand for a division's products can change, marginal costs can change, and the value of opportunities forgone can change. Also, to the extent that a selling division customizes the products or services it transfers to other divisions in a diversified firm, the value of the opportunities forgone by this selling division become even more difficult to calculate.

Even if this information could be obtained and updated rapidly, division general managers in selling divisions have strong incentives to manipulate the information in ways that increase the perceived value of the opportunities forgone by their division. These division general managers can thus increase the transfer price for the products or services they sell to internal customers and thereby appropriate for their division profits that should have been allocated to buying divisions.

Setting Transfer Prices in Practice

Because it is rarely possible for firms to establish an optimal transfer-pricing scheme, most diversified firms must adopt some form of transfer pricing that attempts to approximate optimal prices. Several of these transfer-pricing schemes are described in Table 8.3. However, no matter what particular scheme a firm uses, the transfer prices it generates will, at times, create inefficiencies and conflicts in a diversified firm. Some of these inefficiencies and conflicts are described in Table 8.4.[21]

The inefficiencies and conflicts created by transfer-pricing schemes that only approximate optimal transfer prices mean that few diversified firms are ever fully satisfied with how they set transfer prices. Indeed, one study found that as the level of resource sharing in a diversified firm increases (thereby increasing the importance of transfer-pricing mechanisms) the level of job satisfaction for division general managers decreases.[22]

TABLE 8.3 Alternative Transfer-Pricing Schemes

Exchange autonomy	■ Buying and selling division general managers are free to negotiate transfer price without corporate involvement. ■ Transfer price is set equal to the selling division's price to external customers.
Mandated full cost	■ Transfer price is set equal to the selling division's actual cost of production. ■ Transfer price is set equal to the selling division's standard cost (i.e., the cost of production if the selling division were operating at maximum efficiency).
Mandated market based	■ Transfer price is set equal to the market price in the selling division's market.
Dual pricing	■ Transfer price for the buying division is set equal to the selling division's actual or standard costs. ■ Transfer price for the selling division is set equal to the price to external customers or to the market price in the selling division's market.

Source: R. Eccles (1985). *The transfer pricing problem: A theory for practice.* Lexington Books: Lexington, MA. Used with permission of Rowman and Littlefield Publishing Group.

1. Buying and selling divisions negotiate transfer price.
   - What about the negotiating and haggling costs?
   - The corporation risks not exploiting economies of scope if the right transfer price cannot be negotiated.
2. Transfer price is set equal to the selling division's price to external customers.
   - Which customers? Different selling division customers may get different prices.
   - Shouldn't the volume created by the buying division for a selling division be reflected in a lower transfer price?
   - The selling division doesn't have marketing expenses when selling to another division. Shouldn't that be reflected in a lower transfer price?
3. Transfer price is set equal to the selling division's actual costs.
   - What are those actual costs and who gets to determine them?
   - *All* the selling division's costs or only the costs relevant to the products being purchased by the buying division?
4. Transfer price is set equal to the selling division's standard costs.
   - Standard costs are the costs the selling division would incur if it were running at maximum efficiency. This hypothetical capacity subsidizes the buying division.
5. Transfer price is set equal to the market price.
   - If the product in question is highly differentiated, there is no simple "market price."
   - Shouldn't the volume created by the buying division for a selling division be reflected in a lower transfer price?
   - The selling division doesn't have marketing expenses when selling to a buying division. Shouldn't that be reflected in a lower transfer price?
6. Transfer price is set equal to actual costs for the selling division and to market price for the buying division.
   - This combination of schemes simply combines other problems of setting transfer prices.

It is not unusual for a diversified firm to change its transfer-pricing mechanisms every few years in an attempt to find the "right" transfer-pricing mechanism. Economic theory tells us what the "right" transfer-pricing mechanism is: Transfer prices should equal opportunity cost. However, this "correct" transfer-pricing mechanism cannot be implemented in most firms. Firms that continually change their transfer-pricing mechanisms generally find that all these systems have some weaknesses. In deciding which system to use, a firm should be less concerned about finding the right transfer-pricing mechanism and more concerned about choosing a transfer-pricing policy that creates the fewest management problems—or at least the kinds of problems that the firm can manage effectively. Indeed, some scholars have suggested that the search for optimal transfer pricing should be abandoned in favor of treating transfer pricing as a conflict-resolution process. Viewed in this way, transfer pricing highlights differences between divisions and thus makes it possible to begin to resolve those differences in a mutually beneficial way.[23]

Overall, the three management control processes described here—measuring divisional performance, allocating corporate capital, and transferring intermediate products—suggest that the implementation of a corporate diversification strategy requires a great deal of management skill and experience. They also suggest that sometimes diversified firms may find themselves operating businesses that no

Strategy in the Emerging Enterprise

A **corporate spin-off** exists when a large, typically diversified firm divests itself of a business in which it has historically been operating and the divested business operates as an independent entity. Thus, corporate spin-offs are different from asset divestitures, where a firm sells some of its assets, including perhaps a particular business, to another firm. Spin-offs are a way that new firms can enter into the economy.

Spin-offs can occur in numerous ways. For example, a business might be sold to its managers and employees who then manage and work in this independently operating firm. Alternatively, a business unit within a diversified firm may be sold to the public through an **initial public offering (IPO)**. Sometimes, the corporation spinning off a business unit will retain some ownership stake in the spin-off; other times, this corporation will sever all financial links with the spun-off firm.

In general, large diversified firms might spin off businesses they own for three reasons. First, the efficient management of these businesses may require very specific skills that are not available in a diversified firm. For example, suppose a diversified manufacturing firm finds itself operating in an R&D-intensive industry. The management skills required to manage manufacturing efficiently can be very different from the management skills required to manage R&D. If a diversified firm's skills do not match the skills required in a particular business, that business might be spun off.

Second, anticipated economies of scope between a business and the rest

Transforming Big Business into Entrepreneurship

of a diversified firm may turn out to not be valuable. For example, PepsiCo acquired Kentucky Fried Chicken, Pizza Hut, and Taco Bell, anticipating important marketing synergies between these fast-food restaurants and PepsiCo's soft drink business. Despite numerous efforts to realize these synergies, they were not forthcoming. Indeed, several of these fast-food restaurants began losing market share because they were forced to sell Pepsi rather than Coca-Cola products. After a few years, PepsiCo spun off its restaurants into a separate business.

Finally, it may be necessary to spin a business off in order to fund a firm's other businesses. Large diversified firms may face capital constraints due to, among other things, their high level of debt. In this setting, firms may need to spin off a business in order to raise capital to invest in other parts of the firm. Moreover, spinning off a part of the business that is particularly costly in terms of the capital it consumes may not only be a source of funds for other parts of this firm's business, it can also reduce the demand for that capital within a firm.

Research in corporate finance suggests that corporations are most likely to spin off businesses that are unrelated to a firm's corporate diversification strategy; those that are performing poorly compared with other businesses a firm operates in; and relatively small businesses. Also, the amount of merger and acquisition activity in a particular industry will determine which businesses are spun off. The greater the level of this activity in an industry, the more likely that a business owned by a corporation in such an industry will be spun off. This is because the level of merger and acquisition activity in an industry is an indicator of the number of people and firms that might be interested in purchasing a spun-off business. However, when there is not much merger and acquisition activity in an industry, businesses in that industry are less likely to be spun off, even if they are unrelated to a firm's corporate diversification strategy, are performing poorly, or are small. In such settings, large firms are not likely to obtain the full value associated with spinning off a business and thus are reluctant to do so.

Whatever the conditions that lead a large diversified firm to spin off one of its businesses, this process is important for creating new firms in the economy.

Sources: F. Schlingemann, R. M. Stulz, and R. Walkling (2002). "Divestitures and the liquidity of the market for corporate assets." *Journal of Financial Economics*, 64, pp. 117–144; G. Hite, J. Owens, and R. Rogers (1987). "The market for inter-firm asset sales: Partial sell-offs and total liquidations." *Journal of Financial Economics*, 18, pp. 229–252; P. Berger and E. Ofek (1999). "Causes and consequences of corporate focusing programs." *Review of Financial Studies*, 12, pp. 311–345.

longer fit with the firm's overall corporate strategy. What happens when a division no longer fits with a firm's corporate strategy is described in the Strategy in the Emerging Enterprise feature.

Compensation Policies and Implementing Corporate Diversification

A firm's compensation policies constitute a final set of tools for implementing diversification. Traditionally, the compensation of corporate managers in a diversified firm has been only loosely connected to the firm's economic performance. One important study examined the relationship between executive compensation and firm performance and found that differences in CEO cash compensation (salary plus cash bonus) are not very responsive to differences in firm performance.[24] In particular, this study showed that a CEO of a firm whose equity holders lost, collectively, $400 million in a year earned average cash compensation worth $800,000, while a CEO of a firm whose equity holders gained, collectively, $400 million in a year earned average cash compensation worth $1,040,000. Thus, an $800 million difference in the performance of a firm only had, on average, a $204,000 impact on the size of a CEO's salary and cash bonus. Put differently, for every million dollars of improved firm performance, CEOs, on average, get paid an additional $255. After taxes, increasing a firm's performance by a million dollars is roughly equal in value to a good dinner at a nice restaurant.

However, this same study was able to show that if a substantial percentage of a CEO's compensation came in the form of stock and stock options in the

Ethics and Strategy

Nothing in business gets as much negative press as CEO salaries. In 2012, for example, Larry Ellison, CEO of Oracle, was paid $96.2 million; Robert Kotick, CEO of Activision Blizzard, was paid $64.9 million; Leslie Moonves of CBS $60.3 million; David Zaslay of Discovery Communications $49.9 million; and James Crowe, CEO of Level 3 Communications, $40.7 million. Marissa Mayer, CEO of Yahoo, was the highest-compensated woman in 2012—she was paid $36.6 million (ranked ninth on the list). Reasonable people ask: Is anyone worth this much money?

But determining what CEOs "should" be paid is a difficult question.

Do CEOs Get Paid Too Much?

Some firms adopt policies that state that their CEOs cannot make more than some multiple of the lowest-paid employee in a firm. In Chapter 1, it was suggested that such a compensation policy at Ben & Jerry's Ice Cream may have cost its shareholders millions of dollars because it prevented Ben & Jerry's from recruiting a CEO who would have facilitated Ben & Jerry's acquisition by a firm that could effectively leverage the Ben & Jerry's brand.

Many firms delegate the responsibility of determining CEO salary to the compensation committee on the board of directors. The compensation committee often identifies a set of comparable firms (i.e., firms about the same size and in the same industry) as its firm and firm, changes in compensation would be closely linked with changes in the firm performance. In particular, the $800 million difference in firm performance just described would be associated with a $1.2 million difference in the value of CEO compensation if CEO compensation included stock and stock options in addition to cash compensation. In this setting, an additional million dollars of firm performance increases a CEO's salary by $667.

These and similar findings reported elsewhere have led more and more diversified firms to include stock and stock options as part of the compensation package for the CEO. As important, many firms now extend this non-cash compensation to other senior managers in a diversified firm, including division general managers. For example, the top 1,300 managers at General Dynamics receive stock and stock options as part of their compensation package. Moreover, the cash bonuses of these managers also depend on General Dynamics' stock market performance. At Johnson & Johnson, all division general managers receive a five-component compensation package. The level of only one of those components, salary, does not vary with the economic profitability of the business over which a division general manager presides. The level of the other four components—a cash bonus, stock grants, stock options, and a deferred income package—varies with the economic performance of a particular division. Moreover, the value of some of these variable components of compensation also depends on Johnson & Johnson's long-term economic performance.[25]

To the extent that compensation in diversified firms gives managers incentives to make decisions consistent with stockholders' interests, they can be an important part of the process of implementing corporate diversification. However, the sheer size of the compensation paid to some CEOs raises ethical issues for some. These ethical issues are discussed in the Ethics and Strategy feature.

then calculates the average compensation of CEOs in these firms. Of course, because no firm wants to think that its CEO is in the "bottom half" of its comparable firms, most firms pay their CEOs something over this average—a decision-making process that ensures that, in the long run, CEO pay will continue to rise.

The mix of compensation also makes it difficult to know how much a CEO should get paid. For example, most of the "big bucks" in CEO compensation come not from salary but from bonuses, stock, stock options, and other perquisites. Most of these non-salary forms of compensation depend on the performance of a firm and are designed to align the financial interests of CEOs and a firm's shareholders. This is the case at Berkshire Hathaway, where a key operating principle is that most of the personal wealth of Warren Buffett and his senior management team is held in Berkshire Hathaway stock. In fact, one study showed that, on average, CEO compensation in excess of what would be expected based on a CEO's business experience is positively correlated with a firm's performance.

Of course, correlation is not causation. The question remains open: Does a CEO have to receive massive incentive compensation—literally hundreds of millions of dollars over time—just so he (or she) will do his (or her) job: to maximize returns to shareholders? And what are the implications of this compensation for the other employees in a firm—does it encourage their ambitions to seek employment among the senior ranks of a firm, or does it discourage and demoralize them that one person can get paid so much while they get paid so little?

Sources: Russell, Karl. "Executive Pay by the Numbers" www.nytimes.com/interactive/2013/06/30/business/executive/compensation. Accessed August 23, 2013; A. Mackey (2006). "Dynamics in executive labor markets: CEO effects, executive-firm matching, and rent sharing." Dissertation, The Ohio State University.

Summary

To be valuable, diversification strategies must exploit valuable economies of scope that cannot be duplicated by outside investors at low cost. However, to realize the value of these economies of scope, firms must organize themselves appropriately. A firm's organizational structure, its management control processes, and its compensation policies are all relevant in implementing a corporate diversification strategy.

The best organizational structure for implementing a diversification leveraging strategy is the multidivisional, or M-form, structure. The M-form structure has several critical components, including the board of directors, institutional investors, the senior executive, corporate staff, division general managers, and shared activity managers.

This organizational structure is supported by a variety of management control processes. Three critical management control processes for firms implementing diversification strategies are (1) evaluating the performance of divisions, (2) allocating capital across divisions, and (3) transferring intermediate products between divisions. The existence of economies of scope in firms implementing corporate diversification strategies significantly complicates the management of these processes.

Finally, a firm's compensation policies are also important for firms implementing a diversification strategy. Historically, management compensation has been only loosely connected to a firm's economic performance, but recently the increased popularity of using stock and stock options to help compensate managers. Such compensation schemes help reduce conflicts between managers and outside investors, but the absolute level of CEO compensation is still very high, at least in the United States.

MyManagementLab®

Go to **mymanagementlab.com** to complete the problems marked with this icon ✪.

Challenge Questions

8.1. Agency theory has been criticized for assuming that managers, left on their own, will behave in ways that reduce the wealth of outside equity holders when, in fact, most managers are highly responsible stewards of the assets they control. This alternative view of managers has been called *stewardship theory*. Why would you agree with this criticism of agency theory?

✪ **8.2.** Suppose that the concept of the stewardship theory is correct and that most managers, most of the time, behave responsibly and make decisions that maximize the present value of the assets they control. What implications, if any, would this

supposition have on organizing to implement diversification strategies?

8.3. The M-form structure enables firms to pursue complex corporate diversification strategies by delegating different management responsibilities to different individuals and groups within a firm. Based on the concept of the M-form structure is there a natural limit to the efficient size of a diversified firm?

8.4. Most observers agree that centrally planned economies fail because it is impossible for bureaucrats in large government hierarchies to coordinate different sectors of an economy as efficiently as market mechanisms

do. Many diversified firms, however, are as large as some economies and use private sector hierarchies to coordinate diverse business activities in a firm. Why would you consider these large, private sector hierarchies somehow different from the government hierarchies of centrally planned economies?

8.5. Most observers agree that centrally planned economies fail because it is impossible for bureaucrats in large government hierarchies to coordinate different sectors of an economy as efficiently as market mechanisms do. Many diversified firms, however, are as large as some economies and use private sector hierarchies to coordinate diverse business activities in a firm. If you do not consider these large, private sector hierarchies as different from the government hierarchies of centrally planned economies, then why do they continue to exist?

⭐ **8.6.** Suppose that the optimal transfer price between one business and all other business activities in a firm is the market price. What does this condition say about whether this firm should own this business?

Problem Set

8-7. Which elements of the M-form structure (the board of directors, the office of the CEO, corporate staff, division general managers, shared activity managers) should be involved in the following business activities? If more than one of these groups should be involved, indicate their relative level of involvement (e.g., 20 percent office of the CEO, 10 percent shared activity manager, 70 percent division general manager). Justify your answers.

(a) Determining the compensation of the CEO
(b) Determining the compensation of the corporate vice president of human resources
(c) Determining the compensation of a vice president of human resources in a particular business division
(d) Deciding to sell a business division
(e) Deciding to buy a relatively small firm whose activities are closely related to the activities of one of the firm's current divisions
(f) Deciding to buy a larger firm that is not closely related to the activities of any of a firm's current divisions
(g) Evaluating the performance of the vice president of sales, a manager whose sales staff sells the products of three divisions in the firm
(h) Evaluating the performance of the vice president of sales, a manager whose sales staff sells the products of only one division in the firm
(i) Determining how much money to invest in a corporate R&D function
(j) Deciding how much money to invest in an R&D function that supports the operations of two divisions within the firm
(k) Deciding whether to fire an R&D scientist
(l) Deciding whether to fire the vice president of accounting in a particular division
(m) Deciding whether to fire the corporation's vice president of accounting
(n) Deciding whether to take a firm public by selling stock in the firm to the general public for the first time

8-8. Consider the following facts. Division A in a firm has generated $847,000 of profits on $24 million worth of sales, using $32 million worth of dedicated assets. The cost of capital for this firm is 9 percent, and the firm has invested $7.3 million in this division.

(a) Calculate the Return on Sales (ROS) and Return on Total Assets (ROA) of Division A. If the hurdle rates for ROS and ROA in this firm are, respectively, 0.06 and 0.04, has this division performed well?
(b) Calculate the EVA of Division A (assuming that the reported profits have already been adjusted). Based on this EVA, has this division performed well?
(c) Suppose you were CEO of this firm. How would you choose between ROS/ROA and EVA for evaluating this division?

8-9. Suppose that Division A sells an intermediate product to Division B. Choose one of the ways of determining transfer prices described in this chapter (not setting transfer prices equal to the selling firm's opportunity costs) and show how Division Manager A can use this mechanism to justify a higher transfer price while Division Manager B can use this mechanism to justify a lower transfer price. Repeat this exercise with another approach to setting transfer prices described in the chapter.

MyManagementLab®

Go to **mymanagementlab.com** for Auto-graded writing questions as well as the following Assisted-graded writing questions:

⭐ **8.10.** How are the roles of senior executives and shared activity managers different in making the M-form structure work?

⭐ **8.11.** What are the implications for a multidivisional firm when the corporate staff become too involved in the day-to-day operations of divisions?

End Notes

1. The structure and function of the multidimensional firm were first described by Chandler, A. (1962). *Strategy and structure: Chapters in the history of the industrial enterprise.* Cambridge, MA: MIT Press. The economic logic underlying the multidimensional firm was first described by Williamson, O. E. (1975). *Markets and hierarchies: Analysis and antitrust implications.* New York: Free Press. Empirical examinations of the impact of the M-form or firm performance include Armour, H. O., and D. J. Teece. (1980). "Vertical integration and technological innovation." *Review of Economics and Statistics,* 60, pp. 470–474. There continues to be some debate about the efficiency of the M-form structure. See Freeland, R. F. (1966). "The myth of the M-form? Governance, consent, and organizational change." *American Journal of Sociology,* 102(2), pp. 483–626; and Shanley, M. (1996). "Straw men and M-form myths: Comment on Freeland." *American Journal of Sociology,* 102(2), pp. 527–536.
2. See Finkelstein, S., and R. D'Aveni. (1994). "CEO duality as a double-edged sword: How boards of directors balance entrenchment avoidance and unity of command." *Academy of Management Journal,* 37, pp. 1079–1108.
3. Kesner, I. F. (1988). "Director's characteristics and committee membership: An investigation of type, occupation, tenure and gender." *Academy of Management Journal,* 31, pp. 66–84; and Zahra, S. A., and J. A. Pearce II. (1989). "Boards of directors and corporate financial performance: A review and integrative model." *Journal of Management,* 15, pp. 291–334.
4. Investor Relations Business. (2000). "Reversal of fortune: Institutional ownership is declining." *Investor Relations Business,* May 1, pp. 8–9; and Federal Reserve Board. (2006). "Flow of funds report." www.corpgov.net.
5. See Hansen, G. S., and C. W. L. Hill. (1991). "Are institutional investors myopic? A time-series study of four technology-driven industries." *Strategic Management Journal,* 12, pp. 1–16.
6. See Bergh, D. (1995). "Size and relatedness of units sold: An agency theory and resource-based perspective." *Strategic Management Journal,* 16, pp. 221–239; and Bethel, J., and J. Liebeskind. (1993). "The effects of ownership structure on corporate restructuring." *Strategic Management Journal,* 14, pp. 15–31.
7. Burdens that are well described by Westley, F., and H. Mintzberg. (1989). "Visionary leadership and strategic management." *Strategic Management Journal,* 10, pp. 17–32.
8. See Dumaine, B. (1992). "Is big still good?" *Fortune,* April 20, pp. 50–60.
9. See Golden, B. (1992). "SBU strategy and performance: The moderating effects of the corporate–SBU relationship." *Strategic Management Journal,* 13, pp. 145–158; Berger, P., and E. Ofek. (1995). "Diversification effect on firm value." *Journal of Financial Economics,* 37, pp. 36–65;

Lang, H. P., and R. M. Stulz. (1994). "Tobin's q, corporate diversification, and firm performance." *Journal of Political Economy,* 102, pp. 1248–1280; and Rumelt, R. (1991). "How much does industry matter?" *Strategic Management Journal,* 12, pp. 167–185.
10. See Halal, W. (1994). "From hierarchy to enterprise: Internal markets are the new foundation of management." *The Academy of Management Executive,* 8(4), pp. 69–83.
11. Bartlett, C., and S. Ghoshal. (1993). "Beyond the M-form: Toward a managerial theory of the firm." *Strategic Management Journal,* 14, pp. 23–46.
12. See Simons, R. (1994). "How new top managers use control systems as levers of strategic renewal." *Strategic Management Journal,* 15, pp. 169–189.
13. Bethel, J. E. (1990). "The capital allocation process and managerial mobility: A theoretical and empirical investigation." Unpublished doctoral dissertation, UCLA.
14. Some of these are described in Duffy, M. (1989). "ZBB, MBO, PPB, and their effectiveness within the planning/marketing process." *Strategic Management Journal,* 12, pp. 155–160.
15. See Stern, J., B. Stewart, and D. Chew. (1995). "The EVA financial management system." *Journal of Applied Corporate Finance,* 8, pp. 32–46; and Tully, S. (1993). "The real key to creating wealth." *Fortune,* September 20, pp. 38–50.
16. Applications of EVA are described in Tully, S. (1993). "The real key to creating wealth." *Fortune,* September 20, pp. 38–50; Tully, S. (1995). "So, Mr. Bossidy, we know you can cut. Now show us how to grow." *Fortune,* August 21, pp. 70–80; and Tully, S. (1995). "Can EVA deliver profits to the post office?" *Fortune,* July 10, p. 22.
17. A special issue of the *Journal of Applied Corporate Finance* in 1994 addressed many of these issues.
18. See Priem, R. (1990). "Top management team group factors, consensus, and firm performance." *Strategic Management Journal,* 11, pp. 469–478; and Wooldridge, B., and S. Floyd. (1990). "The strategy process, middle management involvement, and organizational performance." *Strategic Management Journal,* 11, pp. 231–241.
19. A point made by Westley, F. (1900). "Middle managers and strategy: Microdynamics of inclusion." *Strategic Management Journal,* 11, pp. 337–351; Lamont, O. (1997). "Cash flow and investment: Evidence from internal capital markets." *The Journal of Finance,* 52(1), pp. 83–109; Shin, H. H., and R. M. Stulz. (1998). "Are internal capital markets efficient?" *Quarterly Journal of Economics,* May, pp. 531–552; and Stein, J. C. (1997). "Internal capital markets and the competition for corporate resources." *The Journal of Finance,* 52(1), pp. 111–133.
20. See Brickley, J., C. Smith, and J. Zimmerman. (1996). *Organizational architecture and managerial economics approach.* Homewood, IL: Irwin;

and Eccles, R. (1985). *The transfer pricing problem: A theory for practice.* Lexington, MA: Lexington Books.

21. See Cyert, R., and J. G. March. (1963). *A behavioral theory of the firm.* Upper Saddle River, NJ: Prentice Hall; Swieringa, R. J., and J. H. Waterhouse. (1982). "Organizational views of transfer pricing." *Accounting, Organizations & Society*, 7(2), pp. 149–165; and Eccles, R. (1985). *The transfer pricing problem: A theory for practice.* Lexington, MA: Lexington Books.

22. Gupta, A. K., and V. Govindarajan. (1986). "Resource sharing among SBUs: Strategic antecedents and administrative implications." *Academy of Management Journal*, 29, pp. 695–714.

23. A point made by Swieringa, R. J., and J. H. Waterhouse. (1982). "Organizational views of transfer pricing." *Accounting, Organizations and Society*, 7(2), pp. 149–165.

24. Jensen, M. C., and K. J. Murphy. (1990). "Performance pay and top management incentives." *Journal of Political Economy*, 98, pp. 225–264.

25. See Dial, J., and K. J. Murphy. (1995). "Incentive, downsizing, and value creation at General Dynamics." *Journal of Financial Economics*, 37, pp. 261–314, on General Dynamics' compensation scheme; and Aguilar, F. J., and A. Bhambri. (1983). "Johnson & Johnson (A)." Harvard Business School Case No. 9-384-053, on Johnson & Johnson's compensation scheme.

9 Strategic Alliances

1. Define a strategic alliance and give three specific examples of strategic alliances.

2. Describe nine different ways that alliances can create value for firms and how these nine sources of value can be grouped into three large categories.

3. Describe how adverse selection, moral hazard, and holdup can threaten the ability of alliances to generate value.

4. Describe the conditions under which a strategic alliance can be rare and costly to duplicate.

5. Describe the conditions under which "going it alone" and acquisitions are not likely to be substitutes for alliances.

6. Describe how contracts, equity investments, firm reputations, joint ventures, and trust can all reduce the threat of cheating in strategic alliances.

MyManagementLab®
⭐ **Improve Your Grade!**
Over 10 million students improved their results using the Pearson MyLabs.
Visit **mymanagementlab.com** for simulations, tutorials, and end-of-chapter problems.

Breaking Up Is Hard to Do: Apple and Samsung

On the one hand, Samsung and Apple are very close business partners. Apple depends on technologies developed and built by Samsung to build its smart phones, iPods, and iPads. In turn, Apple is one of Samsung's largest, and most profitable, customers. In 2012, Samsung sold $10 billion in electronic components to Apple, one-sixth of Samsung's total component sales.

On the other hand, Apple and Samsung have sued and countersued each other over the look and feel of their respective smart phones and related products. Courts around the world are weighing in on these issues. Initially, Samsung was ordered to pay $1 billion (later reduced to $500 million) to Apple for infringing on some Apple patents. Then the U.S. International Trade Commission concluded that Apple had infringed on a Samsung patent and ordered a ban on some older model Apple smart phones (later rescinded by the Obama administration). Not a great way to maintain a business partnership.

For many years, Samsung and Apple had a very functional alliance. Samsung made the kinds of technologies—including microprocessors, memory chips, and displays—that Apple needed to fuel its growth in smart phones and related products. Not only did Samsung supply these technologies to Apple, it was the best supplier of these technologies—both in terms of quality and cost—in the world. Apple was only too happy to source its components to such a supplier.

Then Samsung entered the smart phone market and began to produce phones that ran Google's Android system. Apple and Samsung became competitors. Indeed, there are now more Android phones sold each year—mostly made by Samsung—than Apple iPhones.

Not surprisingly, Apple is looking around the world to find alternative suppliers of its essential electronic components. The problem is: Finding suppliers that are as competent as Samsung in providing these state-of-the-art technologies has turned out to be quite difficult. While Apple has found second sources for memory chips and some displays, Samsung continues to be an almost exclusive supplier of the microprocessors that run Apple's iPods, iPhones, and iPads.

For example, Apple began working with Taiwan Semiconductor Manufacturing Company (TSMC) to create a new source for microprocessors in 2011. It took two years for TSMC to develop chips that met Apple's (and Samsung's) standards. It will take at least another year for TSMC to ramp up its production of this new technology, all while Samsung remains the only viable supplier of this critical component for Apple.

And Samsung isn't just standing pat, waiting for Apple to find new suppliers. For example, Apple tried to develop a contract with the Japanese firm Sharp for certain displays it currently buys from Samsung. This may have become more difficult since Samsung purchased 3 percent of Sharp's stock and became Sharp's fifth-largest shareholder!

Sometimes, breaking up really is hard to do.

© MaxPayne/Alamy

Sources: J. Lessin, L. Luk, and J. Osawa (2013). "Apple finds it difficult to divorce Samsung." *The Wall Street Journal,* August 16, 2013//online.wsj.com/articles/SB10 0014241278873246822040457851518823499405000 Accessed August 25, 2013; B. Kendall and I. Sherr (2013). "Patent war adds front in U.S." *The Wall Street Journal,* online, August 23, online.wsj.com/article/SB10001424127887324170004578633702773124388 Accessed August 25, 2013; P. Elias (2013). "Apple's Samsung verdict nearly cut in half by federal judge." *Huffington Post,* January 3, huffingtonpost.com/2013/03/01/half-a-billion-cut-from-Apple. Accessed November 4, 2013.

The use of strategic alliances to manage economic exchanges has grown substantially over the past several years. In the early 1990s, strategic alliances were relatively uncommon, except in a few industries. However, by the late 1990s they had become much more common in a wide variety of industries. Indeed, more than 20,000 alliances were created worldwide in 2000 and 2001. In the computer technology–based industries, more than 2,200 alliances were created between 2001 and 2005. This, the complex web of relationships that characterizes the links between Apple and Samsung, is becoming increasingly more common.[1]

What Is a Strategic Alliance?

A **strategic alliance** exists whenever two or more independent organizations cooperate in the development, manufacture, or sale of products or services. As shown in Figure 9.1, strategic alliances can be grouped into three broad categories: nonequity alliances, equity alliances, and joint ventures.

In a **nonequity alliance,** cooperating firms agree to work together to develop, manufacture, or sell products or services, but they do not take equity positions in each other or form an independent organizational unit to manage their cooperative efforts. Rather, these cooperative relations are managed through the use of various contracts. **Licensing agreements** (where one firm allows others to use its brand name to sell products), **supply agreements** (where one firm agrees to supply others), and **distribution agreements** (where one firm agrees to distribute the products of others) are examples of nonequity strategic alliances. Most of the alliances between Tony Hawk and his partners take the form of nonequity licensing agreements.

In an **equity alliance,** cooperating firms supplement contracts with equity holdings in alliance partners. For example, when GM began importing small cars manufactured by Isuzu, not only did these partners have supply contracts in place, but GM purchased 34.2 percent of Isuzu's stock. Ford had a similar relationship with Mazda, and Chrysler had a similar relationship with Mitsubishi.[2] Equity alliances are also very common in the biotechnology industry. Large pharmaceutical firms such as Pfizer and Merck often own equity positions in several startup biotechnology companies.

Figure 9.1 Types of Strategic Alliances

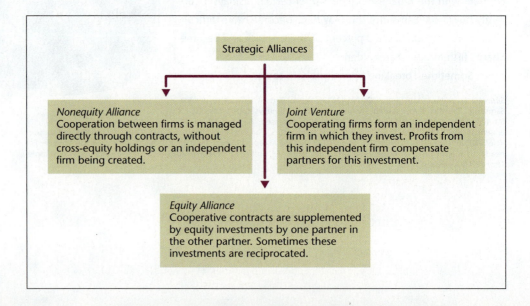

Strategic Alliances

Nonequity Alliance
Cooperation between firms is managed directly through contracts, without cross-equity holdings or an independent firm being created.

Joint Venture
Cooperating firms form an independent firm in which they invest. Profits from this independent firm compensate partners for this investment.

Equity Alliance
Cooperative contracts are supplemented by equity investments by one partner in the other partner. Sometimes these investments are reciprocated.

In a **joint venture,** cooperating firms create a legally independent firm in which they invest and from which they share any profits that are created. Some of these joint ventures can be very large. For example, Dow and Corning's joint venture, Dow-Corning, is a *Fortune 500* company on its own. Before they merged, AT&T and BellSouth were co-owners of the joint venture Cingular, one of the largest wireless phone companies in the United States. And CFM—a joint venture between General Electric and SNECMA (a French aerospace firm)—is one of the world's leading manufacturers of jet engines for commercial aircraft. If you have ever flown on a Boeing 737, then you have placed your life in the hands of this joint venture because it manufactures the engines for virtually all of these aircraft.

How Do Strategic Alliances Create Value?

Like all the strategies discussed in this book, strategic alliances create value by exploiting opportunities and neutralizing threats facing a firm. Some of the most important opportunities that can be exploited by strategic alliances are listed in Table 9.1. Threats to strategic alliances are discussed later in this chapter.

Strategic Alliance Opportunities

Opportunities associated with strategic alliances fall into three large categories. First, these alliances can be used by a firm to improve the performance of its current operations. Second, alliances can be used to create a competitive environment favorable to superior firm performance. Finally, they can be used to facilitate a firm's entry into or exit from new markets or industries.

Improving Current Operations

One way that firms can use strategic alliances to improve their current operations is to use alliances to realize economies of scale. The concept of economies of scale was first introduced in Chapter 2. **Economies of scale** exist when the per-unit cost of production falls as the volume of production increases. Thus, for example, although the per-unit cost of producing one BIC pen is very high, the per-unit cost of producing 50 million BIC pens is very low.

To realize economies of scale, firms have to have a large volume of production, or at least a volume of production large enough so that the cost advantages

Helping firms improve the performance of their current operations
1. Exploiting economies of scale
2. Learning from competitors
3. Managing risk and sharing costs
4. Creating a competitive environment favorable to superior performance
5. Facilitating the development of technology standards
6. Facilitating tacit collusion
7. Facilitating entry and exit
8. Low-cost entry into new industries and new industry segments
9. Low-cost exit from industries and industry segments
10. Managing uncertainty
11. Low-cost entry into new markets

TABLE 9.1 Ways Strategic Alliances Can Create Economic Value

associated with scale can be realized. Sometimes—as was described in Chapters 2 and 4—a firm can realize these economies of scale by itself; other times, it cannot. When a firm cannot realize the cost savings from economies of scale all by itself, it may join in a strategic alliance with other firms. Jointly, these firms may have sufficient volume to be able to gain the cost advantages of economies of scale.

But why wouldn't a firm be able to realize these economies all by itself? A firm may have to turn to alliance partners to help realize economies of scale for a number of reasons. For example, if the volume of production required to realize these economies is very large, a single firm might have to dominate an entire industry in order to obtain these advantages. It is often very difficult for a single firm to obtain such a dominant position in an industry. And even if it does so, it may be subject to anti-monopoly regulation by the government. Also, although a particular part or technology may be very important to several firms, no one firm may generate sufficient demand for this part or technology to realize economies of scale in its development and production. In this setting as well, independent firms may join together to form an alliance to realize economies of scale in the development and production of the part or technology.

Firms can also use alliances to improve their current operations by learning from their competitors. As suggested in Chapter 3, different firms in an industry may have different resources and capabilities. These resources can give some firms competitive advantages over others. Firms that are at a competitive disadvantage may want to form alliances with the firms that have an advantage in order to learn about their resources and capabilities.

General Motors formed this kind of alliance with Toyota. In the early 1990s, GM and Toyota jointly invested in a previously closed GM plant in Fremont, California. This joint venture—called NUMI—was to build compact cars to be distributed through GM's distribution network. But why did GM decide to build these cars in an alliance with Toyota? Obviously, it could have built them in any of its own plants. However, GM was very interested in learning about how Toyota was able to manufacture high-quality small cars at a profit. Indeed, in the NUMI plant, Toyota agreed to take total responsibility for the manufacturing process, using former GM employees to install and operate the "lean manufacturing" system that had enabled Toyota to become the quality leader in the small-car segment of the automobile industry. However, Toyota also agreed to let GM managers work in the plant and directly observe how Toyota managed this production process. Since its inception, GM has rotated thousands of its managers from other GM plants through the NUMI plant so that they can be exposed to Toyota's lean manufacturing methods.

It is clear why GM would want this alliance with Toyota. But why would Toyota want this alliance with GM? Certainly, Toyota was not looking to learn about lean manufacturing, per se. However, because Toyota was contemplating entering the United States by building its own manufacturing facilities, it did need to learn how to implement lean manufacturing in the United States with U.S. employees. Thus, Toyota also had something to learn from this alliance.

When both parties to an alliance are seeking to learn something from that alliance, an interesting dynamic called a **learning race** can evolve. This dynamic is described in more detail in the Strategy in Depth feature.

Finally, firms can use alliances to improve their current operations through sharing costs and risks. For example, HBO produces most of its original programs in alliances with independent producers. Most of these alliances are created to share costs and risks. Producing new television shows can be costly. Development and production costs can run into the hundreds of millions of dollars, especially for long and complicated series like HBO's *Deadwood, Entourage,* and *The Sopranos.* And, despite audience testing and careful market analyses, the production of these new shows is also very risky. Even a bankable star like Johnny Depp—remember *The Lone Ranger*—cannot guarantee success.

In this context, it is not surprising that HBO decides to not "go it alone" in its production efforts. If HBO was to be the sole producer of its original programming, not only would it have to absorb all the production costs, but it would also bear all the risk if a production turned out not to be successful. Of course, by getting other firms involved in its production efforts, HBO also has to share whatever profits a particular production generates. Apparently, HBO has concluded that sharing this upside potential is more than compensated for by sharing the costs and risks of these productions.

Creating a Favorable Competitive Environment

Firms can also use strategic alliances to create a competitive environment that is more conducive to superior performance. This can be done in at least two ways. First, firms can use alliances to help set technology standards in an industry. With these standards in place, technology-based products can be developed and consumers can be confident that the products they buy will be useful for some time to come.

Such technological standards are particularly important in what are called **network industries.** Such industries are characterized by **increasing returns to scale.** Consider, for example, fax machines. How valuable is one fax machine, all by itself? Obviously, not very valuable. Two fax machines that can talk to each other are a little more valuable, three that can talk to each other are still more valuable, and so forth. The value of each individual fax machine depends on the total number of fax machines in operation that can talk to each other. This is what is meant by increasing returns to scale—the value (or returns) on each product increases as the number of these products (or scale) increases.

If there are 100 million fax machines in operation but none of these machines can talk to each other, none of these machines has any value whatsoever—except as a large paperweight. For their full value to be realized, they must be able to talk to each other. And to talk to each other, they must all adopt the same—or at least compatible—communication standards. This is why setting technology standards is so important in network industries.

Standards can be set in two ways. First, different firms can introduce different standards, and consumers can decide which they prefer. This is how the standard for high-definition DVDs was set. Initially, two formats competed: HD DVD (supported by Toshiba) and Blu-ray DVD (supported by the Blu-ray Disc Association, a group of 50 or so electronics firms and content providers). Both formats had attractive features, but they could not be played on each other's players. Competition between the two formats continued for some time, until firms like Panasonic (in 2004), Samsung (in 2005), Disney (in 2004), and Paramount (in 2005) committed to the Blu-ray Disc format. By 2008, even Toshiba had to acknowledge the dominance of Blu-ray Discs. Toshiba released its own Blu-ray Disc player in 2009.[3]

Of course, the biggest problem with letting customers and competition set technology standards is that customers may end up purchasing technologies that are incompatible with the standard that is ultimately set in the industry. What about all those consumers who purchased HD products? For this reason, customers may be unwilling to invest in a new technology until the standards of that technology are established.

Strategy in Depth

A learning race exists in a strategic alliance when both parties to that alliance seek to learn from each other but the rate at which these two firms learn varies. In this setting, the first firm to learn what it wants to learn from an alliance has the option to begin to underinvest in, and perhaps even withdraw from, an alliance. In this way, the firm that learns faster is able to prevent the slower-learning firm from learning all it wanted from an alliance. If, outside of this alliance, these firms are competitors, winning a learning race can create a sustained competitive advantage for the faster-learning firm over the slower-learning firm.

Firms in an alliance may vary in the rate they learn from each other for a variety of reasons. First, they may be looking to learn different things, some of which are easier to learn than others. For example, in the GM–Toyota example, GM wanted to learn about how to use "lean manufacturing" to build high-quality small cars profitably. Toyota wanted to learn how to apply the "lean manufacturing" skills it already possessed in the United States. Which of these is easier to learn—"lean manufacturing" or how to apply "lean manufacturing" in the United States?

An argument can be made that GM's learning task was much more complicated than Toyota's. At the very least, in order for GM to apply knowledge about "lean manufacturing" gleaned from Toyota it would have to transfer that knowledge to several of its currently operating plants. Using this knowledge would require these plants to change their current operations—a difficult and time-consuming process. Toyota, however, only had to transfer its knowledge of how to operate a

Winning Learning Races

"lean manufacturing" operation in the United States to its other U.S. plants— plants that at the time this alliance was first created had yet to be built. Because GM's learning task was more complicated than Toyota's, it is very likely that Toyota's rate of learning was greater than GM's.

Second, firms may differ in terms of their ability to learn. This ability has been called a firm's **absorptive capacity.** Firms with high levels of absorptive capacity will learn at faster rates than firms with low levels of absorptive capacity, even if these two firms are trying to learn exactly the same things in an alliance. Absorptive capacity has been shown to be an important organizational capability in a wide variety of settings.

Third, firms can engage in activities to try to slow the rate of learning of their alliance partners. For example, although a firm might make its technology available to an alliance partner—thereby fulfilling the alliance agreement—it may not provide all the know-how necessary to

exploit this technology. This can slow a partner's learning. Also, a firm might withhold critical employees from an alliance, thereby slowing the learning of an alliance partner. All these actions, to the extent that they slow the rate of a partner's learning without also slowing the rate at which the firm engaging in these activities learns, can help this firm win a learning race.

Although learning race dynamics have been described in a wide variety of settings, they are particularly common in relations between entrepreneurial and large firms. In these alliances, entrepreneurial firms are often looking to learn about all the managerial functions required to bring a product to market, including manufacturing, sales, distribution, and so forth. This is a difficult learning task. Large firms in these alliances often are only looking to learn about the entrepreneurial firm's technology. This is a less difficult learning task. Because the learning task facing entrepreneurial firms is more challenging than that facing their large-firm partners, larger firms in these alliances typically win the learning race. Once these large firms learn what they want from their alliance partners, they often underinvest or even withdraw from these alliances. This is why, in one study, almost 80 percent of the managers in entrepreneurial firms felt unfairly exploited by their large-firm alliance partners.

Sources: S. A. Alvarez and J. B. Barney (2001). "How entrepreneurial firms can benefit from alliances with large partners." *Academy of Management Executive,* 15, pp. 139–148; G. Hamel (1991). "Competition for competence and inter-partner learning within international alliances." *Strategic Management Journal,* 12, pp. 83–103; W. Cohen and D. Levinthal (1990). "Absorptive capacity: A new perspective on learning and innovation." *Administrative Science Quarterly,* 35, pp. 128–152.

This is where strategic alliances come in. Sometimes, firms form strategic alliances with the sole purpose of evaluating and then choosing a technology standard. With such a standard in place, technologies can be turned into products that customers are likely to be more willing to purchase because they know that they will be compatible with industry standards for at least some period of time. Thus, in this setting, strategic alliances can be used to create a more favorable competitive environment.

Another incentive for cooperating in strategic alliances is that such activities may facilitate the development of tacit collusion. As explained in Chapter 3, **collusion** exists when two or more firms in an industry coordinate their strategic choices to reduce competition in an industry. This reduction in competition usually makes it easier for colluding firms to earn high levels of performance. A common example of collusion is when firms cooperate to reduce the quantity of products being produced in an industry in order to drive prices up. **Explicit collusion** exists when firms directly communicate with each other to coordinate their levels of production, their prices, and so forth. Explicit collusion is illegal in most countries.

Because managers that engage in explicit collusion can end up in jail, most collusion must be tacit in character. **Tacit collusion** exists when firms coordinate their production and pricing decisions not by directly communicating with each other, but by exchanging signals with other firms about their intent to cooperate. Examples of such signals might include public announcements about price increases, public announcements about reductions in a firm's productive output, public announcements about decisions not to pursue a new technology, and so forth.

Sometimes, signals of intent to collude are very ambiguous. For example, when firms in an industry do not reduce their prices in response to a decrease in demand, they may be sending a signal that they want to collude, or they may be attempting to exploit their product differentiation to maintain high margins. When firms do not reduce their prices in response to reduced supply costs, they may be sending a signal that they want to collude, or they may be individually maximizing their economic performance. In both these cases, a firm's intent to collude or not, as implied by its activities, is ambiguous at best.

In this context, strategic alliances can facilitate tacit collusion. Separate firms, even if they are in the same industry, can form strategic alliances. Although communication between these firms cannot legally include sharing information about prices and costs for products or services that are produced outside the alliance, such interaction does help create the social setting within which tacit collusion may develop.[4] As suggested in the Research Made Relevant feature, most early research on strategic alliances focused on their implications for tacit collusion. More recently, research suggests that alliances do not usually facilitate tacit collusion.

Facilitating Entry and Exit

A final way that strategic alliances can be used to create value is by facilitating a firm's entry into a new market or industry or its exit from a market or industry. Strategic alliances are particularly valuable in this context when the value of market entry or exit is uncertain. Entry into an industry can require skills, abilities, and products that a potential entrant does not possess. Strategic alliances can help a firm enter a new industry by avoiding the high costs of creating these skills, abilities, and products.

For example, DuPont wanted to enter into the electronics industry. However, building the skills and abilities needed to develop competitive products in this industry can be very difficult and costly. Rather than absorb these costs, DuPont developed a strategic alliance (DuPont/Philips Optical) with an established electronics firm, Philips, to distribute some of Philips's products in the United States. In this way, DuPont was able to enter into a new industry (electronics) without having to absorb all the costs of creating electronics resources and abilities from the ground up.

Of course, for this joint venture to succeed, Philips must have had an incentive to cooperate with DuPont. Whereas DuPont was looking to reduce its cost of entry into a new industry, Philips was looking to reduce its cost of continued entry into a new market—the United States. Philips used its alliance with DuPont to sell in the United States the compact discs it already was selling in Europe.[5] The role of alliances in facilitating entry into new geographic markets will be discussed in more detail later in this chapter.

Alliances to facilitate entry into new industries can be valuable even when the skills needed in these industries are not as complex and difficult to learn as skills in the electronics industry. For example, rather than develop their own frozen novelty foods, Welch Foods, Inc., and Leaf, Inc. (maker of Heath candy bars) asked Eskimo Pie to formulate products for this industry. Eskimo Pie developed Welch's frozen grape juice bar and the Heath toffee ice cream bar. These firms then split the profits derived from these products.[6] As long as the cost of using an alliance to enter a new industry is less than the cost of learning new skills and capabilities, an alliance can be a valuable strategic opportunity.

Some firms use strategic alliances as a mechanism to withdraw from industries or industry segments in a low-cost way. Firms are motivated to withdraw from an industry or industry segment when their level of performance in that business is less than expected and when there are few prospects of it improving. When a firm desires to exit an industry or industry segment, often it will need to dispose of the assets it has developed to compete in that industry or industry segment. These assets often include tangible resources and capabilities, such as factories, distribution centers, and product technologies, and intangible resources and capabilities, such as brand name, relationships with suppliers and customers, a loyal and committed workforce, and so forth.

Firms will often have difficulty in obtaining the full economic value of these tangible and intangible assets as they exit an industry or industry segment. This reflects an important information asymmetry that exists between the firms that currently own these assets and firms that may want to purchase these assets. By forming an alliance with a firm that may want to purchase its assets, a firm is giving its partner an opportunity to directly observe how valuable those assets are. If those assets are actually valuable, then this "sneak preview" can lead the assets to be more appropriately priced and thereby facilitate the exit of the firm that is looking to sell its assets. These issues will be discussed in more detail in Chapter 10's discussion of mergers and acquisitions.

One firm that has used strategic alliances to facilitate its exit from an industry or industry segment is Corning. In the late 1980s, Corning entered the medical diagnostics industry. After several years, however, Corning concluded that its resources and capabilities could be more productively used in other businesses. For this reason, it began to extract itself from the medical diagnostics business. However, to ensure that it received the full value of the assets it had created in the medical diagnostics business upon exiting, it formed a strategic alliance with the Swiss specialty chemical company Ciba-Geigy. Ciba-Geigy paid $75 million to purchase half of Corning's medical diagnostics business. A couple of years later, Corning finished exiting from the medical diagnostics business by selling its remaining assets in this industry to Ciba-Geigy. However, whereas Ciba-Geigy had paid $75 million for the first half of Corning's assets, it paid $150 million for the second half. Corning's alliance with Ciba-Geigy had made it possible for Ciba-Geigy to fully value Corning's medical diagnostics capabilities. Any information asymmetry that might have existed was reduced, and Corning was able to get more of the full value of its assets upon exiting this industry.[7]

Finally, firms may use strategic alliances to manage **uncertainty.** Under conditions of high uncertainty, firms may not be able to tell at a particular point in time which of several different strategies they should pursue. Firms in this setting have an incentive to retain the flexibility to move quickly into a particular market

Research Made Relevant

Several authors have concluded that joint ventures, as a form of alliance, do increase the probability of tacit collusion in an industry. As reviewed in books by Scherer and Barney, one study found that joint ventures created two industrial groups, besides U.S. Steel, in the U.S. iron and steel industry in the early 1900s. In this sense, joint ventures in the steel industry were a substitute for U.S. Steel's vertical integration and had the effect of creating an oligopoly in what (without joint ventures) would have been a more competitive market. Other studies found that more than 50 percent of joint venture parents belong to the same industry. After examining 885 joint venture bids for oil and gas leases, yet another study found only 16 instances where joint venture parents competed with one another on another tract in the same sale. These results suggest that joint ventures might encourage subsequent tacit collusion among firms in the same industry.

In a particularly influential study, Pfeffer and Nowak found that joint ventures were most likely in industries of moderate concentration. These authors argued that in highly

Do Strategic Alliances Facilitate Tacit Collusion?

concentrated industries—where there were only a small number of competing firms—joint ventures were not necessary to create conditions conducive to collusion. In highly fragmented industries, the high levels of industry concentration conducive to tacit collusion could not be created by joint ventures. Only when joint venture activity could effectively create concentrated industries—that is, only when industries were moderately concentrated—were joint ventures likely.

Scherer and Barney also reviewed more recent work that disputes these

findings. Joint ventures between firms in the same industry may be valuable for a variety of reasons that have little or nothing to do with collusion. Moreover, by using a lower level of aggregation, several authors have disputed the finding that joint ventures are most likely in moderately concentrated industries. The original study defined industries using very broad industry categories— "the electronics industry," "the automobile industry," and so forth. By defining industries less broadly—"consumer electronics" and "automobile part manufacturers"—subsequent work found that 73 percent of the joint ventures had parent firms coming from different industries. Although joint ventures between firms in the same industry (defined at this lower level of aggregation) may have collusive implications, subsequent work has shown that these kinds of joint ventures are relatively rare.

Sources: F. M. Scherer (1980). *Industrial market structure and economic performance.* Boston: Houghton Mifflin; J. B. Barney (2006). *Gaining and sustaining competitive advantage,* 3rd ed. Upper Saddle River, NJ: Prentice Hall; J. Pfeffer and P. Nowak (1976). "Patterns of joint venture activity: Implications for anti-trust research." *Antitrust Bulletin,* 21, pp. 315–339.

or industry once the full value of that strategy is revealed. In this sense, strategic alliances enable a firm to maintain a point of entry into a market or industry, without incurring the costs associated with full-scale entry.

Based on this logic, strategic alliances have been analyzed as **real options.**[8] In this sense, a joint venture is an option that a firm buys, under conditions of uncertainty, to retain the ability to move quickly into a market or industry if valuable opportunities present themselves. One way in which firms can move quickly into a market is simply to buy out their partner(s) in the joint venture. Moreover, by investing in a joint venture a firm may gain access to the information it needs to evaluate full-scale entry into a market. In this approach to analyzing strategic alliances, firms that invest in alliances as options will acquire their alliance partners only after the market signals an unexpected increase in value of the venture; that is, only after uncertainty is reduced and the true, positive value of entering into a market is known. Empirical findings are consistent with these expectations.[9]

Given these observations, it is not surprising to see firms in new and uncertain environments develop numerous strategic alliances. This is one of the reasons that strategic alliances are so common in the biotechnology industry. Although there is relatively little uncertainty that at least some drugs created through biotechnology will ultimately prove to be very valuable, which specific drugs will turn out to be the most valuable is very uncertain. Rather than investing in a small number of biotechnology drugs on their own, pharmaceutical companies have invested in numerous strategic alliances with small biotechnology firms. Each of these smaller firms represents a particular "bet" about the value of biotechnology in a particular class of drugs. If one of these "bets" turns out to be valuable, then the large pharmaceutical firm that has invested in that firm has the right, but not the obligation, to purchase the rest of this company. In this sense, from the point of view of the pharmaceutical firms, alliances between large pharmaceutical firms and small biotechnology firms can be thought of as real options.

Alliance Threats: Incentives to Cheat on Strategic Alliances

Just as there are incentives to cooperate in strategic alliances, there are also incentives to cheat on these cooperative agreements. Indeed, research shows that as many as one-third of all strategic alliances do not meet the expectations of at least one alliance partner.[10] Although some of these alliance "failures" may be due to firms forming alliances that do not have the potential for creating value, some are also due to parties to an alliance cheating—that is, not cooperating in a way that maximizes the value of the alliance. Cheating can occur in at least the three different ways presented in Table 9.2: adverse selection, moral hazard, and holdup.[11]

TABLE 9.2 Ways to Cheat in Strategic Alliances

- *Adverse selection*: Potential partners misrepresent the value of the skills and abilities they bring to the alliance.
- *Moral hazard*: Partners provide to the alliance skills and abilities of lower quality than they promised.
- *Holdup*: Partners exploit the transaction-specific investments made by others in the alliance.

Adverse Selection

Potential cooperative partners can misrepresent the skills, abilities, and other resources that they will bring to an alliance. This form of cheating, called **adverse selection,** exists when an alliance partner promises to bring to an alliance certain resources that it either does not control or cannot acquire. For example, a local firm engages in adverse selection when it promises to make available to alliance partners a local distribution network that does not currently exist. Firms that engage in adverse selection are not competent alliance partners.

Adverse selection in a strategic alliance is likely only when it is difficult or costly to observe the resources or capabilities that a partner brings to an alliance. If potential partners can easily see that a firm is misrepresenting the resources and capabilities it possesses, they will not create a strategic alliance with that firm. Armed with such understanding, they will seek a different alliance partner, develop the needed skills and resources internally, or perhaps forgo this particular business opportunity.

However, evaluating the veracity of the claims of potential alliance partners is often not easy. The ability to evaluate these claims depends on information that a firm may not possess. To fully evaluate claims about a potential partner's political contacts, for example, a firm needs its own political contacts; to fully evaluate claims about potential partners' market knowledge, a firm needs significant market knowledge. A firm that can completely, and at low cost, evaluate the resources and capabilities of potential alliance partners probably does not really need these partners in a strategic alliance. The fact that a firm is seeking an alliance partner is in some sense an indication that the firm has limited abilities to evaluate potential partners.

In general, the less tangible the resources and capabilities that are to be brought to a strategic alliance, the more costly it will be to estimate their value before an alliance is created, and the more likely it is that adverse selection will occur. Firms considering alliances with partners that bring intangible resources such as "knowledge of local conditions" or "contacts with key political figures" will need to guard against this form of cheating.

Moral Hazard

Partners in an alliance may possess high-quality resources and capabilities of significant value in an alliance but fail to make those resources and capabilities available to alliance partners. This form of cheating is called **moral hazard.** For example, a partner in an engineering strategic alliance may agree to send only its most talented and best-trained engineers to work in the alliance but then actually send less talented, poorly trained engineers. These less qualified engineers may not be able to contribute substantially to making the alliance successful, but they may be able to learn a great deal from the highly qualified engineers provided by other alliance partners. In this way, the less qualified engineers effectively transfer wealth from other alliance partners to their own firm.[12]

Often both parties in a failed alliance accuse each other of moral hazard. This was the case in the abandoned alliance between Disney and Pixar, described in the Strategy in the Emerging Enterprise feature.

The existence of moral hazard in a strategic alliance does not necessarily mean that any of the parties to that alliance are malicious or dishonest. Rather, what often happens is that market conditions change after an alliance is formed, requiring one or more partners to an alliance to change their strategies.

For example, in the early days of the personal computer industry Compaq Computer Corporation relied on a network of independent distributors to sell its computers. However, as competition in the personal computer industry increased, Internet, mail order, and so-called computer superstores became much more valuable distribution networks, and alliances between Compaq and its traditional distributors became strained. Over time, Compaq's traditional distributors were unable to obtain the inventory they wanted in a timely manner. Indeed, to satisfy the needs of large accounts, some traditional distributors actually purchased Compaq computers from local computer superstores and then shipped them to their customers. Compaq's shift from independent dealers to alternative distributors looked like moral hazard—at least from the point of view of the independent dealers. However, from Compaq's perspective, this change simply reflected economic realities in the personal computer industry.[13]

Holdup

Even if alliance partners do not engage in either adverse selection or moral hazard, another form of cheating may evolve. Once a strategic alliance has been created, partner firms may make investments that have value only in the context of that alliance and in no other economic exchanges. These are the transaction-specific investments mentioned in Chapter 6. For example, managers from one alliance partner may have to develop close, trusting relationships with managers from other alliance partners. These close relationships are very valuable in the context of the alliance, but they have limited economic value in other economic exchanges. Also, one partner may have to customize its manufacturing equipment, distribution network, and key organizational policies to cooperate with other partners. These modifications have significant value in the context of the alliance, but they do not help the firm, and may even hurt it, in economic exchanges outside the alliance. As was the case in Chapter 6, whenever an investment's value in its first-best use (in this case, within the alliance) is much greater than its value in its second-best use (in this case, outside the alliance), that investment is said to be **transaction specific**.[14]

When one firm makes more transaction-specific investments in a strategic alliance than partner firms make, that firm may be subject to the form of cheating called **holdup**. Holdup occurs when a firm that has not made significant transaction-specific investments demands returns from an alliance that are higher than the partners agreed to when they created the alliance.

For example, suppose two alliance partners agree to a 50–50 split of the costs and profits associated with an alliance. To make the alliance work, Firm A has to customize its production process. Firm B, however, does not have to modify itself to cooperate with Firm A. The value to Firm A of this customized production process, if it is used in the strategic alliance, is $5,000. However, outside the alliance, this customized process is only worth $200 (as scrap).

Obviously, Firm A has made a transaction-specific investment in this alliance and Firm B has not. Consequently, Firm A may be subject to holdup by Firm B. In particular, Firm B may threaten to leave the alliance unless Firm A agrees to give Firm B part of the $5,000 value that Firm A obtains by using the modified production process in the alliance. Rather than lose all the value that could be generated by its investment, Firm A may be willing to give up some of its $5,000 to avoid gaining only $200. Indeed, if Firm B extracts up to the value of Firm A's production process in its next-best use (here, only $200), Firm A will still be better off continuing in this relationship rather than dissolving it. Thus, even though Firm A and Firm B initially agreed on a 50–50 split from this strategic alliance, the agreement may be modified if one party to the alliance makes significant transaction-specific investments. Research on international joint ventures suggests that the existence of transaction-specific investments in these relationships often leads to holdup problems.[15]

Strategy in the Emerging Enterprise

In 1994, Pixar was a struggling startup company in northern California that was trying to compete in an industry that really didn't yet exist—the computer graphics animated motion picture industry. Headed by the founder of Apple Computer, Steve Jobs, Pixar was desperately looking for a partner that could help finance and distribute its new brand of animated movies. Who better, Pixar thought, than the world's leader in animated feature-length films: Disney. And, thus, a strategic alliance between Pixar and Disney was formed.

In the alliance, Disney agreed to help finance and distribute Pixar's films. In return, it would share in any profits these films generated. Also, Disney would retain the right to produce any sequels to Pixar's films—after first offering Pixar the right to make these sequels. This agreement gave Disney a great deal of control over any characters that Pixar created in movies distributed through Pixar's alliance with Disney. Of course, at the time the alliance was originally formed there were no such characters. Indeed, Pixar had yet to produce any movies. So, because Pixar was a weak alliance partner, Disney was able to gain control of any characters Pixar developed in the future. Disney, after all, had the track record of success.

A funny thing happened over the next 10 years. Pixar produced blockbuster animated features such as *Toy Story* (total revenues of $419.9 million); *A Bug's Life* (total revenues of $358 million); *Toy Story 2* (total revenues of

Disney and Pixar

$629.9 million); *Monsters, Inc.* (total revenues of $903.1 million); *Finding Nemo* (total revenues of $1,281.4 million); *The Incredibles* (total revenues of $946.6 million); and *Cars* (total revenues of $331.9 million). And these revenue numbers do not include sales of merchandise associated with these films. During this same time period, Disney's traditional animated fare performed much more poorly—*Treasure Planet* generated only $112 million in revenues, *The Emperor's New Groove* only $169 million, and *Brother Bear* only $126 million. Disney's "big hit" during this time period was *Lilo & Stitch*, with revenues of $269 million—less than any of the movies produced by Pixar.

Oops! The firm with the "proven track record" of producing hit animated features—Disney—stumbled badly, and the upstart company with no track record—Pixar—had all the success. Because Disney did not have many of its own characters upon which to base sequels, it began to eye Pixar's characters.

Fast-forward to 2004. It's time to renew this alliance. But now Pixar has the upper hand because it has the track record. Disney comes knocking and asks Pixar to redo the alliance. What does Pixar say? "OK, but ... we want control of our characters, we want Disney to act just as a distributor"—in other words, "We want Disney out of our business!" Disney balks at these demands, and Pixar—well, Pixar just canceled the alliance.

But Pixar still needed a distribution partner. Pixar simply does not produce enough films to justify the expense of building its own distribution system. After a several-month search, Pixar found what it considered to be its best distribution partner. The only problem was—it was Disney.

Reestablishing the alliance between Pixar and Disney seemed out of the question. After all, such an alliance would have all the same challenges as the previous alliance.

Instead, Disney decided to buy Pixar. On January 25, 2006, Disney announced that it was buying Pixar in a deal worth $7.4 billion. Steve Jobs became Disney's single largest investor and became a member of Disney's board of directors. John Lasseter—the creative force behind Pixar's success—became chief creative officer at Disney.

Sources: S. Levy and D. Jefferson (2004). "Hey Mickey, buzz off!" *BusinessWeek*, February 9, p. 4; T. Lowry et al. (2004). "Megamedia mergers: How dangerous?" *BusinessWeek*, February 23, pp. 34+; and money.cnn.com/2006/01/24/newscompanies/disney_pixar_deal.

Although holdup is a form of cheating in strategic alliances, the threat of holdup can also be a motivation for creating an alliance. Bauxite-smelting companies often join in joint ventures with mining companies in order to exploit economies of scale in mining. However, these firms have another option: They could choose to operate large and efficient mines by themselves and then sell the excess bauxite (over and above their needs for their own smelters) on the open market. Unfortunately, bauxite is not a homogeneous commodity. Moreover, different kinds of bauxite require different smelting technologies. In order for one firm to sell its excess bauxite on the market, other smelting firms would have to make enormous investments, the sole purpose of which would be to refine that particular firm's bauxite. These investments would be transaction specific and subject these other smelters to holdup problems.

In this context, a strategic alliance can be thought of as a way of reducing the threat of holdup by creating an explicit management framework for resolving holdup problems. In other words, although holdup problems might still exist in these strategic alliances, the alliance framework may still be a better way in which to manage these problems than attempting to manage them in arm's-length market relationships. Some of the ethical dimensions of adverse selection, moral hazard, and holdup are discussed in the Ethics and Strategy feature.

Strategic Alliances and Sustained Competitive Advantage

The ability of strategic alliances to be sources of sustained competitive advantage, like all the other strategies discussed in this book, can be analyzed with the VRIO framework developed in Chapter 3. An alliance is economically valuable when it exploits any of the opportunities listed in Table 9.1 but avoids the threats in Table 9.2. In addition, for a strategic alliance to be a source of sustained competitive advantage it must be rare and costly to imitate.

The Rarity of Strategic Alliances

The rarity of strategic alliances does not only depend on the number of competing firms that have already implemented an alliance. It also depends on whether the benefits that firms obtain from their alliances are common across firms competing in an industry.

Consider, for example, the U.S. automobile industry. Over the past several years, strategic alliances have become very common in this industry, especially with Japanese auto firms. General Motors developed an alliance with Toyota that has already been described; Ford developed an alliance with Mazda before it purchased this Japanese firm outright; and Chrysler developed an alliance with Mitsubishi. Given the frequency with which alliances have developed in this industry, it is tempting to conclude that strategic alliances are not rare and thus not a source of competitive advantage.

Closer examination, however, suggests that these alliances may have been created for different reasons. For example, until recently, GM and Toyota have cooperated only in building a single line of cars, the Chevrolet Nova. General Motors has been less interested in learning design skills from Toyota and has been more interested in learning about manufacturing high-quality small cars profitably. Ford and Mazda, in contrast, worked closely together in designing new cars and had joint manufacturing operations. Indeed, Ford and Mazda worked so closely together that Ford finally once purchased 33 percent of Mazda's stock. Since 2008, Ford has reduced its investment in Mazda dramatically. Mitsubishi has acted primarily as a supplier to Chrysler, and (until recently) there has been relatively little joint development or manufacturing. Thus, although all three U.S. firms have strategic alliances, the alliances serve different purposes, and therefore each may be rare.[16]

One of the reasons why the benefits that accrue from a particular strategic alliance may be rare is that relatively few firms may have the complementary resources and abilities needed to form an alliance. This is particularly likely when an alliance is formed to enter into a new market, especially a new foreign market. In many less-developed economies, only one local firm or very few local firms may exist with the local knowledge, contacts, and distribution network needed to facilitate entry into that market. Moreover, sometimes the government acts to limit the number of these local firms. Although several firms may seek entry into this market, only a very small number will be able to form a strategic alliance with the local entity, and therefore the benefits that accrue to the allied firms will likely be rare.

The Imitability of Strategic Alliances

As discussed in Chapter 3, the resources and capabilities that enable firms to conceive and implement valuable strategies may be imitated in two ways: direct duplication and substitution. Both duplication and substitution are important considerations in analyzing the imitability of strategic alliances.

Direct Duplication of Strategic Alliances

Research suggests that successful strategic alliances are often based on socially complex relations among alliance partners.[17] In this sense, successful strategic alliances often go well beyond simple legal contracts and are characterized by socially complex phenomena such as a trusting relationship between alliance partners, friendship, and even (perhaps) a willingness to suspend narrow self-interest for the longer-term good of the relationship.

Some research has shown that the development of trusting relationships between alliance partners is both difficult and essential to the success of strategic alliances. In one study, the most common reason that alliances failed to meet the expectations of partner firms was the partners' inability to trust one another. Interpersonal communication, tolerance for cultural differences, patience, and willingness to sacrifice short-term profits for longer-term success were all important determinants of the level of trust among alliance partners.[18]

Of course, not all firms in an industry are likely to have the organizational and relationship-building skills required for successful alliance building. If these skills and abilities are rare among a set of competing firms and costly to develop, then firms that are able to exploit these abilities by creating alliances may gain competitive advantages. Examples of firms that have developed these specialized skills include Corning and Cisco, with several hundred strategic alliances each.[19]

Ethics and Strategy

Firms in strategic alliances can cheat on their alliance partners by engaging in adverse selection, moral hazard, or holdup. These three activities all have at least one thing in common—they all involve one alliance partner lying to another. And these lies can often pay off big in the form of the lying firm appropriating more than its "fair share" of the value created in an alliance. Are alliances one place in the economy where the adage "cheaters never prosper" does not hold?

There is little doubt that, in the short run, firms that cheat on their alliance partners can gain some advantages. But research suggests that cheating does not pay in the long run because firms that cheat on their alliance partners will find it difficult to form alliances with new partners and thus have many valuable exchange opportunities foreclosed to them.

One study that examined the long-term return to "cheaters" in strategic alliances analyzed alliances using a simple game called the "Prisoner's Dilemma." In a "Prisoner's Dilemma" game, firms have two options: to continue cooperating in a strategic alliance or to "cheat" on that alliance through adverse selection, moral hazard, or holdup. The payoffs to firms in this game depend on the decisions made by both firms. As shown in Table 9.3, if both firms decide to cooperate, they

**When It Comes to Alliances,
Do "Cheaters Never Prosper"?**

each get a good size payoff from the alliance ($3,000 in Table 9.3); if they both decide to cheat on the alliance, they each get a very small payoff ($1,000 in Table 9.3); and if one decides to cheat while the other decides to cooperate, then the cheating firm gets a very big payoff ($5,000 in Table 9.3) while the cooperating firm gets a very small payoff ($0 in Table 9.3).

If Firm 1 and Firm 2 in this game are going to engage in only one strategic alliance, then they have a very strong incentive to "cheat." The worst that could happen if they cheat is that they earn a $1,000 payoff, but there is a possibility of a $5,000 payoff. However, research has shown that if

a firm is contemplating engaging in multiple strategic alliances over time, then the optimal strategy is to cooperate in all its alliances. This is true even if all these alliances are not with the same partner firm.

The specific "winning" strategy in repeated "Prisoner Dilemma" games is called a "tit-for-tat" strategy. "Tit-for-tat" means that Firm 1 will cooperate in an alliance as long as Firm 2 cooperates. However, as soon as Firm 2 cheats on an alliance, Firm 1 cheats as well. "Tit-for-tat" works well in this setting because adopting a cooperative posture in an alliance ensures that, most of the time, the alliance will generate a high payoff (of $3,000 in Table 9.3). However, by immediately responding to cheaters by cheating, the firm implementing a "tit-for-tat" strategy also minimizes the times when it will earn the lowest payoff in the table ($0). So, "tit-for-tat" maximizes the upside potential of an alliance while minimizing its downside.

All this analysis suggests that although cheating on an alliance can give a firm competitive advantages in the short to medium term, in the long run, "cheaters never prosper."

Sources: R. M. Axelrod (1984). *The evolution of cooperation.* New York: Basic Books; D. Ernst and J. Bleeke (1993). *Collaborating to compete.* New York: Wiley.

TABLE 9.3 Returns from Cooperating and Cheating in a "Prisoner's Dilemma"

		Strategic Alliance	
Firm 1			
		Cooperates	Cheats
	Cooperates	1: $3,000	1: $5,000
		2: $3,000	2: $0
Firm 2			
	Cheats	1: $0	1: $1,000
		2: $5,000	2: $1,000

Substitutes for Strategic Alliances

Even if the purpose and objectives of a strategic alliance are valuable and rare and even if the relationships on which an alliance is created are socially complex and costly to imitate, that alliance will still not generate a sustained competitive advantage if low-cost substitutes are available. At least two possible substitutes for strategic alliances exist: "going it alone" and acquisitions.[20]

"Going It Alone."   Firms "go it alone" when they attempt to develop all the resources and capabilities they need to exploit market opportunities and neutralize market threats by themselves. Sometimes "going it alone" can create the same—or even more—value than using alliances to exploit opportunities and neutralize threats. In these settings, "going it alone" is a substitute for a strategic alliance. However, in other settings using an alliance can create substantially more value than "going it alone." In these settings, "going it alone" is not a substitute for a strategic alliance.

So, when will firms prefer an alliance over "going it alone"? Not surprisingly, the three explanations of vertical integration, discussed in Chapter 6, are relevant here as well. These three explanations focused on the threat of opportunism, the impact of firm resources and capabilities, and the role of uncertainty. If you need to review these three explanations, they are described in detail in Chapter 6. They are relevant here because "going it alone"—as a potential substitute for a strategic alliance—is an example of vertical integration. The implications of these three explanations for when strategic alliances will be preferred over "going it alone" are summarized in Table 9.4. If any of the conditions listed in Table 9.4 exist, then "going it alone" will not be a substitute for strategic alliances.

Recall from Chapter 6 that opportunism-based explanations of vertical integration suggest that firms will want to vertically integrate an economic exchange when they have made high levels of transaction-specific investment in that exchange. That is, using language developed in this chapter, firms will want to vertically integrate an economic exchange when using an alliance to manage that exchange could subject them to holdup. Extending this logic to strategic alliances suggests that strategic alliances will be preferred over "going it alone" and other alternatives when the level of transaction-specific investment required to complete an exchange is moderate. If the level of this specific investment is low, then market forms of exchange will be preferred; if the level of this specific investment is high, then "going it alone" in a vertically integrated way will be preferred; if the level of this specific investment is moderate, then some sort of strategic alliance will be preferred. Thus, when the level of specific exchange in a transaction is moderate, then "going it alone" is not a substitute for a strategic alliance.

TABLE 9.4 When Alliances Will Be Preferred Over "Going It Alone"

Alliances will be preferred over "going it alone" when:

1. The level of transaction-specific investment required to complete an exchange is moderate.
2. An exchange partner possesses valuable, rare, and costly-to-imitate resources and capabilities.
3. There is great uncertainty about the future value of an exchange.

Capabilities-based explanations suggest that an alliance will be preferred over "going it alone" when an exchange partner possesses valuable, rare, and costly-to-imitate resources and capabilities. A firm without these capabilities may find them to be too costly to develop on its own. If a firm must have access to capabilities it cannot develop on its own, it must use an alliance to gain access to those capabilities. In this setting, "going it alone" is not a substitute for a strategic alliance.[21]

Finally, it has already been suggested that, under conditions of high uncertainty, firms may be unwilling to commit to a particular course of action by engaging in an exchange within a firm. In such settings, firms may choose the strategic flexibility associated with alliances. As suggested earlier in this chapter, alliances can be thought of as real options that give a firm the right, but not the obligation, to invest further in an exchange—perhaps by bringing it within the boundaries of a firm—if that exchange turns out to be valuable sometime in the future. Thus, under conditions of high uncertainty, "going it alone" is not a substitute for strategic alliances.

Acquisitions.   The acquisition of other firms can also be a substitute for alliances. In this case, rather than developing a strategic alliance or attempting to develop and exploit the relevant resources by "going it alone," a firm seeking to exploit the opportunities listed in Table 9.1 may simply acquire another firm that already possesses the relevant resources and capabilities. However, such acquisitions have four characteristics that often limit the extent to which they can act as substitutes for strategic alliances. These are summarized in Table 9.5.[22]

First, there may be legal constraints on acquisitions. These are especially likely if firms are seeking advantages by combining with other firms in their own industry. Thus, for example, using acquisitions as a substitute for strategic alliances in the aluminum industry would lead to a very concentrated industry and subject some of these firms to serious antitrust liabilities. These firms have acquisitions foreclosed to them and must look elsewhere to gain advantages from cooperating with their competition.

Second, as has already been suggested, strategic alliances enable a firm to retain its flexibility either to enter or not to enter into a new business. Acquisitions limit that flexibility because they represent a strong commitment to engage in a certain business activity. Consequently, under conditions of high uncertainty firms may choose strategic alliances over acquisitions as a way to exploit opportunities while maintaining the flexibility that alliances create.

Third, firms may choose strategic alliances over acquisitions because of the unwanted organizational baggage that often comes with an acquisition. Sometimes, the value created by combining firms depends on combining particular functions, divisions, or other assets in the firms. A strategic alliance can focus on exploiting the value of combining just those parts of firms that create the most

TABLE 9.5 Reasons Why Strategic Alliances May Be More Attractive Than Acquisitions to Realize Exchange Opportunities

Alliances will be preferred to acquisitions when:
1. There are legal constraints on acquisitions.
2. Acquisitions limit a firm's flexibility under conditions of high uncertainty.
3. There is substantial unwanted organizational "baggage" in an acquired firm.
4. The value of a firm's resources and capabilities depends on its independence.

value. Acquisitions, in contrast, generally include the entire organization, both the parts of a firm where value is likely to be created and parts of a firm where value is not likely to be created.

From the point of view of the acquiring firm, parts of a firm that do not create value are essentially unwanted baggage. These parts of the firm may be sold off subsequent to an acquisition. However, this sell-off may be costly and time consuming. If enough baggage exists, firms may determine that an acquisition is not a viable option, even though important economic value could be created between a firm and a potential acquisition target. To gain this value, an alternative approach—a strategic alliance—may be preferred. These issues will be explored in more detail in Chapter 10.

Finally, sometimes a firm's resources and capabilities are valuable because that firm is independent. In this setting, the act of acquiring a firm can actually reduce the value of a firm. When this is the case, any value between two firms is best realized through an alliance, not an acquisition. For example, the international growth of numerous marketing-oriented companies in the 1980s led to strong pressures for advertising agencies to develop global marketing capabilities. During the 1990s, many domestic-only advertising firms acquired nondomestic agencies to form a few large international advertising agencies. However, one firm that was reluctant to be acquired in order to be part of an international advertising network was the French advertising company Publicis. Over and above the personal interests of its owners to retain control of the company, Publicis wanted to remain an independent French agency in order to retain its stable of French and French-speaking clients—including Renault and Nestlé. These firms had indicated that they preferred working with a French advertising agency and that they would look for alternative suppliers if Publicis were acquired by a foreign firm. Because much of the value that Publicis created in a potential acquisition depended on obtaining access to its stable of clients, the act of acquiring Publicis would have had the effect of destroying the very thing that made the acquisition attractive. For this reason, rather than allowing itself to be acquired by foreign advertising agencies, Publicis developed a complex equity strategic alliance and joint venture with a U.S. advertising firm, Foote, Coyne, and Belding. Although, ultimately, this alliance was not successful in providing an international network for either of these two partner firms, an acquisition of Publicis by Foote, Coyne, and Belding would almost certainly have destroyed some of the economic value that Publicis enjoyed as a stand-alone company.

Organizing to Implement Strategic Alliances

VRIO

One of the most important determinants of the success of strategic alliances is their organization. The primary purpose of organizing a strategic alliance is to enable partners in the alliance to gain all the benefits associated with cooperation while minimizing the probability that cooperating firms will cheat on their cooperative agreements. The organizing skills required in managing alliances are, in many ways, unique. It often takes some time for firms to learn these skills and realize the full potential of their alliances. This is why some firms are able to gain competitive advantages from managing alliances more effectively than their competitors. Indeed, sometimes firms may have to choose alternatives to alliances—including "going it alone" and acquisitions—even when those alternatives are not preferred, simply because they do not have the skills required to organize and manage alliances.

A variety of tools and mechanisms can be used to help realize the value of alliances and minimize the threat of cheating. These include contracts, equity investments, firm reputations, joint ventures, and trust.

Explicit Contracts and Legal Sanctions

One way to avoid cheating in strategic alliances is for the parties to an alliance to anticipate the ways in which cheating may occur (including adverse selection, moral hazard, and holdup) and to write explicit contracts that define legal liability if cheating does occur. Writing these contracts, together with the close monitoring of contractual compliance and the threat of legal sanctions, can reduce the probability of cheating. Earlier in this chapter, such strategic alliances were called nonequity alliances.

However, contracts sometimes fail to anticipate all forms of cheating that might occur in a relationship—and firms may cheat on cooperative agreements in subtle ways that are difficult to evaluate in terms of contractual requirements. Thus, for example, a contract may require parties in a strategic alliance to make available to the alliance certain proprietary technologies or processes. However, it may be very difficult to communicate the subtleties of these technologies or processes to alliance partners. Does this failure in communication represent a clear violation of contractual requirements, or does it represent a good-faith effort by alliance partners? Moreover, how can one partner tell whether it is obtaining all the necessary information about a technology or process when it is unaware of all the information that exists in another firm? Hence, although contracts are an important component of most strategic alliances, they do not resolve all the problems associated with cheating.

Although most contracts associated with strategic alliances are highly customized, these different contracts do have some common features. These common features are described in detail in Table 9.6. In general, firms contemplating a strategic alliance that will be at least partially governed by a contract will have to include clauses that address the issues presented in Table 9.6.

Equity Investments

The effectiveness of contracts can be enhanced by having partners in an alliance make equity investments in each other. When Firm A buys a substantial equity position in its alliance partner, Firm B, the market value of Firm A now depends, to some extent, on the economic performance of that partner. The incentive of Firm A to cheat Firm B falls, for to do so would be to reduce the economic performance of Firm B and thus the value of Firm A's investment in its partner. These kinds of strategic alliances are called equity alliances.

Many firms use cross-equity investments to help manage their strategic alliances. These arrangements are particularly common in Japan, where a firm's largest equity holders often include several of its key suppliers, including its main banks. These equity investments, because they reduce the threat of cheating in alliances with suppliers, can reduce these firms' supply costs. In turn, not only do firms have equity positions in their suppliers, but suppliers often have substantial equity positions in the firms to which they sell.[23]

TABLE 9.6 Common Clauses in Contracts Used to Govern Strategic Alliances

Establishment Issues

Shareholdings: Percentage of JV owned by various partners

Voting rights: Votes held by various partners

Dividend percentage: How profits are to be allocated

Minority protection: How minority owner interests are protected

Board of directors: Initial board and rules for modifying the board

Articles of association: Processes for making decisions

Place of incorporation

Accountants, lawyers, and other advisors

Operating Issues

Performance expectations

Noncompete agreements

Nonsolicitation clauses: Partners cannot recruit employees from each other

Confidentiality clauses

Licensing intellectual property rights: Who owns the intellectual property created by a joint venture?

Liability of the alliance and liability of cooperating partners

Process of changing the contract

Process of resolving disputes

Termination Issues

Preemption rights: If one partner wishes to sell its shares, it must first offer them to the other partner

When one partner can force the other partner to sell its shares to it

When a partner has the right to force another partner to buy its alliance shares

Drag-along rights: When one partner can arrange a sale to an outside firm and force the other partner to sell shares as well

Tag-along rights: When one partner can prevent the sale of the second partner's shares to an outside firm unless that outside firm also buys the first partner's shares

When an initial public offering (IPO) will be pursued

Termination: When the JV can be terminated

Source: Based on E. Campbell and J. Reuer (2001). "Note on the legal negotiation of strategic alliance agreements." Copyright © 2000 INSEAD.

Firm Reputations

A third constraint on incentives to cheat in strategic alliances exists in the effect that a reputation for cheating has on a firm's future opportunities. Although it is often difficult to anticipate all the different ways in which an alliance partner may cheat, it is often easier to describe after the fact how an alliance partner has cheated. Information about an alliance partner that has cheated is likely to become widely known. A firm with a reputation as a cheater is not likely to be able to develop strategic alliances with other partners in the future, despite any special resources or capabilities that it might be able to bring to an alliance. In this way, cheating in a current alliance may foreclose opportunities for developing other valuable alliances. For this reason, firms may decide not to cheat in their current alliances.[24]

Substantial evidence suggests that the effect of reputation on future business opportunities is important. Firms go to great lengths to make sure that they do not develop a negative reputation. Nevertheless, this reputational control of cheating in strategic alliances does have several limitations.[25]

First, subtle cheating in a strategic alliance may not become public, and if it does become public, the responsibility for the failure of the strategic alliance may be very ambiguous. In one equity joint venture attempting to perfect the design of a new turbine for power generation, financial troubles made one partner considerably more anxious than the other partner to complete product development. The financially healthy, and thus patient, partner believed that if the alliance required an additional infusion of capital, the financially troubled partner would have to abandon the alliance and would have to sell its part of the alliance at a relatively low price. The patient partner thus encouraged alliance engineers to work slowly and carefully in the guise of developing the technology to reach its full potential. The financially troubled, and thus impatient, partner encouraged alliance engineers to work quickly, perhaps sacrificing some quality to develop the technology sooner. Eventually, the impatient partner ran out of money, sold its share of the alliance to the patient partner at a reduced price, and accused the patient partner of not acting in good faith to facilitate the rapid development of the new technology. The patient partner accused the other firm of pushing the technology too quickly, thereby sacrificing quality and, perhaps, worker safety. In some sense, both firms were cheating on their agreement to develop the new technology cooperatively. However, this cheating was subtle and difficult to spot and had relatively little impact on the reputation of either firm or on the ability of either firm to establish alliances in the future. It is likely that most observers would simply conclude that the patient partner obtained a windfall because of the impatient partner's bad luck.[26]

Second, although one partner to an alliance may be unambiguously cheating on the relationship, one or both of the firms may not be sufficiently connected into a network with other firms to make this information public. When information about cheating remains private, public reputations are not tarnished and future opportunities are not forgone. This is especially likely to happen if one or both alliance partners operate in less-developed economies where information about partner behavior may not be rapidly diffused to other firms or to other countries.

Finally, the effect of a tarnished reputation, as long as cheating in an alliance is unambiguous and publicly known, may foreclose future opportunities for a firm, but it does little to address the current losses experienced by the firm that was cheated. Moreover, any of the forms of cheating discussed earlier—adverse selection, moral hazard, or holdup—can result in substantial losses for a firm currently in an alliance. Indeed, the wealth created by cheating in a current alliance may be large enough to make a firm willing to forgo future alliances. In this case, a tarnished reputation may be of minor consequence to a cheating firm.[27]

Joint Ventures

A fourth way to reduce the threat of cheating is for partners in a strategic alliance to invest in a joint venture. Creating a separate legal entity, in which alliance partners invest and from whose profits they earn returns on their investments, reduces some of the risks of cheating in strategic alliances. When a joint venture is created, the ability of partners to earn returns on their investments depends on the economic success of the joint venture. Partners in joint ventures have limited interests in behaving in ways that hurt the performance of the joint venture because such behaviors end up hurting both partners. Moreover, unlike reputational consequences of cheating, cheating in a joint venture does not just foreclose future alliance opportunities; it can hurt the cheating firm in the current period as well.

Given the advantages of joint ventures in controlling cheating, it is not surprising that when the probability of cheating in a cooperative relationship is greatest, a joint venture is usually the preferred form of cooperation. For example, bauxite mining has some clear economies of scale. However, transaction-specific investments would lead to significant holdup problems in selling excess bauxite in the open market, and legal constraints prevent the acquisition of other smelter companies to create an intraorganizational demand for excess bauxite. Holdup problems would continue to exist in any mining strategic alliances that might be created. Nonequity alliances, equity alliances, and reputational effects are not likely to restrain cheating in this situation because the returns on holdup, once transaction-specific investments are in place, can be very large. Thus, most of the strategic alliances created to mine bauxite take the form of joint ventures. Only this form of strategic alliance is likely to create incentives strong enough to significantly reduce the probability of cheating.[28]

Despite these strengths, joint ventures are not able to reduce all cheating in an alliance without cost. Sometimes the value of cheating in a joint venture is sufficiently large that a firm cheats even though doing so hurts the joint venture and forecloses future opportunities. For example, a particular firm may gain access to a technology through a joint venture that would be valuable if used in another of its lines of business. This firm may be tempted to transfer this technology to this other line of business even if it has agreed not to do so and even if doing so would limit the performance of its joint venture. Because the profits earned in this other line of business may have a greater value than the returns that could have been earned in the joint venture and the returns that could have been earned in the future with other strategic alliances, cheating may occur.

Trust

It is sometimes the case that alliance partners rely only on legalistic and narrowly economic approaches to manage their alliance. However, recent work seems to suggest that although successful alliance partners do not ignore legal and economic disincentives to cheating, they strongly support these narrower linkages with a rich set of interpersonal relations and trust. Trust, in combination with contracts, can help reduce the threat of cheating. More important, trust may enable partners to explore exchange opportunities that they could not explore if only legal and economic organizing mechanisms were in place.[29]

At first glance, this argument may seem far-fetched. However, some research offers support for this approach to managing strategic alliances, suggesting that successful alliance partners typically do not specify all the terms and conditions in their relationship in a legal contract and do not specify all possible forms of cheating and their consequences. Moreover, when joint ventures are formed, partners do not always insist on simple 50–50 splits of equity ownership and profit sharing. Rather, successful alliances involve trust, a willingness to be flexible, a willingness to learn, and a willingness to let the alliance develop in ways that the partners could not have anticipated.[30]

Commitment, coordination, and trust are all important determinants of alliance success. Put another way, a strategic alliance is a relationship that evolves over time. Allowing the lawyers and economists to too rigorously define, a priori, the boundaries of that relationship may limit it and stunt its development.[31]

This "trust" approach also has implications for the extent to which strategic alliances may be sources of sustained competitive advantage for firms. The ability to move into strategic alliances in this trusting way may be very valuable over the long run. There is strong reason to believe that this ability is not uniformly distributed across all firms that might have an interest in forming strategic alliances and that this ability may be history-dependent and socially complex and thus costly to imitate. Firms with these skills may be able to gain sustained competitive advantages from their alliance relationships. The observation that just a few firms, including Corning and Cisco, are well-known for their strategic alliance successes is consistent with the observation that these alliance management skills may be valuable, rare, and costly to imitate.

Summary

Strategic alliances exist whenever two or more organizations cooperate in the development, manufacture, or sale of products or services. Strategic alliances can be grouped into three large categories: nonequity alliances, equity alliances, and joint ventures.

Firms join in strategic alliances for three broad reasons: to improve the performance of their current operations, to improve the competitive environment within which they are operating, and to facilitate entry into or exit from markets and industries. Just as there are incentives to cooperate in strategic alliances, there are also incentives to cheat. Cheating generally takes one or a combination of three forms: adverse selection, moral hazard, or holdup.

Strategic alliances can be a source of sustained competitive advantage. The rarity of alliances depends not only on the number of competing firms that have developed an alliance, but also on the benefits that firms gain through their alliances.

Imitation through direct duplication of an alliance may be costly because of the socially complex relations that underlie an alliance; however, imitation through substitution is more likely. Two substitutes for alliances may be "going it alone," where firms develop and exploit the relevant sets of resources and capabilities on their own, and acquisitions. Opportunism, capabilities, and uncertainty all have an impact on when "going it alone" will be a substitute for a strategic alliance. Acquisitions may be a substitute for strategic alliances when there are no legal constraints, strategic flexibility is not an important consideration, when the acquired firm has relatively little unwanted "organizational baggage," and when the value of a firm's resources and capabilities does not depend on its remaining independent. However, when these conditions do not exist, acquisitions are not a substitute for alliances.

The key issue facing firms in organizing their alliances is to facilitate cooperation while avoiding the threat of cheating. Contracts, equity investments, firm reputations, joint ventures, and trust can all reduce the threat of cheating in different contexts.

MyManagementLab®
Go to **mymanagementlab.com** to complete the problems marked with this icon ⭐.

Challenge Questions

9.1. One reason firms might want to pursue a strategic alliance strategy is to exploit economies of scale. Exploiting economies of scale should reduce a firm's costs. Why would this mean that a firm pursuing an alliance strategy to exploit economies of scale is actually pursuing a cost leadership strategy?

9.2. Consider the joint venture between General Motors and Toyota. GM has been interested in learning how to profitably manufacture high-quality small cars from its alliance with Toyota. Toyota has been interested in gaining access to GM's U.S. distribution network and in reducing the political liability associated with local content laws. Which of these firms do you think is more likely to accomplish its objectives, and why?

9.3. Consider the joint venture between General Motors and Toyota. GM has been interested in learning how to profitably manufacture high-quality small cars from its alliance with Toyota. Toyota has been interested in gaining access to GM's U.S.

distribution network and in reducing the political liability associated with local content laws. What implications, if any, does this alliance have for a possible "learning race?"

9.4. Some researchers have argued that strategic alliances are one way in which firms can help facilitate the development of a tacit collusion strategy. In your view, what are the critical differences between tacit collusion strategies and strategic alliance strategies?

⭐ **9.5.** How can one tell whether two firms are engaging in an alliance to facilitate collusion or are engaging in an alliance for other purposes?

9.6. Some researchers have argued that alliances can be used to help firms evaluate the economic potential of entering into a new industry or market. Under what conditions will a firm seeking to evaluate these opportunities need to invest in an alliance to accomplish this evaluation?

9.7. Some researchers have argued that alliances can be used to help firms

evaluate the economic potential of entering into a new industry or market. Why couldn't such a firm simply hire some smart managers, consultants, and industry experts to evaluate the economic potential of entering into a new industry?

⭐ **9.8.** Some researchers have argued that alliances can be used to help firms evaluate the economic potential of entering into a new industry or market. What, if anything, about an alliance makes this a better way to evaluate entry opportunities than alternative methods?

9.9. If adverse selection, moral hazard, and holdup are such significant problems for firms pursuing alliance strategies, why do firms even bother with alliances?

9.10. If adverse selection, moral hazard, and holdup are such significant problems for firms pursuing alliance strategies, why don't they instead adopt a "go it alone" strategy to replace strategic alliances?

Problem Set

9.11. Which of the following firms faces the greater threat of "cheating" in the alliances described, and why?

(a) Firm I and Firm II form a strategic alliance. As part of the alliance, Firm I agrees to build a new plant right next to Firm II's primary facility. In return, Firm II promises to buy most of the output of this new plant. Which is at risk, Firm I or Firm II?

(b) Firm A and Firm B form a strategic alliance. As part of the alliance, Firm A promises to begin selling products it already sells around the world in the home country of Firm B. In return, Firm B promises to provide Firm A with crucial contacts in its home country's government. These contacts are essential if Firm A is going to be able to sell in Firm B's home country. Which is at risk, Firm A or Firm B?

(c) Firm 1 and Firm 2 form a strategic alliance. As part of the alliance, Firm 1 promises to provide Firm 2 access to some new and untested technology that Firm 2 will use in its products. In return, Firm 2 will share some of the profits from its sales with Firm 1. Which is at risk, Firm 1 or Firm 2?

9.12. For each of the strategic alliances described in the above question, what actions could be taken to reduce the likelihood that partner firms will "cheat" in these alliances?

9.13. Examine the Web sites of the following strategic alliances and determine which of the sources of value presented in Table 9.1 are present:

(a) Dow-Corning (an alliance between Dow Chemical and Corning)
(b) CFM (an alliance between General Electric and SNECMA)
(c) NCAA (an alliance among colleges and universities in the United States)
(d) Visa (an alliance among banks in the United States)
(e) The alliance among United, Delta, Singapore Airlines, AeroMexico, Alitalia, and Korean Air

MyManagement**Lab**®

Go to **mymanagementlab.com** for Auto-graded writing questions as well as the following Assisted-graded writing questions:

⭐ **9.14.** How would a firm's reputation reduce the threat of cheating in a strategic alliance?

⭐ **9.15.** How can holdup be considered a form of cheating in strategic alliances and threat of holdup be considered a motivation for creating an alliance?

End Notes

1. See www.pwc.com/extweb/exccps.nsf/docid; www.addme.com/issue208; McCracken, J. (2006). "Ford doubles reported loss for second quarter." *The Wall Street Journal*, August 3, p. A3; and www.msnbc.msn.com/id/13753688.
2. Badaracco, J. L., and N. Hasegawa. (1988). "General Motors' Asian alliances." Harvard Business School Case No. 9-388-094.
3. See www.blu-ray.com.
4. See Burgers, W. P., C. W. L. Hill, and W. C. Kim. (1993). "A theory of global strategic alliances: The case of the global auto industry." *Strategic Management Journal*, 14, pp. 419–432.
5. See Freeman, A., and R. Hudson. (1980). "DuPont and Philips plan joint venture to make, market laser disc products." *The Wall Street Journal*, December 22, p. 10.
6. Teitelbaum, R. S. (1992). "Eskimo pie." *Fortune*, June 15, p. 123.
7. Nanda, A., and C. A. Bartlett. (1990). "Corning Incorporated: A network of alliances." Harvard Business School Case No. 9-391-102.
8. See Knight, F. H. (1965). *Risk, uncertainty, and profit.* New York: John Wiley & Sons, Inc., on uncertainty; Kogut, B. (1991). "Joint ventures and the option to expand and acquire." *Management Science*, 37, pp. 19–33; Burgers, W. P., C. W. L. Hill, and W. C. Kim. (1993). "A theory of global strategic alliances: The case of the global auto industry." *Strategic Management Journal*, 14, pp. 419–432; Noldeke, G., and K. M. Schmidt. (1998). "Sequential investments and options to own." *Rand Journal of Economics*, 29(4), pp. 633–653; and Folta, T. B. (1998). "Governance and uncertainty: The tradeoff between administrative control and commitment." *Strategic Management Journal*, 19, pp. 1007–1028.
9. See Kogut, B. (1991). "Joint ventures and the option to expand and acquire." *Management Science*, 37, pp. 19–33; and Balakrishnan, S., and M. Koza. (1993). "Information asymmetry, adverse selection and joint-ventures." *Journal of Economic Behavior & Organization*, 20, pp. 99–117.
10. See, for example, Ernst, D., and J. Bleeke. (1993). *Collaborating to compete: Using strategic alliances and acquisition in the global marketplace.* New York: John Wiley & Sons, Inc.
11. These terms are defined in Barney, J. B., and W. G. Ouchi. (1986). *Organizational economics.* San Francisco: Jossey-Bass; and Holmstrom, B. (1979). "Moral hazard and observability." *Bell Journal of Economics*, 10(1), pp. 74–91. Problems of cheating in economic exchanges in general, and in alliances in particular, are discussed by Gulati, R., and H. Singh. (1998). "The architecture of cooperation: Managing coordination costs and appropriation concerns in strategic alliances." *Administrative Science Quarterly*, 43, pp. 781–814; Williamson, O. E. (1991). "Comparative economic organization: The analysis of discrete structural alternatives." *Administrative Science Quarterly*, 36, pp. 269–296; Osborn, R. N., and C. C. Baughn. (1990). "Forms of interorganizational governance for multinational alliances." *Academy of Management Journal*, 33(3), pp. 503–519; Hagedoorn, J., and R. Narula. (1996). "Choosing organizational modes of strategic technology partnering: International and sectoral differences." *Journal of International Business Studies*, second quarter, pp. 265–284; Hagedorn, J. (1996). "Trends and patterns in strategic technology partnering since the early seventies." *Review of Industrial Organization*, 11, pp. 601–616; Kent, D. H. (1991). "Joint ventures vs. non-joint ventures: An empirical investigation." *Strategic Management Journal*, 12, pp. 387–393; and Shane, S. A. (1998). "Making new franchise systems work." *Strategic Management Journal*, 19, pp. 697–707.
12. Such alliance difficulties are described in Ouchi, W. G. (1984). *The M-form society: How American teamwork can capture the competitive edge.* Reading, MA: Addison-Wesley; and Bresser, R. K. (1988). "Cooperative strategy." *Strategic Management Journal*, 9, pp. 475–492.
13. Pope, K. (1993). "Dealers accuse Compaq of jilting them." *The Wall Street Journal*, February 26, pp. 8, B1+.
14. Williamson, O. E. (1975). *Markets and hierarchies: Analysis and antitrust implications.* New York: Free Press; Klein, B., R. Crawford, and A. Alchian. (1978). "Vertical integration, appropriable rents, and the competitive contracting process." *Journal of Law and Economics*, 21, pp. 297–326.
15. See, for example, Yan, A., and B. Gray. (1994). "Bargaining power, management control, and performance in United States–China joint ventures: A comparative case study." *Academy of Management Journal*, 37, pp. 1478–1517.
16. See Badaracco, J. L., and N. Hasegawa. (1988). "General Motors' Asian alliances." Harvard Business School Case No. 9-388-094, on GM and Toyota; Patterson, G. A. (1991). "Mazda hopes to crack Japan's top tier." *The Wall Street Journal*, September 20, pp. B1+; and Williams, M., and M. Kanabayashi. (1993). "Mazda and Ford drop proposal to build

cars together in Europe." *The Wall Street Journal*, March 4, p. A14, on Ford and Mazda; and Ennis, P. (1991). "Mitsubishi group wary of deeper ties to Chrysler." *Tokyo Business Today*, 59, July, p. 10, on DaimlerChrysler and Mitsubishi.

17. See, for example, Ernst, D., and J. Bleeke. (1993). *Collaborating to compete: Using strategic alliances and acquisition in the global marketplace.* New York: John Wiley & Sons, Inc.; and Barney, J. B., and M. H. Hansen. (1994). "Trustworthiness as a source of competitive advantage." *Strategic Management Journal*, 15, winter (special issue), pp. 175–190.

18. Ernst, D., and J. Bleeke. (1993). *Collaborating to compete: Using strategic alliances and acquisition in the global marketplace.* New York: John Wiley & Sons, Inc.

19. Bartlett, C., and S. Ghoshal. (1993). "Beyond the M-form: Toward a managerial theory of the firm." *Strategic Management Journal*, 14, pp. 23–46.

20. See Nagarajan, A., and W. Mitchell. (1998). "Evolutionary diffusion: Internal and external methods used to acquire encompassing, complementary, and incremental technological changes in the lithotripsy industry." *Strategic Management Journal*, 19, pp. 1063–1077; Hagedoorn, J., and B. Sadowski. (1999). "The transition from strategic technology alliances to mergers and acquisitions: An exploratory study." *Journal of Management Studies*, 36(1), pp. 87–107; and Newbury, W., and Y. Zeira. (1997). "Generic differences between equity international joint ventures (EIJVs), international acquisitions (IAs) and International Greenfield investments (IGIs): Implications for parent companies." *Journal of World Business*, 32(2), pp. 87–102, on alliance substitutes.

21. Barney, J. B. (1999). "How a firm's capabilities affect boundary decisions." *Sloan Management Review*, 40(3), pp. 137–145.

22. See Hennart, J. F. (1988). "A transaction cost theory of equity joint ventures." *Strategic Management Journal*, 9, pp. 361–374; Kogut, B. (1988). "Joint ventures: Theoretical and empirical perspectives." *Strategic Management Journal*, 9, pp. 319–332; and Barney, J. B. (1999). "How a firm's capabilities affect boundary decisions." *Sloan Management Review*, 40(3), pp. 137–145, for a discussion of these limitations.

23. See Ouchi, W. G. (1984). *The M-form society: How American teamwork can capture the competitive edge.* Reading, MA: Addison-Wesley; and Barney, J. B. (1990). "Profit sharing bonuses and the cost of debt: Business finance and compensation policy in Japanese electronics firms." *Asia Pacific Journal of Management*, 7, pp. 49–64.

24. This is an argument developed by Barney, J. B., and M. H. Hansen. (1994). "Trustworthiness as a source of competitive advantage." *Strategic Management Journal*, 15, winter (special issue), pp. 175–190; Weigelt, K., and C. Camerer. (1988). "Reputation and corporate strategy: A review of recent theory and applications." *Strategic Management Journal*, 9, pp. 443–454; and Granovetter, M. (1985). "Economic action and social structure: The problem of embeddedness." *American Journal of Sociology*, 3, pp. 481–510.

25. See, for example, Eichenseher, J., and D. Shields. (1985). "Reputation and corporate strategy: A review of recent theory and applications." *Strategic Management Journal*, 9, pp. 443–454; Beatty, R., and R. Ritter. (1986). "Investment banking, reputation, and the underpricing of initial public offerings." *Journal of Financial Economics*, 15, pp. 213–232; Kalleberg, A. L., and T. Reve. (1992). "Contracts and commitment: Economic and Sociological Perspectives on Employment Relations." *Human Relations*,

45(9), pp. 1103–1132; Larson, A. (1992). "Network dyads in entrepreneurial settings: A study of the governance of exchange relationships." *Administrative Science Quarterly*, March, pp. 76–104; Stuart, T. E., H. Hoang, and R. C. Hybels. (1999). "Interorganizational endorsements and the performance of entrepreneurial ventures." *Administrative Science Quarterly*, 44, pp. 315–349; Stuart, T. E. (1998). "Network positions and propensities to collaborate: An investigation of strategic alliance formation in a high-technology industry." *Administrative Science Quarterly*, 43(3), pp. 668–698; and Gulati, R. (1998). "Alliances and networks." *Strategic Management Journal*, 19, pp. 293–317.

26. Personal communication, April 8, 1986.

27. This same theoretic approach to firm reputation is discussed in Tirole, J. (1988). *The theory of industrial organization.* Cambridge, MA: MIT Press.

28. Scherer, F. M. (1980). *Industrial market structure and economic performance.* Boston: Houghton Mifflin.

29. See, again, Ernst, D., and J. Bleeke. (1993). *Collaborating to compete: Using strategic alliances and acquisition in the global marketplace.* New York: John Wiley & Sons, Inc.; and Barney, J. B., and M. H. Hansen. (1994). "Trustworthiness as a source of competitive advantage." *Strategic Management Journal*, 15, winter (special issue), pp. 175–190. In fact, there is a great deal of literature on the role of trust in strategic alliances. Some of the most interesting of this work can be found in Holm, D. B., K. Eriksson, and J. Johanson. (1999). "Creating value through mutual commitment to business network relationships." *Strategic Management Journal*, 20, pp. 467–486; Lorenzoni, G., and A. Lipparini. (1999). "The leveraging of interfirm relationships as a distinctive organizational capability: A longitudinal study." *Strategic Management Journal*, 20(4), pp. 317–338; Blois, K. J. (1999). "Trust in business to business relationships: An evaluation of its status." *Journal of Management Studies*, 36(2), pp. 197–215; Chiles, T. H., and J. F. McMackin. (1996). "Integrating variable risk preferences, trust, and transaction cost economics." *Academy of Management Review*, 21(1), pp. 73–99; Larzelere, R. E., and T. L. Huston. (1980). "The dyadic trust scale: Toward understanding interpersonal trust in close relationships." *Journal of Marriage and the Family*, August, pp. 595–604; Butler, J. K., Jr. (1983). "Reciprocity of trust between professionals and their secretaries." *Psychological Reports*, 53, pp. 411–416; Zaheer, A., and N. Venkatraman. (1995). "Relational governance as an interorganizational strategy: An empirical test of the role of trust in economic exchange." *Strategic Management Journal*, 16, pp. 373–392; Butler, J. K., Jr., and R. S. Cantrell. (1984). "A behavioral decision theory approach to modeling dyadic trust in superiors and subordinates." *Psychological Reports*, 55, pp. 19–28; Carney, M. (1998). "The competitiveness of networked production: The role of trust and asset specificity." *Journal of Management Studies*, 35(4), pp. 457–479.

30. Ernst, D., and J. Bleeke. (1993). *Collaborating to compete: Using strategic alliances and acquisition in the global marketplace.* New York: John Wiley & Sons, Inc.

31. See Mohr, J., and R. Spekman. (1994). "Characteristics of partnership success: Partnership attributes, communication behavior, and conflict resolution techniques." *Strategic Management Journal*, 15, pp. 135–152; and Zaheer, A., and N. Venkatraman. (1995). "Relational governance as an interorganizational strategy: An empirical test of the role of trust in economic exchange." *Strategic Management Journal*, 16, pp. 373–392.

10 Mergers and Acquisitions

LEARNING OBJECTIVES *After reading this chapter, you should be able to:*

1. Describe different types of mergers and acquisitions.

2. Estimate the return to the stockholders of bidding and target firms when there is no strategic relatedness between firms.

3. Describe different sources of relatedness between bidding and target firms.

4. Estimate the return to stockholders of bidding and target firms when there is strategic relatedness between firms.

5. Describe five reasons why bidding firms might still engage in acquisitions, even if, on average, they do not create value for a bidding firm's stockholders.

6. Describe three ways that bidding firms might be able to generate high returns for their equity holders through implementing mergers or acquisitions.

7. Describe the major challenges that firms integrating acquisitions are likely to face.

MyManagementLab®
⭐ **Improve Your Grade!**
Over 10 million students improved their results using the Pearson MyLabs.
Visit **mymanagementlab.com** for simulations, tutorials, and end-of-chapter problems.

The Google Acquistion Machine

Google spent almost $6.8 billion on research and development in 2012. More than 19,700 of its 54,000 employees work in R&D, which generated 13.5 percent of all of its costs in 2012 and constituted the largest expense item on its annual income statement. In public statements, Google justified this expense as necessary to keep up with the rapidly changing technological environment within which it competes.

But Google also uses another strategy to try to keep up with technological change: acquisitions. Since 2010, Google has acquired other companies at the rate of one company per week. These acquisitions ranged from extremely small to very large, the largest being the $12.5 billion acquisition of Motorola's mobile phone business. Some other large Google acquisitions included YouTube (in 2006 for $1.65 billion), DoubleClick (in 2007 for $3.2 billion), and Waze (in 2013 for $1 billion).

If Google is spending so much money on R&D, why does it also have to spend so much money on acquisitions? After all, if Google is inventing lots of cool technology internally, why does it also have to buy technology on the market? Or, alternatively, if Google is buying lots of cool technology on the market—by buying other companies—why does it have to spend so much money on R&D?

Of course, for Google, there is a direct link between its external acquisitions and its internal R&D. In particular, Google's internal R&D not only develops new products from scratch—like the Android operating system for smart phones—it also invests in integrating the technologies it purchases into upgrading established Google products. Indeed, some observers believe that Google is unusually skilled in creating economic value by integrating the technologies it acquires into its products. Of the hundred or so technologies that Google has gained access to through its acquisitions, only a handful have not been integrated into current Google products—including, to name just a few, Google Wallet, Google Docs, Gmail, Google+, and Google TV—or have become established as new products within the Google portfolio—including, for example, YouTube.

In fact, Google has only divested three of its hundreds of acquisitions: Dodgeball (a mobile phone service divested in 2005), Slide (a social gaming company divested in 2010), and Frommer's (a travel guide company divested in 2012). These three acquisitions are widely seen as failures.

But three "failures" out of hundreds of deals is a much higher success rate than other firms in high-technology industries. It is even a higher success rate than firms in other industries. While the corporate strategy of acquisitions often does not generate superior performance for acquiring firms, Google seems to have found a way to create enough value from its acquisitions to justify their prices while still investing in its own research and development projects. Of course, the big question mark fac-

© incamerastock/Alamy

ing Google is its acquisition of Motorola. Recently, Motorola introduced its first new line of mobile phones designed and manufactured under Google's ownership—the Moto X. Reviews of these phones were mixed. Commentators were particularly surprised that Motorola's latest phones did not run the most up-to-date version of Android, Google's smart phone operating system. Perhaps Google did not want to disadvantage other users of its Android system, including Samsung, by making the latest version available on the Moto X. At the very least, that Motorola's most advanced phone did not use Android's most advanced system suggests some challenges in integrating Motorola into Google's technology family.

Sources: Google 2013 10K http://www.sec.gov/Archives/edgar/data/1288776/000119312513028362/d452134d10k.htm; A. Efrati (2013). "Google nears deal for Waze." *The Wall Street Journal*, June 10, pp. B1+; R. Knutson and S. Ante (2013). "Google leans on Motorola with hardware push." *The Wall Street Journal*, April 1, p. B2.

Google is not the only firm that engages in mergers and acquisitions. Indeed, mergers and acquisitions are one very common way that a firm can accomplish its vertical integration and diversification objectives. However, although a firm may be able to accomplish its vertical integration and diversification objectives through mergers or acquisitions, it is sometimes difficult to generate real economic profit from doing so. Indeed, one of the strongest empirical findings in the fields of strategic management and finance is that, on average, the equity holders of target firms in mergers and acquisitions make money while the equity holders of bidding firms in these same mergers and acquisitions usually only "break even."

What Are Mergers and Acquisitions?

The terms *mergers* and *acquisitions* are often used interchangeably, even though they are not synonyms. A firm engages in an **acquisition** when it purchases a second firm. The form of this purchase can vary. For example, an acquiring firm can use cash it has generated from its ongoing businesses to purchase a target firm; it can go into debt to purchase a target firm; it can use its own equity to purchase a target firm; or it can use a mix of these mechanisms to purchase a target firm. Also, an acquiring firm can purchase all of a target firm's assets; it can purchase a majority of those assets (greater than 51 percent); or it can purchase a **controlling share** of those assets (i.e., enough assets so that the acquiring firm is able to make all the management and strategic decisions in the target firm).

Acquisitions also vary on several other dimensions. For example, **friendly acquisitions** occur when the management of the target firm wants the firm to be acquired. **Unfriendly acquisitions** occur when the management of the target firm does not want the firm to be acquired. Some unfriendly acquisitions are also known as **hostile takeovers**. Some acquisitions are accomplished through direct negotiations between an acquiring firm's managers and the managers of a target firm. This is especially common when a target firm is **privately held** (i.e., when it has not sold shares on the public stock market) or **closely held** (i.e., when it has not sold very many shares on the public stock market). Other acquisitions are accomplished by the acquiring firm publicly announcing that it is willing to purchase the outstanding shares of a potential target for a particular price. This price is normally greater than the current market price of the target firm's shares. The difference between the current market price of a target firm's shares and the price a potential acquirer offers to pay for those shares is known as an **acquisition premium**. This approach to purchasing a firm is called a **tender offer**. Tender offers can be made either with or without the support of the management of the target firm. Obviously, tender offers with the support of the target firm's management are typically friendly in character; those made without the support of the target firm's management are typically unfriendly.

It is usually the case that larger firms—in terms of sales or assets—acquire smaller firms. For example, Google has been larger than all of its intended targets, including Motorola Mobile. In contrast, when the assets of two similar-sized firms are combined, this transaction is called a **merger**. Mergers can be accomplished in many of the same ways as acquisitions, that is, using cash or stock to purchase a percentage of another firm's assets. Typically, however, mergers will not be unfriendly. In a merger, one firm purchases some percentage of a second firm's assets while the second firm simultaneously purchases some percentage of the first firm's assets. For example, DaimlerChrysler was created as a merger between Daimler-Benz (the maker of Mercedes-Benz) and Chrysler. Daimler-Benz invested some of its capital in Chrysler, and Chrysler invested some of its capital in Daimler-Benz. More recently, these merged companies split into two firms again. Then, after the financial crisis of 2007, Chrysler merged with Fiat.

Although mergers typically begin as a transaction between equals—that is, between firms of equal size and profitability—they often evolve after a merger such that one firm becomes more dominant in the management of the merged firm than the other. For example, most observers believe that Daimler (the German part of DaimlerChrysler) became more dominant in the management of the combined firm than Chrysler (the American part). And now, most believe that Fiat is more dominate.[1] Put differently, although mergers usually start out as something different from acquisitions, they usually end up looking more like acquisitions than mergers.

The Value of Mergers and Acquisitions

That merger and acquisition strategies are an important strategic option open to firms pursuing diversification and vertical integration strategies can hardly be disputed. The number of firms that have used merger and acquisition strategies to become diversified over the past few years is staggering. This is the case even though the credit crunch crisis in 2008 reduced M&A activity somewhat. For example, in 2010, there were 10,108 acquistions or mergers in the United States, valued at $898 billion. In 2011, there were 10,518 deals valued at $1 trillion, and in 2012, 12,192 deals valued at $482 billion.[2]

The list of firms that have recently engaged in mergers and acquisitions is long and varied. For example, in 2012 SAP (an enterprise software company) purchased Ariba (a cloud computing firm) for $4.3 billion; Cisco (a computer server company) bought NDS Group (a video software and security company) for $5 billion; and Softbank (the third-largest mobile phone company in Japan) bought SprintNextel (a U.S. mobile provider) for $20.1 billion.

That mergers and acquisitions are common is clear. What is less clear is that they actually generate value for firms implementing these strategies. Two cases will be examined here: mergers and acquisitions between strategically unrelated firms and mergers and acquisitions between strategically related firms.

Mergers and Acquisitions: The Unrelated Case

Imagine the following scenario: One firm (the target) is the object of an acquisition effort, and 10 firms (the bidders) are interested in making this acquisition. Suppose the **current market value** of the target firm is $10,000—that is, the price of each of this firm's shares times the number of shares outstanding equals $10,000. Also, suppose the current market value of each of the bidding firms is $15,000.[3] Finally, suppose there is no strategic relatedness between these bidding firms and the target. This means that the value of any one of these bidding firms when combined with the target firm exactly equals the sum of the value of these firms as separate entities. In this example, because the current market value of the target is $10,000 and the current market value of the bidding firms is $15,000, the value of this target when combined with any of these bidders would be $25,000 ($10,000 + $15,000). Given this information, at what price will this target be acquired, and what are the economic performance implications for bidding and target firms at this price?

In this and all acquisition situations, bidding firms will be willing to pay a price for a target up to the value that the target firm adds to the bidder once it is acquired. This price is simply the difference between the value of the two firms combined (in this case, $25,000) and the value of the bidding firm by itself (in this case, $15,000). Notice that this price does not depend on the value of the target firm acting as an independent business; rather, it depends on the value that the target firm creates when it is combined with the bidding firm. Any price for a target less than this value (i.e., less than $10,000) will be a source of economic profit for a bidding firm; any price equal to this value (i.e., equal to $10,000) will be a source of zero economic profits; and any price greater than this value (i.e., greater than $10,000) will be a source of economic losses for the bidding firm that acquires the target.

It is not hard to see that the price of this acquisition will quickly rise to $10,000 and that at this price the bidding firm that acquires the target will earn zero economic profits. The price of this acquisition will quickly rise to $10,000 because any bid less than $10,000 will generate economic profits for a successful bidder. These potential profits, in turn, will generate entry into the bidding war for a target. Because entry into the acquisition contest is very likely, the price of the acquisition will quickly rise to its value, and economic profits will not be created.

Moreover, at this $10,000 price the target firm's equity holders will also gain zero economic profits. Indeed, for them, all that has occurred is that the market value of the target firm has been capitalized in the form of a cash payment from the bidder to the target. The target was worth $10,000, and that is exactly what these equity holders will receive.

Mergers and Acquisitions: The Related Case

The conclusion that the acquisition of strategically unrelated targets will generate only zero economic profits for both the bidding and the target firms is not surprising. It is very consistent with the discussion of the economic consequences of unrelated diversification in Chapter 7. There it was argued that there is no economic justification for a corporate diversification strategy that does not build on some type of economy of scope across the businesses within which a firm operates, and therefore unrelated diversification is not an economically viable corporate strategy. So, if there is any hope that mergers and acquisitions will be a source of superior performance for bidding firms, it must be because of some sort of strategic relatedness or economy of scope between bidding and target firms.

Types of Strategic Relatedness

Of course, bidding and target firms can be strategically related in a wide variety of ways. Three particularly important lists of these potential linkages are discussed here.[4]

The Federal Trade Commission Categories.   Because mergers and acquisitions can have the effect of increasing (or decreasing) the level of concentration in an industry, the Federal Trade Commission (FTC) is charged with the responsibility of evaluating the competitive implications of proposed mergers or acquisitions. In principle, the FTC will disallow any acquisition involving firms with headquarters in the United States that could have the potential for generating monopoly

- Vertical merger — A firm acquires former suppliers or customers.
- Horizontal merger — A firm acquires a former competitor.
- Product extension merger — A firm gains access to complementary products through an acquisition.
- Market extension merger — A firm gains access to complementary markets through an acquisition.
- Conglomerate merger — There is no strategic relatedness between a bidding and a target firm.

TABLE 10.1 Federal Trade Commission Categories of Mergers and Acquisitions

(or oligopoly) profits in an industry. To help in this regulatory effort, the FTC has developed a typology of mergers and acquisitions (see Table 10.1). Each category in this typology can be thought of as a different way in which a bidding firm and a target firm can be related in a merger or acquisition.

According to the FTC, a firm engages in a **vertical merger** when it vertically integrates, either forward or backward, through its acquisition efforts. Vertical mergers could include a firm purchasing critical suppliers of raw materials (backward vertical integration) or acquiring customers and distribution networks (forward vertical integration). eBay's acquisition of Skype is an example of a backward vertical integration as eBay tries to assemble all the resources to compete in the Internet telephone industry. Disney's acquisition of Capital Cities/ABC can be understood as an attempt by Disney to forward vertically integrate into the entertainment distribution industry, and its acquisition of ESPN can be seen as backward vertical integration into the entertainment production business.[5]

A firm engages in a **horizontal merger** when it acquires a former competitor; Adidas's acquisition of Reebok is an example of a horizontal merger, as the number 2 and number 3 sneaker manufacturers in the world combined their efforts. Obviously, the FTC is particularly concerned with the competitive implications of horizontal mergers because these strategies can have the most direct and obvious anticompetitive implications in an industry. For example, the FTC raised antitrust concerns in the $10 billion merger between Oracle and PeopleSoft because these firms, collectively, dominated the enterprise software market. Similar concerns were raised in the $16.4 billion merger between ChevronTexaco and Unocal and the merger between Mobil and Exxon.

The third type of merger identified by the FTC is a **product extension merger**. In a product extension merger, firms acquire complementary products through their merger and acquisition activities. Examples include Google's acquisition of Motorola Mobile.

The fourth type of merger identified by the FTC is a **market extension merger**. Here the primary objective is to gain access to new geographic markets. Examples include SABMiller's acquisition of Bavaria Brewery Company in Columbia, South America.

The final type of merger or acquisition identified by the FTC is a **conglomerate merger**. For the FTC, conglomerate mergers are a residual category. If there are no vertical, horizontal, product extension, or market extension links between firms, the FTC defines the merger or acquisition activity between firms as a conglomerate merger. Given our earlier conclusion that mergers or acquisitions between strategically *unrelated* firms will not generate economic profits for either bidders or targets, it should not be surprising that there are currently relatively few examples of conglomerate mergers or acquisitions; however, at various times in history, they have been relatively common. In the 1960s, for example, many acquisitions took the form of conglomerate mergers. Research has shown that the fraction of single-business firms in the Fortune 500 dropped from 22.8 percent in 1959 to 14.8 percent in 1969, while the fraction of firms in the *Fortune 500* pursuing unrelated diversification strategies rose from 7.3 to 18.7 percent during the same time period. These findings are consistent with an increase in the number of conglomerate mergers and acquisitions during the 1960s.[6]

Despite the popularity of conglomerate mergers in the 1960s, many mergers or acquisitions among strategically unrelated firms are divested shortly after they are completed. One study estimated that more than one-third of the conglomerate mergers of the 1960s were divested by the early 1980s. Another study showed that more than 50 percent of these acquisitions were subsequently divested. These results are all consistent with our earlier conclusion that mergers or acquisitions involving strategically unrelated firms are not a source of economic profits.[7]

Other Types of Strategic Relatedness.   Although the FTC categories of mergers and acquisitions provide some information about possible motives underlying these corporate strategies, they do not capture the full complexity of the links that might exist between bidding and target firms. Several authors have attempted to develop more complete lists of possible sources of relatedness between bidding and target firms. One of these lists, developed by Professor Michael Lubatkin, is summarized in Table 10.2. This list includes **technical economies** (in marketing, production, and similar forms of relatedness), **pecuniary economies** (market power), and **diversification economies** (in portfolio management and risk reduction) as possible bases of strategic relatedness between bidding and target firms.

A second important list of possible sources of strategic relatedness between bidding and target firms was developed by Michael Jensen and Richard Ruback after a comprehensive review of empirical research on the economic returns to mergers and acquisitions. This list is summarized in Table 10.3 and includes the following factors as possible sources of economic gains in mergers and acquisitions: potential reductions in production or distribution costs (from economies of scale, vertical integration, reduction in agency costs, and so forth); the realization of financial opportunities (such as gaining access to underutilized tax shields, avoiding bankruptcy costs); the creation of market power; and the ability to eliminate inefficient management in the target firm.

TABLE 10.2 Lubatkin's List of Potential Sources of Strategic Relatedness Between Bidding and Target Firms

Technical economies	Scale economies that occur when the physical processes inside a firm are altered so that the same amounts of input produce a higher quantity of outputs. Sources of technical economies include marketing, production, experience, scheduling, banking, and compensation.
Pecuniary economies	Economies achieved by the ability of firms to dictate prices by exerting market power.
Diversification economies	Economies achieved by improving a firm's performance relative to its risk attributes or lowering its risk attributes relative to its performance. Sources of diversification economies include portfolio management and risk reduction.

Source: M. Lubatkin (1983). "Mergers and the performance of the acquiring firm." *Academy of Management Review,* 8, pp. 218–225. © 1983 by the Academy of Management. Reproduced with permission.

To reduce production or distribution costs:
1. Through economies of scale.
2. Through vertical integration.
3. Through the adoption of more efficient production or organizational technology.
4. Through the increased utilization of the bidder's management team.
5. Through a reduction of agency costs by bringing organization-specific assets under common ownership.

Financial motivations:
1. To gain access to underutilized tax shields.
2. To avoid bankruptcy costs.
3. To increase leverage opportunities.
4. To gain other tax advantages.
5. To gain market power in product markets.
6. To eliminate inefficient target management.

Source: Reprinted from Jensen, M. C., and R. S. Ruback (1983). "The Market for Corporate Control: The Scientific Evidence." *Journal of Financial Economics*, 11, pp. 5–50. Vol. II. Copyright © with permission from Elsevier.

TABLE 10.3 Jensen and Ruback's List of Reasons Why Bidding Firms Might Want to Engage in Merger and Acquisition Strategies

To be economically valuable, links between bidding and target firms must meet the same criteria as diversification strategies (see Chapter 7). First, these links must build on real economies of scope between bidding and target firms. These economies of scope can reflect either cost savings or revenue enhancements that are created by combining firms. Second, not only must this economy of scope exist, but it must be less costly for the merged firm to realize than for outside equity holders to realize on their own. As is the case with corporate diversification strategies, by investing in a diversified portfolio of stocks, outside equity investors can gain many of the economies associated with a merger or acquisition on their own. Moreover, investors can realize some of these economies of scope at almost zero cost. In this situation, it makes little sense for investors to "hire" managers in firms to realize these economies of scope for them through a merger or acquisition. Rather, firms should pursue merger and acquisition strategies only to obtain valuable economies of scope that outside investors find too costly to create on their own.

Economic Profits in Related Acquisitions

If bidding and target firms are strategically related, then the economic value of these two firms combined is greater than their economic value as separate entities. To see how this changes returns to merger and acquisition strategies, consider the following scenario: As before, there is one target firm and 10 bidding firms. The market value of the target firm as a stand-alone entity is $10,000, and the market value of the bidding firms as stand-alone entities is $15,000. However, unlike the earlier scenario in this chapter, the bidding and target firms are strategically related. Any of the types of relatedness identified in Table 10.1, Table 10.2, or Table 10.3 could be the source of these economies of scope. They imply that when any of the bidding firms and the target are combined, the market value of this combined entity will be $32,000—note that $32,000 is greater than the sum of $15,000 and $10,000. At what price will this target firm be acquired, and what are the economic profit implications for bidding and target firms at this price?

As before, bidding firms will be willing to pay a price for a target up to the value that a target firm adds once it is acquired. Thus, the maximum price bidding firms are willing to pay is still the difference between the value of the combined entity (here, $32,000) and the value of a bidding firm on its own (here, $15,000), or $17,000.

As was the case for the strategically unrelated acquisition, it is not hard to see that the price for actually acquiring the target firm in this scenario will rapidly rise to $17,000 because any bid less than $17,000 has the potential for generating profits for a bidding firm. Suppose that one bidding firm offers $13,000 for the target. For this $13,000, the bidding firm gains access to a target that will generate $17,000 of value once it is acquired. Thus, to this bidding firm, the target is worth $17,000, and a bid of $13,000 will generate $4,000 economic profit. Of course, these potential profits will motivate entry into the competitive bidding process. Entry will continue until the price of this target equals $17,000. Any price greater than $17,000 would mean that a bidding firm is actually losing money on its acquisition.[8]

At this $17,000 price, the successful bidding firm earns zero economic profits. After all, this firm has acquired an asset that will generate $17,000 of value and has paid $17,000 to do so. However, the owners of the target firm will earn an economic profit worth $7,000. As a stand-alone firm, the target is worth $10,000; when combined with a bidding firm, it is worth $17,000. The difference between the value of the target as a stand-alone entity and its value in combination with a bidding firm is the value of the economic profit that can be appropriated by the owners of the target firm.

Thus, the existence of strategic relatedness between bidding and target firms is not a sufficient condition for the equity holders of bidding firms to earn economic profits from their acquisition strategies. If the economic potential of acquiring a particular target firm is widely known and if several potential bidding firms can all obtain this value by acquiring a target, the equity holders of bidding firms will, at best, earn only zero economic profits from implementing an acquisition strategy. In this setting, a "strategically related" merger or acquisition will create economic value, but this value will be distributed in the form of economic profits to the equity holders of acquired target firms.

Because so much of the value created in a merger or acquisition is appropriated by the stockholders of the target firm, it is not surprising that many small and entrepreneurial firms look to be acquired as one way to compensate their owners for taking the risks associated with founding these firms. This phenomenon is discussed in more detail in the Strategy in the Emerging Enterprise feature.

What Does Research Say About Returns to Mergers and Acquisitions?

The empirical implications of this discussion of returns to bidding and target firms in strategically related and strategically unrelated mergers and acquisitions have been examined in a variety of academic literatures. One study reviewed more than 40 empirical merger and acquisition studies in the finance literature. This study concluded that acquisitions, on average, increased the market value of target firms by about 25 percent and left the market value of bidding firms unchanged. The authors of this report concluded that "corporate takeovers generate positive gains,...target firm equity holders benefit, and...bidding firm equity holders do not lose."[9] The way these studies evaluate the return to acquisition strategies is discussed in the Strategy in Depth feature.

Strategy in the Emerging Enterprise

Imagine you are an entrepreneur. You have mortgaged your home, taken out loans, run up your credit cards, and put all you own on the line in order to help grow a small company. And, finally, after years of effort, things start going well. Your product or service starts to sell, customers start to appreciate your unique value proposition, and you actually begin to pay yourself a reasonable salary. What do you do next to help grow your company?

Cashing Out

Some entrepreneurs in this situation decide that maintaining control of the firm is very important. These entrepreneurs may compensate certain critical employees with equity in the firm, but typically limit the number of outsiders who make equity investments in their firm. To grow these closely held firms, these entrepreneurs must rely on capital generated from their ongoing operations (called **retained earnings**) and debt capital provided by banks, customers, and suppliers. Entrepreneurs who decide to maintain control of their companies are compensated for taking the risks associated with starting a firm through the salary they pay themselves.

Other entrepreneurs get more outside equity investors involved in providing the capital a firm needs to grow. These outside investors might include wealthy individuals—called **business angels**—looking to invest in entrepreneurial ventures or **venture capital firms**. Venture capital firms typically raise money from numerous smaller investors that they then invest in a portfolio of entrepreneurial firms. Over time, many of these firms decide to "go public" by engaging in what is called an **initial public offering (IPO).** In an IPO, a firm, typically working with an investment banker, sells its equity to the public at large. Entrepreneurs who decide to sell equity in their firm are compensated for taking the risks associated with starting a firm through the sale of their equity on the public markets through an IPO. An entrepreneur who receives compensation for risk-taking in this manner is said to be **cashing out.**

Finally, still other entrepreneurs may decide to not use an IPO to cash out, but rather to have their firm acquired by another, typically larger firm. In this scenario, entrepreneurs are compensated by the acquiring firm for taking the risks associated with starting a firm. Indeed, because the demand for IPOs has been volatile since the technology-bubble burst of 2000, more and more small and entrepreneurial firms are looking to be acquired as a way for their founders to cash out. Moreover, because the stockholders of target firms typically appropriate a large percentage of the total value created by an acquisition and because the founders of these entrepreneurial firms are also often large stockholders, being acquired is often a source of great wealth for an entrepreneurial firm's founders.

The choice between keeping a firm private, going public, or being acquired is a difficult and multidimensional one. Issues such as the personal preferences of a firm's founders, demand for IPOs, how much capital a firm will need in order to continue to grow its business, and what other resources—besides capital—the firm will need to create additional value all play a role. In general, firms that do not need a great deal of money or other resources to grow will choose to remain private. Those that need only money to grow will choose IPOs, whereas those that need managerial or technical resources controlled by another firm to grow will typically be acquired. Of course, this changes if the entrepreneurs decide to maintain control of their firms because they want to.

Sources: R. Hennessey (2004). "Underwriters cut prices on IPOs as market softens." *The Wall Street Journal,* May 27, p. C4; F. Vogelstein (2003). "Can Google grow up?" *Fortune,* December 8, pp. 102+.

Strategy researchers have also attempted to examine in more detail the sources of value creation in mergers and acquisitions and the question of whether these sources of value creation affect whether bidders or targets appropriate this value. For example, two well-known studies examined the impact of the type and degree of strategic relatedness (defined using the FTC typology summarized in Table 10.1) between bidding and target firms on the economic consequences of mergers and acquisitions.[10] These studies found that the more strategically related bidding and target firms are, the more economic value mergers and acquisitions create. However, like the finance studies, this work found that this economic value was appropriated by the owners of the target firm, regardless of the type or degree of relatedness between the bidding and target firms. Bidding firms—even when they attempt to acquire strategically related targets—earn, on average, zero economic profits from their merger and acquisition strategies.

Why Are There So Many Mergers and Acquisitions?

Given the overwhelming empirical evidence that most of the economic value created in mergers and acquisitions is appropriated by the owners of the target firm most of the time, an important question becomes: "Why do managers of bidding firms continue to engage in merger and acquisition strategies?" Some possible explanations are summarized in Table 10.4 and discussed in this section.

To Ensure Survival

Even if mergers and acquisitions, on average, generate only zero economic profits for bidding firms, it may be necessary for bidding firms to engage in these activities to ensure their survival. In particular, if all of a bidding firm's competitors have been able to improve their efficiency and effectiveness through a particular type of acquisition, then failing to make such an acquisition may put a firm at a competitive disadvantage. Here the purpose of a merger or acquisition is not to gain competitive advantages, but rather to gain competitive parity.

Many recent mergers among banks in the United States seem to have competitive parity and normal economic profits as an objective. Most bank managers recognize that changing bank regulations, increased competition from nonbanking financial institutions, and soft demand are likely to lead to a consolidation of the U.S. banking industry. To survive in this consolidated industry, many U.S. banks will have to merge. As the number of banks engaging in mergers and acquisitions goes up, the ability to earn superior profits from those strategies goes down. These lower returns from acquisitions have already reduced the economic value of some of the most aggressive acquiring banks. Despite these lower returns, acquisitions are likely to continue for the foreseeable future, as banks seek survival opportunities in a consolidated industry.[11]

Free Cash Flow

Another reason why firms may continue to invest in merger and acquisition strategies is that these strategies, on average, can be expected to generate at least competitive parity for bidding firms. This zero economic profit may be a more attractive investment for some firms than alternative strategic investments. This is particularly the case for firms that generate free cash flow.[12]

TABLE 10.4 Possible Motivations to Engage in Mergers and Acquisitions Even Though They Usually Do Not Generate Profits for Bidding Firms

1. To ensure survival
2. Free cash flow
3. Agency problems
4. Managerial hubris
5. The potential for above-normal profits

Free cash flow is simply the amount of cash a firm has to invest after all positive net present-value investments in its ongoing businesses have been funded. Free cash flow is created when a firm's ongoing business operations are very profitable but offer few opportunities for additional investment. One firm that seems to have generated a great deal of free cash flow over the past several years is Philip Morris. Philip Morris's retail tobacco operations are extremely profitable. However, regulatory constraints, health concerns, and slowing growth in demand limit investment opportunities in the tobacco industry. Thus, the amount of cash generated by Philip Morris's ongoing tobacco business has probably been larger than the sum of its positive net present-value investments in that business. This difference is free cash flow for Philip Morris.[13]

A firm that generates a great deal of free cash flow must decide what to do with this money. One obvious alternative would be to give it to stockholders in the form of dividends or stock buybacks. However, in some situations (e.g., when stockholders face high marginal tax rates), stockholders may prefer a firm to retain this cash flow and invest it for them. When this is the case, how should a firm invest its free cash flow?

Because (by definition) no positive net present-value investment opportunities in a firm's ongoing business operations are available, firms have only two investment options: to invest their free cash flow in strategies that generate competitive parity or in strategies that generate competitive disadvantages. In this context, merger and acquisition strategies are a viable option because bidding firms, on average, can expect to generate at least competitive parity. Put differently, although mergers and acquisitions may not be a source of superior profits, there are worse things you could do with your free cash flow.

Agency Problems

Another reason why firms might continue to engage in mergers and acquisitions, despite earning only competitive parity from doing so, is that mergers and acquisitions benefit managers directly, independent of any value they may or may not create for a bidding firm's stockholders. As suggested in Chapter 8, these conflicts of interest are a manifestation of agency problems between a firm's managers and its stockholders.

Merger and acquisition strategies can benefit managers—even if they do not directly benefit a bidding firm's equity holders—in at least two ways. First, managers can use mergers and acquisitions to help diversify their human capital investments in their firm. As discussed in Chapter 7, managers have difficulty diversifying their firm-specific human capital investments when a firm operates in a narrow range of businesses. By acquiring firms with cash flows that are not perfectly correlated with the cash flows of a firm's current businesses, managers can reduce the probability of bankruptcy for their firm and thus partially diversify their human capital investments in their firm.

Second, managers can use mergers and acquisitions to quickly increase firm size, measured in either sales or assets. If management compensation is closely linked to firm size, managers who increase firm size are able to increase their compensation. Of all the ways to increase the size of a firm quickly, growth through mergers and acquisitions is perhaps the easiest. Even if there are no economies of scope between a bidding and a target firm, an acquisition ensures that the bidding firm will grow by the size of the target (measured in either sales or assets). If there are economies of scope between a bidding and a target firm, the size of the bidding firm can grow at an even faster rate, as can the value of management's compensation, even though, on average, acquisitions do not generate wealth for the owners of the bidding firm.

Strategy in Depth

By far, the most popular way to evaluate the performance effects of acquisitions for bidding firms is called **event study analysis**. Rooted in the field of financial economics, event study analysis compares the actual performance of a stock after an acquisition has been announced with the expected performance of that stock if no acquisition had been announced. Any performance greater (or less) than what was expected in a short period of time around when an acquisition is announced is attributed to that acquisition. This **cumulative abnormal return (CAR)** can be positive or negative depending on whether the stock in question performs better or worse than expected without an acquisition.

The CAR created by an acquisition is calculated in several stages. First, the expected performance of a stock, without an acquisition, is estimated with the following regression equation:

$$E(R_{j,t}) = a_j + b_j R_{m,t} + e_{j,t}$$

where $E(R_{j,t})$ is the expected return of stock j during time t; a_j is a constant (approximately equal to the rate of return on risk-free equities); b_j is an empirical estimate of the financial parameter β (equal to the covariance between the returns of a particular firm's stock and the average return of all stocks in the market, over time); $R_{m,t}$ is the actual average rate of return of all stocks in the market over time; and $e_{j,t}$ is an error term. The form of this equation is derived from the capital asset pricing model in finance. In this model, $E(R_{j,t})$ is simply the expected

Evaluating the Performance Effects of Acquisitions

performance of a stock, given the historical relationship between that stock and the overall performance of the stock market.

To calculate the unexpected performance of a stock, this expected level of performance is simply subtracted from the actual level of performance for a stock. This is done in the following equation:

$$XR_{j,t} = R_{j,t} - (a_j + b_j R_{m,t})$$

where $R_{j,t}$ is the actual performance of stock j during time t, and $XR_{j,t}$ is the unexpected performance of stock j during time t.

In calculating the CAR for a particular acquisition, it is necessary to sum the unexpected returns ($XR_{j,t}$) for a stock across the t periods when the stock market is responding to news about this acquisition. Most analyses of acquisitions examine the market's reaction one day before an acquisition is formally announced to three days after it is announced. The sum of these unexpected returns over this

time period is the CAR attributable to this acquisition.

This methodology has been applied to literally thousands of acquisition episodes. For example, when Manulife Financial purchased John Hancock Financial, Manulife's CAR was –10 percent, whereas John Hancock's CAR was 6 percent; when Anthem acquired Wellpoint, Anthem's CAR was –10 percent, and Wellpoint's was 7 percent; when Bank of America acquired FleetBoston Financial, Bank of America's CAR was –9 percent, and FleetBoston's was 24 percent; and when UnitedHealth acquired Mid Atlantic Medical, UnitedHealth's CAR was –4 percent, and Mid Atlantic Medical's was 11 percent.

Although the event study method has been used widely, it does have some important limitations. First, it is based entirely on the capital asset pricing model, and there is some reason to believe that this model is not a particularly good predictor of a firm's expected stock price. Second, it assumes that a firm's equity holders can anticipate all the benefits associated with making an acquisition at the time that acquisition is made. Some scholars have argued that value creation continues long after an acquisition is announced as parties in this exchange discover value-creating opportunities that could not have been anticipated.

Sources: A. Arikan (2004). "Long-term returns to acquisitions: The case of purchasing tangible and intangible assets." Unpublished, Fisher College of Business, Ohio State University; S. J. Brown and J. B. Warner (1985). "Using daily stock returns: The case of event studies." *Journal of Financial Economics*, 14, pp. 3–31; D. Henry, M. Der Hovanseian, and D. Foust (2003). "M&A deals: Show me." *BusinessWeek*, November 10, pp. 38+.

Managerial Hubris

Another reason why managers may choose to continue to invest in mergers and acquisitions, despite the fact that, on average, they gain no profits from doing so, is the existence of what has been called **managerial hubris**.[14] This is the unrealistic belief held by managers in bidding firms that they can manage the assets of a target firm more efficiently than the target firm's current management. This notion can lead bidding firms to engage in acquisition strategies even though there may not be positive economic profits from doing so.

The existence of managerial hubris suggests that the economic value of bidding firms will fall once they announce a merger or acquisition strategy. Although managers in bidding firms might truly believe that they can manage a target firm's assets more efficiently than the target firm's managers, investors in the capital markets are much less likely to be caught up in this hubris. In this context, a commitment to a merger or acquisition strategy is a strong signal that a bidding firm's management has deluded itself about its abilities to manage a target firm's assets. Such delusions will certainly adversely affect the economic value of the bidding firm.

Of course, empirical work on mergers and acquisitions discussed earlier in this chapter has concluded that although bidding firms do not obtain profits from their merger and acquisition strategies, they also do not, on average, reduce their economic value from implementing these strategies. This is inconsistent with the "hubris hypothesis." However, the fact that, on average, bidding firms do not lose economic value does not mean that some bidding firms do not lose economic value. Thus, although it is unlikely that all merger and acquisition strategies are motivated by managerial hubris, it is likely that at least some of them are.[15]

The Potential for Economic Profits

A final reason why managers might continue to pursue merger and acquisition strategies is the potential that these strategies offer for generating profits for at least some bidding firms. The empirical research on returns to bidding firms in mergers and acquisitions is very strong. On average, bidding firms do not gain profits from their merger and acquisition strategies. However, the fact that bidding firms, *on average*, do not earn profits on these strategies does not mean that *all* bidding firms will *always* fail to earn profits. In some situations, bidding firms may be able to gain competitive advantages from merger and acquisition activities. These situations are discussed in the following section.

Mergers and Acquisitions and Sustained Competitive Advantage

We have already seen that the economies of scope that motivate mergers and acquisitions between strategically related bidding and target firms can be valuable. However, the ability of these economies to generate profits and competitive advantages for bidding firms depends not only on their economic value, but also on the competitiveness of the market for corporate control through which these valuable economies are realized. The **market for corporate control** is the market that is created when multiple firms actively seek to acquire one or several firms. Only when the market for corporate control is imperfectly competitive might it be possible for bidding firms to earn profits from implementing a merger or acquisition strategy. To see how the competitiveness of the market for corporate control can affect returns to merger and acquisition strategies, we will consider three scenarios involving bidding and target firms and examine their implications for the managers of these firms.[16]

Valuable, Rare, and Private Economies of Scope

An imperfectly competitive market for corporate control can exist when a target is worth more to one bidder than it is to any other bidders and when no other firms—including bidders and targets—are aware of this additional value. In this setting, the price of a target will rise to reflect public expectations about the value of the target. Once the target is acquired, however, the performance of the special bidder that acquires the target will be greater than generally expected, and this level of performance will generate profits for the equity holders of the bidding firm.

Consider a simple case. Suppose the market value of bidder Firm A combined with target firms is $12,000, whereas the market value of all other bidders combined with targets is $10,000. No other firms (bidders or targets) are aware of Firm A's unique relationship with these targets, but they are aware of the value of all other bidders combined with targets (i.e., $10,000). Suppose also that the market value of all bidding firms, as stand-alone entities, is $7,000. In this setting, Firm A will be willing to pay up to $5,000 to acquire a target ($12,000 − $7,000), and all other bidders will only be willing to pay up to $3,000 to acquire a target ($10,000 − $7,000).

Because publicly available information suggests that acquiring a target is worth $3,000 more than the target's stand-alone price, the price of targets will rapidly rise to this level, ensuring that, if bidding firms, apart from Firm A, acquire a target, they will obtain no profits. If there is only one target in this market for corporate control, then Firm A will be able to bid slightly more than $3,000 (perhaps $3,001) for this target. No other firms will bid higher than Firm A because, from their point of view, the acquisition is simply not worth more than $3,000. At this $3,001 price, Firm A will earn a profit of $1,999—Firm A had to spend only $3,001 for a firm that brings $5,000 in value above its stand-alone market price. Alternatively, if there are multiple targets, then several bidding firms, including Firm A, will pay $3,000 for their targets. At this price, these bidding firms will all earn zero economic profits, except for Firm A, which will earn an economic profit equal to $2,000. That is, only Firm A will gain a competitive advantage from acquiring a target in this market.

In order for Firm A to obtain this profit, the value of Firm A's economy of scope with target firms must be greater than the value of any other bidding firms with that target. This special value will generally reflect unusual resources and capabilities possessed by Firm A—resources and capabilities that are more valuable in combination with target firms than are the resources and capabilities that other bidding firms possess. Put differently, to be a source of economic profits and competitive advantage, Firm A's link with targets must be based on resources and capabilities that are rare among those firms competing in this market for corporate control.

However, not only does Firm A have to possess valuable and rare links with bidding firms to gain economic profits and competitive advantages from its acquisition strategies, but information about these special economies of scope must not be known by other firms. If other bidding firms know about the additional value associated with acquiring a target, they are likely to try to duplicate this value for themselves. Typically, they would accomplish this by imitating the type of relatedness that exists between Firm A and its targets by developing the resources and capabilities that enabled Firm A to have its valuable economies of scope with targets. Once other bidders developed the resources and capabilities necessary to obtain this more valuable economy of scope, they would be able to enter into bidding, thereby increasing the likelihood that the equity holders of successful bidding firms would earn no economic profits.

Target firms must also be unaware of Firm A's special resources and capabilities if Firm A is to obtain competitive advantages from an acquisition. If target firms were aware of this extra value available to Firm A, along with the sources of this value, they could inform other bidding firms. These bidding firms could then adjust their bids to reflect this higher value, and competitive bidding would reduce profits to bidders. Target firms are likely to inform bidding firms in this way because increasing the number of bidders with more valuable economies of scope increases the likelihood that target firms will extract all the economic value created in a merger or acquisition.[17]

Valuable, Rare, and Costly-to-Imitate Economies of Scope

The existence of firms that have valuable, rare, and private economies of scope with targets is not the only way that the market for corporate control can be imperfectly competitive. If other bidders cannot imitate one bidder's valuable and rare economies with targets, then competition in this market for corporate control will be imperfect, and the equity holders of this special bidding firm will earn economic profits. In this case, the existence of valuable and rare economies does not need to be private because other bidding firms cannot imitate these economies, and therefore bids that substantially reduce the profits for the equity holders of the special bidding firm are not forthcoming.

Typically, bidding firms will be unable to imitate one bidder's valuable and rare economies of scope with targets when the strategic relatedness between the special bidder and the targets stems from some rare and costly-to-imitate resources or capabilities controlled by the special bidding firm. Any of the costly-to-imitate resources and capabilities discussed in Chapter 3 could create costly-to-imitate economies of scope between a firm and a target. If, in addition, these economies are valuable and rare, they can be a source of profits to the equity holders of the special bidding firm. This can happen even if all firms in this market for corporate control are aware of the more valuable economies of scope available to this firm and its sources. Although information about this special economy of scope is publicly available, equity holders of special bidding firms will earn a profit when acquisition occurs. The equity holders of target firms will not obtain all of this profit because competitive bidding dynamics cannot unfold when the sources of a more valuable economy of scope are costly to imitate.

Of course, it may be possible for a valuable, rare, and costly-to-imitate economy of scope between a bidding and a target firm to also be private. Indeed, it is often the case that those attributes of a firm that are costly to imitate are also difficult to describe and thus can be held as proprietary information. In that case, the analysis of profits associated with valuable, rare, and private economies of scope presented earlier applies.

Unexpected Valuable Economies of Scope Between Bidding and Target Firms

Thus far, this discussion has adopted, for convenience, the strong assumption that the present value of the strategic relatedness between bidders and targets is known with certainty by individual bidders. This is, in principle, possible, but certainly not likely. Most modern acquisitions and mergers are massively complex, involving numerous unknown and complicated relationships between firms. In these settings, unexpected events after an acquisition has been completed may make an acquisition or merger more valuable than bidders and targets anticipated it would be. The price that bidding firms will pay to acquire a target will equal the expected value of the target only when the target is combined with the bidder. The difference between the unexpected value of an acquisition actually obtained by a bidder and the price the bidder paid for the acquisition is a profit for the equity holders of the bidding firm.

Of course, by definition, bidding firms cannot expect to obtain unexpected value from an acquisition. Unexpected value, in this context, is a surprise, a manifestation of a bidding firm's good luck, not its skill in acquiring targets. For example, when the British advertising firm WPP acquired J. Walter Thompson for $550 million, it discovered some property owned by J. Walter Thomson in Tokyo. No one knew of this property when the firm was acquired. It turned out to be worth more than $100 million after taxes, a financial windfall that helped offset the high cost of this acquisition. When asked, Martin Sorrel, president of WPP and the architect of this acquisition, admitted that this $100 million windfall was simply good luck.[18]

Implications for Bidding Firm Managers

The existence of valuable, rare, and private economies of scope between bidding and target firms and of valuable, rare, and costly-to-imitate economies of scope between bidding and target firms suggests that although, on average, most bidding firms do not generate competitive advantages from their acquisition strategies, in some special circumstances it may be possible for them to do so. Thus, the task facing managers in firms contemplating merger and acquisition strategies is to choose strategies that have the greatest likelihood of being able to generate profits for their equity holders. Several important managerial prescriptions can be derived from this discussion. These "rules" for bidding firm managers are summarized in Table 10.5.

TABLE 10.5 Rules for Bidding Firm Managers

1. Search for valuable and rare economies of scope.
2. Keep information away from other bidders.
3. Keep information away from targets.
4. Avoid winning bidding wars.
5. Close the deal quickly.
6. Operate in "thinly traded" acquisition markets.

Search for Valuable and Rare Economies of Scope

One of the main reasons why bidding firms do not obtain competitive advantages from acquiring strategically related target firms is that several other bidding firms value the target firm in the same way. When multiple bidders all value a target in the same way, competitive bidding is likely. Competitive bidding, in turn, drives out the potential for superior performance. To avoid this problem, bidding firms should seek to acquire targets with which they enjoy valuable and rare linkages.

Operationally, the search for rare economies of scope suggests that managers in bidding firms need to consider not only the value of a target firm when combined with their own company, but also the value of a target firm when combined with other potential bidders. This is important because it is the difference between the value of a particular bidding firm's relationship with a target and the value of other bidding firms' relationships with that target that defines the size of the potential economic profits from an acquisition.

In practice, the search for valuable and rare economies of scope is likely to become a search for valuable and rare resources already controlled by a firm that are synergistically related to a target. For example, if a bidding firm has a unique reputation in its product market and if the target firm's products could benefit by association with that reputation, then the target firm may be more valuable to this particular bidder than to other bidders (firms that do not possess this special reputation). Also, if a particular bidder possesses the largest market share in its industry, the best distribution system, or restricted access to certain key raw materials and if the target firm would benefit from being associated with these valuable and rare resources, then the acquisition of this target may be a source of economic profits.

The search for valuable and rare economies of scope as a basis of mergers and acquisitions tends to rule out certain interfirm linkages as sources of economic profits. For example, most acquisitions can lead to a reduction in overhead costs because much of the corporate overhead associated with the target firm can be eliminated subsequent to acquisition. However, the ability to eliminate these overhead costs is not unique to any one bidder, and thus the value created by these reduced costs will usually be captured by the equity holders of the target firm.

Keep Information Away from Other Bidders

One of the keys to earning superior performance in an acquisition strategy is to avoid multiple bidders for a single target. One way to accomplish this is to keep information about the bidding process, and about the sources of economies of scope between a bidder and target that underlie this bidding process, as private as possible. In order for other firms to become involved in bidding for a target, they must be aware of the value of the economies of scope between themselves and that target. If only one bidding firm knows this information and if this bidding firm can close the deal before the full value of the target is known, then it may gain a competitive advantage from completing this acquisition.

Of course, in many circumstances, keeping all this information private is difficult. Often, it is illegal. For example, when seeking to acquire a publicly traded firm, potential bidders must meet disclosure requirements that effectively reduce the amount of private information a bidder can retain. In these circumstances, unless a bidding firm has some valuable, rare, and costly-to-imitate economy of scope with a target firm, the possibility of economic profits coming from an acquisition is very low. It is not surprising that the research conducted on mergers and acquisitions of firms traded on public stock exchanges governed by the U.S. Securities and Exchange Commission (SEC) disclosure rules suggests that, most of the time, bidding firms do not earn economic profits from implementing their acquisition strategies.

However, not all potential targets are publicly traded. Privately held firms may be acquired in an information environment that can create opportunities for above-normal performance for bidding firms. Moreover, even when acquiring a publicly traded firm, a bidder does not have to release all the information it has about the potential value of that target in combination with itself. Indeed, if some of this value reflects a bidding firm's taken-for-granted "invisible" assets, it may not be possible to communicate this information. In this case, as well, there may be opportunities for competitive advantages for bidding firms.

Keep Information Away from Targets

Not only should bidding firms keep information about the value of their economy of scope with a target away from other bidders, they should also keep this information away from target firms. Suppose that the value of a target firm to a bidding firm is $8,000, but the bidding firm, in an attempt to earn economic profits, has bid only $5,000 for the target. If the target knows that it is actually worth $8,000, it is very likely to hold out for a higher bid. In fact, the target may contact other potential bidding firms and tell them of the opportunity created by the $5,000 bid. As the number of bidders goes up, the possibility of superior economic performance for bidders goes down. Therefore, to keep the possibility of these profits alive, bidding firms must not fully reveal the value of their economies of scope with a target firm. Again, in some circumstances, it is very difficult, or even illegal, to attempt to limit the flow of information to target firms. In these settings, superior economic performance for bidding firms is very unlikely.

Limiting the amount of information that flows to the target firm may have some other consequences as well. For example, it has been shown that a complete sharing of information, insights, and perspectives before an acquisition is completed increases the probability that economies of scope will actually be realized once it is completed.[19] By limiting the flow of information between itself and a target, a bidding firm may actually be increasing the cost of integrating the target into its ongoing business, thereby jeopardizing at least some of the superior economic performance that limiting information flow is designed to create. Bidding firms will need to carefully balance the economic benefits of limiting the information they share with the target firm against the costs that limiting information flow may create.

Avoid Winning Bidding Wars

It should be reasonably clear that if a number of firms bid for the same target, the probability that the firm that successfully acquires the target will gain competitive advantages is very low. Indeed, to ensure that competitive bidding occurs, target firms can actively encourage other bidding firms to enter into the bidding process. The implications of these arguments are clear: Bidding firms should generally avoid winning a bidding war. To "win" a bidding war, a bidding firm will often have to pay a price at least equal to the full value of the target. Many times, given the emotions of an intense bidding contest, the winning bid may actually be larger than the true value of the target. Completing this type of acquisition will certainly reduce the economic performance of the bidding firm.

The only time it might make sense to "win" a bidding war is when the winning firm possesses a rare and private or a rare and costly-to-imitate economy of scope with a target that is more valuable than the strategic relatedness that exists between any other bidders and that target. In this setting, the winning firm may be able to earn a profit if it is able to fully realize the value of its relationship with the target.

Close the Deal Quickly

Another rule of thumb for obtaining superior performance from implementing merger and acquisition strategies is to close the deal quickly. All the economic processes that make it difficult for bidding firms to earn economic profits from acquiring a strategically related target take time to unfold. It takes time for other bidders to become aware of the economic value associated with acquiring a target; it takes time for the target to recruit other bidders; information leakage becomes more of a problem over time; and so forth. A bidding firm that begins and ends the bidding process quickly may forestall some of these processes and thereby retain some superior performance for itself.

The admonition to close the deal quickly should not be taken to mean that bidding firms need to make their acquisition decisions quickly. Indeed, the search for valuable and rare economies of scope should be undertaken with great care. There should be little rush in isolating and evaluating acquisition candidates. However, once a target firm has been located and valued, bidding firms have a strong incentive to reduce the period of time between the first bid and the completion of the deal. The longer this period of negotiation, the less likely it is that the bidding firm will earn economic profits from the acquisition.

Complete Acquisitions in "Thinly Traded" Markets

Finally, an acquisition strategy can be a source of economic profits to bidding firms if these firms implement this corporate strategy in what could be described as "thinly traded markets." In general, a **thinly traded market** is a market where there are only a small number of buyers and sellers, where information about opportunities in this market is not widely known, and where interests besides purely maximizing the value of a firm can be important. In the context of mergers and acquisitions, thinly traded markets are markets where only a few (often only one) firms are implementing acquisition strategies. These unique firms may be the only firms that understand the full value of the acquisition opportunities in this market. Even target firm managers may not fully understand the value of the economic opportunities in these markets, and, if they do, they may have other interests besides maximizing the value of their firm if it becomes the object of a takeover.

In general, thinly traded merger and acquisition markets are highly fragmented. Competition in these markets occurs at the local level, as one small local firm competes with other small local firms for a common group of geographically defined customers. Most of these small firms are privately held. Many are sole proprietorships. Examples of these thinly traded markets have included, at various points in history, the printing industry, the fast-food industry, the used-car industry, the dry-cleaning industry, and the barber shop/hair salon industry.

As was suggested in Chapter 2, the major opportunity in all highly fragmented industries is consolidation. In the context of mergers and acquisitions, consolidation can occur by one firm (or a small number of firms) buying numerous independent firms to realize economies of scope in these industries. Often, these economies of scope reflect economies of scale in these industries—economies of scale that were not realized in a highly fragmented setting. As long as the number of firms implementing this consolidation strategy is small, then the market for corporate control in these markets will probably be less than perfectly competitive, and opportunities for profits from implementing an acquisition strategy may be possible.

More generally, if a merger or acquisition contest is played out through full-page ads in *The Wall Street Journal*, the ability of bidding firms to gain competitive advantages from their acquisitions is limited. Such highly public acquisitions are likely to lead to very competitive markets for corporate control. Competitive markets for corporate control, in turn, assure that the equity holders of the target firm will appropriate any value that could be created by an acquisition. However, if these contests occur in obscure, out-of-the-way industries, it is more likely that bidding firms will be able to earn profits from their acquisitions.

Service Corporation International: An Example

Empirical research on mergers and acquisitions suggests that it is not easy for bidding firms to earn economic profits from these strategies. However, it may be possible for some bidding firms, some of the time, to do so. One firm that has been successful in gaining competitive advantages from its merger and acquisition strategies is Service Corporation International (SCI). Service Corporation International is in the funeral home and cemetery business. It grew from a collection of five funeral homes in 1967 to being the largest owner of cemeteries and funeral homes in the United States today. It has done this through an aggressive and what was until recently a highly profitable acquisitions program in this historically fragmented industry.

The valuable and rare economy of scope that SCI brought to the funeral home industry is the application of traditional business practices in a highly fragmented and not often professionally managed industry. Service Corporation International–owned funeral homes operate with gross margins approaching 30 percent, nearly three times the gross margins of independently owned funeral homes. Among other things, higher margins reflected savings from centralized purchasing services, centralized embalming and professional services, and the sharing of underutilized resources (including hearses) among funeral homes within geographic regions. Service Corporation International's scale advantages made a particular funeral home more valuable to SCI than to one of SCI's smaller competitors and more valuable than if a particular funeral home was left as a stand-alone business.

Moreover, the funeral homes that SCI targeted for acquisition were, typically, family-owned and lacked heirs to continue the business. Many of the owners or operators of these funeral homes were not fully aware of the value of their operations to SCI (they are morticians more than business managers), nor were they just interested in maximizing the sale price of their funeral homes. Rather, they were often looking to maintain continuity of service in a community, secure employment for their loyal employees, and ensure a comfortable (if not lavish) retirement for themselves. Being acquired by SCI was likely to be the only alternative to closing the funeral home once an owner or operator retired. Extracting less than the full value of the funeral home when selling to SCI often seemed preferable to other alternatives.

Because SCI's acquisition of funeral homes exploited real and valuable economies of scope, this strategy had the potential for generating superior economic performance. Because SCI was, for many years, the only firm implementing this strategy in the funeral home industry, because the funeral homes that SCI acquired were generally not publicly traded, and because the owners or operators of these funeral homes often had interests besides simply maximizing the price of their operations when they sold them, it seems likely that SCI's acquisition strategy generated superior economic performance for many years. However, information about SCI's acquisition strategy has become widely known. This has led other funeral homes to begin bidding to acquire formerly independent funeral homes. Moreover, independent funeral home owners have become more aware of their full value to SCI. Although SCI's economy of scope with independent funeral homes is still valuable, it is no longer rare, and thus it is no longer a source of economic profits to SCI. Put differently, the imperfectly competitive market for corporate control that SCI was able to exploit for almost 10 years has become more perfectly competitive. Future acquisitions in this market by SCI are not likely to be a source of sustained competitive advantage and economic profit. In response, SCI now focuses on managing its more than 1,800 funeral homes in the United States.[20]

Implications for Target Firm Managers

Although bidding firm managers can do several things to attempt to maximize the probability of earning economic profits from their merger and acquisition strategies, target firm managers can attempt to counter these efforts to ensure that the owners of target firms appropriate whatever value is created by a merger or acquisition. These "rules" for target firm managers are summarized in Table 10.6.

Seek Information from Bidders

One way a bidder can attempt to obtain superior performance from implementing an acquisition strategy is to keep information about the source and value of the strategic relatedness that exists between the bidder and target private. If that relationship is actually worth $12,000, but targets believe it is only worth $8,000, then a target might be willing to settle for a bid of $8,000 and, thereby, forgo the extra $4,000 it could have extracted from the bidder. Once the target knows that its true value to the bidder is $12,000, it is in a much better position to obtain this full value when the acquisition is completed. Therefore, not only should a bidding firm inform itself about the value of a target, target firms must inform themselves about their value to potential bidders. In this way, they can help obtain the full value of their assets.

TABLE 10.6 Rules for Target Firm Managers

1. Seek information from bidders.
2. Invite other bidders to join the bidding competition.
3. Delay, but do not stop, the acquisition.

Invite Other Bidders to Join the Bidding Competition

Once a target firm is fully aware of the nature and value of the economies of scope that exist between it and current bidding firms, it can exploit this information by seeking other firms that may have the same relationship with it and then inform-ing these firms of a potential acquisition opportunity. By inviting other firms into the bidding process, the target firm increases the competitiveness of the market for corporate control, thereby increasing the probability that the value created by an acquisition will be fully captured by the target firm.

Delay, but Do Not Stop, the Acquisition

As suggested earlier, bidding firms have a strong incentive to expedite the acqui-sition process in order to prevent other bidders from becoming involved in an acquisition. Of course, the target firm wants other bidding firms to enter the pro-cess. To increase the probability of receiving more than one bid, target firms have a strong incentive to delay an acquisition.

The objective, however, should be to delay an acquisition to create a more competitive market for corporate control, not to stop an acquisition. If a valu-able economy of scope exists between a bidding firm and a target firm, the merger of these two firms will create economic value. If the market for corporate control within which this merger occurs is competitive, then the equity hold-ers of the target firm will appropriate the full value of this economy of scope. Preventing an acquisition in this setting can be very costly to the equity holders of the target firm.

Target firm managers can engage in a wide variety of activities to delay the completion of an acquisition. Some common responses of target firm manage-ment to takeover efforts, along with their economic implications for the equity holders of target firms, are discussed in the Research Made Relevant feature.

Organizing to Implement a Merger or Acquisition

To realize the full value of any strategic relatedness that exists between a bidding firm and a target firm, the merged organizations must be organized appropri-ately. The realization of each of the types of strategic relatedness discussed ear-lier in this chapter requires at least some coordination and integration between the bidding and target firms after an acquisition has occurred. For example, to realize economies of scale from an acquisition, bidding and target firms must coordinate in the combined firm the functions that are sensitive to economies of scale. To realize the value of any technology that a bidding firm acquires from a target firm, the combined firm must use this technology in developing, manufac-turing, or selling its products. To exploit underutilized leverage capacity in the target firm, the balance sheets of the bidding and target firms must be merged, and the resulting firm must then seek additional debt funding. To realize the opportunity of replacing the target firm's inefficient management with more efficient management from the bidding firm, these management changes must actually take place.

Post-acquisition coordination and integration is essential if bidding and target firms are to realize the full potential of the strategic relatedness that drove the acquisition in the first place. If a bidding firm decides not to coor-dinate or integrate any of its business activities with the activities of a target firm, then why was this target firm acquired? Just as corporate diversification requires the active management of linkages among different parts of a firm, mergers and acquisitions (as one way in which corporate diversification strategies can be created) require the active management of linkages between a bidding and a target firm.

Post-Merger Integration and Implementing a Diversification Strategy

Given that most merger and acquisition strategies are used to create corporate diversification strategies, the organizational approaches previously described for implementing diversification are relevant for implementing merger and acquisition strategies as well. Thus, mergers and acquisitions designed to create diversification strategies should be managed through the M-form structure. The management control systems and compensation policies associated with implementing diversification strategies should also be applied in organizing to implement merger and acquisition strategies. In contrast, mergers and acquisitions designed to create vertical integration strategies should be managed through the U-form structure and have management controls and compensation policies consistent with this strategy.

Special Challenges in Post-Merger Integration

Although, in general, organizing to implement merger and acquisition strategies can be seen as a special case of organizing to implement corporate diversification strategies or vertical integration strategies, implementing merger and acquisition strategies can create special problems. Most of these problems reflect the fact that operational, functional, strategic, and cultural differences between bidding and target firms involved in a merger or acquisition are likely to be much greater than these same differences between the different parts of a diversified or vertically integrated business that was not created through acquisition. The reason for this difference is that the firms involved in a merger or acquisition have had a separate existence, separate histories, separate management philosophies, and separate strategies.

Differences between bidding and target firms can manifest themselves in a wide variety of ways. For example, the firms may own and operate different computer systems, different telephone systems, and other conflicting technologies. These firms might have very different human resource policies and practices. One firm might have a very generous retirement and health care program; the other, a less generous program. One firm's compensation system might focus on high salaries; the other firm's compensation system might focus on large cash bonuses and stock options. Also, these firms might have very different relationships with customers. At one firm, customers might be thought of as business partners; in another, the relationship with customers might be more arm's-length in character. Integrating bidding and target firms may require the resolution of numerous differences.

Perhaps the most significant challenge in integrating bidding and target firms has to do with cultural differences.[21] In Chapter 3, it was suggested that it can often be difficult to change a firm's organizational culture. The fact that a firm has been acquired does not mean that the culture in that firm will rapidly change to become more like the culture of the bidding firm; cultural conflicts can last for very long periods of time.

Research Made Relevant

Managers in potential target firms can respond to takeover attempts in a variety of ways. As suggested in Table 10.7, some of these responses increase the wealth of target firm shareholders, some have no impact on target firm shareholders, and others decrease the wealth of target firm shareholders.

Management responses that have the effect of reducing the value of target firms include greenmail, standstill agreements, and "poison pills." Each of these is an anti-takeover action that target firm managers can take to reduce the wealth of target firm equity holders. **Greenmail** is a maneuver in which a target firm's management purchases any of the target firm's stock owned by a bidder and does so for a price that is greater than the current market value of that stock. Greenmail effectively ends a bidding firm's effort to acquire a particular target and does so in a way that can greatly reduce the wealth of a target firm's equity holders. Not only do these equity holders not appropriate any economic value that could have been created if

The Wealth Effects of Management Responses to Takeover Attempts

an acquisition had been completed, but they have to bear the cost of the premium price that management pays to buy its stock back from the bidding firm.

Not surprisingly, target firms that resort to greenmail substantially reduce the economic wealth of their equity holders. One study found that the value of target firms that pay greenmail drops, on average, 1.76 percent. Another study reported a 2.85 percent drop in the value of such firms. These reductions in value are greater if

greenmail leads to the cancellation of a takeover effort. Indeed, this second study found that such episodes led to a 5.50 percent reduction in the value of target firms. These reductions in value as a response to greenmail activities stand in marked contrast to the generally positive market response to efforts by a firm to repurchase its own shares in nongreenmail situations.

Standstill agreements are often negotiated in conjunction with greenmail. A standstill agreement is a contract between a target and a bidding firm wherein the bidding firm agrees not to attempt to take over the target for some period of time. When a target firm negotiates a standstill agreement, it prevents the current acquisition effort from being completed, and it reduces the number of bidders that might become involved in future acquisition efforts. Thus, the equity holders of this target firm forgo any value that could have been created if the current acquisition had occurred, and they also lose some of the value that they could have appropriated in future acquisition episodes by the

TABLE 10.7 The Wealth Effects of Target Firm Management Responses to Acquisition Efforts

1. Responses that reduce the wealth of target firm equity holders:
   - Greenmail
   - Standstill agreements
   - Poison pills
2. Responses that do not affect the wealth of target firm equity holders:
   - Shark repellents
   - Pac Man defense
   - Crown jewel sale
   - Lawsuits
3. Responses that increase the wealth of target firm equity holders:
   - Search for white knights
   - Creation of bidding auctions
   - Golden parachutes

target's inviting multiple bidders into a market for corporate control.

Standstill agreements, either alone or in conjunction with greenmail, reduce the economic value of a target firm. One study found that standstill agreements that were unaccompanied by stock repurchase agreements reduced the value of a target firm by 4.05 percent. Such agreements, in combination with stock repurchases, reduced the value of a target firm by 4.52 percent.

So-called **poison pills** include any of a variety of actions that target firm managers can take to make the acquisition of the target prohibitively expensive. In one common poison-pill maneuver, a target firm issues rights to its current stockholders indicating that if the firm is acquired in an unfriendly takeover, it will distribute a special cash dividend to stockholders. This cash dividend effectively increases the cost of acquiring the target and can discourage otherwise interested bidding firms from attempting to acquire this target. Another poison-pill tactic substitutes the distribution of additional shares of a target firm's stock, at very low prices, for the special cash dividend. Issuing this low-price stock to current stockholders effectively undermines the value of a bidding firm's equity investment in a target and thus increases the cost of the acquisition. Other poison pills involve granting current stockholders other rights—rights that effectively increase the cost of an unfriendly takeover.

Although poison pills are creative devices that target firms can use to prevent an acquisition, they generally have not been very effective. If a bidding firm and a target firm are strategically related, the value that can be created in an acquisition can be substantial, and most of this value will be appropriated by the stockholders of the target firm. Thus, target firm stockholders have a strong incentive to see that the target firm is acquired, and they are amenable to direct offers made by a bidding firm to them as individual investors; these are called **tender offers**. However, to the extent that poison pills actually do prevent mergers and acquisitions, they are usually bad for the equity holders of target firms.

Target firm management can also engage in a wide variety of actions that have little or no impact on the wealth of a target firm's equity holders. One class of these responses is known as shark repellents. **Shark repellents** include a variety of relatively minor corporate governance changes that, in principle, are supposed to make it somewhat more difficult to acquire a target firm. Common examples of shark repellents include **supermajority voting rules** (which specify that more than 50 percent of the target firm's board of directors must approve a takeover) and state incorporation laws (in some states, incorporation laws make it difficult to acquire a firm incorporated in that state). However, if the value created by an acquisition is sufficiently large, these shark repellents will neither slow an acquisition attempt significantly nor prevent it from being completed.

Another response that does not affect the wealth of target firm equity holders is known as the **Pac Man defense**. Targets using this tactic fend off an acquisition by taking over the firm or firms bidding for them. Just as in the old video game, the hunted becomes the hunter; the target turns the tables on current and potential bidders. It should not be too surprising that the Pac Man defense does not, on average, either hurt or help the stockholders of target firms. In this defense, targets become bidders, and we know from empirical literature that, on average, bidding firms earn only zero economic profits from their acquisition efforts. Thus, one would expect that, on average, the Pac Man defense would generate only zero economic profits for the stockholders of target firms implementing it.

Another ineffective and inconsequential response is called a **crown jewel sale**. The idea behind a crown jewel sale is that sometimes a bidding firm is interested in just a few of the businesses currently being operated by the target firm. These businesses are the target firm's "crown jewels." To prevent an acquisition, the target firm can sell off these crown jewels, either directly to the bidding firm or by setting up a separate company to own and operate these businesses. In this way, the bidding firm is likely to be less interested in acquiring the target.

A final, relatively ineffective defense that most target firm managers pursue is filing lawsuits against bidding firms. Indeed, at least in the United States, the filing of a lawsuit has been almost automatic as soon as an acquisition effort is announced. These suits, however, usually do not delay or stop an acquisition or merger.

(Continued)

Finally, as suggested in Table 10.7, some of the actions that the management of target firms can take to delay (but not stop) an acquisition actually benefit target firm equity holders. The first of these is the search for a **white knight**—another bidding firm that agrees to acquire a particular target in the place of the original bidding firm. Target firm management may prefer to be acquired by some bidding firms over others. For example, it may be that some bidding firms possess much more valuable economies of scope with a target firm than other bidding firms. It may also be that some bidding firms will take a longer-term view in managing a target firm's assets than other bidding firms. In both cases, target firm managers are likely to prefer some bidding firms over others.

Whatever motivation a target firm's management has, inviting a white knight to bid on a target firm has the effect of increasing the number of firms bidding for a target by at least one. If there is currently only one bidder, inviting a white knight into the bidding competition doubles the number of firms bidding for a target. As the number of bidders increases, the competitiveness of the market for corporate control and the likelihood that the equity holders of the target firm will appropriate all the value created by an acquisition also increase. On average, the entrance of a white knight into a competitive bidding contest for a target firm increases the wealth of target firm equity holders by 17 percent.

If adding one firm into the competitive bidding process increases the wealth of target firm equity holders some, then adding more firms to the process is likely to increase this wealth even more. Target firms can accomplish this outcome by creating an **auction** among bidding firms. On average, the creation of an auction among multiple bidders increases the wealth of target firm equity holders by 20 percent.

A third action that the managers of a target firm can take to increase the wealth of their equity holders from an acquisition effort is the institution of **golden parachutes.** A golden parachute is a compensation arrangement between a firm and its senior management team that promises these individuals a substantial cash payment if their firm is acquired and they lose their jobs in the process. These cash payments can appear to be very large, but they are actually quite small in comparison to the total value that can be created if a merger or acquisition is completed. In this sense, golden parachutes are a small price to pay to give a potential target firm's top managers incentives not to stand in the way of completing a takeover of their firm. Put differently, golden parachutes reduce agency problems for the equity holders of a potential target firm by aligning the interests of top managers with the interests of that firm's stockholders. On average, when a firm announces golden parachute compensation packages for its top management team, the value of this potential target firm's equity increases by 7 percent.

Overall, substantial evidence suggests that delaying an acquisition long enough to ensure that a competitive market for corporate control emerges can significantly benefit the equity holders of target firms. One study found that when target firms did not delay the completion of an acquisition, their equity holders experienced, on average, a 36 percent increase in the value of their stock once the acquisition was complete. If, however, target firms did delay the completion of the acquisition, this average increase in value jumped to 65 percent.

Of course, target firm managers can delay too long. Delaying too long can create opportunity costs for their firm's equity holders because these individuals do not actually realize the gain from an acquisition until it has been completed. Also, long delays can jeopardize the completion of an acquisition, in which case the equity holders of the target firm do not realize any gains from the acquisition.

Sources: R. Walkling and M. Long (1984). "Agency theory, managerial welfare, and takeover bid resistance." *Rand Journal of Economics*, 15(1), pp. 54–68; R. D. Kosnik (1987). "Greenmail: A study of board performance in corporate governance." *Administrative Science Quarterly*, 32, pp. 163–185; J. Walsh (1989). "Doing a deal: Merger and acquisition negotiations and their impact upon target company top management turnover." *Strategic Management Journal*, 10, pp. 307–322; L. Y. Dann and H. DeAngelo (1983). "Standstill agreements, privately negotiated stock repurchases, and the market for corporate control." *Journal of Financial Economics*, 11, pp. 275–300; M. Bradey and L. Wakeman (1983). "The wealth effects of targeted share repurchases." *Journal of Financial Economics*, 11, pp. 301–328; H. Singh and F. Haricento (1989). "Top management tenure, corporate ownership and the magnitude of golden parachutes." *Strategic Management Journal*, 10, pp. 143–156; T. A. Turk (1987). "The determinants of management responses to interfirm tender offers and their effect on shareholder wealth." Unpublished doctoral dissertation, Graduate School of Management, University of California at Irvine.

The failures of what some observers believe are some of the worst acquisitions ever have all been attributed to cultural clashes.[22] For example, the merger between Daimler (the maker of Mercedes-Benz) and Chrysler pitted the culture of a German company that focused on luxury vehicles with a midwestern U.S. company that sold lower-prestige cars and Jeeps. The merger became the source of a widely known joke: "How do you pronounce DaimlerChrysler? Daimler. The Chrysler is silent." These two firms split after only a few painful years.

Also, Novell's acquisition of Word Perfect brought together two management teams that refused to cooperate. While Novell and Word Perfect managers fought each other, Microsoft emerged as the dominant firm in the word processing industry with Microsoft Word. After two years, Novell sold Word Perfect for $1 billion less than its purchase price.

Another disastrous acquisition involved the combination of America Online (AOL) and Time Warner. In 2000, before the merger, AOL's shares sold for more than $75; in 2008, after the merger, they sold for $15. The problem: the clash between the "new media" AOL culture with the "old media" Time Warner culture.

Sprint's acquisition of Nextel was also a spectacular failure. In 2005, the deal cost Sprint $35 billion. Within three years, 80 percent of Sprint's investment in Nextel was written off. The culprit, once again, was the clash between the cultures of these two firms: Sprint was a "button-down" bureaucratic culture that could not tolerate Nextel's more freewheeling entrepreneurial culture. The two management teams fought about everything from advertising strategy to cell phone technology. Not surprisingly, in 2012, SprintNextel was purchased by the third-largest Japanese mobile phone company, Softbank, for $20.1 billion—almost $15 billion less than Sprint had paid for Nextel seven years earlier.

Finally, HP's acquisition of Compaq reduced the market capitalization of HP by approximately $13 billion. HP's engineering- and consensus-driven culture clashed with Compaq's quick-decision, sales-driven culture. After several years, HP has been able to make cultural and leadership changes that have improved the performance of this acquisition, but this integration has been long in coming.

Operational, functional, strategic, and cultural differences between bidding and target firms can all be compounded by the merger and acquisition process— especially if that process was unfriendly. Unfriendly takeovers can generate anger and animosity among the target firm management that is directed toward the management of the bidding firm. Research has shown that top management turnover is much higher in firms that have been taken over compared with firms not subject to takeovers, reflecting one approach to resolving these management conflicts.[23]

The difficulties often associated with organizing to implement a merger and acquisition strategy can be thought of as an additional cost of the acquisition process. Bidding firms, in addition to estimating the value of the strategic relatedness between themselves and a target firm, also need to estimate the cost of organizing to implement an acquisition. The value that a target firm brings to a bidding firm through an acquisition should be discounted by the cost of organizing to implement this strategy. In some circumstances, it may be the case that the cost of organizing to realize the value of strategic relatedness between a bidding firm and a target may be greater than the value of that strategic relatedness, in which case the acquisition should not occur. For this reason, many observers argue that potential economies of scope between bidding and target firms are often not fully realized.

Although organizing to implement mergers and acquisitions can be a source of significant cost, it can also be a source of value and opportunity. Some scholars have suggested that value creation can continue to occur in a merger or acquisition long after the formal acquisition is complete.[24] As bidding and target firms continue to coordinate and integrate their operations, unanticipated opportunities for value creation can be discovered. These sources of value could not have been anticipated at the time a firm was originally acquired (and thus are, at least partially, a manifestation of a bidding firm's good luck), but bidding firms can influence the probability of discovering these unanticipated sources of value by learning to cooperate effectively with target firms while organizing to implement a merger or acquisition strategy.

Summary

Firms can use mergers and acquisitions to create corporate diversification and vertical integration strategies. Mergers or acquisitions between strategically unrelated firms can be expected to generate only competitive parity for both bidders and targets. Thus, firms contemplating merger and acquisition strategies must search for strategically related targets.

Several sources of strategic relatedness have been discussed in literature. On average, the acquisition of strategically related targets does create economic value, but most of that value is captured by the equity holders of target firms. The equity holders of bidding firms generally gain competitive parity even when bidding firms acquire strategically related targets. Empirical research on mergers and acquisitions is consistent with these expectations. On average, acquisitions do create value, but that value is captured by target firms, and acquisitions do not hurt bidding firms.

Given that most mergers and acquisitions generate only zero economic profits for bidding firms, an important question becomes: "Why are there so many mergers and acquisitions?" Explanations include (1) the desire to ensure firm survival, (2) the existence of free cash flow, (3) agency problems between bidding firm managers and equity holders, (4) managerial hubris, and (5) the possibility that some bidding firms might earn economic profits from implementing merger and acquisition strategies.

To gain competitive advantages and economic profits from mergers or acquisitions, these strategies must be either valuable, rare, and private or valuable, rare, and costly to imitate. In addition, a bidding firm may exploit unanticipated sources of strategic relatedness with a target. These unanticipated sources of relatedness can also be a source of economic profits for a bidding firm. These observations have several implications for the managers of bidding and target firms.

Organizing to implement a merger or acquisition strategy can be seen as a special case of organizing to implement a corporate diversification or vertical integration strategy. However, historical differences between bidding and target firms may make the integration of different parts of a firm created through acquisitions more difficult than if a firm is not created through acquisitions. Cultural differences between bidding and target firms are particularly problematic. Bidding firms need to estimate the cost of organizing to implement a merger or acquisition strategy and discount the value of a target by that cost. However, organizing to implement a merger or acquisition can also be a way that bidding and target firms can discover unanticipated economies of scope.

Challenge Questions

10.1. Consider the following scenario: A firm acquires a strategically related target after successfully fending off four other bidding firms. Under what conditions, if any, can the firm that acquired this target expect to earn an economic profit from doing so?

⭐ **10.2.** Consider this scenario: A firm acquires a strategically related target; there were no other bidding firms. Under what conditions, if any, can the firm that acquired this target expect to earn an economic profit from doing so?

10.3. Some researchers have argued that the existence of free cash flow can lead managers in a firm to make inappropriate acquisition decisions. To avoid these problems, these authors have argued that firms should increase their debt-to-equity ratio and "soak up" free cash flow through interest and principal payments. Is free cash flow a significant problem for many firms?

10.4. What are the strengths and weaknesses of increased leverage as a response to free cash flow problems in a firm?

10.5. The hubris hypothesis suggests that managers continue to engage in acquisitions, even though, on average, they do not generate economic profits, because of the unrealistic belief on the part of these managers that they can manage a target firm's assets more efficiently than that firm's current management. This type of systematic nonrationality usually does not last too long in competitive market conditions: Firms led by managers with these unrealistic beliefs change, are acquired, or go bankrupt in the long run. What are the attributes of the market for corporate control that suggest that managerial hubris could exist in this market, despite its performance-reducing implications for bidding firms?

10.6. The hubris hypothesis suggests that managers continue to engage in acquisitions, even though, on average, they do not generate economic profits, because of the unrealistic belief on the part of these managers that they can manage a target firm's assets more efficiently than that firm's current management. This type of systematic nonrationality usually does not last too long in competitive market conditions: Firms led by managers with these unrealistic beliefs change, are acquired, or go bankrupt in the long run. Can the hubris hypothesis be a legitimate explanation for continuing acquisition activity?

⭐ **10.7.** It has been shown that so-called poison pills rarely prevent a takeover from occurring. In fact, sometimes when a firm announces that it is instituting a poison pill, its stock price goes up. Why?

Problem Set

10.8. For each of the following scenarios, estimate how much value an acquisition will create, how much of that value will be appropriated by each of the bidding firms, and how much of that value will be appropriated by each of the target firms. In each of these scenarios, assume that firms do not face significant capital constraints.

(a) A bidding firm, A, is worth $27,000 as a stand-alone entity. A target firm, B, is worth $12,000 as a stand-alone entity, but $18,000 if it is acquired and integrated with Firm A. Several other firms are interested in acquiring Firm B, and Firm B is also worth $18,000 if it is acquired by these other firms. If Firm A acquired Firm B, would this acquisition create value? If yes, how much? How much of this value would the equity holders of Firm A receive? How much would the equity holders of Firm B receive?

(b) The same scenario as above except that the value of Firm B, if it is acquired by the other firms interested in it, is only $12,000.

(c) The same scenario in part (a), except that the value of Firm B, if it is acquired by the other firms interested in it, is $16,000.

(d) The same scenario as in part (b), except that Firm B contacts several other firms and explains to them how they can create the same value with Firm B that Firm A does.

(e) The same scenario as in part (b), except that Firm B sues Firm A. After suing Firm A, Firm B installs a "supermajority" rule in how its board of directors operates. After putting this new rule in place, Firm B offers to buy back any stock purchased by Firm A for 20 percent above the current market price.

MyManagementLab®

Go to **mymanagementlab.com** for Auto-graded writing questions as well as the following Assisted-graded writing questions:

⭐ **10.9.** How can product differentiation be used to neutralize environmental threats and exploit environmental opportunities?

⭐ **10.10.** How would a firm's investment in merger and acquisition strategies, on average, be expected to generate at least competitive parity for bidding firms?

End Notes

1. See Welch, D., and G. Edmondson. (2004). "A shaky automotive *ménage à trois.*" *BusinessWeek*, May 10, pp. 40–41.
2. (2013). "S&P, Nasdaq set marks as merger activity boosts stocks." *Salt Lake Tribune*, February 20, p. E3.
3. Here, and throughout this chapter, it is assumed that capital markets are semi-strong efficient, that is, all publicly available information about the value of a firm's assets is reflected in the market price of those assets. One implication of semi-strong efficiency is that firms will be able to gain access to the capital they need to pursue any strategy that generates positive present value. See Fama, E. F. (1970). "Efficient capital markets: A review of theory and empirical work." *Journal of Finance*, 25, pp. 383–417.
4. See Trautwein, I. (1990). "Merger motives and merger prescriptions." *Strategic Management Journal*, 11, pp. 283–295; and Walter, G., and J. B. Barney. (1990). "Management objectives in mergers and acquisitions." *Strategic Management Journal*, 11, pp. 79–86. The three lists of potential links between bidding and target firms were developed by the Federal Trade Commission; Lubatkin, M. (1983). "Mergers and the performance of the acquiring firm." *Academy of Management Review*, 8, pp. 218–225; and Jensen, M. C., and R. S. Ruback. (1983). "The market for corporate control: The scientific evidence." *Journal of Financial Economics*, 11, pp. 5–50.
5. See Huey, J. (1995). "Eisner explains everything." *Fortune*, April 17, pp. 44–68; and Lefton, T. (1996). "Fitting ABC and ESPN into Disney: Hands in glove." *Brandweek*, 37(18), April 29, pp. 30–40.
6. See Rumelt, R. (1974). *Strategy, structure, and economic performance.* Cambridge, MA: Harvard University Press.
7. The first study was by Ravenscraft, D. J., and F. M. Scherer. (1987). *Mergers, sell-offs, and economic efficiency.* Washington, DC: Brookings Institution. The second study was by Porter, M. E. (1987). "From competitive advantage to corporate strategy." *Harvard Business Review*, 3, pp. 43–59.
8. This is because if the combined firm is worth $32,000 the bidder firm is worth $15,000 on its own. If a bidder pays, say, $20,000 for this target, it will be paying $20,000 for a firm that can only add $17,000 in value. So, a $20,000 bid would lead to a $3,000 economic loss.
9. This is Jensen, M. C., and R. S. Ruback. (1983). "The market for corporate control: The scientific evidence." *Journal of Financial Economics*, 11, pp. 5–50.
10. See Lubatkin, M. (1987). "Merger strategies and stockholder value." *Strategic Management Journal*, 8, pp. 39–53; and Singh, H., and C. A. Montgomery. (1987). "Corporate acquisition strategies and economic performance." *Strategic Management Journal*, 8, pp. 377–386.
11. See Grant, L. (1995). "Here comes Hugh." *Fortune*, August 21, pp. 43–52; Serwer, A. E. (1995). "Why bank mergers are good for your savings account." *Fortune*, October 2, p. 32; and Deogun, N. (2000). "Europe catches merger fever as global volume sets record." *The Wall Street Journal*, January 3, p. R8.
12. The concept of free cash flow has been emphasized in Jensen, M. C. (1986). "Agency costs of free cash flow, corporate finance, and takeovers." *American Economic Review*, 76, pp. 323–329; and Jensen, M. (1988). "Takeovers: Their causes and consequences." *Journal of Economic Perspectives*, 2, pp. 21–48.
13. See Miles, R. H., and K. S. Cameron. (1982). *Coffin nails and corporate strategies.* Upper Saddle River, NJ: Prentice Hall.
14. Roll, R. (1986). "The hubris hypothesis of corporate takeovers." *Journal of Business*, 59, pp. 205–216.
15. See Dodd, P. (1980). "Merger proposals, managerial discretion and stockholder wealth." *Journal of Financial Economics*, 8, pp. 105–138; Eger, C. E. (1983). "An empirical test of the redistribution effect in pure exchange mergers." *Journal of Financial and Quantitative Analysis*, 18, pp. 547–572; Firth, M. (1980). "Takeovers, shareholder returns, and the theory of the firm." *Quarterly Journal of Economics*, 94, pp. 235–260; Varaiya, N. (1985). "A test of Roll's hubris hypothesis of corporate takeovers." Working paper, Southern Methodist University, School of Business; Ruback, R. S., and W. H. Mikkelson. (1984). "Corporate investments in common stock." Working paper, Massachusetts Institute of Technology, Sloan School of Business; and Ruback, R. S. (1982). "The Conoco takeover and stockholder returns." *Sloan Management Review*, 14, pp. 13–33.
16. This section of the chapter draws on Barney, J. B. (1988). "Returns to bidding firms in mergers and acquisitions: Reconsidering the relatedness hypothesis." *Strategic Management Journal*, 9, pp. 71–78.
17. See Turk, T. A. (1987). "The determinants of management responses to interfirm tender offers and their effect on shareholder wealth." Unpublished doctoral dissertation, Graduate School of Management, University of California at Irvine. In fact, this is an example of an anti-takeover action that can increase the value

of a target firm. These anti-takeover actions are discussed later in this chapter.

18. See Bower, J. (1996). "WPP-integrating icons." Harvard Business School Case No. 9-396-249.

19. See Jemison, D. B., and S. B. Sitkin. (1986). "Corporate acquisitions: A process perspective." *Academy of Management Review*, 11, pp. 145–163.

20. Blackwell, R. D. (1998). "Service Corporation International." Presented to The Cullman Symposium, October, Columbus, OH.

21. Cartwright, S., and C. Cooper. (1993). "The role of culture compatibility in successful organizational marriage." *The Academy of Management Executive*, 7(2), pp. 57–70; Chatterjee, S., M. Lubatkin, D. Schweiger,

and Y. Weber. (1992). "Cultural differences and shareholder value in related mergers: Linking equity and human capital." *Strategic Management Journal*, 13, pp. 319–334.

22. Jacobsen, D. (2012). "Six big mergers killed by culture." *Globoforce*, September 22.

23. See Walsh, J., and J. Ellwood. (1991). "Mergers, acquisitions, and the pruning of managerial deadwood." *Strategic Management Journal*, 12, pp. 201–217; and Walsh, J. (1988). "Top management turnover following mergers and acquisitions." *Strategic Management Journal*, 9, pp. 173–183.

24. See Haspeslagh, P., and D. Jemison. (1991). *Managing acquisitions: Creating value through corporate renewal*. New York: Free Press.

11 International Strategies

LEARNING OBJECTIVES *After reading this chapter, you should be able to:*

1. Define international strategy.

2. Describe the relationship between international strategy and other corporate strategies, including vertical integration and diversification.

3. Describe five ways that international strategies can create economic value.

4. Discuss the trade-off between local responsiveness and international integration and transnational strategies as a way to manage this trade-off.

5. Discuss the political risks associated with international strategies and how they can be measured.

6. Discuss the rarity and imitability of international strategies.

7. Describe four different ways to organize to implement international strategies.

MyManagementLab®

⭐ **Improve Your Grade!**
More than 10 million students improved their results using the Pearson MyLabs.
Visit **mymanagementlab.com** for simulations, tutorials, and end-of-chapter problems.

The Baby Formula Problem

It began in 2008, when most of the domestic dairy producers in China were found to be selling baby formula tainted with the toxic chemical melamine. Melamine—a chemical used in plastics and fertilizers—makes baby formula appear less watery than it actually is. Six babies died, and 300,000 became sick. Not surprisingly, demand among Chinese consumers for baby formula produced by Chinese firms dropped dramatically.

Enter foreign companies. Recognizing a market opportunity, companies headquartered outside China began importing baby formula into China. These included Mead Johnson, Dumex, Abbott Laboratories, Royal FrieslandCampina, and Fonterra. By 2012, non-Chinese producers of baby formula had 60 percent of the Chinese market, even though they charged prices that were 30 percent higher than formula produced by Chinese firms.

Even at these prices, supply of non-Chinese formula was not enough to satisfy Chinese demand. Visitors from China to Hong Kong began loading up on non-Chinese formula and bringing it into the mainland, where they used it for their own children or sold it. This continued until quotas on importing formula from Hong Kong to China were implemented. Shortages of non-Chinese formula began showing up around the world. In the United Kingdom, Tesco and Sainsbury—two leading grocery store chains—had to put restrictions on the amount of baby formula that could be purchased because people were buying numerous boxes of non-Chinese formula and selling it online to consumers in China.

Apparently, even though the melamine poisonings took place in 2008, Chinese consumers still don't trust Chinese producers—and with some reason. Most of the dairy companies that put melamine in their milk in 2008 are still operating. Mengniu Dairy, a state-owned dairy, discovered cancer-causing toxins in its milk in 2011. Yili Dairy had to recall some of its formula, tainted with mercury, in 2012, and in 2013, it sold formula with more trans-fat than is deemed safe.

In this setting, the decision taken by the National Development and Reform Commission was a bit surprising—it levied fines amounting to $108 million on five international producers of baby formula—the five listed earlier—and one domestic producer. This agency concluded that these producers set minimum resale prices and punished distributors who sold at lower prices. Xu Kunlin, a spokesperson for the commission, was quoted as saying, "These practices caused milk powder prices to remain at a high level, restricted competition in the market, and harmed the interests of consumers."

© tulpahn/Fotolia

Another interpretation of the commission's decision was that it concluded it was time for China to "reclaim" the domestic baby formula market and that one way to do this would be to punish foreign producers. Indeed, this motive was hinted at in an article published in *The People's Daily* that emphasized that Chinese firms needed to take advantage of this situation by producing "high-quality low-cost products." The article went on to say, "In fact, it is very possible for China-made milk powder to replace imported ones or even defeat their foreign counterparts and sell their products to the overseas market by improving the quality and regaining consumer confidence."

Did non-Chinese producers engage in anticompetitive activities to artificially inflate the price of baby formula in China? Did the Chinese government, for its own reasons, decide to help reestablish the domestic baby formula industry by fining non-Chinese producers? It is difficult to know, but this kind of interaction between business and industry is the kind of thing that can make international strategies very complicated.

Sources: E. Wong (2013). "China says foreign makers of baby formula may be fixing prices." *The New York Times,* July 3, www.nytimes.com/2013/07/04/business/global/china-says-its-investigating-price-fixing. Accessed August 26, 2013; B. Demick (2013). "China fines baby formula companies $108 million in price-fixing case." *The Los Angeles Times,* August 7, www.latimes.com/new/world/worldnow/la-fg-china-fines-babyformula-companies. Accessed August 26, 2013; C. Riley (2013). "China fines six companies for baby formula price fixing." *CNN Money,* August 7, money.cnn.com/2013/08/07/news/china-baby-formula/index.html. Accessed August 26, 2013; L. Kuo (2013). "Why Chinese parents are still so paranoid about made-in-China baby formula." *Quartz,* August 9, qz.com/113508/why-chinese-parents-are-still-so-paranoid-about-made-in-china-babyformula. Accessed August 26, 2013.

As the five non-Chinese baby formula firms have discovered, operating internationally can sometimes create unexpected strategic challenges.

Firms that operate in multiple countries simultaneously are implementing **international strategies**. International strategies are actually a special case of the corporate strategies already discussed in Part 3 of this book. That is, firms can vertically integrate, diversify, form strategic alliances, and implement mergers and acquisitions, all across national borders. Thus, the reasons why firms might want to pursue these corporate strategies identified in Chapters 6 through 10 also apply to firms pursuing international strategies. For this reason, this chapter emphasizes the unique characteristics of international strategies.

At some level, international strategies have existed since before the beginning of recorded time. Certainly, trade across country borders has been an important determinant of the wealth of individuals, companies, and countries throughout history. The search for trading opportunities and trade routes was a primary motivation for the exploration of much of the world. Therefore, it would be inappropriate to argue that international strategies are an invention of the late twentieth century.

Strategy in the Emerging Enterprise

Logitech is a leader in peripheral devices for personal computers and related digital technology. With 2013 sales of $2.1 billion, Logitech sells computer pointing devices (e.g., computer mice and trackballs), regular and cordless computer keyboards, webcam cameras, PC headsets and VoIP (voice over Internet protocol) handsets, PC game controllers, and speakers and headphones for PCs in virtually every country in the world. Headquartered in Switzerland and with offices in California, Switzerland, China, Hong Kong, Taiwan, and Japan, Logitech is a classic example of a firm pursuing an international strategy.

And it has always been this way—not that Logitech had sales of $2.1 billion when it was first founded, in 1981. But Logitech was one of the first entrepreneurial firms that began its operations—way back in 1981—by pursuing an international strategy. At its founding, for example, Logitech had offices in Switzerland and the United States. Within two years of its founding, it had research and development

International Entrepreneurial Firms: The Case of Logitech

and manufacturing operations in Taiwan and Ireland. In short, Logitech was "born global."

Of course, not all entrepreneurial firms pursue international strategies from their inception. But this is less unusual for firms in high-technology industries, where global technical standards make it possible for products made in one market to be sold as "plug and play" products in markets around the world. Because Logitech's pointing devices and other peripherals could be used by any personal computer

around the world, their market—from day one—was global in scope. Indeed, in one study of firms that were "born global," most of these firms were operating in high-technology markets with well-developed technical standards.

More recently, entrepreneurial firms have begun exploiting international opportunities in sourcing the manufacturing of their products. The rise of low-cost manufacturing in China, Vietnam, and the Philippines—among other places—has led increased numbers of firms, including many small and entrepreneurial firms, to outsource their manufacturing operations to these countries. In this global environment, even the smallest entrepreneurial firms must become aware of and manage the challenges associated with implementing international strategies discussed in this chapter.

Sources: www.logitech.com; (2013). Logitech 10 K Report; B. Oviatt and P. McDougall (1995). "Global start-ups: Entrepreneurs on a worldwide stage." *Academy of Management Executive,* 9, pp. 30–44.

In the past, however, the implementation of international strategies was limited to relatively small numbers of risk-taking individuals and firms. Today these strategies are becoming remarkably common. For example, in 2012, almost a third of Wal-Mart's sales revenues came from outside the United States; only about a third of ExxonMobil's profits came from its U.S. operations; almost 50 percent of General Motors' automobile sales came from outside the United States; and about half of General Electric's revenues came from non-U.S. operations. And it's not only U.S-based firms that have invested in non-U.S. operations. Numerous non-U.S. firms have invested around the world as well. For example, the U.S. market provides the largest percentage of the sales of such firms as Nestlé (a Swiss food company), Toyota (a Japanese car company), and Royal Dutch/Shell Group (an energy company headquartered in both the United Kingdom and the Netherlands). Moreover, as described in the Strategy in the Emerging Enterprise feature, international strategies are not limited to just huge multinational companies.

The increased use of international strategies by both large and small firms suggests that the economic opportunities associated with operating in multiple geographic markets can be substantial. However, to be a source of sustained competitive advantages for firms, these strategies must exploit a firm's valuable, rare, and costly to imitate resources and capabilities. Moreover, a firm must be appropriately organized to realize the full competitive potential of these resources and capabilities. This chapter examines the conditions under which international strategies can create economic value, as well as the conditions under which they can be sources of sustained competitive advantages.

The Value of International Strategies

As suggested earlier, international strategies are an example of corporate strategies. So to be economically valuable, they must meet the two value criteria originally introduced in Chapter 7: They must exploit real economics of scope, and it must be costly for outside investors to realize these economies of scope on their own. Many of the economies of scope discussed in the context of vertical integration, corporate diversification, strategic alliances, and merger and acquisition strategies can be created when firms operate across multiple businesses. These same economies can also be created when firms operate across multiple geographic markets.

More generally, like all the strategies discussed in this book, to be valuable, international strategies must enable a firm to exploit environmental opportunities or neutralize environmental threats. To the extent that international strategies enable a firm to respond to its environment, they will also enable a firm to reduce its costs or increase the willingness of its customers to pay compared to what would have been the case if that firm did not pursue these strategies. Several potentially valuable economies of scope particularly relevant for firms pursuing international strategies are summarized in Table 11.1.

1. To gain access to new customers for current products or services
2. To gain access to low-cost factors of production
3. To develop new core competencies
4. To leverage current core competencies in new ways
5. To manage corporate risk

TABLE 11.1 Potential Sources of Economies of Scope for Firms Pursuing International Strategies

To Gain Access to New Customers for Current Products or Services

The most obvious economy of scope that may motivate firms to pursue an international strategy is the potential new customers for a firm's current products or services that such a strategy might generate. To the extent that customers outside a firm's domestic market are willing and able to buy a firm's current products or services, implementing an international strategy can directly increase a firm's revenues.

Internationalization and Firm Revenues

If customers outside a firm's domestic market are willing and able to purchase its products or services, then selling into these markets will increase the firm's revenues. However, it is not always clear that the products and services that a firm sells in its domestic market will also sell in foreign markets.

Are Nondomestic Customers Willing to Buy?

It may be the case that customer preferences vary significantly in a firm's domestic and foreign markets. These different preferences may require firms seeking to internationalize their operations to substantially change their current products or services before nondomestic customers are willing to purchase them.

This challenge faced many U.S. home appliance manufacturers as they looked to expand their operations into Europe and Asia. In the United States, the physical size of most home appliances (washing machines, dryers, refrigerators, dishwashers, and so forth) has become standardized, and these standard sizes are built into new homes, condominiums, and apartments. Standard sizes have also emerged in Europe and Asia. However, these non-U.S. standard sizes are much smaller than the U.S. sizes, requiring U.S. manufacturers to substantially retool their manufacturing operations in order to build products that might be attractive to Asian and European customers.[1]

Different physical standards can require a firm pursuing international opportunities to change its current products or services to sell them into a nondomestic market. Physical standards, however, can easily be measured and described. Differences in tastes can be much more challenging for firms looking to sell their products or services outside the domestic market.

The inability to anticipate differences in tastes around the world has sometimes led to very unfortunate, and often humorous, marketing blunders. For example, General Motors once introduced the Chevrolet Nova to South America, even though "No va" in Spanish means "it won't go." When Coca-Cola was first introduced in China, it was translated into Ke-kou-ke-la, which turns out to mean either "bite the wax tadpole" or "female horse stuffed with wax," depending on which dialect one speaks. Coca-Cola reintroduced its product with the name Ke-kou-ko-le, which roughly translates into "happiness in the mouth."

Coca-Cola is not the only beverage firm to run into problems internationally. Pepsi's slogan "Come alive with the Pepsi generation" was translated into "Pepsi will bring your ancestors back from the dead" in Taiwan. In Italy, a marketing campaign for Schweppes tonic water was translated into Schweppes toilet water—not a terribly appealing drink. Bacardi developed a fruity drink called "Pavian." Unfortunately, "Pavian" means baboon in German. Coors used its "Turn it loose" slogan when selling beer in Spain and Latin America. Unfortunately, "Turn it loose" was translated into "Suffer from diarrhea."

Food companies have had similar problems. Kentucky Fried Chicken's slogan "Finger-lickin' good" translates into "eat your fingers off" in Chinese. In Arabic, the "Jolly Green Giant" translates into "Intimidating Green Ogre." Frank Perdue's famous catch phrase—"It takes a tough man to make a tender chicken"—takes on a slightly different meaning when translated into Spanish— "It takes a sexually stimulated man to make a chicken affectionate." And Gerber found that it was unable to sell its baby food in Africa—with pictures of cute babies on the jar—because the tradition in Africa is to put pictures of what is inside the jar on the label. Think about it.

Other marketing blunders include Colgate's decision to introduce Cue toothpaste in France, even though Cue is the name of a French pornographic magazine; an American T-shirt manufacturer that wanted to print T-shirts in Spanish that said "I saw the Pope" (el Papa) but instead printed T-shirts that said "I saw the potato" (la papa); and Salem cigarettes, whose slogan "Salem—feeling free" translated into Japanese as "When smoking Salem, you feel so refreshed that your mind seems to be free and empty." What were they smoking?

However, of all these blunders, perhaps none tops Electrolux—a Scandinavian vacuum cleaner manufacturer. While its marketing slogan for the U.S. market does rhyme—"Nothing sucks like an Electrolux"—it doesn't really communicate what the firm had in mind.[2]

It's not just these marketing blunders that can limit sales in nondomestic markets. For example, Yugo had difficulty selling its automobiles in the United States. Apparently, U.S. consumers were unwilling to accept poor-performing, poor-quality automobiles, despite their low price. Sony, despite its success in Japan, was unable to carve out significant market share in the U.S. video market with its Betamax technology. Most observers blame Sony's reluctance to license this technology to other manufacturers, together with the shorter recording time available on Betamax, for this product failure. The British retail giant Marks and Spencer's efforts to enter the Canadian and U.S. retail markets with its traditional mix of clothing and food stores also met with stiff consumer resistance.[3]

In order for the basis of an international strategy to attract new customers, those products or services must address the needs, wants, and preferences of customers in foreign markets at least as well as, if not better than, alternatives. Firms pursuing international opportunities may have to implement many of the cost-leadership and product differentiation business strategies discussed in Chapters 4 and 5, modified to address the specific market needs of a nondomestic market. Only then will customers in nondomestic markets be willing to buy a firm's current products or services.

Are Nondomestic Customers Able to Buy?

Customers in foreign markets might be willing to buy a firm's current products or services but be unable to buy them. This can occur for at least three reasons: inadequate distribution channels, trade barriers, and insufficient wealth to make purchases.

Inadequate distribution channels may make it difficult, if not impossible, for a firm to make its products or services available to customers outside its domestic market. In some international markets, adequate distribution networks exist but are tied up by firms already operating in these markets. Many European firms face this situation as they try to enter the U.S. market. In such a situation, firms pursuing international opportunities must either build their own distribution networks from scratch (a very costly endeavor) or work with a local partner to utilize the networks that are already in place.

However, the problem facing some firms pursuing international opportunities is not that distribution networks are tied up by firms already operating in a market. Rather, the problem is that distribution networks do not exist or operate in ways that are very different from the operation of the distribution networks in a firm's domestic market. This problem can be serious when firms seek to expand their operations into developing economies. Inadequate transportation, warehousing, and retail facilities can make it difficult to distribute a firm's products or services into a new geographic market. These kinds of problems have hampered investment in Russia, China, and India. For example, when Nestlé entered the Chinese dairy market, it had to build a network of gravel roads connecting the villages where dairy farmers produce milk and factory collection points. Obtaining the right to build this network of roads took 13 years of negotiations with Chinese government officials.[4]

Such distribution problems are not limited to developing economies. For example, Japanese retail distribution has historically been much more fragmented, and much less efficient, than the system that exists in either the United States or Western Europe. Rather than being dominated by large grocery stores, discount retail operations, and retail superstores, the Japanese retail distribution network has been dominated by numerous small "mom-and-pop" operations. Many Western firms find this distribution network difficult to use because its operating principles are so different from what they have seen in their domestic markets. However, Procter & Gamble and a few other firms have been able to crack open this Japanese distribution system and exploit significant sales opportunities in Japan.[5]

Even if distribution networks exist in nondomestic markets and even if international firms can operate through those networks if they have access to them, it still might be the case that entry into these markets can be restricted by various tariff and nontariff trade barriers. A list of such trade barriers is presented in Table 11.2. Trade barriers, no matter what their specific form, have the effect

TABLE 11.2 Tariffs, Quotas, and Nontariff Trade Barriers

Tariffs: Taxes levied on imported goods or services	Quotas: Quantity limits on the number of products or services that can be imported	Nontariff barriers: Rules, regulations, and policies that increase the cost of importing products or services
Import duties	Voluntary quotas	Government policies
Supplemental duties	Involuntary quotas	Government procurement policies
Variable levies	Restricted import licenses	Government-sponsored exports
Subsidies	Minimum import limits	Domestic assistance programs
Border levies	Embargoes	Custom policies
Countervailing duties		Valuation systems
		Tariff classifications
		Documentation requirements
		Fees
		Quality standards
		Packaging standards
		Labeling standards

of increasing the cost of selling a firm's current products or services in a new geographic market and thus make it difficult for a firm to realize this economy of scope from its international strategy.

Despite a worldwide movement toward free trade and reduction in trade barriers, trade barriers are still an important economic phenomenon for many firms seeking to implement an international strategy. Japanese automobile manufacturers have faced voluntary quotas and various other trade barriers as they have sought to expand their presence in the U.S. market; U.S. automobile firms have argued that Japan has used a series of tariff and nontariff trade barriers to restrict their entry into the Japanese market. Kodak once asked the U.S. government to begin negotiations to facilitate Kodak's entry into the Japanese photography market—a market that Kodak argued was controlled, through a government-sanctioned monopoly, by Fuji. Historically, beginning operations in India was hampered by a variety of tariff and nontariff trade barriers. Tariffs in India had averaged more than 80 percent; foreign firms have been restricted to a 40 percent ownership stake in their operations in India; and foreign imports had required government approvals and licenses that could take up to three years to obtain. Many of these trade barriers in India have been reduced but not eliminated. The same is true for the United States. The tariff on imported goods and services imposed by the U.S. government reached an all-time high of 60 percent in 1932. It averaged from 12 to 15 percent after the Second World War and now averages about 5 percent for most imports into the United States. Thus, U.S. trade barriers have been reduced but not eliminated.[6]

Governments create trade barriers for a wide variety of reasons: to raise government revenue, to protect local employment, to encourage local production to replace imports, to protect new industries from competition, to discourage foreign direct investment, and to promote export activity. However, for firms seeking to implement international strategies, trade barriers, no matter why they are erected, have the effect of increasing the cost of implementing these strategies. Indeed, trade barriers can be thought of as a special case of artificial barriers to entry, as discussed in Chapter 2. Such barriers to entry can turn what could have been economically viable strategies into nonviable strategies.

Finally, customers may be willing but unable to purchase a firm's current products or services even if distribution networks are in place and trade barriers are not making internationalization efforts too costly. If these customers lack the wealth or sufficient hard currency to make these purchases, then the potential value of this economy of scope can go unrealized.

Insufficient consumer wealth limits the ability of firms to sell products into a variety of markets. For example, per capita gross national product is $270 in Bangladesh, $240 in Chad, and $110 in the Congo. In these countries, it is unlikely that there will be significant demand for many products or services originally designed for affluent Western economies. This situation also exists in India. The middle class in India is large and growing (164 million people with the highest 20 percent of income in 1998), but the income of this middle class is considerably lower than the income of the middle class in other economies. These income levels are sufficient to create demand for some consumer products. For example, Gillette estimates the market in India for its shaving products could include 240 million consumers, and Nestlé believes that the market in India for its noodles, ketchup, and instant coffee products could include more than 100 million people. However, the potential market for higher-end products in India is somewhat smaller. For example, Bausch & Lomb believes that only about 30 million consumers in India can afford to purchase its high-end sunglasses and soft contact lenses. The level of consumer wealth is such an important determinant of the economic potential of beginning operations in a new country that McDonald's adjusts the number of restaurants it expects to build in a new market by the per capita income of people in that market.[7]

Even if there is sufficient wealth in a country to create market demand, lack of hard currency can hamper internationalization efforts. **Hard currencies** are currencies that are traded, and thus have value, on international money markets. When an international firm does business in a country with hard currency, the firm can take whatever after-tax profits it earns in that country and translate those profits into other hard currencies—including the currency of the country in which the firm has headquarters. Moreover, because the value of hard currencies can fluctuate in the world economy, firms can also manage their currency risk by engaging in various hedging strategies in world money markets.

When firms begin operations in countries without hard currency, they are able to obtain few of these advantages. Indeed, without hard currency, cash payments to these firms are made with a currency that has essentially no value

Strategy in Depth

When international firms engage in countertrade, they receive payment for the products or services they sell into a country, but not in the form of currency. They receive payment in the form of other products or services that they can sell on the world market. Countertrade has been a particularly important way by which firms have tried to gain access to the markets in the former Soviet Union. For example, Marc Rich and Company (a Swiss commodity-trading firm) once put together the following deal: Marc Rich purchased 70,000 tons of raw sugar from Brazil on the open market; shipped this sugar to Ukraine, where it was refined; then transported 30,000 tons of refined sugar (after using some profits to pay the refineries) to Siberia, where it was sold for 130,000 tons of oil products that, in turn, were shipped to Mongolia in exchange for 35,000 tons of copper concentrate, which was moved to Kazakhstan, where it was refined into copper and, finally, sold on the world

Countertrade

market to obtain hard currency. This complicated countertrade deal is typical of the kinds of actions that international firms must take if they are to engage in business in countries without hard currency and if they desire to extract their profits out of those countries. Indeed, countertrade in various forms is actually quite common. One estimate suggests that countertrade accounts for between 10 and 20 percent of world trade.

Although countertrade can enable a firm to begin operations in countries without hard currency, it can create difficulties as well. In particular, in order to do business, a firm must be willing to accept payment in the form of some good or commodity that it must sell in order to obtain hard currency. This is not likely to be a problem for a firm that specializes in buying and selling commodities. However, a firm that does not have this expertise may find itself taking possession of natural gas, sesame seeds, or rattan in order to sell its products or services in a country. If this firm has limited expertise in marketing these kinds of commodities, it may have to use brokers and other advisers to complete these transactions. This, of course, increases the cost of using countertrade as a way to facilitate international operations.

Source: A. Ignatius (1993). "Commodity giant: Marc Rich & Co. does big deals at big risk in former U.S.S.R." *The Wall Street Journal*, May 13, p. A1; D. Marin (1990). "Tying in trade: Evidence on countertrade." *World Economy*, 13(3), p. 445.

outside the country where the payments are made. Although these payments can be used for additional investments inside that country, an international firm has limited ability to extract profits from countries without hard currencies and even less ability to hedge currency fluctuation risks in this context. The lack of hard currency has discouraged firms from entering a wide variety of countries at various points in time despite the substantial demand for products and services in those countries.[8] One solution to this problem, called **countertrade**, is discussed in the Strategy in Depth feature.

Internationalization and Product Life Cycles

Gaining access to new customers not only can directly increase a firm's revenues but also can enable a firm to manage its products or services through their life cycle. A typical **product life cycle** is depicted in Figure 11.1. Different stages in this life cycle are defined by different growth rates in demand for a product. Thus, in the first emerging stage (called **introduction** in the figure), relatively few firms are producing a product, there are relatively few customers, and the rate of growth in demand for the product is relatively low. In the second stage (**growth**) of the product life cycle, demand increases rapidly, and many new firms enter to begin producing the product or service. In the third phase of the product life cycle (**maturity**), the number of firms producing a product or service remains stable, demand growth levels off, and firms direct their investment efforts toward refining the process by which a product or service is created and away from developing entirely new products. In the final phase of the product life cycle (**decline**), demand drops off when a technologically superior product or service is introduced.[9]

From an international strategy perspective, the critical observation about product life cycles is that a product or service can be at different stages of its life cycle in different countries. Thus, a firm can use the resources and capabilities it developed during a particular stage of the life cycle in its domestic market during that same stage of the life cycle in a nondomestic market. This can substantially enhance a firm's economic performance.

One firm that has been very successful in managing its product life cycles through its international efforts is Crown Cork & Seal. This firm had a traditional

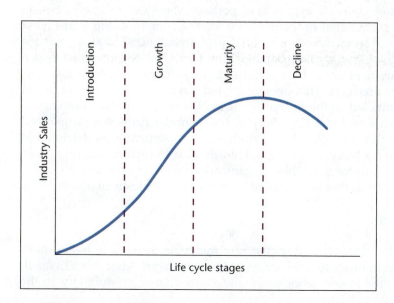

Figure 11.1 The Product Life Cycle

strength in the manufacturing of three-piece metal containers when the introduction of two-piece metal cans into the U.S. market rapidly made three-piece cans obsolete. However, rather than abandoning its three-piece manufacturing technology, Crown Cork & Seal moved many of its three-piece manufacturing operations overseas into developing countries where demand for three-piece cans was just emerging. In this way, Crown Cork & Seal was able to extend the effective life of its three-piece manufacturing operations and substantially enhance its economic performance.[10]

Internationalization and Cost Reduction

Gaining access to new customers for a firm's current products or services can increase a firm's sales. If aspects of a firm's production process are sensitive to economies of scale, this increased volume of sales can also reduce the firm's costs and enable the firm to gain cost advantages in both its nondomestic and its domestic markets.

Many firms in the worldwide automobile industry have attempted to realize manufacturing economies of scale through their international operations. According to one estimate, the minimum efficient scale of a single compact-car manufacturing plant is 400,000 units per year.[11] Such a plant would produce approximately 20 percent of all the automobiles sold in Britain, Italy, or France. Obviously, to exploit this 400,000 car-per-year manufacturing efficiency, European automobile firms have had to sell cars in more than just a single country market. Thus, the implementation of an international strategy has enabled these firms to realize an important manufacturing economy of scale.[12]

To Gain Access to Low-Cost Factors of Production

Just as gaining access to new customers can be an important economy of scope for firms pursuing international opportunities, so is gaining access to low-cost factors of production such as raw materials, labor, and technology.

Raw Materials

Gaining access to low-cost raw materials is, perhaps, the most traditional reason why firms begin international operations. For example, in 1600, the British East India Company was formed with an initial investment of $70,000 to manage trade between England and the Far East, including India. In 1601, the third British East India Company fleet sailed for the Indies to buy cloves, pepper, silk, coffee, saltpeter, and other products. This fleet generated a return on investment of 234 percent. These profits led to the formation of the Dutch East India Company in 1602 and the French East India Company in 1664. Similar firms were organized to manage trade in the New World. The Hudson Bay Company was chartered in 1670 to manage the fur trade, and the rival North West Company was organized in 1784 for the same purpose. All these organizations were created to gain access to low-cost raw materials that were available only in nondomestic markets.[13]

Labor

In addition to gaining access to low-cost raw materials, firms also begin international operations in order to gain access to low-cost labor. After World War II, Japan had some of the lowest labor costs, and highest labor productivity, in the

Ethics and Strategy

There is little doubt that globalization has improved lives of both producers in developing economies and consumers in more developed economies. Individuals working in companies that make, for example, clothing in countries like Bangladesh, China, the Philippines, and Vietnam have jobs that pay good wages—compared to alternatives in those countries—and are able to move their families out of abject poverty. Consumers in developed economies are able to buy good quality clothes at relatively low prices.

But this seemingly virtuous trade is not without its personal and social costs. A series of disasters in factories in Bangladesh reminds us that low-cost clothes for consumers in developed countries can sometimes be manufactured in grossly unsafe factories in less-developed countries. One fire in a Bangladeshi factory killed 112 workers. At least some of the fire escape doors built in this factory had been locked to prevent workers from taking unauthorized breaks. Then a complex of clothing factories in Bangladesh collapsed, killing 892 workers. It turns out that the top four floors of this complex had been built illegally without the proper permits. And even though cracks in the building led the manager of a bank located on the first floor to close and send all his employees home for their safety, the owners of the factories in the top floors insisted that their employees go to work. Shortly thereafter,

Manufacturing Tragedies and International Business

the building collapsed, and almost 900 people died.

These factories all produced clothing for well-known U.S. and Western European stores, including H&M, Wal-Mart, Target, Benetton, Primark (in the United Kingdom), and Mango (in Spain)—to name just a few. Indeed, because Bangladesh is the second-largest producer of garments in the world, behind China, it is very likely that at least some of the clothing that each of us wear each day is made by Bangladeshi workers operating in marginally safe factories.

Of course, these Western firms do not have managers on site at these factories insisting that fire doors are locked and unsafe buildings are built. Indeed, after the building collapse, many firms in developed economies pledged to work with suppliers to ensure safer

working conditions. This will take some time, of course. And, in the meantime, at least some workers' lives may be at risk. For example, shortly after these firms announced their commitment to improved worker safety, a fire in another Bangladeshi factory that makes clothing for Wal-Mart, Benetton, and other companies killed eight employees.

Some have argued that the intense cost pressures put on Bangladeshi factory owners by their developed economy customers force these factory owners to locate their factories in inexpensive but dangerous locations. It would be convenient for these factory owners if all the blame for these terrible tragedies could be placed on their customers from developed countries—and by implication on all who purchase clothes from these retailers. Of course, things are rarely that simple. While these retail firms do put cost pressures on their suppliers, it is the factory owners and factory managers who lock fire doors and insist on production in a building that appears likely to collapse at any time.

Nevertheless, the growing number of tragedies in Bangladesh, China, and elsewhere in garment manufacturing may require firms in developed economies to rethink at least some aspects of their international business strategies.

Sources: J. Yardley (2013). "Fire at Bangladeshi factory kills eight." *NYTimes,* May 9; J. Juliflar, A. Monik, and J. Yardley (2013). "Building collapses in Bangladesh, leaves scores dead." *NYTimes,* April 24.

world. Over time, however, the improving Japanese economy and the increased value of the yen have had the effect of increasing labor costs in Japan, and South Korea, Taiwan, Singapore, and Malaysia all emerged as geographic areas with inexpensive and highly productive labor. More recently, China, Mexico, and Vietnam have taken this role in the world economy.[14]

Numerous firms have attempted to gain the advantages of low labor costs by moving their manufacturing operations. For example, Minebea, a Japanese ball-bearing and semiconductor manufacturer, attempted to exploit low labor costs by manufacturing ball bearings in Japan in the 1950s and early 1960s, in Singapore in the 1970s, and since 1980 has been manufacturing them in Thailand. Hewlett-Packard operates manufacturing and assembly operations in Malaysia and Mexico, Japan's Mitsubishi Motors opened an automobile assembly plant in Vietnam, General Motors operates assembly plants in Mexico, and Motorola has begun operations in China. All these investments were motivated, at least partly, by the availability of low-cost labor in these countries.[15] Some of the ethical issues associated with the search for low-cost labor are discussed in the Ethics and Strategy feature.

Although gaining access to low-cost labor can be an important determinant of a firm's international efforts, this access by itself is usually not sufficient to motivate entry into particular countries. After all, relative labor costs can change over time. For example, South Korea used to be the country in which most sports shoes were manufactured. In 1990, Korean shoe manufacturers employed 130,000 workers in 302 factories. However, by 1993, only 80,000 Koreans were employed in the shoe industry, and only 244 factories (most employing fewer than 100 people) remained. A significant portion of the shoe-manufacturing industry had moved from Korea to China because of the labor-cost advantages of China (approximately $40 per employee per month) compared with Korea (approximately $800 per employee per month).[16]

Moreover, low labor costs are not beneficial if a country's workforce is not able to produce high-quality products efficiently. In the sport shoe industry, China's access to some of the manufacturing technology and supporting industries (for example, synthetic fabrics) to efficiently produce high-end sports shoes and high-technology hiking boots was delayed for several years. As a result, Korea was able to maintain a presence in the shoe-manufacturing industry—even though most of that industry had been outsourced to China.

One interesting example of firms gaining access to low-cost labor through their international strategies is maquiladoras—manufacturing plants that are owned by non-Mexican companies and operated in Mexico near the U.S. border. The primary driver behind maquiladora investments is lower labor costs than similar plants located in the United States. In addition, firms exporting from maquiladoras to the United States have to pay duties only on the value added that was created in Mexico; maquiladoras do not have to pay Mexican taxes on the goods processed in Mexico; and the cost of land on which plants are built in Mexico is substantially lower than would be the case in the United States. However, a study by the Banco de Mexico suggests that without the 20 percent cost-of-labor advantage, most maquildoras would not be profitable.[17]

Technology

Another factor of production that firms can gain low-cost access to through operations is technology. Historically, Japanese firms have tried to gain access to technology by partnering with non-Japanese firms. Although the non-Japanese firms have often been looking to gain access to new customers for their current products or services by operating in Japan, Japanese firms have used this entry into the Japanese market to gain access to foreign technology.[18]

To Develop New Core Competencies

One of the most compelling reasons for firms to begin operations outside their domestic markets is to refine their current core competencies and to develop new core competencies. By beginning operations outside their domestic markets, firms can gain a greater understanding of the strengths and weaknesses of their core competencies. By exposing these competencies to new competitive contexts, traditional competencies can be modified, and new competencies can be developed.

Of course, for international operations to affect a firm's core competencies, firms must learn from their experiences in nondomestic markets. Moreover, once these new core competencies are developed, they must be exploited in a firm's other operations in order to realize their full economic potential.

Learning from International Operations

Learning from international operations is anything but automatic. Many firms that begin operations in a nondomestic market encounter challenges and difficulties and then immediately withdraw from their international efforts. Other firms continue to try to operate internationally but are unable to learn how to modify and change their core competencies.

One study examined several strategic alliances in an effort to understand why some firms in these alliances were able to learn from their international operations, modify their core competencies, and develop new core competencies while others were not. This study identified the intent to learn, the transparency of business partners, and receptivity to learning as determinants of a firm's ability to learn from its international operations (see Table 11.3).

The Intent to Learn

A firm that has a strong intent to learn from its international operations is more likely to learn than a firm without this intent. Moreover, this intent must be communicated to all those who work in a firm's international activities. Compare, for example, a quote from a manager whose firm failed to learn from its international operations with a quote from a manager whose firm was able to learn from these operations.[19]

> *Our engineers were just as good as [our partner's]. In fact, theirs were narrower technically, but they had a much better understanding of what the company was trying to accomplish. They knew they were there to learn; our people didn't.*
>
> *We wanted to make learning an automatic discipline. We asked the staff every day, "What did you learn from [our partner] today?" Learning was carefully monitored and recorded.*

Obviously, the second firm was in a much better position than the first to learn from its international operations and to modify its current core competencies and

1. The intent to learn
2. The transparency of business partners
3. Receptivity to learning
Source: G. Hamel (1991). "Competition for competence and inter-partner learning within international strategic alliances." *Strategic Management Journal*, 12, pp. 83–103.

TABLE 11.3 Determinants of the Ability of a Firm to Learn from Its International Operations

develop new core competencies. Learning from international operations takes place by design, not by default.

Transparency and Learning

It has also been shown that firms were more likely to learn from their international operations when they interacted with what have been called **transparent business partners**. Some international business partners are more open and accessible than others. This variance in accessibility can reflect different organizational philosophies, practices, and procedures, as well as differences in the culture of a firm's home country. For example, knowledge in Japanese and most other Asian cultures tends to be context specific and deeply embedded in the broader social system. This makes it difficult for many Western managers to understand and appreciate the subtlety of Japanese business practices and Japanese culture. This, in turn, limits the ability of Western managers to learn from their operations in the Japanese market or from their Japanese partners.[20]

In contrast, knowledge in most Western cultures tends to be less context specific, less deeply embedded in the broader social system. Such knowledge can be written down, can be taught in classes, and can be transmitted, all at a relatively low cost. Japanese managers working in Western economies are more likely to be able to appreciate and understand Western business practices and thus are more able to learn from their operations in the West and from their Western partners.

Receptivity to Learning

Firms also vary in their receptiveness to learning. A firm's receptiveness to learning is affected by its culture, its operating procedures, and its history. Research on organizational learning suggests that, before firms can learn from their international operations, they must be prepared to unlearn. **Unlearning** requires a firm to modify or abandon traditional ways of engaging in business. Unlearning can be difficult, especially if a firm has a long history of success using old patterns of behavior and if those old patterns of behavior are reflected in a firm's organizational structure, its management control systems, and its compensation policies.[21]

Even if unlearning is possible, a firm may not have the resources it needs to learn. If a firm is using all of its available managerial time and talent, capital, and technology just to compete on a day-to-day business, the additional task of learning from international operations can go undone. Although managers in this situation often acknowledge the importance of learning from their international operations in order to modify their current core competencies or build new ones, they simply may not have the time or energy to do so.[22]

The ability to learn from operations can also be hampered if managers perceive that there is too much to be learned. It is often difficult for a firm to understand how it can evolve from its current state to a position where it operates with new and more valuable core competencies. This difficulty is exacerbated when the distance between where a firm is and where it needs to be is large. One Western manager who perceived this large learning gap after visiting a state-of-the-art manufacturing facility operated by a Japanese partner was quoted as saying:[23]

> It's no good for us to simply observe where they are today, what we have to find out is how they got from where we are to where they are. We need to experiment and learn with intermediate technologies before duplicating what they've done.

Leveraging New Core Competencies in Additional Markets

Once a firm has been able to learn from its international operations and modify its traditional core competencies or develop new core competencies, it must then leverage those competencies across its operations, both domestic and international, in order to realize their full value. Failure to leverage these "lessons learned" can substantially reduce the return associated with implementing an international strategy.

To Leverage Current Core Competencies in New Ways

International operations can also create opportunities for firms to leverage their traditional core competencies in new ways. This ability is related to, though different from, using international operations to gain access to new customers for a firm's current products or services. When firms gain access to new customers for their current products, they often leverage their domestic core competencies across country boundaries. When they leverage core competencies in *new* ways, they not only extend operations across country boundaries but also leverage their competencies across products and services in ways that would not be economically viable in their domestic market.

Consider, for example, Honda. There is widespread agreement that Honda has developed core competencies in the design and manufacture of power trains. Honda has used this core competence to facilitate entry into a variety of product markets—including motorcycles, automobiles, and snow blowers—both in its domestic Japanese market and in nondomestic markets such as the United States. However, Honda has begun to explore some competence-leverage opportunities in the United States that are not available in the Japanese market. For example, Honda has begun to design and manufacture lawn mowers of various sizes for the home in the U.S. market—lawn mowers clearly build on Honda's traditional power train competence. However, given the crowded living conditions in Japan, consumer demand for lawn mowers in that country has never been very great. Lawns in the United States, however, can be very large, and consumer demand for high-quality lawn mowers in that market is substantial. The opportunity for Honda to begin to leverage its power train competencies in the sale of lawn mowers to U.S. homeowners exists only because Honda operates outside its Japanese home market.

To Manage Corporate Risk

The value of risk reduction for firms pursuing a corporate diversification strategy was evaluated previously. It was suggested that, although diversified operations across businesses with imperfectly correlated cash flows can reduce a firm's risk, outside equity holders can manage this risk more efficiently on their own by investing in a diversified portfolio of stocks. Consequently equity holders have little direct interest in hiring managers to operate a diversified portfolio of businesses, the sole purpose of which is risk diversification.

Similar conclusions apply to firms pursuing international strategies—with two qualifications. First, in some circumstances, it may be difficult for equity holders in one market to diversify their portfolio of investments across multiple markets. To the extent that such barriers to diversification exist for individual equity holders but not for firms pursuing international strategies, risk reduction can directly benefit equity holders. In general, whenever barriers to international capital flows exist, individual investors may not be able to diversify their portfolios across country boundaries optimally. In this context, individual investors can indirectly diversify their portfolio of investments by purchasing shares in diversified multinationals.[24]

Research Made Relevant

Firms whose ownership is dominated by a single family are surprisingly common around the world. In the United States, for example, Marriott, Walgreens, Wrigley, Alberto-Culver, Campbell Soup, Dell, and Wal-Mart are all family dominated. However, only four of the 20 largest firms in the United States are family dominated, and only one of the 20 largest firms in the United Kingdom is family dominated.

Though not uncommon in the United States and the United Kingdom, family-dominated firms are the rule, not the exception, in most economies around the world. For example, in New Zealand, nine of the 20 largest firms are family dominated; in Argentina, 13 of the 20 largest firms are family dominated; and in Mexico, all 20 of the 20 largest firms are family dominated. In many countries, including Argentina, Belgium, Canada, Denmark, Greece, Hong Kong, Israel, Mexico, New Zealand, Portugal, Singapore, South Korea, Sweden, and Switzerland, more than one-third of the largest 20 firms are dominated by family owners.

A variety of explanations of why family-dominated firms continue to be an important part of the world economy have been proposed. For example, some researchers have argued that family owners obtain private benefits of ownership—over and above the financial benefits they might receive. Such private benefits include high social status in their countries. Other researchers

Family Firms in the Global Economy

have argued that family ownership helps guarantee that family members will be able to control their property in countries with less-well-developed property rights. And still others have argued that concentrated family owners help a firm gain political clout in its negotiations with the government.

On the positive side, family ownership may reduce conflicts that might otherwise arise between a firm's managers and its outside equity holders—the agency costs discussed in the Strategy in Depth feature in Chapter 8. Managers of family firms are "playing with" their own money, not "other people's money," and thus are less likely to pursue strategies that benefit themselves but hurt the firm's owners because they are the firm's owners.

On the negative side, family firms may become starved for capital, and especially equity capital. Non-family

members will often be reluctant to invest in family firms because the interests of the family are often likely to take precedence over the interests of outsiders. Also, family firms must limit their search for senior leadership to family members. It may well be the case that the best leaders of a family firm are not members of the family, but family ownership can prevent a firm from gaining access to the entire labor market. Finally, for reasons explained in the text, family firms may need to pursue a broad diversification strategy in order to reduce the risk borne by their family owners. As suggested in Chapter 8, such unrelated diversification strategies can sometimes be difficult to manage.

From a broader perspective, the importance of family-dominated firms throughout the world suggests that the "standard" model of corporate governance—with numerous anonymous stockholders, an independent board of directors, and senior managers chosen only for their ability to lead and create economic value—may not apply that broadly. This approach to corporate governance, so dominant in the United States and the United Kingdom, may actually be the exception, not the rule.

Sources: R. Morck and B. Yeung (2004). "Family control and the rent-seeking society." *Entrepreneurship: Theory and Practice*, Summer, pp. 391–409; R. LaPorta, F. Lopez-de-salina, A. Shleifer, and R. Vishny (1999). "Corporate ownership around the world." *Journal of Finance*, 54, pp. 471–520; J. Weber, L. Lavelle, T. Lowry, W. Zellner, and A. Barrett (2003). "Family, Inc.," *BusinessWeek*, November 10, pp. 100+.

Second, large privately held firms may find it in their wealth maximizing interests to broadly diversify to reduce risk. In order to gain the risk reduction advantages of diversifying their investments by owning a portfolio of stocks, the owners of these firms would have to "cash out" their ownership position in their firm—by, for example, taking their firm public—and then use this cash to invest in a portfolio of stocks. However, these individuals may gain other advantages from owning their firms and may not want to cash out. In this setting, the only way that owners can gain the risk-reducing benefits of broad diversification is for the firm that they own to broadly diversify.

This justification of diversification for risk reduction purposes is particularly relevant in the international context because, as described in the Research Made Relevant feature, many of the economies of countries around the world are dominated by private companies owned by large families. Not surprisingly, these family-owned firms tend to be much more diversified than the publicly traded firms that are more common in the United States and the United Kingdom.

The Local Responsiveness/International Integration Trade-Off

As firms pursue the economies of scope listed in Table 11.1, they constantly face a trade-off between the advantages of being responsive to market conditions in their nondomestic markets and the advantages of integrating their operations across the multiple markets in which they operate.

On the one hand, **local responsiveness** can help firms be successful in addressing the local needs of nondomestic customers, thereby increasing demand for a firm's current products or services. Moreover, local responsiveness enables a firm to expose its traditional core competencies to new competitive situations, thereby increasing the chances that those core competencies will be improved or will be augmented by new core competencies. Finally, detailed local knowledge is essential if firms are going to leverage their traditional competencies in new ways in their nondomestic markets. Honda was able to begin exploiting its power train competencies in the U.S. lawn mower market only because of its detailed knowledge of, and responsiveness to, that market.

On the other hand, the full exploitation of the economies of scale that can be created by selling a firm's current products or services in a nondomestic market often can occur only if there is tight integration across all the markets in which a firm operates. Gaining access to low-cost factors of production can not only help a firm succeed in a nondomestic market but also help it succeed in all its markets—as long as those factors of production are used by many parts of the international firm. Developing new core competencies and using traditional core competencies in new ways can certainly be beneficial in a particular domestic market. However, the full value of these economies of scope is realized only when they are transferred from a particular domestic market into the operations of a firm in all its other markets.

Traditionally, it has been thought that firms have to choose between local responsiveness and international integration. For example, firms like CIBA-Geigy (a Swiss chemical company), Nestlé (a Swiss food company), and Phillips (a Dutch consumer electronics firm) have chosen to emphasize local responsiveness. Nestlé, for example, owns nearly 8,000 brand names worldwide. However, of those 8,000 brands, only 750 are registered in more than one country, and only 80 are registered in more than 10 countries. Nestlé adjusts its product attributes to the needs of local consumers, adopts brand names that resonate with those consumers, and builds its brands for long-run profitability by country. For example, in the United States, Nestlé's condensed milk carries the brand name "Carnation" (obtained through the acquisition of the Carnation Company); in Asia, this same product carries the brand name "Bear Brand." Nestlé delegates brand management authority to country managers, who can (and do) adjust traditional marketing and manufacturing strategies in accordance with local tastes and preferences. For example, Nestlé's Thailand management group dropped traditional coffee-marketing efforts that focused on taste, aroma, and stimulation and instead began selling coffee as a drink that promotes relaxation and romance. This marketing strategy resonated with Thais experiencing urban stress, and it prompted Nestlé coffee sales in Thailand to jump from $25 million to $100 million four years later.[25]

Of course, all this local responsiveness comes at a cost. Firms that emphasize local responsiveness are often unable to realize the full value of the economies of scope and scale that they could realize if their operations across country borders were more integrated. Numerous firms have focused on appropriating this economic value and have pursued a more integrated international strategy. Examples of such firms include IBM, General Electric, Toyota Motor Corporation, and most major pharmaceutical firms, to name just a few.

Internationally integrated firms locate business functions and activities in countries that have a comparative advantage in these functions or activities. For example, the production of components for most consumer electronics is research intensive, capital intensive, and subject to significant economies of scale. To manage component manufacturing successfully, most internationally integrated consumer electronics firms have located their component operations in technologically advanced countries like the United States and Japan. Because the assembly of these components into consumer products is labor intensive, most internationally integrated consumer electronics firms have located their assembly operations in countries with relatively low labor costs, including Mexico and China.

Of course, one of the costs of locating different business functions and activities in different geographic locations is that these different functions and activities must be coordinated and integrated. Operations in one country might very efficiently manufacture certain components. However, if the wrong components are shipped to the assembly location or if the right components are shipped at the wrong time, any advantages that could have been obtained from exploiting the comparative advantages of different countries can be lost. Shipping costs can also reduce the return on international integration.

To ensure that the different operations in an internationally integrated firm are appropriately coordinated, these firms typically manufacture more standardized products, using more standardized components, than do locally responsive firms. Standardization enables these firms to realize substantial economies of scale and scope, but it can limit their ability to respond to the specific needs of individual markets. When international product standards exist, as in the personal computer industry and the semiconductor chip industry, such standardization is not problematic. Also, when local responsiveness requires only a few modifications of a standardized product (for example, changing the shape of the electric plug or changing the color of a product), international integration can be very effective. However, when local responsiveness requires a great deal of local knowledge and product modifications, international integration can create problems for a firm pursuing an international strategy.

The Transnational Strategy

Recently, it has been suggested that the traditional trade-off between international integration and local responsiveness can be replaced by a **transnational strategy** that exploits all the advantages of both international integration and local responsiveness.[26] Firms implementing a transnational strategy treat their international operations as an integrated network of distributed and interdependent resources and capabilities. In this context, a firm's operations in each country are not simply independent activities attempting to respond to local market needs; they are also repositories of ideas, technologies, and management approaches that the firm might be able to use and apply in its other international operations. Put differently, operations in different countries can be thought of as "experiments" in the creation of new core competencies. Some of these experiments will work and generate important new core competencies; others will fail to have such benefits for a firm.

When a particular country operation develops a competence in manufacturing a particular product, providing a particular service, or engaging in a particular activity that can be used by other country operations, the country operation with this competence can achieve international economies of scale by becoming the firm's primary supplier of this product, service, or activity. In this way, local responsiveness is retained as country managers constantly search for new competencies that enable them to maximize profits in their particular markets, and international integration and economies are realized as country operations that have developed unique competencies become suppliers for all other country operations.

Managing a firm that is attempting to be both locally responsive and internationally integrated is not an easy task. Some of these organizational challenges are discussed later in this chapter.

Financial and Political Risks in Pursuing International Strategies

There is little doubt that the realization of the economies of scope listed in Table 11.1 can be a source of economic value for firms pursuing international strategies. However, the nature of international strategies can create significant risks that these economies of scope will never be realized. Beyond the implementation problems (to be discussed later in this chapter), both financial circumstances and political events can significantly reduce the value of international strategies.

Financial Risks: Currency Fluctuation and Inflation

As firms begin to pursue international strategies, they may begin to expose themselves to financial risks that are less obvious within a single domestic market. In particular, currency fluctuations can significantly affect the value of a firm's international investments. Such fluctuations can turn what had been a losing investment into a profitable investment (the good news). They can also turn what had been a profitable investment into a losing investment (the bad news). In addition to currency fluctuations, different rates of inflation across countries can require very different managerial approaches, business strategies, and accounting practices. Certainly, when a firm first begins international operations, these financial risks can seem daunting.

Fortunately, it is now possible for firms to hedge most of these risks through the use of a variety of financial instruments and strategies. The development of money markets, together with growing experience in operating in high-inflation economies, has substantially reduced the threat of these financial risks for firms pursuing international strategies. Of course, the benefits of these financial tools and experience in high-inflation environments do not accrue to firms automatically. Firms seeking to implement international strategies must develop the resources and capabilities they will need to manage these financial risks. Moreover, these hedging strategies can do nothing to reduce the business risks that firms assume when they enter into nondomestic markets. For example, it may be the case that consumers in a nondomestic market simply do not want to purchase a firm's products or services, in which case this economy of scope cannot be realized. Moreover, these financial strategies cannot manage political risks that can exist for firms pursuing an international strategy.

Political Risks

The political environment is an important consideration in all strategic decisions. Changes in the political rules of the game can have the effect of increasing some environmental threats and reducing others, thereby changing the value of a firm's resources and capabilities. However, the political environment can be even more problematic as firms pursue international strategies.

Types of Political Risks

Politics can affect the value of a firm's international strategies at the macro and micro levels. At the macro level, broad changes in the political situation in a country can change the value of an investment. For example, after the Second World War, nationalist governments came to power in many countries in the Middle East. These governments expropriated for little or no compensation many of the assets of oil and gas companies located in their countries. Expropriation of foreign company assets also occurred when the Shah of Iran was overthrown, when a communist government was elected in Chile, and when new governments came to power in Angola, Ethiopia, Peru, Zambia, and, more recently, Venezuela and Bolivia.[27]

Government upheaval and the attendant risks to international firms are facts of life in some countries. Consider, for example, oil-rich Nigeria. From 1960–1999, Nigeria has experienced several successful coups d'états, one civil war, two civil governments, and six military regimes.[28] The prudent course of action for firms engaging in business activities in Nigeria is to expect the current government to change and to plan accordingly.

Quantifying Political Risks

Political scientists have attempted to quantify the political risk that firms seeking to implement international strategies are likely to face in different countries. Although different studies vary in detail, the country attributes listed in Table 11.4

Increments to Country		
Risk If Risk Factor Is:	**Low**	**High**
The political economic environment		
1. Stability of the political system	3	14
2. Imminent internal conflicts	0	14
3. External threats to stability	0	12
4. Degree of control of the economic system	5	9
5. Reliability of country as a trade partner	4	12
6. Constitutional guarantees	2	12
7. Effectiveness of public administration	3	12
8. Labor relations and social peace	3	15
Domestic economic conditions		
1. Size of the population	4	8
2. Per capita income	2	10
3. Economic growth over the past five years	2	7
4. Potential growth over the next three years	3	10
5. Inflation over the past two years	2	10
6. Availability of domestic capital markets to outsiders	3	7
7. Availability of high-quality local labor force	2	8
8. Possibility of employing foreign nationals	2	8
9. Availability of energy resources	2	14
10. Environmental pollution legal requirements	4	8
11. Transportation and communication infrastructure	2	14
External economic relations		
1. Import restrictions	2	10
2. Export restrictions	2	10
3. Restrictions on foreign investments	3	9
4. Freedom to set up or engage in partnerships	3	9
5. Legal protection for brands and products	3	9
6. Restrictions on monetary transfers	2	8
7. Revaluation of currency in the past five years	2	7
8. Balance-of-payments situation	2	9
9. Drain on hard currency through energy imports	3	14
10. Financial standing	3	8
11. Restrictions on the exchange of local and foreign currencies	2	8

TABLE 11.4 Quantifying Political Risks from International Operations

Source: Adapted from E. Dichtl and H. G. Koeglmayr (1986). "Country risk ratings." *Management Review,* 26(4), pp. 2–10. Reprinted with permission.

summarize most of the important determinants of political risk for firms pursuing international strategies.[29] Firms can apply the criteria listed in the table by evaluating the political and economic conditions in a country and by adding up the scores associated with these conditions. For example, a country that has a very unstable political system (14 points), a great deal of control of the economic system (9 points), and significant import restrictions (10 points) represents more political risk than a country that does not have these attributes.

Managing Political Risk

Unlike financial risks, there are relatively few tools for managing the political risks associated with pursuing an international strategy. Obviously, one option would be to pursue international opportunities only in countries where political risk is very small. However, it is often the case that significant business opportunities exist in politically risky countries precisely because they are politically risky. Alternatively, firms can limit their investment in politically risky environments. However, these limited investments may not enable a firm to take full advantage of whatever economies of scope might exist by engaging in business in that country.

Another approach to managing political risk is to see each of the determinants of political risk, listed in Table 11.4, as negotiation points as a firm enters into a new country market. In many circumstances, those in a nondomestic market have just as much an interest in seeing a firm begin doing business in a new market as does the firm contemplating entry. International firms can sometimes use this bargaining power to negotiate entry conditions that reduce, or even neutralize, some of the sources of political risk in a country. Of course, no matter how skilled a firm is in negotiating these entry conditions, a change of government or changes in laws can quickly nullify any agreements.

A third approach to managing political risk is to turn this risk from a threat into an opportunity. One firm that has been successful in this way is Schlumberger, an international oil services company. Schlumberger has headquarters in New York, Paris, and the Caribbean; it is a truly international company. Schlumberger management has adopted a policy of strict neutrality in interactions with governments in the developing world. Because of this policy, Schlumberger has been able to avoid political entanglements and continues to do business where many firms find the political risks too great. Put differently, Schlumberger has developed valuable, rare, and costly-to-imitate resources and capabilities in managing political risks and is using these resources to generate high levels of economic performance.[30]

Research on the Value of International Strategies

Overall, research on the economic consequences of implementing international strategies is mixed. Some research has found that the performance of firms pursuing international strategies is superior to the performance of firms operating only in domestic markets.[31] However, most of this work has not examined the particular economies of scope that a firm is attempting to realize through its internationalization efforts. Moreover, several of these studies have attempted to evaluate the impact of international strategies on firm performance by using accounting measures of performance. Other research has found that the risk-adjusted performance of firms pursuing an international strategy is not different from the risk-adjusted performance of firms pursuing purely domestic strategies.[32]

These ambivalent findings are not surprising because the economic value of international strategies depends on whether a firm pursues valuable economies of scope when implementing this strategy. Most of this empirical work fails to examine the economies of scope that a firm's international strategy might be based on. Moreover, even if a firm is able to realize real economies of scope from its international strategies, to be a source of sustained competitive advantage, this economy of scope must also be rare and costly to imitate, and the firm must be organized to fully realize it.

International Strategies and Sustained Competitive Advantage

As suggested earlier in this chapter, much of the discussion of rarity and imitability in strategic alliance, diversification, and merger and acquisition strategies also applies to international strategies. However, some aspects of rarity and imitability are unique to international strategies.

The Rarity of International Strategies

In many ways, it seems likely that international strategies are becoming less rare among most competing firms. Consider, for example, the increasingly international strategies of many telephone companies around the world. Through much of the 1980s, telecommunications remained a highly regulated industry around the world. Phone companies rarely ventured beyond their country borders and had few, if any, international aspirations. However, as government restrictions on telecommunications firms around the world began to be lifted, these firms began exploring new business alternatives. For many firms, this originally meant exploring new telecommunications businesses in their domestic markets. Thus, for example, many formerly regulated telecommunications firms in the United States began to explore business opportunities in less-regulated segments of the U.S. telecommunications market, including cellular telephones and paging. Over time, these same firms began to explore business opportunities overseas.

In the past several years, the telecommunications industry has begun to consolidate on a worldwide basis. For example, in the early 1990s, Southwestern Bell (now AT&T) purchased a controlling interest in Mexico's government-owned telecommunications company. Ameritech (now a division of AT&T), Bell Atlantic, U.S. West, BellSouth, and Pacific Telesis (now a division of AT&T) also engaged in various international operations. In the late 1990s, MCI (a U.S. firm) and British Telecom (a British company) merged. In 1999, the Vodafone Group (a British-headquartered telecommunications company) purchased AirTouch Cellular (a U.S. firm) for $60.29 billion, formed a strategic alliance with U.S. West (another U.S. firm), purchased Mannesmann (a German telecommunications firm) for $127.76 billion, and increased its ownership interest in several smaller telecommunications companies around the world. Also, in 1999, Olivetti (the Italian electronics firm) successfully beat back Deutsche Telephone's effort to acquire ItaliaTelecom (the Italian telephone company). And, in 2012, the Japanese mobile phone company Softbank purchased the U.S. phone company SprintNextel. Obviously, international strategies are no longer rare among telecommunications companies.[33]

There are, of course, several reasons for the increased popularity of international strategies. Not the least of these are the substantial economies of scope that internationalizing firms can realize. In addition, several changes in the organization of the international economy have facilitated the growth in popularity of international strategies. For example, the General Agreement on Tariff and Trade (GATT) treaty, in conjunction with the development of the European Community (EC), the Andean Common Market (ANCOM), the Association of Southeast Asian Nations (ASEAN), the North American Free Trade Agreement (NAFTA), and other free-trade zones, has substantially reduced both tariff and nontariff barriers to trade. These changes have helped facilitate trade among countries included in an agreement; they have also spurred firms that wish to take advantage of these opportunities to expand their operations into these countries.

Improvements in the technological infrastructure of business are also important contributors to the growth in the number of firms pursuing international strategies. Transportation (especially air travel) and communication (via computers, fax, telephones, pagers, cellular telephones, and so forth) have evolved to the point where it is now much easier for firms to monitor and integrate their international operations than it was just a few years ago. This infrastructure helps reduce the cost of implementing an international strategy and thus increases the probability that firms will pursue these opportunities.

Finally, the emergence of various communication, technical, and accounting standards is facilitating international strategies. For example, there is currently a de facto world standard in personal computers. Moreover, most of the software that runs off these computers is flexible and interchangeable. Someone can write a report on a PC in India and print that report out on a PC in France with no real difficulties. There is also a world de facto standard business language: English. Although fully understanding a non-English–speaking culture requires managers to learn the native tongue, it is nevertheless possible to manage international business operations by using English.

Even though it seems that more and more firms are pursuing international strategies, it does not follow that these strategies will never be rare among a set of competing firms. Rare international strategies can exist in at least two ways. Given the enormous range of business opportunities that exist around the globe, it may very well be the case that huge numbers of firms can implement international strategies and still not compete head to head when implementing these strategies.

Even if several firms are competing to exploit the same international opportunity, the rarity criterion can still be met if the resources and capabilities that a particular firm brings to this international competition are themselves rare. Examples of these rare resources and capabilities might include unusual marketing skills, highly differentiated products, special technology, superior management talent, and economies of scale.[34] To the extent that a firm pursues one of the economies of scope listed in Table 11.1 using resources and capabilities that are rare among competing firms, that firm can gain at least a temporary competitive advantage, even if its international strategy, per se, is not rare.

The Imitability of International Strategies

Like all the strategies discussed in this book, both the direct duplication of and substitutes for international strategies are important in evaluating the imitability of these actions.

Direct Duplication of International Strategies

In evaluating the possibility of the direct duplication of international strategies, two questions must be asked: (1) Will firms try to duplicate valuable and rare international strategies? and (2) Will firms be able to duplicate these valuable and rare strategies?

There seems little doubt that, in the absence of artificial barriers, the profits generated by one firm's valuable and rare international strategies will motivate other firms to try to imitate the resources and capabilities required to implement these strategies. This is what has occurred in the international telecommunications industry. This rush to internationalization has occurred in numerous other industries as well. For example, the processed-food industry at one time had a strong home-market orientation. However, because of the success of Nestlé and Procter & Gamble worldwide, most processed-food companies now engage in at least some international operations.

However, simply because competing firms often try to duplicate a successful firm's international strategy does not mean that they are always able to do so. To the extent that a successful firm exploits resources or capabilities that are path dependent, uncertain, or socially complex in its internationalization efforts, direct duplication may be too costly, and thus international strategies can be a source of sustained competitive advantage. Indeed, there is some reason to believe that at least some of the resources and capabilities that enable a firm to pursue an international strategy are likely to be costly to imitate.

For example, the ability to develop detailed local knowledge of nondomestic markets may require firms to have management teams with a great deal of foreign experience. Some firms may have this kind of experience in their top management teams; other firms may not. One survey of 433 chief executive officers from around the world reported that 14 percent of U.S. chief executive officers (CEOs) had no foreign experience and that the foreign experience of 56 percent of U.S. CEOs was limited to vacation travel. Another survey showed that only 22 percent of the CEOs of multinational companies had extensive international experience.[35] Of course, it can take a great deal of time for a firm that does not have much foreign experience in its management team to develop that experience. Firms that lack this kind of experience will have to bring managers in from outside the organization, invest in developing this experience internally, or both. Of course, these activities are costly. The cost of creating this experience base in a firm's management team can be thought of as one of the costs of direct duplication.

Substitutes for International Strategies

Even if direct duplication of a firm's international strategies is costly, substitutes might still exist that limit the ability of that strategy to generate sustained competitive advantages. In particular, because international strategies are just a special case of corporate strategies in general, any of the other corporate strategies discussed in this book—including some types of strategic alliances, diversification, and mergers and acquisitions—can be at least partial substitutes for international strategies.

For example, it may be possible for a firm to gain at least some of the economies of scope listed in Table 11.1 by implementing a corporate diversification strategy within a single country market, especially if that market is large and geographically diverse. One such market, of course, is the United States. A firm that originally conducted business in the northeastern United States can gain many of the benefits of internationalization by beginning business operations in the southern United States, on the West Coast, or in the Pacific Northwest. In this sense, geographic diversification within the United States is at least a partial substitute for internationalization and is one reason why many U.S. firms have lagged behind European and Asian firms in their international efforts.

There are, however, some economies of scope listed in Table 11.1 that can be gained only through international operations. For example, because there are usually few limits on capital flows within most countries, risk management is directly valuable to a firm's equity holders only for firms pursuing business opportunities across countries where barriers to capital flow exist.

The Organization of International Strategies

To realize the full economic potential of a valuable, rare, and costly-to-imitate international strategy, firms must be appropriately organized.

Becoming International: Organizational Options

A firm implements an international strategy when it diversifies its business operations across country boundaries. However, firms can organize their international business operations in a wide variety of ways. Some of the most common, ranging from market forms of governance to manage simple export operations to the use of wholly owned subsidiaries to manage **foreign direct investment**, are listed in Table 11.5.

Market Exchanges and International Strategies

Firms can maintain traditional arm's-length market relationships between themselves and their nondomestic customers and still implement international strategies. They do this by simply exporting their products or services to nondomestic markets and limiting any foreign direct investment into nondomestic markets. Of course, exporting firms generally have to work with some partner or partners to receive, market, and distribute their products in a nondomestic setting. However, it is possible for exporting firms to use contracts to manage their relationship with these foreign partners and thereby maintain arm's-length relationships with them—all the time engaging in international operations.

The advantages of adopting exporting as a way to manage an international strategy include its relatively low cost and the limited risk exposure that firms pursuing international opportunities in this manner face. Firms that are just beginning to consider international strategies can use market-based exporting to test international waters—to find out if there is demand for their current products or services, to develop some experience operating in nondomestic markets, or to begin to develop relationships that could be valuable in subsequent international strategy efforts. If firms discover that there is not much demand for their products or services in a nondomestic market or if they discover that they do not have the resources and capabilities to effectively compete in those markets, they can simply cease their exporting operations. The direct cost of ceasing export operations can be quite low, especially if a firm's volume of exports is small and the firm has not invested in plant and equipment designed to facilitate exporting. Certainly, if a firm has limited its foreign direct investment, it does not risk losing this investment if it ceases export operations.

However, the opportunity costs associated with restricting a firm's international operations to exporting can be significant. Of the economies of scope listed in Table 11.1, only gaining access to new customers for a firm's current products

TABLE 11.5 Organizing Options for Firms Pursuing International Strategies

Market Governance	Intermediate Market Governance	Hierarchical Governance
Exporting	Licensing	Mergers
	Non-equity alliances	Acquisitions
	Equity alliances	Wholly owned subsidiaries
	Joint ventures	

or services can be realized through exporting. Other economies of scope that hold some potential for firms exploring international business operations are out of the reach of firms that restrict their international operations to exporting. For some firms, realizing economies from gaining access to new customers is sufficient, and exporting is a long-run viable strategy. However, to the extent that other economies of scope might exist for a firm, limiting international operations to exporting can limit the firm's economic profit.

Intermediate Market Exchanges and International Strategies

If a firm decides to move beyond exporting in pursuing international strategies, a wide range of **strategic alliances** are available. These alliances range from simple licensing arrangements, where a domestic firm grants a firm in a nondomestic market the right to use its products and brand names to sell products in that nondomestic market, to full-blown joint ventures, where a domestic firm and a nondomestic firm create an independent organizational entity to manage international efforts. As suggested in Chapter 9, the recent growth in the number of firms pursuing strategic alliance strategies is a direct result of the growth in popularity of international strategies. Strategic alliances are one of the most common ways that firms manage their international efforts.

Most of the discussion of the value, rarity, imitability, and organization of strategic alliances in Chapter 9 applies to the analysis of strategic alliances to implement an international strategy. However, many of the opportunities and challenges of managing strategic alliances as cooperative strategies, discussed in Chapter 9, are exacerbated in the context of international strategic alliances.

For example, it was suggested that opportunistic behavior (in the form of adverse selection, moral hazard, or holdup) can threaten the stability of strategic alliances domestically. Opportunistic behavior is a problem because partners in a strategic alliance find it costly to observe and evaluate the performance of alliance partners. Obviously, the costs and difficulty of evaluating the performance of an alliance partner in an international alliance are greater than the costs and difficulty of evaluating the performance of an alliance partner in a purely domestic alliance. Geographic distance, differences in traditional business practices, language barriers, and cultural differences can make it very difficult for firms to accurately evaluate the performance and intentions of international alliance partners.

These challenges can manifest themselves at multiple levels in an international strategic alliance. For example, one study has shown that managers in U.S. organizations, on average, have a negotiation style very different from that of managers in Chinese organizations. Chinese managers tend to interrupt each other and ask many more questions during negotiations than do U.S. managers. As U.S. and Chinese firms begin to negotiate collaborative agreements, it will be difficult for U.S. managers to judge whether the Chinese negotiation style reflects Chinese managers' fundamental distrust of U.S. managers or is simply a manifestation of traditional Chinese business practices and culture.[36]

Similar management style differences have been noted between Western and Japanese managers. One Western manager was quoted:[37]

Whenever I made a presentation [to our partner], I was one person against 10 or 12. They'd put me in front of a flip chart, and then stop me while they went into a conversation in Japanese for 10 minutes. If I asked them a question they would break into Japanese to first decide what I wanted to know, and then would discuss options in terms of what they might tell me, and finally would come back with an answer.

During those 10-minute breaks in the conversation, it would be very difficult for this manager to know whether the Japanese managers were trying to develop a complete and accurate answer to his question or scheming to provide an incomplete and misleading answer. In this ambiguous setting, to prevent potential opportunism, Western managers might demand greater levels of governance than were actually necessary. In fact, one study has shown that differences in the perceived trustworthiness of international partners have an impact on the kind of governance mechanisms that are put into place when firms begin international operations. If partners are not perceived as being trustworthy, then elaborate governance devices, including joint ventures, are created—even if the partners are in fact trustworthy.[38]

Cultural and style conflicts leading to perceived opportunism problems are not restricted to alliances between Asian and Western organizations. U.S. firms operating with Mexican partners often discover numerous subtle and complex cultural differences. For example, a U.S. firm operating a steel conveyor plant in Puebla, Mexico, implemented a three-stage employee grievance policy. An employee who had a grievance first went to the immediate supervisor and then continued up the chain of command until the grievance was resolved one way or another. U.S. managers were satisfied with this system and pleased that no grievances had been registered—until the day the entire plant walked out on strike. It turns out that there had been numerous grievances, but Mexican workers had felt uncomfortable directly confronting their supervisors with these problems. Such confrontations are considered antisocial in Mexican culture.[39]

Although significant challenges are associated with managing strategic alliances across country boundaries, there are significant opportunities as well. Strategic alliances can enable a firm pursuing an international strategy to realize any of the economies of scope listed in Table 11.1. Moreover, if a firm is able to develop valuable, rare, and costly to imitate resources and capabilities in managing strategic alliances, the use of alliances in an international context can be a source of sustained competitive advantage.

Hierarchical Governance and International Strategies

Firms may decide to integrate their international operations into their organizational hierarchies by acquiring a firm in a nondomestic market or by forming a new wholly owned subsidiary to manage their operations in a nondomestic market. Obviously, both of these international investments involve substantial direct foreign investment by a firm over long periods of time. These investments are subject to both political and economic risks and should be undertaken only if the economy of scope that can be realized through international operations is significant and other ways of realizing this economy of scope are not effective or efficient.

Although full integration in international operations can be expensive and risky, it can have some important advantages for internationalizing firms. First, like strategic alliances, this approach to internationalization can enable a firm to realize any of the economies of scope listed in Table 11.1. Moreover, integration enables managers to use a wider range of organizational controls to limit the threat of opportunism that are normally not available in market forms of international governance or intermediate market forms of international governance. Finally, unlike strategic alliances, where any profits from international operations must be shared with international partners, integrating into international operations enables firms to capture all the economic profits from their international operations.

Managing the Internationally Diversified Firm

Not surprisingly, the management of international operations can be thought of as a special case of managing a diversified firm. Thus, many of the issues discussed in Chapter 8 apply here. However, managing an internationally diversified firm does create some unique challenges and opportunities.

Organizational Structure.   Firms pursuing an international strategy have four basic organizational structural alternatives, listed in Table 11.6 and discussed later. Although each of these structures has some special features, they are all special cases of the multidivisional structure first introduced in Chapter 8.[40]

Some firms organize their international operations as a **decentralized federation**. In this organizational structure, each country in which a firm operates is organized as a full profit-and-loss division headed by a division general manager who is typically the president of the company in a particular country. In a decentralized federation, there are very few shared activities or other relationships among different divisions/country companies, and corporate headquarters plays a limited strategic role. Corporate staff functions are generally limited to the collection of accounting and other performance information from divisions/country companies and to reporting this aggregate information to appropriate government officials and to the financial markets. Both strategic and operational decision making are delegated to division general managers/country company presidents in a decentralized federation organizational structure. There are relatively few examples of pure decentralized federations in today's world economy, but firms like Nestlé, CIBA-Geigy, and Electrolux have many of the attributes of this type of structure.[41]

A second structural option for international firms is the **coordinated federation**. In a coordinated federation, each country operation is organized as a full profit-and-loss center, and division general managers can be presidents of country companies. However, unlike the case in a decentralized federation, strategic and operational decisions are not fully delegated to division general managers. Operational decisions are delegated to division general managers/country presidents, but broader strategic decisions are made at corporate headquarters. Moreover, coordinated federations attempt to exploit various shared activities and other relationships among their divisions/country companies. It is

Decentralized federation	Strategic and operational decisions are delegated to divisions/country companies.
Coordinated federation	Operational decisions are delegated to divisions/country companies; strategic decisions are retained at corporate headquarters.
Centralized hub	Strategic and operational decisions are retained at corporate headquarters.
Transnational structure	Strategic and operational decisions are delegated to those operational entities that maximize responsiveness to local conditions and international integration.

TABLE 11.6 Structural Options for Firms Pursuing International Strategies

Source: Adapted from C. A. Bartlett and S. Ghoshal (1989). *Managing across borders: The transnational solution.* Boston: Harvard Business School Press.

not uncommon for coordinated federations to have corporately sponsored central research and development laboratories, corporately sponsored manufacturing and technology development initiatives, and corporately sponsored management training and development operations. There are numerous examples of coordinated federations in today's world economy, including General Electric, General Motors, IBM, and Coca-Cola.

A third structural option for international firms is the **centralized hub**. In centralized hubs, operations in different companies may be organized into profit-and-loss centers, and division general managers may be country company presidents. However, most of the strategic and operational decision making in these firms takes place at the corporate center. The role of divisions/country companies in centralized hubs is simply to implement the strategies, tactics, and policies that have been chosen at headquarters. Of course, divisions/country companies are also a source of information for headquarters staff when these decisions are being made. However, in centralized hubs, strategic and operational decision rights are retained at the corporate center. Many Japanese and Korean firms are managed as centralized hubs, including Toyota, Mitsubishi, and NEC in Japan and Goldstar, Daewoo, and Hyundai in Korea.[42]

A fourth structural option for international firms is the **transnational structure**. This structure is most appropriate for implementing the transnational strategy described earlier in this chapter. In many ways, the transnational structure is similar to the coordinated federation. In both, strategic decision-making responsibility is largely retained at the corporate center, and operational decision making is largely delegated to division general managers/country presidents. However, important differences also exist.

In a coordinated federation structure, shared activities and other cross-divisional/cross-country economies of scope are managed by the corporate center. Thus, for many of these firms, if research and development is seen as a potentially valuable economy of scope, a central research and development laboratory is created and managed by the corporate center. In the transnational structure, these centers of corporate economies of scope may be managed by the corporate center. However, they are more likely to be managed by specific divisions/country companies within the corporation. Thus, for example, if one division/country company develops valuable, rare, and costly-to-imitate research-and-development capabilities in its ongoing business activities in a particular country, that division/country company could become the center of research-and-development activity for the entire corporation. If one division/country company develops valuable, rare, and costly-to-imitate manufacturing technology development skills in its ongoing business activities in a particular country, that division/country company could become the center for manufacturing technology development for the entire corporation.

The role of corporate headquarters in a transnational structure is to constantly scan business operations across different countries for resources and capabilities that might be a source of competitive advantage for other divisions/country companies in the firm. Once these special skills are located, corporate staff must then determine the best way to exploit these economies of scope—whether they should be developed within a single division/country company (to gain economies of scale) and then transferred to other divisions/country companies, or developed through an alliance between two or more divisions/country companies (to gain economies of scale) and then transferred to other divisions/country companies, or developed for the entire firm at corporate headquarters. These options are not available to decentralized federations (which always let individual divisions/country companies develop their own competencies), coordinated federations, or centralized hubs (which always develop corporate-wide economies of scope at the corporate level). Firms that have been successful in adopting this transnational structure include Ford (Ford Europe has become a leader for automobile design in all of the Ford Motor Company) and Ericson (Ericson's Australian subsidiary developed this Swedish company's first electronic telecommunication switch, and corporate headquarters was able to help transfer this technology to other Ericson subsidiaries).[43]

Organizational Structure, Local Responsiveness, and International Integration. It should be clear that the choice among these four approaches to managing international strategies depends on the trade-offs that firms are willing to make between local responsiveness and international integration. Firms that seek to maximize their local responsiveness will tend to choose a decentralized federation structure. Firms that seek to maximize international integration in their operations will typically opt for centralized hub structures. Firms that seek to balance the need for local responsiveness and international integration will typically choose centralized federations. Firms that attempt to optimize both local responsiveness and international integration will choose a transnational organizational structure.

Management Control Systems and Compensation Policies. Like the multidivisional structure discussed in Chapter 8, none of the organizational structures described in Table 11.5 can stand alone without the support of a variety of management control systems and management compensation policies. All the management control processes discussed in Chapter 8, including evaluating the performance of divisions, allocating capital, and managing the exchange of intermediate products among divisions, are also important for firms organizing to implement an international strategy. Moreover, the same management compensation challenges and opportunities discussed in that chapter apply in the organization of international strategies as well.

However, as is often the case when organizing processes originally developed to manage diversification within a domestic market are extended to the management of international diversification, many of the management challenges highlighted in Chapter 8 are exacerbated in an international context. This puts an even greater burden on senior managers in an internationally diversified firm to choose control systems and compensation policies that create incentives for division general managers/country presidents to appropriately cooperate to realize the economies of scope that originally motivated the implementation of an international strategy.

Summary

International strategies can be seen as a special case of diversification strategies. Firms implement international strategies when they pursue business opportunities that cross country borders. Like all diversification strategies, international strategies must exploit real economies of scope that outside investors find too costly to exploit on their own in order to be valuable. Five potentially valuable economies of scope in international strategies are (1) to gain access to new customers for a firm's current products or services, (2) to gain access to low-cost factors of production, (3) to develop new core competencies, (4) to leverage current core competencies in new ways, and (5) to manage corporate risk.

As firms pursue these economies of scope, they must evaluate the extent to which they can be responsive to local market needs and obtain the advantages of international integration. Firms that attempt to accomplish both these objectives are said to be implementing a transnational strategy. Both economic and political risks can affect the value of a firm's international strategies.

To be a source of sustained competitive advantage, a firm's international strategies must be valuable, rare, and costly to imitate, and the firm must be organized to realize the full potential of its international strategies. Even though more and more firms are pursuing international strategies, these strategies can still be rare, for at least two reasons: (1) Given the broad range of international opportunities, firms may not compete head to head with other firms pursuing the same international strategies that they are pursuing; and (2) firms may bring valuable and rare resources and capabilities to the international strategies they pursue. Both direct duplication and substitution can affect the imitability of a firm's international strategy. Direct duplication is not likely when firms bring valuable, rare, and costly to imitate resources and capabilities to bear in their international strategies. Several substitutes for international strategies exist, including some strategic alliances, vertical integration, diversification, and mergers and acquisitions, especially if these strategies are pursued in a large and diverse single country market. However, some potential economies of scope from international strategies can be exploited only by operating across country borders.

Firms have several organizational options as they pursue international strategies, including market forms of exchange (for example, exports), strategic alliances, and vertical integration (for example, wholly owned subsidiaries). Four alternative structures, all special cases of the multidivisional structure introduced in Chapter 8, can be used to manage these international operations: a decentralized federation structure, a coordinated federation structure, a centralized hub structure, and a transnational structure. These structures need to be consistent with a firm's emphasis on being responsive to local markets, on exploiting international integration opportunities, or both.

MyManagementLab®

Go to **mymanagementlab.com** to complete the problems marked with this icon ⭐.

Challenge Questions

⭐11.1. Are international strategies always just a special case of diversification strategies that a firm might pursue?

11.2. What, if anything, is different about international strategies and diversification strategies?

11.3. In your view, is gaining access to low-cost labor a sufficient reason for a firm to pursue an international strategy? Why or why not? In your view, is gaining access to special tax breaks a sufficient reason for a firm to pursue an international strategy? Why or why not?

11.4. The transnational strategy is often seen as one way in which firms can avoid the limitations inherent in the local responsiveness/international integration trade-off. However, given the obvious advantages of being both locally responsive and internationally integrated, why are apparently only a relatively few firms implementing a transnational strategy?

11.5. Can a firm's transnational strategy be a source of sustained competitive advantage?

⭐ **11.6.** On average, why is the threat of adverse selection and moral hazard in strategic alliances greater for firms pursuing an international strategy or a domestic strategy?

11.7. How are the organizational options for implementing an international strategy related to the M-form structure described in Chapter 8?

11.8. Are international organizational options for implementing an international strategy just special cases of the M-form structure, with slightly different emphases, or are these international organizational options fundamentally different from the M-form structure?

Problem Set

11.9. In which country is it riskiest to begin international operations: Mexico, Argentina, or Poland? Justify your conclusions.

11.10. Your firm has decided to begin selling its mining machinery products in Ghana. Unfortunately, there is not a highly developed trading market for currency in Ghana. However, Ghana does have significant exports of cocoa. Describe a process by which you would be able to sell your machines in Ghana and still translate your earnings into a tradable currency (e.g., dollars or euros).

11.11. Match the actions of these firms with their sources of potential value.

(a) Tata Motors (India) acquires Jaguar (United Kingdom).
(b) Microsoft (United States) opens four research and development centers in Europe.
(c) Disney opens Disney–Hong Kong.
(d) Merck forms a research and development alliance with an Indian pharmaceutical firm.
(e) Lenovo purchases IBM's laptop computer business.
(f) Honda Motor Company opens an automobile manufacturing plant in southern China. Most of the cars it produces are sold in China.
(g) Honda starts exporting cars made in its China plant to Japan.
(h) A Canadian gold mining company acquires an Australian opal mining company.

1. Managing corporate risk
2. New core competencies
3. Leveraging current core competencies in new ways
4. Gaining access to low-cost factors of production
5. New customers for current products or services

MyManagementLab®

Go to **mymanagementlab.com** for Auto-graded writing questions as well as the following Assisted-graded writing questions:

⭐ **11.12.** How can we measure the political risks associated with international strategies?

⭐ **11.13.** How does internationalization affect product life cycles?

End Notes

1. See Yoshino, M., S. Hall, and T. Malnight. (1991). "Whirlpool Corp." Harvard Business School Case no. 9-391-089.
2. 258marketing.wordpress.com/2008/02/27/bad-ads-nothing-sucks-like-an-electrolux/. Accessed June 17, 2009.
3. See Perry, N. J. (1991). "Will Sony make it in Hollywood?" *Fortune*, September 9, pp. 158–166; and Montgomery, C. (1993). "Marks and Spencer Ltd. (A)," Harvard Business School Case no. 9-391-089.
4. See Rapoport, C. (1994). "Nestlé's brand building machine." *Fortune*, September 19, pp. 147–156.
5. See Yoshino, M. Y., and P. Stoneham. (1992). "Procter & Gamble Japan (A)." Harvard Business School Case no. 9-793-035.
6. See Davis, B. (1995). "U.S. expects goals in pact with Japan to be met even without overt backing." *The Wall Street Journal*, June 30, p. A3; Bounds, W., and B. Davis. (1995). "U.S. to launch new case against Japan over Kodak." *The Wall Street Journal*, June 30, p. A3; Jacob, R. (1992). "India is opening for business." *Fortune*, November 16, pp. 128–130; and Rugman, A., and R. Hodgetts. (1995). *Business: A strategic management approach.* New York: McGraw-Hill.
7. See Jacob, R. (1992). "India is opening for business." *Fortune*, November 16, pp. 128–130; Serwer, A. E. (1994). "McDonald's conquers the world." *Fortune*, October 17, pp. 103–116; and World Bank (1999). *World development report.* Oxford: Oxford University Press.
8. See Jacob, R. (1992). "India is opening for business." *Fortune*, November 16, pp. 128–130; Ignatius, A. (1993). "Commodity giant: Marc Rich & Co. does big deals at big risk in former U.S.S.R." *The Wall Street Journal*, May 13, p. A1; and Kraar, L. (1995). "The risks are rising in China." *Fortune*, March 6, pp. 179–180.
9. The life cycle is described in Utterback, J. M., and W. J. Abernathy. (1975). "A dynamic model of process and product innovation." *Omega*, 3, pp. 639–656; Abernathy, W. J., and J. M. Utterback. (1978). "Patterns of technological innovation." *Technology Review*, 80, pp. 40–47; and Grant, R. M. (1991). *Contemporary strategy analysis.* Cambridge, MA: Basil Blackwell.
10. See Bradley, S. P., and S. Cavanaugh. (1994). "Crown Cork and Seal in 1989." Harvard Business School Case no. 9-793-035; and Hamermesh, R. G., and R. S. Rosenbloom. (1989). "Crown Cork and Seal Co., Inc." Harvard Business School Case no. 9-388-096. Of course, this strategy works only until nondomestic markets mature. This occurred for Crown Cork & Seal during the 1990s. Since then, it has had to search elsewhere for growth opportunities.
11. Porter, M. E. (1986). "Competition in international industries: A conceptual framework." In M. E. Porter (ed.), *Competition in International Industries.* Boston: Harvard Business School Press, p. 43; and Ghoshal, S. (1987). "Global strategy: An organizing framework." *Strategic Management Journal*, 8, p. 436.
12. See Kobrin, S. (1991). "An empirical analysis of the determinants of global integration." *Strategic Management Journal*, 12, pp. 17–31.
13. See Trager, J. (1992). *The people's chronology.* New York: Henry Holt.
14. Kraar, L. (1992). "Korea's tigers keep roaring." *Fortune*, May 4, pp. 108–110.
15. See Collis, D. J. (1991). "A resource-based analysis of international competition: The case of the bearing industry." *Strategic Management Journal*, 12 (Summer Special Issue), pp. 49–68; and Engardio, P. (1993). "Motorola in China: A great leap forward." *Business Week*, May 17, pp. 58–59.
16. Gain, S. (1993). "Korea is overthrown as sneaker champ." *The Wall Street Journal*, October 7, p. A14.
17. See Reibstein, L., and M. Levinson. (1991). "A Mexican miracle?" *Newsweek*, May 20, p. 42; and de Forest, M. E. (1994). "Thinking of a plant in Mexico?" *Academy of Management Executive*, 8(1), pp. 33–40.
18. See Zimmerman, M. (1985). *How to do business with the Japanese.* New York: Random House; and Osborn, R. N., and C. C. Baughn. (1987). "New patterns in the formation of US/Japan cooperative ventures: The role of technology." *Columbia Journal of World Business*, 22, pp. 57–65.
19. Ibid.
20. See Benedict, R. (1946). *The chrysanthemum and the sword.* New York: New American Library; Peterson, R. B., and H. F. Schwind. (1977). "A comparative study of personnel problems in companies and joint ventures in Japan." *Journal of Business Studies*, 8(1), pp. 45–55; Peterson, R. B., and J. Y. Shimada. (1978). "Sources of management problems in Japanese-American joint ventures." *Academy of Management Review*, 3, pp. 796–804; and Hamel, G. (1991). "Competition for competence and inter-partner learning within strategic alliances." *Strategic Management Journal*, 12, pp. 83–103.
21. See Burgleman, R. A. (1983). "A process model of internal corporate venturing in the diversified major firm." *Administrative Science Quarterly*, 28(2), pp. 223–244; Hedberg, B. L. T. (1981). "How organizations learn and unlearn." In P. C. Nystrom and W. H. Starbuck (eds.), *Handbook of Organizational Design.* London: Oxford University Press; Nystrom, P. C., and W. H. Starbuck. (1984). "To avoid organizational crisis, unlearn." *Organizational Dynamics*, 12(4), pp. 53–65; and Argyris, C., and D. A. Schon. (1978). *Organizational learning.* Reading, MA: Addison-Wesley.
22. A problem described in Burgleman, R. A. (1983). "A process model of internal corporate venturing in the diversified major firm." *Administrative Science Quarterly*, 28(2), pp. 223–244.
23. Quoted in Hamel, G. (1991). "Competition for competence and inter-partner learning within strategic alliances." *Strategic Management Journal*, 12, p. 97.
24. See Agmon, T., and D. R. Lessard. (1977). "Investor recognition of corporate diversification." *The Journal of Finance*, 32, pp. 1049–1056.
25. Rapoport, C. (1994). "Nestlé's brand building machine." *Fortune*, September 19, pp. 147–156.
26. See Bartlett, C. A., and S. Ghoshal. (1989). *Managing across borders: The transnational solution.* Boston, MA: Harvard Business School Press.
27. See Rugman, A., and R. Hodgetts. (1995). *International business: A strategic management approach.* New York: McGraw-Hill.
28. Glynn, M. A. (1993). "Strategic planning in Nigeria versus U.S.: A case of anticipating the (next) coup." *Academy of Management Executive*, 7(3), pp. 82–83.
29. Dichtl, E., and H. G. Koeglmayr. (1986). "Country risk ratings." *Management International Review*, 26(4), pp. 2–10.
30. See Auletta, K. (1983). "A certain poetry—Parts I and II." *The New Yorker*, June 6, pp. 46–109; and June 13, pp. 50–91.
31. See, for example, Leftwich, R. B. (1974). "U.S. multinational companies: Profitability, financial leverage and effective income tax rates." *Survey of Current Business*, 54, May, pp. 27–36; Dunning, J. H. (1973). "The determinants of production." *Oxford Economic Papers*, 25, November, pp. 289–336; Errunza, V., and L. W. Senbet. (1981). "The effects of international operations on the market value of the firm: Theory and evidence." *The Journal of Finance*, 36, pp. 401–418; Grant, R. M. (1987). "Multinationality and performance among British manufacturing companies." *Journal of International Business Studies*, 18 (Fall), pp. 78–89; and Rugman, A. (1979). *International diversification and the multinational enterprise.* Lexington, MA: Lexington Books.
32. See, for example, Brewer, H. L. (1981). "Investor benefits from corporate international diversification," *Journal of Financial and Quantitative Analysis*, 16, March, pp. 113–126; and Michel, A., and I. Shaked. (1986). "Multinational corporations vs. domestic corporations: Financial performance and characteristics," *Journal of Business*, 17 (Fall), pp. 89–100.
33. Kirkpatrick, D. (1993). "Could AT&T rule the world?" *Fortune*, May 17, pp. 54–56; Deogun, N. (2000). "Europe catches merger fever as international volume sets record." *The Wall Street Journal*, January 3, p. R8.
34. See Caves, R. E. (1971). "International corporations: The industrial economics of foreign investment." *Economica*, 38, Feb. pp. 1–28; Dunning, J. H. (1973). "The determinants of production." *Oxford Economic Papers*, 25, Nov., pp. 289–336; Hymer, S. (1976). *The international operations of national firms: A study of direct foreign investment.* Cambridge, MA: The MIT Press; Errunza, V., and L. W. Senbet. (1981). "The effects of international operations on the market value of the firm: Theory and evidence." *The Journal of Finance*, 36, pp. 401–418.
35. Anders, G. (1989). "Going global: Vision vs. reality." *The Wall Street Journal*, September 22, p. R21; Carpenter, M., G. Sanders, and H. Gregerson. (2001). "Building human capital with organizational context: The impact of assignment experience on multinational firm performance and CEO pay." *Academy of Management Journal*, vol. 44 no. 3, pp. 493–511.

36. Adler, N., J. R. Brahm, and J. L. Graham. (1992). "Strategy implementation: A comparison of face-to-face negotiations in the People's Republic of China and the United States." *Strategic Management Journal*, 13, pp. 449–466.

37. Hamel, G. (1991). "Competition for competence and inter-partner learning within international strategic alliances." *Strategic Management Journal*, 12, p. 95.

38. Shane, S. (1994). "The effect of national culture on the choice between licensing and direct foreign investment." *Strategic Management Journal*, 15, pp. 627–642.

39. See de Forest, M. E. (1994). "Thinking of a plant in Mexico?" *Academy of Management Executive*, 8(1), pp. 33–40.

40. See Bartlett, C. A. (1986). "Building and managing the transnational: The new organizational challenge." In M. E. Porter (ed.), *Competition in international industries.* Boston: Harvard Business School Press, pp. 367–401; and Bartlett, C. A., and S. Ghoshal. (1989). *Managing across borders; The transnational solution.* Boston: Harvard Business School Press.

41. See Baden-Fuller, C. W. F., and J. M. Stopford. (1991). "Globalization frustrated: The case of white goods." *Strategic Management Journal*, 12, pp. 493–507.

42. See Kraar, L. (1992). "Korea's tigers keep roaring." *Fortune*, May 4, pp. 108–110.

43. Bartlett, C. A., and S. Ghoshal. (1989). *Managing across borders: The transnational solution.* Boston: Harvard Business School Press; Grant, R. M. (1991). *Contemporary strategy analysis.* Cambridge, MA: Basil Blackwell.

Appendix

Analyzing Cases and Preparing for Class Discussions

This book, properly understood, is really about how to analyze cases. Just reading the book, however, is no more likely to fully develop one's skills as a strategist than reading a book about golf will make one a golfer. Practice in applying the concepts and tools is essential. Cases provide the opportunity for this necessary practice.

Why the Case Method?

The core of many strategic management courses is the case method of instruction. Under the case method, you will study and discuss the real-world challenges and dilemmas that face managers in firms. Cases are typically accounts of situations that a firm or manager has faced at a given point in time. By necessity, cases do not possess the same degree of complexity that a manager faces in the real world, but they do provide a concrete set of facts that suggest challenges and opportunities that real managers have faced. Very few cases have clear answers. The case method encourages you to engage problems directly and propose solutions or strategies in the face of incomplete information. To succeed at the case method, you must develop the capability to analyze and synthesize data that are sometimes ambiguous and conflicting. You must be able to prioritize issues and opportunities and make decisions in the face of ambiguous and incomplete information. Finally, you must be able to persuade others to adopt your point of view.

In an applied field like strategic management, the real test of learning is how well you can apply knowledge to real-world situations. Strategic management cases offer you the opportunity to develop judgment and wisdom in applying your conceptual knowledge. By applying the concepts you have learned to the relatively unstructured information in a case, you develop judgment in applying concepts. Alfred North Whitehead discussed the importance of application to knowledge:

> This discussion rejects the doctrine that students should first learn passively, and then, having learned, should apply knowledge....For the very meaning of the things known is wrapped up in their relationship beyond themselves. This unapplied knowledge is knowledge shorn of its meaning.

Alfred North Whitehead (1947). *Essays in Science and Philosophy*. New York: Philosophical Library, Inc. pp. 218–219.

Thus, you gain knowledge as you apply concepts. With the case method, you do not passively absorb wisdom imparted from your instructor, but actively develop it as you wrestle with the real-world situations described in the cases.

How to Analyze Cases

Before discussing how to analyze a case, it may be useful to comment on how *not* to prepare a case. We see two common failings in case preparation that often go hand-in-hand. First, students often do not apply conceptual frameworks in a rigorous and systematic manner. Second, many students do not devote sufficient time to reading, analyzing, and discussing a case before class. Many students succumb to the temptation to quickly read a case and latch on to the most visible issues that present themselves. Thus, they come to class prepared to make only a few superficial observations about a case. Often, they entirely miss the deeper issues around why a firm is in the situation that it is in and how it can better its performance. Applying the frameworks systematically may take more time and effort in the beginning, but it will generally lead to deeper insights about the cases and a more profound understanding of the concepts in the chapters. As you gain experience in this systematic approach to analyzing cases, many of you will find that your preparation time will decrease. This appendix offers a framework that will assist you as you analyze cases. The framework is important, but no framework can substitute for hard work. There are no great shortcuts to analyzing cases, and there is no single right method for preparing a case. The following approach, however, may help you develop your ability to analyze cases.

1. **Skim through the case very quickly.** Pay particular attention to the exhibits. The objective in this step is to gain familiarity with the broad facts of the case. What apparent challenges or opportunities does the company face? What information is provided? You may find it especially useful to focus on the first and last few paragraphs of the case in this step.

2. **Read the case more carefully and make notes, underline, etc.** What appear to be important facts? The conceptual frameworks in the chapters will be essential in helping you identify the key facts. Throughout the course, you will want to address central questions such as the following:

   - What is the firm's performance?
   - What is the firm's mission? strategy? goals?
   - What are the resources involved in the firm's value chain? How do they compare to competitors on cost and differentiation?
   - Does the firm have a competitive advantage?
   - Are the firm's advantages and disadvantages temporary or sustainable?
   - What is the value of the firm's resources?
   - Are the firm's resources rare?
   - Are the firm's resources costly to imitate?
   - Is the firm organized sufficiently to exploit its resources?

Depending on the case, you may also want to consider other frameworks and questions, where appropriate. Each chapter provides concepts and frameworks that you may want to consider. For example:

■ What are the five forces? How do they influence industry opportunities and threats? (Chapter 2)
■ What are the sources of cost differences in an industry? (Chapter 4)
■ What are the bases and potential bases for product differentiation in an industry? (Chapter 5)

Each chapter suggests more specific questions and concepts than those above. You will want to consider these concepts in detail. In some cases, the instructor may offer direction about which concepts to apply to a given case. In other instances, you may be left to use your judgment in choosing which concepts to focus on in analyzing a case.

3. **Define the basic issues.** This is perhaps the most important step and also the stage of analysis that requires the most wisdom and judgment. Cases are rarely like tidy problem sets where the issues or problems are explicitly stated and the tools needed to address those issues are prescribed. Generally, you need to determine what the key issues are. In doing this, it may help for you to begin by asking: What are the fundamental issues in the case? Which concepts matter most in providing insight into those issues? One trap to avoid in defining basic issues is doing what some decision-making scholars label "plunging-in," which is drawing conclusions without first thinking about the crux of the issues involved in a decision.[1] Many students have a tendency to seize the first issues that are prominently mentioned in a case. As an antidote to this trap, you may want to consider a case from the perspective of different conceptual frames.

4. **Develop and elaborate your analysis of the key issues.** As with all of the steps, there is no substitute for painstaking work in this stage. You need to take the key issues you have defined in Step 3, examine the facts that you have noted in Step 2, and assess what are the key facts. What does quantitative analysis reveal? Here it is not just ratio analysis that we are concerned with. Just as body temperature, blood pressure, and pulse rate may reveal something about a person's health but little about the causes of a sickness, ratio analysis typically tells us more about the health of a company than the causes of its performance. You should assemble facts and analysis to support your point of view. Opinions unsupported by factual evidence and analysis are generally not persuasive. This stage of the analysis involves organizing the facts in the case. You will want to develop specific hypotheses about what factors relate to success in a particular setting. Often, you will find it helpful to draw diagrams to clarify your thinking.

5. **Draw conclusions and formulate a set of recommendations.** You may be uncomfortable drawing conclusions and making recommendations because you do not have complete information. This is an eternal dilemma for managers. Managers who wait for complete information to do something, however, usually act too late. Nevertheless, you should strive to do the most complete analysis that you can under reasonable time constraints. Recommendations should also

---

[1] J. E. Russo and P. J. H. Schoemaker (1989). *Decision Traps: The Ten Barriers to Brilliant Decision-Making and How to Overcome Them*. New York: Fireside.

flow naturally from your analysis. Too often, students formulate their recommendations in an ad hoc way. In formulating recommendations, you should be clear about priorities and the sequence of actions that you recommend.

6. **Prepare for class discussion.** Students who diligently work through the first five steps and rigorously examine a case should be well prepared for class discussion. You may find it helpful to make some notes and bring them to class. Over the years, we have observed that many of the students who are low contributors to class discussions bring few or no notes to class. Once in class, a case discussion usually begins with a provocative question from the instructor. Many instructors will "cold call"—direct a question to a specific student who has not been forewarned. Students who have thoroughly analyzed and discussed the case before coming to class will be much better prepared for these surprise calls. They will also be better prepared to contribute to the analysis, argument, and persuasion that will take place in the class discussion. Discussions can move rapidly. You will hear new insights from fellow students. Preparation helps you to absorb, learn, and contribute to the insights that emerge from class discussion.

Summary

Students who embark in the case method soon learn that analyzing cases is a complex process. Having a clear conceptual approach such as the VRIO framework does not eliminate the complexity. This systematic approach, however, does allow the analyst to manage the complexity of real-world business situations. In the end, though, neither cases nor real-world businesses conclude their analyses with tidy solutions that resolve all the uncertainties and ambiguities a business faces. However, the case method coupled with a good theory such as the VRIO approach and hard work do make it more likely that you will generate valuable insights into the strategic challenges of firms and develop the strategic skills needed to lead a firm.

Glossary

above average accounting performance when a firm's accounting performance is greater than the industry average

above normal economic performance when a firm earns above its cost of capital

absorptive capacity the ability of firms to learn

accounting performance a measure of a firm's competitive advantage; calculated from information in the firm's published profit and loss and balance sheet statements

accounting ratios numbers taken from a firm's financial statements that are manipulated in ways that describe various aspects of the firm's performance

acquisition a firm purchases another firm

acquisition premium the difference between the current market price of a target firm's shares and the price a potential acquirer offers to pay for those shares

activity ratios accounting ratios that focus on the level of activity in a firm's business

adverse selection an alliance partner promises to bring to an alliance certain resources that it either does not control or cannot acquire

agency problems parties in an agency relationship differ in their decision-making objectives

agency relationship one party to an exchange delegates decision-making authority to a second party

agent a party to whom decision-making authority is delegated

architectural competence the ability of a firm to use organizational structure and other organizing mechanisms to facilitate coordination among scientific disciplines to conduct research

auction in mergers and acquisitions, a mechanism for establishing the price of an asset when multiple firms bid for a single target firm

audit committee subgroup of the board of directors responsible for ensuring the accuracy of accounting and financial statements

average accounting performance when a firm's accounting performance is equal to the industry average

backward vertical integration a firm incorporates more stages of the value chain within its boundaries and those stages bring it closer to gaining access to raw materials

barriers to entry attributes of an industry's structure that increase the cost of entry

below average accounting performance when a firm's accounting performance is less than the industry average

below normal economic performance when a firm earns less than its cost of capital

board chair the person who presides over the board of directors; may or may not be the same person as a firm's senior executive also known as Chairman of the Board

board of directors a group of 10 to 15 individuals drawn from a firm's top management and from people outside the firm whose primary responsibilities are to monitor decisions made in the firm and to ensure that they are consistent with the interests of outside equity holders

business angels wealthy individuals who act as outside investors typically in an entrepreneurial firm

business cycle the alternating pattern of prosperity followed by recession followed by prosperity

business-level strategies actions firms take to gain competitive advantages in a single market or industry

business model the set of activities that a firm engages in to create and appropriate economic value

business plan a document that summarizes how an entrepreneur will organize a firm to exploit an opportunity, along with the economic implications of exploiting that opportunity

business strategy a firm's theory of how to gain competitive advantage in a single business or industry

buyers those who purchase a firm's products or services

capabilities a subset of a firm's resources, defined as tangible and intangible assets, that enable a firm to take full advantage of other resources it controls

cashing out the compensation paid to an entrepreneur for risk-taking associated with starting a firm

causally ambiguous imitating firms do not understand the relationship between the resources and capabilities controlled by a firm and that firm's competitive advantage

centralized hub each country in which a firm operates is organized as a full profit-and-loss division headed by a division general manager; strategic and operational decisions are retained at headquarters

chairman of the board the person who presides over the board of directors; may or may not be the same person as a firm's senior executive

chief executive officer (CEO) person to whom all functional managers report in a U-form organization; the person to whom all divisional personal and corporate staff report to in an M-form organization: responsible for strategy formulation and implementation

chief operating officer (COO) reports to CEO; primary responsibility is strategy implementation

closely held firm a firm that has not sold many of its shares on the public stock market

collusion two or more firms in an industry coordinate their strategic choices to reduce competition in that industry

compensation policies the ways that firms pay employees

competitive advantage a firm creates more economic value than rival firms

competitive disadvantage a firm generates less economic value than rival firms

competitive dynamics how one firm responds to the strategic actions of competing firms

competitive parity a firm creates the same economic value as rival firms

competitor any firm, group, or individual trying to reduce a firm's competitive advantage

complementary resources and capabilities resources and capabilities that have limited ability to generate competitive advantage in isolation but in combination with other resources can enable a firm to realize its full potential for competitive advantage

complementor when the value of a firm's products increases in the presence of another firm's products

conduct (as in structured conduct performance model) the strategies that firms in an industry implement

conglomerate merger a merger or acquisition where there are no vertical, horizontal, product extension, or market extension links between the firms

consolidation strategy strategy that reduces the number of firms in an industry by exploiting economies of scale

controlling share when an acquiring firm purchases enough of a target firm's assets to be able to make all the management and strategic decisions in the target firm

coordinated federation each country in which a firm operates is organized as a full profit-and-loss division headed by a division general manager; operational decisions are delegated to these divisions or countries, but strategic decisions are retained at headquarters

core competence the collective learning in an organization, especially how to coordinate diverse production skills and integrate multiple streams of technologies

corporate diversification strategy when a firm operates in multiple industries or markets simultaneously

corporate-level strategies actions firms take to gain competitive advantages by operating in multiple markets or industries simultaneously

corporate spin-off exists when a large, typically diversified firm divests itself of a business in which it has historically been operating and the divested business operates as an independent entity

corporate staff upper-level managers who provide information about a firm's external and internal environments to the firm's senior executive

corporate strategy a firm's theory of how to gain competitive advantage by operating in several businesses simultaneously

cost centers divisions are assigned a budget and manage their operations to that budget

cost leadership business strategy focuses on gaining advantages by reducing costs below those of competitors

cost of capital the rate of return that a firm promises to pay its suppliers of capital to induce them to invest in a firm

cost of debt the interest that a firm must pay its debt holders to induce them to lend money to the firm

cost of equity the rate of return a firm must promise its equity holders to induce them to invest in the firm

countertrade international firms receiving payment for the products or services they sell into a country not in the form of currency, but in the form of other products or services that they can sell on the world market

crown jewel sale a bidding firm is interested in just a few of the most highly regarded businesses being operated by the target firm, known as its *crown jewels*, and the target firm sells these businesses

culture the values, beliefs, and norms that guide behavior in a society and in a firm

cumulative abnormal return (CAR) performance that is greater (or less) than what was expected in a short period of time around when an acquisition is announced

current market value the price of each of a firm's shares multiplied by the number of shares outstanding

customer-switching costs customers make investments in order to use a firm's particular products or services that are not useful in using other firms' products

debt capital from banks and bondholders

decentralized federation each country in which a firm operates is organized as a full profit-and-loss division headed by a division general manager and strategic and operational decisions are delegated to these country managers

decline the final phase of the product life cycle during which demand drops off when a technologically superior product or service is introduced

declining industry an industry that has experienced an absolute decline in unit sales over a sustained period of time

deep-pockets model a firm that takes advantage of its monopoly power in one business to subsidize several different businesses

demographics the distribution of individuals in a society in terms of age, sex, marital status, income, ethnicity, and other personal attributes that may determine their buying patterns

depression a severe recession that lasts for several years

direct duplication the attempt to imitate other firms by developing resources that have the same strategic effects as the resources controlled by those other firms

diseconomies of scale a firm's costs begin to rise as a function of the volume of production

distinctive competence a valuable and rare resource or capability

distribution agreement one firm agrees to distribute the products of others

diversification economies sources of relatedness in a diversified firm

divestment a firm sells a business in which it had been operating

division   each business that a firm engages in, also called a strategic business unit (SBU)

dominant-business firms   firms with between 70 percent and 95 percent of their total sales in a single product market

dominant logic   common theory of how to gain competitive advantages shared by each business in a diversified firm

economic climate   the overall health of the economic systems within which a firm operates

economic measures of competitive advantage   measures that compare a firm's level of return to its cost of capital instead of to the average level of return in the industry

economic value   the difference between the perceived benefits gained by a customer who purchases a firm's products or services and the full economic cost of these products or services

economic value added (EVA)   worth calculated by subtracting the cost of the capital employed in a division from that division's earnings

economies of scale   the per-unit cost of production falls as the volume of production increases

economies of scope   the value of a firm's products or services increases as a function of the number of different businesses in which that firm operates

emerging industries   newly created or newly re-created industries formed by technological innovations, change in demand, or the emergence of new customer needs

emergent strategies   theories of how to gain competitive advantage in an industry that emerge over time or have been radically reshaped once they are initially implemented

environmental threat   any individual, group, or organization outside a firm that seeks to reduce the level of that firm's performance

equity   capital from individuals and institutions that purchase a firm's stocks

equity alliance   cooperating firms supplement contracts with equity holdings in alliance partners

escalation of commitment   an increased commitment by managers to an incorrect course of action, even as its limitations become manifest

event study analysis   evaluates the performance effects of acquisitions for bidding firms

executive committee   typically consists of the CEO and two or three functional senior managers

explicit collusion   firms directly communicate with each other to coordinate levels of production, prices, and so forth (illegal in most countries)

external analysis   identification and examination of the critical threats and opportunities in a firm's competitive environment

finance committee   subgroup of the board of directors that maintains the relationship between the firm and external capital markets

financial resources   all the money, from whatever source, that firms use to conceive and implement strategies

firm-specific human capital investments   investments made by employees in a particular firm over time, including understanding the culture, policies, and procedures and knowing the people to contact to complete a task, that have limited value in other firms

firm-specific investments   the value of stakeholders' investments in a particular firm is much greater than the value those same investments would be in other firms

first-mover advantages   advantages that come to firms that make important strategic and technological decisions early in the development of an industry

flexibility   how costly it is for a firm to alter its strategic and organizational decisions

foreign direct investment   investing in operations located in a foreign country

formal management controls   a firm's budgeting and reporting activities that keep people higher up in a firm's organizational chart informed about the actions taken by people lower down in the organizational chart

formal reporting structure   a description of who in the organization reports to whom

forward vertical integration   a firm incorporates more stages of the value chain within its boundaries and those stages bring it closer to interacting directly with final customers

fragmented industries   industries in which a large number of small or medium-sized firms operate and no small set of firms has dominant market share or creates dominant technologies

free cash flow   the amount of cash a firm has to invest after all positive net present-value investments in its ongoing businesses have been funded

friendly acquisition   the management of a target firm wants the firm to be acquired

functional manager   a manager who leads a particular function within a firm, such as manufacturing, marketing, finance, accounting, or sales

functional organizational structure   the structure a firm uses to implement business-level strategies it might pursue where each function in the firm reports to the CEO

general environment   broad trends in the context within which a firm operates that can have an impact on a firm's strategic choices

generic business strategies   another name for business-level strategies, which are cost leadership and product differentiation

geographic market diversification strategy   when a firm operates in multiple geographic markets simultaneously

golden parachutes   incentive compensation paid to senior managers if the firm they manage is acquired

greenmail   a target firm's management purchases any of the target firm's stock owned by a bidder for a price that is greater than its current market value

growth   the second stage of the product life cycle during which demand increases rapidly and many new firms enter to begin producing the product or service

hard currencies   currencies that are traded globally and thus have value on international money markets

harvest strategy   a firm engages in a long, systematic, phased withdrawal from a declining industry, extracting as much value as possible

hedonic price   that part of the price of a product or service that is attributable to a particular characteristic of that product or service

holdup   one firm makes more transaction-specific investments in an exchange than partner firms make and the firm that has not made these investments tries to exploit the firm that has made the investments

horizontal merger   a firm acquires a former competitor

hostile takeover   the management of a target firm does not want the firm to be acquired

human capital resources   the training, experience, judgment, intelligence, relationships, and insight of individual managers and workers in a firm

imperfectly imitable   resources and capabilities that are more costly for other firms to imitate, compared to firms that already possess them

increasing returns to scale   in network industries, the value of a product or service increases as the number of people using those products or services increases

inelastic in supply   the quantity of supply is fixed and does not respond to price increases, such as the total supply of land, which is relatively fixed and cannot be significantly increased in response to higher demand and prices

informal management controls   include a firm's culture and the willingness of employees to monitor each other's behavior

initial public offering (IPO)   the initial sale of stock of a privately held firm or a division of a corporation to the general public

institutional owners   pension funds, corporations, and others that invest other peoples' money in firm equities

intermediate products or services   products or services produced in one division that are used as inputs for products or services produced by a second division

internal analysis   identification of a firm's organizational strengths and weaknesses and of the resources and capabilities that are likely to be sources of competitive advantage

internal capital market   when businesses in a diversified firm compete for corporate capital

international strategies   operations in multiple geographic markets: vertical integration, diversification, the formation of strategic alliances, or implementation of mergers and acquisitions, all across national borders

introduction   the first stage of a product's life cycle when relatively few firms are producing a product, there are relatively few customers, and the rate of growth in demand for the product is relatively low

invented competencies   illusory inventions by creative managers to justify poor diversification moves by linking intangible core competencies to completely unrelated businesses

joint venture   cooperating firms create a legally independent firm in which they invest and from which they share any profits that are created

learning curve   a concept that formalizes the relationship between cumulative volumes of production and falling per-unit costs

learning race   both parties to an alliance seek to learn from each other, but the rate at which these two firms learn varies; the first party to learn "wins" the race and may withdraw from the alliance

legal and political conditions   the laws and the legal system's impact on business, together with the general nature of the relationship between government and business

leverage ratios   accounting ratios that focus on the level of a firm's financial flexibility

licensing agreement   one firm allows others to use its brand name to sell products in return for some fee or percentage of profits

limited corporate diversification   all or most of a firm's business activities fall within a single industry and geographic market

liquidity ratios   accounting ratios that focus on the ability of a firm to meet its short-term financial obligations

local responsiveness   in an international strategy, the ability a firm has to respond to the consumer preferences in a particular geographic market

management control systems   a range of formal and informal mechanisms to ensure that managers are behaving in ways consistent with a firm's strategies

managerial hubris   the unrealistic belief held by managers in bidding firms that they can manage the assets of a target firm more efficiently than the target firm's current management

managerial know-how   the often-taken-for-granted knowledge and information that are needed to compete in an industry on a day-to-day basis

managerial perquisites   activities that do not add economic value to the firm but directly benefit the managers who make them

managerial risk aversion   managers unable to diversify their firm-specific human capital investments may engage in less risky business decisions than what would be preferred by equity holders

market extension merger   firms make acquisitions in new geographical markets

market for corporate control   the market that is created when multiple firms actively seek to acquire one or several firms

market leader   the firm with the largest market share in an industry

matrix structures   one employee reports to two or more people

mature industries   an industry in which, over time, ways of doing business have become widely understood, technologies have diffused through competitors, and the rate of innovation in new products and technologies drops

maturity   third phase of the product life cycle during which the number of firms producing a product or service remains stable, demand growth levels off, and firms direct their investment efforts toward refining the process by which a product or service is created and away from developing entirely new products

merger   the assets of two similar-sized firms are combined

M-form (multidivisional form)   an organizational structure for implementing a corporate diversification strategy whereby each business a firm engages in is managed through a separate profit-and-loss division

mission   a firm's long-term purpose

mission statement   written statement defining both what a firm aspires to be in the long run and what it wants to avoid in the meantime

monopolistic competition   a market structure where within the market niche defined by a firm's differentiated product, a firm possesses a monopoly

monopolistic industries   industries that consist of only a single firm

monopolistically competitive industries   industries in which there are large numbers of competing firms and low-cost entry and exit, but products are not homogeneous with respect to cost or product attributes; firms are said to enjoy a "monopoly" in that part of the market they dominate

moral hazard   partners in an exchange possess high-quality resources and capabilities of significant value to the exchange but fail to make them available to the other partners

mutual forbearance   a form of tacit collusion whereby firms tacitly agree to not compete in one industry in order to avoid competition in a second industry

network industries   industries in which a single technical standard and increasing returns to scale tend to dominate; competition in these industries tends to focus on which of several competing standards will be chosen

new competitors   firms that have either recently started operating in an industry or that threaten to begin operations in an industry soon

niche strategy   a firm reduces its scope of operations and focuses on narrow segments of a declining industry

nominating committee   subgroup of the board of directors that nominates new board members

nonequity alliance   cooperating firms agree to work together to develop, manufacture, or sell products or services, but they do not take equity positions in each other or form an independent organizational unit to manage the cooperative efforts

normal economic performance   a firm earns its cost of capital

objectives   specific, measurable targets a firm can use to evaluate the extent to which it is realizing its mission

office of the president   together, the roles of chairman of the board, CEO, and COO

oligopolies   industries characterized by a small number of competing firms, by homogeneous products, and by costly entry and exit

operational economies of scope   shared activities and shared core competencies in a diversified firm

operations committee   typically meets monthly and usually consists of the CEO and each of the heads of the functional areas included in the firm

opportunism   a firm is unfairly exploited in an exchange

organizational chart   a depiction of the formal reporting structure within a firm

organizational resources   a firm's formal reporting structure; its formal and informal planning, controlling, and coordinating systems; its culture and reputation; and informal relations among groups within a firm and between a firm and those in its environment

Pac Man defense   fending off an acquisition by a firm acquiring the firm or firms bidding for it

path dependence   events early in the evolution of a process have significant effects on subsequent events

pecuniary economies   sources of relatedness in market power between bidding and target firms

perfectly competitive industry   when there are large numbers of competing firms, the products being sold are homogeneous with respect to cost and product attributes, and entry and exit costs are very low

performance   (in the structure-conduct-performance model) performance of individual firms and performance of the industry

personnel and compensation committee   subgroup of the board of directors that evaluates and compensates the performance of a firm's senior executive and other senior managers

physical resources   all the physical technology used in a firm

poison pills   a variety of actions that target firm managers can take to make the acquisition of the target prohibitively expensive

policy choices   choices firms make about the kinds of products or services they will sell—choices that have an impact on relative cost and product differentiation position

policy of experimentation   exists when firms are committed to engage in several related product differentiation efforts simultaneously

predatory pricing   setting prices so that they are less than a business's costs

price takers   where the price of the products or services a firm sells is determined by market conditions and not by the decisions of firms

principal   the party who delegates the decision-making authority

privately held   a firm that has stock that is not traded on public stock markets and that is not a division of a larger company

processes   the activities a firm engages in to design, produce, and sell its products or services

process innovation   a firm's effort to refine and improve its current processes

process manufacturing   when manufacturing is accomplished in a continuous system; examples include manufacturing in chemical, oil refining, and paper and pulp industries

product differentiation   a business strategy whereby firms attempt to gain a competitive advantage by increasing the perceived value of their products or services relative to the perceived value of other firms' products or services

product diversification strategy   a firm operates in multiple industries simultaneously

product extension merger   firms acquire complementary products through merger and acquisition activities

product life cycle   naturally occurring process that occurs when firms begin offering a product or service; the stages consist of introduction, growth, maturity, and decline

productive inputs   any supplies used by a firm in conducting its business activities, such as labor, capital, land, and raw materials, among others

product-market diversification strategy   a firm implements both product and geographic market diversification simultaneously

profitability ratios   accounting ratios with some measure of profit in the numerator and some measure of firm size or assets in the denominator

profit-and-loss centers   profits and losses are calculated at the level of the division in a firm

proprietary technology   secret or patented technology that gives incumbent firms important advantages over potential entrants

question of imitability   "Do firms without a resource or capability face a cost disadvantage in obtaining or developing it compared to firms that already possess it?"

question of organization   "Is a firm organized to exploit the full competitive potential of its resources and capabilities?"

question of rarity   "How many competing firms already possess particular valuable resources and capabilities?"

question of value   "Does a resource enable a firm to exploit an external opportunity or neutralize an external threat?"

real options   investments in real assets that create the opportunity for additional investments in the future

recession   a period of relatively low prosperity; demand for goods and services is low and unemployment is high

related-constrained diversification   all the businesses in which a firm operates share a significant number of inputs, product technologies, distribution channels, similar customers, and so forth

related corporate diversification   less than 70 percent of a firm's revenue comes from a single product market and its multiple lines of business are linked

related-linked diversification strategy   the different businesses that a single firm pursues are linked on only a couple of dimensions or different sets of businesses are linked along very different dimensions

reputation   beliefs customers hold about a firm

resource-based view (RBV)   a model of firm performance that focuses on the resources and capabilities controlled by a firm as sources of competitive advantage

resource heterogeneity   for a given business activity, some firms may be more skilled in accomplishing the activity than other firms

resource immobility   resources controlled by some firms may not diffuse to other firms

resources   the tangible and intangible assets that a firm controls, which it can use to conceive and implement its strategies

retained earnings   capital generated from a firm's ongoing operations that is retained by a firm

seemingly unrelated diversified   diversified firms that exploit core competencies as an economy of scope, but are not doing so with any shared activities

senior executive   the president or CEO of a firm

shakeout period   period during which the total supply in an industry is reduced by bankruptcies, acquisitions, and business closings

shared activities   potential sources of operational economies of scope for diversified firms

shark repellents   a variety of relatively minor corporate governance changes that, in principle, are supposed to make it somewhat more difficult to acquire a target firm

single-business firms   firms with greater than 95 percent of their total sales in a single product market

"skunk works"   temporary teams whose creative efforts are intensive and focused

socially complex   resources and capabilities that involve interpersonal, social, or cultural links among individuals

social welfare   the overall good of society

specific international events   events such as civil wars, political coups, terrorism, wars between countries, famines, and country or regional economic recessions, all of which can have an enormous impact on the ability of a firm's strategies to generate competitive advantage

stakeholders   all groups and individuals who have an interest in how a firm performs

standstill agreement   contract between a target and a bidding firm wherein the bidding firm agrees not to attempt to take over the target for some period of time

stock grants   payments to employees in a firm's stock

stock options   employees are given the right, but not the obligation, to purchase a firm's stock at predetermined prices

strategic alliance   whenever two or more independent organizations cooperate in the development, manufacture, or sale of products or services; a form of exchange governance between market exchanges and hierarchical exchanges; examples include licensing arrangements, manufacturing agreements, and joint ventures

strategic management process   a sequential set of analyses that can increase the likelihood of a firm's choosing a strategy that generates competitive advantages

strategically valuable assets   resources required to successfully compete in an industry, including access to raw materials, particularly favorable geographic locations, and particularly valuable product market positions

strategy   a firm's theory about how to gain competitive advantage

strategy implementation   a firm adopting organizational policies and practices that are consistent with its strategy

structure   (in the structure-conduct-performance model) industry structure measured by such factors as the number of competitors in an industry, the heterogeneity of products in an industry, the cost of entry and exit in an industry, and so forth

structure-conduct-performance model (S-C-P)   theory suggesting that industry structure determines a firm's conduct, which in turn determines its performance

substitutes   products or services that meet approximately the same customer needs but do so in different ways

substitution   developing or acquiring strategically equivalent, but different, resources as a competing firm

supermajority voting rules   an example of a shark repellent that specifies that more than 50 percent of the target firm's board of directors must approve a takeover

suppliers   firms that make a wide variety of raw materials, labor, and other critical assets available to firms

supply agreements   one firm agrees to supply others

sustainable distinctive competencies   valuable, rare, and costly-to-imitate resources or capabilities

sustained competitive advantage   a competitive advantage that lasts for a long period of time; an advantage that is not competed away through strategic imitation

tacit collusion   firms coordinate their production and pricing decisions not by directly communicating with each other, but by exchanging signals with other firms about their intent to cooperate; special case of tacit cooperation

tacit cooperation   actions a firm takes that have the effect of reducing the level of rivalry in an industry and that do not require firms in an industry to directly communicate or negotiate with each other

tactics   the specific actions a firm takes to implement its strategies

technical economies   sources of relatedness in marketing, production, and similar activities between bidding and target firms

technological hardware   the machines and other hardware used by firms

technological leadership strategy   firms make early investments in particular technologies in an industry

technological software   the quality of labor–management relations, an organization's culture, and the quality of managerial controls in a firm

temporary competitive advantage   a competitive advantage that lasts for a short period of time

tender offer   a bidding firm offers to purchase the shares of a target firm directly by offering a higher-than-market price for those shares to current shareholders

thinly traded market   a market where there are only a small number of buyers and sellers, where information about opportunities in this market is not widely known, and where interests besides purely maximizing the value of a firm can be important

transaction-specific investment   the value of an investment in its first-best use is much greater than its value in its second-best use; any investment in an exchange that has significantly more value in the current exchange than it does in alternative exchanges

transfer-pricing system   using internally administered "prices" to manage the movement of intermediate products or services among divisions within a firm

transnational strategy   actions in which a firm engages to gain competitive advantages by investing in technology across borders

transnational structure   each country in which a firm operates is organized as a full profit-and-loss division headed by a division general manager and strategic and operational decisions are delegated to operational entities that maximize local responsiveness and international integration

transparent business partners   international business partners that are open and accessible

U-form structure   organization where different functional heads report directly to CEO; used to implement business-level strategies

uncertainty   the future value of an exchange cannot be known when investments in that exchange are being made

unfriendly acquisition   the management of the target firm does not want the firm to be acquired

unlearning   when a firm tries to modify or abandon traditional ways of engaging in business

unrelated corporate diversification   less than 70 percent of a firm's revenues is generated in a single product market and a firm's businesses share few, if any, common attributes

value added as a percentage of sales   measures the percentage of a firm's sales that are generated by activities done within the boundaries of a firm; a measure of vertical integration

value chain that set of activities that must be accomplished to bring a product or service from raw materials to the point that it can be sold to a final customer

venture capital firms outside investment firms looking to invest in entrepreneurial ventures

vertical integration the number of steps in the value chain that a firm accomplishes within its boundaries

vertical merger when a firm vertically integrates, either forward or backward, through its acquisition efforts

visionary firms firms whose mission is central to all they do

VRIO framework four questions that must be asked about a resource or capability to determine its competitive potential: the questions of value, rarity, imitability, and organization

weighted average cost of capital (WACC) the percentage of a firm's total capital that is debt multiplied by the cost of debt plus the percentage of a firm's total capital; that is, equity times the cost of equity

white knight another bidding firm that agrees to acquire a particular target in place of the original bidding firm

zero-based budgeting corporate executives create a list of all capital allocation requests from divisions in a firm, rank them from most important to least important, and then fund all the projects the firm can afford, given the amount of capital it has available

Company Index

In the page references, the number after "n" refers to the number of the end note in which the name is cited.

Name Index

In the page references, the number after "n" refers to the number of the end note in which the name is cited.

Subject Index

In the page references, the number after "n" refers to the number of the end note in which the name is cited.

Generation Y, 29
Generic business strategies, 102. *See also*
    Cost leadership strategies; Product
    differentiation strategies
Generic value chains. *See* Value chains
Geographic location, 64
Geographic market diversification
    strategies, 188
Germany, cultural trends in, 30
Globalization. *See also* International
    strategies
  cost reduction and, 316
  family firms and, 322
  firm revenues and, 310–315
  multinational firms and, 208
  opposition to, 20
  product life cycles and, 315–316
GM. *See* General Motors
"Going it alone" strategies, 263–264
Golden parachutes, 300
"Gold standard" of drug approval, 141
Google
  acquisitions by, 274–275
  resources and capabilities, 62–63
  smartphone applications, 2–3
Gore-Tex, 199
Governance, corporate, 322
Government policy as barrier to entry, 40
Gravity Games, 74
Greece, family-dominated firms in, 322
Greenmail, 298
Grocery store industry, 51, 84, 196
Gross profit margin ratio, 14
Growth stage of product life cycles, 315
Guitar string industry, 199

H
Hair salon industry, 293
Hard currencies, 314–315
Hardware, technological, 110, 115, 117
Harpo, Inc., 177
Harvest strategies, 55–56
HBO, 250–251
Health care industry. *See also* Medical in-
    dustry; Pharmaceutical industry
    costs, 71
    marketing strategies for product differ-
        entiation, 148
    product claims and ethical dilemmas,
        141
Hedonic prices, 133
Height of barriers to entry, 36, 60n10, 86
Herbal treatments, 141
Hewlett-Packard (HP)
    international strategies, 318
    mergers, 301
    mission, 5
    multipoint competition used by,
        204–205
    shared activities used by, 194
Hierarchical governance, 334
High-quality objectives, 6
Hispanics, demographic trends among, 29
Historical conditions, 75–76
Holdups, 256, 258–260
Home appliance industry, 52, 310
Home detergent industry, 52
Home financial planning, 41

Honda, 321, 323
Hong Kong, family-dominated firms
    in, 322
Horizontal mergers, 279
Hostile takeovers, 276
Hotel/motel industry, 49, 145
HP. *See* Hewlett-Packard
Hub-and-spoke systems, 41
Hubris hypothesis, 287
Human capital investments, 210, 211
Human resources, 64–65, 79

I
IBM
    international strategies, 324
    mission, 5
    product differentiation by, 144, 147
    shared activities used by, 194
Illegal immigrants, 111
Imitation. *See also* Direct duplication;
    Substitutes
    causal ambiguity and, 75, 76–77, 96n16
    of corporate diversification strategies,
        212–213
    of cost leadership strategies, 115–119
    direct duplication and substitution,
        74–75
    of international strategies, 330–331
    patents and, 75, 78, 143
    of product differentiation strategies,
        142–147
    of resources and capabilities, 73–78
    as response to competitive
        advantages, 87
    social complexity and, 75, 77–79, 91–92
    sources of costly imitation, 75–78
    of strategic alliances, 261, 263–265
    unique historical conditions and, 75–76
    of vertical integration strategies, 175
Immigrants, 111
Imperfectly imitable resources, 73
Implementation. *See* Strategy
    implementation
Incentives, 207
Increasing returns to scale, 251
India
    outsourcing to, 160–161, 167, 168
    trade barriers in, 313
Industry structure. *See also specific*
    industries
    competitive dynamics in, 84–88
    conduct and performance impacted
        by, 33
    declining, 54–56, 140
    emerging, 49–51, 140
    environmental opportunities and,
        47–56
    firm performance, impact on, 47
    fragmented, 48–49, 139, 294
    mature, 51–54, 140
Inelastic in supply, 66, 67
Inflation, 325–326
Informal management controls, 79
Information technologies, 110, 135–136,
    144, 171
Initial public offerings (IPOs), 239, 283
Innovation, 52–54
Institutional investors, 226

Institutional owners, 225–226
Intangible assets, 60n18, 64, 257
Intended strategies, 18–21
Intent to learn, 319–320
Intermediate market exchanges, 333–334
Intermediate products, 236–238
Internal analysis, defined, 6–7
Internal capabilities. *See* Resources and
    capabilities
Internal capital markets, 201–203, 216n21,
    235–236
Internal management committees,
    178–179
International events, 31
International integration, 323–325, 337
International operations, learning from,
    319–320
International strategies, 306–341. *See also*
    Globalization
    compensation policies and
        implementation of, 337
    core competencies, development and
        leveraging of, 319–321
    defined, 308
    direct duplication of, 330–331
    ethical considerations, 317
    financial risks of, 325–326
    hierarchical governance and, 334
    history of, 308–309
    imitation of, 330–331
    implementation of, 332–337
    local responsiveness/international
        integration trade-off, 323–325, 337
    low-cost production factors, gaining
        access to, 316–318
    to manage corporate risk, 321–323
    management control systems and
        implementation of, 337
    market exchanges and, 332–334
    new customers, gaining access to,
        310–316
    organizational structure and
        implementation of, 335–337
    political risks of, 326–328
    rarity of, 329–330
    research on, 328
    strategic alliances and, 333–334
    substitutes for, 331
    sustained competitive advantages and,
        329–331
    transnational strategies, 325
    value of, 309–323
Internet
    search engines, 62–63
    smartphone applications and, 2–3
Introduction stage of product life
    cycles, 315
Invented competencies, 201
Inventory turnover ratio, 15
Investments
    equity, 266
    firm-specific, 179–180, 210–211
    human capital, 210, 211
    transaction-specific, 165–167, 170–171,
        174, 179, 258–260
Invisible hand, 163
iPhones, 2
IPOs (initial public offerings), 239, 283